Social Psychology of Gender, Race, and Ethnicity

Readings and Projects

Kelli A. Keough and Julio Garcia

McGraw-Hill Higher Education

A Division of The McGraw-Hill Companies

SOCIAL PSYCHOLOGY OF GENDER, RACE AND ETHNICITY:
READINGS AND PROJECTS

RECYCLED

1 2 3 4 5 6 7 8 9 0 QPD/QPD 0 9 8 7 6 5 4 3 2 1 0

ISBN 0–07–365484–1

Editorial director: *Jane E. Vaicunas*
Executive editor: *Mickey Cox*
Editorial coordinator: *Sarah C. Thomas*
Senior marketing manager: *James Rozsa*
Project manager: *Susan J. Brusch*
Production supervisor: *Enboge Chong*
Coordinator of freelance design: *Rick D. Noel*
Typeface: *12/14 Book Antiqua*
Printer: *Quebecor Printing Book Group/Dubuque, IA*

Cover designer: *Jamie O'Neal*
Cover image: ©SuperStock, Inc. Market Place, Guatemala 1979, by John Hollis Kaufmann

www.mhhe.com

About the Authors

KELLI A. KEOUGH is an Assistant Professor of Psychology at the University of Texas at Austin. She received her B.A. psychology from Yale University and her Masters and Ph.D. from Stanford University. She has conducted research in a number of areas, including stereotype threat, self-esteem processes, and stress and illness prevention.

JULIO GARCIA, an Assistant Professor of Psychology at Tufts University, received his B.A. from the University of California at Davis, and went on to complete his Ph.D. at Stanford University. His research interests include stereotyping and social communication, decision-making in interracial situations, and identity formation in multicultural environments.

To Tony and my family for all of their support.

- K. A. K.

To those that matter most, my family and friends.

- J. G.

Brief Table of Contents

The Social Psychology of Gender, Race, and Ethnicity
Readings and Projects

Kelli A. Keough and Julio Garcia

CONTENTS

Chapter 7: The Prejudiced Mind: Biased Attitudes and Gender, Race, and Ethnicity

Chapter 8: The Problem of Discrimination

Foreword

By Philip G. Zimbardo
Series Consulting Editor

The traditional focus of psychology has made the individual the target of our investigations, which social psychology has broadened to include dyads and small groups. Yet much of what is vital in our lives comes in big categories not in small packages. We interact with individuals, but they are typically dealt with as tokens of a type of gender, or a racial group, or any of hundreds of ethnic groups. The cognitive construction of categories work to help simplify the complexity of our world, sparing us from having to process each stimulus composite as a totally novel experience. They aid us in the daily challenge of "people processing" by providing neatly stored models that are rich with expectations, which in turn guide and shape ready reactions. However, these learned categories are not merely descriptive summaries of objective features of the members of the group they represent. Often they come studded with subjective appraisals, with narratives, anecdotes, fears, anticipations, distorted construal of the typical member of the category, and frequently with action-sequence intentions tightly correlated with their identification mechanisms.

At its best, this categorization advances the categorical imperative of loving and sacrificing self for others, at its worst the categorical imperative promotes prejudice, sexism, racism, discrimination, segregation, dehumanization, "ethnic cleansing," and genocide. We have all seen each of these sides of human nature not only "out there" in society -- among martyrs and perpetrators of evil in crimes against humanity -- but deep in our personal makeup. Whom do you love without question, and whom do you fear or maybe even hate without similar rational inquiry? According to Alexander Solzenitsyn, a fine line between good and evil lies in the center of every human heart. But how and why? What are the social psychological mechanisms and processes underlying the operation of the categories of gender, race, and ethnicity?

This important new book by **Kelli Keough** and **Julio Garcia** offers some provocative analyses and answers to these significant questions, questions that define a social psychology engaged with society and dedicated to generating knowledge that helps to resolve social conflict in the world. **The Social Psychology of Gender, Race, and Ethnicity: Readings and Projects** is a masterful travel guide into this territory of diversity, controversy, and adventure. Using it will enrich the experiences of every traveler.

This unique book emerged from several courses taught by the authors, Kelli and Julio, at Stanford University and then refined in their recent courses at the University of Texas, Austin and Tufts University, respectively. They wanted their students to be exposed to seminal, classic articles and contemporary, "cutting edge" analyses by experts in these areas who had thought hard and well about the many underlying issues raised by the serious study of gender, race, ethnicity. But they wanted more than just a book of readings. They wanted to excite students with the possibility of conducting research into each of these domains by providing a series of projects that were interesting and offered a closer, more personal engagement with basic aspects within these three primary categories. Each of their well chosen readings are bolstered by excerpts from speeches, news articles, essays, and three research projects on each of the following topics: group processes, the self, identity, roles, stereotypes, prejudice, and discrimination. What may be an even more valuable contribution to the education of today's students are the two final sections informing students of how to think critically and creatively about the IQ debate in society and the affirmative action debate in the workplace. How do we apply what we have learned to clarifying the confusing and obscuring aspects of these recurring, spirited debates? Because many of the students most likely to use this book are beginning social psychology students, the authors provide an invaluable appendix that is chock full of resources for learning how to read and how to conduct research, along with a series of appropriate projects to assess their mastery with each component of the research process and research article.

I welcome Kelli Keough and Julio Garcia, as the newest authors to contribute to **The McGraw-Hill Social Psychology Series**, and you, our reader, to enjoy and benefit from their scholarship and dedication to the science of social psychology.

Preface

We live in a world which is said to be growing more connected with each passing moment. At the same time as we are growing closer to one another, a paradox has arisen. Coming closer to one another often leads us to become more aware of our differences. The differences that we often focus on are those based on gender, race, and ethnicity. Because these differences are at the basis of many of the ways in which people interact with one another and how they have interacted in the past, it is important for everyone to gain an understanding of the psychological creation, maintenance, and impact of gender, racial, and ethnic differences.

From early on in their discipline, social psychologists have engaged in the study of gender, race, and ethnicity. They have wrestled with a host of issues, ranging from how one defines the terms gender, race, and ethnicity, to how gender, race, and ethnicity affect us in school and on the job. The goal of this Workbook is to give students the opportunity to explore gender, race, and ethnicity primarily from a social psychological view. Our goal has at its center the desire to provide students and instructors the material, in the form of articles and projects, that will allow them to struggle together toward a clearer understanding of these issues.

The articles and projects in this Workbook are organized into ten chapters and an Appendix. Each of the chapters deals with a key theme in the study of gender, race, and ethnicity from a social psychological perspective. Chapter 1 is an introduction to the subject area focusing primarily on the definitions of the terms gender, race, and ethnicity. The second chapter offers readings and projects exploring the impact, which can often be negative, that being in a group can have on us. Chapter 3 presents a series of pieces and activities designed to expose you to another side of group processes — creating cooperation between groups.

In Chapter 4 you will read articles and do projects involving the role that gender, race, and ethnicity play when we attempt to answer thequestion "Who am I?" The pieces and activities in the fifth chapter then go on to explore how social roles influence our thinking about how we should act and our actual behavior.

Chapter 6 consists of articles and activities examining stereotyping as it relates to gender, race, and ethnicity. Chapter 7 then explores why and how our prejudgments or biased attitudes based on gender, race, and ethnicity are formed and maintained. And, in the eighth chapter the articles and projects deal with how our prejudicial attitudes based on gender, race, and ethnicity often lead to negative outcomes, especially discrimination.

The selections and activities in Chapter 9 and 10 deal with gender, race, and ethnicity at a more pragmatic level. The articles and projects in Chapter 9 focus generally on issues involving education and, more specifically, intelligence. Chapter

10 takes a look at the social psychology of gender, race, and ethnicity as it applies to the workplace and to the affirmative action debate.

Each of the chapters is introduced by a short essay that briefly discusses the key themes and articles in it. In addition, each of the articles is preceded by an Editors' note, which briefly describes the article and highlights the major points of the article. We would also like to draw your attention to the Appendix. In it you will find articles that we think will be helpful. It contains selections on how experiments are conducted and how one should read the research literature, along with a project which takes you through the various stages of the development of a research proposal. Whether or not you are asked to do this proposal, it will help you understand many of the articles that you will be reading if you spend time examining the material in the Appendix.

In selecting and organizing the articles and projects for this Workbook, our goal was to offer a diverse collection focusing on the key themes traditionally addressed in the study of gender, race, and ethnicity by social psychologists. While most of the articles in it were written by social psychologists we thought it appropriate to reach out to the wider community of individuals who have dealt with these issues. Included among these are public figures like Dr. Martin Luther King Jr., journalists, sociologists, and non academics. While the articles and projects in this Workbook can serve as the main text for a course, this Workbook can also serve as a source of materials that instructors can draw on and use as a basis for further exploration into any of the issues discussed in the Workbook. Because each of the chapters offers diverse readings and projects, both in terms of their approach and format, they can be used to highlight important points raised in lectures and in the class text or they can be used to replace a particular chapter in that text. Also, while the perspective it takes is clearly grounded in social psychology, the Workbook will be useful as an adjunct text for introductory psychology, cultural psychology, developmental psychology, the sociology of gender, race, and ethnicity, and introductory women's studies.

The research articles presented in this Workbook may prove challenging for students, but we think that their rigor and the seriousness with which they approach the issues of gender, race, and ethnicity can be a source of much stimulating interaction between student and instructor. Not all of the articles in the Workbook are of this type, but the research articles are a fundamental teaching tool.

The articles and projects in this Workbook have undergone the toughest and truest of tests. They have been used, and in some cases abused, by students in classes at Stanford University, the University of Texas at Austin, and Tufts University. We are grateful to these students for their honest input by way of their written responses to the articles and their feedback on the effectiveness of the projects. In this process articles have been rejected and projects abandoned or refined so that it is with a sense of confidence that we offer the material in this Workbook to students as a tool to use in their attempt to gain more knowledge about the important issues involving gender, race, and ethnicity.

In addition to the students who have helped us refine this Workbook, we would like to thank all of those who have helped us make this Workbook happen. This manuscript is much better due to the efforts of the following reviewers: Judy Addelston at Rollins College, FL; Julie Allison at Pittsburg State University, KS; Matthew Berent at Idaho State University, Pocatello, ID; Brad Bushman at Iowa State University, IA; Rodney Coates at Miami University, OH; Chante L. Cox-Boyd at Mississippi State University, MS; Cynthia Crown at Xavier University, OH; Susan Dutch at Westfield State College, MA; Steve Ellyson at Youngstown State University, OH; Angela R. Gillen at Beaver College, PA; Dr. John Greenwood at Lewis University, IL; James Johnson at University of North Carolina, Wilmington, NC; Saera Khan at Washington University, MO; Marie McKenall at Grand Valley State University, MI; Willie Melton at Michigan Technological University, MI; John Phalen at Western Oklahoma State College, OK; and Judith A. Warner at Texas A&M International University, TX.

Without Philip Zimbardo, this project would never have happened. We thank him for his continual support, enthusiasm, and the opportunities he has given us. We would also like to thank Brian McKean, Mickey Cox, and Sarah Thomas for their guidance throughout the publication process. Penny Riha, Michelle Cutbirth, Jason Rentfrow, and Sampson Gardner were great helpers pulling the actual text together. Finally, we would like to thank our mentor—Claude Steele. He has shown us that through psychology, you can make a difference in the world.

C h a p t e r   1

Introduction To The Social Psychology Of Gender, Race, And Ethnicity

The social psychology of gender, race, and ethnicity is a complex scientific field. This complexity is even reflected in the title of this Workbook. Because each of us have both unique and shared experiences tied to our membership in gender, racial, and ethnic groups, these terms can and do mean different things to different people. The articles in this introductory chapter will expose you to some of the differences in how these terms have been conceived and defined. They also examine how these different definitions have influenced the way in which gender, race, and ethnicity have been viewed by society and researched by the scientific community.

In the first of the articles, Ruth Hubbard discusses how scientific work examining biological differences between groups has often been influenced by our society's views on gender, race, and ethnicity. She also analyzes how this work in turn has been used to sustain our cultural views of groups and the biases that we have of them. Jean Phinney, in the next piece, begins by acknowledging that thinking of ethnic groups as unique categories can aid us in understanding certain psychological processes. However, she goes on to make the case that because ethnicity is a complex concept it would be more productive to explore the complex factors comprising ethnicity rather than viewing it as simple categories in order to more fully comprehend its role in psychology. Continuing the discussion of the definition of terms, Kay Deaux comments on her strategies for deciding on the appropriate use of the terms "sex" and "gender" in psychological research. This article is followed by Paula and Jeremy Caplan's call for us to become active consumers of scientific research. They advocate developing critical thinking skills that can aid us in identifying the biases that can be present, often unintentionally, in such research and in the inferences that are drawn from it.

The study of psychology by definition should include all of us. In her article, Sandra Graham discusses a major limitation of current work in all areas of psychology, the lack of variety in who is studied. In analyzing a sampling of top journals in psychology Graham shows a decline in the inclusion of African Americans in research, and she makes recommendations for remedying this problem. The final piece in this chapter is not by a psychologist, rather it by Dr. Martin Luther King, Jr. who challenged psychologists to reach out to society at large with their questions and findings.

The articles in this chapter discuss several major issues that people who are concerned with gender, race, and ethnicity must consider. These articles offer the first formulation of questions that you will encounter repeatedly in one form or another throughout this Workbook. Among these are "What is the relationship of biological differences to psychological differences?" and "What does it mean to say that groups are different from one another?"

Race And Sex As Biological Categories

Ruth Hubbard

---

*𝓔*ditors' Note: In this article, Ruth Hubbard discusses how biological differences have been used to justify our culture's views of women and minorities. She points out that socially constructed categories that fit our cultural preoccupation are often at the root of scientific research that uncovers "inherent, biological differences" between groups. She also notes the negative impressions of groups that can be created when we exaggerate biological differences between groups, and that we "need to be wary of scientific descriptions and interpretations that sustain or enhance the prevailing political realities." It is important that you keep this warning in mind as you read through this Workbook. It is especially critical to consider it when we are examining work investigating differences between gender, race, and ethnic groups.

The laws made of skin and hair fill the statute books in Pretoria. . . .Skin and hair. It has mattered more than anything else in the world.

—*Nadine Gordimer*, A Sport of Nature

Scientists, whose business it is to investigate things that matter in the world, have put a good deal of effort into examining the biological basis of differences not only in skin and hair but also in other characteristics that are assigned cultural and political significance. And they have sometimes made it appear as though the differences in power, encoded in the statute books (and not only those in Pretoria), were no more than the natural outcomes of biological differences. This became critically important in the eighteenth century, when support for the aims of the revolutions fought for liberty, equality, fraternity and for the Rights of Man needed to be reconciled with the obvious inequalities between nations, the "races," and the sexes.

As late as the sixteenth century some authors described the peoples of Africa as superior in wit and intelligence to the inhabitants of northern climes, arguing that the hot, dry climate "enlivened their temperament,"[1] and two centuries later Rousseau still rhapsodized about the Noble Savage. Yet beginning in the fifteenth century Africans became human chattel, hunted and sold as part of the resources Europeans extracted from that "dark and primitive"

continent. The industrialization of Europe and North America depended on the exploitation of the native populations of the Americas and Africa, and so it became imperative to draw distinctions between that small number of men who were created equal and everyone else. By the nineteenth century the Noble Savage was a lying, thieving Indian, and Africans and their enslaved descendants were ugly, slow, stupid, and in every way inferior to Caucasians. Distinctions also needed to be drawn between women and men, since, irrespective of class and race, women were not included among "all men" who had been created equal.

Although there are many similarities in the ways biologists have rationalized the inequalities between the races and sexes (and continue to do so to this day), this discussion will be clearer if we look at the arguments separately.

The Races of Man

Allan Chase[2] dates scientific racism from the publication of Malthus's *Essay on Population* in 1798 and argues that it focused on class distinctions among Caucasians rather than on distinctions between Caucasians and the peoples of Africa, America, and Asia. On the other hand, Stephen Jay Gould[3] points to Linnaeus (1758) for the first scientific ranking of races. Linnaeus arranged the races into different subspecies and claimed that Africans, whom he called *Homo sapiens afer,* are "ruled by caprice," whereas Europeans *(Homo sapiens europaeus)* are "ruled by customs." He also wrote that African men are indolent and that African women are shameless and lactate profusely.

Both dates occur more than two centuries after the beginning of the European slave trade, which became an important part of the economies of Europe and the Americas. But they are contemporary with the intellectual and civic ferment that led to the American and French revolutions (1776 and 1789, respectively) and to the revolution that overthrew slavocracy in Haiti (1791). As Walter Rodney has pointed out,[4] it is wrong to think "that Europeans enslaved Africans for racist reasons." They did so for economic reasons, since without a supply of free African labor they would not have been able "to open up the New World and to use it as a constant generator of wealth. Then, having become utterly dependent on African labour, Europeans at home and abroad found it necessary to rationalize that exploitation in racist terms."

Nineteenth-century physicians and biologists helped with that effort by constructing criteria, such as skull volume and brain size, by which they tried to prove scientifically that Africans are inferior to Caucasians. Gould's *Mismeasure of Man* describes some of the measurements and documents their often patently racist intent. Gould also illustrates the apparent naiveté with which, for example, the famous French scientist Paul Broca discarded criteria (such as the ratio of lengths of the long bones in the lower and upper arm, because it is greater in apes than humans) when he could not make them rank white men at the top. And he shows how Broca and the U.S. craniometer Samuel George Morton fudged and fiddled with their data in order to make the rankings come out as these men knew they must: white men on top, next Native American men, then African-American men. Women were problematic: though clearly white women ranked below white men, were they to be above or below men of the other races? A colleague of Broca's wrote in 1881, "Men of

the black races have a brain scarcely heavier than that of white women."[5]

In 1854 an American physician, Dr. Cartwright, wrote in an article entitled "Diseases and Peculiarities of the Negro" that a defect in the "atmospherization of the blood conjoined with a deficiency of cerebral matter in the cranium . . . led to that debasement of mind which has rendered the people of Africa unable to take care of themselves."[6] And racialist biologisms did not end with slavery. Jim Crow theorizing and practices survived until past the passage of the Civil Rights Act of 1957. Writing during World War II, Gunnar Myrdal marveled that the American Red Cross "refused to accept Negro blood donors. After protests it now accepts Negro blood but segregates it to be used exclusively for Negro soldiers. This is true at a time when the United States is at war, and the Red Cross has a semi-official status."[7] The American Red Cross continued to separate the blood of whites and African Americans until December 1950, when the binary classification into "Negro" and "white" was deleted from donor forms. As Howard Zinn remarks, "It was, ironically, a black physician named Charles Drew who developed the blood bank system."[8]

What can we in the 1990s say about the biology of race differences? Looking at all the evidence, there are none.[9] Demographers, politicians, and social scientists may continue to use "race" to sort people, but, as a biological concept, it has no meaning. The fact is that, genetically, human beings *(Homo sapiens)* are a relatively homogeneous species. If Caucasians were to disappear overnight, the genetic composition of the species would hardly change. About 75 percent of known genes are the same in all humans. The remaining 25 percent exist in more than one form, but all these forms occur in all groups, only sometimes in different proportions.[10] Another way is that, because of the extent of interbreeding that has happened among human populations over time, our genetic diversity is pretty evenly distributed over the entire species. The occasional, relatively recent mutation may still be somewhat localized within a geographic area, but about 90 percent of the variations known to occur among humans as a whole occur also among individuals of any one national or racial group.[11]

Another important point is that, for any scientific measurement of race difference, we first have to construct what we mean by race. Does the least trace of African origins make someone black, or does the least trace of Caucasian origins make someone white? The U.S. census for 1870 contained a third category, "Mulatto," for "all persons having any perceptible trace of African blood" and warned that "important scientific results depend on the correct determination of this class."[12] The U.S. census for 1890 collected information separately for "quadroons and octoroons"—that is, people who have one grandparent or one great-grandparent who is African, respectively, "while in 1930, any mixture of white and some other race was to be reported according to the race of the parent who was not white." Finally, in 1970 the Statistical Policy Division of the Office of Management and Budget warned that racial "classifications should not be interpreted as being scientific or anthropological in nature."[13] We need only look at the morass of legalisms in apartheid South Africa to abandon any notion that there are clear racial differences.

Yet we read such statistics as that "black men under age 45 are ten times more likely to die from the effects of high blood pressure than white men," that "black women suffer twice as many heart attacks as white women," and that "a variety of common cancers are more frequent among blacks . . . than whites."[14] At the same time some scientists and the media keep stressing the genetic origin of these diseases. So, must we not believe once again that there are inherent, biological differences between blacks and whites, as groups?

A closer look again leads us to answer no. What is misleading is that U.S. health statistics are usually presented in terms of the quasibiological triad of age, race, and sex,

without providing data about employment, income, housing, and the other prerequisites for healthful living. Even though there are genetic components to skin color, as there are to eye or hair color, there is no biological reason to assume that any one of these is more closely related to health status than any other. Skin color ("race") is no more likely to be related biologically to the tendency to develop high blood pressure than is eye color.

On the other hand, the median income of African Americans since 1940 has been less than two-thirds that of whites. Disproportionate numbers of African Americans live in more polluted and rundown neighborhoods, work in more polluted and stressful workplaces, and have fewer escape routes out of these living and work situations than whites have. Therefore, it is not surprising to find large discrepancies in health outcomes between these groups.

Mary Bassett and Nancy Kneger, looking at mortality risks from breast cancer, have found that the black-white differential of 1.35 drops to 1.10 when they look at African-American and white women of comparable social class, as measured by a range of social indicators.[15] And within each "racial" group social class is correlated with mortality risk. Thus, although it is true that African-American women, as a group, are at greater risk of dying from breast cancer than white women are, women of comparable class standing face a similar risk within these groups as well as between them. In other words, because of racial oppression, being black is a predictor of increased health risk, but so is being poor, no matter what one's skin color may be.

Sex Difference

That having been said, what about sex? Here, too, it can be argued that, since in our society any muting of differences between women and men is intolerable, this insistence may exaggerate biological differences and, therefore, enhance our impressions of them.[16] (Note the use of the phrase "the opposite sex" instead of "the other sex.") In fact, women and men exhibit enormous overlaps in body shape and form, strength, and most other parameters. The diversity within the two groups is often as large as the differences between them. Yet biological differences exist as regards women's and men's procreative capacities. Our society may exaggerate and overemphasize them, but the fact is that people who procreate need to be of two kinds. Therefore, the question I want to look at is to what extent ideological commitments to the differences our society ascribes to women and men in the social and political spheres influence the ways biologists describe the differences that are involved in procreation.

To do this it is useful to start with a quick look at Darwin's theory of sexual selection, which embedded Victorian preconceptions about the differences between women and men in modern biology. Sex is important to Darwin's theory of evolution by natural selection because the direction evolution takes is assumed to depend crucially on who mates with whom. This is why Darwin needed to invent the concept of sexual selection—the ways sex partners choose each other. Given the time in which he was writing, it is not surprising that he came up with the Victorian paradigm of the active, passionate, sexually undiscriminating male who competes with every other male in his pursuit of every available female, while females, though passive, coy, and sexually unenthusiastic, are choosy and go for "the winner." Darwin theorized that this makes for greater competition among males than females, and, since competition is what drives evolution by natural selection, males are in the vanguard of evolution. Females get pulled along by mating with the most successful males. The essentials of this interpretation have been incorporated into modern sociobiology.[17] Only in the last few years feminist sociobiologists, such as Sarah Blaffer Hrdy, have revised this canon and pointed out that females also can be active, sexually aggressive, and competitive and that males can nurture and be passive. Among animals as well as among people

females do not just stand by and wait for the most successful males to come along.[18]

I have criticized the Darwinian paradigm of looking at sex differences elsewhere.[19] The point I want to stress here is that, until quite recently, the active male-passive female dyad has been part of biological dogma and is the metaphor that informs standard descriptions of procreative biology at every level.

For example, the differentiation of the sex organs during embryonic development is said to proceed as follows: the embryo starts out sexually bipotential and ambiguous, but early during embryonic development in future males something happens under the influence of the Y chromosome which makes part of the undifferentiated, primitive gonads turn into fetal testes. These then begin to secrete fetal androgens (called male hormones), which are instrumental in masculinizing one set of embryonic ducts so that they develop into the sperm ducts and external male genitalia (the scrotal sac and penis), whereas another set of ducts atrophies. The story goes on to say that, if at this critical point no Y chromosome is present, then *nothing happens*. In that case somewhat later, and without special hormonal input, another part of the undifferentiated fetal gonad differentiates into ovaries, and, since these do *not* secrete androgens, the other set of fetal ducts differentiates into the fallopian tubes, uterus, vagina, and the external female genitalia (the labia and clitoris).

Notice that in this description male differentiation is active and triggered by the Y chromosome and by so-called male hormones; female differentiation happens because these triggering mechanisms are absent.[20] Of course, this cannot be true. All differentiation is active and requires multiple inputs and decision points. Furthermore, the so-called sex hormones are interconvertible, and both males and females secrete all of them and, for considerable parts of our lives, in not very different proportions. Diana Long Hall has described the history of the discovery of these hormones and the ways gender ideology was incorporated into designating them "male" and "female."[21] Anne Fausto-Sterling has noted that the Greek names that scientists gave them are also ideology laden. The "male" hormone is called androgen, the "generator of males," but there is no gynogen, or generator of females. Instead, the "female" analogue of androgen is called estrogen, from *oeastrus,* which means "frenzy" or "gadfly."[22]

The standard description of fertilization again follows the traditional script.[23] Ejaculation launches sperm on its dauntless voyage up the female reproductive tract. In contrast, eggs are "released," or "shed," from the ovary to sit patiently in the fallopian tubes until a sperm "penetrates" and "activates" them. Given that fertilization is an active process in which two cells join together and their nuclei fuse, why is it that we say that a sperm *fertilizes* the egg, whereas eggs are fertilized? In 1948 Ruth Herschberger caricatured this scenario in her delightful book *Adam's Rib,*[24] but that did not change the standard biological descriptions.

Of course, both sessile eggs and sprightly sperm are fabrications. Eggs, sperm, and the entire female reproductive tract must participate if fertilization is to take place, and infertility can result from the malfunctioning of any one of them. Also, a good deal goes on in eggs both before and after fertilization. It is interesting that modern biologists have been so focused on the role of the sperm and on chromosomes and genes that they have paid much more attention to the fact that, during fertilization, eggs and sperm contribute the same number of chromosomes than to the important part the egg's cytoplasm plays in the differentiation and development of the early embryo. The egg contributes much more than its nuclear chromosomes; it contributes all its cell contents—the cytoplasm, with its complement of cytoplasmic DNA and its subcellular structure and metabolic apparatus.

Finally, let us turn to the surely objective realm of DNA molecules. Here we find an article, published in December 1987 in the professional journal *Cell* and immediately publicized in the weekly scientific magazine *Science* and in the daily press, entitled "The Sex-Determining Region of the Human Y Chromosome Encodes a Finger Protein."[25] The authors claimed, and the magazines and newspapers promptly reported, that sex is determined by a single gene, located on the Y chromosome. The X chromosome, the authors wrote, has a similar gene, but it has nothing to do with sex differentiation. Reading the article more closely, we see that the authors identified a region of the Y chromosome which seemed to be correlated with the differentiation of testes. When this region was missing no testes developed; when it was present they did. By this argument the presence or absence of testes determines sex: people who have testes are male; people who don't are female.

More recently, in December 1989, two other groups of scientists claimed that the region on the Y chromosome which the previous group had identified as "determining sex" does not "determine" either maleness or sex because males can develop testes in its absence,[26] but that has simply refocused the search for *the sex* gene elsewhere on the Y chromosome. None of these authors points out that being female implies more than not having testes and that the differentiation of sex organs, whether female or male, requires processes of differentiation in which many genes as well as other metabolites must be involved.

Conclusions

I have selected these examples to illustrate the ways in which our particular cultural preoccupations with race and sex penetrate the biological sciences. But I do not want this analysis to suggest that it is useless to attempt to describe nature or, indeed, society in scientific ways. In fact, throughout this article I have drawn on scientific work to argue against scientific claims that exhibit racial or gender bias. Science remains one of the better ways we have of trying to understand what goes on in the world. But when we use it to investigate subjects such as race and sex, which are suffused with cultural meanings and embedded in power relationships, we need to be wary of scientific descriptions and interpretations that sustain or enhance the prevailing political realities.

To look critically at these kinds of data and interpretations, we need to bear in mind that in any society that is stratified by gender or race the fact that we are born with "female" or "male" genitals and "black" or "white" skin means that we will live different lives. Yet our biology and how we live are dialectically related and interpenetrate each other. The differences in our genital anatomy or in the color of our skin affect the ways we live, and our ways of life affect our biology.

For these reasons the scientific methodology of research into sex or race differences is intrinsically flawed. Scientists cannot vary genital anatomy or skin color and hold the environment constant, nor can they switch the cultural conditions that differentiate the environments of African Americans and whites or of women and men. Therefore, scientists cannot sort the effects of biology from societal influences. Scientists can catalog similarities and differences between women and men and between African Americans and whites, but they cannot establish their causes.[27]

One last point: I have looked at race and sex as separate categories, but we must not forget that they have also been combined to generate the cultural images of the eroticized, exotic African, male and female, and of the debased, sexualized African American, the black rapist, pimp, and whore. Social scientists and philosophers have only begun to explore the significance and ramifications of this melding of racism and sexism.[28] Scientists, and indeed all of us, need to become aware of the multiple meanings of these images and metaphors and to grasp the extent to which they penetrate our consciousness, collectively and as individuals, if we are to free the ways we think about race, sex, and gender from the subtle as well as the more blatant stereotypes that permeate our culture.

Notes

1. Londa Schiebinger, *The Mind Has No Sex? Women and the Origins of Modem Science* (Cambridge: Harvard University Press, 1989), 165.

2. Allan Chase, *The Legacy of Malthus: The Social Costs of the New Scientific Racism* (New York: Alfred Knopf, 1977).

3. Stephen Jay Gould, *The Mismeasure of Man* (New York: W.W. Norton, 1981), 35.

4. Walter Rodney, *How Europe Underdeveloped Africa* (Dar-es-Salaam: Tanzania Publishing House, 1972), 99-100.

5. Gould, *Mismeasure of Man,* 103.

6. Cited in Dorothy Buinham, "Black Women as Producers and Reproducers for Profit," in *Woman's Nature: Rationalizations of Inequality,* ed. Marian Lowe and Ruth Hubbard (New York: Pergamon Press, 1983), 35.

7. Gunnar Myrdal, *An American Dilemma: The Negro Problem and Modern Democracy* (New York: Harper and Brothers, 1944), 1367.

8. Howard Zinn, *A People's History of the United States* (New York: Harper and Row, 1980), 406.

9. Leo Kuper, ed., *Race, Science and Society* (Paris: UNESCO Press, 1975).

10. R. C. Lewontin, Steven Rose, and Leon J. Kamin, *Not in Our Genes: Biology, Ideology, and Human Nature* (New York: Pantheon, 1984), esp.119-29.

11. Richard Lewontin, *Human Diversity* (New York: Scientific American Books, 1982).

12. Janet L. Norwood and Deborah P. Klein, "Developing Statistics to Meet Society's Needs," *Monthly Labor Review* (October 1989).

13. Norwood and Klein, "Developing Statistics."

14. Nancy Krieger and Mary Bassett, "The Health of Black Folk: Disease, Class, and Ideology in Science," *Monthly Review* 38, no.3 (July-August 1986): 74.

15. Mary T. Bassett and Nancy Krieger, "Social Class and Black-White Differences in Breast Cancer Survival," *American Journal of Public Health* 76, no. 12 (1986): 1400-1403.

16. Suzanne J. Kessler and Wendy McKenna, *Gender: An Ethnomethodological Approach* (Chicago: University of Chicago Press, 1978).

17. Edward O. Wilson, *Sociobiology: The Modern Synthesis* (Cambridge: Harvard University Press, 1975).

18. Sarah Blaffer Hrdy, "Empathy, Polyandry, and the Myth of the Coy Female," in *Feminist Approaches to Science,* ed. Ruth Bleier (New York: Pergamon Press, 1986).

19. Ruth Hubbard, *The Politics of Women's Biology* (New Brunswick, N.J.: Rutgers University Press, 1990), 87-118.

20. Anne Fausto-Sterling, *Myths of Gender: Biological Theories about Women and Men* (New York: Basic Books, 1985).

21. Diana Long Hall, "Biology, Sex Hormones, and Sexism in the 1920s," in *Women and Philosophy: Toward a Theory of Liberation,* ed. Carol C. Gould and Marx W. Wartofsky (New York: G. P. Putnam's Sons, 1976), 81-96.

22. Anne Fausto-Sterling, "Society Writes Biology/ Biology Constructs Gender," *Daedalus* 116 (1987): 61-76.

23. Emily Martin, "The Egg and the Sperm," *Signs* 16 (1991): 485-501.

24. Ruth Herschberger, *Adam's Rib* (New York: Harper and Row, 1948).

25. David C. Page et al., "The Sex-Determining Region of the Human Y Chromosome Encodes a Finger Protein." *Cell* 51 (24 December 1987): 1091-1104.

26. M. S. Palmer et al., "Genetic Evidence that ZFY Is Not the Testis-Determining Factor," *Nature* 342, nos. 21-28 (December 1989): 937-39; Peter Koopman et al., "Zfy Gene Expression Patterns Are Not Compatible with a Primary Role in Mouse Sex Determination," *Nature* 342, nos. 21-28 (December 1989): 940-42.

27. Hubbard, *Politics of Women's Biology,* 128-29, 136-40.

28. Angela Y. Davis, *Women, Race, and Class* (New York: Random House, 1981); Henry Louis Gates, Jr., ed. *Race, Writing, and Difference* (Chicago: University of Chicago Press, 1986); Sander Gilman, *Difference and Pathology: Stereotypes of Sexuality, Race, and Madness* (Ithaca: Cornell University Press, 1985); Donna Haraway, *Primate Visions: Gender, Race, and Nature in the World of Modern Science* (New York: Routledge, 1989); Nancy Stepan, "Race and Gender: The Role of Analogy in Science," *Isis* 77: 261-77.

When We Talk About American Ethnic Groups, What Do We Mean?

Jean S. Phinney

Editors' Note: We are often in situations in which we are asked to indicate our race and ethnicity. Such questions are posed by the United States Census Bureau and many psychological researchers. These seemingly innocuous requests can tell us much about the assumptions that underlie the way that race and ethnicity are viewed by those doing research. These questions often presuppose that people fit into just one racial or ethnic category. Jean Phinney challenges these assumptions in this article. The questions and insights that she offers about ethnicity and race are things that we must keep in mind when studying these topics.

American ethnic groups are often thought of as discrete categories to which people belong and that explain some aspects of psychological functioning. However, ethnicity is a complex multidimensional construct that, by itself explains little. To understand its psychological implications, it is necessary to identify and assess those aspects of ethnicity that may have an impact on outcomes of interest. In this article, the author examines 3 key aspects of ethnicity: cultural norms and values; the strength, salience, and meaning of ethnic identity; and the experiences and attitudes associated with minority status. These aspects are best understood in terms of dimensions along which individuals and samples vary, rather than as categories into which individuals can be classified.

Ethnicity is becoming an increasingly important topic in psychology. The American Psychological Association (1994) recommended description of samples by ethnic group, and concern with ethnicity as a variable is evident across all areas of the field. Increased interest in and attention to ethnicity promises important benefits to psychology. The growth of psychological information about American ethnic groups can help to fill in theoretical and empirical gaps that have resulted from the focus of mainstream research on largely White middle-class samples (Graham, 1992). Greater awareness of ethnic issues can bring increased sensitivity to the treatment of clients from diverse backgrounds (Rogler, Cortes, & Malgady, 1991). However, the increased attention to ethnicity poses complex problems that are often ignored. Although ethnic group membership clearly has important psychological implications for individuals, the exact nature of the relationship between ethnicity and psychological outcomes is unclear. Simply knowing the ethnicity of an individual or group of individuals does little to explain specific social, emotional, cognitive, and mental health outcomes.

To achieve a better understanding of the implications of ethnic group membership, it is necessary to unpack the packaged variable of ethnicity, as has been recommended in the case of culture (Poortinga, van de Vijver, Joe, & van de Koppel, 1989; Whiting 1976); that is, we must identify and assess the variables associated with ethnicity that may explain its influence. Although this point has been made by various writers (e.g., Betancourt & Lopez, 1993; Phinney & Landin, in press), it remains unclear what variables should be considered in attempting to understand ethnicity. My first goal in this article is to examine three aspects of ethnicity that are assumed to account for its psychological importance: culture, ethnic identity, and minority status. In addition, although each of these aspects contributes something to the understanding of ethnicity, they are not categorical variables that differentiate clearly among groups. My second goal is to demonstrate that these aspects are best understood in terms of dimensions along which individuals and samples vary, rather than as categories into which individuals can be classified.

The focus in this article is on ethnic groups of color in the United States, that is, groups of non-European origin, primarily African Americans, Asian and Pacific Islander Americans, Latinos, and Native Americans.

Americans of European descent can of course also be considered as members of ethnic groups. However, in this article, I use the term ethnic group to refer only to members of nondominant groups, in order to avoid the repeated use of the term minority to distinguish non-European groups (which in many places are no longer minorities) from the dominant White majority. The discussion also does not include ethnic groups in other parts of the world, where ethnic conflicts have escalated into internecine wars (see Calhoun, 1993; Williams, 1994). Although American ethnic groups are not without conflict, most Americans support the idea of a multiethnic society in principle, even though they may differ in how to attain it.

The term ethnicity is also used here to encompass race. The term race is avoided because of the wide disagreement on its meanings and usage for psychology (Jones, 1991; Wilkinson & King, 1987; Yee, Fairchild, Weizmann, & Wyatt, 1993; Zuckerman, 1990). The psychological importance of race derives largely from the way in which one is responded to by others, on the basis of visible racial characteristics, most notably skin color and facial features. and in the implications of such responses for one's life chances and sense of identity. In this discussion, these implications of race are subsumed as aspects of ethnicity that are of psychological importance. Thus, the term ethnicity is used to refer to broad groupings of Americans on the basis of both race and culture of origin.

There are at least three aspects of ethnicity that may account for its psychological importance. These include (a) the cultural values, attitudes, and behaviors that distinguish ethnic groups; (b) the subjective sense of ethnic group membership (i.e., ethnic identity) that is held by group members; and (c) the experiences associated with minority status, including powerlessness, discrimination, and prejudice. There are certainly other important aspects of ethnicity, such as political, economic, and historical factors, that are relevant in other contexts. However, the three named components are the critical features from a psychological perspective. They correspond closely to the three defining criteria for ethnic groups identified by Sue (1991), and they provide the

focus for this discussion. These three aspects are not independent; rather, they are overlapping and confounded. However, they can be separated conceptually for purposes of discussion. Before examining these three aspects of ethnicity in detail, I explore the categories and labels that have been commonly used to designate ethnic groups.

Ethnic Categories and Labels

Categories are necessary for human discourse, and without categorical labels, discussion of psychological phenomena is virtually impossible. Similarly, ethnic groups need to be defined and labeled for purposes of discussion.

However, many psychologists, perhaps because of the typical training in experimental research methods, tend to think of ethnicity as a categorical variable, either an independent variable that is assumed to influence psychological outcomes or as a nuisance variable to be controlled. Sociologists, who have a longer tradition of studying ethnicity (e.g., Yinger, 1985), tend to see more clearly the problems of ethnic categories. Sociologists who have wrestled with problems of categorization to describe ethnic differences in indexes, such as self-esteem (Porter & Washington, 1993), mental health (Vega & Rumbaut, 1991), or economic well-being (Waters & Eschbach, 1995) generally agree that ethnic categories are imprecise and arbitrary, "social constructions rather than natural entities that are simply 'out there' in the world" (Waters & Eschbach, 1995, p. 421). Both ethnic categories and the labels for these categories vary over time, context and individuals. . . .

[E]ven within an ethnic group whose members share a relatively precise ethnic label there is tremendous heterogeneity. Many writers have pointed out that there is greater variation within than between groups (e.g., Jones, 1991; Reid, 1994; Zuckerman, 1990). . . . Because of this within-group variation, ethnic group membership alone cannot predict behaviors or attitudes in any psychologically meaningful way. . . .

There are additional problems with ethnic category labels. Many groups have several alternative labels available, and these various labels have different meanings both for members and nonmembers of a particular group (Huddy & Virtanen, 1995). The different connotations of ethnic labels have been well documented. For example, Larkey, Hecht, and Martin (1993) have demonstrated the diversity of meanings associated with the terms Black and African-American. The diverse labels used by individuals of Mexican origin, such as Mexican, Chicano, Latino, Hispanic, and Mexican American, have different psychological correlates (Buriel, 1987). Not only do different labels for the same group have different meanings, but also the same label can have varied meanings for different individuals. Ferdman (1995) provided descriptions of the various ways in which a group of individuals, all of whom described themselves as Mexican American and were of similar social position, interpreted that label.

Because of these varied meanings associated with ethnic labels, individuals may use different labels in different situations to convey a particular sense of themselves (Waters, 1990). . . . Use of self-labels changes depending on circumstance. Labels can, for example, become a political choice, particularly in cases where resources are allotted on the basis of membership in particular groups. A recent study found that of 259 university students who claimed to be American Indian or Alaska Native, only 52 were able to verify their status as a member of one of those groups (Pavel, Sanchez, & Machamer, 1994).

However, although there is some choice as to self-label, usage is constrained to varying degrees by the way one is perceived by others. . . . For some individuals, the two definitions differ; also some individuals have dual or multiple ethnic identities. When distinct racial features are evident, individuals have less freedom as to the self-label they can choose (Chung, 1991).

An additional problem in the use of ethnic categories involves the growing number of individuals of mixed ethnicity (Root, 1992). In a recent report on high school and college students in several ethnically diverse settings, researchers found that over one tenth of adolescent and young adult respondents were of mixed backgrounds when parental ethnicity was assessed (Phinney & Alipuria, 1996). . . . [I]f self-labels alone are used to categorize research participants, the categories may include individuals from mixed backgrounds. The implications of such blurring of categories are unclear, but they are likely to differ depending on the particular combination involved and the phenotypic appearance of the individual (Phinney & Alipuria, 1996).

In summary, it is increasingly clear that for a number of reasons ethnic categories and labels are problematic. Labels are not consistent indicators of group membership; rather, they vary over time and situations, carry different connotations among individuals and groups, and gloss over within-group variation. To get beyond simplistic ethnic categories, we need to examine the meanings associated with ethnicity, specifically culture, identity, and minority status.

Ethnicity as Culture

Ethnicity is perhaps most often thought of as culture. A common assumption about the meaning of ethnicity focuses on the cultural characteristics of a particular group, that is, the norms, values, attitudes, and behaviors that are typical of an ethnic group and that stem from a common culture of origin transmitted across generations. American ethnic groups of color are assumed to reflect the cultures of Africa, Asia, Latin America, and the indigenous peoples of North America. To understand the psychological implications of ethnicity, it is essential to identify the specific cultural characteristics associated with an ethnic group and with the outcomes of interest such as educational achievement or mental health (Betancourt & Lopez, 1993; Phinney & Landin, in press). . . .

In spite of the long-standing recognition of the need to identify cultural variables that distinguish ethnic groups, little has been done to accomplish this. A number of articles and books have appeared in recent years that attempt to describe and characterize the culture of particular ethnic groups (e.g., Gibbs & Huang. 1989; Harrison et al., 1990; McAdoo, 1993; McGoldrick, Pearce, & Giordano, 1982; Mindel & Habenstein, 1988). Writers who are attempting to generalize about ethnic cultures typically qualify their descriptions by pointing out that research is limited, that groups are heterogeneous, and that many conclusions are based on informal observations or clinical experience rather than on empirical data (e.g., Uba, 1994). Nevertheless, there appear to be core characteristics that many accounts agree on. . . .

A theme running through many of these descriptions is the broad cultural difference between individualism and collectivism that has been observed to distinguish mainstream American and Western European cultures from the cultures of Asia, Africa, Latin America, and many indigenous peoples (Greenfield & Cocking, 1994; Markus & Kitayama, 1991; Triandis, 1990). Western industrialized countries are said to emphasize the importance of the individual over the group and to construe the individual as independent, autonomous, and self-contained. Many non-Western countries emphasize the group over the individual and view persons as interdependent and connected. Members of American ethnic groups from collectivistic cultures, such as Asian, African, or Latin American, are assumed to reflect this difference, that is, to emphasize inter-dependence and orientation toward the group, in contrast to the mainstream American tendency toward independence. Recent research provides support for the greater interdependence among ethnic minority children in the United States (Greenfield & Cocking, 1994). There is, in addition, a tradition of cross-cultural research aimed at identifying broad dimensions of cultural differences across nations worldwide (Hofstede, 1980; Schwartz & Bilsky, 1990).

In spite of some agreement both on descriptions of specific ethnic cultures and on broad differences between Western and non-Western cultures, there are serious problems in using culture as a basis for understanding the psychological implications of ethnicity. The most obvious problem is the tremendous heterogeneity among members of American ethnic groups, as noted earlier with regard to ethnic labels. Ethnic cultures differ in terms of particular country of origin within a broad cultural group (e.g., Asian Americans of Japanese vs. Korean ancestry) generation of immigration region of settlement in the United States, socioeconomic status, and community structure (Marin & Marin, 1991; Reid, 1994). Furthermore, because of their

dispersion and mixing with both mainstream American culture and with other ethnic groups in the United States, ethnic cultures are not discrete entities but rather part of a diverse cultural mix (Phinney & Devich-Navarro, in press; Szapocznik & Kurtines, 1993). Finally, even if particular subcultures can be described with some accuracy, cultures are not static, but continually evolving and changing (Roosens, 1989; Vega, 1992).

Because of this heterogeneity, cultural blending, and cultural change, it is not clear whether particular individuals or samples actually reflect the culture they are thought to represent. A common practice is to interpret empirical results or clinical observations in terms of cultural characteristics that are assumed to exist but that are not directly assessed (Betancourt & Lopez, 1993; Phinney & Landin, in press). In such cases, group membership is used as a "social address" (Bronfenbrenner, 1986) that is assumed to be linked to particular traits or behaviors.

To make sense of the cultural implications of ethnicity, it is important to determine whether cultural attributes of particular samples in fact conform to broad descriptions of the group and whether these attributes can be linked to psychological outcomes. . . .

In summary, although cultural norms and values are an important component of the construct of ethnicity, they cannot alone explain the role of ethnicity in particular psychological outcomes. The problem is in part methodological; at present, there is a lack of reliable measures of cultural characteristics. However, in cases where such measures exist and have been used, they often do not clearly distinguish between members and nonmembers of particular groups. Because of the overlap and blending of cultures, measures of culture yield continuous scores that reveal differing degree of adherence to particular cultural norms and values (e.g., Triandis, Marin, Lisansky, & Betancourt, 1984). Ethnic cultures, rather than unified structures to which one belongs, can be thought of as clusters of dimensions along which individuals or samples vary. Although these dimensions are typically correlated in the group as a whole, individuals differ in the extent to which they adhere to any given value or attitude.

Ethnicity as Identity

In addition to variation in the adherence to cultural values and practices, individuals differ in the strength of identification with their ethnic group, that is, their ethnic identity. Ethnic identity may remain strong even when there is little direct cultural involvement, a phenomenon that has been termed symbolic ethnicity or ethnic loyalty (Keefe, 1992; Keefe & Padilla, 1987). To understand the role of ethnicity in human behavior, it is therefore important to consider individuals' ethnic identities.

The term ethnic identity is sometimes used to refer simply to ethnic group membership or label. However, ethnic identity is not a categorical variable, something that one does or does not have. Rather, it is a complex, multidimensional construct that, like culture, varies across members of a group. Ethnic identity has been conceptualized as an enduring, fundamental aspect of the self that includes a sense of membership in an ethnic group and the attitudes and feelings associated with that membership (Bernal & Knight, 1993; Keefe, 1992; Phinney, 1990). The view of ethnic identity as the link between ethnicity and psychological outcomes is based on the assumption that ethnicity is a meaningful psychological variable to the extent that it has salience and centrality for the individuals involved. . . .

[E]thnicity is salient in cases where one's group membership is evident, as in the case of ethnic groups of color and specifically in the case of racial differences (Deaux, 1992). Ethnic identity has been shown to be a more important component of the self for these individuals than for most White Americans (Aries & Moorehead, 1989; Phinney & Alipuria, 1990). In addition, ethnic identity varies in importance and strength among ethnic group members (Keefe & Padilla, 1987). Research suggests that the stronger one's ethnic identity, the greater the contribution that that identity makes to one's self-concept. For example, in a study of Black, White, and Asian college students, Crocker, Luhtanen, Blaine, and Broadnax (1994) found that the Black students who rated their group identity as being of greatest importance also showed the highest correlation between self-

esteem and their evaluation of their group and of themselves as group members. These results indicate, at least at the group level, that identification with one's ethnic group may be more important than group membership per se in understanding the psychological role of ethnicity.

Furthermore, ethnic identity comprises a number of different components, including self-labeling, a sense of belonging, positive evaluation, preference for the group, ethnic interest and knowledge, and involvement in activities associated with the group (Phinney, 1990, 1995). The various components of ethnic identity relate differently to psychological outcomes; a recent meta-analysis showed that some aspects of ethnic identity, notably preference and evaluation, contributed to self-esteem, but others, such as self-identification, did not (Bat-Chava & Steen, 1995). The components of ethnic identity may be combined in different ways across individuals. Gurin, Hurtado, and Peng (1994) documented different identity structures among individuals of Mexican descent depending on their place of birth and language usage. . . .

Differences among individuals in the quality of their ethnic identity are also related to developmental changes over time, as people explore and evaluate the meaning and implications of their group membership. The research on ethnic identity development (Phinney, 1989, 1993) and racial identity attitudes (Cross, 1991; Helms, 1990) suggests that ethnic identity can be conceptualized as a process: Individuals progress from an early stage in which one's ethnicity is taken for granted, on the basis of attitudes and opinions of others or of society; through a period of exploration into the meaning and implications of one's group membership; to an achieved ethnic identity that reflects a secure, confident sense of oneself as member of a group. Furthermore, an achieved ethnic identity is not necessarily a static end point of development; individuals are likely to reexamine their ethnicity throughout their lives and thus may reexperience earlier developmental stages (Parham, 1989). Different stages of ethnic or racial identity have different mental health correlates (Phinney & Kohatsu, in press). Thus, the psychological implications of ethnicity will vary over the life cycle, with changes in one's identification with the group.

In summary, ethnic identity is a complex cluster of factors that define the extent and type of involvement with one's ethnic group. It differs both qualitatively and quantitatively among ethnic group members; two individuals who belong to the same group may differ widely on their identification with the group and their commitment to it. They may vary in how salient the group is for them and in what it means subjectively. Furthermore, ethnic identity can vary within one individual over time. The psychological correlates of ethnicity are likely to differ depending on the quality of this identity.

Ethnicity as Minority Status

The importance and centrality of ethnic identity are strongly associated with one's situation and experiences within society. For members of groups of color, the significance of their group membership may lie in part in the struggle to gain equality, recognition, and acceptance within a predominantly White society. Therefore, a final variable to examine in order to understand the meaning and impact of ethnicity is the status of the ethnic group within the larger society.

For ethnic groups of color, ethnicity implies less power and status and often the experience of prejudice and discrimination. . . . For Sue (1991), the term minority group carries with it the connotation of the unequal relationships among groups within society, in which some groups are subjected to greater prejudice and discrimination. He suggested that to fully understand ethnic groups, it is necessary to analyze patterns of exploitation. This theme has been developed in greatest depth with reference to African Americans. Boykin and Toms (1985) suggested that the minority experience is one part of the "triple quandary" (p. 39) faced by African Americans. In addition to issues related to being Black and to being American, Blacks must deal with a third aspect of their ethnicity, namely, racism and oppression.

The fact that the minority experience has a psychological impact has been documented in various ways. Gaines and Reed (1995) made the case that there are predictable

psychological outcomes of "belonging to a group that has been oppressed or exploited throughout an historical period" (p. 97). They noted that one effect is the tendency to emphasize collective values over individualistic values. (Thus, the greater collectivism of ethnic group members may be as much a product of their experience in the United States as a result of transmission from their culture of origin.) . . .

Another obvious correlate of minority status is the presence of negative stereotypes. Although all groups are subject to stereotypes, the effects of such stereotypes are likely to be more detrimental for groups with less power and status (Fiske, 1993). Stereotypes can both restrict the way other people view ethnic group members and make the group members themselves vulnerable to believing or acting on them (Steele, 1992; Steele & Aronson, 1995). . . .

As with other aspects of ethnicity that have been discussed, the impact of minority status is not uniform across individuals or groups. This diversity is due in part to varying historical experiences that differentiate groups, including slavery, internment, relocation, and immigrant or refugee status. There is, in addition, variation within groups. . . .

Furthermore, there is individual variation in the extent to which discrimination is perceived and in the way it is responded to. Stable personal characteristics such as self-esteem can influence the extent to which discrimination is perceived (Phinney, Santos, & Madden, 1996). Also, as discussed earlier with reference to ethnic identity, there are changes over time in the ways in which individuals interpret and respond to the experience of prejudice and racism (Cross, 1991; Helms, 1990; Phinney, 1989); the impact of ethnicity varies in relation to the extent to which one has examined and resolved issues related to one's ethnic or racial group membership (Phinney & Kohatsu, in press).

In summary, minority status, defined by lower status and the experience of discrimination, involves a number of complex variables. As with the other aspects of ethnicity that have been discussed, it cannot be considered a categorical variable that does or does not apply, rather, its psychological impact on any given individual and group will vary along a number of dimensions. The history and present status of one's ethnic group in society, personal experiences with prejudice, and one's response to perceptions of stereotypes and discrimination are among the factors likely to interact in complex ways in influencing psychological outcomes.

Implications and Recommendations

Given the wide variation in the ways in which ethnicity is expressed, there is a need for new approaches to understanding ethnic groups among both researchers and practitioners. Ethnic categories will continue to be needed because of the importance of exploring and understanding the many differences associated with aspects of ethnicity, but they should be used with caution (Azibo, 1988).

First, ethnic categories need to be used in describing research samples, as required by American Psychological Association (1994) guidelines. However, for all the reasons discussed, a simple label is not sufficient. Authors should describe ethnic samples thoroughly in terms of all variables that may be relevant, such as social class, geographic region, and level of acculturation (Azibo, 1988), so that readers can determine the particular subgroups involved. It is important also to indicate how participants were assigned to an ethnic category, for example, on the basis of school records, appearance, last name, self-report, or some other means. In the case of self-report, the options given to respondents should be described, including whether the option "mixed" was included, and whether parental ethnicity was solicited and used in classification.

Ethnic categories are also necessary for making descriptive comparisons of societal indexes such as income, health status, mental disorders, and educational achievement. However, such comparisons can only serve as a starting point, with the recognition that these descriptions do not explain anything. The important question for psychologists is why the differences exist. To answer this question, we need more information on the variables that may explain variation among groups. The present article suggests that these differences can be found in the areas of culture, identity, and status in society.

Thus, an additional appropriate use of categories is as a basis for describing group differences along the dimensions of culture, identity, and status. Research is needed to identify precisely the cultural norms and values that distinguish ethnic groups, as well as differences related to a group's status in society and variations in response to such experiences. For example, there is considerable evidence that ethnic identity is stronger and more salient among African Americans than among other ethnic groups or among Whites (e.g., Phinney, Cantu, & Kurtz, in press); the basis for the strength and salience of this identity may lie in experiences associated with a group's status in society. For exploring such differences, comparisons can be made between minority and White groups and among minority groups.

In cases of group comparisons, all possible efforts should be made to match the groups being compared, to minimize confounding with the many demographic variables that covary with ethnicity. However, because of the many ways in which ethnic groups differ, groups can never be exactly matched. Thus, ethnicity cannot be treated like an independent variable that explains an outcome, and a comparison group cannot be a control group.

Therefore, the best way to control for ethnicity is to hold it constant, that is, to study processes within groups, rather than make comparisons across groups. Researchers should consider carefully which dimensions associated with ethnicity may be germane to their particular concerns and then assess them, in order to be able to link specific predictors to outcomes of interest within groups. As ethnic variables are described and linked to psychological processes, it becomes possible to consider to what extent the processes are similar or different across groups.

Finally, it is important to recognize that as in other areas of human functioning, ethnicity is far more complex than most of our models allow. The three dimensions that have been identified are likely to interact in complex ways that will challenge researchers and clinicians to develop more sophisticated models. For example, the particular form that one's ethnic identity takes is likely to reflect an interaction of cultural socialization, experience in society, the way one is perceived by others, and one's own construction of these experiences. Simple research designs are not adequate for studying such phenomena. There is need both for in-depth qualitative studies that can describe processes in detail and for large-scale multivariate studies that can include and examine a wide range of factors.

Conclusion

Although there is increasing recognition that ethnicity is a complex multidimensional construct, it continues to be treated in many cases as a categorical variable. For the study of ethnicity to progress, it is important to recognize that the psychological implications of ethnicity can be best understood in terms of clusters of dimensions: "Race [and] ethnicity. . . are dimensions, not categories, of human experience" (Goodchilds, 1991, p. 1). These dimensions clearly cluster together in ways that make ethnicity a highly salient and meaningful construct in American society. Yet the boundaries are blurred and flexible, and the implications of ethnicity vary widely across individuals.

Therefore, to explain outcomes that are influenced by ethnicity, we need to explore at least three dimensions of difference that vary within and across ethnic groups. First, cultural norms and attitudes that may be influential in psychological processes need to be identified and measured to determine the extent to which they covary with membership in a particular group or sample and have an impact on specific outcomes. Second, the strength, salience, and meaning of individuals' ethnic identities, that is, their sense of belonging to their group, need to be assessed as variables that may impact psychological outcomes. Third, individuals' experiences as members of a minority group with lower status and power need to be considered, together with the ways in which individuals respond to and deal with such experiences. As these dimensions are more clearly defined and studied within and across groups, we will begin to get a better comprehension of the role of ethnicity for psychology. Furthermore, a greater awareness that individuals vary along a number of

underlying human dimensions and cannot simply be categorized by group membership could help to break down stereotypes and contribute to understanding among all people.

References

American Psychological Association. (1994). *Publication manual of the American Psychological Association* (4th ed.). Washington, DC: Author.

Aries, E., & Moorehead, K. (1989). The importance of ethnicity in the development of identity of Black adolescents. *Psychological Reports. 65*, 75-82.

Azibo, D. (1988). Understanding the proper and improper usage of the comparative research framework. *Journal of Black Psychology: 15*, 81-91.

Bat-Chava, Y., & Steen. E. (1995). *Ethnic identity and self-esteem: A meta-analytic review:* Manuscript submitted for publication.

Bernal, M., & Knight, G. (Eds). (1993). *Ethnic identity: Formation and transmission among Hispanics and other minorities.* Albany: State University of New York Press.

Betancourt, H., & Lopez, S. (1993). The study of culture, ethnicity, and race in American psychology. *American Psychologist, 48*, 629-637.

Boykin, A.W., & Toms, F. (1985). Black child socialization: A conceptual framework. In H. McAdoo & McAdoo (Eds.), *Black children: Social, educational, and parental environments* (pp. 32-51). Newbury Park, CA: Sage.

Bronfenbrenner, U. (1986). Ecology of the family as a context for human development. *Developmental Psychology, 22*, 723-742.

Buriel, R. (1987). Ethnic labeling and identity among Mexican Americans. In J. Phinney & M. Rotheram (Eds.). *Children's ethnic socialization: Pluralism and development* (pp. 134-152). Newbury Park, CA: Sage.

Calhoun, C. (1993). Nationalism and ethnicity. *Annual Review of Sociology, 19*, 211-239.

Chung, L. (1991). Ethnic identity: A book review essay. *International Journal of Intercultural Relations, 15*, 491-500.

Crocker, J., Luhtanen, R., Blaine, B., & Broadnax, S. (1994). Collective self-esteem and psychological well-being among White, Black, and Asian college students. *Personality and Social Psychology Bulletin, 20*, 503-513.

Cross, W. (1991). *Shades of Black: Diversity in African-American identity.* Philadelphia: Temple University Press.

Deaux, K. (1992). Personalizing identity and socializing self. In G. Breakwell (Ed). *Social psychology of identity and the self concept* (pp. 9-33). San Diego. CA: Academic Press.

Ferdman, B. (1995). Cultural identity and diversity in organizations: Bridging the gap between group differences and individual uniqueness. In M. Chemers, S. Oskamp, & M. Costanzo (Eds.), *Diversity in organizations: New perspectives for a changing workplace* (pp. 37-61). Thousand Oaks, CA: Sage.

Fiske, S. (1993). Controlling other people: The impact of power on stereotyping. *American Psychologist,* 48, 621-628.

Gaines, S., Jr., & Reed, E. (1995). Prejudice from Allport to DuBois. *American Psychologist,* 50, 96-103.

Gibbs, J. & Juang, L. (1989). *Children of color: psychological interventions with minority youth.* San Francisco: Jossey-Bass.

Goodchilds, J. (Ed.). (1991). *Psychological perspectives on human diversity in America.* Washington, DC: American Psychological Association.

Graham, S. (1992). Most of the subjects were White and middle class: Trends in published research on African Americans in selected APA journals, 1970-1989. *American Psychologist,* 47, 629-639.

Greenfield, P., & Cocking, R. (1994). *Cross-cultural roots of minority child development.* Hillsdale, NJ Erlbaum.

Gurin, P., Hurtado, A., & Peng. T. (1994). Group contacts and ethnicity in the social identities of Mexicanos and Chicanos. *Personality and Social Psychology Bulletin,* 20, 521-532.

Harrison, A., Wilson, M., Pine, C., Chan, S., & Buriel, R. (1990). Family ecologies of ethnic minority children. *Child Development,* 61, 347-362.

Helms, J. (1990). *Black and White racial identity: Theory, research, and practice.* New York: Greenwood.

Hofstede, G. (1980*).   Culture's consequences; International differences in work-related values.* Beverly Hills, CA: Sage.

Huddy, L., & Virtanen, S. (1995). Subgroup differentiation and subgroup bias among Latinos as a function of familiarity and positive distinctiveness. *Journal of Personality and Social Psychology,* 68, 97-108.

Jones, J. (1991). Psychological models of race: What have they been and what should they be? In. J. Goodchilds (Ed.). *Psychological perspectives on human diversity in America* (pp. 3-46). Washington, DC: American Psychological Association.

Keefe, S. (1992). Ethnic identity: The domain of perceptions of and attachment to ethnic groups and cultures. *Human Organizations,* 51, 35-43.

Keefe, S., & Padilla, A. (1987). *Chicano ethnicity*: Albuquerque: University of New Mexico Press.

Larkey, L., Hecht, M., & Martin, J. (1993). What's in a name? African American ethnic identity terms and self-determination. *Journal of Language and Social Psychology,* 12, 302-317.

Marin, G., & Marin, B. (1991). *Research with Hispanic populations.* Newbury Park, CA: Sage.

Markus, H., Kitayama, S. (1991). Culture and the self: Implications for cognition, emotion, and motivation. *Psychological Review,* 98, 224-253.

McAdoo, H. (Ed.) (1993). *Family ethnicity: Strength in diversity.* Thousand Oaks, CA: Sage.

McGoldrick, M., Pearce, J., & Giordano, J. (Eds). (1992). *Ethnicity and family therapy.* New York: Guilford Press.

Mindel, C., & Habenstein, P. (1988). *Ethnic families in America: Patterns and variations* (3rd ed.). New York: Elsevier.

Parham, T. (1989). Cycles of psychological Nigrescence. *The Counseling Psychologist,* 17, 187-226.

Pavel, D., Sanchez, T., & Machamer, A. (1994). Ethnic fraud. Native peoples, and higher education. *Thought and Action,* 10, 91-100.

Phinney, J. (1989). Stages of ethnic identity development in minority group adolescents. *Journal of Early Adolescence,* 9, 34-49.

Phinney, J. (1990). Ethnic identity in adolescents and adults: A review of research. *Psychological Bulletin,* 108, 499-514.

Phinney, J. (1993). A three-stage model of ethnic identity development. In M. Bernal & G. Knight (Eds.). *Ethnic identity: Formation and transmission among Hispanics and other minorities* (pp. 61-79). Albany: State University of New York Press.

Phinney, J. (1995). Ethnic identity and self-esteem: A review and integration. In A. Padilla (Ed.) *Hispanic psychology: Critical issues in theory and research* (pp. 57-70). Thousand Oaks, CA: Sage.

Phinney, J., & Alpuria, L. (1990). Ethnic identity in college students from four ethnic groups. *Journal of Adolescence,* 13, 171-184.

Phinney, J., & Alipuria, L. (1996). At the interface of culture: Multiethnic/multiracial high school and college students. *Journal of Social Psychology,* 136, 139-158.

Phinney, J., Cantu, C., & Kurtz, D. (in press). Ethnic and American identity as predictors of self-esteem among African American, Latino, and White adolescents. *Journal of Youth and Adolescence.*

Phinney, J., & Devich-Navarro, M. (in press). Variations in bicultural identification among African American and Mexican American adolescents. *Journal of Research on Adolescence.*

Phinney, J., & Kohatsu, E. (in press). Ethnic and racial identity and mental health. In J. Schulenberg, J. Maggs, & K. Hurrelman (Eds.), *Health risks and developmental transitions during adolescence.* New York: Cambridge University Press.

Phinney, J., & Landin, J. (in press). Research paradigms for studying ethnic minority families within and across groups. In V. McLoyd & L. Steinberg (Eds.). *Research on minority adolescents: Conceptual, methodological, and theoretical issues.* Hillsdale, NJ: Erlbaum.

Phinney, J., Santos, L., & Madden, T. (1996, August). *Individual differences in perceived discrimination among minority and immigrant adolescents.* Paper presented at the meeting of the International Society for the Study of Behavioral Development. Quebec, Canada.

Poortinga, Y., van de Vijver, F., Joe, R., & van de Koppel, J. (1989). Peeling the onion called culture: A synopsis. In C. Kagitcibasi (Ed.). *Growth and progress in cross-cultural psychology* (pp. 22-34). Berwyn. PA: Swets North American.

Porter, J., & Washington, R. (1993). Minority identity and self-esteem. *Annual Review of Sociology*, 19, 139-161.

Reid, P. (1994, August). *Gender and class identities: African Americans in context.* Paper presented at the American Psychological Association Annual Convention, Los Angeles.

Rogler, L., & Malgady, R. (1991). Acculturation and mental health status among Hispanics: Convergence and new directions for research. *American Psychologist*, 46, 585-597.

Roosens, E. (1989). *Creating ethnicity: The process of ethnogenesis.* Thousand Oaks, CA: Sage.

Root, M. (1992). *Racially mixed people in America.* Newbury Park, CA: Sage.

Schwartz, S., & Bilsky, W. (1990). Toward a theory of the universal content and structure of values: Extensions and cross-cultural replications. *Journal of Personality and Social Psychology*, 58, 878-891.

Steele, C. (1992, April). Race and the schooling of Black Americans. *The Atlantic Monthly*, pp. 68-78.

Steele, C., & Aronson, J. (1995) Stereotype threat and the intellectual test performance of African Americans. *Journal of Personality and Social Psychology*, 69, 797-811.

Sue, S. (1991). Ethnicity and culture and psychological research and practice. In J. Goodchilds (Ed.), *Psychological perspectives on human diversity in America* (pp. 51-85). Washington, DC: American Psychological Association.

Szapocznik, J., & Kurtines, W. (1993). Family psychology and cultural diversity. *American Psychologist*, 48, 400-407.

Triandis, H. (1990). *Cross-cultural studies of individualism and collectivism.* In J. Berman (Ed.). Nebraska Symposium on Motivation: Vol. 37. Cross-cultural perspectives (pp. 41-133). Lincoln: University of Nebraska Press.

Triandis, H., Marin, G., Lisansky, J., & Betancourt, H. (1984). Simpatia as a cultural script of Hispanics. *Journal of Personality and Social Psychology*, 47, 1363-1375.

Uba, L. (1994). *Asian Americans: Personality patterns, identity and mental health.* New York: Guilford Press.

Vega, W. (1992). Theoretical and pragmatic implications of cultural diversity for community research. *American Journal of Community Psychology*, 23, 375-391.

Vega, W., & Rumbaut, R. (1991). Ethnic minorities and mental health. *Annual Review of Sociology*, 17, 351-383.

Waters, M. (1990). *Ethnic options: Choosing identities in America.* Berkeley: University of California Press.

Waters, M., & Eschbach, K. (1995). Immigration and ethnic and racial inequality in the United States. *Annual Review of Sociology*, 21, 419-446.

Whiting, B. (1976). The problem of the packaged variable. In K. Riegel & J. Meacham (Eds.). *The developing individual in a changing world* (pp. 303-309). Chicago: Aldine.

Wilkinson, D., & King, G. (1987). Conceptual and methodological issues in the use of race as a variable: Policy implications. *The Milbank Quarterly*, 65, 56-71.

Williams, R. (1994). The sociology of ethnic conflicts: Comparative international perspectives. *Annual Review of Sociology*, 20, 49-79.

Yee, A., Fairchild, H., Weizmann, F., & Wyatt, G. (1993). Addressing psychology's problems with race. *American Psychologist*, 48, 1132-1140.

Yinger, J. (1985). Ethnicity. *Annual Review of Sociology*, 11, 151-180.

Zuckerman, M. (1990). Some dubious premises in research and theory on racial differences. *American Psychologist*, 45, 1297-1303.

Commentary: Sorry, Wrong Number—A Reply To Gentile's Call

Kay Deaux

> **Editors' Note:** In psychological research, there is an ongoing debate about when it is appropriate to use the terms "sex" or "gender." In the following commentary, Kay Deaux weighs in on this debate, discussing her strategies for determining when and why she has used each term in her extensive research in the field. Why is this debate important? As Deaux points out, the terms used in studying behaviors can contain assumptions about their causes. Her article underscores a fundamental issue in scientific research—the importance of the clarity of terminology.

Gentile (1993) calls for a new terminological standard for the use of the terms sex and gender, suggesting that current usage is inconsistent, confusing, and scientifically uninformative. . . .

My own preference, first stated in 1985, is to use sex when one is referring to any study or finding in which people are selected on the basis of the demographic categories of male and female. Thus, if one compares women with men, girls with boys, or male with female rats, one is making a sex comparison.[1] However, I advocate the use of gender when one is making judgments or inferences about the nature of femaleness and maleness, of masculinity and femininity. Thus, I argue for terms such as gender identity, gender stereotypes, and gender roles. Unger (1979) made a similar distinction in discussing differences between sex as a subject variable and as a stimulus variable. As she noted, "Gender may be used for those traits for which sex acts as a stimulus variable, independently of whether those traits have their origin with the subject or not" (1979, p. 1086).

Neither of these analyses presupposes the origins of any observed similarities or differences. For many people, however, the sex-versus-gender debate does connote causal assumptions. Thus, some would restrict the term sex to those behaviors that are biologically determined, and gender to those that are societally influenced.[2] This desire to identify causal factors also motivates Gentile to offer his resolution. Whatever appeal such a state of certainty may have, it is fundamentally unattainable. . . .

Science is a dynamic process, and the certainty of yesterday can easily be replaced by ambiguity today, or vice versa. In Gentile's scheme, such shifts in understanding would require changes in terminology. Thus, the biologically sex-linked behavior of one decade could be the gender-linked behavior of another, and the sex- and gender-linked behavior of yet another period. Or consider the case in which a difference thought to be biologically determined is modified by training (e.g., Conner, Schackman, & Serbin, 1978). Should such a pattern be called a biologically linked difference before training and a gender-linked similarity after training?

I believe there is some value in using a term such as sex-correlated or sex-related (as distinct from sex-linked, which as Gentile shows is defined by the *Oxford English Dictionary* in terms of chromosomes). As an alternative to the term sex differences, the use of the term sex-related, as well as such conceptually similar terms as age-related, should signal the reader that sex is being used as a marker rather than a causal statement. Scientific caution would thus prevail over deterministic theories. The field of sex and gender has had more than its share of simplistic and wrongheaded assumptions over the past 100 years (e.g., Shields, 1975, 1982). Arguing for specific terminology on an assumption of scientific certainty risks adding to the record of misguided pronouncements.

Footnotes

[1] This distinction ignores, but does not preclude the existence of, individuals whose sex categorization is more ambiguous.

[2] A similar debate is possible with regard to the use of race versus ethnicity. Again, these terms have often been used interchangeably although there is some tendency to use race when biological factors are implicated, and ethnicity when socialization is the dominant explanation (P. T. Reid, personal communication, September 23, 1992).

References

Conner, J. M., Schackman, M., & Serbin, L. A. (1978). Sex-related differences in response to practice on a visual-spatial test and generalization to a related test. Child Development, 49, 24-29.

Shields, S. A. (1975). Functionalism, Darwinism, and the psychology of women: A study in social myth. American Psychologist, 30, 739-754.

Unger, R. K. (1979). Toward a redefinition of sex and gender. American Psychologist, 34, 1085-1094.

Keeping Sex Differences In Perspective

P. J. Caplan and J. B. Caplan

Editors' Note: Although science appears to be objective, it, like all human endeavors, is susceptible to many biases. Bias can intrude at any point in the scientific enterprise. It can influence which questions are asked or not asked. It can also color the conclusions that are drawn from the data that is gathered by researchers. Paula and Jeremy Caplan draw our attention to a few of these biases, and they go on to warn us to guard against the unthinking acceptance of scientific findings as "truth." The application of the critical thinking skills that the Caplans offer will help you better evaluate the research presented in this Workbook and to aid you in formulating the questions you have about it.

When we study the research on sex differences, we can get so absorbed in thinking about the details of the studies that we lose sight of the larger perspective. Part of the larger perspective that we need to keep in mind is that, since each scientist will be able to explore only a limited number of research questions, there must be a reason that some choose to spend their lives trying to find sex and gender differences.

Since most "proof" of differences between groups is usually used to "prove" that one group is *better than* the other, and scientists are aware of this, we need to ask what motivates them to pursue such research. A few hope to prove that there are fewer sex differences than people thought there were; many, however, seem to be intent on justifying the treatment of females as inferior in terms of being, for instance, less intelligent, "overly emotional," or more dependent than males. Scientists who try to prove that there are important differences between members of different *races* are usually recognized, these days, as racist, but those who try to prove that there are important sex differences are not usually recognized as sexist.

Another part of the perspective that we need to maintain involves a clear view of *which* research questions become the focus of the greatest amount of research. For example, although early sex-difference researchers reported that females were superior to males in various verbal abilities (e.g., learning to speak at younger ages, developing greater vocabularies) and that males were superior to females in spatial abilities, *most* of the research effort has gone into work on spatial abilities. So has most of the attention from the media. The research effort has included trying to document how great the male superiority is and developing theories to explain why males are so superior in this regard. If we become caught up in exploring the details of the spatial abilities research, we fall into the trap of *assuming* that males are superior, forgetting that there is also evidence that females are superior to males. The goal should not be to reverse the pattern and focus on areas where females outperform males; rather, it should be to take care not to let our beliefs be shaped by the research topics that receive the most attention from scientists and from the media reports about them.

We do not claim that there are definitely no sex differences in humans' behavior. What we do believe is that, since so much of the research is deeply flawed, and since males and females have nowhere been treated identically from birth, it is virtually impossible to know what inevitable sex differences there might be. And if it seems to you, . . . that most sex-difference research is riddled with problems, you are right. This is partly because of the difficulty of studying human behavior, which is so variable and complex, and partly because of researchers' biases and failures to plan their studies as carefully as they might.

We do not believe that most or all sex-difference researchers have consciously and purposely set out to do research that is harmful or demeaning to one sex or the other. We do believe, however, that it is hard, if not impossible, for any of us to be aware of all our biases and unquestioned assumptions, and those of us who do research will bring those factors into our research, like it or not. We are all products of our time and culture. . . .

A word of warning is in order. Some students have been accustomed to believing that scientists and teachers are always right, and they sometimes find it upsetting to be shown that the so-called experts have often made significant mistakes, unintentional as they may have been. It can feel like the rug of certainty pulled from under us when we start to question what we read or what we are taught. To be sure, we cannot promise to give you new, absolute truths to replace some of the certainty you may lose, but we believe that it is important to know when what we thought was absolute truth is only partial or even nonexistent. Better, we feel, to know the limits of our knowledge than to believe we know more than we actually do.

Furthermore, developing critical thinking skills does *not* leave you with nothing. Instead, it leaves you with a wealth of important abilities which enable you to grapple with research in an active way. And by approaching research with an active mind, you will be in a good position to see which research *is* reasonably done and which researchers try to identify and freely acknowledge their own biases.

When we encounter experimental errors, we should not be surprised; after all, we cannot know anything in this world with absolute certainty. Naturally, error should be minimized, but we can go only so far. The important thing for researchers is to be as accurate as possible but to make sure the conclusions that they draw do not go beyond what the study's method and results, combined with the experimenters' biases, really show. . . .

"Most Of The Subjects Were White And Middle Class" Trends In Published Research On African Americans In Selected APA Journals, 1970-1989

Sandra Graham

𝓔ditors' Note: Psychology, as a discipline, should engage the concerns of all groups. And, if it is to make claims about the general nature of psychological functioning, its research must include participants from every segment of the population in its studies. In this article, Sandra Graham examines the representation of African-Americans in psychological research over time. Her findings are not encouraging. As you read this Workbook, consider the issues raised by Graham by taking note of whether or not the studies you read are more inclusive than those she examined. Also, think about ways in which all the studies you are exposed to could be more inclusive.

Six APA journals (Developmental Psychology, Journal of Applied Psychology, Journal of Consulting and Clinical Psychology, Journal of Counseling Psychology, Journal of Educational Psychology, *and* Journal of Personality and Social Psychology) *were content analyzed for the presence of empirical articles on African Americans during the 1970-1989 publication period. The analysis revealed a declining representation of African-American research in the six journals. In addition, the empirical literature that does exist was found to be lacking in methodological rigor, as defined by characteristics such as the reporting of the socioeconomic status of subjects and experimenter race. Explanations for the decline were suggested, and recommendations were proposed for alleviating the growing marginalization of African-American research in the journals of mainstream psychology.*

With regard to the study of African Americans, academic psychologists face serious challenges as the 1990s unfold. This is a time when social concerns demand increased understanding of the psychological functioning of Black Americans, and pedagogical needs call for cultural diversity in our academic curricula. As difficult and complex as these challenges are, they are not likely to be met without a strong empirical literature on African Americans from which psychologists can draw. It therefore seems appropriate to stop and take stock of the status of African-American research in the journals of mainstream psychology.

In this article, I will argue that there has been a growing exclusion of research on African Americans in some of the major journals of our discipline, and this has resulted in a shrinking empirical base from which to pursue the challenges stated above. Just as mainstream psychology was once accused of being "womanless" (see Crawford & Marecek, 1989), so too in the 1990s it is in danger of becoming "raceless." This state of affairs has serious intellectual and pedagogical implications for the discipline that have not, in my judgment, been adequately acknowledged.

To document the status of African-American research in mainstream psychology, I conducted a content analysis of six American Psychological Association (APA) journals for the presence of empirical articles on African-Americans. . . . Although skeptics may question whether empirical journals are the best indicator of a discipline's intellectual focus, there can be little doubt that these journals depict the current zeitgeist, mirror the scholarly interests of our academic leadership, and disseminate the products of what funding agencies deem worthy of support.

It could be argued, of course, that basic research journals concerned with so-called universal principles of human behavior might be less likely to publish research on African Americans than those oriented more toward application. To examine this possibility and to ensure a broader sampling of journals, two APA publications with a more applied research focus were included in the analysis. . . .

The representation of research on African Americans in the six APA journals was explored in two ways. The journals were first examined for the presence of studies on African-American subjects, and total counts were tabulated. Because my interest was in publication *trends,* as well as the current status of research, the journals were examined over a 20-year period beginning in 1970. This appeared to be a reasonable starting point inasmuch as the social unrest of the 1960s stimulated psychologists to turn their attention toward the study of socially relevant topics, particularly ethnic minority groups (see Caplan & Nelson, 1973).

Next, studies on African Americans were further examined for specific content and for selected methodological features that are pertinent to empirical research on Blacks, yet general enough for an analysis covering the range of journals and topics of psychology sampled here. Specifically, I was interested in how many studies were conducted within a comparative racial framework and whether or not socioeconomic status (SES) of subjects and race of experimenter (E; examiner; therapist) were reported. . . . In sum, the two broad goals of the journal content analysis were based on the belief that understanding the status of African-American research in mainstream psychology involves issues of both quantity (e.g., How large is the literature?) and quality (e.g., How can we ascertain its relative merit?).

Before launching into the specifics of the analysis, it might be useful to anchor our expectations about quantity by considering what would constitute an adequate representation of research on African Americans in APA journals. More specifically, if one were to calculate the percentage of African-American articles relative to the total empirical output of the six target journals during the past 20 years, within what range of values would this percentage be expected to fall? Perhaps the best source of information for answering this question can be found in the results of prior journal content analyses on this topic. . . . Extrapolating from data reported by J. M. Jones (1983), roughly 5% of the articles published in *JPSP* between 1968 and 1980 were race relevant. About the same percentages emerge for research on African-American children in *DP* and *JEP* during the 1973-1975 time period (McLoyd & Randolph, 1984). Similarly, Ponterotto (1988) reported that close to 6% of the articles in *JCP* deal with ethnic minority research, with African American being the most frequently studied

ethnic group. Thus we are guided by prior quantitative summaries of trend in published research, we might expect at least 5% of the articles published in four of the six target journals to be about African Americans.

This estimate assumes that there have been no discernible changes in publication trends in recent years One might ask, however, whether the representation of African Americans in mainstream psychology has increased, decreased, or remained relatively constant over the past decade or so. The 20-year time period over which the journals were examined allowed this question to be explored.

Method

The data for this study consisted of the empirical article published in *Developmental Psychology, Journal of Applied Psychology, Journal of Consulting and Clinical Psychology, Journal of Counseling Psychology, Journal of Educational Psychology,* and *Journal of Personality and Social Psychology* between 1970 and 1989. . . . Because the goal of this article was to examine research specifically *about* African Americans, two additional selection criteria were imposed. First, empirical articles that addressed race-relevant issues (i.e., prejudice stereotyping) were discounted if the subjects were not African American. Thus, for example, a number of articles on the racial attitudes of Whites toward Blacks, published largely in *JPSP* during the time period under review, were not included in the total count. Although one could certainly argue that studies of racial attitudes and prejudice are pertinent to understanding the psychological functioning of African Americans, they were deemed less central to this analysis, which focused on the subjective experiences of Black research participants. Second, articles that included African Americans as subjects were not counted unless (a) the researchers specifically stated that Blacks were the population of interest or (b) the data were analyzed by race. . . .

To identify those articles that fit these criteria, I read the titles and abstracts and scanned the method sections of all empirical articles published in the six journals during the

20 years under review. Articles about African Americans, identified on the basis of these criteria, were then retrieved, read in detail, and coded for content (topics covered) as well as for selected methodological characteristics (number of comparative racial studies, SES of subjects, and experimenter race). . . .

Results and Discussion

A total of 14,542 empirical articles were published in the six target journals between 1970 and 1989. With 12 issues a year; *JPSP* produced the greatest number of articles (4,037), followed by *JCCP* (2,946) and *DP* (2,399), the two bimonthly publications. The three remaining journals began as bimonthlies but became quarterly publications in the mid-1980s and therefore accounted for the fewest empirical articles: *JAP* (1,810), *JEP* (1,768), and *JCP* (1,582).[1]

. . . 526 articles on African Americans were published between 1970 and 1989, or 3.6% of these journals' entire empirical output. This is not altogether surprising, in light of the less conservatively based estimates in the range of 5% inferred from the earlier journal content analyses by J. M. Jones (1983), McLoyd and Randolph (1984), and Ponterotto (1988). It nonetheless remains disheartening to uncover such a poor representation of studies on African Americans across this range of APA journals and particular time period sampled.

Rise and Fall of Research on African Americans

It has been documented that the overall percentage of studies on African Americans is low (3.6%). But how has this percentage fluctuated during the past 20 years, both within and across journals? . . . Most striking is the steady decrease in both the number and percentage of African-American articles across the four publication periods: from 203 articles (5.2%) in 1970-1974 to 65 articles (2.0%) in 1985-1989. Furthermore, this pattern of decline is evident in all of the target journals except *JCP,* in which there appeared to be some recovery by the fourth publication period. . . .

This trend is perhaps more clearly illustrated in Figure 1, which displays the number of African-American articles in each of the 20 years between 1970 and 1989, combined over all six journals. (The same trend is exhibited when the numbers are expressed as percentages.) Figure 1 reveals a linear increase from 1970 to 1974, the year in which the greatest number (49) and percentage (5.5%) of articles were published. Thereafter these numbers and percentages steadily drop. In 1989 the six journals combined published only 11 articles (1.8%) on African Americans. . . .

Having documented the declining status of published research on African Americans, relative to the total empirical output in six target APA journals, I will now attend to the 526 articles that compose this African American empirical literature. . . .

Figure 1:   Number of African-American Articles as a Function of Publication Year, Combined Across Six APA Journals

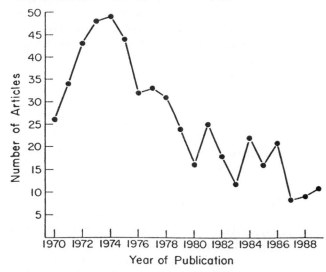

African-American Empirical Literature: Topics Covered

Among the six journals sampled, *Journal of Applied Psychology* and *Journal of Counseling Psychology* were the most specialized and therefore published articles specific to particular topical domains. Most of the 77 African-American articles in *JAP* were concerned with job training and performance (26%); occupational and vocational attitudes (21%); test bias, particularly in instruments for employment selection (17%); or leadership and managerial styles (9%). These topics are consistent with the general emphasis in *JAP* on organizational behavior. With its focus on the practice of counseling, *JCP* published 75 African-American empirical articles that dealt primarily with counselor characteristics, such as their perceived trustworthiness (35%), vocational aspirations (16%), evaluations of counseling interventions (16%), or general attitudes toward counseling (9%). . . .

[S]ome topics appeared to be specific to particular journals. For example, African-American research on infant development was published only in *DP*, academic achievement and teacher-student interaction were topics of interest mostly to *JEP*, and studies involving clinical diagnosis or treatment of African Americans were logically the purview of *JCCP*. Within the more general topics of psychology, the most popular domains of inquiry and those represented in all of the journals, have been social behavior, particularly aggression and interracial cooperation and competition; intelligence, as assessed by standardized measures of IQ; and personality, largely studied as individual differences in locus of control, self esteem, and psychopathology. . . .

Methodological Factors

How have these topics been studied in the 526 articles sampled across six APA journals? In terms of subject population, empirical studies of African Americans are typically one of two types: A psychological variable such as intelligence might be examined among Black subjects only. Thus, for example, Moore (1986) examined IQ (WISC) performance of young African-American children who had been either traditionally or transracially adopted. Such studies are labeled *intrasubcultural* by J. M. Jones (1983) and *race homogeneous* by McLoyd and Randolph (1984, 1985). Alternatively, Black subjects can be contrasted on the relevant variable with one or more other racial groups, typically Whites. Reynolds and Jensen (1983), for example, compared the subscale scores of African-American and White school-aged children on the revised WISC. This type of investigation has been classified as *cross subcultural* by J. M. Jones (1983) and *race*

comparative by McLoyd and Randolph (1984, 1985).

. . . [This study examined] the number and percentage of African-American articles in each journal that were race comparative. Note that in all cases comparative investigations predominated, and in four of the six journals, there were about three times as many race-comparative as race-homogeneous studies.

Much criticism has been voiced about this comparative approach. Quite a few years ago, Donald Campbell (1967) warned psychologists about the risks of ethnic stereotyping, if the field were to become inundated with racial comparisons. And a number of African-American psychologists have been particularly critical of the scientific basis of a comparative racial paradigm that both reinforces interpretations of African-American behavior as deviant and ignores within-group variation (e.g., Azibo, 1988). . . .

Socioeconomic status of subjects. Because African Americans are overrepresented among economically disadvantaged groups in this society, researchers who make Black-White comparisons need to incorporate SES in their designs in order to disentangle race and social class effects. Furthermore, with the growing gap between the affluent and the impoverished within the population American Blacks, it is just as important that race-homogeneous studies not err in the direction of ignoring socioeconomic distinctions between African-America subjects. Despite these obvious (and oft-stated) potential confoundings, empirical studies involving African Americans have remained remarkably insensitive to the complexities of race and social class in this society. It is evident that this is true for research published in APA journals as well. . . . These findings show the number and percentage studies (race homogeneous and race comparative) in the six target journals that included a measure of subject SES. Acceptable measures included not only the standard social class indices (e.g., Hollingshead, Warner, and Duncan scales), but also indirect measures such as census data information contained in school records, or participation in a compensatory education program, such as Headstart. . . .

[F]ewer than one half of the African-American articles appearing in *DP, JEP, JAP,* and *JCP* and fewer than one third of those in

JCCP and *JPSP*, specified SES of participants in an acceptable manner. . . .

There is nothing ambiguous about this pattern of findings: Race and social class have been seriously confounded in much of the African-American empirical literature published in prestigious APA journals.

Experimenter race. Yet another important methodological concern in this literature is the race of the experimenter (examiner; interviewer; therapist). By experimenter I mean the individual who actually participates in data collection, as opposed to a study's authors, whose racial identity cannot ordinarily be ascertained from the information accompanying a published article. Are these studies telling us whether African-American subjects were tested by Black or White experimenters? . . . In terms of percentages, *JPSP* and *JCP* fared somewhat better than did the other journals in this category; a number of *JPSP*'s comparative racial articles were studies of race-of-examiner effects, as were *JCP*'s studies on race of counselor. But in none of the journals did even one half of the studies mention experimenter race. . . .

Failure to take into account experimenter race is certainly an issue, whether an article is race homogeneous or race comparative. The problem is not so much that White experimenters have well-documented negative effects on African-American subjects. In fact, two reviews indicate that White experimenters do *not* negatively influence Black subjects' intellectual performance, the domain in which most of the criticism of White experimenters and examiners has been voiced (Graziano, Varca, & Levy, 1982; Sattler & Gwynne, 1982). The crux of the problem is really the unknown—given the range of experimental contexts, some novel but some frankly threatening—to which African-American subjects have been exposed. In the absence of careful controls on race of E, we simply do not know what effect a White experimenter has on an African-American child who is required, for example, to read a passage in perfect Standard English, choose between a Black and a White doll, solve a puzzle in the wake of induced failure, or realistically estimate the likelihood of going to college. . . .

General Discussion

African Americans have been increasingly marginalized in mainstream psychological research, as methodologically sound empirical articles on Blacks have all but vanished from the pages of major APA journals. This trend prevailed across six diverse journals, with both basic and applied research foci and over numerous individual editorships. Thus no single journal or editorial tenure can be singled out as particularly blameworthy. Why has this literature undergone such a steady decline since the early 1970s? Five possible explanations are offered, although in my view the first two are less plausible than the last three.

1. *Diminishing pool of African-American psychologists.* Psychologists often choose research topics based on their own life experiences or personal concerns. Hence, the volume of the research on African Americans might be expected to covary to some degree with the number of same-race investigators. If the number of Black doctoral psychologists has been declining over the past two decades, as popular wisdom seems to suggest, then it logically follows that the empirical fruits of their collective efforts would similarly decline. One flaw in this argument is that the recent past has *not* produced such a diminished pool of African-American doctoral psychologists. According to data compiled by APA (Kohout & Pion, 1990), during the 1977-1987 decade, the percentage of doctorates psychology earned by African Americans remained relatively constant. In 1977, 95 (3.5%) of the new PhDs psychology were Black, and in 1987 there were 92 (3.4%) such new graduates.[2]

Presently, of course, the waning enrollment of African-American students in all levels of higher education is well documented (see Thomas, 1987). This declining participation in the educational pipeline represents the *current* state of affairs and portends poorly for the future. But it cannot be considered a very plausible explanation for the 1970-1989 trends discussed earlier.

2. *Preference for non-APA journals.* As journals have arisen that more directly address issues pertinent to African-American psychology, these specialized publications might be viewed as more receptive and thus

preferred over the mainstream APA alternatives. If this argument is correct, then one might expect to find a growing empirical focus in, for example, *Journal of Black Psychology,* the publication arm of the Association of Black psychologists. The journal, which began in 1974, states that one of its primary goals is "to promote psychological research, theory, and writing that is for and about blacks." Yet, only two issues a year are published, each consisting of from three to five articles. Furthermore, because the journal must serve so many functions, this small sampling of articles includes not only empirical investigations, but also literature reviews, theoretical analyses, and position papers as well. During the past 10 years, a total of 35 empirical articles appeared in the *Journal of Black Psychology.* Thus the overall number of empirical articles found in this journal is now, and always has been, relatively small.

Perhaps other mainstream journals examined in previous content analyses are perceived as more receptive. J. M. Jones (1983) reported that *Journal of Social Psychology (JSP)* had published the most race-relevant articles of the seven social psychology journals included in this analysis. To get a sense of whether this is still true, I scanned the titles and in some cases read abstracts of the empirical articles published in *JSP* over the last five years (1985-1989). Although the journal continues to have a strong crosscultural focus, I identified only 13 articles, or 3.7%, that specifically were concerned with African Americans. Similarly with *Child Development,* the non-APA journal analyzed by McLoyd and Randolph (1985), scanning the titles and abstracts for the same publication period revealed 10 African-American articles, or 1.6% of that journal's total. In sum, African-American research does not appear to have found a more receptive audience in other mainstream journals. My sense is that one has to turn to the more specialized publications with an interdisciplinary focus, such as *Journal of Black Studies,* to find an adequate representation of empirical work on the psychological functioning of African Americans. Needless to say, such journals do not have the readership or the visibility of the more mainstream variety.

3. *Fears associated with conducting socially sensitive research.* There are ethical and moral risks associated with studying the psychological functioning of African Americans. Many researchers are drawn to this topic out of concern for the social problems associated with ethnic minority status in this society. Thus, for example, one may investigate intelligence because of the chronic school failure of many African-American children; aggression due to the higher incidence of violent crimes among urban Black males; helping behavior; given the negative consequences associated with welfare dependency; and so on. Often the study of such phenomena leads to unpopular findings or, even worse, to accusations of "victim blame" (Caplan & Nelson, 1973; Ryan, 1971). Many committed researchers may be unwilling to risk the kind of reprisal leveled against Jensen (1969), for example, following the publication of his monograph on racial differences in IQ. They may instead opt for the safer alternative of scientifically acceptable, but socially noncontroversial, research topics (see Scarr, 1988; Sieber & Stanley, 1988). More often than not, such choices will foster the decision to avoid or abandon the study of African Americans.

4. *Bandwagon effects.* Over the years, some psychological topics pertinent to African Americans have been subject to "bandwagon" effects (cf. E. E. Jones, 1985). By this I mean the tendency for particular issues to rapidly emerge as timely, to dominate an empirical literature for some period, and to just as quickly fade from view. For example, the study of language in the developmental and educational journals largely grew from the attention surrounding the use of the Black English Vernacular (BEV). During the early 1970s, a flurry of research studies were conducted to explore whether economically disadvantaged African-American children actually spoke a language that was structurally different from Standard English (Labov, 1972). The study of the BEV also became the rallying cry for psychologists' recognition of the "differences versus deficits" and "performance versus competence" distinctions (e.g., Baratz & Baratz, 1970; Cole & Bruner; 1971). But once these distinctions became part of the conventional wisdom of psychology, and without a strong theoretical

basis for conducting the research, studies of the Black English Vernacular faded from the scene.

5. *Changes in the zeitgeist.* As reflected in their journals, the intellectual foci of the subdisciplines of psychology examined here have shifted to topics less relevant to the study of Black Americans. In recent years, developmental psychology's adoption of life-span perspectives has yielded more articles in *DP* on populations at both ends of the life cycle, but this conceptual shift has yet to embrace published research on African-American infants and older adults. Similarly, educational psychology's concern with sociocultural influences on achievement has narrowed of late, with the growing emphasis in *JEP* on the psychology of subject matter.

Perhaps the clearest example of shifts in dominant research themes that undermine the study of African Americans has occurred in social psychology. As social psychology has become increasingly cognitive, the traditional concerns of the discipline—that is, the social influences on psychological functioning—have gradually been displaced. Even a cursory glance at the titles in the Attitudes and Social Cognition section of *JPSP* reveals an increasing emphasis on information-processing metaphors in social psychology that rely on principles and methodologies borrowed from cognitive psychology. For some this may signal progress in the field; others may lament a perceived loss of identity (e.g., Carlson, 1984). But it is clear that as the intellectual focus of the subdiscipline has become the effect of priming, reaction time, or other indicators of process, the traditionally social psychological issues pertinent to the study of African Americans have receded from view. Of course, this need not (and should not) be the case. But academic psychologists in social psychology, as well as those in the other subdisciplines of the field, appear to implicitly assume that the study of basic process transcends the need to examine within- or between-group variation.

Independent of one's preferred causal explanation, the trends documented in this article do not bode well for mainstream psychology in the 1990s. Whether personal research agendas are affected by the demise of an African-American literature, as academic psychologists most of us will have to confront

this issue, if for no reason other than the vociferous demands for greater diversity in the undergraduate curriculum. Diversifying the psychology curriculum is interpreted to mean more than the creation of courses for and about ethnic minorities, including African Americans. Substantive changes are also demanded in the discipline's core programs of study to eradicate what often amounts to mere token reference to the psychological functioning of these groups. Yet how will we be able to meet these challenges in the absence of a strong empirical base of research on ethnic minorities from which we can confidently draw? How will we be able to avoid oversimplifying complex topics, citing outdated findings, or perpetuating incorrect beliefs if a relevant database remains so unfamiliar and inaccessible? As an African-American psychologist, I find it disconcerting, for example, to hear and read so often in the popular press that Black children have a unique learning style or that they prefer cooperation to competition, when the empirical evidence supporting these conclusions is so thin. What we need from our major journals is a substantive African-American psychological literature that is both accurate and current. What we have instead are sets of isolated and outdated findings, often of questionable methodological soundness.

What Can Be Done?

Steps must be taken to rectify this perilous state of affairs. Much of what is needed will require major shifts in priorities of the research enterprise, such as greater access to training opportunities for minority scholars, enhanced funding initiatives for minority research, and more sensitivity to the diversity of paths that scholarship can follow, given the enormous complexity underlying the psychological study of ethnic minority populations. Rather than tackle these broad issues, I wish to remain closer to the focus of this article and conclude with some specific recommendations to those who regulate the dissemination of knowledge in APA journals.

First, some of the methodological problems noted for published research on African Americans might be corrected if editors required authors to report complete descriptions of method. These more detailed accounts should then enter into the publication decision. *Any* study in which substantial numbers of the subjects are Black should routinely report the race of the experimenter (examiner, therapist), and investigations that use only White experimenters to interview, test or otherwise interact with African-American research participants should acknowledge this potential drawback. Socioeconomic information should just as routinely be reported, although I recognize that such data are often difficult to secure, particularly in research with children. But in comparative racial studies, the reporting of SES information should be mandatory, along with analyses or experimental controls that reveal sensitivity to possible interactions.

Second, editors should be more open to alternative (nonexperimental) methodologies when the research pertains to African Americans. Many Black psychologists express dismay that the requirements of a so-called proper scientific psychology (cf. Sampson, 1978) seem to place disproportional value on studies with "control group" of White subjects and with experimental manipulations in laboratory settings. The well-conducted field investigation of a particular African-American population rarely finds its way into mainstream APA journals.

Third, special issues and special sections of journals are a good forum for enhancing the visibility of particular areas of psychological research, and all of the journals examined here have used this format during the year under review. With a structure already in place, this may be an appropriate time for APA journal editors to initiate a special section or special issue on African-American research. A good model for such an undertaking has recently been provided by *Child Development,* which devoted its entire April 1990 issue to research on ethnic minorities, under the guest editorship of two African-American developmental psychologists.

Finally, APA journal editors must attend to the new generation of African-American psychologists by finding ways to enhance their access to the production of knowledge. In addition to encouraging submission of articles, journal editors should take steps to foster mentorships whereby young Black scholars can benefit from the expertise of established researchers, both Black and White, who have successfully mastered the publication process. Progress along these lines has already been achieved—*JEP,* under the editorship of Robert Calfee, with the establishment in 1987 of its Underrepresented Groups Project (UGP). The UGP sponsors a mentoring program whereby junior minority scholars are "linked with a mentor who will provide substantive or methodology guidance, or both, *before* the manuscript is submitted to the Journal for regular review" (Calfee & Valencia, 1987, p. 362). Although it is evident that the fruits of this labor have yet to be reaped (Calfee, 1990), editors of other APA journals should follow the *JEP* lead so that this kind of program can be further nurtured.

Academic psychology cannot maintain its integrity by continuing to allow ethnic minorities to remain marginalized in mainstream research. In contemporary society, most of the population is not White and middle class. Neither should the subject populations in the journals of our discipline continue to be so disproportionally defined.

Footnotes

[1] *Journal of Applied Psychology* resumed its status as a bimonthly publication in 1989.

[2] I acknowledge that there are additional complexities underlying this issue. Because clinical psychology continues to be the most popular subdiscipline among Black doctoral psychologists (Kohout & Pion, 1990), it is difficult to estimate how the African-American empirical literature has been influenced by the preferences of Black clinical psychologists to seek nonacademic positions.

References

Azibo, D.A. (1988). Understanding the proper and improper usage of the comparative research framework. *Journal of Black Psychology*, 15, 81-91.

Baratz, S., & Baratz, J. (1970). Early childhood intervention: The social science base of institutional racism. *Harvard Educational Review*, 40, 29-49.

Calfee, R.C. (1990). Educational psychology: The journal and the discipline. *Journal of Educational Psychology*, 82, 613-615.

Calfee, R.C., & Valencia, R.R. (1987). Editorial. *Journal of Educational Psychology*, 79, 362.

Campbell, D.T. (1967). Stereotypes and the perception of group differences. *American Psychologist*, 22, 817-829.

Caplan, N., & Nelson, S.D. (1973). On being useful: The nature and consequences of psychological research on social problems. *American Psychologist*, 28, 199-211.

Carlson, R. (1984). What's social about social psychology? Where's the person in personality research? *Journal of Personality and Social Psychology*, 47, 1304-1309.

Cole, M., & Bruner, J.S. (1971). Cultural differences and inferences about psychological process. *American Psychologist*, 26, 867-876.

Crawford, M., & Marecek, J. (1989). Psychology reconstructs the female. *Psychology of Women Quarterly*, 13, 147-165.

Graziano, W., Varca, P., & Levy, J. (1982). Race of examiner effects and the validity of intelligence tests. *Review of Educational Research*, 52, 469-498.

Jensen, A.R. (1969). How much can we boost IQ and scholastic achievement? *Harvard Educational Review*, 39, 1-123.

Jones, E.E. (1985). Major developments in social psychology during the past five decades. In G. Lindzey & E. Aronson (Eds), *The handbook of social psychology* (Vol. 3, pp. 47-107). New York: Random House.

Jones, J.M. (1983). The concept of race in social psychology. In L. Wheeler & P. Shaver (Eds), *Review of personality and social psychology* (Vol. 4, pp. 117-150). Beverly Hills, CA: Sage.

Kohout, J., & Pion, G. (1990). Participation of ethnic minorities in psychology: Where do we stand today? In G. Striker, E. Davis-Russell, E. Bourg, E. Duran, W. Hammond, J. McHolland, K. Polite, & B. Vaughn (Eds), *Toward ethnic diversification in psychology education and training* (pp. 153-165). Wash., DC: American Psychological Association.

Labov, W. (1972). *Language in the inner city: Studies in the Black English Vernacular*. Philadelphia: University of Pennsylvania Press.

McLoyd, V.C., & Randolph, S.M. (1984). The conduct and publication of research on Afro-American children. *Human Development*, 27, 65-75.

McLoyd, V.C., & Randolph, S.M. (1985). Secular trends in the study of Afro-American children: *A review of Child Development*, 1936-1980. *Monographs of the Society for Research in Child Development*, 50, 78-92.

Moore, E. (1986). Family socialization and the IQ test performance of traditionally and transracially adopted black children. *Developmental Psychology*, 22, 327-326.

Ponterotto, J.G. (1988). Racial/ethnic minority research in the Journal of Counseling Psychology: A content analysis and methodological critique. *Journal of Counseling Psychology*, 35, 410-418.

Reynolds, C.R., & Jensen, A.R. (1983). WISC-R subscale patterns of abilities of Blacks and Whites matched on full scale IQ. *Journal of Educational Psychology*, 75, 207-214.

Ryan, W. (1971). *Blaming the victim*. New York: Pantheon.

Sampson, E.E. (1978). Scientific paradigms and social values: Wanted—A scientific revolution. *Journal of Personality and Social Psychology*, 36, 1332-1343.

Sattler, J.M., & Gwynne, J. (1982). White examiners generally do not impede the intelligence test performance and Black children: To debunk a myth. *Journal of Consulting and Clinical Psychology*, 50, 196-208.

Scarr, S. (1988). Race and gender as psychological variables. *American Psychologist*, 43, 56-59.

Sieber, J.E., & Stanley, B. (1988). Ethical and professional dimensions of socially sensitive research. *American Psychologist*, 43, 49-55.

Thomas, G.E. (1987). Black students in U.S. graduate and professional schools in the 1980s: A national and institutional assessment. *Harvard Educational Review*, 57, 261-282.

The Role Of The Behavioral Scientist
In The Civil Rights Movement

Martin Luther King, Jr.

> **Editors' Note:** The following excerpts are taken from a 1961 address by Dr. Martin Luther King, Jr., made to the Society for the Psychological Study of Social Issues, calling on those in the social sciences, particularly those in psychology, to take part in the struggle for civil rights. When you are reading the articles in this Workbook, try applying Dr. King's challenge to yourself. Attempt to discover ways of using the questions and findings presented in these readings in your daily life. Ask yourself how they could help make for a better life, not just for you, but for everyone in society.

It is always a very rich and rewarding experience when I can take a brief break from the day-to-day demands of our struggle for freedom and human dignity and discuss the issues involved in that struggle with concerned friends of good will all over this nation. It is particularly a great privilege to discuss these issues with members of the academic community, who are constantly writing about and dealing with the problems that we face and who have the tremendous responsibility of molding the minds of young men and women all over our country.

In the preface to their book, *Applied Sociology,* S.M. Miller and Alvin Gouldner (1965) state: "It is the historic mission of the social sciences to enable mankind to take possession of society." It follows that for Negroes who substantially are excluded from society this science is needed even more desperately than for any other group in the population.

For social scientists, the opportunity to serve in a life-giving purpose is a humanist challenge of rare distinction. Negroes too are eager for a rendezvous with truth and discovery. We are aware that social scientists, unlike some of their colleagues in the physical sciences, have been spared the grim feelings of guilt that attended the invention of nuclear weapons of destruction. Social scientists, in the main, are fortunate to be able to extirpate evil, not to invent it.

If the Negro needs social science for direction and for self-understanding, the white society is in even more urgent need. White America needs to understand that it is poisoned to its soul by racism and the understanding needs to be carefully documented and consequently more difficult to reject. The present crisis arises because, although it is historically imperative that our society take the next step to equality, we find ourselves psychologically and socially imprisoned. All too many white Americans are horrified not with conditions of Negro life but with the product of these conditions—the Negro himself. . . .

What other areas are there for social scientists to assist the Civil Rights movement? There are many, but I would like to suggest three because they have an urgent quality.

Social science may be able to search out some answers to the problem of Negro leadership. E. Franklin Frazier (1957), in his profound work, *Black Bourgeoisie,* laid painfully bare the tendency of the upwardly mobile Negro to separate from his community, divorce himself from responsibility to it, while failing to gain acceptance into the white community. There has been significant improvement from the days Frazier researched, but anyone knowledgeable about Negro life knows its middle class is not yet bearing its weight. Every riot has carried strong overtones of hostility of lower class Negroes toward the affluent Negro and vice versa. No contemporary study of scientific depth has totally studied this problem. Social science should be able to suggest mechanisms to create a wholesome black unity and a sense of peoplehood while the process of integration proceeds.

As one example of this gap in research, there are no studies, to my knowledge, to explain adequately the absence of Negro trade union leadership. Eighty-five percent of Negroes are working people. Some 2,000,000 are in trade unions, but in 50 years we have produced only one national leader—A. Philip Randolph.

Discrimination explains a great deal, but not everything. The picture is so dark even a few rays of light may signal a useful direction.

The second area for scientific examination is political action. In the past 2 decades, Negroes have expended more effort in quest of the franchise than they have in all other campaigns combined. Demonstrations, sit-ins, and marches, though more spectacular, are dwarfed by the enormous number of man-hours expended to register millions, particularly in the South. Negro organizations from extreme militant to conservative persuasion, Negro leaders who would not even talk to each other, all have been agreed on the key importance of voting. Stokely Carmichael said black power means the vote and Roy Wilkins, while saying black power means black death, also energetically sought the power of the ballot.

A recent major work by social scientists Matthews and Prothro (1966) concludes that "The concrete benefits to be derived from the franchise—under conditions that prevail in the South—have often been exaggerated," . . . that voting is not the key that will unlock the door to racial equality because "the concrete measurable payoffs from Negro voting in the South will not be revolutionary."

James A. Wilson (1965) supports this view, arguing, "Because of the structure of American politics as well as the nature of the Negro community, Negro politics will accomplish only limited objectives."

If their conclusion can be supported, then the major effort Negroes have invested in the past 20 years has been in the wrong direction and the major pillar of their hope is a pillar of sand. My own instinct is that these views are essentially erroneous, but they must be seriously examined.

The need for a penetrating massive scientific study of this subject cannot be overstated. Lipsit (1959) in 1957 asserted that a limitation in focus in political sociology has resulted in a failure of much contemporary research to consider a number of significant theoretical questions. The time is short for social science to illuminate this critically important area. If the main thrust of Negro effort has been, and remains, substantially irrelevant, we may be facing an agonizing crisis of tactical theory.

The third area for study concerns psychological and ideological changes in Negroes. It is fashionable now to be pessimistic. Undeniably, the freedom movement has encountered setbacks. Yet I still believe there are significant aspects of progress.

Negroes today are experiencing an inner transformation that is liberating them from ideological dependence on the white majority. What has penetrated substantially all strata of Negro life is the revolutionary idea that the philosophy and morals of the dominant white society are not holy or sacred but in all too many respects are degenerate and profane.

Negroes have been oppressed for centuries not merely by bonds of economic and political servitude. The worst aspect of their oppression was their inability to question and defy the fundamental percepts of the larger society. Negroes have been loath in the past to hurl any fundamental challenges because they were coerced and conditioned into thinking within the context of the dominant white ideology. This is changing and new radical trends are appearing in Negro thought. I use radical in its broad sense to refer to reading into roots.

Ten years of struggle have sensitized and opened the Negro's eyes to reaching. For the first time in their history, Negroes have become aware of the deeper causes for the crudity and cruelty that governed white society's responses to their needs. They discovered that their plight was not a consequence of superficial prejudice but was systemic.

The slashing blows of backlash and frontlash have hurt the Negro, but they have also awakened him and revealed the nature of the oppressor. To lose illusions is to gain truth. Negroes have grown wiser and more mature and they are hearing more clearly those who are raising fundamental questions about our society whether the critics be Negro or white. When this process of awareness and independence crystallizes, every rebuke, every evasion, become hammer blows on the wedge that splits the Negro from the larger society.

Social science is needed to explain where this development is going to take us. Are we moving away, not from integration, but from the society which made it a problem in the first place? How deep and at what rate of speed is this process occurring? These are some vital questions to be answered if we are to have a clear sense of our direction.

We know we have not found the answers to all forms of social change. We know, however, that we did find some answers. We have achieved and we are confident. We also know we are confronted now with far greater complexities and we have not yet discovered all the theory we need.

And may I say together, we must solve the problems right here in America. As I have said time and time again, Negroes still have faith in America. Black people still have faith in a dream that we will all live together as brothers in this country of plenty one day. . . .

References

Frazier, E. F. (1956) *Black bourgeoisie*. Glencoe, Ill.: Free Press.

Lipsit, M. (1959) Political sociology. In *Sociology today*. New York: Basic Books.

Matthews, D. R., and Prothro, J. W. (1966) *Negroes and the new southern politics*. New York: Harcourt & Brace.

Miller, S. M., and Gouldner, A. (1965) *Applied sociology*. New York: Free Press.

Wilson, J. A. (1965) The Negro in politics. *Daedalus*, Fall.

C h a p t e r   2

The Power Of Groups

The articles in Chapter 1 introduced the key issues of gender, race, and ethnicity. They discussed how these concepts are, to a significant degree, defined by society and how these definitions influence how psychologists study them. Acknowledging that people may have differing definitions of what these categories mean for them serves as a starting point for examining the role they play in our lives. However, to gain a better understanding, we must explore the relationship of the individual to the groups to which she or he belongs. Whether we choose to be in a group, or simply find ourself placed in it, group membership can play a major role in determining how we act, think, and feel.

We have all witnessed the positive consequences of being in a group. We may have experienced the pride that comes from knowing that someone in our community or school has accomplished something positive, perhaps they rescued a child from a dangerous situation or won a major competition. We also know that behavior that occurs between groups can lead to negative outcomes. Many of us have seen the evening news or read in our daily newspaper reports of violent acts carried out by one group on their neighbors. You may have even been a member of a group perpetrating such an act or of a group targeted by such an act.

Each of the articles in this section discusses ways in which a group can influence psychological states and behavior. Ron Jones, a high school teacher, gives us a first-hand account of a demonstration he carried out that is a dramatic display of the power of the group. It shows how rapidly group-based behavior can come to dominate an individual's life. The second article in this chapter presents a more theoretical perspective on group-based behavior. In it, Henri Tajfel and John Turner discuss how ready we are to form groups. They show how we will even form groups using the flimsiest of criteria, for instance, whether we prefer blue or green. They go on to talk about how we employ our group membership to reinforce our self-esteem by using it as basis for making comparisons that help us look better.

Delia Saenz, in her article, explores the negative impact of being the sole member of a group in certain situations. She shows how token status can have an adverse effect on performance. David Matsumoto's article highlights some of the issues raised in Chapter 1. He explains how being in a group can lead people in different groups to behave in opposite ways in a situation which appears to be the same.

All of these authors are dealing with the effects that belonging to a group can have on an individual. In reading them we would urge you to think about how the groups in your life impact you.

The Third Wave

Ron Jones

€ditors' Note: Historically, one of the driving forces behind social psychology has been the attempt to understand how events like the Holocaust could have happened. Research on group processes is one area that has addressed this question. As the title of this chapter indicates, groups can powerfully affect our behavior. The following reading vividly demonstrates how leaders can quickly form groups and how group behaviors can rapidly take on a life of their own. Though this essay by Ron Jones is not based on psychological research, it presents a number of psychological processes that highlight the power of groups. These group process will be discussed in a number of the other readings in this Workbook.

For years I kept a strange secret. I shared this silence with 200 students. Yesterday I ran into one of those students, and it all rushed back.

Steve Coniglio had been a sophomore in my World History class. We ran into each other quite by accident. It's one of those occasions experienced by teachers when they least expected it. You're walking down the street, eating at a secluded restaurant, or buying some underwear, when all of a sudden an ex-student pops up to say hello. In this case it was Steve, running down the street shouting, "Mr. Jones! Mr. Jones!" We greeted with an embarrassed hug.

I had to stop for a minute to remember. Who is this young man hugging me? He calls me Mr. Jones. Must be a former student. What's his name?

In the split second of my race back in time, Steve sensed my questioning and backed up. Then he smiled, and slowly raised a hand in a cupped position.

My God. He's a member of the Third Wave. It's Steve, Steve Coniglio. He sat in the second row. He was a sensitive and bright student. Played guitar and enjoyed drama.

We just stood there exchanging smiles when, without a conscious command, I raised my hand in curved position. The salute was given. Two comrades had met long after the war. The Third Wave was still alive.

"Mr. Jones, do you remember the Third Wave?"

I sure do. It was one of the most frightening events I ever experienced in the classroom. It was also the genesis of a secret that I and 200 students would share for the rest of our lives.

We talked about the Third Wave for the next few hours. Then it was time to part. It's strange, you meet a past student in these chance ways. You catch a few moments of your life. Hold them tight. Then say goodbye, not knowing when and if you'll ever see each other again. Oh, you make promises to call each other, but it won't happen. Steve will continue to grow and change. I will remain an ageless benchmark in his life—a presence that will not change. I am Mr. Jones. Steve turns and gives a silent salute, his hand raised upward in a shape of a curling wave. Hand curved in a similar fashion, I return the gesture.

The Third Wave. Well, at last it can be talked about. Here I've met a student and we've talked for hours about this nightmare. The secret must finally be waning. It's taken a dozen years. It's now just a dream, something to remember—no, it's something we tried to forget. That's how it all started. By strange coincidence, I think it was Steve who started the Third Wave with a question.

We were studying Nazi Germany and, in the middle of a lecture, I was interrupted by the question. How could the German populace claim ignorance of the slaughter of the Jewish people? How could the townspeople—railroad conductors, teachers, doctors—claim that they knew nothing about concentration camps and human carnage? How could people who were neighbors and maybe even friends of the Jewish citizens say they weren't there when it happened? It was a good question. I didn't know the answer.

Inasmuch as there were several months still to go in the school year and I was already at World War II, I decided to take a week and explore the question.

Strength Through Discipline

On Monday, I introduced my sophomore history students to one of the experiences that characterized Nazi Germany. Discipline. I lectured about the beauty of discipline. How an athlete feels having worked hard and regularly to be successful at a sport. How a ballet dancer or painter works hard to perfect a movement. The dedicated patience of a scientist in pursuit of an idea. It's discipline. That self-training. Control. The power of the will. The exchange of physical hardships for superior mental and physical facilities. The ultimate triumph.

To experience the power of discipline, I invited, no, I commanded the class to exercise and use a new seating posture. I described how proper sitting posture assists concentration and strengthens the will. In fact, I instructed the class in a mandatory sitting posture. This posture started with feet flat on the floor, hands placed flat across the small of the back to force a straight alignment of the spine. "There—can't you breathe more easily? You're more alert. Don't you feel better?"

We practiced this new attention position over and over. I walked up and down the aisles of seated students pointing out small flaws, making improvements. Proper seating became the most important aspect of learning. I would dismiss the class, allowing them to leave their desks, and then call them abruptly back to an attention sitting position. In speed drills the class learned to move from standing position to attention sitting in fifteen seconds. In focus drills I concentrated attention on the feet being parallel and flat, ankles locked, knees bent at ninety-degree angles, hands flat and crossed against the back, spine straight, chin down, head forward. We did noise drills in which talking was allowed only to be shown as a detraction. Following minutes of progressive drill assignments the class could move from standing positions outside the room to attention sitting positions at their desks without making a sound. The maneuver took five seconds.

It was strange how quickly the students took to this uniform code of behavior. I began to wonder just how far they could be pushed. Was this display of obedience a momentary game we were all playing, or was it something else? Was the desire for discipline and uniformity a natural need—a societal instinct we hide within our franchise restaurants and TV programming?

I decided to push the tolerance of the class for regimented action. In the final twenty-five minutes of the class I introduced some new rules. Students must be sitting in class at the attention position before the late bell; all students must carry pencils and paper for note taking; when asking or answering questions students must stand at the side of their desks; and the first word given in answering or asking a question must be "Mr. Jones!"

Students who responded to questions in a sluggish manner were reprimanded and in every case made to repeat their behavior until it was a model of punctuality and respect. The intensity of the response became more important than the content. To accentuate this, I requested that answers be given in three words or less. Students were rewarded for making an effort at answering questions. They were also acknowledged for doing this in a crisp and attentive manner. Soon everyone in the class began popping up with answers and questions. The involvement level in the class moved from the few who always dominated discussions to the entire class. Even stranger was the gradual improvement in the quality of answers. Everyone seemed to be listening more intently. New people were speaking. Answers started to stretch out as students who were usually hesitant to speak found support for their efforts.

As for my part in this exercise, I had nothing but questions. Why hadn't I thought of this technique before? Students seemed intent on the assignment and displayed accurate recitation of facts and concepts. They even seemed to be asking better questions and treating each other with more compassion. How could this be? Here I was enacting an authoritarian learning environment and it seemed very productive. I began to ponder not just how far this class could be pushed, but how much I would change my basic beliefs toward an open classroom and self-directed learning. Was all my belief in Carl Rogers to shrivel and die? Where was this experiment leading?

Strength Through Community

On Tuesday, the second day of the exercise, I entered the classroom to find everyone sitting in silence at the attention position. Some of their faces were relaxed with smiles that come from pleasing the teacher. But most of the students looked straight ahead in earnest concentration. Neck muscles rigid. No sign of a smile or a thought or even a question. Every fiber strained to perform the deed. To release the tension, I went to the chalkboard and wrote in big letters: STRENGTH THROUGH DISCIPLINE. Below this I wrote a second law: STRENGTH THROUGH COMMUNITY.

While the class sat in stern silence I began to talk, lecture, sermonize about the value of community. At this stage of the game I was debating in my own mind whether to stop the experiment or to continue. I hadn't planned such intensity or compliance. In fact, I was surprised to find the ideas on discipline enacted at all. While pondering whether to stop or go on with the experiment, I talked on and on about community. I made up stories from my experiences as an athlete, coach, and historian. It was easy. Community is that bond between individuals who work and struggle together. It's raising a barn with your neighbors, it's feeling that you are a part of something beyond yourself—a movement, a team, La Raza, a cause.

It was too late to step back. I now can appreciate why the astronomer turns relentlessly to the telescope. I was probing deeper and deeper into my own perceptions and the motivations for group and individual action. There was much more to see and try to understand. Many questions haunted me. Why did the students accept the authority I was imposing? Where was their curiosity or resistance to this martial behavior? When and how would this end?

Following my description of community, I once again told the class that community-like discipline must be experienced if it is to be understood. To provide an encounter with community I had the class recite in unison: "Strength through discipline"; "Strength through community." First I would have two students stand and call out our motto. Then

I'd add two more, and two more, until finally the whole class was standing and reciting.

It was fun. The students began to look at each other and sense the power of belonging. Everyone was capable and equal. They were doing something together. We worked on this simple act for the entire class period. We would repeat the mottoes in a rotating chorus, or say them with various degrees of loudness. Always we said them together, emphasizing the proper way to sit, stand, and talk.

I began to think of myself as a part of the experiment. I enjoyed the unified action demonstrated by the students. It was rewarding to see their satisfaction and excitement to do more. I found it harder and harder to extract myself from the momentum and identity that the class was developing. I was following the group dictate as much as I was directing it.

As the class period was ending, and without forethought, I created a class salute. It was for class members only. To make the salute you brought your right hand up toward the right shoulder in a curled position. I called it the Third Wave salute because the hand resembled a wave about to top over. The idea for the three came from beach lore that waves travel in chains, the third wave being the last and largest of each series. Since we had a salute, I made it a rule to salute all class members outside the classroom. When the bell sounded, ending the period, I asked the class for complete silence. With everyone sitting at attention I slowly raised my arm and, with a cupped hand, I saluted. It was a silent signal of recognition. They were something special. Without command the entire group of students returned the salute.

Throughout the next few days students in the class would exchange this greeting. You would be walking down the hall when all of a sudden three classmates would turn your way, each flashing a quick salute. In the library or in gym students would be seen giving this strange hand jive. You would hear a crash of cafeteria food, only to have it followed by two classmates saluting each other. The mystique of thirty individuals doing this strange gyration soon brought more attention to the class and its experiment into the Nazi personality. Many students outside the class asked if they could join.

Strength Through Action

On Wednesday, I decided to issue membership cards to every student who wanted to continue what I now called the experiment. Not a single student elected to leave the room. In this, the third day of activity, there were forty-three students in the class. Thirteen students had cut some other class to be a part of the experiment. While the class sat at attention, I gave each person a card. I marked three of the cards with a red X and informed the recipients that they had a special assignment to report any students not complying with class rules.

I then proceeded to talk about the meaning of action. I discussed the beauty of taking full responsibility for one's actions. Of believing so thoroughly in yourself and your community or family that you will do anything to preserve, protect, and extend that being. I stressed how hard work and allegiance to each other would allow accelerated learning and accomplishment. I reminded students of what it felt like to be in classes where competition caused pain and degradation— situations in which students were pitted against each other in everything from gym to reading. The feeling of never acting, never being a part of something, never supporting each other.

At this point students stood without prompting and began to give what amounted to testimonials.

"Mr. Jones, for the first time I'm learning lots of things."

"Mr. Jones, why don't you teach like this all the time?"

I was shocked! Yes, I had been pushing information at them in an extremely controlled setting, but the fact that they found it comfortable and acceptable was startling. It was equally disconcerting to realize that complex and time-consuming written homework assignments on German life were being completed and even expanded by students. Performance in academic skill areas was improving significantly. They were learning more. And they seemed to want more. I began to think that the students might do anything I assigned. I decided to find out.

To allow students the experience of direct action, I gave each individual a specific verbal assignment.

"It's your task to design a Third Wave banner."

"You are responsible for stopping any student who is not a Third Wave member from entering this room."

"I want you to remember and be able to recite by tomorrow the name and address of every Third Wave member."

"You are assigned the problem of training and convincing at least twenty children in the adjacent elementary school that our sitting posture is necessary for better learning."

"It's your job to read this pamphlet and report its entire content to the class before the period ends."

"I want each of you to give me the name and address of one reliable friend who you think might want to join the Third Wave."

To conclude the session on direct action, I instructed students in a simple procedure for initiating new members. It went like this. A new member had only to be recommended by an existing member and issued a card by me. Upon receiving this card the new member had to demonstrate knowledge of our rules and pledge obedience to them. My announcement unleashed a fervor.

The school was alive with conjecture and curiosity. It affected everyone. The school cook asked what a Third Wave cookie looked like. I said chocolate chip, of course. Our principal came into an afternoon faculty meeting and gave me the Third Wave salute. I saluted back. The librarian thanked me for the thirty-foot banner on learning, which she placed above the library entrance. By the end of the day more than 200 students were admitted into the order. I felt very alone and a little scared.

Most of my fear emanated from the incidence of tattletaling. Although I formally appointed only three students to report deviant behavior, approximately twenty students came to me with reports about how Allan didn't salute, or Georgene was talking critically about our experiment. This incidence of monitoring meant that half the class now considered it their duty to observe and report on members of their class. Within this avalanche of reporting, one legitimate conspiracy did seem to be under way.

Three women in the class had told their parents all about our classroom activities. These young women were by far the most intelligent students in the class. As friends, they chummed together. They possessed a silent confidence and took pleasure in a school setting that gave them academic and leadership opportunity. During the days of the experiment I was curious about how they would respond to the egalitarian and physical reshaping of the class. The rewards they were accustomed to winning just didn't exist in the experiment. The intellectual skills of questioning and reasoning were nonexistent. In the martial atmosphere of the class they seemed stunned and pensive. Now that I look back, they appeared much like the child with a so-called learning disability. They watched the activities and participated in a mechanical fashion. Others jumped in, whereas they held back, watching.

In telling their parents of the experiment, I set off a brief chain of events. The rabbi for one of the parents called me at home. He was polite and condescending. I told him we were merely studying the Nazi personality. He seemed delighted and told me not to worry; he would talk to the parents and calm their concerns. In concluding this conversation, I envisioned similar conversations throughout history in which the clergy accepted and apologized for untenable conditions. If only he would have raged in anger or simply investigated the situation, I could point the students to an example of righteous rebellion. But no—the rabbi became a part of the experiment. In remaining ignorant of the oppression in the experiment, he became an accomplice and advocate.

By the end of the third day I was exhausted. I was tearing apart. The balance between role-playing and directed behavior became indistinguishable. Many of the students were completely into being Third Wave members. They demanded strict obedience of the rules from other students and bullied those who took the experiment lightly. Others simply sunk into the activity and took self-assigned roles.

I particularly remember Robert. Robert was big for his age and displayed very few academic skills. Oh, he tried harder than anyone I know to be successful. He handed in elaborate weekly reports copied word for word from the reference books in the library. Robert is like so many kids in school who don't excel or cause trouble. They aren't bright, they can't make athletic teams, and they don't strike out for attention. They are lost, invisible. The only reason I came to know Robert at all is that I found him eating lunch in my classroom. He always ate lunch alone.

Well, the Third Wave gave Robert a place in school. At least he was equal to everyone. He could do something. Take part, be meaningful. That's just what Robert did. Late Wednesday afternoon I found Robert following me and asked what in the world was he doing.

He smiled—I don't think I had ever seen him smile—and announced, "Mr. Jones, I'm your bodyguard. I'm afraid something will happen to you. Can I do it, Mr. Jones? Please?"

Given that assurance and smile, I couldn't say no. I had a bodyguard. All day long Robert opened and closed doors for me. He always walked on my right, smiling and saluting other class members. He followed me everywhere. In the faculty room (closed to students) he stood at silent attention while I gulped some coffee. When an English teacher reminded him that students weren't permitted in the teachers' room, he just smiled and informed the faculty member that he wasn't a student, he was a bodyguard.

Strength Through Pride

On Thursday I began to draw the experiment to a conclusion. I was exhausted and worried. Many students were over the line. The Third Wave had become the center of their existence. I was in pretty bad shape myself. I was now acting instinctively as a dictator. Oh, I was benevolent. And I daily argued to myself on the benefits of the learning experience.

By this, the fourth day of the experiment, I was beginning to lose my own arguments. As I spent more time playing the role, I had less time to remember its rational origins and purpose. I found myself sliding into the role even when it wasn't necessary. I wondered if this doesn't happen to lots of people. We get or take an ascribed role and then bend our life to fit the image. Soon the image is the only identity people will accept. So we become the image. The trouble with the situation and role

I had created was that I didn't have time to think where it was leading. Events were crushing around me. I worried for students doing things they would regret. I worried for myself.

Once again I faced the thoughts of closing the experiment or letting it go its own course. Both options were unworkable. If I stopped the experiment a great number of students would be left hanging. They had committed themselves in front of their peers to radical behavior. Emotionally and psychologically they had exposed themselves. If I suddenly jolted them back to classroom reality, I would face a confused student body for the remainder of the year. It would be too painful and demeaning for Robert and the students like him to be twisted back into their seats and told it's just a game. They would take the ridicule from the brighter students who had participated in a measured and cautious way. I couldn't let the Roberts lose again.

The other option—letting the experiment run its course—was also out of the question. Things were already getting out of control. Wednesday evening someone had broken into the room and ransacked the place. I later found out it was the father of one of the students. He was a retired Air Force colonel who had spent time in a German prisoner-of-war camp. Upon hearing of our activity he simply lost control. Late in the evening he broke into the room and tore it apart. I found him propped up against the classroom door the next morning. He told me about his friends who had been killed in Germany. He was holding on to me and shaking. In staccato words he pleaded that I understand and help him get home. I called his wife and, with the help of a neighbor, walked him home. Later we spent hours talking about what he felt and did, but from that moment on Thursday morning I was more concerned with what might be happening at school.

I was increasingly worried about how our activity was affecting the faculty and other students in the school. The Third Wave was disrupting normal learning. Students were cutting class to participate and the school counselors were beginning to question every student in the class. The real gestapo in the school was at work. Faced with this experiment exploding in a hundred directions, I decided to try an old basketball strategy.

When you're playing against all the odds, the best action to take is to try the unexpected. That's what I did.

By Thursday the class had swollen in size to more than eighty students. The only thing that allowed them all to fit was the enforced discipline of sitting in silence at attention. A strange calm is in effect when a room full of people sit in quiet observation and anticipation. It helped me approach them in a deliberate way. I talked about pride. "Pride is more than banners or salutes. Pride is something no one can take from you. Pride is knowing you are the best. . . . It can't be destroyed. . .."

In the midst of this crescendo I abruptly changed and lowered my voice to announce the real reason for the Third Wave. In a slow, methodic tone I explained: "The Third Wave isn't just an experiment or classroom activity. It's far more important than that. The Third Wave is a nationwide program to find students who are willing to fight for political change in this country. That's right. This activity we have been doing has been practice for the real thing. Across the country teachers like myself have been recruiting and training a youth brigade capable of showing the nation a better society through discipline, community, pride, and action. If we can change the way the school is run, we can change the way that factories, stores, universities, and all the other institutions are run. You are a selected group of young people chosen to help in this cause. If you will stand up and display what you have learned in the past four days, we can change the destiny of this nation. We can bring it a new sense of order, community, pride, and action. A new purpose. Everything rests with you and your willingness to take a stand."

To validate the seriousness of my words I turned to the three women in the class whom I knew had questioned the Third Wave. I demanded that they leave the room. I explained why I acted and then assigned four guards to escort the women to the library and to restrain them from entering the class on Friday. Then in dramatic style I informed the class of a special noon rally to take place on Friday. This would be a rally for Third Wave members only.

It was a wild gamble. I just kept talking, afraid that if I stopped, someone would laugh or ask a question and the grand scheme would dissolve in chaos. I explained how at noon on Friday a national candidate for president would announce the formation of a Third Wave Youth Program. Simultaneous to this announcement more than a thousand youth groups from every part of the country would stand up and display their support for such a movement.

I confided that they were the students selected to represent our area. I also asked if they could make a good showing, because the press had been invited to record the event. No one laughed. There was not a murmur of resistance—quite the contrary, in fact. A fever pitch of excitement swelled across the room. "We can do it!" "Should we wear white shirts?" "Can we bring friends?" "Mr. Jones, have you seen this advertisement in *Time* magazine?"

The clincher came quite by accident. It was a full-page color advertisement in the current issue of *Time* for some lumber products. The advertiser identified his product as the Third Wave. The ad proclaimed in big red, white, and blue letters, "The Third Wave is coming. " "Is this part of the campaign, Mr. Jones?" "Is it a code or something?"

"Yes. Now listen carefully. It's all set for tomorrow. Be in the small auditorium ten minutes before noon. Be seated. Be ready to display the discipline, community, and pride you have learned. Don't talk to anyone about this. This rally is for members only."

Strength Through Understanding

On Friday, the final day of the exercise, I spent the early morning preparing the auditorium for the rally. At eleven-thirty students began to trickle into the room—at first a few, scouting the way, and then more. Row after row began to fill. A hushed silence shrouded the room. Third Wave banners hung like clouds over the assembly.

At twelve o'clock sharp I closed the room and placed guards at each door. Several friends of mine, posing as reporters and photographers, began to interact with the crowd, taking pictures and jotting frantic descriptive notes. A group photograph was taken. More than 200 students were crammed into the room. Not a vacant seat could be found. The group seemed to be composed of students from many persuasions. There were the athletes, the social prominents, the student leaders, the loners, the group of kids who always left school early, the bikers, the pseudo-hip, a few representatives of the school's dadaist clique, and some of the students who hung out at the laundromat. The entire collection, however, looked like one force as they sat in perfect attention. Every person was focusing on the TV set I had in the front of the room. No one moved. The room was empty of sound. It was like we were all witnesses to a birth. The tension and anticipation were beyond belief.

"Before turning on the national press conference, which begins in five minutes, I want to demonstrate to the press the extent of our training." With that, I gave the salute, which was followed automatically by 200 arms stabbing a reply. I then said the words "Strength through discipline," again followed by a repetitive chorus. We did this again and again. Each time the response was louder. The photographers were circling the ritual, snapping pictures, but by now they were ignored. I reiterated the importance of this event and asked once more for a show of allegiance. It was the last time I would ask anyone to recite. The room rocked with a guttural cry, "Strength through discipline."

It was 12:05. I turned off the lights in the room and walked quickly to the television set. The air in the room seemed to be drying up. It felt hard to breathe and even harder to talk. It was as if the climax of shouting souls had pushed everything out of the room. I switched the television set on. I was now standing next to the television, directly facing the room full of people. The machine came to life, producing a luminous field of phosphorous light.

Robert was at my side. I whispered to him to watch closely and pay attention to the next few minutes. The only light in the room was coming from the television, and it played against the faces in the room. Eyes strained and pulled at the light, but the pattern didn't change. The room stayed deadly still. Waiting. There was a mental tug-of-war between the people in the room and the television. The television won. The white glow of the test pattern didn't snap into the vision of a political candidate. It just whined on. Still the viewers persisted. There must be a program. It must be coming on. Where is it? The trance with the television continued for what seemed like hours. It was 12:07. Nothing. A blank field of white. It's not going to happen. Anticipation turned to anxiety and then to frustration. Someone stood up and shouted.

"There isn't any leader, is there?" Everyone turned in shock, first to the despondent student and then back to the television. Their faces held looks of disbelief.

In the confusion of the moment I moved slowly toward the television. I turned if off. I felt air rush back into the room. The room remained in fixed silence, but for the first time I could sense people breathing. Students were withdrawing their arms from behind their chairs. I expected a flood of questions but got intense silence. I began to talk. Every word seemed to be taken and absorbed.

"Listen closely, I have something important to tell you. Sit down. There is no leader! There is no such thing as a national youth movement called the Third Wave. You have been used. Manipulated. Shoved by your own desires into the place you now find yourselves. You are no better or worse than the German Nazis we have been studying. You thought that you were the elect, that you were better than those outside this room. You bargained your freedom for the comfort of discipline and superiority. You chose to accept the group's will and the Big Lie over your own convictions. Oh, you think to yourselves that you were just going along for the fun, that you could have extricated yourselves at any moment. But where were you heading? How far would you have gone? Let me show you your future."

With that I switched on a rear-screen projector. It quickly illuminated a white dropcloth hanging behind the television. Large numbers appeared in a countdown. The roar of the Nurenburg Rally blasted into vision. My heart was pounding. In ghostly images the history of the Third Reich paraded into the room. The discipline, the march of super race. The Big Lie. Arrogance, violence, terror. People being pushed into vans. The visual stench of death camps. Faces without eyes. The trials. The plea of ignorance. I was only doing my job. My job. As abruptly as it started, the film froze to a halt on a single written frame: "Everyone must accept the blame—no one can claim that he didn't in some way take part."

The room stayed dark as the final footage of film flapped against the projector. I felt sick to my stomach. The room sweated and smelled like a locker room. No one moved. It was as if everyone wanted to dissect the moment, figure out what had happened. As if awakening from a dream and deep sleep, the entire room of people took one last look back into their consciousness. I waited for several minutes to let everyone catch up.

In the still-darkened room I began the explanation. I confessed my feeling of sickness and remorse. I told the assembly that a full explanation would take quite a while. But I'd start. I sensed myself moving from an introspective participant in the event toward the role of teacher. It's easier being a teacher. In objective terms I began to describe the past events.

"Through the experience of the past week we have all tasted what it was like to live and act in Nazi Germany. We learned what it felt like to create a disciplined social environment. To build a special society. Pledge allegiance to that society. Replace reason with rules. Yes, we would all have made good Germans. We would have put on the uniform. Turned our heads as friends and neighbors were cursed and then persecuted. Pulled the locks shut. Worked in the 'defense' plants. Burned ideas. Yes, we know in a small way what it feels like to find a hero. To grab quick solutions. Feel strong and in control of destiny. We know the fear of being left out. The pleasure of doing something right and being rewarded. To be number one. To be right. Taken to an extreme, we have seen and perhaps felt what these actions will lead to. We have seen that fascism is not just something those other people did. No, it's right here. In this room. In our own personal habits and way of life. Scratch the surface and it appears. Something in all of us. We carry it like a disease. The belief that human beings are basically evil and therefore unable to act well toward each other. A belief that demands a strong leader and discipline to preserve social order. And there is something else. The act of apology."

"This is the final lesson to be experienced. This last lesson is perhaps the one of greatest importance. This lesson was the question that started our plunge into studying Nazi life. Do you remember the question? It concerned a bewilderment at the German populace claiming ignorance and noninvolvement in the Nazi movement. If I remember the question, it went something like this. How could the German soldier, teacher, railroad conductor, purse, tax collector, the average citizen, claim at the end of the Third Reich that they knew nothing of what was going on? How can a people be a part of something and then claim at the demise that they were not really involved? What causes people to blank out their own history? In the next few minutes—and perhaps years—you will have an opportunity to answer this question.

"If our enactment of the fascist mentality is complete, not one of you will ever admit to being at this final Third Wave rally. Like the Germans, you will have trouble admitting to yourselves that you came this far. You will not allow your friends and parents to know that you were willing to give up individual freedom and power for the dictates of order and unseen leaders. You can't admit to being manipulated. Being a follower. To accepting the Third Wave as a way of life. You won't admit to participating in this madness. You will keep this day and this rally a secret. It's a secret I shall share with you."

I took the film from the three cameras in the room and pulled the celluloid into the exposing light. The deed was concluded. The trial was over. The Third Wave had ended.

I glanced over my shoulder. Robert was crying. Students slowly rose from their chairs and, without words, filed into the outdoor light. I walked over to Robert and threw my arms around him. Robert was sobbing—taking in large uncontrollable gulps of air, and saying, "It's over."

"It's all right." In our consoling each other we became a rock in the stream of exiting students. Some swirled back to momentarily hold Robert and me. Others cried openly and then brushed away tears to carry on. Human beings circling and holding each other. Moving toward the door and the world outside.

For a week in the middle of a school year we had shared fully in life. And as predicted, we also shared a deep secret. In the four years I taught at Cubberley High School no one ever admitted to attending the Third Wave rally. Oh, we talked and studied our actions intently. But the rally itself—no. It was something we all wanted to forget.

NOTE: *THE WAVE* IS AVAILABLE ON VIDEOTAPE. CONTACT DIRK DIRKSEN AT (415) 206-1621.

The Social Identity Theory Of Intergroup Behavior

Henri Tajfel and John C. Turner

Editors' Note: This excerpt from Henri Tajfel and John Turner describes how dividing people into groups based on the most arbitrary of criteria, such as whether their social security number ends in an even or odd number, or whether they prefer green or blue, can result in people treating those in their group differently from those who are not. It also discusses how people use their group to bolster their self-esteem by comparing their group to other groups. These group processes can help explain behaviors as common as a school rivalry. After all, everyone knows that your school is much better than your rival, right? More importantly, many of the group processes discussed in this article play significant roles in stereotyping, prejudice, and discrimination.

Social Categorization and Intergroup Discrimination

The initial stimulus for the theorizing presented here was provided by certain experimental investigations of intergroup behavior. The laboratory analogue of real-world ethnocentrism is in-group bias—that is, the tendency to favor the in-group over the out-group in evaluations and behavior. Not only are incompatible group interests not always sufficient to generate conflict. . . , but there is a good deal of experimental evidence that these conditions are not always necessary for the development of competition and discrimination between groups (Brewer, 1979; Turner, 1981), although this does not mean, of course, that in-group bias is not influenced by the goal relations between the groups.

All this evidence implies that in-group bias is a remarkably omnipresent feature of intergroup relations. The phenomenon in its extreme form has been investigated by Tajfel and his associates. There have now been in addition to the original studies (Tajfel, 1970; Tajfel, et al., 1971) a large number of other experiments employing a similar procedure (methodological and conceptual issues concerning the experimental paradigm are discussed by Aschenbrenner and Schaefer, 1980; Bornstein, et al., 1983a; Bornstein, et al., 1983b; Branthwaite, Doyle, & Lightbown, 1979; Brown, Tajfel, & Turner, 1980; Turner, 1980, 1983a, 1983b; and the results of the relevant studies are summarized most recently by Turner, 1983a, and in a wider theoretical and empirical context by Brewer, 1979; Brown & Turner, 1981; Turner, 1981, 1982), all showing that the mere perception of belonging to two distinct groups—that is, social categorization per se—is sufficient to trigger intergroup discrimination favoring the in-group. In other words, the mere awareness of the presence of an out-group is sufficient to provoke intergroup competitive or discriminatory responses on the part of the in-group.

In the basic paradigm the subjects (both children and adults have acted as subjects in the various studies) are randomly classified as members of two nonoverlapping groups—ostensibly on the basis of some trivial performance criterion. They then make "decisions," awarding amounts of money to pairs of other subjects (excluding self) in specially designed booklets. The recipients are anonymous, except for their individual code numbers and their group membership (for example, member number 51 of the X group and member number 33 of the Y group). The subjects, who know their own group membership, award the amounts individually and anonymously. The response format of the booklets does not force the subjects to act in terms of group membership.

In this situation, there is neither a conflict of interests nor previously existing hostility between the "groups." No social interaction takes place between the subjects, nor is there any rational link between economic self-interest and the strategy of in-group favoritism. Thus, these groups are purely cognitive, and can be referred to as "minimal."

The basic and highly reliable finding is that the trivial, ad hoc intergroup categorization leads to in-group favoritism and discrimination against the out-group. Fairness is also an influential strategy. There is also a good deal of evidence that, within the pattern of responding in terms of in-group favoritism, maximum difference (MD) is more important to the subjects than maximum in-group profit (MIP). Thus, they seem to be competing with the out-group, rather than following a strategy of simple economic gain for members of the in-group. Other data from several experiments also show that the subjects' decisions were significantly nearer to the maximum joint payoff (MJP) point when these decisions applied to the division of money between two anonymous members of the in-group than when they applied to two members of the out-group; that is, relatively less was given to the out-group, even when giving more would not have affected the amounts for the in-group. Billig and Tajfel (1973) have found the same results even when the assignment to groups was made explicitly random. This eliminated the similarity on the performance criterion within the in-group as an alternative explanation of the results. An explicitly random classification into groups proved in this study to be a more potent determinant of discrimination than perceived interpersonal similarities and dissimilarities not associated with categorization into groups. Billig (1973), Brewer and Silver (1978), Locksley, Ortiz, & Hepburn (1980) and Turner, Sachder, & Hogg (1983) have all replicated this finding that even explicitly arbitrary social categorizations are sufficient for discrimination, and Allen and Wilder (1975) have provided additional evidence for the importance of group classification compared to similarities between people without such classification.

The question that arises is whether in-group bias in these minimal situations is produced by some form of the experimenter effect or of the demand characteristics of the experimental situation—in other words, whether explicit references to group membership communicate to the subjects that they are expected to, or ought to, discriminate. The first point to be made about this interpretation of the results is that explicit references to group membership are logically necessary for operationalizing in these minimal situations the major independent variable—that is, social categorization per se. This requires not merely that the subjects perceive themselves as

similar to or different from others as individuals, but that they are members of discrete and discontinuous categories—that is, "groups." Second, a detailed analysis of the subjects' postsession reports (Billig, 1972; Turner, 1975a) shows that they do not share any common conception of the "appropriate" or "obvious" way to behave, that only a tiny minority have some idea of the hypothesis, and that this minority does not always conform to it. Thirdly, the relevant experimental data do not support this interpretation. St. Claire and Turner (1982) exposed observer-subjects to exactly the same experimental cues as normal categorized subjects; the former were required to predict the responses of the latter in the standard decision booklets. The categorized subjects did discriminate significantly, but the observers failed to predict it and in fact expected significantly more fairness than was actually displayed.

The more general theoretical problem has been referred to elsewhere by one of us as follows:

Simply and briefly stated, the argument (e.g., Gerard and Hoyt, 1974) amounts to the following: the subjects acted in terms of the intergroup categorization provided or imposed by the experimenters not necessarily because this has been successful in inducing any genuine awareness of membership in separate and distinct groups, but probably because they felt that this kind of behavior was expected of them by the experimenters, and therefore they conformed to this expectation. The first question to ask is why should the subjects be expecting the experimenters to expect of them this kind of behavior? The Gerard and Hoyt answer to this is that the experimental situation was rigged to cause this kind of expectation in the subjects. This answer retains its plausibility only if we assume that what was no more than a hint from the experimenters about the notion of "groups" being relevant to the subjects' behavior had been sufficient to determine, powerfully and consistently, *a particular form* of intergroup behavior. In turn if we assume this—and the assumption is by no means unreasonable—we must also assume that this particular form of intergroup behavior is one which is capable of being induced by the experimenters much more easily than other forms (such as cooperation between the groups in extorting the maximum total amount of money from the experimenters, or a fair division of the spoils between the groups, or simply random responding). And this last assumption must be backed up in its turn by another presupposition: namely, that for some reasons (whatever they may be) competitive behavior between groups, at least in our culture, is extraordinarily easy to trigger off—at which point we are back where we started from. The problem then must be restated in terms of the need to specify why a certain *kind* of intergroup behavior can be elicited so much more easily than other kinds; and this specification is certainly not made if we rest content with the explanation that the behavior occurred because it was very easy for the experimenters to make it occur. (Tajfel, 1978, pp. 35-36)

Two points stand out: first, minimal intergroup discrimination is not based on incompatible group interests; second, the baseline conditions for intergroup competition seem indeed so minimal as to cause the suspicion that we are dealing here with some factor or process inherent in the intergroup situation itself. Our theoretical orientation was developed initially in response to these clues from our earlier experiments. We shall not trace the history of its development, however, but shall describe its present form.

Social Identity and Social Comparison

Many orthodox definitions of "social groups" are unduly restrictive when applied to the context of intergroup relations. For example, when members of two national or ethnic categories interact on the basis of their reciprocal beliefs about their respective categories and of the general relations between them, this is clearly intergroup behavior in the everyday sense of the term. The groups to which the interactants belong need not depend upon the frequency of intermember interaction, systems of role relationships, or

interdependent goals. From the social-psychological perspective, the essential criteria for group membership, as they apply to large-scale social categories, are that the individuals concerned define themselves and are defined by others as members of a group.

We can conceptualize a group, in this sense, as a collection of individuals who perceive themselves to be members of the same social category, share some emotional involvement in this common definition of themselves, and achieve some degree of social consensus about the evaluation of their group and of their membership in it. Following from this, our definition of intergroup behavior is basically identical to that of Sherif (1967, p. 62): any behavior displayed by one or more actors toward one or more others that is based on the actors' identification of themselves and the others as belonging to different social categories.

Social categorizations are conceived here as cognitive tools that segment, classify, and order the social environment, and thus enable the individual to undertake many forms of social action. But they do not merely systematize the social world; they also provide a system of orientation for *self-reference:* they create and define the individual's place in society. Social groups, understood in this sense, provide their members with an identification of themselves in social terms. These identifications are to a very large extent relational and comparative: they define the individual as similar to or different from, as "better" or worse than, members of other groups. It is in a strictly limited sense, arising from these considerations, that we use the term *social identity.* It consists, for the purposes of the present discussion, of those aspects of an individual's self-image that derive from the social categories to which he perceives himself as belonging. With this limited concept of social identity in mind, our argument is based on the following general assumptions:

1. Individuals strive to maintain or enhance their self-esteem: they strive for a positive self-concept.

2. Social groups or categories and the membership of them are associated with positive or negative value connotations. Hence, social identity may be positive or negative according to the evaluations (which

tend to be socially consensual, either within or across groups) of those groups that contribute to an individual's social identity.

3. The evaluation of one's own group is determined with reference to specific other groups through social comparisons in terms of value-laden attributes and characteristics. Positively discrepant comparisons between in-group and out-group produce high prestige; negatively discrepant comparisons between in-group and out-group result in low prestige.

From these assumptions, some related theoretical principles can be derived:

1. Individuals strive to achieve or to maintain positive social identity.

2. Positive social identity is based to a large extent on favorable comparisons that can be made between the in-group and some relevant out-groups: the in-group must be perceived as positively differentiated or distinct from the relevant out-groups.

3. When social identity is unsatisfactory, individuals will strive either to leave their existing group and join some more positively distinct group and/or to make their existing group more positively distinct.

The basic hypothesis, then, is that pressures to evaluate one's own group positively through in-group/out-group comparisons lead social groups to attempt to differentiate themselves from each other (Tajfel, 1978a; Turner, 1975b). There are at least three classes of variables that should influence intergroup differentiation in concrete social situations. First, individuals must have internalized their group membership as an aspect of their self-concept: they must be subjectively identified with the relevant in-group. It is not enough that the others define them as a group, although consensual definitions by others can become, in the long run, one of the most powerful causal factors determining a group's self-definition. Second, the social situation must be such as to allow for intergroup comparisons that enable the selection and evaluation of the relevant relational attributes. Not all between-group differences have evaluative significance (Tajfel, 1959), and those that do vary from group to group. Skin color, for instance, is apparently a more salient attribute in the United States than in Hong Kong (Morland,

1969); whereas language seems to be an especially salient dimension of separate identity in French Canada, Wales, and Belgium (Giles & Johnson, 1981; Giles & Powesland, 1975). Third, in-groups do not compare themselves with every cognitively available out-group: the out-group must be perceived as a relevant comparison group. Similarity, proximity, and situational salience are among the variables that determine out-group comparability, and pressures toward ingroup distinctiveness should increase as a function of this comparability. It is important to state at this point that, in many social situations, comparability reaches a much wider range than a simply conceived "similarity" between the groups.

The aim of differentiation is to maintain or achieve superiority over an out-group on some dimensions. Any such act, therefore, is essentially competitive. Fully reciprocal competition between groups requires a situation of mutual comparison and differentiation on a shared value dimension. In these conditions, intergroup competition, which may be unrelated to the objective goal relations between the groups, can be predicted to occur. Turner (1975b) has distinguished between social and instrumental or "realistic" competition. The former is motivated by self-evaluation and takes place through social comparison, whereas the latter is based on "realistic" self-interest and represents embryonic conflict. Incompatible group goals are necessary for realistic competition, but mutual intergroup comparisons are necessary, and often sufficient, for social competition. The latter point is consistent with the data from the minimal group experiments that mere awareness of an out-group is sufficient to stimulate in-group favoritism, and the observations (Doise & Weinberger, 1973; Ferguson & Kelley, 1964; Rabbie & Wilkens, 1971) that the possibility of social comparison generates "spontaneous" intergroup competition. . . .

References

Allen, V.L. & Wilder, D.A. (1975). Categorization, belief similarity and intergroup discrimination. *Journal of Personality and Social Psychology, 32,* 971-977.

Aschenbrenner, K.M., & Schaefer, R.E. (1980). Minimal intergroup situations: Comments on a mathematical model and on the research paradigm. *European Journal of Social Psychology, 10,* 389-398.

Billig, M. (1972). *Social categorization in intergroup relations.* Unpublished doctoral dissertation, University of Bristol.

Billig, M. (1973). Normative communication in a minimal intergroup situation. *European Journal of Social Psychology, 3,* 339-343.

Billig, M., & Tajfel, H. (1973). Social categorization and similarity in intergroup behavior. *European Journal of Social Psychology, 3,* 27-52.

Bornstein, G., Crum, L., Wittenbraker, J., Harring, K., Insko, C.A., & Thibaut, J. (1983a). On the measurement of social orientations in the minimal group paradigm. *European Journal of Social Psychology, 13.*

Bornstein, G., Crum, L., Wittenbraker, J., Harring, K., Insko, C.A., & Thibaut, J. (1983b). Reply to Turner's comments. *European Journal of Social Psychology, 13.*

Branthwaite, A., Doyle, S., & Lightbown, N. (179). The balance between fairness and discrimination. *European Journal of Social Psychology, 9,* 149-163.

Brewer, M.B. (1979a). In-group bias in the minimal intergroup situation: A cognitive-motivational analysis. *Psychological Bulletin, 86,* 307-327.

Brown, R. J., Tajfel, H., & Turner, J.C. (1980). Minimal group situations and intergroup discrimination. Comments on the paper by Aschenbrenner and Schaefer. *European Journal of Social Psychology, 10,* 399-424.

Brown, R.J., & Turner, J.C. (1981). Interpersonal and intergroup behaviour. In J.C. Turner and H. Giles (Eds.), *Intergroup behaviour.* Oxford: Basil Blackwell.

Doise, W., & Weinberger, M. (1973). Representations masculines dans differentes situation de recontres mixtes. *Bulletin de Psychologie, 26,* 649-657.

Ferguson, C.K., & Kelley, H.H. (1964). Significant factors in overevaluation of own group's product. *Journal of Abnormal and Social Psychology, 69,* 223-228.

Gerard, H.B. & Hoyt, M.F. (1974). Distinctiveness of social categorization and attitude toward in-group members. *Journal of Personality and Social Psychology, 29,* 836-842.

Giles, H., & Johnson, P. (1981). The role of language in ethnic group relations, In J.C. Turner and H. Giles (Eds.), Intergroup behavior. Oxford: Basil Blackwell.

Giles, H., & Powesland, P.F. (1975). *Speech style and social evaluation.* European Monographs in Social Psychology. London: Academic Press.

Locksley, A., Ortiz, V., & Hepburn, C. (1980). Social categorization and discrimination behaviour: Extinguishing the minimal intergroup discrimination effect. *Journal of Personality and Social Psychology, 39,* 773-783.

Morland, J.K. (1969). Race awareness among American and Hong Kong Chinese children. *American Journal of Sociology, 75,* 360-374.

Rabbie, J., & Wilkens, C. (1971). Intergroup competition and its effect on intra- and intergroup relations. *European Journal of Social Psychology, 1,* 215-234.

Sherif, M. (1967). *Group Conflict and Co-operation.* London: Routledge and Kegan Paul.

St. Claire, L., and Turner, J.C. (1982). The role of demand characteristics in the social categorization paradigm. *European Journal of Social Psychology, 12,* 307-314.

Tajfel, H. (1959). Quantitative judgement in social perception. *British Journal of Psychology, 10,* 16-29.

Tajfel, H. (1970). Experiments in intergroup discrimination. *Scientific American, 223,* 96-102.

Tajfel, H. (1978a). The achievement of group differentiation. In H. Tajfel (Ed.), *Differentiation between social groups: Studies in the social psychology of intergroup relations.* London: Academic Press.

Turner, J.C. (1975a). *Social Categorization of social comparison in intergroup relations.* Unpublished doctoral dissertation, University of Bristol.

Turner, J.C. (1975b). Social comparison and social identity: Some prospects for intergroup behavior. *European Journal of Social Psychology, 5,* 5-34.

Turner, J.C. (1980). Fairness or discrimination in intergroup behavior? A reply to Branthwaite, Doyle & Lightbrown. *European Journal of Social Psychology, 10,* 131-147.

Turner, J.C. (1982). Towards a cognitive redefinition of the social group. In H. Tajfel (Ed.), *Social identity and intergroup relations.* Cambridge: Cambridge University Press.

Turner, J.C. (1983a). A second reply to Bornstein, Crum, Wittenbraker, Harring, Insko, and Thibaut on the measurement of social orientations. *European Journal of Social Psychology, 13.*

Turner, J.C. (1983b). Some comments on "...the measurement of social orientations in the minimal group paradigm." *European Journal of Social Psychology, 13.*

Turner, J.C., & Giles, H. (Eds.). (1981). *Intergroup behavior.* Oxford: Basil Blackwell.

Turner, J.C., Sachdev, I., & Hogg, M.A. (1983). Social categorization, interpersonal attraction, and group formation. *British Journal of Social Psychology, 22,* 227-239.

Token Status And Problem-Solving Deficits: Detrimental Effects Of Distinctiveness And Performance Monitoring*

Delia S. Saenz

$\mathcal{E}$ditors' Note: In this article Delia Saenz describes a tightly-controlled laboratory experiment that examines what can occur when a person is in a group situation and thinks they are the only member of their group present, that is, when they think they hold token status. This reading is more technical in nature than others presented so far in this Workbook. We included it because we think it is important that you be exposed to a good example of how laboratory experiments in social psychology are carried out, and then written up for psychology journals. We are aware that without some background in statistics the article may be a bit confusing. However, we ask you to be patient in your reading of it as the text will describe the results even if you are not able to understand the statistics.

The present experiment examined whether extra-task worry is associated with performance deficits in token individuals, and also examined whether deficits occur in the ongoing performance of group members who are distinctive along a nonvisual dimension. Female subjects took turns solving anagrams with three other same-sex participants who were identified as students belonging to the same school as the subject (nontoken condition) or as students from a rival institution (token condition). The three other participants were actually confederates who had been videotaped previously, thus ensuring that all subjects received the same standard treatment. The primary dependent measure of ongoing performance was the percentage of anagrams solved. Extra-task worry was assessed by examining how well subjects monitored the successes/failures of group participants. The principle hypothesis was that, relative to nontokens, tokens would display poorer problem-solving capability and enhanced performance monitoring behavior. The results corroborated past work and demonstrated that even nonperceptual distinctiveness is detrimental to the individual's cognitive capabilities: token subjects solved significantly fewer anagrams than nontokens. Moreover, the data on the monitoring task revealed that tokens were more adept than nontokens at tracking the performance of group members. Theoretical implications regarding the role of self-presentational concern in promoting cognitive deficits among tokens are discussed.

Distinctive persons, by definition, attract disproportionate attention (Kanter, 1977; Lord & Saenz, 1985; Saenz & Lord, 1989; Taylor, Fiske, Etcoff, & Ruderman, 1978). Under certain conditions, this heightened social attention can lead to improved performance (e.g., Crocker & McGraw, 1984; Mullen & Baumeister, 1987; Ott, 1989). Numerically distinctive male nurses, for example, report receiving special treatment and this, in turn, increases their outcomes and motivation in the work setting (Ott, 1989). . . . Distinctiveness, however, can also engender negative consequences. Token women and minorities, for example, evince lowered job proficiency relative to their nontoken counterparts, and display diminished levels of involvement and contributions to the central task (Kanter, 1977; Wolman & Frank, 1975).

Often, the nature of differential outcomes that tokens attain is a function of the treatment they receive from majority group

* From Saenz, Delia S., *Token Status and Problem-Solving Deficits: Detrimental Effects of Distinctiveness and Performance Monitoring*. **Social Cognition,** Vol. 12, No. 1 (1994) pp. 61-74. Copyright ©1994 by The Guilford Press. Reprinted with permission.

members. In some cases, being distinctive is associated with favorable treatment, and not surprisingly these conditions result in positive outcomes for the token person (e.g., Crocker & McGraw, 1984; Ott, 1989). Conversely, unfavorable treatment of the distinctive group member can result in poor outcomes for him/her. Negative expectancies held by employers, for example, may lead them to assign the token to low responsibility positions (Kanter, 1977); also, prejudicial attitudes can result in biased evaluations of tokens' successes and failures (Garland & Price, 1977). . . .

Most research on token status suggests that forces external to the distinctive individual are responsible for the nature of outcomes (deficits, surfeits) that the token attains (Yoder, 1991). There is some work, however, which suggests that the performance of tokens may be affected even in the absence of differential treatment from majority group members. In one laboratory study, for example, subjects exchanged opinions with three other group participants who were either of the same gender as the subject or of the opposite gender (Lord & Saenz, 1985). Following the group conversation, tokens remembered less of what was said than their nontoken counterparts. . . .

The investigators suggested that the cognitive deficits incurred by tokens might be due to one of several underlying mechanisms. First, tokens might be influenced by heightened arousal. Specifically, being the token might induce the individual to believe that he/she is the center of attention (cf. Kanter, 1977; Taylor et al., 1978). This awareness might increase arousal and anxiety, which in turn, might narrow the token's range of attention and reduce his/her level of incidental learning (Easterbrook, 1959; Wine, 1971; Zajonc, 1980). Alternatively, token deficits might be due to an increase in self-focused attention (cf. Mullen & Chapman, 1989). Hence, tokens might turn attention inward and pay less attention to environmental information (Wicklund, 1982). Differential attention might impair processing of information relevant to the group task, particularly information relevant to majority members. In parallel fashion, processing of self-relevant information might be enhanced. Finally, it is possible that cognitive deficits

might be due to competing demands on the tokens' attentional resources. That is, tokens—like majority members—might be concerned with performing the central group task. This is often the explicit goal of the group interaction. However, and unlike majority members, tokens might also become acutely aware of their own salience relative to the other group members. Their self-perceived distinctiveness might engender heightened self-presentational concern. Ruminations such as: "I'm different." "What do they think of me?" "How am I coming across?" could divert the token's attention from the group task, thereby impairing performance.

Two features of the putative mediators identified by Lord and Saenz (1985) are noteworthy. First, the mechanisms listed might be concomitant effects of distinctiveness. Accordingly, concern with evaluation could engender increased physiological arousal (e.g., Cottrell, 1972; Geen, 1980; Wicklund, 1975), which in turn, might inform the individual about important elements in the environment on which to focus (Bond, 1982; Carver & Scheier, 1981). To the extent that one or more of these processes is activated, tokens' attentional resources might be either narrowed in range or divided between the central task and irrelevant concerns. These attentional consequences, whether produced independently or jointly, would result in the same outcome: impaired performance for the token.

A second feature of the mediators identified above is that they all involve strictly intrapsychic, as compared to interpersonal, processes. That is, the cognitive and motivational reactions of tokens described above are rooted in the tokens' perceptions of their own numerical status, and not in the actions of the majority group members. This line of reasoning suggests that simply knowing that one is distinctive can generate cognitive deficits in tokens, independent of majority members' behavior. Therefore, it may be the case that individual group members who believe they are distinctive but who possess no perceptually distinguishable features might also suffer performance deficits. If sheer distinctiveness leads to disproportionate concern about one's status, then the tokens' mere awareness of their numerical status should be sufficient to generate attention-based deficits.

Related work in the area of marginal status suggests that impression management concerns preoccupy the stigmatized participants of dyadic interactions, even when they possess a nonvisible blemish (Frable, Blackstone, & Scherbaum, 1990; Goffman, 1963; Jones, Farina, Hastorf, Markus, Miller, & Scott, 1984). Although the nonperceptual stigmas that produce such pervasive concern with self-presentation are typically attributes that are inherent in the marginal person and relatively permanent in nature (e.g., emotional handicap, alcohol/drug addiction, crime victim status), it is possible that temporary and situationally induced marginal status may evoke a similar response. Thus, token status—which is a function of the situational configuration, rather than a stable cross-situational condition—may also engender divided attention. The research conducted to date, however, has focused primarily on perceptual operationalizations of distinctiveness such as gender or race (e.g., Crocker & McGraw, 1984; Kanter, 1977; Lord & Saenz, 1985; 1989; Yoder, 1985). Whether or not nonperceptual tokens also incur costs as a function of their nonvisible distinctiveness remains unknown, and is one of the primary purposes for conducting the present experiment.

On-Going Task Performance

In addition to examining the consequences of nonperceptual distinctiveness, the present research tested whether *ongoing* performance is impaired in token individuals. In previous studies, the primary dependent measure (e.g., memory) has typically been assessed after subjects are no longer in the group (e.g., Lord & Saenz, 1985). Although such measures are expected to parallel the degree of attention directed at the central group task, the possibility remains that token deficits occur at the retrieval, rather than at the encoding of information. The distinction between deficits occurring at either stage is important. If errors occur only at retrieval, for example, token deficits are likely to be temporary. Given sufficient time, tokens might recover from their period of information loss and regain

access to information presented previously (cf. Gilbert & Osborne, 1989). By comparison, errors incurred at encoding are likely to have more detrimental and long-term consequences.

It is necessary to assess whether token status affects ongoing performance adversely, particularly if this work is to have any implications for outcomes attained by token women and minorities in the workplace or for token students in the classroom. After all, their performance based evaluations will depend primarily on how they perform while the group is intact. In an effort to capture the impact of token status as it occurs during the group interaction, thus, the current study employed a problem-solving activity (to be described below) as the central group task. By measuring ongoing performance while the token is in the "group" the present demonstration was intended to more closely parallel the experience faced by tokens in nonlaboratory situations, relative to previous studies. Additionally, by using a task different from previous demonstrations, the present work would expand the range of performance behaviors affected by the group member's distinctiveness.

Nature of Extra-Task Worry

Finally, the present study also attempted to assess one of the putative mediators of token deficits—distraction due to extra-task worry. If, as Lord and Saenz (1985) suggest, tokens are concerned with how they are coming across, then they should be engaged in cognitive activity that reflects this self-presentational concern. . . . The prediction was that tokens would display greater concern for the level of their performance than nontokens, and that consequently, they would be more accurate in recalling how well and how poorly they performed.

In sum, the present experiment sought to examine whether tokens who are of a different social category, but who *look no different* from the majority group members, display the typical token deficit effect on a problem-solving task. The experiment also attempted to capture the nature of distraction that putatively occupies tokens' attention.

Research Overview

Subjects were led to believe that they would take turns solving anagrams with three other persons, each located in a separate room, and that participants would be able to see and hear each other on television monitors. In reality, the three other participants were not live, but were instead confederates who had been recorded previously on videotape. All subjects "interacted" with the same videotaped female confederates. However, half of the subjects (tokens) believed that the other group participants were from a rival institution, whereas the other half (nontokens) believed that the others were from the same institution as themselves. Because tokens and nontokens saw the same videotaped others, any effects of the manipulation could not be attributed to differential treatment, verbal or nonverbal, on the part of the group members.

After the group interaction, subjects were asked to recall the number of anagrams that each participant had solved correctly. This measure was expected to capture self-presentational concern, in that it represented the extent to which subjects were aware of how they were performing relative to the other participants. "Keeping track" of their own and other participants' performance was expected to interfere with solving the anagrams.

Method

Subjects

Eighteen undergraduate women at a private midwestern university were recruited for a study ostensibly investigating problem-solving behavior in groups. The women received course credit for participating in the study. Half of the subjects were randomly assigned to the token condition, the other half to the nontoken condition. . . .

Procedure

Instructions. Upon arriving at the lab, the subject was given a description of the study and informed consent documents. As the subject read these forms, the experimenter left

and could be heard opening doors to adjacent rooms and addressing the other participants. After enough time had passed to allow subjects to complete the forms, the experimenter returned and explained that subjects would be participating in a group problem-solving task. They would take turns with three other students introducing themselves and then solving a series of anagrams. Group participants would be seated in separate rooms, each equipped with a camera, monitor, and microphone. They were told that the interaction would take place via closed-circuit TV in order to avoid embarrassment and distractions that might occur if group participants were placed in the same room. Additionally, subjects were told, the use of cameras and monitors would allow the experimenter to have a good view of each participant during the group exchange. In reality, of course, the adjacent rooms were empty and each subject participated individually.

The experimenter handed the subject a name tag and a deck of 72 sequentially numbered index cards—each with a different anagram typed on it. He explained that the group session would be comprised of 72 individual trials. Thus, for trial 1, one of the participants would be called on to solve the anagram on card 1. Regardless of whether she solved the anagram correctly or not, the experimenter would proceed to the next trial and call on a different participant to solve the anagram on card 2. Throughout the 72 trials, participants would be called on in random order and each would be prompted 18 times. The experimenter further indicated that each participant should respond whenever he called out her room number. Hence, because the subject was in Room 3, as designated by a large numeral "3" on the wall behind her, she should respond whenever the experimenter called on room 3. The other individuals, who were also given name tags, and were identified by room numbers would be called on in similar fashion.

The experimenter further requested that subjects not jump ahead in looking at subsequent anagrams, but rather that they turn the cards as the experimenter called out the trial number and prompted each participant in turn. Finally, subjects were instructed to look into the camera as they gave their responses, to watch their monitors as the other participants responded, and to refrain from making extraneous remarks. The experimenter explained that each participant's image would appear on the screen for 12 seconds as she attempted to solve the anagram in question, and that whatever image the subject saw on her screen was the same image seen by all participants. At this point, the experimenter responded to inquiries that the subject might have had about the procedure, and indicated that the group session would begin.

Group Interaction. The group session began with introductions, and then proceeded to the anagram portion. The experimenter called on each group participant, in turn, and asked her to state her name, class, major, and hobbies. When it was the subject's turn to respond, the experimenter switched from videotape to live. The subject was able to see and hear herself through the monitor, and believed that the other participants could also. When the subject's turn ended, the experimenter switched back to videotape. Introductions were followed by the group interaction, during which the experimenter again switched from videotape to live, as described above. After the anagram-solving task, subjects completed the performance monitoring measure, as well as manipulation checks on the institutional affiliation of the majority members. Then, they were debriefed, thanked, and given credit slips for their participation.

Dependent Measures and Predictions

The primary dependent measure of ongoing cognitive performance was the percentage of anagrams solved. Tokens were expected to solve fewer anagrams than were nontokens. In addition to the anagram performance measure, the experiment included a dependent variable representing self-presentational concern. This measure, presented on a separate questionnaire following the group interaction, asked subjects to recall the number of anagrams that each participant solved correctly. As mentioned previously, the central hypothesis was that tokens were expected to monitor their relative performance more closely than nontokens; hence, in comparison to task performance,

tokens were expected to out-perform nontokens on this measure.

Results

... Task Performance.... The main prediction for problem-solving performance was that tokens would perform more poorly then nontokens. . . .[T]he data confirmed this prediction: token subjects solved fewer anagrams (55%) than nontoken subjects (75%), F (1,16) 7.64, p <.05.[1] This result replicated the token deficit effect reported in previous work, and demonstrated that being the only one of a social category in an otherwise homogeneous group is detrimental to the subject's ongoing cognitive performance.

Performance Monitoring. If these deficits are associated, as previously argued, with heightened concern over performance, then tokens should have been more inclined to keep track of hits and misses than nontokens. . . .

The results revealed that tokens made fewer errors than nontokens in recalling the performance of both self (token X = 9.5%; nontoken X = 24.1%) and others (token X = 8.6%; nontoken X = 13.4%). . . .[O]verall error scores were 9.1% for tokens and 18.7% for nontokens, F (1,14) =4.81, p <.05. Only the main effect for token status emerged; neither the main effect of participant nor the interaction was statistically reliable.

Relationship Between Monitoring of Errors and Task Performance. Two additional analyses were conducted to assess the relationship between errors in performance monitoring and anagram solving capability. First, the correlation between these measures was assessed. As might be expected, the association between number of errors in recalling self and other performance and the number of anagrams solved was positive and significant, r = .51, p < .05. Hence, increased errors—which reflected inattention to performance of the group participants—were associated with better performance in solving anagrams. . . .

In sum, the pattern of means for the two dependent measures suggested that token subjects direct more attention toward extra-task worries than toward central group tasks, relative to nontoken subjects. Moreover, these performance tracking tendencies appear to be associated with problem-solving deficits.

Discussion

The current set of results extends previous work on token status in several ways. First, the present study demonstrates that a token need not look different from majority members to incur deficits. Knowing you are different is sufficient to divert your attention from the central task. This finding is in keeping with both classic and recent discussions on the behavioral consequences of marginal status (Frable et al., 1990; Goffman, 1963; Lewin, 1935). It emphasizes the social nature of self-definition and illustrates how one's self-view is often constructed in negotiation with the social context. In group settings, individuals respond not only to the behavior of others, but also to their own expectations of how others will perceive them. In the present study, token subjects were aware of their distinctive status despite the fact that they looked no different from majority members. Their awareness may have induced them to believe that they were being evaluated by the majority outgroup members. This worry, in turn, diverted their attention from the central task. By comparison, nontokens-who were not expected to have competing demands on their attention—did not show the same amount of concern, and consequently solved more anagrams. In general, then, nonperceptual distinctiveness produced deficits that parallel those found in experiments wherein a visible categorization attribute was used as the token variable.

A second contribution of the present work lies in its demonstration that deficits associated with token status are not limited to memory. Ongoing problem-solving capabilities are also impaired in distinctive persons. Previous work measured performance after the individual was no longer in the group (e.g., memory in the Lord & Saenz, 1985 study). The current study, in contrast, captured the impact of token status as it occurred during the group interaction. As predicted, tokens experienced decrements in performance relative to nontokens, suggesting that the detrimental consequences of token status are not limited to cognitive performance as measured via memory.

Finally, and perhaps most importantly, the current set of results provides evidence for the nature of self-preoccupation that diverts the token's attention from the central group task. The measure of performance monitoring indicated that rather than allocating their attention to solving the anagrams, tokens were thinking about how well or how poorly they were doing relative to majority members. The data suggested that they were busy counting hits and misses instead of simply generating solutions to the anagrams; ironically, this preoccupation proved to be detrimental.

It is notable that tokens were attuned not only to their own performance, but also to that of majority members. Such a pattern is consistent with a self-presentational analysis in that social comparison information might be particularly critical to the token's concern with evaluation. After all, "worrying about the image one is projecting" implicates the evaluation of others. When those others are participating in the same exercise as oneself, a natural response would be to compare one's own performance with that of the other group members. The results on the performance-monitoring measure indicate that this is exactly what tokens did—they focused on how well (or poorly) they and the majority members were doing.

Such a tendency, furthermore, might have been intensified in the present study by elements of the methodology. Specifically, tokens believed they were dissimilar along the dimension of school affiliation, and they were asked to find the correct solutions to an objective set of problems. It might have been that these features led them to see the group task as a competition between students of the two institutions. Even though the group interaction was described as simply a "group problem-solving task," and no explicit reference was made to school affiliation, the presence of rival school members could have heightened social comparison processes. This perception of competition would have applied equally to nontokens and tokens, however, the latter may have had the added burden of believing that they were "the sole representative" of their school in the group. Further, given their distinctive status, tokens may have felt the vulnerability associated with worrying that they might represent their ingroup poorly (Steele, 1993). Although no data were collected directly to assess this type of concern, the results were consistent with such an explanation: token status produced deficits in task performance, along with surfeits in social comparison tendencies.

Interestingly, the putative role of social comparison has not been explicitly highlighted in previous work on token status, possibly because the group tasks which have been employed previously have focused on expression of preferences rather than on objective performance. . . . The present work underscored the role of one form of extra-task worry that may impair a token's performance—social comparison. Additional work is needed. . . . For now, there is at least one thing that we can be certain of: distinctiveness has its costs.

Footnote

[1] Raw anagram scores were 9.9 for tokens, and 13.5 for nontokens, out of a possible score of 18.

References

Bond, C.F. (1982). Social facilitation: A self-presentational view. *Journal of Personality and Social Psychology*, 42, 1042-1050.

Carver, C.S., & Scheier, M.F. (1981). *Attention and self-regulation: A control theory approach to human behavior*. New York: Springer-Verlag.

Cottrell, N.B. (1972). Social facilitation. In C.G. McClintock (Ed.), *Experimental social psychology*. New York: Holt.

Crocker, J., & McGraw, K.M. (1984). What's good for the goose is not good for the gander. *American Behavioral Scientist*, 27, 357-369.

Easterbrook, J.A. (1959). The effect of emotion on cue utilization and the organization of behavior. *Psychological Review*, 66, 183-199.

Frable, D.E., Blackstone, T., & Scherbaum, C. (1990). Marginal and mindful: Deviants in social interaction. *Journal of Personality and Social Psychology*, 140-149.

Garland, H. & Price, K.H. (1977). Attributions toward women in management and attributions for their success and failure in managerial positions. *Journal of Applied Psychology*, 62, 29-33.

Geen, R.C. (1980). The effects of being observed on performance. In P.B. Paulus (Ed.), *Psychology of group influence* (pp. 61-98). Hillsdale, NJ: Lawrence Erlbaum Associates.

Gilbert, D.T., & Osborne, R.E. (1989). Thinking backward: Some curable and incurable consequences of cognitive busyness. *Journal of Personality and Social Psychology*, 57, 940-949.

Goffman, E. (1963). *Stigma: Notes on the management of a spoiled identity*. Englewood Cliffs, NJ: Prentice Hall.

Jones, E.E., Farina, A., Hastorf, A.H., Markus, H., Miller, D.T., & Scott, R.A. (1984). *Social stigma: The psychology of marked relationships*. New York: W.H. Freeman.

Kanter, R.M. (1977). *Men and women of the corporation*. New York: Basic Books.

Lewin, K. (1935). Psycho-sociological problems of a minority group. *Character and Personality*, 3, 175-187.

Lord, C.G., & Saenz, D.S. (1985). Memory deficits and memory surfeits: Differential cognitive consequences of tokenism for tokens and observers. *Journal of Personality and Social Psychology*, 49, 918-925.

Mullen, B., & Baumeister, R.F. (1987). Group effects on self-attention and performance: Social loafing, social facilitation, and social impairment. In C. Hendrick (Ed.), *Review of Personality and Social Psychology* (vol. 9), pp. 189-206. Sage.

Mullen, B., & Chapman, J.G. (1989). Focus of attention in groups: A self-attention perspective. *Journal of Social Psychology*, 129, 807-817.

Ott, E.M. (1989). Effects of the male-female ratio at work. *Psychology of Women Quarterly*, 13, 41-57.

Saenz, D.S., & Lord, C.G. (1989). Reversing roles: A cognitive strategy for undoing memory deficits associated with token status. *Journal of Personality and Social Psychology*, 56, 698-708.

Steele, C. (1993). *Collective prejudice: How stereotypes shape achievement and performance in American schools*. Invited address presented at the Western Psychological Association Convention, Phoenix, AZ.

Taylor, S.E., Fiske, S.T., Etcoff, N.L., & Ruderman, A.J. (1978). Categorical and contextual bases of person memory and stereotyping. *Journal of Personality and Social Psychology*, 36, 778-793.

Wicklund, R.A. (1975). Objective self-awareness. In L. Berkowitz (Ed.), *Advances in Experimental Social Psychology* (vol. 8, pp. 233-275). New York: Academic Press.

Wicklund, R.A. (1982). How society uses self-awareness. In J. Suls (Ed.), *Psychological Perspectives on the Self* (Vol. 1, pp. 209-230). Hillsdale, NJ: Erlbaum.

Wine, J. (1971). Text anxiety and direction of attention. *Psychological Bulletin*, 76, 92-104.

Wolman, C., & Frank, H. (1975). The token woman in a profession peer group. *American Journal of Orthopsychiatry*, 45, 164-171.

Yoder, J.D. (1985). An academic woman as a token: A case study. *Journal of Social Issues*, 41, 61-72.

Yoder (1991). Rethinking tokenism: Looking beyond the numbers. *Gender and Society*, 5, 178-192.

Zajonc, R.B. (1980). Compresence. In P.B. Paulus (Ed.), *Psychology of group influence* (pp. 35-60). Hillsdale, NJ: Erlbaum.

Social Loafing Across Cultures
David Matsumoto

℮ditors' Note: Until recently it was common practice among American social psychologists to assume that findings obtained using white, middle-class, American college students applied to everyone. This reading by David Matsumoto demonstrates that this may not always be the case. He describes research that shows that people in the U.S. tend to work less when in a group than if they are alone, while people in Japan and the People's Republic of China tend to work more when in a group than when alone. This article reinforces Graham's point in Chapter 1 that it is critical to consider a variety of populations if we want to understand how we function psychologically.

Knowledge Based on Research in the United States

Research on group productivity has typically shown that individual productivity often declines in larger groups (Latane, Williams, & Harkins, 1979). These findings have contributed to the coining of the term, *social loafing.* Two factors appear to contribute to this phenomenon. One is the reduced efficiency resulting from the loss of coordination among workers' efforts. As group membership increases, presumably the lack of coordination among the people tends to reduce efficiency, resulting in lack of activity or duplicate activity. This consequently results in loss of productivity.

The second factor typically identified as a contributor to lack of group productivity involves the reduction in effort by individuals when they work in groups as compared to when they work by themselves (social loafing). Latane and his colleagues (Latane, 1981; Latane, Williams, & Harkins, 1979) have conducted a number of studies investigating group size, coordination, and effort. They have found that larger groups produced lack of both coordination and effort, resulting in decreased productivity. Latane (1981) attributed these findings to a diffusion of responsibility in groups. That is, as group size increases, the responsibility for getting a job done is divided among more people, and many group members slack off because their individual contribution is less recognizable.

Cross-Cultural Findings on Group Productivity

Several cross-cultural studies suggest that social loafing is definitely *not* generalizable across other cultures. Earley (1989), for example, examined social loafing in an organizational setting among managerial trainees in the United States and the People's Republic of China. Subjects in both cultures worked on a task under conditions of low or high accountability and low or high shared responsibility. The results were clear, indicating that social loafing was observed only among the American subjects, whose individual performances in a group were less than when working alone, but not among the Chinese.

Shirakashi (1985) and Yamaguchi, Okamoto, and Oka (1985) conducted studies involving Japanese participants in several tasks. They showed that not only did social loafing not occur, but exactly the opposite occurred. That is, being in a group enhanced individual performance of their subjects rather than diminished it. Gabrenya, Wang, and Latane (1985) also demonstrated this *social striving*, not social loafing, in a sample of Chinese schoolchildren.

Several authors have offered some speculations concerning why social striving has been observed in other cultures. These explanations center on the culture's degree of collectivism, or group orientation. Cultures that are more collectivistic—such as China and Japan—foster interpersonal interdependence and group collective functioning more than does the individualistic American culture. As a result, groups tend to be more productive in these cultures, precisely because they foster coordination among ingroup members. They also place higher value on individual contributions in group settings.

Interestingly, a trend toward social striving may also be occurring within the United States. Several studies involving American subjects have begun to challenge the traditional notions of social loafing (for example, Harkins, 1987; Harkins & Petty, 1982; Shepperd & Wright, 1989; Weldon & Gargano, 1988; Zaccaro, 1984). Jackson and Williams (1985), for instance, showed that Americans working collectively indeed improved performance and productivity. Thus, our notions of social loafing and group productivity are challenged not only cross-culturally, but within our own American culture as well. With increased American interest in the organizational and management styles of other countries, particularly Japan, this topic is sure to gain even more attention in the future.

References

Earely, P.C. (1989). Social loafing and collectivism: A comparison of the United States and the People's Republic of China. *Administrative Science Quarterly, 34*, 565-581.

Gabrenya, W.K., Jr., Wang, Y., & Latane, B. (1985). Social loafing on an optimizing task: Cross-cultural differences among Chinese and Americans. *Journal of Cross-Cultural Psychology, 16*, 223-242.

Harkins, S.G. (1987). Social loafing and social facilitation. *Journal of Experimental Social Psychology, 23*, 1-18.

Harkins, S.G., & Petty, R.E. (1982). Effects of task difficulty and task uniqueness on social loafing. *Journal of Personality and Social Psychology, 43*, 1214-1229.

Jackson, J.M., & Williams, K.D. (1985). Social loafing on difficult task: Working collectively can improve performance. *Journal of Personality and Social Psychology, 49*, 937-942.

Latane, B. (1981). The psychology of social impact. *American Psychologist, 36*, 343-356.

Latane, B., Williams, K., & Harkins. (1979). Many hands make light the work: The causes and consequences of social loafing. *Journal of Personality and Social Psychology, 37*, 322-332.

Shepperd, J., & Wright, R. (1989). Individual contributions to a collective effort: An incentive analysis. *Personality and Social Psychology Bulletin, 15*, 141-149.

Shirakashi, S. (1985). Social loafing of Japanese students. *Hiroshima Forum for Psychology, 10*, 35-40.

Weldon, E., & Gargano, G.M. (1988). Cognitive loafing: The effects of accountability and shared responsibility on cognitive effort. *Personality and Social Psychology Bulletin, 14*, 159-171.

Yamaguchi, Okamoto, K., & Oka, T. (1985). Effects of coactor's presence: Social loafing and social facilitation. *Japanese Psychological Research, 27*, 215-222.

Zaccaro, S.J. (1984). The role of task attractiveness. *Personality and Social Psychology Bulletin, 10*, 99-106.

✓ PROJECT 2.1
What Is A Group?

I.   The term "group" has been defined in a number of ways. How "group" is defined can affect the types of research questions people ask, including which collections of people even constitute a group. Three definitions of a group are listed below.
   A.   *People who share a common fate*
   B.   *A collection of people who have face-to-face interactions on a regular basis*
   C.   *Two or more people who decide that they are a group*

II.   For this project, give one of these definitions of a group to an individual, and after they read the definition, ask this person to list all of the groups to which he or she belongs. You will need 3 different people. Each person will read one of the three definitions. Try to ask people who are members of different groups.

III. After 3 people complete your project, examine their responses. Do their responses vary according to how a group was defined? How do they vary (if they do)? What do their responses say about the definitions? What is your definition of a group? Does it matter for psychological research which definition is used? What if no definition had been used, and you asked your participants to list the groups to which they belong? Write a one-page description of the responses you received and how these responses were affected by the definition that individuals were given.

✂---

A group is: *People who share a common fate*

Using this definition of a group, please list all of the groups to which you belong.

_____

_____

_____

_____

_____

_____

_____

_____

_____

_____

A group is: *A collection of people who have face-to-face interactions on a regular basis*

Using this definition of a group, please list all of the groups to which you belong.

_____

_____

_____

_____

_____

_____

_____

_____

_____

✂---

A group is: *Two or more people who decide that they are a group*

Using this definition of a group, please list all of the groups to which you belong.

_____

_____

_____

_____

_____

_____

_____

_____

_____

✓ PROJECT 2.2
In-group And Out-group Behaviors

I.   As you read, according to Tajfel's social identity theory (Tajfel & Turner, 1986), our self-esteem is in part based on our membership in positively-viewed groups. This is a major benefit of being a part of a group, but there are other benefits that come from group membership.

II.   This project investigates the benefits people derive from being members of groups. For this project, choose three people in the same gender, racial, or ethnic group, and ask them about the benefits they derive from their group membership. Conduct your interview with each of the individuals so that you can answer the following questions:

• To what group do these people belong?

_____

_____

• Did these group members perceive their group as positive or negative? Were they in agreement in their evaluation of the group?

_____

_____

_____

_____

• How much did they identify with their group? Were the individuals equal in their level of identification with their group?

_____

_____

_____

_____

• What benefits did the members say they derived from the group?

_____

_____

_____

- Which benefits were mentioned most frequently?

  _____

  _____

- What were some of the negative consequences of being part of the group?

  _____

  _____

  _____

  _____

- Were there any benefits some members spoke positively of that were seen as disadvantages for others? _____ If yes, which ones?

  _____

  _____

  _____

  _____

- After interviewing these people and answering these questions, what do you think belonging to this group provided for these group members? Do your findings fit with social identity theory? If yes, how? If no, why not?

  _____

  _____

  _____

  _____

  _____

  _____

  _____

  _____

  _____

  _____

  _____

✓ PROJECT 2.3
Deindividuation

I.   Another effect that groups can have on us is called "deindividuation." This occurs when we are in a group, and we lose sight of ourselves and our concern for what others think of us. This loss of self-awareness and evaluation apprehension is especially likely to happen in group situations that foster anonymity and that draw attention away from the individual. The reading by Ron Jones on the "Third Wave" dramatically illustrates how group forces can foster deindividuation. There are also examples in our everyday lives. A mob scene is an obvious example of this behavior, and this behavior also occasionally occurs at sporting events or in situations in which all of those in a group wear the same clothing, chant the same phrases, or engage in some impulsive group action. Being part of a group can create a feeling of anonymity, freeing people from the social constraints they would normally experience. This leads them to commit acts that they would not normally do when they are not part of the group. Racial or ethnic violence often takes place when those committing the violence are in states of deindividuation.

II.   This project will examine deindividuation. Find and copy 2 articles in a newspaper or magazine that describe events in which deindividuation took place. If possible, try to find articles that discuss deindividuated behaviors against different gender, racial, or ethnic groups.

III.   Then, discuss why being anonymous in this group situation led to the aggressive or non-normative behavior described in each of the articles. Also discuss how you would change the situation to decrease deindividuation and to possibly decrease the occurrence of non-normative or aggressive behaviors. Write your answers below and on the back of this sheet, and turn in your responses to your instructor.

C h a p t e r   3

Creating Cooperation Through Group Processes

Chapter 2 examined some of the processes that occur when people are members of existing or newly created groups. It contained an example of how quickly groups can become the center of our lives, along with discussions of how easily groups can be formed, how we use our group membership for self-enhancement purposes, the consequence of holding solo or token status, and of the dangers in assuming that all groups function psychologically in the same way. Chapter 3 continues our discussion of groups by focusing on the research that can help groups cooperate and to achieve common goals.

A thread linking each of the articles in this section is the question, "How can our knowledge of group processes foster cooperation between gender, racial, and ethnic groups?" The section begins with a brief description of a famous study conducted by Muzafer Sherif and his colleagues, which explores the conditions for group competition and cooperation. The following article presents work by Elliot Aronson and his colleagues that led to a technique for increasing cooperation in the classroom between students of differing ethnic and racial backgrounds.

While increasing contact between conflicting groups can lead to a lessening of conflict, this does not always occur. In the next piece Samuel Gaertner, John Dovidio, and Betty Bachman present a refinement of the contact hypothesis that explores a more complex view of the processes involved when groups interact with one another. The final article is by Herbert Kelman, and it provides a glimpse into how research on group processes can be applied to an ongoing and long-standing ethnic conflict. Kelman has applied group processes in the Israeli-Palestinian conflict to help promote social change.

This chapter, like the previous two, raises both pragmatic and theoretical issues about the relationship of the individual to the group. These articles present actual solutions to vexing social problems. Again, as you read the articles in this section of the Workbook think about how you might be able to apply these solutions and approaches to the conflicts in your daily life and to the conflicts between gender, race, and ethnic groups.

Research Highlight

Eagles vs. Rattlers

Editors' Note: The readings in the previous chapter demonstrated the power of the group. One outcome of group processes can be an increase in conflict when groups are competing with one another, but there are also certain circumstances in which groups will cooperate with each other. This Research Highlight describes a famous study by Muzafer Sherif in which he and his colleagues studied behaviors relating to group processes at a boys' summer camp. Among these behaviors were conflicts such as food fights and acts that were primarily competitive such as tug-of-war contests. Most importantly, this study shed light on ways in which these competing and occasionally fighting groups of boys could be brought together to cooperate with one another. Perhaps, this article can show us how we can bring gender, racial, and ethnic groups together.

What are the foundations of group conflict? How can we overcome it? Muzafer Sherif and his associates asked these questions in a field study they carried out in the summer of 1954. They wanted to study how informal groups would develop and interact. In order to do this they set up a summer camp for eleven- and twelve-year-old boys. Prior to the start of the camp twenty-two boys, all white males who did not know one another, were recruited and divided into two groups. The two groups were brought to the camp separately and placed in separate housing. Over the course of the first week the boys, who were unaware that they had been divided into groups, took part in regular camp activities and games. During this period they formed close bonds with their housemates and a sense of group identity developed in each of the two groups.

Sherif and his colleagues thought that one reason that group conflicts arise is that groups often have competing aims. To test their hypothesis, they brought the two groups together in a series of competitive situations—the groups played games such as baseball, football, and tug-of-war. As the competitions progressed, the groups became more and more antagonistic toward one another. They began calling one another names, and even after the games were done these antagonistic feelings carried over to their subsequent interactions with one another. The groups, who had come to call themselves the "Eagles" and the "Rattlers," carried out a series of raids on each others' camps and several more name calling episodes occurred between the groups. Along with this increased antagonism, the experimenters also saw an

increase in solidarity, morale, and cooperation within each of the groups.

Sherif and his associates then focused on what might reduce this group antagonism by testing whether pleasant social contact between members of the two groups would lessen the hostility between them. The experimenters arranged a series of social events that brought members of the two groups together—going to the movies, eating their meals together, and so on. Instead of reducing the friction between the two groups, these activities increased the conflict. Food fights broke out, spit wads and dirty words flew, and shoving matches occurred between members of the two groups.

It was clear to Sherif and his colleagues that simply having the two groups interact with one another was no way to reduce group conflict. They then decided to test whether or not they could increase harmony between the groups by having them work at some common task that would benefit both, and that could not be accomplished if only one group took part in the task. The experimenters first had the two groups help repair a breakdown in the water supply. Later, when the boys asked for a movie they were told that the camp could not afford to rent them one. The two groups responded by pooling their money and choosing a film they then watched together. Finally, while on an outing, the two groups were told that the truck that was to go back to town to pick up their food would not start. The two groups joined together to pull the truck until it started up again.

Having the boys work together in situations where they had superordinate goals—goals that benefited all of them and that required cooperation—did not immediately lead to harmony between members of the two groups. Initially, the boys went back to their antagonistic ways, but gradually the cooperative acts began reducing the conflict between them. Shoving matches became less frequent, there was less name calling heard, and new friendships that crossed group boundaries began to develop. By the end of the camp, the boys had overcome their group-based antagonisms. In fact, when given the chance to name their best friends at the camp, they were now much more likely to name a member of the other group than they had been before participating in the situations with superordinate goals. As Sherif and his associates put it, "hostility gives way when groups pull together to achieve overriding goals which are real and compelling to all concerned."

Sherif's research dramatically illustrated the principle that cooperation reduces conflict. However, because the study only involved middle-class white boys, we are left with this question: Could this principle help reduce conflict between gender, racial, and ethnic groups?

Based on material in Sherif, M. (1966). *In common predicament: Social psychology of intergroup conflict and cooperation.* Boston: Houghton Mifflin.

Cooperation And Interdependence:
The Jigsaw Classroom

Elliot Aronson, Timothy D. Wilson, and Robin M. Akert

ditors' Note: As was shown in the description of Sherif's research, social psychological researchers have sought ways for reducing group conflict. Reducing conflict between groups in the classroom is clearly important as it will lead to a more welcoming and productive environment for all. The following piece describes experiments conducted by Elliot Aronson and his collaborators in which they developed a technique that led to an interdependent classroom environment. The authors go on to discuss the positive influence that this "jigsaw" classroom environment had on the relationships between students of various racial and ethnic backgrounds.

. . . Let's paint a typical scenario. Imagine a sixth-grader of Mexican American origin, whom we will call Carlos. Carlos has been attending schools in an underprivileged neighborhood for his entire life. Because the schools in his neighborhood were not well equipped or well staffed, his first five years of education were somewhat deficient. Suddenly, without much warning or preparation, he is bused to a school in a predominantly white middle-class neighborhood.

As you know from experience, the traditional classroom is a highly competitive, factorylike environment. The typical scene involves the teacher asking a question; immediately, several hands go into the air as the children strive to show the teacher that they know the answer. When a teacher calls on one child, several others groan, because they've missed an opportunity to show the teacher how smart they are. If the child who is called on hesitates or comes up with the wrong answer, there is a renewed and intensified flurry of hands in the air, perhaps even accompanied by whispered, derisive comments directed at the student who failed. Thus, Carlos finds he must compete against white middle-class students who have had better preparation than he and who have been reared to hold white middle-class values, which include working hard in pursuit of good grades, raising one's hand enthusiastically whenever the teacher asks a question, and so on. In effect, Carlos has been thrust into a highly competitive situation for which he is unprepared and in which payoffs are made for abilities he has not yet developed. He is virtually guaranteed to lose. After a few failures, Carlos, feeling defeated, humiliated, and dispirited, stops raising his hand and can hardly wait for the bell to ring to signal the end of the school day.

In the typical desegregated classroom, to use Allport's (1954) terms, the students were not of equal status and were not pursuing common goals. Indeed, one might say that they were in a tug-of-war on an uneven playing field. When one examines the situation closely, it is easy to see why Stephan (1978) found a general decrease in the self-esteem of minority youngsters following desegregation. Moreover, given the competitive atmosphere of the classroom, it is likely that the situation would have exacerbated whatever stereotypes were present in the youngsters' minds prior to desegregation. Specifically, given that the minority kids were ill-prepared for the competitiveness of the classroom, it is not surprising that some of the white kids quickly concluded that the minority kids were stupid, unmotivated, and sullen—just as they had suspected (Wilder & Shapiro, 1989). Moreover, it is likely that the minority kids might conclude that the white kids were arrogant show-offs. This is an example of the self-fulfilling prophecy.

How could we change the atmosphere of the classroom so that it comes closer to Gordon Allport's prescription for the effectiveness of contact? Specifically, how could we get white students and minority students to be of equal status, mutually dependent, and in pursuit of common goals? One of the authors of this textbook got to find out. In 1971, the school system of Austin, Texas, was desegregated. Within a few weeks, the schools were in turmoil. African American, white, and Mexican American children were in open conflict; fistfights broke out between the various racial groups in the corridors and school yards. The school superintendent invited Elliot Aronson, who was then a professor at the University of Texas, to enter the system with the mandate to do anything within reason to create a more harmonious environment. After spending a few days observing the dynamics of several classrooms, Aronson and his graduate students were strongly reminded of the situation that existed in the Sherif (1966) camp experiment. With the findings of that study in mind, they developed a technique that created an interdependent classroom atmosphere, designed to place the students of various racial and ethnic groups in pursuit of common goals. They called it the jigsaw classroom, because it resembled the assembling of a jigsaw puzzle (Aronson & Bridgeman, 1979; Aronson & Gonzalez, 1988; Aronson, Stephan, Sikes, Blaney, & Snapp, 1978; Aronson & Thibodeau, 1992).

Here is how the jigsaw classroom works: Students are placed in six-person learning groups. The day's lesson is divided into six paragraphs, so that each student has one segment of the written material. For example, if the students are to learn the life of Eleanor Roosevelt, her biography is arranged in six parts. Each student has possession of a unique and vital part of the information, which, like the pieces of a jigsaw puzzle, must be put together before anyone can learn the whole picture. The individual must learn his or her own section and teach it to the other members of the group—who do not have any other access to that material. Thus, if Debbie wants to do well on the ensuing exam about the life of Eleanor Roosevelt, she must pay close attention to Carlos (who is reciting on Roosevelt's girlhood years), to Natalie (who is reciting on Roosevelt's years in the White House), and so on.

Unlike the traditional classroom, where students are competing against each other, the jigsaw classroom has students depending on each other. In the traditional classroom, if Carlos, because of anxiety and discomfort, is having difficulty reciting, the other students can easily ignore him (or even put him down) in their zeal to show the teacher how smart they are. But in the jigsaw classroom, if Carlos is having difficulty reciting, it is now in the best interests of the other students to be

patient, make encouraging comments, and even ask friendly, probing questions to make it easier for Carlos to bring forth the knowledge within him.

Through the jigsaw process, the children begin to pay more attention to each other and to show respect for each other. As you might expect, a child like Carlos would respond to this treatment by simultaneously becoming more relaxed and more engaged; this would inevitably produce an improvement in his ability to communicate. In fact, after a couple of weeks the other students were struck by their realization that Carlos was a lot smarter than they had thought he was. They began to like him. Carlos began to enjoy school more and began to see the Anglo students in his group not as tormentors but as helpful and responsible teammates. Moreover, as he began to feel increasingly comfortable in class and started to gain more confidence in himself, Carlos's academic performance began to improve. As his academic performance improved, so did his self-esteem. The vicious circle had been broken; the elements that had been causing a downward spiral were changed—the spiral moved dramatically upward.

The formal data that Aronson and his colleagues gathered from the jigsaw experiments were clear and striking. Compared to students in traditional classrooms, students in jigsaw groups showed a decrease in prejudice and stereotyping, as well as an increase in their liking for their groupmates, both within and across ethnic boundaries. In addition, children in the jigsaw classrooms performed better on objective exams and showed a significantly greater increase in self-esteem than children in traditional classrooms. Children in the jigsaw classrooms also showed far greater liking for school than those in traditional classrooms. Moreover, children in schools where the jigsaw technique was practiced showed substantial evidence of true integration—that is, in the school yard there was far more intermingling among the various races and ethnic groups than in the yards of schools using more traditional classroom techniques. Finally, children in the jigsaw classrooms developed a greater ability to empathize with others and to see the world through the perspective of others than children in traditional classrooms did (Aronson & Bridgeman, 1979).

The jigsaw approach was first tested in 1971; since then, several similar cooperative techniques have been developed (see Cook, 1985; Johnson & Johnson, 1987, 1989; Sharan, 1980; Slavin, 1980). The striking results described above have been successfully replicated in thousands of classrooms in all regions of the country and abroad. The cooperative movement in education, as a way of achieving the goals of school desegregation, has grown by leaps and bounds and now constitutes something of a revolution within the field of public education. Alfie Kohn (1986) estimated that by the mid-1980s more than 25,000 teachers were using some form of cooperative learning in the United States alone--and hundreds more have been adopting it every year. John McConahay (1981), one of our nation's foremost experts on race relations, has called the cooperative learning revolution the single most effective practice for improving race relations in desegregated schools. According to Samuel Gaertner and his colleagues (1990), the process of cooperation is effective in part because the mere act of participating in a cooperative group succeeds in breaking down in-group versus out-group perceptions and allows the individual to develop the cognitive category of "one group."

In recent years, cooperative strategies have been extended from students in the classroom to teachers working together to sharpen their teaching abilities (Hammerman, 1995). And an even more radical departure from the factorylike competitiveness of the traditional classroom to a more cooperative, nonbureaucratic, student-centered approach is beautifully documented by Deborah Meier (1995) in her recent book *The Power of Their Ideas*. Meier, as founder and director of a cluster of cooperatively run public schools in East Harlem, has succeeded, over the years, in dramatically raising the performance and lowering the dropout rate of her students.

In sum, although the initial optimism about eliminating prejudice that occurred after the 1954 Supreme Court decision was a bit premature, we now have good evidence that we are on the right track. Research on cooperative learning groups is extremely encouraging and demonstrates beyond a doubt that, with proper care and in a sensible environment, integrated contact can produce a significant decrease in prejudice and marked improvements in students' self-esteem and classroom performance. The jigsaw experiments have taught us that under the proper conditions, contact is a viable and powerful tool in the battle against prejudice.

References

Allport, G. (1954). *The nature of prejudice*. Reading, MA: Addison-Wesley.

Aronson, E., & Bridgeman, D. (1979). Jigsaw groups and the desegregated classroom: In pursuit of common goals. *Personality and Social Psychology Bulletin, 5*, 438-446.

Aronson, E., & Gonzalez, A. (1988). Desegregation, jigsaw, and the Mexican-American experience. In P. A. Katz & D. Taylor (Eds.), *Towards the elimination of racism: Profiles in controversy*. New York: Plenum.

Aronson, E., Stephan, C., Siekes, J., Blaney, N., & Snapp, M. (1978). *The jigsaw classroom*. Beverly Hills, CA: Sage.

Aronson, E., & Thibodeau, R. (1992). The jigsaw classroom: A cooperative strategy for reducing prejudice. In J. Lynch, C. Modgil, & S. Modgil (Eds.), *Cultural diversity in the schools*. London: Falmer Press.

Cook, S. W. (1985). Experimenting on social issues: The case of school desegregation. *American Psychologist, 40*, 452-460.

Gaertner, S. L., Mann, J. A., Dovidio, J. F., & Murrell, A. J. (1990). How does cooperation reduce intergroup bias? *Journal of Personality and Social Psychology, 59*, 692-704.

Johnson, D. W., & Johnson, R. T. (1987). *Learning together and alone: Cooperative, competitive, and individualistic learning* (2nd ed.). Englewood Cliffs, NJ: Prentice Hall.

Johnson, D. W., & Johnson, R. T. (1989). *A meta-analysis of cooperative, competitive, and individualistic goal structures*. Hillsdale, NJ: Erlbaum.

Kohn, A. (1986). *No contest*. Boston: Houghton Mifflin.

McConahay, J. B. (1981). Reducing racial prejudice in desegregated schools. In W. D. Hawley (Ed.), *Effective school desegregation*. Beverly Hills, CA: Sage.

Meier, D. (1995). *The power of their ideas*. New York: Beacon.

Sharan, S. (1980). Cooperative learning in small groups. *Review of Educational Research, 50*, 241-271.

Sherif, M. (1966). *In common predicament: Social psychology of intergroup conflict and cooperation*. Boston: Houghton Mifflin.

Slavin, R. E. (1980). Cooperative learning and desegregation. Paper presented at the meeting of the American Psychological Association.

Stephan, W. G. (1979). School desegregation: An evaluation of predictions made in Brown vs. Board of Education. *Psychological Bulletin, 85*, 217-238.

Wilder, D. A., & Shapiro, P. N. (1989). Role of competition-induced anxiety in limiting the beneficial impact of positive behavior by an out-group member. *Journal of Personality and Social Psychology, 56,* 60-69.

Revisiting The Contact Hypothesis: The Induction Of A Common Ingroup Identity

Samuel L. Gaertner, John F. Dovidio, and Betty A. Bachman

ℰditors' Note: Under certain conditions intergroup bias and conflict can be reduced through contact between groups. In the following piece, Gaertner, Dovidio, and Bachman discuss their research showing how the creation of a superordinate identity for members of separate groups can decrease bias between groups. They present a series of studies in which they examine the conditions that can lead to such an identity, and show that it is possible to do this without necessarily undermining an individual's original group identity. This work is important as it speaks to how individuals can be brought together without the threat that they will be asked to surrender an important social identity as a condition of resolving a conflict or overcoming a bias.

This paper reviews evidence pertaining to the Common Ingroup Identity Model for reducing intergroup bias. This model proposes that intergroup bias and conflict can be reduced by factors that transform members' cognitive representations of the memberships from two groups to one more inclusive social entity. Theoretically, a common ingroup identity extends or redirects the cognitive and motivational processes that produce positive feelings toward ingroup members to former outgroup members. It is proposed that the prerequisite features specified by the Contact Hypothesis (Allport, 1954; Cook, 1985), such as equal status between the memberships, cooperative interdependence, opportunity for self-revealing interactions and egalitarian norms, successfully reduce bias, in part, because they help transform members' perceptions of the memberships from "Us" and "Them" to a more inclusive "We." Evidence from a laboratory experiment, two survey studies involving students attending a multi-ethnic high school and executives who have experienced a corporate merger, and a field experiment involving fans attending a college football game are summarized. In general, across these diverse settings, greater perceptions of a superordinate identity predicted lower levels of intergroup bias toward original outgroup members. . . .

One of the more persistent problems in the study of social conflict has been the identification of strategies that promote more positive intergroup attitudes and behaviors. The more we discover about the cognitive and motivational processes related to prejudice, discrimination and racism, for example, the more pessimistic the picture becomes (Rothbart & John, 1985). Even people with liberal, egalitarian values, who regard themselves as nonprejudiced and nondiscriminatory do not entirely escape these cognitive and motivational dynamics (see Gaertner & Dovidio, 1986; Crosby, Bromley & Saxe, 1980; Devine, 1989). Gaertner and Dovidio (1986) reported a series of studies about a contemporary form of racism, *aversive racism,* that revealed that many whites with genuinely liberal, egalitarian values discriminate against blacks in subtle, rationalizable ways that preclude them from recognizing their behaviors as racially biased (see also, Dovidio & Gaertner, 1991; Murrell, Dietz-Uhler, Dovidio, Gaertner & Drout, 1993). The major goals of our subsequent research have been to develop interventions for improving intergroup relations; to identify strategies that can specifically bring the attitudes and behaviors of aversive racists into a closer alignment with their nonprejudiced, nondiscriminatory self-images; and to understand theoretically the processes by which these interventions and strategies may change intergroup attitudes.

Perspective on Reducing Bias

. . . [F]or the past half-century, the revised Contact Hypothesis (Allport, 1954; Amir, 1969; Cook, 1985) has been social science's major contribution to reducing intergroup bias and conflict. It proposes that simple contact between groups is not sufficient to improve intergroup relations. Rather, to reduce bias, the contact situation must contain certain conditions, including, for example: equal status between the groups, cooperative intergroup interactions, opportunities for personal acquaintance between outgroup members and supportive egalitarian norms. Contact under these conditions does reduce bias (see Cook, 1985), presumably by producing more favorable impressions of outgroup members. Nevertheless, it has not been clear theoretically just how or through what processes they produce this positive effect.

Coincident with our search for strategies to reduce bias, we have been reconsidering whether the behavior we observed earlier pertaining to aversive racism was driven primarily by pro-ingroup biases initiated by social categorization processes, rather than by unconscious anti-outgroup attitudes as we originally believed (Gaertner, Dovidio, Banker, Rust, Nier, Mottola & Ward, in press a). While it may not matter very much to the targets of discrimination whether they are disadvantaged because of pro-ingroup or anti-outgroup biases, this may be an important consideration when identifying strategies that could reduce bias and discrimination.

If portions of contemporary interracial behavior are driven by pro-ingroup biases, it may suggest that the racial biases of some people may be driven, at least in part, by an inability to expand their circle of inclusion when considering other people's ingroup and outgroup status. Therefore, strategies that expand the inclusiveness of one's ingroup to include people who would otherwise be regarded as outgroup members may have beneficial consequences for promoting more positive intergroup attitudes and behaviors. This is the fundamental idea of the Common Ingroup Identity Model (see Gaertner, Dovidio, Anastasia, Batman & Rust, 1993) that has been guiding our current research. From this perspective, the reason why the features specified by the Contact Hypothesis (Allport, 1954; Cook, 1985) reduce intergroup bias and conflict is because, in part, they transform members' cognitive representations of the memberships from two groups to one group. This change in perception of the memberships is proposed to produce more positive views of outgroup members.

Common Ingroup Identity Model

In the Common Ingroup Identity Model, we propose that the causal relation between the conditions of contact and reduced intergroup bias is mediated by changes in members' perceptions of the aggregate from two groups to one more inclusive group. . ..

Theoretically, the process by which a revised, more inclusive common ingroup identity can reduce intergroup bias rests partially on two conclusions of Brewer's (1979) analysis and upon propositions of social identity theory (Tajfel & Turner, 1979) and self-categorization theory (Turner, 1985). First, intergroup bias usually begins with (see Allport, 1954), and frequently takes the form of, ingroup enhancement rather than outgroup devaluation. Second, group formation brings ingroup members closer to the self, while the distance between the self and outgroup members remains unchanged. Thus, circumstances that induce a more inclusive one-group representation may extend or redirect the cognitive and motivational processes that usually produce positive feelings toward ingroup members to former outgroup members.

While equal status, cooperative interdependence, self-revealing interactions and egalitarian norms are proposed to induce a common ingroup identity between the members of different groups, they may provide somewhat different routes to a common identity. For example, cooperative interdependence concretely redefines the functional relations between groups, whereas the other features (e.g., egalitarian norms) may influence a common identity through more subtle, perceptual or contextual factors. In addition, other contextual variables may also contribute to the perception of shared ingroup status. Some factors simply increase the salience of existing common superordinate group memberships rather than creating new, possibly less stable ingroup identities. For example, people are not usually cognizant of their national or state identities as they perform the routines of everyday behavior. These identities, however, often become very salient when traveling, especially when other travelers are recognized as sharing these national or state identities. It is also interesting that these travelers, recognizing their common identity, feel not only closer to one another than to others, but also closer to one another than they would if they were at home. In other instances, a common ingroup identity may be achieved by introducing factors (e.g., common tasks or common fate) that are perceived to be shared by the memberships. If each of these elements is efficacious, then agents of social change would have an increased range of strategies for calming intergroup tensions. For example, whereas it may be especially difficult to induce conflicting groups to interact and work cooperatively together (Worchel, 1979), agents of social change with the power to dispense desirable resources could impose common fate among these groups.

The Benefits of a Dual Identity

We believe that the development of a common ingroup identity does not necessarily require each group to forsake its subgroup identity. It is possible for people to conceive of two groups (for example, parents and children) as operating interdependently with the context of a superordinate (family) entity. Furthermore, in some contexts, it would be undesirable or impossible for people to relinquish their ethnic or racial subgroup identities. Thus, it is proposed that if members of different groups merely regarded themselves as though they were members of different groups but all playing in the same team, that the intergroup consequences of this dual identity would be more positive than if members regarded themselves as only separate groups, perhaps playing in different teams. The dual identity in which members' subgroup and superordinate group identities are salient simultaneously (e.g., African-American) is especially interesting because of its potential to permit the positive benefits of contact to generalize to outgroup members not present in the contact situation. In contrast to a purely one group representation, the dual identity maintains the associative link to these additional outgroup members (see Anastasio, 1993; Anastasio, Bachman, Gaertner & Dovidio, in press).

... The value of the dual identity relative to that of a single, more homogenous, superordinate identity may depend upon contextual factors involving the functional utility for maintaining the original subgroup identities. In contexts involving ethnic and racial subgroups, for example, maintaining original identities may be very rewarding, rather than threatening, as when, for example, people are expected to be color blind (see Schofield, 1986) and subgroup identities are regarded as unimportant. In other situations, such as a corporate merger, however, maintaining the salience of the original subgroup identities may signal problems that can undermine the goals of the new organization.

In the next section, we describe some research that illustrates the benefits of a common ingroup identity as well as the complexity of the effects for the dual identity. Thus, we will describe a laboratory study, two survey studies involving different domains: a multi-ethnic high school and corporate mergers, and finally, a field experiment in which members of different racial groups were induced to share a common ingroup identity.

EMPIRICAL INVESTIGATIONS

The specific purpose of the first three studies was to test the hypothesis that the causal relationship between the favorable conditions of intergroup contact and reduced intergroup bias is mediated by changes in members' representations of the memberships from separate groups to either a purely one-group, social entity, or a dual identity—when subgroup and superordinate identities are salient simultaneously. The purpose of the last study was to test experimentally the implications of these processes for improving relations between racial groups in a natural setting.

Study 1. How Does Cooperation Reduce Intergroup Bias?

The purpose of a study by Gaertner, Mann, Dovidio, Murrell & Pomare (1990) was to test experimentally the idea that cooperation, for example, among Sherif and Sherif's (1969) groups of summer campers increased positive attitudes toward outgroup members because it changed members' perceptions of one another from "Us" and "Them" to a more inclusive "We." Two three-person laboratory groups were brought together under conditions designed to vary independently the members representations of the aggregate as one group or two groups (by varying factors such as seating arrangement) and the presence or absence of intergroup cooperative interaction. In the absence of cooperative interaction, subjects induced to feel like one group relative to those in the two group conditions reported that the aggregate did feel more like one group (using 1-7 ratings) and they also had lower degrees of intergroup bias in their evaluations (likable, cooperative, honest, trustworthy) of ingroup and outgroup members.

. . . [T]he introduction of cooperative interaction increased subjects' perceptions of one group and also reduced their bias in evaluative ratings relative to those who did not cooperate during the contact period. As expected, reduced bias associated with introducing cooperation was due to enhanced favorable evaluations of outgroup members. Consistent with Brewer's (1979) analysis, cooperation appeared to move ingroup members closer to the self. Consistent with our mediation hypothesis, cooperation induced a sense of group formation between the members of the two groups and also reduced bias. . .

Because this study used an experimental design, we know that cooperation preceded changes in members' conceptual representations of the aggregate from two groups to one group and also changes in intergroup bias. Therefore, this experimental study is useful for establishing the overall plausibility of the direction of causality among the variables specified by the Common Ingroup Identity Model. Whereas the next two studies use a correlational design and were undertaken to conceptually replicate the laboratory work in more naturalistic settings, the direction of causality among the variables would be even more ambiguous, if not for the evidence obtained from the laboratory study that demonstrates the plausibility of the direction of causality proposed by the model.

Study 2: Intergroup Relations in a Multi-Ethnic High School

A survey study was conducted in a multi-ethnic high school in the northeastern United States in which a sample of 1,357 Black, Chinese, Hispanic, Japanese, Korean, Vietnamese and Caucasian students, closely matching the school's diversity, participated (see Gaertner, Rust, Dovidio, Bachman & Anastasio, 1994; Gaertner, Rust, Dovidio, Bachman & Anastasio, in press b). The primary theoretical question we pursued in this study was whether students' perceptions of a student body as one group or separate groups would mediate the proposed relation between their perceptions of the favorableness of the conditions of contact (e.g., cooperation and equal status) and their degrees of intergroup bias. Also, we explored the effects of the dual identity (in which subgroup identities are maintained within the context of a superordinate entity) using two different strategies. First, we included in the survey an item designed to tap this representation (i.e., "Although there are different groups at school, it feels like we are playing on the same team"). Second, we compared students who identified themselves in the survey using a dual identity (e.g., some students indicated they were Korean and American) with those who used only a single, subgroup identity (e.g., Korean). We expected that, for both strategies, a dual identity would be associated with lower intergroup bias.

Questionnaire items that were modifications of those developed by Green, Adams and Turner (1988) were designed to measure four distinct conditions hypothesized by the Contact Hypothesis (see Allport, 1954; Cook, 1984) to be necessary for successful intergroup contact: equal status, cooperative interdependence, the degree of interaction between the groups and egalitarian norms. Scores on these four scales were combined to form an overall measure of intergroup contact. Additional items, similar to those used in our laboratory work, were included to measure students' perceptions of the student body as one group ("Despite the different groups at school, there is frequently the sense that we are just one group"), separate groups ("At school, it usually feels as though we belong to different groups"), and separate individuals ("At school, it usually feels as though we are individuals and not members of a particular group"). Also, we included the dual-identity item.

An index of intergroup bias was obtained by including several items designed to assess feelings towards one's own ethnic group and towards each of the other ethnic groups [e.g., "How often do XXXXXXXX make you feel (good, uneasy, badly, respectful)?"]. Evaluation of the "outgroups" was indexed by averaging feelings towards all ethnic groups to which students did not indicate membership. The index measuring bias in affective reactions was then obtained by calculating the difference between feelings for one's ingroup and feelings for the "outgroups." In addition, students rated the "Overall Favorability" (1-9) of each ethnic/racial group on a modified "Feelings Thermometer" (see Abelson, Kinder, Peters & Fiske, 1982), and an index of ingroup and outgroup overall favorability was derived in a manner similar to that for bias in affective feelings. Both affective feelings and overall favorability were included because there is converging support for the idea that overall attitudinal favorability toward groups is strongly determined by the affect (Abelson et al., 1982; Stangor, Sullivan & Ford, 1991).

...[T]he results of this study ... closely paralleled the findings from the laboratory. The conditions of contact significantly predicted both cognitive representations of the groups and intergroup bias in affective feelings. Cognitive representations, in turn, predicted bias. The more the student body was perceived to be "one group" or "on the same team," the lower the bias in affective feelings (betas = .08 and .09, respectively). While these relationships are relatively weak, they are statistically reliable. Furthermore, the relationship between conditions of contact and bias in affective feelings was significantly reduced (from beta = -.32 to beta = .24) when cognitive representations were statistically controlled, which provides further evidence of the mediating role of the cognitive representations. ...

These results nicely support the ideas of Abelson et al. (1982) and Stangor et al. (1991) that overall attitudinal favorability may be determined by affective feelings. Also, the results are consistent with those of our laboratory study and indicate the applicability of the Common Ingroup Identity Model to naturalistic settings. In this multi-ethnic context, the "one-group" and the "the same team" representations each related positively to the conditions of contact and to lower degrees of bias in affective feelings. In addition, the lower the bias in affective feelings and the weaker the perceptions of the student body as "different groups," the lower the bias in overall favorability.

The beneficial effects of a superordinate identity is further revealed by the effects of a dual identity. Students who identified themselves on the survey as being members of a minority group and also American had a lower bias in affective reactions than minority students who did not use a superordinate American identity (means = 0.88 vs. 1.16, $p <$ .03). Whereas there may be many differences between these two groups of students (e.g., American citizenship), they did have different cognitive representations of the student body. As we might expect, if the item "different groups but on the same team" did measure a dual identity, minority students, who identified themselves both as an American and as a member of a minority group, endorsed this "same team" item (but no other item) more strongly than students who only identified themselves using their minority group identities (means = 3.22 and 3.01, $p <$ .04), These findings suggest that minority students who *did not* use a dual identity should more strongly perceive the student body as "different groups, relative to each of the other representations of the aggregate"; whereas students who used the dual identity should most strongly perceive the student body as "different groups playing on the same team." Separate analyses conducted for these groups of students indicated that this expectation was generally supported. Thus, the perceptions of the student body by students who used a dual identity involving a minority subgroup and an American superordinate identity were generally less differentiated than students who used only a minority group identity. ...

Overall, the findings of the mediation analyses and also the comparisons involving students, who use both their ethnic subgroup and superordinate American identity in this multi-ethnic setting, converge with those of the laboratory study in offering support for the Common Ingroup Identity Model. Perceptions of more favorable conditions of contact predicted less differentiated, more superordinate representations of the memberships that, in part, seemed to contribute to reduced intergroup bias in affective feelings and overall favorability. The next study considers the utility of the Common Ingroup Identity Model for explaining the reactions of executives involved in corporate mergers.

Study 3: The Bank Mergers

Betty Bachman (1993) surveyed 229 banking executives who had been involved in a corporate merger representing a wide variety of different banks across the United States. The survey instrument contained 126 items designed to examine a more complicated intergroup model of corporate mergers (including several organizational and job related variables) than we will address at this time. However, we will focus here only on those elements most relevant to the general Common Ingroup Identity Model and those discussed in the laboratory and the multi-ethnic high school studies.

The merger survey measured (among other constructs) variables akin to those examined in the high school study: (1) the banking executives assessment of contact conditions (i.e., the degree to which partners to the merger held equal status, the degree to which egalitarian norms existed, perceptions of positive interdependence among the banks, opportunities for interaction), and (2) the executive's mental representations of the merged organization [one group, two subgroups within a larger group (the dual identity item), two separate groups, or separate individuals]. The affective reactions component measured in this model was somewhat different from that used in the high school setting, and was based on Stephan and Stephan's (1984, 1985) construct of intergroup anxiety. Here, respondents were asked to rate their reactions to interacting with members of the "other" organization relative to how they felt when interacting with their own (including how awkward, self-conscious, accepted, confident, irritated,

impatient, defensive and happy). As a measure of intergroup bias, participants rated the members of their original group relative to members of the other group on characteristics related to the corporate setting. Factor analysis indicated that our bias measure actually was composed of two distinct factors, which we interpreted as a "sociability" factor (sociable, helpful and cliquish) and a "work-related" factor (intelligent, hard-working, reliable, organized, skilled and creative. . .

Overall, . . . analysis assessing the effects of contact conditions, mental representations of the group, and affective reactions (intergroup anxiety) on sociability bias . . . revealed a pattern of findings that closely mirrored the results of the high school study. . . . The more the organization was perceived to be one group and the less as separate individuals, the lower the intergroup anxiety. Also, as in the high school study, the relation between perceptions of the contact conditions and bias was mediated by affective feelings involving intergroup anxiety (beta = .30); the lower the intergroup anxiety, the lower the bias in sociability. Thus, supportive of the Common Ingroup Identity Model, the superordinate, one-group representation is associated with favorable perceptions of the conditions of contact, and lower intergroup anxiety. Also, as intergroup anxiety decreases, bias in sociability decreases as well.

. . . [T]he results across these two field studies offer support for the hypothesis that the relation between conditions of contact and intergroup bias is mediated by changes in members' representations of the memberships. The purpose of the next experiment was to examine the possibility experimentally that inducing a common ingroup identity among racial groups will elicit more favorable treatment to people who would otherwise be regarded as outgroup members.

Study 4: The Football Game Study

On a sunny Saturday afternoon in September, our research team, composed of several black and white, male and female students, visited the University of Delaware football stadium prior to a game between the University of Delaware and its local rival,

Westchester State University (see Ward, Rust, Nier, Gaertner & Carpenter, 1995). Armed with clipboards and survey forms, members of the research team attempted to engage white fans (n = 193) in a 5-min survey about their food preferences. In addition to carrying the survey materials, our black and white interviewers systematically varied whether they wore University of Delaware or Westchester State University signature hats. By selecting fans who similarly wore clothing that identified their university affiliation, we could systematically vary whether fans were approached by an interviewer who had a common or different university identity as themselves. We assumed that university identities would be particularly salient in this setting. We expected that, when fans were approached by black or white interviewers with different university identity than themselves (i.e., Delaware fans approached by a Westchester interviewer or Westchester fans approached by a Delaware interviewer), white interviewers would gain greater compliance than black interviewers. In this condition, black interviewers could be regarded as outgroup members with regard to both race and university affiliation. When interviewers and fans shared common university identities, however, we expected that compliance would be increased generally—and that black and white interviewers would be equally successful in gaining fans' compliance to be interviewed.

The results were not quite what we expected. Nevertheless, they speak favorably of the benefit of a common ingroup identity for improving interracial behavior. Contrary to expectations, when the interviewer was white, fans were not significantly more compliant in the Common University Identity than in the Different University Identity condition (43% vs. 40%). However, supportive of the potential benefits of a common ingroup identity for racial outgroup members, black interviewers gained reliably more compliance in the Common (59.6%) than in the Different (37.8%) University Identity condition. Whereas there are several interpretations for this pattern of results, these findings are generally consistent with the major idea of the model. Indeed, black outgroup members were treated more favorably under the umbrella of a common

ingroup identity than they were when they were only regarded as outgroup members.

CONCLUSION

In the present paper, we have presented one laboratory experiment, two field studies and one field experiment, each testing propositions of the Common Ingroup Identity Model. Although field studies should most cautiously be interpreted as correlational, the converging evidence provided by the experimental studies supports the directions of causality proposed in the model. Also, the evidence obtained in the field studies suggests that the laboratory findings are generalizable to naturalistic settings.

The findings, as we observed them in the laboratory and the field settings, offer continued support for the utility of the Contact Hypothesis as a strategic framework for reducing intergroup bias. Furthermore, when viewed in the context of the Common Ingroup Identity Model, the present research demonstrates how different variations in the nature of intergroup contact might operate to reduce intergroup bias through common processes—specifically by influencing group representations. In general, across four diverse research settings, greater perceptions of a superordinate identity predicted lower levels of intergroup bias toward original outgroup members.

The present set of studies also extends our previous formulations of the Common Ingroup Identity Model in two fundamental ways. First, the present research highlights the importance of affective reactions in intergroup relations. The findings for affective reactions in the high school study and for intergroup anxiety in the bank merger study support the ideas of Stangor, Abelson and colleagues, and Stephan and Stephan, regarding the important role played by affect in influencing intergroup attitudes. Indeed, in both the high school and the bank merger studies, these affective reactions mediated the relation between the conditions of contact and intergroup bias. Furthermore, whereas the present work focused on the hypothesized effect of group representations on affective reactions, other research suggests a potential reciprocal relationship between affect and subsequent group representations. We have found, for example, that positive affect, induced incidentally in an intergroup setting, can produce more inclusive, one-group representations and thereby reducing intergroup bias (Dovidio, Gaertner, Isen & Lowrance, 1995). Thus, understanding how affective reactions are influenced by, and can in turn influence, group representations is critical for understanding the processes of reducing intergroup bias. Because theories of contemporary forms of racism, such as Modern (McConahay, 1986) and Symbolic (Sears, 1988) racism, emphasize the negative effects of unconscious negative feelings, despite conscious egalitarian beliefs, further examination of the mediating role of affective reactions represents a promising approach for eliminating subtle biases, such as aversive racism.

... While we do not regard inducing a common, superordinate identity to be a panacea, we have reviewed some evidence suggesting that it does seem to encourage more positive intergroup behaviors.

References

Abelson, R. P., Kinder, D. R., Peters, M. D. (1982). Affective and semantic components in political person perception. *Journal of Personality and Social Psychology*, 42, 619-630.

Allport, G.W. (1954). *The nature of prejudice.* Cambridge, MA: Addison-Wesley.

Amir, Y. (1969). Contact Hypothesis in ethnic relations. *Psychological Bulletin*, 71, 319-342.

Anastasio, P. A. (1993). *Generalization of positive impressions from individual to outgroup: Interpersonal vs. intergroup interactions.* Unpublished Doctoral Dissertation, University of Delaware.

Anastasio, P. A., Bachman, B. A., Gaertner, S. L., & Dovidio, J. F. (in press). In R. Spears, P. J. Oakes, N. Ellemers & S. A. Haslam (Eds.), *The social psychology of stereotyping and group life.* Oxford: Blackwell.

Bachman, B. A. (1993). *An intergroup model of organizational mergers.* Unpublished Doctoral Dissertation, University of Delaware, Newark.

Bachman, B. A., Gaertner, S., Anastasio, P., & Rust, M. (1993). *When corporations merge: Organizational identification among employees of acquiring and acquired organizations.* Paper presented at the 64th Eastern Psychological Association Convention, Crystal City, VA.

Brewer, M. B. (1979). Ingroup bias in the minimal intergroup situation: A cognitive-motivational analysis. *Psychological Bulletin*, 86, 307-324.

Cook, S. W. (1985). Experimenting on social issues: The case of school desegregation. *American Psychologist*, 40, 452-460.

Crosby, F., Bromely, S., & Saxe, L. (1980). Recent unobtrusive studies of black and white discrimination and prejudice: A literature review. *Psychological Bulletin*, 87, 546-563.

Devine, P. (1989). Stereotypes and prejudice: Their automatic and controlled components. *Journal of Personality and Social Psychology*, 56, 5-18.

Dovidio, J. F., & Gaertner, S. L. (1991). Changes in the expression and assessment of racial prejudice. In H. J. Knopke, R. J. Norrell & R. W. Rogers (Eds.), *Opening doors: Perspectives of race relations in contemporary America.* Tuscaloosa, Alabama: University of Alabama Press.

Dovidio, J. F., Gaertner, S. L., Isen, A. M., & Lowrance, R. (1995). Group representations and intergroup bias: Positive affect, similarity and group size. *Personality and Social Psychology Bulletin*, 21, 856-865.

Gaertner, S. L., & Dovidio, I. F. (1986). The aversive form of racism. In J. F. Dovidio & S. L. Gaertner (Eds.), *Prejudice, discrimination, and racism* (pp. 61-89). Orlando, FL: Academic Press.

Gaertner, S. L., Dovidio, I. F., Anastasio, P. A., Bachman, B. A., & Rust, M. C. (1993). The Common Ingroup Identity Model: Recategorization and the reduction of intergroup bias. In W. Stroebe and M. Hewstone (Eds.), *The European review of social psychology*, (Vol. 4, pp. i -126). London: Wiley.

Gaertner, S. L., Dovidio, I. F., Banker, B., Rust, M. C., Nier, J., Mottola, C., & Ward, C. (in press a). Does pro-whiteness necessarily mean anti-blackness? In M. Fine, L. Powell, L. Weis & M. Wong (Eds.), *Off white.* London: Routledge.

Gaertner, S. L., Mann, J. A., Dovidio, J. F., Murrel, A. J., & Pomare, M. (1990). How does cooperation reduce intergroup bias? *Journal of Personality and Social Psychology*, 59, 692-704.

Gaertner, S. L., Rust, M. C., Dovidio, J. F., Bachman, B. A., & Anastasio, P. A. (1994). The Contact Hypothesis: The role of a common ingroup identity on reducing intergroup bias. *Small Groups Research*, 25, 224-249.

Gaertner, S. L., Rust, M. C., Dovidio, J. F., Bachman, B. A., & Anastasio, P. A. (1996). The Contact Hypothesis: The role of a common ingroup identity on reducing intergroup bias among majority and minority group members. In J. L. Nye & A. M. Brower (Eds.), *What's social about social cognition?* (pp. 230-260). Newbury Park, CA: Sage Publications.

Green C. W., Adams, A. M., & Turner, C. W. (1988). Development and validation of the School Interracial Climate Scale. *American Journal of Community Psychology*, 16, 241-259.

McConahay, J. B. (1986). Modern racism, ambivalence, and the modern racism scale. In I. F. Dovidio & S. L. Gaertner (Eds.), *Prejudice, discrimination, and racism* (pp. 91-125). Orlando, FL: Academic Press.

Marcus-Newhall, A., Miller, N., Holtz, R., & Brewer, M. B. (1993). Crosscutting category membership with role assignment: A means of reducing intergroup bias. *British Journal of Social Psychology*, 32, 125-146.

Murell, A. J., Dietz-Uhler, B. L., Dovidio, I. F., Gaertner, S. L, & Drout, C. E. (1993). Aversive racism and resistance to affirmative action: Perceptions of justice are not necessarily color blind. *Basic and Applied Social Psychology* 15, 71-86.

Rothbart, M., & John, O. P. (1985). Social categorization and behavioral episodes: A cognitive analysis of the effects of intergroup contact. *Journal of Social Issues*, 4l, 81-104.

Sears, D. O. (1988). Symbolic racism. In P. Katz & D. Taylor (Eds.), *Towards the elimination of racism: Profiles in controversy* (pp. 53-84). New York: Plenum Press.

Schofield, J. W. (1986). Causes and consequences of the colorblind perspective. In J. F. Dovidio & S. L. Gaertner (Eds.), *Prejudice, discrimination, and racism* (pp. 231-250). Orlando, FL: Academic Press.

Sherif, M., & Sherif, C. W. (1969). *Social psychology.* New York: Harper & Row.

Stangor, C., Sullivan, L. A., & Ford, T. E. (1991). Affective and cognitive determinants of prejudice. *Social Cognition*, 9, 359-380.

Stephan, W. G., & Stephan, C. W. (1984). The role of ignorance in intergroup relations. In N. Miller & M. B. Brewer (Eds.), *Groups in contact: The psychology of desegregation* (pp. 229-257). Orlando, FL: Academic Press.

Stephan, W. G., & Stephan, C. W. (1985). Intergroup anxiety. *Journal of Social Issues*, 41, 157-175.

Tajfel, H., & Turner, J. C. (1979). An integrative theory of intergroup conflict. In W. G. Austin & S. Worchel (Eds.), *The social psychology of intergroup relations* (pp. 33-48). Monterey, CA: Brooks/Cole.

Turner, J. C. (1985). Social categorization and the self-concept: A social cognitive theory of group behavior. In E. J. Lawler (Ed.), *Advances in group processes* (Vol. 2, pp. 77-122). Greenwich, CT: JAI Press.

Ward, C., Rust, M. C., Nier, J., Gaertner, S. L., & Carpenter, I. (1995). *A game they came to watch: A study of compliance and team membership.* Poster presented at the annual meeting of the Eastern Psychological Association Convention, Boston, MA, 2 April.

Worchel, S. (1979). Cooperation and the reduction of intergroup conflict: Some determining factors. In W. C. Austin & S. Worchel (Eds.), *The social psychology of intergroup relations* (pp. 262-273). Monterey, CA: Brooks/Cole.

Group Processes In The Resolution Of International Conflicts: Experiences From The Israeli-Palestinian Case

Herbert C. Kelman

*E*ditors' Note: Throughout history ethnic conflicts have been among the most difficult to resolve. For example, the Israeli-Palestinian conflict has perplexed those striving to achieve peace in the Middle East for quite some time. Herbert Kelman, the author of this reading, was extensively involved in peace talks between these groups. In the process he discovered a number of ways in which small group workshops could help promote change within the larger society. His work is an excellent example of applying research in group processes to larger social problems in a way that leads to positive outcomes.

For over 20 years, politically influential Israelis and Palestinians have met in private, unofficial, academically based, problem-solving workshops designed to enable the parties to explore each other's perspective, generate joint ideas for mutually satisfactory solutions to their conflict, and transfer insights and ideas derived from their interaction into the policy process. Most of the work takes place in small groups, but the focus is on promoting change in the larger system. This article discusses 5 ways in which the workshop group serves as a vehicle for change at the macrolevel. It does so by functioning as a microcosm of the larger system, as a laboratory for producing inputs into the larger system, as a setting for direct interaction, as a coalition across conflict lines, and as a nucleus for a new relationship.

The Israeli-Palestinian conflict has long been cited as a typical case of a protracted, intractable conflict. The origins of the conflict go back to the birth of modern political Zionism at the end of the 19th century. Violence first erupted in the 1920s, and, in various forms and with varying degrees of intensity, it has pervaded the relationship between the two peoples since that time. The psychological core of the conflict has been its perception by the two sides as a zero-sum conflict around national identity and national existence, which has led over the years to mutual denial of the other's identity and systematic efforts to delegitimize the other (Kelman, 1978, 1987). Under the circumstances, the parties had been reluctant for a long time to go to the negotiation table and, indeed, to offer each other the assurances

and enticements that would make negotiations safe and promising in their eyes.

Nevertheless, in response to a strong initiative from the U.S. administration, Israelis and Palestinians finally entered into a process of direct negotiations, starting with the Madrid Conference in the fall of 1991. The mere fact that the parties were negotiating represented a significant departure in the history of the conflict, but the official talks themselves, which continued in Washington, DC, for nearly two years, did not develop their own momentum and seemed to arrive at an impasse (cf. Kelman, 1992a). In the meantime, however, secret talks between representatives of Israel's Labor Party-led government (elected in June 1992) and the Palestine Liberation Organization, held in Oslo in 1993, produced a dramatic agreement that was signed by the parties on the White House lawn in September 1993. The Oslo accord took the form of an exchange of letters of mutual recognition between the official representatives of the two peoples, followed by a Declaration of Principles (DOP) that stipulated the establishment of a Palestinian authority in Gaza and Jericho as the first step in Palestinian self-rule. Despite the shortcomings of the DOP and despite the fact that the most difficult political issues were left to be resolved in the final-status negotiations, which were scheduled to begin in May 1996, the Oslo accord represents a fundamental breakthrough in the Israeli-Palestinian conflict. That breakthrough derives, in my view, from the mutual recognition of the other's nationhood and each side's commitment to negotiate and make peace with the body that symbolizes and legitimates that nationhood.

It would be foolhardy to insist that the peace process set into motion by the Oslo accords is irreversible. At this writing (October 1996), the indications are that, under the current Likud-led government in Israel, the process will be slowed down but neither reversed nor entirely halted. . . .

What are the forces that led to this breakthrough? On a long-term basis, the Six-Day War of 1967 created a new geopolitical and strategic situation in the Middle East, which led to the gradually evolving recognition on all sides that a historic compromise of the Palestine problem in the form of some version of a two-state solution would best serve their national interests (cf. Kelman, 1988). . . . [A] significant factor contributing to the breakthrough was the conclusion, on both sides, that negotiations were not only necessary but also possible— that they could yield an acceptable agreement without jeopardizing their national existence. This sense of possibility evolved out of interactions between the two sides that produced the individuals, the ideas, and the political atmosphere required for productive negotiations.

A variety of unofficial contacts between the two sides played a significant role in creating this sense of possibility and the climate conducive to negotiations. It is in this context that the third-party efforts in which my colleagues and I have been engaged since the early 1970s contributed to the evolving peace process (Kelman, 1995). Our work illustrates the potential contributions of social psychology and the scholar-practitioner model (Kelman 1992b) to the interdisciplinary, multifaceted task of analyzing and resolving protracted international and ethnic conflicts.

This article focuses on the ways in which the microprocess of the small-group meetings that my colleagues and I organize can serve as a vehicle for change at the macrolevel. To set the stage for this discussion, the article briefly (a) places our work in the context of the emerging field of conflict resolution, (b) describes our particular approach to conflict resolution at the international level, and (c) discusses our efforts to contribute to the Israeli-Palestinian peace process.

The Conflict Resolution Field

In the past two decades or so, the world has witnessed the development and proliferation of a variety of new approaches to conflict resolution, which together constitute a new field of theory and practice (see Kelman, 1993b). The precise boundaries of this emerging field are difficult to draw, and practitioners differ in their view of what should be included and what should be excluded.

Practitioners of conflict resolution work at different levels—ranging from the interpersonal to the international. . . . Despite the diversity in level, domain, and intellectual origins that characterizes the work in this field, there are certain common insights and approaches to practice that run through all of its manifestations. Thus, with different degrees of emphasis, they all call for a nonadversarial framework for conflict resolution, an analytic approach, a problem-solving orientation, direct participation by the parties in conflict in jointly shaping a solution, and facilitation by a third party trained in the process of conflict resolution.

Interaction among scholar-practitioners working at different levels and in different domains is instructive and enriching and contributes significantly to the refinement of theory and technique. At the same time, it is important to keep in mind that the application of general principles requires sensitivity to the unique features of the context in which they are applied. Thus, in my own work over the years on international and intercommunal conflict, I have called attention to the need for knowledge about and experience with the particular features and issues of conflict at these levels and to the danger of direct transfer of experiences from the interpersonal and interorganizational levels to the international arena.

Interactive Problem Solving

The unofficial third-party approach to international and ethnic conflict resolution that my colleagues and I have been developing and applying derives from the pioneering efforts of Burton (1969, 1979, 1984). I have used the term *interactive problem solving* to describe the approach, which finds its fullest expression in problem solving workshops (Kelman, 1972, 1979, 1986, 1991, 1992b, 1996; Kelman & Cohen, 1986). . . .

Problem-solving workshops are intensive meetings between politically involved but entirely unofficial representatives of conflicting parties—for example, Israelis and Palestinians or Greek and Turkish Cypriots (see Kelman, 1993a). Workshop participants are often politically influential members of their communities. Thus, in our Israeli-Palestinian work, participants have included parliamentarians; leading figures in political parties or movements; former military officers or government officials; journalists or editors specializing in the Middle East; and academic scholars who are major analysts of the conflict for their societies and some of whom have served in advisory, official, or diplomatic positions.[1] The workshops take place under academic auspices and are facilitated by a panel of social scientists who are knowledgeable about international conflict, group process, and the Middle East region.

The discussions are completely private and confidential. There is no audience, no publicity, and no record, and one of the central ground rules specifies that statements made in the course of a workshop cannot be cited with attribution outside of the workshop setting. These and other features of the workshop are designed to enable and encourage workshop participants to engage in a type of communication that is usually not available to parties involved in an intense conflict relationship. The third party creates an atmosphere, establishes norms, and makes occasional interventions, all conducive to free and open discussion, in which the parties address each other rather than third parties or their own constituencies and in which they listen to each other in order to understand their differing perspectives. They are encouraged to deal with the conflict analytically rather than polemically—to explore the ways in which their interaction helps to exacerbate and perpetuate the conflict, rather than to assign blame to the other side while justifying their own. This analytic discussion helps the parties penetrate each other's perspective and understand each other's concerns, needs, fears, priorities, and constraints.

Once both sets of concerns are on the table and have been understood and acknowledged, the parties are encouraged to engage in a process of joint problem solving. They are asked to work together in developing new ideas for resolving the conflict in ways that would satisfy the fundamental needs and allay the existential fears of both parties. They are then asked to explore the political and psychological constraints that stand in the way of such integrative, win-win solutions and that, in fact, have prevented the parties from moving to (or staying at) the negotiating table. Again, they are asked to engage in a process of joint problem solving, designed to generate ideas for "getting from here to there." A central feature of this process is the identification of steps of mutual reassurance—in the form of acknowledgments, symbolic gestures, or confidence-building measures—that would help reduce the parties' fears of engaging in negotiations in which the outcome is uncertain and risky. Problem-solving workshops also contribute to mutual reassurance by helping the parties develop—again, through collaborative effort—a non-threatening, deescalatory language and a shared vision of a desirable future.

Workshops have a dual purpose. First, they are designed to produce changes in the workshop participants themselves—changes in the form of more differentiated images of the enemy (see Kelman, 1987), a better understanding of the other's perspective and of their own priorities, greater insight into the dynamics of the conflict, and new ideas for resolving the conflict and for overcoming the barriers to a negotiated solution. These changes at the level of individual participants are a vehicle for promoting change at the policy level. Thus, the second purpose of workshops is to maximize the likelihood that the new insights, ideas, and proposals developed in the course of the interaction are fed back into the political debate and the decision-making process in each community. One of the central tasks of the third party is to structure the workshop in such a way that new insights and ideas are likely both to be generated and to be transferred effectively to the policy process.

The composition of the workshop is crucial in this context: Great care must be taken to select participants who, on the one hand, have the interest and capacity to engage in the kind of learning process that workshops provide and, on the other hand, have the positions and credibility in their own communities that enable them to influence the thinking of political leaders, political constituencies, or the general public. It should be noted that the third party's role, although essential to the success of problem-solving workshops, is strictly a facilitative role. The critical work of generating ideas and infusing them into the political process must be done by the participants themselves. A basic assumption of our approach is that solutions emerging out of the interaction between the conflicting parties are most likely to be responsive to their needs and to engender their commitment.[2]

Contributions to the Israeli-Palestinian Peace Process

Most of the Israeli-Palestinian work that my colleagues and I carried out over the years took place during the prenegotiation phase of the conflict. The primary purpose was to help create a political atmosphere that would encourage the parties to move to the negotiating table. Moreover, until 1990, the workshops that we organized were all one-time events. . . .

In 1990, however, we took a major step forward in our work by organizing, for the first time, a continuing workshop (see Rouhana & Kelman, 1994). A group of highly influential Israelis and Palestinians committed themselves initially to a series of three workshop meetings over the course of a year. The first meeting took place in November 1990 and, at the end of the third meeting (in August 1991), the participants decided to continue the process.

In the meantime, external events instigated a second major new development in our work. With the convening of the Madrid Conference in the fall of 1991 and the opening of an official Israeli-Palestinian peace process, our own work moved from the prenegotiation to the negotiation phase of the conflict. We had no doubt—and the participants in the continuing workshop agreed—that there was still a great need for maintaining an unofficial process alongside of

the official one. However with the onset of official negotiations, the purpose and focus of our work had to change (Rouhana & Kelman, 1994). When negotiations are in progress, workshops can contribute to overcoming obstacles to staying at the table and negotiating productively, to creating a momentum for the negotiations, to addressing long-term issues that are not yet on the negotiating table, and to beginning the process of peace-building that must accompany and follow the process of peacemaking. . . .

The meetings of the continuing workshop after the start of the official negotiations focused on the obstacles confronting the peace process at the negotiating table and on the ground but also addressed the question of the functions and composition of the continuing workshop in the new political environment. Altogether, this continuing workshop met over a three-year period. Its final session took place in August 1993, ending just a day or so before the news of the Israeli-Palestinian breakthrough that was achieved in Oslo began to emerge.

In the wake of the Oslo accord, signed in September 1993, there has been general recognition of the role that unofficial efforts have played, directly or indirectly, in laying the groundwork for the Israeli-Palestinian breakthrough. In this context, various observers—within and outside of the Middle East—have acknowledged the contributions of the activities in which my colleagues and I have been engaged over the years. In my own assessment, there are three ways in which our work, along with that of many others, has contributed (Kelman, 1995).

1. Workshops have helped to develop cadres prepared to carry out productive negotiations. Over the years, dozens of Israelis and dozens of Palestinians, many of them political influentials or preinfluentials, have participated in our workshops and related activities, including the continuing workshop in the early 1990s. Many of these individuals were involved in the discussions and negotiations that led up to the Oslo accord. Many have continued to be involved in the peace process, and some have served in the Israeli cabinet, Knesset, and foreign ministry and in leading positions in the various Palestinian political agencies.

2. The sharing of information and the formulation of new ideas in the course of our workshops have provided important substantive inputs into the negotiations. Through the public and private communications of workshop participants— and to some degree also through the communications of members of the third party—some of the insights and ideas on which productive negotiations could be built were injected into the two political cultures. These included shared assumptions, mutual sensitivities, and new conceptions of the process and outcome of negotiations, all of which were developed in the course of workshop interactions.

3. Workshops have fostered a political atmosphere that has made the parties open to a new relationship. Our workshops, along with various other Israeli-Palestinian meetings and projects, have done so by encouraging the development of more differentiated images of the enemy, of a deescalatory language and a new political discourse that is attentive to the other party's concerns and constraints, of a working trust that is based on the conviction that both parties have a genuine interest in a peaceful solution, and of a sense of possibility regarding the ultimate achievement of a mutually satisfactory outcome.

The Oslo agreement, of course, represented only the beginning of what has already been and will almost certainly continue to be a long and difficult process, confronting obstacles and periodic setbacks. Therefore, unofficial efforts alongside the official negotiations continue to be needed. Accordingly, when we decided to close the continuing workshop in the late fall of 1993, we immediately initiated a new project, which built on the experience and achievements of the preceding work. This new project has taken the form of a joint working group on Israeli-Palestinian relations, which held its first meeting in May 1994. The initial emphasis of the group has been on systematic exploration of the difficult political issues— including Israeli settlements, Palestinian refugees, Jerusalem, and the precise nature of Palestinian self-determination—that have been deferred to the final-status negotiations. . . .

The Role of Group Processes in Conflict Resolution

Having presented a brief description of our microlevel approach and its contribution to conflict resolution at the macrolevel, I now want to highlight the role that interaction within the small group plays in the larger process.

Most of our work takes place in the context of small groups, composed of three to six representatives of the two sides and two to four third-party facilitators. The focus of all of our efforts is on promoting change in the larger system, but direct interaction in the small-group setting can produce important inputs into the political thinking, the political debate, and the decision-making processes within the two societies and into the formal negotiations between them. Thus, changes at the individual level resulting from interaction in the small group become vehicles for change at the system level.

In the following sections, I discuss five ways in which the workshop group serves as a vehicle for change in the larger system. . . .

The Group as a Microcosm

The group assembled for a workshop can be viewed as a microcosm of the larger system. It is a microcosm not in the sense of a small-scale *model* that reproduces all of the forces of the larger system but in the sense of an *arena* in which the forces of the larger system may manifest themselves. We make no attempt to reproduce the larger system in our workshops. In fact, we try to create an environment that differs significantly from the one in which the conflicting parties normally interact—an environment governed by a different set of norms, in which participants are both free and obligated to speak openly, listen attentively, and treat each other as equals. Nor do we try to represent the entire political spectrum in our workshops. We look for participants who are part of the mainstream in their communities and close to the political center but who are interested in exploring the possibilities of a negotiated, mutually satisfactory solution to the conflict.

The group is a microcosm of the larger system because, despite their relative moderation, the participants share the fundamental concerns, fears, memories, and aspirations of their respective communities. As they interact with each other around the issues in conflict, they reflect their own community's perspectives, priorities, and limits of what is negotiable, not only in what they say but also in how they say it and how they act toward each other. As a result, some of the dynamics of the larger conflict are acted out in the interactions within the workshop group. Participants' interactions in the group context often reflect the nature of the relationship between their communities— their mutual distrust, their special sensitivities and vulnerabilities, their differences in power and minority-majority status—and demonstrate the self-perpetuating character of interactions among conflicting societies.

The advantage of the workshop is that it creates an atmosphere, a set of norms, and a working trust among the participants that enable them to observe and analyze these conflict dynamics at or very near the moment they occur. Such analyses are facilitated by third-party interventions in the form of process observations, which suggest possible ways in which interactions between the parties "here and now" may reflect the dynamics of the conflict between their communities (Kelman, 1979). . . .

In summary, the character of the workshop group as a microcosm of the larger system makes it a valuable learning experience: It provides opportunities for the participants to gain important insights into the dynamics of the conflict. I turn next to the role of the group in transmitting what is learned into the larger system.

The Group as a Laboratory

The workshop group can also be conceived as a laboratory for producing inputs into the larger system. The metaphor of the laboratory is particularly appropriate because it captures the two roles that workshops play in the macroprocess. A workshop is a specially constructed space in which the parties can engage in a process of exploration, observation, and analysis and in which they can create new products to be fed into the

political debate and decision making in the two societies.

Providing a space for exploring issues in the conflict, mutual concerns, and ideas for conflict resolution is one of the key contributions of problem-solving workshops. The opportunity for joint informal exploration—playing with ideas, trying out different scenarios, obtaining a sense of the range of possible actions and of the limits for each party, and discovering potential trade-offs—enhances the productivity of negotiations and the quality of the outcome. Such opportunities, however, are not readily available in official negotiations, in which the participants operate in representative roles, are instructed and closely monitored by their governments, are concerned about the reactions of various constituencies and third parties, and are in the business of producing binding agreements. Problem-solving workshops, by virtue of their nonbinding character, are ideally suited to fill this gap in the larger diplomatic process. . . .

The process of exploration and joint thinking yields new products, which can be exported into the political process within and between the two communities. This is the second sense in which the laboratory metaphor captures the function of workshops. Indeed the group constitutes a workshop in the literal sense of that term: It is a specially constructed space for shaping products that are then brought back into the two communities. The sharing of perspectives, the conflict analysis, and the joint thinking encouraged in workshops enable the participants to come up with a variety of products in the form of new information, new insights, and new ideas that can advance the negotiation process: differentiated images of the other, which suggest that there is someone to talk to on the other side and something to talk about; understanding of the needs, fears, priorities, and constraints on the other side and, indeed, on one's own side; insight into the escalatory and self-perpetuating dynamics of the conflict relationship; awareness of change and the readiness for change on the other side; ideas for mutual reassurance and other ways of improving the atmosphere for negotiation; ideas for the overall shape of a mutually satisfactory solution; and ideas for redefining the conflict and reframing issues so as to make them more amenable to resolution. These products must then be exported into the political arena. It is essential, therefore, that the individuals selected as workshop participants have not only an interest in mutual exploration and learning, and skills for generating ideas and creative problem solving, but also the capacity and opportunity to utilize what they learn and to inject the workshop products into their respective communities in ways that make a political difference.

In sum, I have described the workshop group as a special space—a laboratory—in which a significant part of the work of peacemaking can be carried out. The unique contribution of the workshop to this larger process is that it provides a carefully designed environment in which constructive social interaction between the parties can take place. Let me, therefore, turn to the third image of the workshop: the group as a setting for direct interaction.

The Group as a Setting for Direct Interaction

Although international conflict and conflict resolution are societal and intersocietal processes, which cannot be reduced to the level of individual behavior, there are certain processes central to conflict resolution—such as empathy or taking the perspective of the other (which is at the heart of social interaction), learning and insight, and creative problem solving—that, of necessity, take place at the level of individuals and interactions between individuals. These psychological processes are by no means the whole of conflict resolution, but they must occur somewhere in the system if there is to be movement toward a mutually satisfactory and stable peace. Problem-solving workshops provide a setting for these processes to occur by bringing together representatives of the conflicting parties for direct interaction under conditions of confidentiality and equality and under an alternative set of norms in contrast to the norms that usually govern interactions between conflicting parties.

The context, norms, ground rules, agenda, procedures, and third-party interventions in workshops are all designed to encourage (and permit) a special kind of interaction, marked by an emphasis on addressing each other

(rather than one's constituencies, third parties, or the record) and on listening to each other, an analytical focus, adherence to a "no-fault" principle, and a problem-solving orientation. This kind of interaction allows the parties to explore each other's concerns, penetrate each other's perspective, and take cognizance of each other's constraints (Kelman, 1992b). As a result, they are able to offer each other the reassurances needed for productive negotiation and mutual accommodation and to come up with solutions responsive to both sides' needs and fears. . . .

An underlying assumption of the workshop process is that products of social interaction have an emergent quality (Kelman, 1992b). In the course of direct interaction, the parties are able to observe firsthand their differing reactions to the same events and the different perspectives these reflect, the differences between the way they perceive themselves and the way the other perceives them, and the impact that their statements and actions have on each other. Out of these observations, they can jointly shape new insights and ideas that could not have been predicted from what they initially brought to the interaction. Certain kinds of solutions to the conflict can emerge only from the confrontation of assumptions, concerns, and identities during face-to-face communication.

The emergence of ideas for solution to the conflict out of the interaction between the parties (in contrast, e.g., to ideas proposed by third parties) has several advantages. Such ideas are more likely to be responsive to the fundamental needs and fears of both parties; the parties are more likely to feel committed to the solutions they produce themselves; and the process of producing these ideas in itself contributes to building a new relationship between the parties, initially between the pronegotiation elements on the two sides and ultimately between the two societies as wholes. Let me turn then to the function of the workshop group in building relationships of both kinds.

The Group as a Coalition Across Conflict Lines

The workshop group can be conceived as a coalition across conflict lines—as part of a process of building a coalition between those elements on each side that are interested in a negotiated solution (Kelman, 1993a). This does not mean that workshop participants are all committed doves. Often, they are individuals who, out of pragmatic considerations, have concluded that a negotiated agreement is in the best interest of their own community. Workshops, then, can be seen as attempts to strengthen the hands of the pronegotiation elements on each side in their political struggle within their own communities and to increase the likelihood that the pronegotiation elements on the two sides will support and reinforce each other in pursuing their common interest in a negotiated solution.

Because the coalition formed by a workshop group (and by the entire array of joint efforts by the pronegotiation forces on the two sides) cuts across a very basic conflict line, it is almost by definition an uneasy coalition. It must function in the face of the powerful bonds that coalition members have to the very groups that the coalition tries to transcend. The coalition may well be perceived as threatening the national community that is so important to the identity, the long-term interests, and the political effectiveness of each coalition partner. As a result, the coalition work is complicated by participants' concern about their self-images as loyal members of their group; by their concern about their credibility at home and, hence, their long-term political effectiveness; by significant divergences in the perspectives of the two sets of coalition partners; and by the fact that even committed proponents of negotiation share the memories, concerns, fears, and sensitivities of their identity group.

Participants' bonds to their national communities create inevitable barriers to coalition work, which require systematic attention if problem-solving workshops are to achieve their goals. Thus, mutual distrust is an endemic condition that complicates coalition work. Even among individuals who have worked together for some time and have achieved a considerable level of working trust, old fears and suspicions that have deep historical roots are easily rearoused by events on the ground or by words and actions of a participant on the other side. Coalition work, therefore, requires a continuing process of mutual testing and reestablishment of working trust. A second impediment to coalition work is alienating language—the use of words or a manner of speaking that the other side finds irritating, patronizing, insulting, threatening, or otherwise oblivious to its sensitivities. One of the valuable outcomes of workshops is growing sensitivity to the meaning of particular words to the other side. Nevertheless, alienating language does crop up, both because participants speak from the perspectives and out of the experiences of their own communities and because the pragmatic terms in which peace is justified to one's domestic audiences (and perhaps to one's self) may appear dehumanizing or delegitimizing to the other side. Examples are the Israeli emphasis on the Palestinian "demographic threat" and the Palestinian emphasis on Israel's superior power as reasons for seeking a compromise. Finally, fluctuations in the political and psychological climate may affect one or the other party, creating a lack of synchronism in the readiness for coalition work between the two sides.

The uneasy quality of a coalition across conflict lines is an inevitable reality, insofar as coalition members are bona fide representatives of their national groups—as they must be if the coalition is to achieve its goal of promoting a negotiated agreement. This reality creates barriers to coalition work, and it is part of the task of the third party to help overcome them. But it is not only difficult to overcome these barriers, it may in fact be counterproductive to overcome them entirely. It is important for the coalition to remain uneasy in order to enhance the value of what participants learn in the course of workshops and of what they can achieve upon reentry into their home communities.

Experimental research by Rothbart and associates (Rothbart & John, 1985; Rothbart & Lewis, 1988) suggests that direct contact between members of conflicting groups may have a paradoxical effect on intergroup stereotypes. If it becomes apparent, in the course of direct interaction with representatives of the other group, that they do not fit one's stereotype of the group, there is a tendency to differentiate these particular individuals from their group: to perceive them as nonmembers. Since they are excluded from the category, the stereotype about the category itself can remain intact. This process of differentiating and excluding individual members of the other group from their category could well take place in workshops in which a high degree of trust develops between the parties. Therefore, it is essential for the participants to reconfirm their belongingness to their national categories—thus keeping the coalition uneasy—if they are to demonstrate the possibility of peace not just between exceptional individuals from the two sides but between the two enemy camps.

An even more important reason why a coalition across conflict lines must, of necessity, remain uneasy relates to what is often called the *reentry problem* (see, e.g., Kelman, 1972; Walton, 1970). If a workshop group became overly cohesive, it would undermine the whole purpose of the enterprise: to have an impact on the political decisions within the two communities. Workshop participants who become closely identified with their counterparts on the other side may become alienated from their own co-nationals, lose credibility, and hence forfeit their political effectiveness and their ability to promote a new consensus within their own communities. One of the challenges for problem-solving workshops, therefore, is to create an atmosphere in which participants can begin to humanize and trust each other and to develop an effective collaborative relationship, without losing sight of their separate group identities and the conflict between their communities (Kelman, 1992b, p. 82).

The Group as a Nucleus for a New Relationship

Our work is based on the proposition that in conflicts such as that between Palestinians and Israelis—conflicts about national identity and national existence between two peoples destined to live together in the same small space—conflict resolution must aim toward the ultimate establishment of a new cooperative and mutually enhancing relationship and must involve a process that paves the way to such a relationship. Nothing less will work in the long run, and, even in the short run, only a process embodying the principle of reciprocity that is at the center of a new relationship is likely to succeed. Perhaps the greatest strength of problem-solving workshops is their potential contribution to transforming the relationship between the conflicting parties.

Interaction in the workshop group both promotes and models a new relationship between the parties. It is based on the principles of equality and reciprocity. The participants are encouraged to penetrate each other's perspective and to gain an understanding of the other's needs, fears, and constraints. They try to shape solutions that are responsive to the fundamental concerns of both sides. They search for ways of providing mutual reassurance. Such ideas often emerge from acknowledgments that participants make to each other in the course of their interaction: acknowledgments of the other's humanity, national identity, view of history, authentic links to the land, legitimate grievances, and commitment to peace.

Out of these interactions, participants develop increasing degrees of empathy, of sensitivity and responsiveness to the other's concerns, and of working trust, which are essential ingredients of the new relationship to which conflict resolution efforts aspire. The working trust and responsiveness both develop out of the collaborative work in which the group is engaged and, in turn, help to enhance the effectiveness of that work. Thus, workshop participants can transmit to their respective communities not only ideas toward transformation of the relationship between the communities but also the results of their own experience: They can testify that a cooperative, mutually enhancing relationship is possible and can point to some of the conditions that promote such a relationship.

The joint working group on Israeli-Palestinian relations, which my colleague Nadim Rouhana and I are currently cochairing, is explicitly based on the conception of the group as the nucleus of a new relationship between the two societies. The main purpose of the working group is to focus on the peace-building processes that must follow successful peacemaking and to explore the nature of the long-term relationship envisaged in the aftermath of the final political agreement. At this point, as I mentioned earlier, we are addressing the difficult political issues— settlements, refugees, Jerusalem, Palestinian self-determination—that have been deferred to the final-status negotiations, in the light of the future relationship between the societies. That is, we try to assess different options for resolving these issues from the point of view of their congruence with a long-term relationship that is based on peaceful coexistence, cooperation, and mutual benefit.

Furthermore, we see the working group itself as a model and perhaps even as the seed of an institutional mechanism that a new relationship calls for. In our view, a mutually beneficial relationship between two units that are as closely linked and as interdependent as the Israeli and Palestinian communities requires the development of a civil society across the political borders. A useful institutional mechanism for such a civil society would be an unofficial joint forum for exploring issues in the relationship between the two communities within a problem-solving framework. It is not entirely unrealistic to hope that our current working group may evolve into or at least serve as a model for such an institution. This scenario thus provides an illustration of the way in which a group like our Israeli-Palestinian working group can serve not only as a means for promoting a new relationship between the parties but also as a model and manifestation of that new relationship.

Footnotes

[1] For a description of the recruitment process, see Kelman (1992b) and Rouhana and Kelman (1994).

[2] For a more detailed discussion of the workshop ground rules, the nature of the interaction between participants, and the role of the third party, see Kelman (1979), Kelman (1992b), and Rouhana and Kelman (1994).

References

Burton, J. W. (1969). *Conflict and communication: The use of controlled communication in international relations.* London: Macmillan.

Burton, J. W. (1979). *Deviance, terrorism, and war: The process of solving unsolved social and political problems.* New York: St. Martin's Press.

Burton, J. W. (1984). *Global conflict: The domestic sources of international crisis.* Brighton, England: Wheatsheaf.

Kelman, H. C. (1972). The problem-solving workshop in conflict resolution. In R. L. Merritt (Ed.), *Communication in international politics* (pp. 168-204). Urbana: University of Illinois Press.

Kelman, H. C. (1978). Israelis and Palestinians: Psychological prerequisites for mutual acceptance. *International Security, 3,* 162-186.

Kelman, H. C. (1979). An interactional approach to conflict resolution and its application to Israeli-Palestinian relations. *International Interactions, 6,* 99-122.

Kelman, H. C. (1986). Interactive problem solving: A social-psychological approach to conflict resolution. In W. Klassen (Ed.), *Dialogue toward interfaith understanding* (pp. 293-314). Tantur/Jerusalem: Ecumenical Institute for Theological Research.

Kelman, H. C. (1987). The political psychology of the Israeli-Palestinian conflict: How can we overcome the barriers to a negotiated solution? *Political Psychology, 8,* 347-363.

Kelman, H. C. (1988, Spring). Palestinianization of the Arab-Israeli conflict. *The Jerusalem Quarterly, 46,* 3-15.

Kelman, H. C. (1991). Interactive problem solving: The uses and limits of a therapeutic model of the resolution of international conflicts. In V. D. Volkan, J. V. Montville, & D. A. Julius (Eds.), *The psychodynamics of international relationships, Volume II: Unofficial diplomacy at work* (pp. 145-160). Lexington, MA: Lexington Books.

Kelman, H. C. (1992a). Acknowledging the other's nationhood: How to create the momentum for the Israeli-Palestinian negotiations. *Journal of Palestine Studies, 22*(1), 18-38.

Kelman, H. C. (1992b). Informal mediation by the scholar/practitioner. In J. Bercovitch & J. Z. Rubin (Eds.), *Mediation in international relations: Multiple approaches to conflict management* (pp. 64-96). New York: St. Martin's Press.

Kelman, H. C. (1993a). Coalitions across conflict lines: The interplay of conflicts within and between the Israeli and Palestinian communities. In S. Worchel & J. Simpson (Eds.), *Conflict between people and groups* (pp. 236-258). Chicago: Nelson-Hall.

Kelman, H. C. (1993b). Foreword. In D. J. D. Sandole & H. van der Merwe (Eds.), *Conflict resolution theory and practice: Integration and application* (pp. ix-xii). Manchester, England: Manchester University Press.

Kelman, H. C. (1995). Contributions of an unofficial conflict resolution effort to the Israeli-Palestinian breakthrough. *Negotiation Journal, 11,* 19-27.

Kelman, H. C. (1996). Negotiation as an interactive problem solving. *International Negotiation, 1,* 99-123.

Kelman, H. C., & Cohen, S. P. (1986). Resolution of international conflict: An interactional approach. In S. Worchel & W. G. Austin (Eds.), *Psychology of intergroup relations* (2nd ed., pp. 323-342). Chicago: Nelson Hall.

Rothbart, M., & John, O. P. (1985). Social categorization and behavioral episodes: A cognitive analysis of the effects of intergroup contact. *Journal of Social Issues, 41*(3), 81-104.

Rothbart, M., & Lewis, S. (1988). Inferring category attributes from exemplar attributes: Geometric shapes and social categories. *Journal of Personality and Social Psychology, 55,* 861-872.

Rouhana, N. N., & Kelman, H. C. (1994). Promoting joint thinking in international conflicts: An Israeli-Palestinian continuing workshop. *Journal of Social Issues, 50*(1), 157-178.

Walton, R. E. (1970). A problem-solving workshop on border conflicts in Eastern Africa. *Journal of Applied Behavioral Science, 6,* 453-489.

✓ PROJECT 3.1
Superordinate Goals In The Real World

I.   The Research Highlight, "Eagles vs. Rattlers," describes how Muzafer Sherif created situations to reduce conflict between groups of boys by having them work toward a superordinate common goal.   The principle that cooperation reduces conflict is extremely powerful, and it can be applied to reducing conflict between real-world groups.

II.   For this project, please collect, from the news media or historical sources, two real-world examples of how the pursuit of superordinate goals has brought together conflicting gender, racial, and/or ethnic groups.   For each of the examples, describe the groups in conflict, the nature of the conflict, the superordinate goal the groups were working toward, and evidence of the lessening of the conflict.

EXAMPLE 1

Which groups were in conflict?

_____

_____

What was the conflict?

_____

_____

_____

What was the superordinate goal toward which they were working?

_____

_____

_____

What evidence exists that the conflict has been reduced or is being reduced?

_____

_____

_____

_____

EXAMPLE 2

Which groups were in conflict?

_____

_____

What was the conflict?

_____

_____

_____

_____

What was the superordinate goal toward which they were working?

_____

_____

_____

_____

What evidence exists that the conflict has been reduced or is being reduced?

_____

_____

_____

_____

✓ PROJECT 3.2
A Jigsaw Workplace

I.   Aronson, Wilson, and Akert described an intervention in which classrooms were redesigned so that students were interdependent and had to cooperate in order to achieve. This "jigsaw" technique proved to be an effective way of reducing tensions between ethnic and racial groups as well as boosting the achievement and self-esteem of all students.

II.   For this project, you will apply the jigsaw techniques discussed by Aronson, Wilson, and Akert to a business setting. Workers in this business are from diverse backgrounds—they are male and female, from many different racial and ethnic groups, and from different education and economic backgrounds. These diverse groups have difficulty working with one another which has caused a high level of tension in the workplace, which in turn, has led to lower levels of productivity. Your overall goals are to reduce tensions between groups, boost the self-esteem of all, and most important to the managers who are employing you as a consultant, you must boost productivity. Please outline your strategies below.

- Identify the problems that exist initially.

        _____

        _____

        _____

        _____

        _____

        _____

        _____

        _____

- What specific goals are you trying to achieve in your workplace redesign?

        _____

        _____

        _____

        _____

        _____

        _____

- What situational changes would you make in the workplace to alleviate the problems you have identified?

  _____

  _____

  _____

  _____

  _____

  _____

  _____

  _____

  _____

  _____

- How would you measure the success of your jigsaw redesign? Be specific. Your manager wants results!

  _____

  _____

  _____

  _____

  _____

  _____

  _____

- What benefits would workers derive from the redesign?

  _____

  _____

  _____

  _____

  _____

  _____

  _____

  _____

✓ PROJECT 3.3
Bringing Groups Together Through Contact

I.　　In Amir's article describing when and how contact can alleviate group conflict, the author describes six different situational components that contribute to improvements in intergroup relations. Those six components are listed below. For this project, pick two conflicting groups, either contemporary or historical. These groups can be groups from your campus, your community, the United States, or another country.

II.　　Once you have chosen two groups, work through Amir's six components with the goal of using these to present ways that conflict between the groups could be reduced. For example, to reduce conflict between the Israelis and the Palestinians using the equal status component of contact, one could create a situation in which the two groups undertake negotiations at a neutral site where they are each given the same diplomatic status.

Which groups are in conflict?_____

What is the nature of the conflict? _____

For each of the following components, describe specific situational changes you would make to create a successful contact situation:

Acquaintance potential

_____
_____
_____
_____

Equal status

_____
_____
_____
_____

Cooperation versus competition

_____
_____
_____
_____

Intimate versus superficial contact

_____
_____
_____
_____

Normative support

_____
_____
_____
_____

Need satisfaction

_____
_____
_____
_____

What are some of the obstacles to applying these components to conflict reduction?

_____
_____
_____
_____

C h a p t e r   4

Who Am I? Gender, Race, And Ethnic Identities

The previous chapters examined the psychological processes that issue out of group situations and their impact on the individual. This chapter addresses a question that is central to all of us. Arriving at an answer to the question, "Who am I?" is often a process involving, in part, a consideration of our gender, racial, and ethnic identities.

We all have ideas about what makes us who we are and how we are different from others. We understand that not everyone has had exactly the same experiences, read the same books, or smiles in exactly the same way. Still, we are aware that we share many things with those around us. If you are a woman, you know that other women have similar biological characteristics and that you have many social roles in common. You also know that many of your core values are shared by those in your ethnic or racial group.

The articles in this chapter highlight the role that our gender, race, and ethnicity can have in developing and maintaining our identities. Kay Deaux, in the first article in this chapter, provides an overview of the psychological research addressing identity creation and maintenance. In it she shows that our personal and social identities are both important psychologically. Sandra Bem, in her article, focuses on the role of gender in identity development by presenting various theories, including her own, for how gender identity develops over the course of time.

William Cross, in the next article, describes his developmental model of African-American identity, "Nigresence Theory." His theory explores the stages of development and the effect that history can have on the formation and maintenance of our identity. Teresa LaFromboise and her collaborators examine several models that speak to how individuals negotiate the process of being bicultural. In addition, they pose the question of whether some ways of acquiring a second culture are more adaptive than others. The last article in this series is a short essay written by Shanlon Wu, an Asian-American male, in which he describes his search for images of Asian men with which to identify and to use as role models.

The articles in this section offer an opportunity to gain a deeper understanding of the relationship of the individual to the groups to which he or she belongs. In examining how our social identities develop, they help us understand some of the reasons for why and how the social groups with which we identify play such pivotal roles in our lives

Reconstructing Social Identity

Kay Deaux

---

ditors' Note: Who am I? Nearly all of us have asked this question. The answers we come up with vary tremendously as they are a reflection of our distinct sense of identity. Our identity is shaped by our experiences and, in part, by our memberships in groups, including gender, racial, and ethnic groups. This article by Kay Deaux provides an overview of the psychological research on identity. It demonstrates that identities can be both personal and social, and that both are very important psychological constructs.

As a concept with a tradition in both social and personality psychology, identity lends itself to a variety of interpretations. In the present analysis, identity refers to social categories in which an individual claims membership as well as the personal meaning associated with those categories. Four key issues for research are discussed: (a) the structure and interrelationships among multiple identities, (b) the several functions that identities serve, (c) the importance of context to the development and enactment of identities, and (d) the need for longitudinal studies of identity change.

As a construct, identity has a rich tradition and offers a multiplicity of possible meanings. One can draw on varied disciplines such as philosophy, sociology and anthropology to define and interpret identity. More immediately, and more important for my purposes, identity has the potential to link concerns of personality and social psychologists in fundamental and heuristic ways.

In proposing to reconstruct identity, I want to draw on both of those traditions, considering how individual motivations and experiences combine with social norms and situations to influence self-definition. In reconstructing, I will hold the concept of identity up to a psychological prism—breaking it apart, looking at its elements, and considering new additive mixtures. In doing so and in introducing issues of subjectivity, context, and change, I believe we can enrich our understanding of social identities.

The term *reconstruction* intentionally evokes associations with the current discourse on construction and deconstruction. Although my analysis deals with neither of these movements directly, I am sympathetic to the underlying themes of both. Constructionists remind us that concepts do not have a reality independent of those who create them (Berger & Luckinan, 1966; Gergen, 1985). Thus identity is a way that we, as cultural observers or social scientists, can describe certain aspects of individual definition and behavior. The term *construction* can also be applied to the individual, recognizing that people make active and often idiosyncratic choices, both in the identities that they claim and in the meanings and experiences associated with those identities. Deconstruction, as literary critics have introduced the term, argues that one must question the text—that categories must be taken apart, examined for their underlying assumptions, and considered in terms of multiple meanings. That spirit, if not the full exercise, is part of this analysis (Parker & Shotter, 1990; Sampson, 1989).

Conceptualizing Identity

People can be categorized in a variety of ways, as studies of stereotyping have shown. Similarly, people can claim membership in a variety of groups in describing themselves. Ascribed categories such as gender, race, and ethnicity are forms of identity that provide a basis for self-definition. So, too, are groups that evolve to provide support or political clout to those who identify with them, such as Gray Panthers or associations of family members of people with Alzheimer's disease.

How are these forms of identity represented in our existing theories? Within Tajfel's (1978) theory of social identity, identity emerges from the context of intergroup relations. Thus one defines oneself as a member of a particular in-group vis-à-vis an out-group—for example, Blacks versus Whites or Nazis versus Jews. In making this presumably favorable distinction between one's own group and some other group, the person is thought to achieve a positive social identity. Turner (1987), in his more recent development of self-categorization theory, moves somewhat away from the intergroup context to consider the basic cognitive process of categorization. His analysis refers to three levels of abstraction in self-categorization, which constitute human identity, social identity, and personal identity.

The use of identity as a concept is not confined to social identity and self-categorization theory. Sociologist and anthropologists studying ethnicity and religion often rely on a concept of ethnic identity (Gleason, 1983). Symbolic interaction theory, though originally using the Meadian language of self, gradually incorporated identity as a central term, as exemplified in Stryker's work (Stryker, 1987; Stryker & Serpe, 1982). In some cases, the key concept is defined as a role-identity (McCall & Simmons, 1978; Thoits, 1991). Typically, the sociological models broaden the domain of identity bringing elements of social structure and system to bear. Within this tradition, multiple identities are assumed whose exercise is influenced by social settings.

Identity has also been conceptualized in a more personological sense. Erikson (1959) is a prime example of this position, which is also reflected in the empirical work of Marcia (1976). From this (often psychodynamic) perspective, identity is conceived as an internal process, holistic and stable across time (Gleason, 1983). Erikson describes the resolution of identity crises as a major stage of development (though one that can be revisited), and Marcia and his followers measure identity integration as a stable personality disposition.

Thus both personality and social psychology are represented in identity's lineage. In the present conceptualization, I recognize this parentage by assuming that both categorical membership and personal meaning must be considered in the analysis of identity. Consider an example drawn from a study of Hispanic students in their first year of college (Ethier & Deaux, 1990). In this research, students first named the identities they claimed and then listed the characteristics they associated with each identity.

Table 1 shows two common identities claimed by many (but not all) of these respondents—that of Hispanic and that of student. Although both these respondents identified themselves in these ways, the meanings that they associated with these identities differed. For one student, being Hispanic was associated with primarily positive feelings; for the other, the Hispanic identity reflected much more ambivalence. Identities as students diverged less, although the positive aspects of intellectual pursuit seem more evident for the student shown on

TABLE 1: Self-Characterized Identities of Two Hispanic Students

Characteristics

Identity	Subject 1	Subject 2
Hispanic	Confused	Proud
	Proud	Loyal
	On guard	Happy
	Representative	Part of a big family
	Questioning	Lucky
	Aware	Cared for
	Token	Stand out in good and bad ways
	Excluded	Social
		Religious
Student	Conscientious	Hard
	Flexible	Big change
	Self-sacrificing	Pressure
	Curious	Freedom
	Assertive	Responsibilities
	Demanding	New environment

the left, whereas more negatively toned pressures appear on the right. Thus the social category is infused with personal meaning.

A number of investigators have proposed distinctions between personal and social identity, although the basis for this distinction is not consensual. Some, such as Brewer (1991) and Turner (1987), posit a temporal trade-off between a sense of personal identity, when one feels different from others, and social identity when one focuses on shared group characteristics. In this analysis, there is no distinctive content of personal and social identity. Rather, what is personal or social depends on the particular fit of individual to context. Others, such as Hogg and Abrams (1988), make a substantive distinction, wherein social identity refers to group membership, such as being English or being a professor, and personal identity encompasses more individual relationships, such as daughter or friend, or lover of Bach.

My view of personal and social identity is somewhat different (see Deaux, 1992, for a more detailed argument). Although I agree with Hogg and Abrams in viewing identities in terms of stable and definable entities, I see the distinction between personal and social as somewhat arbitrary and misleading. Rather than being cleanly separable, social and personal identity are fundamentally interrelated. Personal identity is defined, at least in part, by group memberships, and social categories are infused with personal meaning. [1]

... *Social identities* are those roles *or* membership categories that a person claims as representative. Here I make no distinction between a group such as Asian-Americans and a role such as mother. *Personal identity* refers to those traits and behaviors that the person finds self-descriptive, characteristics that are typically linked to one or more of the identity categories. These two types of identity are linked to each other. Although they can be separated for analysis, each is necessary to give the other meaning. . . .

Key Issues for Identity

The general framework for identity that I propose considers identity in terms of reasonably stable categories of membership to which a person claims to belong, together with sets of personal meanings and experiences linked to the identities. Individuals construct their own identity packages, both in their choice of categories and in the meaning they attach to a category. Taking this perspective suggests at least four sets of issues that need to be addressed.

First, we need to consider how identities are structured and what the significance of different patterns might be. Second, we need to explore the variety of functions that identities serve. Third, the context in which identities are played out must be considered more seriously than it has been. And fourth, in this as in many other areas of social

psychology, there is knowledge to be gained by taking a longitudinal perspective on social identity.

I will discuss each of these issues in more detail, using examples from our recent research to illustrate the kinds of questions and answers that can emerge. These studies include a number of natural membership groups such as ethnicity, deafness, and medical condition. [2]

The Structure of Social Identity

... [I]dentity can be represented as a hierarchical structure in which sets of identities are related to categories of features or attributes. Using this framework, one can address questions of position and salience. For example, one might ask whether categories that are most salient in person perception, such as sex and age (Brewer & Lui, 1989; Hurtig & Pichevin, 1990), also have priority in a typical identity structure. Stryker (1987) has suggested that categories such as these serve as master statuses: Would they be represented at the top of a hierarchy? Or, if the focus is stigma, one could ask whether stigmatized identities are more or less likely to be dominant, a question that Frable (in press) is pursuing.

The position of an identity within the overall structure is more than mere description. Particular positions may have important affective and behavioral correlates, as a recent study of women with lupus suggests (Ouellette, Kobasa, Bochnak, & McKinley, 1991). For patients in this sample, identities as a person with lupus as well as an image of the self before lupus were explored, using the basic hierarchical classification methodology. The resulting identity structures were classified in terms of the position that "me before lupus" occupied. Patients for whom this identity was dominant (and typically was described in very positive terms) showed clinically significant levels of depression, whereas women who did not give priority to this identity showed lower-than-average depression. Ouellette Kobasa and her colleagues also found that people whose identity as a patient was combined with other subjectively negative identities, such as being overweight, were likely to show higher depression.

Thus knowing which identities a person claims is not enough. Information about the position of an identity within the overall structure may be an important predictor of affective state, behavioral choice, and response to interventions.

Functions of Social Identities

A major function of group identification, according to Tajfel, is the enhancement of self-esteem. In social identity theory, self-esteem is enhanced through favorable comparisons between one's own group and an out-group. Yet, as we broaden our conception of identity, so must we broaden our view of the functions that identity plays.

As Abrams and Hogg (Abrams, 1992; Abrams & Hogg, 1988) have noted, the importance of self-esteem as a motivation for social identity may be exaggerated. "Although self-esteem may be involved, it may not merit the status of the prime motivation, especially once one moves beyond the minimal group paradigm" (Abrams, 1992, p. 66). Thus the methodological choice to pit one group against another may foster comparative evaluations and hence activate evaluative concerns of better or worse. Without this explicit comparison, however, other motives may take the forefront.

In moving beyond the minimal group paradigm, Abrams (1992) suggests that the question "Who am I?" may take precedence over "How good am I?" Thus, in claiming to be a professor or a woman or an art collector, I may not be serving any particular self-esteem needs but simply making an existential statement of where I belong in a universe of possibilities. In fact, Tajfel himself discussed the importance of a coherent self-conception in his early analysis of social identity; later, in linking social identity to social comparison processes (Festinger, 1954), he relied more heavily on self-enhancement as a motivational force.

Abrams (1992) suggests that motivations relevant to social identity might include needs for wealth, power, and control; for meaning; and for self-knowledge, cognitive consistency, and self-efficacy. In a related endeavor; Forsyth and his colleagues (Forsyth, Elliott, & Welsh, 1991) have identified 16 functions that group membership can serve. These functions include self-esteem, self-insight, social comparison, social support, and social identity (defined as self-image based on group membership). In each case, people who are highly satisfied with their group see more functional utility in the group membership than people who are less satisfied with the group.

Social identity theory has tended to treat various categories of membership as theoretically equivalent, in keeping with the inclination of social psychology to deal with variables at a generic, rather than a specific, level of analysis. Yet the characteristics of an identity, and in turn the motivational basis of that identity may vary substantially. In a recent analysis of identity variation, Hinkle and Brown (1990) propose two orthogonal dimensions, one a collectivistic versus individualistic orientation and one a comparative versus noncomparative ideology. The first of these dimensions deals with the focus of an individual's concern, on either the self or a group; the second dimension represents the degree to which people are motivated to compare with others. Using the resulting four-category framework, Hinkle and Brown suggest that the emphasis in social identity theory on intergroup comparisons may hold true only when a collectivist orientation is combined with a comparative ideology, as in rival school teams.

Our approach to the question of variability in identities is an empirical one, using methods of cluster analysis and multidimensional scaling to determine what the major categories of identity are and what the psychological dimensions that distinguish them might be.

In earlier research, a diverse set of adults were asked to list identities that they used to characterize themselves. From these lists, we selected a comprehensive set of identities for the cluster analysis study. (To the identities provided by these earlier respondents, we added a number of negative identities, such as alcoholic and homeless person, that might not be readily claimed by respondents but seemed advisable to include in order to assure a range of positive and negative identities.) We then presented the resulting set of 64 identities to 50 experimental participants and asked them to sort the identities into groups on the basis of their perceived similarity to one another (Ethier, Deaux, Addelston, & Reid, 1991).

A cluster analysis of these data showed that a five cluster solution provided the best fit. Table 2 shows these five clusters, together with a few examples of identities falling within each category.

These clusters provide some evidence that there are several types of social identity that can be characterized in distinctive ways. With regard to the motivational issue, we suspect that the primary functions of these identities will differ. Political identities may be associated with power, for example, whereas ethnicity and religion may offer meaning or self-knowledge. Vocations may fulfill needs for self-efficacy.

A second approach to the question of variability among identities is based on multidimensional scaling. Here the aim is to determine what the key psychological dimensions that differentiate the clusters might be. A preliminary analysis suggests at least three dimensions. One refers to whether an identity is achieved, such as an occupation, or whether it is ascribed, such as ethnicity. A distinction can also be made between identities that are clearly defined in a public, organizational context, such as occupation, and those that are more privately defined, such as spouse (possibly related to Hinkle and Brown's, 1990, distinction between collectivist and individualistic orientations). Not surprisingly, an evaluative, good-bad dimension can also be detected.[3] These differences should have important implications not only for the functions that identities serve but also for the functions of activities that identities might predict, including self-proclamation, causal attribution, and perceptions of group homogeneity.

TABLE 2: Identity Clusters and Representative Identities

1. **Relationships**
   Widow
   Friend
   Father
2. **Vocations and avocations**
   Gardener
   Scientist
   Musician
3. **Political affiliations**
   Feminist
   Democrat
   Republican
4. **Stigmatized groups**
   Homeless person
   Deaf person
   Person with AIDS
5. **Ethnic and religious affiliations**
   African-American
   Hispanic
   Christian

The Importance of Context

Sears (1991) recently discussed the "home turf advantage" of social psychology, a domain characterized by laboratory studies that focus on generic variables. In this somewhat rarefied domain, social psychologists are indeed controllers of all they survey. Yet Sears asked a further question regarding ambition: How broadly do we want to cast our nets, how much do we want to explain, how tractable should our theories be? My answers to these questions reflect a belief that we should be broad, that we should tenaciously explore the boundary conditions of our theories, and that we need to find support for those theories in context as well as in the lab.

In literary criticism, the "new historicism" encourages critics to formulate their analyses in terms of the historical events and circumstances that were occurring as the literature was being written (Bernstein, 1991). Traditional literary criticism considered the internal aspects of a text—the use of figurative language, for example—the essential elements for interpretation. In contrast, the "new historicism" criticize analysis in a vacuum and argue that one needs to analyze works in their historical contexts in order to discover their full meaning. Similar arguments are made by the constructionists within social science and by the critical legal theorists within law.

In social psychology, an interesting case for this debate is the discipline's relative emphasis on internal versus external validity. Internal validity has traditionally been the more important concern for social psychologists, somewhat similar to the literary critic's concern with internal structure. In contrast, discussions of external validity are often rather vacuous, merely noting that one needs to know whether laboratory-based findings will generalize to other settings. In casting the issue as a concern with context, however, we change the terms of the discussion. The setting and the dynamics within the setting become important elements of meaning and interpretation, rather than simply a passive foil for the previously framed theory.

Pettigrew (1991) describes contextual social psychology as an approach that considers how individual factors play out in a macrostructural framework and looks for factors that mediate between these levels of analysis. This approach is more associated with sociological social psychology than with psychological social psychology, more linked to the symbolic interaction tradition than to a logical positivist one. Role theory, of course, embedded self-categorizations in terms of relationships with others and a structural setting in which those relationships were carried out. In conceptualizing what they termed role-identities, McCall and Simmons (1978) emphasized the importance of the "when" and "where" of identity—that is, a recognition that each identity has domains in which its influence is most likely to be evident. An even more specific use of context is seen in Proshansky's concept of place identity defined as a sense of self in a particular geographical or environmental context (Proshansky, 1978; Proshansky, Fabian, & Kaminoff, 1983).

A full understanding of social identities calls for the incorporation of some of these sociological concepts. Although the minimal group paradigm uses arbitrary identities created in the laboratory, one needs to remember that the paradigm was an attempt to create an analogue for more durable identities. Thus Tajfel first discussions were not about admirers of Klee and Kandinsky or over- and underestimators of dots but, rather, about Jews and Nazis, about national and ethnic loyalties

and conflicts. This contextualized sense of identity needs to be recaptured in our models.

I offer two examples of the importance of context to identity issues. The first example illustrates how past context can affect current patterns of identity; the second shows how a change in context can affect identity definition.

In recently completed dissertation work, Bat-Chava (1992) studied the conditions in early education and family life that encourage the development of group identity among the deaf. One hypothesis concerned the relationship between group identification[4] and self-esteem, as formulated by Tajfel. The simple correlation between these two variables, though significant, was relatively low at $r = +.18$. Closer inspection of background variables, however, showed important moderating effects of the context in which the now-adult deaf person had grown up.

Figure 1

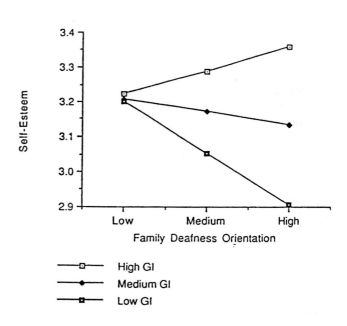

As shown in Figure 1, identity and self-esteem were unrelated for people who had grown up in a household where deaf awareness was low—where parents and siblings could hear and where sign language was not used. In contrast, the relationship between identity and self-esteem is striking when the childhood home was more deaf oriented. Thus context—in this case, past context—has an important moderating effect on a basic theoretical function.

A second example of the role of context comes from a study of Hispanic students interviewed during their first year at Ivy League universities (Ethier & Deaux, 1990, 1992). The selection of this particular group to study the effects of context was based on two assumptions: first, that the transition to college is an important point for possible changes in identity and, second, that for Hispanic students possible discrimination and token status could pose serious threats to ethnic identity (see also Hormuth, 1990; Waters, 1990).

The importance of the students' ethnic identity was assessed, using both a direct rating of importance (a 7-point scale) and the identity subscale from Luhtanen and Crocker's (1992) measure of collective self-esteem. (These two measures were significantly correlated, $r = +.79$.) We predicted that the importance of students' ethnic identity, as assessed during their first 2 months at college, would be related to some features of their family background, such as the use of Spanish in the home and the association with other Hispanics in high school and in their home community. To test this prediction, we created an index of strength of cultural background (SCB) that summarized a number of these background variables. At the initial interview with these students during their first 2 months at college, the expected relationship between cultural background and strength of identity emerged. This was true both for SCB ($r = +.42$, $p < .01$) and for a more specific question about the importance of their identity as a son or daughter ($r = +.30$).

More interesting, and illustrative of the importance of context, are the data obtained when these same students were interviewed at the end of their first year. Overall, there was no change in the frequency of students' claiming a Hispanic identity or in the rated importance of that identity.[5] However, the context in which the Hispanic identity was supported had changed sharply. At the end of the first year, ethnic identity was unrelated to the strength of the student's cultural background. In its place, a relationship emerged between Hispanic identity and cultural

involvement at college, including membership in Hispanic organizations and percentage of Hispanic friends at college ($r = +.62$, $p < .01$). Further, this pattern obtained despite the increasing importance that students gave to their identity as a son or daughter, which rose steadily over the year. One might consider this the lichen model of identity, illustrating how the identity can take hold in a new environment without changing its form substantially.

The point that needs to be made with regard to shifting contexts is that people must continually work at their identities—they need to engage in what I term (shamelessly borrowing from Goffman) *identity work*. Although ethnic identity remained quite steady in its importance, students still had to work actively to reengage the links of the identity to their current context Those who did not do this showed lower ethnic identification.

Longitudinal Perspectives

As context needs to be part of the social psychological perspective, so, too, do we need to pay more attention to long-term issues of development and change. Social psychologists almost always take the cross-sectional cut in their research. These designs yield information about how processes operate at one point in time but tell us little about where they come from or where they are going. In commenting on this disciplinary emphasis, Costanzo (1991) recently likened social psychology to Chapter 4 of an eight-chapter book. That chapter is very thorough; but how about paying a little attention to chapters 1 through 3 and 5 through 8, he asked.

Social identities, as conceptualized here, have stability, duration, and permanence. Although their expression may fluctuate with situation, the basic structure is relatively stable. Against this background of stability, however, important changes occur, precipitated either by a reshuffling of internal priorities or by alterations in the external environment Longitudinal analysis enables us to look at these changing patterns and consequences.

A consideration of longitudinal factors allows us to deal with issues of acquisition and loss. How are identities acquired? How are they modified by experience? How does a person react to the loss of an important identity? Some work has pointed to possible routes. Markus and Nurius (1986), for example, offer possible selves as cognitive/motivational links between present and future. Yet we know relatively little about the movement that occurs between those two time frames. From another perspective, Brewer's (1991) model of optimal distinctiveness suggests some of the psychological conditions that may motivate a change in self-described identity. These ideas, if linked with work on adult socialization and development (Dion, 1985; Ruble, 1987), could substantially enrich our understanding of social identity.

To provide one example of the kind of information that a longitudinal analysis can provide, I turn again to the Ethier and Deaux (1990, 1992) study of Hispanic students. A central question addressed by this study was how people cope with threats to an important identity. In this case, the threats were defined as the negative judgments and discriminatory treatment that members of an ethnic minority group may experience in a primarily White/Anglo environment. We hypothesized that the greater these threats to a student's ethnic identity—or, more accurately, perceptions of threat—the greater would be the impact on identity.

In our longitudinal design, students were interviewed at three points in time over the course of their first year. If we had limited ourselves to a single interview, in the more typical one-shot, cross-sectional approach, we would have found little support for our predictions. At Time 1 there was no relationship ($r = -.15$) between the amount of threat students reported experiencing during their first 2 months in college and their feelings about being Hispanic (as assessed by the Private subscale of the Luhtanen and Crocker [1992] Collective Self-Esteem Scale). Over time, however, the relationship between threat and identity emerges strongly. Students who experienced more threat at Time 1 were more negative about being Hispanic at Time 2 ($r = -.43$, $p< .01$) and at Time 3 ($r =-.60$, $p< .01$). Similarly, amount of threat perceived initially was related to a decrease in the students' tendency to identify with Hispanics.

There are many forms that change can take (Deaux, 1991). Identities can change in their evaluative aspect, as this study showed.

Identity categories themselves can be added or deleted. Or, more simply, the characteristics associated with an identity can shift. All these issues warrant further study.

Conclusions

My objective in this article was to look critically and broadly at the concept of identity and then to provide at least some of the bricks and a portion of the architectural plan for reconstructing the concept. I have not offered a single theory or advocated a single method for engaging in such a project. Indeed, here as elsewhere in psychology, I believe we need to entertain a variety of theories and methods if we want to understand the richness and complexity of social phenomena.

In outlining my view of identity, I draw from both personality and social psychological approaches. Indeed, I argue that analysis of identity provides a common ground for these subdisciplines. Identity exemplifies the interrelationships that are possible, and perhaps inevitable, between social and personality psychology particularly when one seeks to understand behavior in context.

Footnotes

[1] Certainly not all would agree. Trafimow, Triandis, and Goto (1991) recently argued that private and collective aspects of self (similar to personal and social identity, as used here) are stored in separate "baskets." Accordingly, they successfully predicted that the retrieval of private versus collective self-cognitions would be facilitated by different types of retrieval cues.

[2] Students who have been working with me in exploring some of the parameters of social identity include Judi Addelston, Yael Bat-Chava, Beth Brofee, Kathleen Ethier, Kim Mizrahi, and Anne Reid.

[3] Restricting her focus to identity categories that are marked by their deviance, Frable (in press) is also exploring the dimensionality that underlies a variety of social groups.

[4] Group identification was assessed by questions about involvement in the deaf community and percentage of deaf friends.

[5] Ethnic identity is not always so constant. Waters (1990), for example, reports that only 65% of respondents names the same ethnic identity over a 1-year period. This rate varied substantially by ethnic group, however, being higher for groups such as Poles, Mexicans, and Italians and lower for older immigrant groups such as the English, Scottish, and Welsh.

References

Abrahams, D. (1992). Processes of social identification. In G. Breakwell (Ed.), *Social psychology of identity and the self-concept* (pp. 57-99). London: Academic Press.

Abrams, D., & Hoggs, M.A. (1988). Comments on the motivational status of self-esteem in social identity and intergroup discimination. *European Journal of Social Psychology*, 18, 317-334.

Bat-Chava, Y. (1992). *Group identification and self-esteem among members of a non-ethnic minority group: The case of deaf people.* Unpublished doctoral dissertation, City University of New York.

Berger, P.L., & Luckman, T. (1965). *The social construction of reality.* New York: Doubleday.

Bernstein, R. (1991, February 19). It's back to the blackboard for literary criticism. *New York Times*, pp. C11, C16.

Brewer, M.B. (1991). The social self: On being the same and different at the same time. *Personality and Social Psychology Bulletin*, 17, 475-482.

Brewer, M.B., & Lui, L.N. (1989). The primacy of age of sex in the structure of person categories. *Social Cognition*, 7, 262-274.

Costanzo, P. (1991, June). *Socialization and mental health.* Paper presented at the conference of the Society for Personality and Social Psychology, Washington, DC.

Deaux, K. (1991). Social identities: Thoughts on structure and change. In R.C. Curtis (Ed.), *The relational self: Theoretical; convergences in psychoanalysis and social psychology* (pp. 77-93). New York: Guilford.

Deaux, K. (1992). Personalizing identity and socializing self. In G. Breakwell (Ed.), *Social psychology of identity and the self-concept* (pp. 9-33). London: Academic Press.

Dion, K.K. (1985). Socialization in adulthood. In G. Lindzey & E. Aronson (Eds.), *The handbook of social psychology* (3rd ed., Vol. 2, pp. 123-147). New York: Random House.

Erikson, E.H. (1959). Identity and the life cycle. In G.S. Klein (Ed.), *Psychological issues.* New York: International Universities Press.

Ethier, K.A., & Deaux, K. (1990). Hispanics in ivy: Assessing identity and perceived threat. *Sex Roles*, 22, 427-440.

Ethier, K.A., & Deaux, K. (1992). Coping with threats to ethnic identity. Manuscript in preparation, City University of New York.

Ethier, K.A., Deaux, K., Addelston, J., & Reid, A. (1991, June). Dimensions of social identity. Poster presented at the meeting of the American Psychological Society, Washington, DC.

Festinger, L. (1954). A theory of social comparison processes. *Human Relations*, 7, 117-140.

Forsyth, D.R., Elliott, T.R., & Welsh, J.A. (1991, June). Multidimensional model of the function of groups. Poster presented at the meeting of the American Psychological Society, Washington, DC.

Frable, D.E.S. (in press). Being and feeling unique: Statistical deviance and psychological marginality. *Journal of Personality.*

Gergen, K.J. (1985). The social constructionist movement in modern psychology. *American Psychologist*, 40, 266-275.

Gleason, P. (1983). Identifying identity: A semantic history. *Journal of American History*, 69, 910-931.

Hinkle, S., & Brown, R.J. (1990). Intergroup comparison and social identity: Some links and lacunae. In D. Abrams & M.A. Hogg (Eds.), *Social identity theory: Constructive and critical advances* (pp. 48-70). London: Harvester-Wheatsheaf; New York: Springer-Verlag.

Hogg, M.A., & Abrams, D. (1988). *Social identifications.* London and New York: Routledge & Kegan Paul.

Hormuth, S.E. (1990). *The ecology of the self: Relocation and self-concept change.* Cambridge: Cambridge University Press.

Hurtig, M.C., & Pichevin, M.F. (1990). Salience of the sex category system in person perception: Contextual variations. *Sex roles*, 22, 369-395.

Luhtanen, R., & Crocker, J. (1992). A collective self-esteem scale: Self-evaluation of one's social identity. *Personality and Social Psychology Bulletin*, 18, 302-318.

Marcia, J.E. (1976). Ego identity status: Relationship to change in self-esteem, "general maladjustment" and authoritarianism. *Journal of Personality*, 35, 118-133.

Markus, H., & Nurius, P. (1986). Possible selves. *American Psychologist*, 41, 954-969.

McCall, G.J., & Simmons, J.L. (1978). *Identities and interactions* (rev. ed.). New York: Free Press.

Ouellette Kobasa, S.C., Bochnak, B., & McKinley, P.S. (1991, November). *Patient identity in women with systemic lupus erythematosus.* Paper presented at the 26th Arthritis Health Professions Association National Scientific Meeting, Boston.

Parker, I., & Shotter, J. (1990). *Deconstructing social psychology.* London: Routledge & Kegan Paul.

Pettigrew, T.F. (1991). Toward unity and bold theory: Popperian suggestions for two persistent problems of social psychology. In C.W. Stephan, W.G. Stephan, & T.F. Pettigrew (Eds.), *The future of social psychology: Defining the relationship between sociology and psychology* (pp. 13-27). New York: Springer-Verlag.

Proshansky, H.M. (1978). The city and self identity. *Environment and Behavior*, 10, 147-169.

Proshansky, H.M., Fabian, A.K., & Kaminoff, R. (1983). Place-identity: Physical world socialization of the self. *Journal of Environmental Psychology*, 3, 57-83.

Ruble, D.N. (1987). The acquisition of self-knowledge: A self-socialization perspective. In N. Eisenberg (Ed.), *Contemporary topics in developmental psychology* (pp. 243-270). New York: Wiley.

Sampson, E.E. (1989). The deconstruction of self. In J. Shotter & K.J. Gergen (Eds.), *Texts of identity* (pp. 1-19). London: Sage.

Sears, D. (1991, June). *Application and applicability: Social psychology's home turf.* Keynote address at the conference of the Society for Personality and Social Psychology, Washington, DC.

Stryker, S. (1987). Identity theory: Developments and extensions. In K. Yardley & T. Honess (Eds.), *Self and identity: Psychosocial perspectives* (pp. 83-103). New York: Wiley.

Stryker, S., & Serpe, R. (1982). Commitment, identity salience, and role behavior. In W. Ickes & E. Knowles (Eds.), *Personality, roles, and social behavior* (pp. 199-218). New York: Springer-Verlag.

Tajfel, H. (1978). Differentiation between social groups: *Studies in the social psychology of intergroup relations.* London: Academic Press.

Thoits, P. (1991). *Identity structures and psychological well-being: Gender and marital status comparison.* Unpublished manuscript, Vanderbilt University.

Trafimow, D., Triandis, H.C., & Goto, S.G. (1991). Some tests of the distinction between the private self and the collective self. *Journal of Personality and Social Psychology, 60,* 649-655,

Turner, J.C. (1987). *Rediscovering the social group: A self-categorization theory.* Oxford: Basil Blackwell.

Waters, M.C. (1990). *Ethnic options: Choosing identities in America.* Berkeley: University of California Press.

Gender Schema Theory And Its Implications For Child Development: Raising Gender-Aschematic Children In A Gender-Schematic Society

Sandra Lipsitz Bem

ℰditors' Note: When we answer the question, "Who am I?" most of us will undoubtedly include that we are either male or female in our response. In this article, Sandra Bem argues that this indicates that our self-descriptions contain elaborate gender descriptions or gender schemas. After describing different theories of gender identity, including her own gender schema theory, Bem offers suggestions to parents for raising children without a predominant gender identity. Do you think this is possible?

As every parent, teacher, and developmental psychologist knows, male and female children become "masculine" and "feminine," respectively, at a very early age. By the time they are four or five, for example, girls and boys have typically come to prefer activities defined by the culture as appropriate for their sex and also to prefer same-sex peers. The acquisition of sex-appropriate preferences, skills, personality attributes, behaviors, and self-concepts is typically referred to within psychology as the process of sex typing.

The universality and importance of this process is reflected in the prominence it has received in psychological theories of development, which seek to elucidate how the developing child comes to match the template defined as sex appropriate by his or her culture. Three theories of sex typing have been especially influential: psychoanalytic theory, social learning theory, and cognitive-developmental theory. More recently, a fourth theory of sex typing has been introduced into the psychological literature—gender schema theory.

This article is designed to introduce gender schema theory to feminist scholars outside the discipline of psychology. In order to provide a background for the conceptual issues that have given rise to gender schema theory, I will begin with a discussion of the three theories of sex typing that have been dominant within psychology to date.

Psychoanalytic Theory

The first psychologist to ask how male and female are transmuted into masculine and feminine was Freud. Accordingly, in the past virtually every major source book in developmental psychology began its discussion of sex typing with a review of psychoanalytic theory.[1]

Psychoanalytic theory emphasizes the child's identification with the same-sex parent as the primary mechanism whereby children become sex typed, an identification that results from the child's discovery of genital sex differences, from the penis envy and castration anxiety that this discovery produces in females and males, respectively, and from the successful resolution of the Oedipus conflict.[2] Although a number of feminist scholars have found it fruitful in recent years to work within a psychoanalytic framework,[3] the theory's "anatomy is destiny" view has been associated historically with quite conservative conclusions regarding the inevitability of sex typing.

Of the three dominant theories of sex typing, psychoanalytic theory is almost certainly the best known outside the discipline of psychology, although it is no longer especially popular among research psychologists. In part, this is because the theory is difficult to test empirically. An even more important reason, however, is that the empirical evidence simply does not justify emphasizing either the child's discovery of genital sex differences in particular[4] or the child's identification with his or her same-sex parent[5] as a crucial determinant of sex typing.

Social Learning Theory

In contrast to psychoanalytic theory, social learning theory emphasizes the rewards and punishments that children receive for sex-appropriate and sex-inappropriate behaviors, as well as the vicarious learning that observation and modeling can provide.[6] Social learning theory thus locates the source of sex typing in the sex-differentiated practices of the socializing community.

Perhaps the major virtue of social learning theory for psychologists is that it applies to the development of psychological femaleness and maleness the very same general principles of learning that are already known to account for the development of a multitude of other behaviors. Thus, as far as the formal theory is concerned, gender does not demand special consideration; that is, no special psychological mechanisms or processes must be postulated in order to explain how children become sex typed beyond those already used to explain how children learn other socialized behaviors. . . .

Although social learning theory can account for the young child's acquiring a number of particular behaviors that are stereotyped by the culture as sex appropriate, it treats the child as the relatively passive recipient of environmental forces rather than as an active agent striving to organize and thereby to comprehend the social world. This view of the passive child is inconsistent with the common observation that children themselves frequently construct and enforce their own version of society's gender rules. . . .

Cognitive-Developmental Theory

Unlike social learning theory, cognitive-developmental theory focuses almost exclusively on the child as the primary agent of his or her own sex-role socialization, a focus reflecting the theory's basic assumption that sex typing follows naturally and inevitably from universal principles of cognitive development. As children work actively to comprehend their social world, they inevitably "label themselves—call it alpha—and determine that there are alphas and betas in the environment. Given the cognitive-motivational properties of the self,

the child moves toward other alphas and away from betas. That is, it is the child who realizes what gender he or she is, and in what behaviors he or she should engage."[7] In essence, then, cognitive-developmental theory postulates that, because of the child's need for cognitive consistency, self-categorization as female or male motivates her or him to value that which is seen as similar to the self in terms of gender. This gender-based value system, in turn, motivates the child to engage in gender-congruent activities, to strive for gender-congruent attributes, and to prefer gender-congruent peers. "Basic self-categorizations determine basic valuings. Once the boy has stably identified himself as male, he then values positively those objects and acts consistent with his gender identity."[8]

The cognitive-developmental account of sex typing has been so influential since its introduction into the literature in 1966 that many psychologists now seem to accept almost as a given that the young child will spontaneously develop both a gender-based self-concept and a gender-based value system even in the absence of external pressure to behave in a sex-stereotyped manner. Despite its popularity, however, the theory fails to explicate why sex will have primacy over other potential categories of the self such as race, religion, or even eye color. . . .

To understand why children become *sex* typed rather than, say, race or caste typed, we still need a theory that explicitly addresses the question of how and why children come to utilize sex in particular as a cognitive organizing principle.

Gender Schema Theory

Gender schema theory[9] contains features of both the cognitive-developmental and the social learning accounts of sex typing. In particular, gender schema theory proposes that sex typing derives in large measure from gender-schematic processing, from a generalized readiness on the part of the child to encode and to organize information—including information about the self-according to the culture's definitions of maleness and femaleness. Like cognitive-developmental theory, then, gender schema theory proposes that sex typing is mediated by the child's own cognitive processing. However, gender schema theory further proposes that gender-schematic processing is itself derived from the sex-differentiated practices of the social community. Thus, like social learning theory, gender schema theory assumes that sex typing is a learned phenomenon and, hence, that it is neither inevitable nor unmodifiable. In this discussion, I shall first consider in some detail what gender-schematic processing is and how it mediates sex typing; I shall then explore the conditions that produce gender-schematic processing, thereby providing an explicit account of why sex comes to have cognitive primacy over other social categories.

Gender-schematic Processing

Gender schema theory begins with the observation that the developing child invariably learns his or her society's cultural definitions of femaleness and maleness. In most societies, these definitions comprise a diverse and sprawling network of sex-linked associations encompassing not only those features directly related to female and male persons—such as anatomy, reproductive function, division of labor, and personality attributes—but also features more remotely or metaphorically related to sex, such as the angularity or roundedness of an abstract shape and the periodicity of the moon. Indeed, no other dichotomy in human experience appears to have as many entities linked to it as does the distinction between female and male.

But there is more. Gender schema theory proposes that, in addition to learning such content-specific information about gender, the child also learns to invoke this heterogeneous network of sex-related associations in order to evaluate and assimilate new information. The child, in short, learns to encode and to organize information in terms of an evolving gender schema.

A schema is a cognitive structure, a network of associations that organizes and guides an individual's perception. A schema functions as an anticipatory structure, a readiness to search for and to assimilate incoming information in schema-relevant terms. Schematic information processing is thus highly selective and enables the individual to impose structure and meaning onto a vast array of incoming stimuli. More specifically, schematic information processing entails a readiness to sort information into categories on the basis of some particular dimension, despite the existence of other dimensions that could serve equally well in this regard. Gender-schematic processing in particular thus involves spontaneously sorting attributes and behaviors into masculine and feminine categories or "equivalence classes," regardless of their differences on a variety of dimensions unrelated to gender, for example, spontaneously placing items like "tender" and "nightingale" into a feminine category and items like "assertive" and "eagle" into a masculine category. Like schema theories generally,[10] gender schema theory thus construes perception as a constructive process in which the interaction between incoming information and an individual's preexisting schema determines what is perceived.

What gender schema theory proposes, then, is that the phenomenon of sex typing derives, in part, from gender-schematic processing, from an individual's generalized readiness to process information on the basis of the sex-linked associations that constitute the gender schema. Specifically, the theory proposes that sex typing results, in part, from the assimilation of the self-concept itself to the gender schema. As children learn the contents of their society's gender schema, they learn which attributes are to be linked with their own sex and, hence, with themselves. This does not simply entail learning the defined relationship between each sex and each dimension or attribute—that boys are to be strong and girls weak, for example—but involves the deeper lesson that the dimensions themselves are differentially applicable to the two sexes. Thus the strong-weak dimension itself is absent from the schema to be applied to girls just as the dimension of nurturance is implicitly omitted from the schema to be applied to boys. Adults in the child's world rarely notice or remark upon how strong a little girl is becoming or how nurturant a little boy is becoming, despite their readiness to note precisely these attributes in the "appropriate" sex. The child learns to apply this same schematic selectivity to the self, to choose from among the many possible dimensions of human personality only that subset defined as applicable to his or her own sex and thereby eligible for organizing the diverse contents of the self-concept. Thus do children's self-concepts become sex typed, and thus do the two sexes become, in their own eyes, not only different in degree, but different in kind.

Simultaneously, the child also learns to evaluate his or her adequacy as a person according to the gender schema, to match his or her preferences, attitudes, behaviors, and personal attributes against the prototypes stored within it. The gender schema becomes a prescriptive standard or guide,[11] and self-esteem becomes its hostage. Here, then, enters an internalized motivational factor that prompts an individual to regulate his or her behavior so that it conforms to cultural definitions of femaleness and maleness. Thus do cultural myths become self-fulfilling prophecies, and thus, according to gender schema theory, do we arrive at the phenomenon known as sex typing.

It is important to note that gender schema theory is a theory of process, not content. Because sex-typed individuals are seen as processing information and regulating their behavior according to whatever definitions of femininity and masculinity their culture happens to provide, the process of dividing the world into feminine and masculine categories—and not the contents of the categories—is central to the theory. Accordingly, sex-typed individuals are seen to differ from other individuals not primarily in the degree of femininity or masculinity they possess, but in the extent to which their self-concepts and behaviors are organized on the basis of gender rather than on the basis of some other dimension. Many non-sex-typed individuals may describe themselves as, say, nurturant or dominant without implicating the concepts of femininity or masculinity. When sex-typed individuals so describe themselves, however, it is precisely the gender connotations of the attributes or behaviors that are presumed to be salient for them.

Empirical Research on Gender-schematic Processing

Recent empirical research supports gender schema theory's basic contention that sex typing is derived from gender-schematic

processing. In a variety of studies using different subject populations and different paradigms, female and male sex-typed individuals have been found to be significantly more likely than non-sex-typed individuals to process information—including information about the self—in terms of gender [12]

One study, for example, used a memory task to determine whether gender connotations are, in fact, more "cognitively available" to sex-typed individuals than to non-sex-typed individuals, as gender schema theory claims.[13] The subjects in this study were forty-eight male and forty-eight female undergraduates who had described themselves as either sex typed or non-sex typed on the Bem Sex Role Inventory (BSRI).[14]

During the experimental session, subjects were presented with a randomly ordered sequence of sixty-one words that included proper names, animal names, verbs, and articles of clothing. Half of the proper names were female, half were male; one-third of the items within each of the other semantic categories had been consistently rated by undergraduate judges as feminine (e.g., butterfly, blushing, bikini), one-third as masculine (e.g., gorilla, hurling, trousers), and one-third as neutral (e.g., ant, stepping, sweater). The words were presented on slides at three-second intervals, and subjects were told that their recall would later be tested. Three seconds after the presentation of the last word, they were given a period of eight minutes to write down as many words as they could, in whatever order they happened to come to mind.

As expected, the results indicated that although sex-typed and non-sex-typed individuals recalled equal numbers of items overall, the order in which they recalled the items was different. Once having recalled a feminine item, sex-typed individuals were more likely than non-sex-typed individuals to recall another feminine item next rather than a masculine or a neutral item. The same was true for masculine items. In other words, the sequence of recall for sex-typed individuals revealed significantly more runs or clusters of feminine items and of masculine items than the sequence of recall for non-sex-typed individuals. Thinking of one feminine (or masculine) item could enhance the probability of thinking of another feminine (or masculine) item in this way only if the individual spontaneously encodes both items as feminine (or masculine), and the gender schema thereby links the two items in memory. These results thus confirm gender schema theory's claim that sex-typed individuals have a greater readiness than do non-sex-typed individuals to encode information in terms of the sex-linked associations that constitute the gender schema. . . .

Antecedents of Gender-schematic Processing

But how and why do sex-typed individuals develop a readiness to organize information in general, and their self-concepts in particular, in terms of gender? Because gender-schematic processing is considered a special case of schematic processing, this specific question is superseded by the more general question of how and why individuals come to organize information in terms of any social category, that is, how and why a social category becomes transformed into a cognitive schema.

Gender schema theory proposes that the transformation of a given social category into the nucleus of a highly available cognitive schema depends on the nature of the social context within which the category is embedded, not on the intrinsic nature of the category itself. Given the proper social context, then, even a category like eye color could become a cognitive schema. More specifically, gender schema theory proposes that a category will become a schema if: *(a)* the social context makes it the nucleus of a large associative network, that is, if the ideology and/or the practices of the culture construct an association between that category and a wide range of other attributes, behaviors, concepts, and categories; and *(b)* the social context assigns the category broad functional significance, that is, if a broad array of social institutions, norms, and taboos distinguishes between persons, behaviors, and attributes on the basis of this category.

This latter condition is most critical, for gender schema theory presumes that the culture's insistence on the functional importance of the social category is what transforms a passive network of associations into an active and readily available schema for interpreting reality. We all learn many associative networks of concepts throughout life, many potential cognitive schemata, but the centrality or functional importance assigned by society to particular categories and distinctions animates their associated networks and gives these schemata priority and availability over others. . . .

Gender schema theory thus implies that children would be far less likely to become gender schematic and hence sex typed if the society were to limit the associative network linked to sex and to temper its insistence on the functional importance of the gender dichotomy. . . .

Raising Gender-Aschematic Children

Feminist parents who wish to raise gender-aschematic children in a gender-schematic world are like any parents who wish to inculcate their children with beliefs and values that deviate from those of the dominant culture. Their major option is to try to undermine the dominant ideology before it can undermine theirs. Feminist parents are thus in a difficult situation. They cannot simply ignore gender in their child rearing as they might prefer to do, because the society will then have free rein to teach their children the lessons about gender that it teaches all other children. Rather, they must manage somehow to inoculate their children against gender-schematic processing.

Two strategies are suggested here. First, parents can enable their children to learn about sex differences initially without their also learning the culture's sex-linked associative network by simultaneously retarding their children's knowledge of sex's cultural correlates and advancing their children's knowledge of sex's biological correlates. Second, parents can provide alternative or "subversive" schemata that their children can use to interpret the culture's sex-linked associative network when they do learn it. This step is essential if children are not simply to learn gender-schematic processing somewhat later than their counterparts from more traditional homes. Whether one is a child or an adult, such alternative schemata "build up one's resistance" to the lessons of the dominant culture and thereby enable one to remain gender-aschematic even while living in a gender-schematic society.

Teaching Children about Sex Differences

Cultural correlates of sex. Children typically learn that gender is a sprawling associative network with ubiquitous functional importance through their observation of the many cultural correlates of sex existing in their society. Accordingly, the first step parents can take to retard the development of gender-schematic processing is to retard the child's knowledge of these cultural messages about gender. Less crudely put, parents can attempt to attenuate sex-linked correlations within the child's social environment, thereby altering the basic data upon which the child will construct his or her own concepts of maleness and femaleness.

In part, parents can do this by eliminating sex stereotyping from their own behavior and from the alternatives that they provide for their children, just as many feminist parents are already doing. Among other things, for example, they can take turns making dinner, bathing the children, and driving the car; they can ensure that all their children—regardless of sex—have both trucks and dolls, both pink and blue clothing, and both male and female playmates; and they can arrange for their children to see women and men in nontraditional occupations.

When children are quite young, parents can further inhibit cultural messages about gender by actually censoring books and television programs whose explicit or implicit message is that the sexes differ on nonbiological dimensions. At present, this tactic will eliminate many children's books and most television programming. . ..

To compensate for this censorship, parents will need to seek out—and to create—materials that do not teach sex stereotypes. With our own children, my husband and I got into the habit of doctoring books whenever possible so as to remove all sex-linked correlations. We did this, among other ways, by changing the sex of the main character; by drawing longer hair and the outline of breasts onto illustrations of previously male truck drivers, physicians, pilots, and the like; and by deleting or altering sections of the text that described females or males in a sex-stereotyped manner. When reading children's picture books aloud, we also chose pronouns that avoided the ubiquitous implication that all characters without dresses or pink bows must necessarily be male: "And what is this little piggy doing? Why, he or she seems to be building a bridge."

All of these practices are designed to permit very young children to dwell temporarily in a social environment where, if the parents are lucky, the cultural correlations with sex will be attenuated. ... By themselves, however, these practices teach children only what sex is not. But children must also be taught what sex is.

Biological correlates of sex. What remains when all of the cultural correlates of sex are attenuated or eliminated, of course, are two of the undisputed biological correlates of sex: anatomy and reproduction. Accordingly, parents can make these the definitional attributes of femaleness and maleness. By teaching their children that the genitalia constitute the definitive attributes of females and males, parents help them to apprehend the merely probabilistic nature of sex's cultural correlates and thereby restrict sex's associative sprawl. By teaching their children that whether one is female or male makes a difference only in the context of reproduction, parents limit sex's functional significance and thereby retard gender-schematic processing. Because children taught these lessons have been provided with an explicit and clear-cut rule about what sex is and when sex matters, they should be predisposed to construct their own concepts of femaleness and maleness based on biology, rather than on the cultural correlates to which they have been exposed. . . .

The liberation that comes from having an unambiguous genital definition of sex and the imprisonment that comes from not having such a definition are nicely illustrated by the story of what happened to our son Jeremy, then age four, the day he decided to wear barrettes to nursery school. Several times that day, another little boy told Jeremy that he, Jeremy, must be a girl because "only girls wear barrettes." After trying to explain to this child that "wearing barrettes doesn't matter" and that "being a boy means having a penis and testicles," Jeremy finally pulled down his pants as a way of making his point more convincingly. The other child was not impressed. He simply said, "Everybody has a penis; only girls wear barrettes."

In the American context, children do not typically learn to define sex in terms of anatomy and reproduction until quite late, and, as a result, they—like the child in the example above—mistakenly treat many of the cultural correlates of sex as definitional. This confusion is facilitated, of course, by the fact that the genitalia themselves are not usually visible and hence cannot be relied on as a way of identifying someone's sex.

Accordingly, when our children asked whether someone was male or female, we frequently denied certain knowledge of the person's sex, emphasizing that without being able to see whether there was a penis or a vagina under the person's clothes, we had no definitive information. Moreover, when our children themselves began to utilize nonbiological markers as a way of identifying sex, we gently teased them about that strategy to remind them that the genitalia—and only the genitalia—constitute the definition of sex: "What do you mean that you can tell Chris is a girl because Chris has long hair? Does Chris's hair have a vagina?"

We found Stephanie Waxman's picture book *What Is a Girl? What Is a Boy?* to be a superb teaching aid in this context.[15] Each page displays a vivid and attractive photograph of a boy or a girl engaged in some behavior stereotyped as more typical of or more appropriate for the other sex. The accompanying text says such things as, "Some people say a girl is someone with jewelry, but Barry is wearing a necklace and he's a boy." The book ends with nude photographs of both children and adults, and it explicitly defines sex in terms of anatomy.

These particular lessons about what sex is, what sex is not, and when sex matters are designed to make young children far more naive than their peers about the cultural aspects of gender and far more sophisticated than their peers about the biological aspects of sex. Eventually, of course, their naivete will begin to fade, and they too will begin to learn the culture's sprawling network of sex-linked

associations. At that point, parents must take steps to prevent that associative network from itself becoming a cognitive schema.

Providing Alternative Schemata

Let us presume that the feminist parent has successfully produced a child who defines sex in terms of anatomy and reproduction. How is such a child to understand the many sex-linked correlations that will inevitably begin to intrude upon his or her awareness? What alternative schemata can substitute for the gender schema in helping the child to organize and to assimilate gender-related information?

Individual differences schema. The first alternative schema is simply a child's version of the time-honored liberal truism used to counter stereotypic thinking in general, namely, that there is remarkable variability of individuals within groups as compared with the small mean differences between groups. To the child who says that girls do not like to play baseball, the feminist parent can thus point out that although it is true that some girls do not like to play baseball, it is also true that some girls do (e.g., your Aunt Beverly and Alissa who lives across the street) and that some boys do not (e.g., your dad and Alissa's brother Jimmy). It is, of course, useful for parents to supply themselves with a long list of counterexamples well in advance of such occasions.

This individual differences schema is designed to prevent children from interpreting individual differences as sex differences, from assimilating perceived differences among people to a gender schema. Simultaneously, it should also encourage children to treat as a given that the sexes are basically similar to one another and, hence, to view all glib assertions about sex differences as inherently suspect. And it is with this skepticism that feminist consciousness begins.

Cultural relativism schema. As the child's knowledge and awareness grow, he or she will gradually begin to realize that his or her family's beliefs and attitudes about gender are at variance with those of the dominant culture. Accordingly, the child needs some rationale for not simply accepting the majority view as the more valid. One possible rationale is cultural relativism, the notion that "different people believe different things" and that the coexistence of even contradictory beliefs is the rule in society rather than the exception. . . .

Accordingly, before we read our daughter her first volume of fairy tales, we discussed with her the cultural beliefs and attitudes about men and women that the tales would reflect, and while reading the tales, we frequently made such comments as, "Isn't it interesting that the person who wrote this story seems to think that girls always need to be rescued?" If such discussions are not too heavy-handed, they can provide a background of understanding against which the child can thoroughly enjoy the stories themselves, while still learning to discount the sex stereotypes within them as irrelevant both to their own beliefs and to truth. The cultural relativism schema thus brings children an awareness that fairy tales are fairy tales in more than one sense.

Sexism schema. Cultural relativism is fine in its place, but feminist parents will not and should not be satisfied to pretend that they think all ideas—particularly those about gender—are equally valid. At some point, they will feel compelled to declare that the view of women and men conveyed by fairy tales, by the mass media—and by the next-door neighbors—is not only different, but wrong. It is time to teach one's children about sexism.

Moreover, it is only by giving children a sexism schema, a coherent and organized understanding of the historical roots and the contemporaneous consequences of sex discrimination, that they will truly be able to comprehend why the sexes appear to be so different in our society: why, for example, there has never been a female president of the United States; why fathers do not stay home with their children; and why so many people believe these sex differences to be the natural consequence of biology. The child who has developed a readiness to encode and to organize information in terms of an evolving sexism schema is a child who is prepared to oppose actively the gender-related constraints that those with a gender schema will inevitably seek to impose. . . .

A Comment on Psychological Androgyny

The central figure in gender schema theory is the sex-typed individual, a shift in focus from my earlier work in which the non-sex-typed individual—the androgynous individual in particular—commanded center stage.[16] In the early 1970s, androgyny seemed to me and to many others a liberated and more humane alternative to the traditional, sex-biased standards of mental health. And it is true that this concept can be applied equally to both women and men, and that it encourages individuals to embrace both the feminine and the masculine within themselves. But advocating the concept of androgyny can also be seen as replacing a prescription to be masculine or feminine with the doubly incarcerating prescription to be masculine and feminine. The individual now has not one but two potential sources of inadequacy with which to contend. Even more important, however, the concept of androgyny is problematic from the perspective of gender schema theory because it is based on the presupposition that there is a feminine and a masculine within us all, that is, that "femininity" and "masculinity" have an independent and palpable reality and are not cognitive constructs derived from gender-schematic processing. Focusing on androgyny thus fails to prompt serious examination of the extent to which gender organizes both our perceptions and our social world.

In contrast, the concept of gender-schematic processing directs our attention to the promiscuous availability of the gender schema in contexts where other schemata ought to have priority. Thus, if gender schema theory has a political message, it is not that the individual should be androgynous. Rather, it is that the network of associations constituting the gender schema ought to become more limited in scope and that society ought to temper its insistence on the ubiquitous functional importance of the gender dichotomy. In short, human behaviors and personality attributes should no longer be linked with gender, and society should stop projecting gender into situations irrelevant to genitalia.

Notes

1. See, e.g., Paul H. Mussen, "Early Sex-Role Development," in *Handbook of Socialization Theory and Research,* ed. David A. Goslin (Chicago: Rand McNally & Co., 1969), pp. 703-31. For a more recent review that does not even mention psychoanalytic theory, see Aletha C. Ruston, "Sex-Typing," to appear in *Carmichael's Manual of Child Psychology,* ed. Paul H. Mussen, 4th ed. (New York: John Wiley & Sons, in press).

2. Urie Bronfenbrenner, "Freudian Theories of Identification with Their Derivatives," *Child Development* 31, no. 1 (March 1960): ISAC; Sigmund Freud, "Some Psychological Consequences of the Anatomical Distinction between the Sexes (1925)," in *Collected Papers of Sigmund Freud,* ed. Ernest Jones, 5 vols. (New York: Basic Books, 1959), 5:l8-97; Sigmund Freud, "The Passing of the Oedipus Complex (1924)," ibid., 2: 269-76.

3. E.g., Nancy Chodorow, *The Reproduction of Mothering: Psychoanalysis and the Sociology of Gender* (Berkeley: University of California Press, 1978); Gayle Rubin, "The Traffic in Women: Notes on the 'Political Economy' of Sex," in *Toward an Anthropology of Women,* ed. Rayna Reiter (New York: Monthly Review Press, 1975), pp. 157-2l0.

4. Lawrence Kohlberg, "A Cognitive-Developmental Analysis of Children's Sex-Role Concepts and Attitudes," in *The Development of Sex Differences,* ed. Eleanor E. Maccoby (Stanford, CA: Stanford University Press, 1966), pp. 82-173; Maureen J. McConaghy, "Gender Permanence and the Genital Basis of Gender: Stages in the Development of Constancy of Gender Identity," *Child Development* 50, no. 4 (December 1979): 1223-26.

5. Eleanor E. Maccoby and Carol N. Jacklin, *The Psychology of Sex Differences* (Stanford, CA: Stanford University Press, 1974).

6. Walter Mischel, "Sex-Typing and Socialization," in *Carmichael's Manual of Child Psychology,* ed. Paul H. Mussen, 2 vols. (New York: John Wiley & Sons, 1970), 2:3-72.

7. Michael Lewis and Jeanne Brooks-Gunn, *Social Cognition and the Acquisition of Self* (New York: Plenum Publishing Corp., 1979), p. 270.

8. Kohlberg, p. 89.

9. Sandra L. Bem, "Gender Schema Theory: A Cognitive Account of Sex Typing," *Psychological Review* 88, no. 4 (July 1981): 354-64; and "Gender Schema Theory and Self-Schema Theory Compared: A Comment on Markus, Crane, Bernstein, and Siladi's 'Self-Schemas and Gender,' *Journal of Personality and Social Psychology* 43, no. 6 (December 1982): 1192-94.

10. Ulric Neisser, *Cognition and Reality* (San Francisco: W. H. Freeman & Co., 1976); Shelley F. Taylor and Jennifer Crocker, "Schematic Bases of Social Information Processing," in *Social Cognition, the Ontario Symposium,* ed. E. Tory Higgins, C. Peter Herman, and Mark P. Zanna (Hillsdale, N.J.: Lawrence Erlbaum Associates, 1981), 1:89-135.

11. Jerome Kagan, "Acquisition and Significance of Sex Typing and Sex Role Identity," in *Review of Child Development Research,* ed. Martin L. Hoffman and Lois W. Hoffman (New York: Russell Sage Foundation, 1964), 1:137-47.

12. Susan M. Andersen and Sandra L. Bem, "Sex Typing and Androgyny in Dyadic Interaction: Individual Differences in Responsiveness to Physical Attractiveness," *Journal of Personality and Social Psychology* 41, no. 1 (July 1981): 7-86; Bem, "Gender Schema Theory"; Kay Deaux and Brenda Major, "Sex-related Patterns in the Unit of Perception," *Personality and Social Psychology Bulletin* 3, no. 2 (Spring 1977): 297-300; Brenda Girvin, "The Nature of Being Schematic: Sex-Role Self-Schemas and Differential Processing of Masculine and Feminine Information" (Ph.D. diss., Stanford University, 1978); Robert V. Kail and Laura F. Levine, "Encoding Processes and Sex-Role Preferences," *Journal of Experimental Child Psychology* 21, no. 2 (April 1976): 25-43; Lynn S. Liben and Margaret L. Signorella, "Gender-related Schemata and Constructive Memory in Children," *Child Development* 51, no. 1 (March 1980): 11-15; Richard Lippa, "Androgyny, Sex Typing, and the Perception of Masculinity-Femininity in Handwriting," *Journal of Research in Personality* 11, no. 1 (March 1977): 21-37; Hazel Markus et al., "Self-Schemas and Gender," *Journal of Personality and Social Psychology* 42, no. 1 (January 1982): 38-50; Shelley F. Taylor and Hsiao-Ti Falcone, "Cognitive Bases of Stereotyping: The Relationship between Categorization and Prejudice," *Personality and Social Psychology Bulletin* 8, no. 3 (September 1982): 426-32.

13. Bem, "Gender Schema Theory," pp. 356-58.

14. The Bem Sex Role Inventory, or BSRI, is an instrument that identifies sex-typed individuals on the basis of their self-concepts or self-ratings of their personal attributes. The BSRI asks the respondent to indicate on a seven-point scale how well each of sixty attributes describes himself or herself. Although it is not apparent to the respondent, twenty of the attributes reflect the culture's definition of masculinity (e.g., assertive), and twenty reflect its definition of femininity (e.g., tender), with the remaining attributes serving as filler. Each respondent receives both a masculinity and a femininity score, and those who score above the median on the sex-congruent scale and below the median on the sex-incongruent scale are defined as sex typed. That is, men who score high in masculinity and low in femininity are defined as sex typed, as are women who score high in femininity and low in masculinity. The BSRI is described in detail in the following articles: Sandra L. Bem, "The Measurement of Psychological Androgyny," *Journal of Consulting and Clinical Psychology* 42, no. 2 (April 1974): 15-42; "On the Utility of Alternative Procedures for Assessing Psychological Androgyny," *Journal of Clinical and Consulting Psychology,* 45, no. 2 (April 1977): 196-205; "The Theory and Measurement of Androgyny: A Reply to the Pedhazur-Tetenbaum

and Locksley Colten Critiques," *Journal of Personality and Social Psychology* 37, no. 6 (June 1979): 1047-54; and *A Manual for the Bem Sex Role Inventory* (Palo Alto, Calif.: Consulting Psychologists Press, 1981).

15. Stephanie Waxman, What Is a Girl? What Is a Boy? (Culver City, Calif.: Peace Press, 1976).

16. Sandra L. Bem, "Sex-Role Adaptability: One Consequence of Psychological Androgyny," Journal of Personality and Social Psychology 31, no. 4 (April 1975): 634-43; Sandra L. Bem, Wendy Martyna, and Carol Watson, "Sex-Typing and Androgyny: Further Explorations of the Expressive Domain," *Journal of Personality and Social Psychology,* 34, no. 5 (November 1976): 101-23; Sandra L. Bem, "Beyond Androgyny: Some Presumptuous Prescriptions for a Liberated Sexual Identity," in *The Future of Women: Issues in Psychology,* ed. Julia Sherman and Florence Denmark (New York: Psychological Dimensions, Inc., 1978), pp.1-23; Sandra L. Bem and Ellen Lenney, "Sex-Typing and the Avoidance of Cross Sex Behavior," *Journal of Personality and Social Psychology,* 33, no. 1 (January 1976): 48-54.

Nigrescence Theory: Historical And Explanatory Notes

William E. Cross, Jr.

𝓔ditors' Note: A number of researchers have proposed stage theories of identity development. All of the models, whether they apply to gender, race, or ethnicity, assume that people pass through fixed stages in the same order as identity develops. In this article, William Cross describes Nigrescence Theory, which is a theory of identity development for African Americans. Within each stage of his theory, there are common concerns and behaviors. This model, then, illustrates the link between identity and behaviors, and it explores the effect of historical contexts on identity.

Nigrescence Models attempt to capture the stages that African Americans traverse when experiencing a major shift in their racial self-identification. In addition to a description of the key dynamics associated with each stage, this work explores the history of such constructs.

... [M]y objectives are to present a historical perspective on the evolution of the Nigrescence construct and an overview of typical stages.

The Evolution of Nigrescence Models

From the late 1930s to the early 1970s, the discourse on black identity was reduced to notions of self-hatred, as reflected in the identity preferences of young black children taking so-called "racial doll tests." While this rather straight-forward, if not simple-minded, way of viewing the essence of Black peoples' psychology continues to enchant a number of observers (Davison, 1993; Hopson & Hopson, 1990; Russell, Wilson, & Hall, 1992; Steele, 1990), increasingly Black and White scholars alike are moving toward a multidimensional orientation (Cross, 1991; Helms, 1990; Hecht, Collier, & Ribeau, 1993). Contributing to this more nuanced perspective has been the growing theoretical and empirical literature on Nigrescence (Cross, Parham, & Helms, in press).

No less than the great W. E. B. Du Bois proclaimed that he *became* a Negro, while completing his undergraduate studies at Fisk University, between 1883 and 1888. In an otherwise masterful biography on Du Bois, David Levering Lewis admitted having difficulty interpreting Du Bois' assertion, wondering if Du Bois' new identity was a contrivance. Yet a few pages before mulling over Du Bois' self-affirmation, Lewis noted that at the same time Du Bois' religious faith seemed to shrivel in the face of southern hypocrisy and unbridled bigotry, Du Bois ". . . rapidly acquired a faith in his race that was quasi-religious" (Lewis, 1993, p. 66). According to Lewis, Du Bois eventually marked this *oceanic* conversion experience with the phase, "The New Negro," an appellation later made famous by Alain Locke in his book on the Harlem Renaissance. In all likelihood, Du Bois' conversion is one of the earliest written records of Nigrescence.

Nigrescence is a French term which means *the process of becoming Black,* and since the late 1960s, a significant cluster of Black and White scholars have attempted to develop a theoretical and empirical corpus on the stages African American traverse in moving from one identity frame to another. Its parallel can be found in the consciousness-raising process experienced by women in their metamorphosis from non-feminist-to-feminist, or the *coming out* process of gays and lesbians.

While the phenomena itself can be traced back to Du Bois' time, if not farther, the actual appearance of dedicated identity development models is a rather recent event. The Contemporary Black Social Movement, which began with the 1954 U.S. Supreme Court school desegregation decision and spanned the mid-1970s, consisted of two phases: a Civil Rights Phase (1954-1965) followed by a Black Consciousness Phase (1965 through the mid-to-late 1970s). The movement culture and dynamics for the earlier phase were driven by identity constructs that affirmed a Black person's *connection* to America and made possible numerous Black-White coalitions, including shared martyrdom in the aftermath of racist violence.

For reasons that are beyond the scope of this paper, the second phase saw the Black Community go through stages of change, some militantly in opposition to any connection to "Amerika," culminating in later stages, which, paradoxically, allowed for a *re-connection* to Whites and White Institutions. Ironically, the participants in the Black Consciousness Phase were not necessarily strangers to the earlier Civil Rights Phase. Rather, it was often the case that participants in the first phase found themselves experiencing a personal identity transformation (Van Deburg, 1992), a "Negro-to-Black" identity, if you will (Cross, 1971), which made it possible to be prepared for membership and even leadership in the second! Yesterday's integrationist oriented and *deracinated* Negroes became today's Black militants. However, over time, such persons, who at one point may have felt ill at the mere sight of a white person, eventually moved toward still another point in the conversion that valued a re-connection to *some* Whites as well as some *non-racist* and *democratic* aspects of American society.

Early on, independent observers, most of them, but not all, Black Psychologists, started codifying the stages. They did so from every region of the country. . . .

How far the Nigrescence and multicultural emphasis will extend into the future depends, I believe, on the results of empirical studies. To the extent that the theory continues to generate hypotheses, which, in turn, result in studies that expand our understanding of the complexities of being Black (or being Hispanic, Asian American, Native American, etc.), the more lasting will be its credulity.

The Stages

I want to close with a brief comment about the nature of the stages. Most identity models start not at the point of change but with an analysis on the identity *to be changed.* In the case of Blacks, the *pre-change* identity (stage one) accords little salience to race out of denial, self-hatred, or in a more positive light, because the person has an identity grounded in

something *other* than race, such as one's religious orientation. That is, the person may have an intact and functional identity, but one which, in the overall scheme of things, makes being Black somewhat insignificant. This is what ultimately makes them a *set-up* for change, because something may happen, an *encounter,* if you will, that causes them to feel they have been *miseducated.* They discover through the *encounter* (stage two) that they are *not black enough,* and in deciding to change this condition, they move into a middle or transition stage (stage three). All the fireworks of identity metamorphosis are contained in this middle stage, for within its boundaries, the old identity and the emerging identity do battle. For those who undergo a particularly intense conversion, it is a period of extreme highs and lows, reflecting the perturbation that comes from first feeling "I think I'm getting this right," to the next moment when one falls flat on his or her face, mired in confusion. It is a period of high energy, risk taking, racial chauvinism, one-up-manship, hatred, joy, and extreme certitude, interspersed with moments of profound self-doubt. This high energy literally compels the person to seek self-expression, leading to poetry, art, or in more vulgar expressions, fantasies about the defeat and destruction on one's enemy, i.e., White people and White society.

Given that things progress in a predictable fashion, the person eventually develops greater comfort, and the new identity becomes internalized (stage four). Some may progress no further than this "group" centered identity (Black nationalism), but others move to still another level. They may begin to *see and relish* interactions with other groups, including people who are white. Their identity becomes secure enough that they can have intense involvement, at all levels—the personal and the collective—with persons *not generally associated with "their" group.* Finally, as their group connection is embraced with the least degree of defensiveness, they revisit their innermost psychological core—their personal identity—that links them to *all* human beings. Going still further, they may well discover, as Thomas Parham has suggested, that one's identity embellishment does not happen *in one episode of change.* Rather, the challenges of being Black are modified through the exploration of new questions that crop up at different points across the lifespan of development.

I have made it all too pat, which is the problem of any summary of inherently complex and nuanced "things." Not everyone moves "forward." People regress, they become "stuck" in transition—consumed by hatred—they become disillusioned, or may spin off into still another cause and another identity "conversion." Or, they become entrapped in the everyday dysfunctionalities and private demons that haunt us all, from time to time. Many a clinician has notes on clients who came to them with problems concerning their "Blackness," only for it later to be revealed that sexual problems, problems of repressed anger, or problems of self-esteem, all unrelated to race, lie at the core of their interpersonal misery.

In summary Nigrescence models begin with people who place *low* salience on being Black, but in the aftermath of a challenging encounter move to find a way to *change* their identity to make it reflect *high* salience for race. They *immerse* themselves in a transition stage, the core of which reveals a war between the old and old and emergent identities. They may progress to a point where the new identity takes hold and is internalized and habituated. In some cases, they evolve still further to embrace a multicultural perspective, including a *rapprochement* with aspects of white culture. This "first" or "foundational" conversion may support still further growth in the future, as the person makes adjustments to new identity questions that are presented over the course of one's lifespan.

At last count, there have been well over sixty empirical studies on Nigrescence (Cross, Parham, & Helms, in press), and the number is expanding. These studies have explored the relation between Nigrescence and self-esteem, ego-integration, external-internal control, counselor preference, ideology, name change, and value system, among other things . . . .

References

Cross, W. E., Jr. (1971). The Negro-to-Black-Conversion Experience. *Black World, 20,* 13-27.

Cross, W. E., Jr. (1991). *Shades of Black.* Philadelphia: Temple University Press.

Cross, W. E., Jr., Parham, T., and Helms, J. (in press). *Nigrescence Revisited: Theory and research.*

Davison, J., Jr. (1993). *Prisoners of our past.* New York: Birch Lane Press.

Hecht, M. L., Collier, M. J., and Ribeau, S. A. (1993). *African American communications.* Newbury Park: Sage Press.

Helms, J. E. (1990). *Black and white racial identity.* New York: Greenwod Press.

Hopson, D. P., and Hopson, D. S. (1990). *Different and wonderful.* New York: Prentice-Hall.

Lewis, D. L. (1993). W. E. B. Du Bois. New York: Holt.

Russell, K., Wilson, M., and Hall, R. (1992). The color complex. New York: Harcourt Brace Jovanovich.

Steele, S. (1990). The content of our character. New York: St. Martin Press.

Van Deburg, W. L. (1992). *New day in Babylon.* Chicago: University of Chicago Press.

Psychological Impact Of Biculturalism: Evidence And Theory

Teresa LaFromboise, Hardin L. K. Coleman, and Jennifer Gerton

> **ditors' Note:** Many people in the United States are the products of two or more cultures. How do people who are bicultural meet the challenges associated with living under the influence of two cultures? Teresa LaFromboise and her colleagues examine five models of the process of identity negotiation that occurs within and between cultures. They then ask the question, are some ways of acquiring a second culture more adaptive than others? Understanding how we adapt to new cultures will greatly help people from different ethnic groups work to live together.

...The purpose of this article is to review the literature on the psychological impact of being bicultural. We present a definition of cultural competence and discuss models that have been used to describe the psychological processes, social experiences, and individual challenges associated with being bicultural. We identify the various skills we believe are needed to successfully negotiate bicultural challenges and obstacles. Finally, we present a hypothetical model of bicultural competence.

Cultural Competence

There is no single definition of culture on which all scholars can agree (Segall, 1986). Attempts to create a satisfactory definition of culture tend to either omit a salient aspect of it or to generalize beyond any real meaning. Despite these problems, there is an abundance of theories available regarding the meaning of the word *culture*. For the purpose of this article, we use a behaviorally focused definition. Like Levine (1982), we believe that human behavior is not just the product of cultural structure, individual cognitive and affective processes, biology, and social environment. Instead, we believe that behavior is a result of the continuous interaction among all of these components. We also ascribe to Bandura's (1978, 1986) concept of reciprocal determinism, which suggests that behavior is influenced by and influences a person's cognition and social environment.

This behavioral model of culture suggests that in order to be culturally competent, an individual would have to (a) possess a strong personal identity, (b) have knowledge of and facility with the beliefs and values of the culture, (c) display sensitivity to the affective processes of the culture, (d) communicate clearly in the language of the given cultural group, (e) perform socially sanctioned behavior, (f) maintain active social relations within the cultural group, and (g) negotiate the institutional structures of that culture....

Models of Second-Culture Acquisition

Five models that have been used to understand the process of change that occurs in transitions within, between, and among cultures are assimilation, acculturation, alternation, multiculturalism, and fusion. Although each was created to address group phenomena, they can be used to describe the processes by which an individual from one culture, the culture of origin, develops competence in another culture, often the dominant majority culture. Each model has a slightly different emphasis and set of assumptions and focuses on different outcomes for the individual. We describe each one, identify its underlying assumptions, and review a number of hypotheses about the psychological impact of biculturalism that each appears to generate. We present, when available, examples from research literature that clarify the hypotheses implicit within each model.

Assimilation Model

One model for explaining the psychological state of a person living within two cultures assumes an ongoing process of absorption into the culture that is perceived as dominant or more desirable. Gordon (1964, 1978) outlined a number of subprocesses constituting various stages of the assimilation process: (a) cultural or behavioral assimilation, (b) structural assimilation, (c) marital assimilation, (d) identificational assimilation, (e) attitudinal receptional assimilation, (f) behavioral receptional assimilation, and (g) civic assimilation. Ruiz (1981) emphasized that the goal of the assimilation process is to become socially accepted by members of the target culture as a person moves through these stages. The underlying assumption of all assimilation models is that a member of one culture loses his or her original cultural identity as he or she acquires a new identity in a second culture.

This model leads to the hypothesis that an individual will suffer from a sense of alienation and isolation until he or she has been accepted and perceives that acceptance within the new culture (Johnston, 1976; Sung, 1985). This person will experience more stress, be more anxious, and suffer more acutely from social problems such as school failure or substance abuse than someone who is fully assimilated into that culture (Burnam, Telles, Karno, Hough, & Escobar, 1987; Pasquali, 1985). The gradual loss of support derived from the original culture, combined with the initial inability to use the assets of the newly acquired culture, which will cause stress and anxiety. . . .

Assimilation is the process by which an individual develops a new cultural identity. Acquiring this new identity, however, involves some loss of awareness and loyalty to one's culture of origin. Three major dangers are associated with assimilation. The first is the possibility of being rejected by members of the majority culture. The second is the likelihood of being rejected by members of the culture of origin. The third is the likelihood of experiencing excessive stress as one attempts to learn the new behaviors associated with the assimilative culture and to shed the inoperable behaviors associated with the culture of origin.

Acculturation Model

The acculturation model of bicultural contact is similar to the assimilation model in three ways. They both (a) focus on the acquisition of the majority group's culture by members of the minority group, (b) emphasize

a unidirectional relationship between the two cultures, and (c) assume a hierarchical relationship between the two cultures. What differentiates the two models is that the assimilation approach emphasizes that individuals, their offspring, or their cultural group will eventually become full members of the majority group's culture and lose identification with their culture of origin. By contrast, the acculturation model implies that the individual, while becoming a competent participant in the majority culture, will always be identified as a member of the minority culture.

Smither (1982) stated that one of the distinguishing characteristics of the acculturation process is its involuntary nature. Most often, the member of the minority group is forced to learn the new culture in order to survive economically. . . .

[A number of] studies lend credence to the conclusion that minority individuals attempting to acculturate will often do so antagonistically (Vogt, 1957) or resign themselves to accepting second-class citizenship within the majority group. Most studies of minority groups do seem to indicate that minorities are often relegated to lower status positions within the majority group. This phenomenon seems to hold true for divergent groups such as ethnic minorities in the United States, Finns in Sweden, Turks in Germany, and Koreans in Japan. These studies also suggest that the most active agent in this process may be the discriminatory behavior of the majority culture. However, the role of minority group members' economic resources has been relatively unexplored in acculturation studies, prohibiting conclusions about the role of socioeconomic status in second-culture acquisition.

Collectively, these studies indicate that acculturation can be a stressful experience, reinforcing the second-class citizenship and alienation of the individual acclimating to a new culture. These studies do support the conjecture that the primary feature of the acculturation model rests on the notion that the individual will never be allowed to lose identification with the culture of origin. Furthermore, this can have negative economic and psychological effects on the individual. This observation led Taft (1977) to argue that the detrimental effects of acculturation can be ameliorated by encouraging biculturalism. Taft (1977) suggested that "the mature bicultural individual may rise above both cultures by following superordinate social proscriptions that serve to integrate the individual's behavior relative to each culture" (p. 146). Several of the studies cited support the hypothesis that the more control people have over their relationship with the majority culture, the less likely they are to experience the negative effects of acculturation stress.

Alternation Model

The alternation model of second-culture acquisition assumes that it is possible for an individual to know and understand two different cultures. It also supposes that an individual can alter his or her behavior to fit a particular social context. As Ogbu and Matute-Bianchi (1986) have argued, "it is possible and acceptable to participate in two different cultures or to use two different languages, perhaps for different purposes, by alternating one's behavior according to the situation" (p.89). Ramirez (1984) also alluded to the use of different problem-solving, coping, human relational, communication, and incentive motivational styles, depending on the demands of the social context. Furthermore, the alternation model assumes that it is possible for an individual to have a sense of belonging in two cultures without compromising his or her sense of cultural identity. . . .

The alternation model differs from the assimilation and acculturation models in two significant ways. First, it posits a bidirectional and orthogonal relationship between the individual's culture of origin and the second culture in which he or she may be living rather than the linear and unidirectional relationship of the other two models. In fact, the alternation model suggests that it is possible to maintain a positive relationship with both cultures without having to choose between them. Second, this model does not assume a hierarchical relationship between two cultures. Within this framework, it is possible for the individual to assign equal status to the two cultures, even if he or she does not value or prefer them equally.

The alternation model postulates that an individual can choose the degree and manner to which he or she will affiliate with either the second culture or his or her culture of origin. Sodowsky and Carey (1988) described certain dual characteristics of first-generation Asian Indians that appear paradoxical yet support this assumption. Although the groups as a whole reported a high level of proficiency in reading and speaking English, they preferred thinking in an Indian language (e.g., Hindi, Tamil). Many preferred Indian food and dress at home but American food and dress outside of the home. . . .

What we see as the essential strength of the alternation model is that it focuses on the cognitive and affective processes that allow an individual to withstand the negative impact of acculturative stress. It also looks at the role the individual has in choosing how he or she will interact with the second culture and the person's culture of origin. This model forces us to consider the bidirectional impact of cultural contact. In other words, it allows us to consider the impact that individuals from both cultures have on each other.

Multicultural Model

The multicultural model promotes a pluralistic approach to understanding the relationship between two or more cultures. This model addresses the feasibility of cultures maintaining distinct identities while individuals from one culture work with those of other cultures to serve common national or economic needs. In this model it is recognized that it may not be geographic or social isolation per se that is the critical factor in sustaining cultural diversity but the manner of multifaceted and multidimensional institutional sharing between cultures. Berry (1986) claimed that a multicultural society encourages all groups to (a) maintain and develop their group identities, (b) develop other-group acceptance and tolerance, (c) engage in intergroup contact and sharing, and (d) learn each other's language.

The multicultural model generates the hypothesis that an individual can maintain a positive identity as a member of his or her culture of origin while simultaneously developing a positive identity by engaging in complex institutional sharing with the larger political entity comprised of other cultural groups. In this model it is assumed that public and private identities need not become fused and that the tension of solving internal conflicts caused by bicultural stress need not have a negative psychological impact but could instead lead to personal and emotional growth. Kelly's (1971) finding, that with little difficulty the Tohono O'odham (Papago) in Tucson could occupy roles in the urban Tohono O'odham community parallel to their status in the wider Tucson social structure, supports the feasibility of this hypothesis. . . .

It is questionable, however, as to whether such a multicultural society can be maintained. As Fishman (1989) suggested, cultural separation of groups demands institutional protection and ethnocultural compart-mentalization. He suggested that there is little evidence for such structures surviving more than three generations of cross-cultural contact. Examples of this separation being maintained include groups making that choice for ideological reasons, such as the Old Amish and the Hasidim, or groups actively discriminated against by the majority group, such as American Indians, African Americans, or Australian aborigines. In lieu of active discrimination or self-selected separation, it may be difficult to maintain a truly multicultural society over time (Mallea, 1988). Instead, it is more likely that the various groups will intermingle, leading to the evolution of a new culture.

Fusion Model

The fusion model of second-culture acquisition represents the assumptions behind the melting pot theory. This model suggests that cultures sharing an economic, political, or geographic space will fuse together until they are indistinguishable to form a new culture. The respectful sharing of institutional structures will produce a new common culture. Each culture brings to the melting pot strengths and weaknesses that take on new forms through the interaction of cultures as equal partners. Gleason (1979) argued that cultural pluralism inevitably produces this type of fusion if the various cultures share a common political unit. The fusion model is different from the assimilation or acculturation model in that there is no necessary assumption of cultural superiority. The psychological impact of this model is unclear because there are few successful

examples of such a new culture. It seems that minority groups become assimilated into the majority group at the price of their ethnic identity. This would suggest that an individual who is a member of a minority group undergoing fusion would have experiences similar to one undergoing assimilation. Once fused, however, the individual's psychological reality would be indistinguishable from a member of the majority group. . . .

Summary

Each of these models has its own assumptions concerning what happens to a person as he or she undergoes the process of second-culture acquisition. This does not mean, however, that the models are mutually exclusive. Depending on the situation and person, any one of these models may represent an adequate explanation for a person's experience as he or she acquires competency in a new culture. An example would be of an African-American family that has moved from the rural South to an urban area. One member of the family may assimilate into the dominant Anglo-oriented culture, whereas another's attempt to acquire competence in that culture may better be described using the acculturation model. Yet a third member of the same family may choose to actively alternate between the two cultures, and a fourth may seek to live in an environment in which the two cultures exist side by side as described by the multicultural model or have amalgamated as described in the fusion model.

. . .[M]ost of the models assume that an individual will lose identification with his or her culture of origin, a process that can be stressful and disorienting. What seems clear from the literature we have reviewed, however, is that the more an individual is able to maintain active and effective relationships through alternation between both cultures, the less difficulty he or she will have in acquiring and maintaining competency in both cultures.

Bicultural Competence

The construct of bicultural competence as a result of living in two cultures grows out of the alternation model. Although there are a number of behaviors involved in the acquisition of bicultural competence (e.g., shifts in cognitive and perceptual processes, acquisition of a new language) the literature on biculturalism consistently assumes that an individual living within two cultures will suffer from various forms of psychological distress. Although it is clear that ethnic minorities in the United States and elsewhere experience high levels of economic and social discrimination as well as other disadvantages, it is inappropriate to assume that this sociological reality produces a predictable negative psychological outcome. Research suggests that individuals living in two cultures may find the experience to be more beneficial than living a monocultural life-style. The key to psychological well-being may well be the ability to develop and maintain competence in both cultures. . . .

From our reading of the literature, we suggest the following dimensions in which an individual may need to develop competence so as to effectively manage the process of living in two cultures: (a) knowledge of cultural beliefs and values, (b) positive attitudes toward both majority and minority groups, (c) bicultural efficacy, (d) communication ability, (e) role repertoire, and (f) a sense of being grounded.

Knowledge of Cultural Beliefs and Values

Cultural awareness and knowledge involves the degree to which an individual is aware of and knowledgeable about the history, institutions, rituals, and everyday practices of a given culture. This would include an understanding of the basic perspectives a culture has on gender roles, religious practices, and political issues, as well as the rules that govern daily interactions among members of the culture.

A culturally competent person is presumed to be one who knows, appreciates, and internalizes the basic beliefs of a given culture. This would require an acceptance of a particular culture's basic worldview and the ability to act within the constraints of that worldview when interacting with members of that culture. . . .

Schiller's (1987) study lends support to considering cultural awareness and knowledge as an important component of cultural competence. In a survey study investigating the impact of biculturalism, she examined the academic, social, psychological, and cultural adjustment of American Indian college students. Schiller found that bicultural Indian students were better adjusted, particularly in the academic and cultural domains, than were their nonbicultural counterparts. They had higher grade point averages (GPAs), more effective study habits, and demonstrated a stronger commitment to using resources for academic success. Participation in cultural activities and enrollment in American-Indian-oriented courses was significantly higher for bicultural students. Finally, these students perceived their Indian heritage to be an advantage. more so than did nonbicultural students. . . .

Positive Attitudes Toward Both Groups

This aspect of the construct assumes that the individual recognizes bicultural competence as a desirable goal in its own right, holds each cultural group in positive but not necessarily equal regard, and does not endorse positions that promulgate hierarchical relations between two cultural groups.

The inclusion of this component is based on certain theoretical assumptions. Without positive attitudes toward both groups, an individual will be limited in his or her ability to feel good about interacting with a group that is the target of negative feelings. Arguably, the process of interacting with individuals from a culture one does not respect will result in negative psychological and behavioral outcomes. We hypothesize that one reason for the tremendous rate of conduct disorders among ethnic minority adolescents is a result of the negative attitudes those adolescents have toward the dominant Anglo group. This hypothesis is supported by Palleja's (1987) finding that monocultural-affiliated Hispanic young men exhibited more rebellious behavior than did bicultural or Anglo-affiliated monocultural peers and Golden's (1987) finding that Korean-American high school students practicing biculturalism displayed more positive educational outcomes and self-concepts than monoculturally affiliated Korean-American students.

. . . As Berry, Padilla, and Szapocznik and their colleagues have suggested, the length and type of contact individuals from one culture have with the other cultures have a significant impact on their attitudes toward the majority and their own culture.

Information is also an essential element in developing a positive attitude toward both groups. Cultural translators, individuals from a person's own ethnic or cultural group who have successfully undergone the dual socialization experience, can help others in the personal integration process (Brown, 1990). He or she can interpret the values and perceptions of the majority culture in ways that do not compromise the individual's own ethnic values or norms.

Bicultural Efficacy

Rashid (1984) asserted that "biculturalism is an attribute that all Americans should possess because it creates a sense of efficacy within the institutional structure of society along with a sense of pride and identification with one's ethnic roots" (p. 15). As Bandura (1978) has demonstrated, the belief, or confidence, that an individual can perform an action has a hierarchical relationship to the actual performance of that action. In this article, we posit that bicultural efficacy, or the belief that one can develop and maintain effective interpersonal relationships in two cultures, is directly related to one's ability to develop bicultural competence.

We define *bicultural efficacy* as the belief, or confidence, that one can live effectively, and in a satisfying manner, within two groups without compromising one's sense of cultural identity. This belief will support an individual through the highly difficult tasks of developing and maintaining effective support groups in both the minority and the majority culture. It will also enable the person to persist through periods when he or she may experience rejection from one or both of the cultures in which he or she is working to develop or maintain competence (Rozek, 1980). . . .

Communication Ability

Communication ability refers to an individual's effectiveness in communicating ideas and feelings to members of a given culture, both verbally and nonverbally.

Language competency, in fact, may be a major building block of bicultural competence. As Northover (1988) suggested, "each of a bilingual's languages is the mediator between differing cultural identities within one and the same person" (p.207). It is vital, however, to distinguish between the language-acquisition processes, which have the goal of transferring competency from the minority group's language to the majority group's language, and processes oriented toward an individual maintaining the language of origin as well as the acquisition of a second language. Bilingual programs that encourage the maintenance, rather than the transfer, of language skills promote bicultural competence rather than assimilation or acculturation (Edwards, 1981; Fishman, 1989; Thomas, 1983). . . .

Role Repertoire

Role repertoire refers to the range of culturally or situationally appropriate behaviors or roles an individual has developed. The greater the range of behaviors or roles, the higher the level of cultural competence.

In a study of individuals who were working and living in Kenya for 2 years, Ruben and Kealey (1979) found that particular interpersonal and social behaviors led to greater effectiveness at role performance and ease in adjustment. The authors looked at (a) displays of respect, (b) interaction posture (e.g., judgmental or not), (c) orientation to knowledge or worldview, (d) empathy, and (e) role behavior. Coinciding with Smither's (1982) assertions, they found that individuals who had the personal resources to use their social skills in a situationally appropriate manner suffered less cultural shock and were more effective in their vocational duties and social interactions than were those whose behavioral repertoire within the second-culture was more limited. . . .

Groundedness

"Every culture provides the individual some sense of identity, some regulation or belonging and some sense of personal place in the school of things" (Adler, 1975, p.20). The literature indicates that the person most successful at managing a bicultural existence has established some form of stable social networks in both cultures. This suggests that the positive resolution of stress engendered by bicultural living cannot be done on one's own (Hernandez, 1981). One must have the skill to recruit and use external support systems. We have labeled the experience of having a well-developed social support system "a sense of being grounded."

Baker (1987) supported this position when she argued that African Americans are best able to avoid the major problems that affect mental health facing their communities (e.g., Black-on-Black homicide, teenage pregnancy, attempted suicide, substance abuse, postincarceration adjustment) when they can call on the resources of the African-American extended family. Both nuclear and extended family models in American Indian communities facilitate this sense of being grounded (Red Horse, 1980). We argue that it is the sense of being grounded in an extensive social network in both cultures that enhances an individual's ability to cope with the pressures of living in a bicultural environment and that acquiring that sense in the second culture is an important outcome of second-culture acquisition (Lewis & Ford, 1991). Murphy (1977) suggested that the ability to become grounded inoculates against the development of psychopathology among immigrants. . . .

Summary

Research suggests that there is a way of being bicultural without suffering negative psychological outcomes, assimilating, or retreating from contact with the majority culture. We recognize that bicultural competence requires a difficult set of skills to achieve and maintain. We do not doubt that there will be stress involved in the process of acquiring competence in a second culture while maintaining affiliation with one's culture of origin. The question we have for future research is whether these difficulties lead to personal growth and greater psychological well-being, or inevitably lead to . . . [psychological problems.]

Model of Bicultural Competence

The goal of this article was to develop an understanding, on the basis of social science research, of the psychological impact of biculturalism. We wanted to understand which factors facilitate a bicultural role and which ones impede the development of that role. We were particularly interested in identifying the skills that would make it possible for an individual to become a socially competent person in a second culture without losing that same competence in the culture of origin. To focus our exploration, we organized our search around a behavioral model of culture that would allow us to better identify the skills of bicultural competence. We also felt that it was important to describe the different models of second-culture acquisition so that our use of the alternation model could be understood in relation to other theories of biculturalism. . . .

At this point, we want to emphasize that we do not know whether these are the only skills of biculturalism, or whether a person needs to be equally competent in all or a particular subset, in order to be biculturally competent. We do think, however, that the dimensions outlined in this article provide a much needed focus to the research on this phenomenon. We believe that identifying these acquirable skills will allow researchers to focus on the relationship between these skills and an individual's sense of psychological well-being, as well as his or her effectiveness in his or her social and work environments. We also believe that these dimensions can be used as the framework for developing programs designed to facilitate the involvement of minority people in majority institutions such as colleges and corporations (Van Den Bergh, 1991).

. . .[W]e have developed a hypothetical model of the relationships among these skills of bicultural competence. After lengthy consideration, we have come to speculate that these skills may have a rational relationship to each other. We believe that some may be more important than others or that some may have to be developed before others. Furthermore, we developed the assumption that one or more of these skills may be the linchpin between monocultural and bicultural competence. In response to these speculations, in the model we have developed it is assumed that there are hierarchical relations among these skills, not linear ones. By this we mean that some of these skills may be developed before others but that the process of skill acquisition does not have an invariant order. Only empirical study can resolve this issue.

The primary emphasis of the model is on the reciprocal relationship between a person and his or her environment. The model becomes complex when considering the acquisition of second-culture competence because one must include two environments, both the culture of origin and the second culture. An individual's personal and cultural identities are primarily developed through the early biosocial learning experiences that an individual has within his or her culture of origin. These identities will also be influenced by the nature and amount of contact the person has with the second culture. For example, if a person lived in rural El Salvador and had no contact with American culture until forced to emigrate in early adulthood, that person's sense of personal and cultural identity would be much different from his or her U.S.-born child, who has attended public schools since kindergarten. It is our contention that in addition to having a strong and stable sense of personal identity, another affective element of bicultural competence is the ability to develop and maintain positive attitudes toward one's culture of origin and the second culture in which he or she is attempting to acquire competence. In addition, we speculate that an individual will also need to acquire knowledge of both cultures in order to develop the belief that he or she can be biculturally competent, which we have labeled *bicultural efficacy.*

We speculate that these attitudes and beliefs about self, what we think of as the affective and cognitive dimension of the model, will facilitate the individual's acquisition of both communication skills and role repertoire, which are the two facets that make up the behavioral aspect of the model. We hypothesize that the individual who has acquired the attitudes and beliefs in the affective and cognitive dimension and the skills of the behavioral aspect of this model will also be able to develop the effective support systems in both cultures that will allow him or her to feel grounded. Being grounded in both cultures will allow the individual to both maintain and enhance his or her personal and cultural identities in a manner that will enable him or her to effectively manage the challenges of a bicultural existence.

This model represents a departure from previous models in that it focuses on the skills that a person needs to acquire in order to be successful at both becoming effective in the new culture and remaining competent in his or her culture of origin.

. . .[T]he alternation model, on which our model of bicultural competence is based, is the one that best facilitates the acquisition of these skills. It appears that the multicultural model would also be useful in this area, but as mentioned before, there is little evidence of a multicultural perspective being maintained over more than three generations.

Conclusion

We suggest that the ethnic minority people who develop these skills will have better physical and psychological health than those who do not. We also think that they will outperform their monoculturally competent peers in vocational and academic endeavors.

There is widespread agreement that failure to achieve equal partnership for minorities in the academic, social, and economic life of the United States will have disastrous effects for this society A vital step in the development of an effective partnership involves moving away from the assumptions of the linear model of cultural acquisition, which has a negative impact on the minority individual, to a clearer understanding of the process of developing cultural competence as a two-way street. This will require that members of both the minority and majority cultures better understand, appreciate, and become skilled in one another's cultures. We hope that the ideas expressed here will serve to facilitate that process.

References

Adler, P. S. (1975). The transitional experience: An alternative view of cultural shock. *Journal of Humanistic Psychology, 15,* 13-23.

Baker, F. M. (1987). The Afro-American life cycle: Success, failure, and mental health. *Journal of the National Medical Association, 79,* 625-633.

Bandura, A. (1978). The self-system in reciprocal determinism. *American Psychologist, 33,* 344-358.

Bandura, A. (1986). *The foundations of social thought and action.* Englewood Cliffs, NJ: Erlbaum.

Berry, J. W. (1986). Multiculturalism and psychology in plural societies. In L. H. Ekstrand (Ed.), *Ethnic minorities and immigrants in a cross-cultural perspective* (pp. 37-51). Lisse, The Netherlands: Swets & Zeitlinger.

Brown, P. M. (1990). Biracial identity and social marginality. *Child and Adolescent Social Work Journal, 7,* 319-337.

Burnam, M. A., Telles. C. A., Karno, M., Hough, R. L., & Escobar, J. I. (1987). Measurement of acculturation in a community population of Mexican Americans. *Hispanic Journal of Behavioral Sciences, 9,* 105-130.

Edwards, J. R. (1981). The context of bilingual education. *Journal of Multilingual and Multicultural Development, 2,* 25-44.

Fishman, J. A. (1989). Bilingualism and biculturalism as individual and societal phenomena. *Journal of Multilingual and Multicultural Development, 1,* 3-15.

Gleason, P. (1979). Confusion compounded: The melting pot in the 1960's and 1970's. *Ethnicity, 6,* 10-20.

Golden, J. G. (1987). Acculturation, biculturalism and marginality: A study of Korean-American high school students. *Dissertation Abstracts International, 48.* II 35A. (University Microfilms No. DA8716257).

Gordon, M. M. (1964). *Assimilation in American life.* New York: Oxford University Press.

Gordon, M. M. (1978). *Human nature, class, and ethnicity.* New York: Oxford University Press.

Hernandez, S. M. (1981). Acculturation and biculturalism among Puerto Ricans in Lamont, California. *Dissertation Abstracts International, 42.* 428B. (University Microfilms No.8113419).

Johnston, R. (1976). The concept of the "marginal man": A refinement of the term. *Australian and New Zealand Journal of Science, 12,* 145-147.

Kelly, M. C. (1971). Las fiestas como reflejo del order social: El caso de San Xavier del Bac. *America Indigena, 31,* 141-161.

Levine, R. A. (1982). *Culture, behavior and personality* (2nd ed.). Chicago: Aldine.

Lewis, E. A., & Ford, B. (1991). The network utilization project: Incorporating traditional strengths of African-American families into group work practice. *Social Work With Groups, 13,* 7-22.

Mallea, J. (1988). Canadian dualism and pluralism: Tensions, contradictions and emerging resolutions. In J. Berry & R. Annis (Eds.), *Ethnic psychology: Research and practice with immigrant, refugees, Native peoples, ethnic groups and sojourners* (pp. 13-37). Berwyn, PA: Swets North America.

Murphy, H. B. M. (1977). Migration, culture and mental health. *Psychological Medicine, 7,* 677-684.

Northover, M. (1988). Bilingual or "dual linguistic identities"? In J. Berry & R. Annis (Eds.), *Ethnic psychology: Research and practice with immigrants, refugees, Native peoples, ethnic groups and sojourners* (pp. 207-216). Berwyn, PA: Swets North America.

Ogbu, J. U., & Matute-Bianchi, M. A. (1986). Understanding sociocultural factors: Knowledge, identity, and social adjustment. In California State Department of Education, Bilingual Education Office, *Beyond language: Social and cultural factors in schooling* (pp. 73-142). Sacramento, CA: California State University-LA, Evaluation, Dissemination and Assessment Center.

Palleja, J. (1987). The impact of cultural identification on the behavior of second generation Puerto Rican adolescents. *Dissertation Abstracts International, 48.* 1541A. (University Microfilms No. DA87 15043).

Pasquali, E. A. (1985). The impact of acculturation on the eating habits of elderly immigrants: A Cuban example. *Journal of Nutrition for the Elderly 5,* 27-36.

Ramirez, M., III. (1984). Assessing and understanding biculturalism-multiculturalism in Mexican-American adults. In J. L. Martinez & R. H. Mendoza (Eds.), *Chicano psychology* (pp. 77-94). San Diego, CA: Academic Press.

Rashid, H. M. (1984). Promoting biculturalism in young African-American children. *Young Children, 39,* 13-23.

Red Horse, J. (1980). Family structure and value orientation in American Indians. *Social Casework, 61,* 462-467.

Rozek, F. (1980). The role of internal conflict in the successful acculturation of Russian Jewish immigrants. *Dissertation Abstracts International, 41,* 2778B. (University Microfilms No.8028799).

Ruben. B. D., & Kealey, D. L. (1979). Behavioral assessment of communication competency and the prediction of cross-cultural adaption. *International Journal of Intercultural Relations, 3,* 15-47.

Ruiz, R. (1981). Cultural and historical perspectives in counseling Hispanics. In D. Sue (Ed.), *Counseling the culturally different* (pp. 186-215). New York: Wiley.

Schiller, P. M. (1987). Biculturalism and psychosocial adjustment among Native American university students. *Dissertation Abstracts International, 48,* I 542A. (University Microfilms No. DA8720632).

Segall, M. M. (1986). Culture and behavior: Psychology in global perspective. *Annual Review of Psychology, 37,* 523-564.

Smither, R. (1982). Human migration and the acculturation of minorities. *Human Relations, 35,* 57-68.

Sodowsky, G. R., & Carey, J. C. (1988). Relationship between acculturation-related demographics and cultural attitudes of an Asian-Indian immigrant group. *Journal of Multicultural Counseling and Development, 16,* 117-136.

Sung, B. L. (1985). Bicultural conflicts in Chinese immigrant children. *Journal of Comparative Family Studies, 16,* 255-269.

Taft, R. (1977). Coping with unfamiliar cultures. In N. Warren (Ed.), *Studies in cross-cultural psychology* (Vol. 1, pp. 121-153). San Diego, CA: Academic Press.

Thomas, G. E. (1983). The deficit, difference, and bicultural theories of Black dialect and nonstandard English. *Urban Review, 15,* 107-118.

Van Den Bergh, N. (1991). Managing biculturalism at the workplace: A group approach. In K. L. Chau (Ed.), *Ethnicity and biculturalism* (pp. 71-84). New York: Haworth Press.

Vogt, E. Z. (1957). The acculturation of American Indians. *Annals of the American Academy of Political and Social Science, 311,* 137-146.

In Search Of Bruce Lee's Grave

Shanlon Wu

Editors' Note: In his short essay Shanlon Wu, an Asian-American male, recounts his psychological journey in search of images of strong Asian men with whom to identify and emulate. The essay illustrates the difficulties of identity formation in cultures in which one is a minority and where there are few role models.

It's Saturday morning in Seattle, and I am driving to visit Bruce Lee's grave. I have been in the city for only a couple of weeks and so drive two blocks past the cemetery before realizing that I've passed it. I double back and turn through the large wrought-iron gate, past a sign that reads: "Open to 9 P.M. or dusk, whichever comes first."

It's a sprawling cemetery, with winding roads leading in all directions. I feel silly trying to find his grave with no guidance. I think that my search for his grave is similar to my search for Asian heroes in America.

I was born in 1959, an Asian-American in Westchester County, N.Y. During my childhood there were no Asian sports stars. On television, I can recall only that most pathetic of Asian characters, Hop Sing, the Cartwright family houseboy on "Bonanza." But in my adolescence there was Bruce.

I was 14 years old when I first saw "Enter the Dragon," the granddaddy of martial-arts movies. Bruce had died suddenly at the age of 32 of cerebral edema, an excess of fluid in the brain, just weeks before the release of the film. Between the ages of 14 and 17, I saw "Enter the Dragon" 22 times before I stopped counting. During those years I collected Bruce Lee posters, putting them up at all angles in my bedroom. I took up Chinese martial arts and spent hours comparing my physique with his.

I learned all I could about Bruce: that he had married a Caucasian, Linda; that he had sparred with Kareem Abdul-Jabbar; that he was a buddy of Steve McQueen and James Coburn, both of whom were his pallbearers.

My parents, who immigrated to America and had become professors at Hunter College, tolerated my behavior, but seemed puzzled at my admiration of an "entertainer." My father jokingly tried to compare my obsession with Bruce to his boyhood worship of Chinese folk-tale heroes.

"I read them just like you read American comic books," he said.

But my father's heroes could not be mine; they came from an ancient literary tradition, not comic books. He and my mother had grown up in a land where they belonged to the majority. I could not adopt their childhood and they were wise enough not to impose it upon me.

Although I never again experienced the kind of blind hero worship I felt for Bruce, my need to find heroes remained strong.

In college, I discovered the men of the 442d Regimental Combat Team, a United States Army all-Japanese unit in World War II. Allowed to fight only against Europeans, they suffered heavy casualties while their families were put in internment camps. Their motto was "Go for Broke."

I saw them as Asians in a Homeric epic, the protagonists of a Shakespearean tragedy; I knew no Eastern myths to infuse them with. They embodied my own need to prove myself in the Caucasian world. I imagined how their American-born flesh and muscle must have resembled mine: epicanthic folds set in strong faces nourished on milk and beef. I thought how much they had proved where there was so little to prove.

After college, I competed as an amateur boxer in an attempt to find my self-image in the ring. It didn't work. My fighting was only an attempt to copy Bruce's movies. What I needed was instruction on how to live. I quit boxing after a year and went to law school.

I was an anomaly there: a would-be Asian litigator. I had always liked to argue and found I liked doing it in front of people even more. when I won the first-year moot court competition in law school, I asked an Asian classmate if he thought I was the first Asian to win. He laughed and told me I was probably the only Asian to even compete.

The law-firm interviewers always seemed surprised that I wanted to litigate.

"Aren't you interested in Pacific Rim trade?" they asked.

"My Chinese isn't good enough," I quipped.

My pat response seemed to please them. It certainly pleased me. I thought I'd found a place of my own—a place where the law would insulate me from the pressure of defining my Asian maleness. I sensed the possibility of merely being myself.

But the pressure reasserted itself. One morning, the year after graduating from law school, I read the obituary of Gen. Minoru Genda—the man who planned the Pearl Harbor attack. I'd never heard of him and had assumed that whoever did that planning was long since dead. But the general had been alive all those years—rising at 4 every morning to do his exercises and retiring every night by 8. An advocate of animal rights, the obituary said.

I found myself drawn to the general's life despite his association with the Axis powers. He seemed a forthright, graceful man who died unhumbled. The same paper carried a front-page story about Congress's failure to pay the Japanese-American internees their promised reparation money. The general, at least, had not died waiting for reparations.

I was surprised and frightened by my admiration for General Genda, by my still-strong hunger for images of powerful Asian men. That hunger was my vulnerability manifested, a reminder of my lack of place.

The hunger is eased this gray morning in Seattle. After asking directions from a policeman—Japanese—I easily locate Bruce's grave. The headstone is red granite with a small picture etched into it. The picture is very Hollywood—Bruce wears dark glasses—and I think the calligraphy looks a bit sloppy. Two tourists stop but leave quickly after glancing at me.

I realize I am crying. Bruce's grave seems very small in comparison to his place in my boyhood. So small in comparison to my need for heroes. Seeing his grave, I understand how large the hole in my life has been, and how desperately I'd sought to fill it.

I had sought an Asian hero to emulate. But none of my choices quite fit me. Their lives were defined through heroic tasks—they had villains to defeat and wars to fight—while my life seemed merely a struggle to define myself.

But now I see how that very struggle has defined me. I must be my own hero even as I learn to treasure those who have gone before.

I have had my powerful Asian male images: Bruce, the men of the 442d and General Genda; I may yet discover others. Their lives beckon like fireflies on a moonless night, and I know that they—like me—may have been flawed by foolhardiness and even cruelty. Still, their lives were real. They were not houseboys on "Bonanza."

Note: Shan Wu is a federal prosecutor in Washington, D. C. His essay, *In Search of Bruce Lee's Grave*, originally appeared in the New York Times Sunday Magazine section *About Men* column.

✓ PROJECT 4.1
Personal And Collective Self-Esteem

I. Researchers interested in identity have often distinguished between personal identity and social or collective identity. Personal identity includes specific attributes of the individual such as competence, talent, and sociability. Social identity, the other part of one's identity, is "that part of an individual's self-concept which derives from his [or her] knowledge of his [or her] membership in a social group (or groups) together with the value and emotional significance attached to that membership" (Tajfel, 1981, p. 255, cited in Luhtanen & Crocker, 1992). People strive to maintain both positive personal and social identities, or in other words, they strive to maintain both high personal and social/collective self-esteem. Psychologists have a long tradition of researching personal self-esteem, but only recently have researchers investigated social or collective self-esteem. This and the next page contain a personal self-esteem scale, the Rosenberg Self-Esteem Scale (1965), which is a widely used measure of personal self-esteem, and a relatively new questionnaire, the Collective Self-Esteem Scale (Luhtanen & Crocker, 1992), which measures the extent to which one's social groups are valued and compared favorably with relevant comparison groups.

II. Please complete both scales and then answer the questions following the scales. The scoring keys to the scales can be found at the end of this project.

Rosenberg Self-Esteem Scale (Personal Self-Esteem)

Circle the number of the response that is most appropriate.

		strongly agree	agree	neutral	disagree	strongly disagree
1.	I feel I am a person of worth, at least on an equal plane with others.	1	2	3	4	5
2.	I feel I have a number of good qualities.	1	2	3	4	5
3.	All in all, I am inclined to feel I am a failure.	1	2	3	4	5
4.	I am able to do things as well as most other people.	1	2	3	4	5
5.	I feel I do not have much to be proud of, compared to most other people.	1	2	3	4	5
6.	I take a positive attitude toward myself.	1	2	3	4	5
7.	On the whole, I am satisfied with myself.	1	2	3	4	5
8.	I wish I could have more respect for myself.	1	2	3	4	5
9.	I certainly feel useless at times.	1	2	3	4	5
10.	At times I think I am no good at all.	1	2	3	4	5

Collective Self-Esteem Scale

We are all members of different social groups or social categories. Some of these social groups or categories pertain to *gender, race, religion, nationality, ethnicity, and socioeconomic class.* We would like you to consider your memberships in *gender, race, religious, national, ethnic, and class* groups or categories, and respond to the following statements on the basis of how you feel about those groups and your memberships in them. There are no right or wrong answers to any of these statements; we are interested in your honest reactions and opinions. Please read each statement carefully, and respond by using the following scale:

1	2	3	4	5	6	7
strongly disagree	disagree	disagree somewhat	neutral	agree somewhat	agree	strongly agree

1.	I am a worthy member of the social groups I belong to.	1	2	3	4	5	6	7
2.	I often regret that I belong to some of the social groups I do.	1	2	3	4	5	6	7
3.	Overall, my social groups are considered good by others.	1	2	3	4	5	6	7
4.	Overall, my group memberships have very little to do with how I feel about myself.	1	2	3	4	5	6	7
5.	I feel I don't have much to offer to the social groups I belong to.	1	2	3	4	5	6	7
6.	In general, I'm glad to be a member of the social groups I belong to.	1	2	3	4	5	6	7
7.	Most people consider my social groups, on the average, to be more ineffective than other social groups.	1	2	3	4	5	6	7
8.	The social groups I belong to are an important reflection of who I am.	1	2	3	4	5	6	7
9.	I am a cooperative participant in the social groups I belong to.	1	2	3	4	5	6	7
10.	Overall, I often feel that the social groups of which I am a member are not worthwhile.	1	2	3	4	5	6	7
11.	In general, others respect the social groups that I am a member of.	1	2	3	4	5	6	7
12.	The social groups I belong to are unimportant to my sense of what kind of a person I am.	1	2	3	4	5	6	7
13.	I often feel I'm a useless member of my social groups.	1	2	3	4	5	6	7
14.	I feel good about the social groups I belong to.	1	2	3	4	5	6	7
15.	In general, others think that the social groups I am a member of are unworthy.	1	2	3	4	5	6	7
16.	In general, belonging to social groups is an important part of my self-image.	1	2	3	4	5	6	7

What kinds of situations or life experiences do you think affect personal self-esteem?

_____

_____

_____

_____

_____

_____

_____

_____

What kinds of situations or life experiences do you think affect social/collective self-esteem?

_____

_____

_____

_____

_____

_____

_____

_____

Do your personal and social/collective self-esteem come from different or similar sources?

_____

_____

_____

_____

_____

_____

_____

Scoring the Rosenberg and Collective Self-Esteem Scales

I.   To score the Rosenberg Self-Esteem Scale: first, reverse code items 1, 2, 4, 6, and 7 (this means to score a response of 5 as 1, 4 as 2, 2 as 4, and 1 as 5); second, add up the items 3, 5, 8, 9, and 10, and the reversed responses to items 1, 2, 4, 6, and 7. Instructors can ask each person to write their score on a piece of paper anonymously, allowing the instructor to calculate the class average on this scale.

II. To score the Collective Self-Esteem Scale: first, reverse code items 2, 4, 5, 7, 10, 12, 13, 15 (score a response of 7 as 1, 6 as 2, 5 as 3, 3 as 5, 2 as 6, and 1 as 7); second, add up the items 1, 3, 6, 8, 9, 11, 14, 16 and the reversed responses to items 2, 4, 5, 7, 10, 12, 13, and 15. Again, instructors can ask each person to write their score on a piece of paper anonymously, allowing the instructor to calculate the class average on this scale.

III. Additionally, the Collective Self-Esteem Scale has 4 subscales. Items 1, 5, 9, and 13 make up the "membership" subscale; items 2, 6, 10, and 14 make up the "private" subscale; items 3, 7, 11, and 15 make up the "public" subscale; and, items 4, 8, 12, and 16 make up the "identity" subscale.

✓ PROJECT 4.2
Who Am I?

I.   Identity researchers will often use the "Twenty Statements Test" to gather information about identity. Merely asking people to list 20 responses to the question "Who am I?" can yield information about the ways they describe themselves using specific attributes (their personal identity), and the groups with which they identify (their social or collective identity). For this project, complete one copy of this questionnaire and give the other copy to one friend to complete. Then, answer the questions on the following page.

Answer the question: "Who am I?" by listing 20 characteristics that describe you.

1.	
2.	
3.	
4.	
5.	
6.	
7.	
8.	
9.	
10.	
11.	
12.	
13.	
14.	
15.	
16.	
17.	
18.	
19.	
20.	

Answer the question: "Who am I?" by listing 20 characteristics that describe you.

1.	
2.	
3.	
4.	
5.	
6.	
7.	
8.	
9.	
10.	
11.	
12.	
13.	
14.	
15.	
16.	
17.	
18.	
19.	
20.	

A. Please look back at the characteristics you and your friend generated in response to the question "Who am I?" Please read over these characteristics and categorize them in a way that separates them by whether they relate to personal or social identity. In the space below, discuss what criteria you used to place the items into one of the two categories. What difficulties did you encounter when separating the responses into these two categories (personal or social identity)?

What criteria did you use to place the items into one of the two categories (personal or social identity)?

_____

_____

_____

_____

_____

_____

Which of the items did you find most difficult to categorize? Why was it difficult?

_____

_____

_____

_____

_____

_____

_____

Do your results tell you anything about the identities you and your friend have? If yes, what did you find?

_____

_____

_____

_____

_____

_____

_____

✓ PROJECT 4.3
Negotiating Identities In *The Joy Luck Club*

I.   For this project you will view the movie, *The Joy Luck Club*. After viewing the movie, write a two-page paper in which you first describe scenes that reflect the influence of culture on identities. Then, discuss how different identities are formed in the characters, how they struggle with multiple identities, how they resolve these identity issues, and how different situations impact their identities.

C h a p t e r   5

How Should I Act? Gender, Racial, And Ethnic Social Roles

People will often assume that you will act in specific ways. If you are a female, Americans will expect you to be friendly to others, and if you are male, they will expect you to hide your emotions. People also expect members of different racial and ethnic groups to act differently from one another. These patterns of expected behaviors that are applied to us when we occupy particular positions in a society are called "social roles" (Myers, 1996). These roles are pervasive, influencing our behavior in nearly every situation in which we find ourselves. They are evident in the workplace in the way a boss and his or her subordinates interact. They are present in the home when a mother and daughter relate to one another. Their effects are seen when young heterosexual boys and girls are attracted to one another and it is assumed that it is the boy that must ask for the first date.

The material in this chapter looks at some of the ways in which social roles impact us, vary by culture, and how they permeate our society. The articles focus primarily on gender roles, since social psychologists have devoted most of their attention to gender rather than ethnic or racial roles. Jacquelynne Eccles' article begins this section with a call for a re-evaluation of the meaning of success instead of relying on a male-centered model. She offers an alternative model for success that allows us more alternatives for having a successful and productive life.

Social psychologists have tended to focus on the social roles of women in their research. Doug Cooper Thompson describes, in his article, the predominant male gender role in the United States and the impact it has on American men. The next article, written by Richard Eisler, investigates the impact that the male role stereotype can have on men. He shows that strongly endorsing the western view of masculinity can, through its influence on affect and physiology, have negative consequences for a male's health. John Williams and Deborah Best go on to explore culture's influence on gender. They demonstrate that not only can gender mean different things to different people, but that what it means to be, for instance, a husband or a wife can also vary from group to group.

The final item in this chapter is a cultural script with which many of us in America are familiar, "The First Date Script." This is a example of a set of expectations that exist in a common social interaction, a heterosexual dating encounter. You will probably recognize some of your behaviors or those of people you know.

Additionally, when reading these articles think about how the articles in the preceding chapters relate to them. Clearly, the definitions of the terms gender, race, and ethnicity raised in Chapter 1 play themselves out in how we construct and assign social roles. The group processes discussed in Chapters 2 and 3 make themselves felt in the area of social roles as social roles are at work any time groups are either in conflict or cooperating with one another. And, just as a group that is important to us can influence our identity, as shown in Chapter 4, social roles can provide the means for linking our social identities to our self-concept.

Gender-Roles And Women's Achievement

Jacquelynne S. Eccles

Editors' Note: Who do you view as more successful—a good parent or a good surgeon? In her article, social psychologist Jacquelynne Eccles calls for a re-evaluation of our ideal standard of achievement, clearly a male center model, that has consistently viewed women's achievement from a perspective that often implies that because a woman "does not achieve like a man," she has failed. Eccles presents an alternative model that tries to create a more balanced and inclusive standard of achievement by legitimizing women's achievement choices while still acknowledging the restrictive influence of gender-role socialization.

Differential participation of the sexes in employment and education has become difficult to ignore. Although increasing numbers of women are working, they are still concentrated in the lower levels of the professional hierarchy and in female-dominated occupations (see Eccles & Hoffman, 1984). Although highly important, institutional barriers are not solely responsible. Psychological factors also contribute to women's underrepresentation in certain high-level and scientific careers. Some of these may limit women's accomplishments through influence on the training young women seek. Successful intervention requires a thorough knowledge of the psychological dynamics themselves. This paper explores these social and psychological processes.

It is important to note that any discussion of sex differences in achievement must acknowledge the problems of societal influence on the very definitions of achievement, as well as on our assessment of the differential worth of various forms of achievement, both of which are value-laden. Too often social scientists adopt a male standard of ideal achievement, seeking to understand why women do not "achieve" like men, without considering the possibility that not engaging in some activity may reflect the choice of an alternate activity rather than avoidance. Focusing on negative at the expense of positive motivational dynamics has perpetuated a distorted view of women's achievement choices (see Parsons & Goff, 1980).

What is needed is a more neutral model that legitimizes women's choices while acknowledging the impact of rigid gender-role socialization on the determinants of these choices. Such a model would provide both a framework for more comprehensive research on achievement and the basis for designing more comprehensive intervention programs to broaden the range of educational and occupational choices considered by both females and males. The approach outlined in this paper is one such model. It analyzes women's "underachievement" from a choice rather than a deficit perspective. We believe that women, like men, select their major life roles and activities from the variety of options they consider to be appropriate and that it is essential to study both approach and avoidance factors if we are to understand women's choices.

Applying decision, achievement, and attribution theories of behavior (see Atkinson, 1964; Crandall, 1969; Weiner, 1974) to academic decisions, my colleagues and I have proposed a model of achievement choice that links academic choices to students' expectations for their performance on various achievement tasks and to their perceptions of the importance of these tasks (see Eccles et al., 1983; Eccles, 1984; Eccles, 1986; Meece, Parsons, Kaczala, Goff, & Futterman, 1982). Applying this model to broader educational and occupational choices, we would predict that such choices are influenced most directly by the value the individual places on the array of choices perceived as appropriate, and by the individual's estimates of the probability of success at these various options. Individual differences on these attitudinal variables, in turn, are assumed to result from socialization experiences, interpretation of one's own performance history at various achievement tasks and one's perceptions of appropriate behaviors and goals.

Several features of our model are particularly important for understanding sex differences in the educational and vocational decisions. The first is the model's assumption that the effects of experience are mediated by the individual's interpretation of the events rather than by the events themselves. For example, doing well in math is presumed to influence one's future expectations for math performance only to the extent that doing well is attributed to one's ability. Past research has shown that girls do as well in math as boys throughout their formative years, yet they do not expect to do as well in the future, nor are they as likely to go in math as are boys. This apparent paradox is less puzzling if we acknowledge that it is the subjective meaning and interpretation of success and failure that determine an individual's perceptions of the task and not the objective outcomes themselves.

The second is our focus on choice as the outcome of interest We believe that individuals continually make choices, both consciously and nonconsciously, regarding how they will spend their time and efforts. Many of the most significant sex differences occur on achievement-related behaviors that involve the element of choice, even if the outcome of that choice is heavily influenced by socialization pressures.

The third important component of our perspective is the issue of what becomes a part of an individual's field of perceived options. Although individuals do choose from among several options, they do not actively or consciously consider the full range of objectively available options. Many options are never considered because the individual is unaware of their existence. Others are not seriously considered because the individual has inaccurate information about them. Still other options may not be considered seriously because they do not fit the individual's gender-role schema.

The fourth feature of our perspective is the explicit assumption that achievement decisions are made within the context of a complex social reality that presents each individual with a wide variety of choices, each of which has both long-range and immediate consequences. The choice is often between two or more positive options or between two or more options that each have both positive and negative components. Too often, theorists have focused attention on the

reasons capable women do not select high status achievement options and have failed to ask why they select the options they do. Complex choices are not made in isolation of one another: It is essential to understand the psychological meaning of the roads taken as well as the roads not taken if we are to understand men's and women's achievement-related choices.

We thus assume that educational and vocational choices are guided by: (a) one's expectations for success on the options perceived as appropriate, (b) the relation of these options both to short and long-range goals and to core self-identity and basic psychological needs, (c) the individual's gender-role and more general self-schema, and (d) the potential costs of investing time in one activity rather than another.

We believe that each of these psychological variables is shaped by experiences, cultural norms, and other external forces. Because we have focused on choice rather than avoidance, we believe our model provides a more positive perspective on women's achievement behavior than is found in most explanations for sex differences in achievement. Beginning with the work associated with need achievement, and continuing to current work in attribution theory, a variety of scholars have considered the origin of sex differences in achievement patterns. There are problems with this body of work that stem from the fact that it has assumed a deficit model of female achievement—the deficit perspective has limited the range of variables studied, and the assumption that the differences uncovered in most studies actually mediate sex differences in achievement behavior has rarely been tested.

Our model provides a different perspective. By assigning a central role to subjective task value, we offer an alternative explanation for sex differences in achievement patterns that puts male and female choices on a more equal footing. Males and females may have been socialized to have different but equally important and valuable goals for their lives. Our model also opens up the possibilities of testing the relative importance of a variety of beliefs in mediating females' occupational decisions and of designing interventions based on value socialization rather than expectancy socialization.

Testing the Model

To test the utility of our model, we have been conducting a series of longitudinal studies of the ontogeny and socialization of precollege students achievement beliefs, attitudes, and behaviors. In support of our predictions, sex differences in students' enrollment in advanced high school math courses and in students' plans to continue taking advanced high school English courses are mediated most strongly by sex differences in the value males and females attach to math and English.

In addition, from the ninth grade on, girls value English more than boys do and more than they value math. From seventh grade on, girls have lower confidence in their math abilities than their English abilities and lower expectations for future success in math than do boys (Eccles, Adler, & Meece, 1984; Eccles, Wigfield, Jayaratne, Meece, & Kaczala, 1986; Wigfield, 1984).

Finally, both mothers and fathers think that math is harder for daughters than for sons, despite the fact that the boys and girls in our samples have earned equivalent math grades, test scores, and teacher ratings (Eccles, 1984). Even more important, parental beliefs have a stronger impact on children's confidence in their ability than do the course grades they receive. Furthermore, parents rate advanced math courses as less important, and English and history courses as more important for daughters than for sons (Eccles et al., 1986; Jayaratne, 1983; Parsons, Adler, & Kaczala, 1982). It is not surprising, then, that girls enroll in approximately one semester less mathematics than boys.

We have also found small but consistent sex differences in the attributional patterns of both children and their parents for success in mathematics. First, parents of boys rate talent as a more important cause of their child's math successes than do parents of girls; parents of girls rate effort as more important (Yee & Eccles, 1983). Similarly, in comparison to girls, boys attribute their successes in mathematics more to ability; in contrast, girls attribute their successes more to unstable factors such as effort or a good teacher (Eccles et al., 1986; Parsons, Adler, Kaczala, & Meece, 1982).

These patterns suggest that males and females of approximately equivalent math ability have a different perception of the causes of success and failure in math that may lead them to different decisions regarding fixture prospects for success in mathematics courses. Both boys and girls think next year's math course will be harder than this year's. The girl who views consistent effort as a more important determinant of her success in this year's math course might have lower expectations of success for next year's math course, precisely because she assumes that future math courses will require even more effort for success than this year's course.

Attributional Process, Perceived Task Value, and Occupational Beliefs

The results above suggest that males and females have differing attributional patterns that may influence academic decisions. Comparable attributional differences may also mediate sex differences in occupational choice. Perhaps the fact that many capable women do not enter male-dominated occupations such as engineering results, in part, from women's perceptions of the causes of success and failure in male versus female stereotyped fields. If women do not attribute success in male stereotyped fields to stable, internal causes and failure to unstable, modifiable causes, then they may be disposed to select other occupations. Similarly, women and men may select different careers because they perceive professions differently.

We have conducted a series of studies to look at these issues. In a study reported earlier, the validity of the attributional approach to career choices was established (Eccles, 1985). Study 1 below assesses the link between attributions and the gender-stereotyping of occupations; Study 2 assesses the links among attributions for math, perceptions of math, and students' math-related occupational aspirations; and Study 3 assesses the link between students' ratings of the characteristics and the gender-stereotyping of occupations.

Study 1

This study assessed the link between attributional patterns and gender-stereotyping of occupations (Eccles, 1985). If women perceive male-stereotyped occupations differently than female-stereotyped occupations of comparable status and required training, then they should respond differently to these career options. Specifically, if women attribute success and failure in male-stereotyped occupations in accord with a low expectancy, low value pattern, but attribute success and failure in female-stereotyped occupations in accord with a high expectancy, high value pattern, then they should be more likely to select female occupations.

To investigate, we had 78 undergraduate women rate the importance of effort, ability, specific help from others, stable help from others, task ease, and interest for success and failure in either three relatively female stereotyped (Pediatrician, Elementary School Teacher, and Nurse) or three male-stereotyped (Surgeon, Secondary School Teacher, and Mechanical Engineer) occupations. These were a subset of a large number of occupations that best matched status and training while varying gender-role stereotyping within each pair of occupations.

Outcome was manipulated within subject, and gender-stereotyping was manipulated between subjects. Separate three-way ANOVA's (gender-stereotyping x status level x outcome) were run for each of the six causes. Gender-stereotyping emerged as either a significant main effect or in a significant three-way interaction for three of the attributions (effort, ability, and task ease). Predicted simple effects were tested with Newman-Keuls at $p<.05$. The most interesting comparisons emerged for the contrasts between Nurse and Mechanical Engineer. Consistent with predictions, success at nursing was seen as due relatively more to effort, ability, and interest; in contrast, failure at mechanical engineering was seen as due relatively more to lack of ability.

More generally, whenever stereotyping effects emerged, the women rated the cause as a more important determinant of success or failure in female than in male occupations. Nevertheless, of the 14 relevant significant differences, twelve supported our predictions.

But of these, only one supported the low expectancy predictions (attributing failure at engineering to lack of ability). In contrast, the other 11 supported the high expectancy, high control predictions (e.g., both success and failure were seen as more due to effort in the three male-typed occupations; similarly, success was seen as more due to ability and to interest in the female-typed occupation for two of the three comparisons).

Thus, although there is support for the prediction that women's success and failure attributions for female-stereotyped occupations are more characteristic of the high expectancy, high control pattern than are their success and failure attributions for male-stereotyped occupations, there was virtually no evidence of a low expectancy attributional pattern in any of the occupations.

These results support our original suggestion that avoidance models of female occupational choices may be painting an unnecessarily negative picture of females' occupational choices. The results from this and other studies suggest that females may select female-stereotyped occupations because they are positively attracted to these occupations and not because they are avoiding male-stereotyped occupations.

Study 2

We next evaluated the attributional patterns of 77 math-able college women (SAT math scores greater than 550 or math ACT scores higher than 28) and related these patterns to their career goals (Kane, 1986). If our model is correct, women's decisions to enter math-related fields should relate to their success attributions more than to their failure attributions for mathematics.

To test this prediction, we asked women to rank the causal importance of talent, unstable effort, stable effort, interest, parent help, teacher help, mood, and task difficulty for success and failure on an imagined math test. These attributions were combined to form the following dimensional categories: internal, external, stable, unstable, internal controllable, and internal uncontrollable.

The women were also asked their career goals, and the following Career Groups were created: (1) engineers, mathematicians, computer scientists, chemists, physicists; (2) biologists, pharmacists, medical professionals; (3) business careers; (4) clinical psychologists, lawyers, other social science professionals; and (5) professions in humanities, education, and social work. Analysis of variance was used to assess the relation between career goals and attributional ratings.

Consistent with our perspective, attributional differences emerged only for success and reflected a high-expectancy pattern. Women planning careers in math-related fields, more than other women, attributed math successes to stable and internal reasons and less to unstable and external reasons ($p < .05$ for all four comparisons).

We also asked these women to rate the interest and utility value of math, their confidence in their math abilities, and their perception of the difficulty of math courses (Freeman, 1986). Consistent with our perspective, the women's career goals related significantly only to their ratings of the value of math ($p < .05$), with women in Career Groups 1 and 2 valuing and enjoying math more than women in Groups 4 and 5. Contrary to what might be expected from a deficit perspective, women selecting relatively low math related careers did not lack confidence in their math ability and did not think math was any harder than did women seeking more highly math related careers.

Study 3

We next turned to a set of attitudinal variables linked to occupational perceptions and subjective task value. Women may select female-stereotyped occupations over male-stereotyped occupations of comparable status and required training if they think that male-stereotyped occupations are more difficult, demand more of the individual, and yet are of no more importance to them than female-stereotyped occupations. Women should thus be more likely to select female-stereotyped, occupations, especially if they also want to devote energy to such non-career pursuits as raising a family.

To test for differential perception of occupational difficulty and importance, we had 48 college women rate six occupations on (a) the difficulty of the occupation, (b) the probability of success, (c) the importance of

success, (d) the amount of effort they would be willing to expend to succeed, (e) how good they would feel if they succeeded, and (f) how bad they would feel if they failed (Eccles, 1985). Four of the occupations represented pairs matched on status and required professional training, but that varied on gender-role stereotyping, surgeon-pediatrician and mechanical engineer-nurse (both B.A. level). Two other occupations were included because of their importance to women: psychologist (a commonly selected occupation) and mother.

Since specific a priori predictions were made, the data were submitted to a series of tests with $p < .05$ as the alpha level. In general, the results support the predictions (see Table 1). The male-stereotyped occupation in each occupational paring was rated as more difficult and the probability of success was rated as lower. Furthermore, success at nursing was seen as more important than success at engineering, and the benefits for success as well as the potential costs of failure were rated as higher in nursing.

Perhaps most interestingly, the occupation of mother was rated as very important, affectively very salient, and moderately difficult. Need-achievement theory (Atkinson, 1964) suggests that activities perceived to be of moderate difficulty and high importance are likely to be seen as especially attractive by people with high need achievement motives. Mothering appears to fit these subjective criteria as well as, if not better than, the other occupations tested.

Comparing the ranking of the six occupations on each of the dependent measures yielded additional interesting information. The amount of effort one would be willing to exert, and the level of affect one would expect to experience if one succeeded or failed in each occupation, correlated significantly with the perceived importance of success ($p < .05$ for each comparison), and not with either the perceived difficulty or perceived probability of success ($p < .05$ for each comparison, except the correlation between positive affect and anticipated difficulty of success, for which $p < .05$). If we consider perceived difficulty, probability of success, and importance of properties primarily of the occupation, and anticipated

Table 1
Mean Ratings for Career Attributes in Study 3

	Careers					
Attributes	Surgeon	Pediatrician	Mechanical Engineer	Nurse	Mother	Psychologist
Difficulty[a]	6.65*	6.00	5.33*	4.73	5.60	5.30
Probability of Success[b]	52.68%	64.49%	42.51%**	70.40%	82.84%	82.76%
Importance of Success[a]	5.73	5.75	4.07*	4.82	6.73	5.32
Effort[a]	5.29	5.27	3.89*	4.60	6.38	5.14
Positive Affect for Success[a]	5.88	5.63	4.25*	4.81	6.49	5.41
Negative Affect for Failure[a]	4.82	4.97	3.39**	4.54	6.31	4.80

Notes: Student *t* tests were used to compare ratings within each career pair for each dependent variable. Significant differences indicated with asterisks (*<.05, **<.01).
[a]Items rated on scale ranging from 1 (low) to 7 (high).
[b]Probability ranges from 0–100%.

effort and affect as personal responses to the occupations, then these data suggest that it is the perceived importance of various occupations that determines one's anticipated personal response to these occupations.

The data from this study support the prediction that male-stereotyped occupations are seen as relatively more difficult, but not more important than, comparable female-stereotyped occupations. The mother role is extremely important to this group of college women and they plan to put great effort into succeeding in this role. It seems likely, given this pattern, that any occupation that seriously threatens these women's ability to become successful mothers would not be seen as very appealing.

General Discussion

Although I would like to conclude that perceived causes of success and failure, confidence in one's abilities, expectations for success, and perceived importance influence educational and occupational choices, the causal direction of these relations cannot be specified unequivocally from the data reported here. It is probable that academic course

selection, career choice, attributional patterns, expectations for success, and perceived importance are all influenced by gender-role stereotyping (as well as other factors like aptitude).

Nonetheless, it seems likely that some of the impact of gender-role socialization is mediated by its impact on expectations, attribution, and subjective task value. Thus, its seems reasonable that once established, the attributional, expectancy, and valuing patterns demonstrated in these studies will influence one's consideration of various occupations. As a result, some occupations may not be considered as viable career alternatives. In turn, without serious consideration of new information, it is unlikely that either the attributional patterns or the perceived importance of occupations will change.

The implications of these results for understanding women's career choices are dear. If we assume that females acquire differential attributional patterns, expectations, and values for success at various occupations, and that these patterns are associated with the gender-role appropriateness of the career and one's other long-range goals, then attributional, expectancy, and valuing patterns can help explain preference for gender-appropriate careers.

Perhaps more importantly this approach provides a mechanism for increasing women's perceived career options. Women's (and men's) perceived career options can be increased by programs targeted to their beliefs that train them to (1) associate different attributions and expectations with various occupations, (2) assess the value they attach to occupations, (3) reevaluate their stereotypes of various occupations and life-roles, and (4) reassess the compatibility between various career options and one's adult-role plans. Actively socializing young women and men to recognize the need to be able to support oneself and one's family is probably as important as helping them select the most "appropriate" profession.

Many effective intervention programs (e.g., EQUALS, see Klein, 1985) incorporate components of this set. Comprehensive career and life-role counseling programs would be most effective at preparing girls to make wise decisions if they incorporated all components (see Eccles & Hoffman, 1984; Eccles, 1985; and Klein, 1985 for further discussions of intervention procedures).

References

Atkinson, J. W. (1964). *An introduction to motivation.* Princeton, NJ: Von Nostrand.

Crandall, V. C. (1969). Sex differences in expectancy of intellectual and academic reinforcement. In C. F. Smith (Ed.), *Achievement-related behaviors in children* (pp. 11-45). New York: Russell Sage Foundation.

Eccles, J. (1984). Sex differences in mathematics participation. In M. Steinkamp & M. Moehr (Eds.), *Women in science* (pp. 93-137). Greenwich, CT: JAI Press.

Eccles, J. (1985). *Female achievement patterns: Attributions, expectancies, values, and choice.* Unpublished manuscript. University of Michigan.

Eccles, J. (1986, April). *Sex differences in achievement.* Paper presented at the annual meeting of the American Educational Research Association, San Francisco.

Eccles, J., & Hoffman, L. W. (1984). Sex roles, socialization, and occupational behavior. In H. W. Stevenson & A. E. Siegel (Eds.), *Research in child development and social policy:* Volume 1 (pp. 367-420). Chicago: University of Chicago Press.

Eccles, J., Jacobs, J., Flanaga, C., Goldsmith, B., Barber, B., Yee, D., & Carlson, E. (1986). *Sex differences in achievement: Parental influences*, Part II. Unpublished manuscript. University of Michigan.

Eccles (Parsons), J., Adler, T. F., Futterman, R., Goff, S. B., Kaczala, C. M., Meece, J. L., & Midgley, C. (1983). Expectations, values, and academic behaviors. In J. T. Spence (Ed.), *Perspective on achievement and achievement motivation* (pp. 75-146). San Francisco: W. H. Freeman.

Eccles (Parsons), J., Adler, T., & Meece, J. L. (1984). Sex differences in achievement: A test of alternate theories. *Journal of Personality ad Social Psychology, 46*, 26-43.

Eccles, J., Wigfield, A., Jayaratne, T., Meece, J., & Kaczala, C. M. (1986). *Ontogeny of achievement-related beliefs and attitudes.* Unpublished manuscript. University of Michigan.

Freedman, D. (1986). *Gender-role identity and the choice of a math-related major.* Unpublished thesis. University of Michigan.

Jayaratne, T. (1983). Sex differences in children's math achievement: Parental attitudes. paper presented at the annual meeting of the Society for Research in Child Development. Detroit.

Klein, S. (Ed.) (1985). Handbook for achieving sex equity education. Baltimore, MD: Johns Hopkins University Press.

Meece, J. L., Parsons, J., Kaczala, C. M., Goff, B., & Futterman, R. (1982). Sex differences in math achievement: Toward a model of academic choice. *Psychological Bulletin, 91*, 324-348.

Parsons, J. E., & Goff, S. G. (1980). Achievement motivation: A dual modality. In L. J. Fyans (Ed.), *Recent trends in achievement motivation: Theory and research* (pp. 349-373). Englewood Cliffs, NJ: Plenum.

Parsons, J. E., Adler, T. F., & Kaczala, C. M (1982). Socialization of achievement attitudes and beliefs: Parental influences. *Child Development, 53*, 310-321.

Parsons, J. E., Adler, T. F., Kaczala, C. M, & Meece, J. (1982). Sex differences in attributional patterns and learned helplessness. *Sex roles, 9*, 322-339.

Weiner, B. (1974). *Achievement motivation and attribution theory.* Morristown, NJ: General Learning Press.

Wigfield, A. (1984, April). *Relationships between ability perceptions, other achievement-related beliefs, and school performance.* Paper presented at the annual meeting of the American Education Research Association. New Orleans.

Yee, D., & Eccles, J. (1983). *A comparison of parents' and children's attributions for successful and unsuccessful math performances.* Paper presented at the annual meeting of the American Psychological Association, Anaheim.

The Male Role Stereotype

Doug Cooper Thompson

Editors' Note: Most social psychological research on roles focuses on roles for women. Few people realize that gender roles also impact men. Doug Cooper Thompson describes the male gender role that is accepted by many in the United States. He also probes the consequences that males face when they do not conform to these roles. Consider how you would respond to a man crying in public. This work points to a larger issue—many psychological processes studies in the psychology of gender also affect men, and we must continually ask ourselves, "How are both genders impacted?"

When you first consider that many men now feel that they are victims of sex role stereotyping, your natural response might be: "Are you kidding? Why should men feel discriminated against? Men have the best jobs; they are the corporation presidents and the political leaders. Everyone says, 'It's a man's world.' What do men have to be concerned about? What are their problems?"

It is obvious that men hold most of the influential and important positions in society, and it does seem that many men "have it made." The problem is that men pay a high cost for the ways they have been stereotyped and for the roles that they play.

To understand why many men and women are concerned, we need to take a look at the male role stereotype. Here is what men who conform to the stereotype must do.

Code of Conduct: The Male Role Stereotype

1. Act "Tough"

    Acting tough is a key element of the male role stereotype. Many boys and men feel that they have to show that they are strong and tough, that they can "take it" and "dish it out" as well. You've probably run into some boys and men who like to push people around, use their strength, and act tough. In a conflict, these males would never consider giving in, even when surrender or compromise would be the smartest or most compassionate course of action.

2. Hide Emotions

    This aspect of the male role stereotype teaches males to suppress their emotions and to hide feelings of fear or sorrow or tenderness. Even as small children, they are warned not to be "crybabies." As grown men they show that they have learned this lesson well, and they become very efficient at holding back tears and keeping a "stiff upper lip."

3. Earn "Big Bucks"

    Men are trained to be the primary source of income for the family. So men try to choose occupations that pay well, and then they stick with those jobs, even when they might prefer to try something else. Boys and men are taught that earning a good living is important. In fact, men are often evaluated not on how kind or compassionate or thoughtful they are, but rather on how much money they make.

4. Get the "Right" Kind of job

    If a boy decides to become a pilot, he will receive society's stamp of approval, for that is the right kind of a job for a man. But if a boy decides to become an airline steward, many people would think that quite strange. Boys can decide to be doctors, mechanics, or business executives, but if a boy wants to become—a nurse, secretary, librarian, ballet dancer, or kindergarten teacher, he will have a tough time. His friends and relatives will probably try to talk him out of his decision, because it's just not part of the male role stereotype.

5. Compete—Intensely

    Another aspect of the male role stereotype is to be super-competitive. This competitive drive is seen not only on athletic fields, but in school and later at work. This commitment to competition leads to still another part of the male stereotype: getting ahead of other people to become a winner.

6. Win—At Almost Any Cost

From the Little League baseball field to getting jobs that pay the most money, boys and men are taught to win at whatever they may try to do. They must work and strive and compete so that they can get ahead of other people, no matter how many personal, and even moral, sacrifices are made along the way to the winner's circle.

Those are some of the major features of the male stereotype. And certainly, some of them may not appear to be harmful. Yet when we look more closely, we find that many males who do "buy" the message of the male role stereotype end up paying a very high price for their conformity.

The Cost of the Code: What Men Give Up

1. Men who become highly involved in competition and winning can lose their perspective and good judgment. Competition by itself is not necessarily bad, and we've all enjoyed some competitive activities. But when a man tries to fulfill the male stereotype, and compete and win at any cost, he runs into problems. You've probably seen sore losers (and even sore winners)—sure signs of overcommitment to competition. Real competitors have trouble making friends because they're always trying to go "one-up" on their friends. And when cooperation is needed, true-blue competitors have a difficult time cooperating.

   The next time you see hockey players hitting each other with their hockey sticks or politicians or businessmen willing to do almost anything for a Senate seat or a big deal, you know that you are seeing some of the problems of the male sex role stereotype: an overcommitment to competition and the need to win at any cost.
2. Hiding emotions can hurt. For one thing, hiding emotions confuses people as to what someone's real feelings are. Men who hide their emotions can be misunderstood by others who might see them as uncaring and insensitive. And men who are always

suppressing their feelings may put themselves under heavy psychological stress. This pressure can be physically unhealthy as well.

3. The heavy emphasis that the male stereotype puts on earning big money also creates problems. Some men choose careers they really do not like, just because the job pays well. Others choose a job which at first they like, only later to find out that they would rather do something else. But they stay with their jobs anyway, because they can't afford to earn less money.

In trying to earn as much as possible, many men work long hours and weekends. Some even take second jobs. When men do this, they begin to lead one-track lives—the track that leads to the office or business door. They drop outside interests and hobbies. They have less and less time to spend with their families. That's one reason why some fathers never really get to know their own children even though they may love them very much.

4. Many men who are absorbed by competition, winning, and earning big bucks pay a terrible price in terms of their physical health. With the continual pressure to compete, be tough, I earn money, with little time left for recreation and other interests, men find themselves much more likely than women to fall victim to serious disease. In fact, on the average, men die 8 years sooner than women. Loss of life is a high cost to pay for following the code of the male role stereotype.
5. Those boys and men who do not follow the male code of conduct may also find their lives more difficult because of this stereotype. For example, some boys choose to become nurses rather than doctors, kindergarten teachers rather than lawyers, artists rather than electricians. Social pressure can make it terribly difficult for males who enter these nonstereotyped careers. Other boys and men feel very uncomfortable with the continual pressure to compete and win.

   And some boys do not want to hide their feelings in order to project an image of being strong and tough. These males may be gentle, compassionate, sensitive human beings who are puzzled with and troubled by the male role stereotype. When society stereotypes any group—by race, religion, or sex—it becomes difficult for individuals to break out of the stereotype and be themselves.

The Relationship Between Masculine Gender Role Stress And Men's Health Risk: The Validation Of A Construct

Richard M. Eisler

> **Editors' Note:** Richard Eisler further examines the male role stereotype Thompson described. This article then presents research in which Eisler and his colleagues measure men's commitment to traditional western views of what it means to be masculine. He goes on to discuss how adherence to these stereotypic views, because of their impact on affect and physiology, may be unhealthy and stress-producing. This article is more technical than many in this Workbook, but it is a good example of research on male gender roles, and it illustrates how to construct a questionnaire and then test questions concerning gender and health in the laboratory.

Masculinity and Health

The wisdom of relying on traditional masculine gender role beliefs and behavior patterns to ensure men's health and adjustment to life has only recently been critically examined by mental and medical health researchers. In 1976 the popular writer and psychologist Herb Goldberg was one of the first to warn of the emotional and health "hazards of being male." Others, notably Doyle (1989) and Fasteau (1975), have theorized about the stressful and unhealthy aspects of adherence to traditional masculine imperatives, including competitiveness, a focus on obtaining power and control, and being successful at all costs. O'Neil (1982) has hypothesized that culturally sanctioned homophobia and antifemininity are central underlying precepts of masculinity that have produced stifling conformity in men's roles.

Recent epidemiological data on gender-linked differences between men's and women's health have documented sex differences in "premature mortality" and hazardous lifestyles or behavior patterns for men (Cleary, 1987; Harrison, Chin, & Ficarrotto, 1989). In the United States, women live, on average, about seven years longer than men; the rate of death is higher for men than for women at all ages, and for all leading causes of death (Verbrugge, 1985). Some of the data suggest that gender-related lifestyles may impact the differential death rates. For example, between the ages of 15 and 24, men die at three times the rate of women, largely because of the higher rates of violent death among male youth (Cleary, 1987).

Men have nearly twice the premature death rate of women from coronary artery disease. The reasons for that particular higher mortality rate among men are hotly debated between those advocating a biogenetic etiology and those adhering to a psychosocial perspective. What is not debated is the fact that men are nearly three times as likely to die in motor vehicle accidents and three times as likely as women to actually commit suicide (Waldron & Johnson, 1976). Higher death rates in men by homicide, suicide, and accidents have been attributed by some to the paucity of acceptable masculine alternatives for aggressive behaviors in coping with stress. Additionally, data compiled by Waldron and Johnson (1976) showed that men's death rate from lung cancer is nearly six times that of women, and twice as high from cirrhosis of the liver, suggesting that masculine coping styles that incorporate higher rates of smoking and drinking are added health risk factors for men.

Mental Health Issues

Large-scale American epidemiological studies conducted by Robins and her colleagues (Robins, Helzer, Weissman, Orvaschel, Gruenberg, Burke, & Regier, 1984) looked at gender differences in vulnerability to psychiatrically diagnosed mental disorders. The results showed that while women are more prone to anxiety disorders and depression, men show more evidence of antisocial personality disorder and alcohol and drug abuse. Also compelling is the evidence that men, compared with women, are far more likely to be involved in violent crime and in spouse or sexual abuse (Widom, 1984). Thus, it appears that our culturally sanctioned masculine coping styles, including repertoires of toughness, combativeness, and reliance on aggressive responses, may have maladaptive consequences for men and their families. In the context of our culture's sports events, military operations, and business competitions, masculine initiative and shows of force are virtuously applauded. In the context of armed robbery, rape, or sexual harassment, masculine imperatives of aggression and daring are clearly less than welcome.

The Concept of Masculine Gender Role Stress

A central impetus for the measurement of—and the research on—masculine gender role stress reported in this chapter was my assumption that our dominant culture's requirement that men adhere to several aspects of culturally approved masculine ideology and role behavior may have dysfunctional health consequences for many men and for those with whom they come into contact. Unlike some who write about men 5 issues, I do not believe there is evidence to conclude that all or even most of our most cherished stereotypic masculine qualities in themselves are necessarily detrimental to men's health. For instance, Cook's (1985) extensive review of research on androgynous, masculine, and feminine characteristics showed that many attributes of traditional masculinity, as opposed to traditional femininity, have positive implications for the psychological adjustment of both men and women.

In this chapter, I (a) discuss the theoretical derivation of the masculine gender role stress construct; (b) detail the empirical development of the Masculine Gender Role Stress Scale (MGRSS); (c) present validation of and research with the MGRSS; and finally, (d) discuss the implications of this research for understanding men's health problems.

Theoretical Notions Underlying Masculine Gender Role Stress

During the last few decades, there has been increasing interest among those doing research on men in viewing "masculinities" as cultural constructions that are imposed on men by particular social groups and organizations rather than as routine outcomes of biopsychosocial development. For example, Franklin (1988) has pointed out that, traditionally, men, as distinct from women, have *shared* a culturally designed and enforced way of seeing things, planning things, and doing things. That is, many American men, whatever their race, politics, ethnic background, and educational or vocational attainment, may have shared a collective "masculine consciousness" or traditional masculinity that is enacted through commitment to socially prescribed masculine gender roles. For example, many men who differ in race or ethnic background commonly value power and dominance in their relationships, approve of a certain degree of aggression and violence in gaining competitive advantage, and disdain "feminine" strategies for coping with life. This antifeminine imperative for men is often manifested through demeaning the importance or utility of self-disclosing emotion or vulnerability in human relationships. Some questions we might ask at this point are: How do men become so deeply committed to particular masculine gender roles? How do these roles become so pervasive among so many men of different ethnic background and status?

Bem's Gender Schema Theory

In contrast to her work on androgynous sex roles (1974), Sandra Bem's more recent theoretical work on cognitive processing differences between sex-typed and non-sex-typed persons (1981) has relevance for our notions about gender role stress. Bem (1981) has proposed a cognitive theory of the development of gender schema to explain the pervasiveness of each sex's affinity for masculine versus feminine gender roles and attitudes. She has proposed that sex-typed masculinity and femininity originate from an individual's general readiness to encode and organize information about the world and himself or herself in terms of the culture's definitions of "maleness" and "femaleness." Thus, a person's self-concept becomes interwoven with culturally approved, sex-typed distinctions.

What Bem's (1981) gender schema theory proposes, then, is that sex-typed attitudes and behaviors are learned when one is willing to process information primarily according to society's mandates of what is appropriate for one's own sex and to ignore information associated with the opposite sex. For example, the adults in a child's world seldom note how nurturant a little boy is or how stoic a little girl is. Therefore, the child learns to apply the same gender schema to himself or herself.

The implications of Bem's gender schema theory for development of the masculine gender role stress model are: (a) men and women to learn to evaluate their adequacy (as persons) based on their ability to regulate their behavior in accord with their learned masculine or feminine gender schema; (b) this self-propagating developmental process becomes stable at an early age; and (c) some men (and some women) become more highly committed than others to regulating their behavior in accord with masculine (or feminine) socially prescribed schema as a way of assessing their self-worth.

One might raise questions at this point about the problems associated with approaching life from such gender-based schemata. Certainly, men acting in predictably masculine ways and women acting in predictably feminine ways provide a certain stable, if not always comfortable, basis for relationships with both the same and the opposite gender. One has to look no further than the current debate about gay men in the military to note the potential havoc many fear will result if some men fail to think or behave in traditionally accepted masculine ways.

To thoroughly explore the complex questions about the disadvantages of men becoming highly committed to culturally stereotypic masculine attitudes and behaviors would require more space than we have here. Certainly, those men and women who have written about and participated in the women's movement against sexism have felt that rigid gender roles were becoming a problem for us all. However, one of the most influential

scholars to portray the stressful and unhealthy implications of traditional masculinity was the psychologist Joseph H. Pleck.

Joseph Pleck's View of Masculinity

In the early 1980s, Pleck critically analyzed what he termed the gender role identification (GRI) paradigm in his book *The Myth of Masculinity* (1981). This paradigm had dominated the social sciences' views of masculine sex typing since the 1930s. According to Pleck, the GRI paradigm held that boys innately need to develop a "masculine" sex role identity to ensure that they develop normally into adult men. From this perspective, mental health problems would arise not from the imposition of culturally inspired gender roles, but rather from the failure of men to learn gender roles appropriate to their biological sex.

To counter the long-held traditional notions that certain features of culturally defined masculinity, such as "dominance," are not only innate but necessary for healthy male development, Pleck (1981) set forth what he termed the gender role strain (GRS) paradigm. Among the assumptions of the GRS paradigm are (a) gender role norms are contradictory and inconsistent; (b) the proportion of individuals who violate traditional gender role norms is high; (c) violating gender role norms leads to social condemnation; (d) violating gender role norms leads to negative and stressful psychological consequences; (e) violating gender role norms has more severe consequences for males than females; and (f) certain consequences prescribed by gender role norms are psychologically dysfunctional. Pleck (1981) also reviewed existing research findings on the effects of gender role violation for men to support his propositions that traditional masculinity often produces deleterious psychological and physical health consequences.

Thus, Pleck's landmark book helped to systematically debunk long-held views that there is something inevitable, natural, or necessary about males developing culturally sanctioned masculine attitudes and role behaviors. On the contrary, the implications of Pleck's work for our notions about masculine gender role stress are that: (a) men have been externally directed by societal expectations to live up to culturally *imposed* definitions of masculinity; (b) the struggle to attain these masculine characteristics may frequently have undesirable consequences for many or even most men; and (c) the routine deployment of masculine strategies for dealing with life's problems may produce dysfunctional solutions and emotional distress for many men.

At this point, we might ask what aspects of traditional masculinity predispose men to being stressed in a manner different from women. Is there something about the way men have been socialized to think and respond differently from women that puts them at greater risk for developing certain types of health problems? How can culturally approved masculine gender role behavior increase or decrease a man's vulnerability to stress? To answer these questions, a measure assessing the kinds of situations that tend to produce more stress in men than in women was needed. But first, a theoretical view of stress that would enable the investigators to focus on gender differences in the cognitive attribution of stress in men compared with women needed to be developed. Richard Lazarus and his colleagues (Lazarus & Folkman, 1984; Lazarus, 1990) provided a model of stress appraisal and coping that we deemed particularly relevant to our development of the notion of masculine gender role stress.

Lazarus's Theory-Based Measurement of Stress

Over time, the concept of stress has evolved as a biopsycho-social construct in which psychological and biological factors interact with environmental events to produce physical and psychological disorders (Goldberger & Breznitz, 1982; Neufeld, 1989; Selye, 1978). Modern theories that describe the way stressful situations produce illness are based on the notion that cognition links events to arousal. It is realized that the impacts of environmental events are cognitively modified by our perceptions, anticipations, and beliefs about a situation, as well as by our appraisal of the efficacy of our coping responses to them. According to Lazarus and Folkman (1984), "psychological stress is a particular relationship between the person and the environment that is appraised

by the person as taxing or exceeding his or her resources and endangering his or her well being" (p.19). Thus, the interaction between cognitive appraisals of situations and evaluations of one's ability to psychologically and emotionally manage those situations defines the stress process.

While many factors can influence one's appraisal of a situation as challenging or threatening, one's vulnerability to a stressor is partly related, as Lazarus and Folkman (1984) pointed out, to the strength of one's *commitment* to that event. Therefore, if a man becomes extremely committed to being successful at a particular enterprise, his vulnerability to stress and emotional upset should be proportional to the strength of his commitment.

Masculine Gender Role Stress Paradigm

Borrowing from Bem's theory that gender role schema predispose men to view the world through masculine-tinted cognitive lenses, from Pleck's view that culturally imposed masculinity predisposes men to masculine gender role strain, and from Lazarus and Folkman's views about the roles of cognitive appraisal and commitment in understanding stress, we have developed the following propositions about the masculine gender role stress paradigm to help explain stress arousal and subsequent health problems in men.

1. The sociocultural contingencies that reward masculine attitudes and behaviors while punishing nonmasculine (i.e., feminine) attitudes result in the development of masculine gender role cognitive schema in the vast majority of individuals with XY chromosome patterns. Thus, little boys develop masculine schema that encourage them to attack rather than cry when someone hurts or threatens them, because the former response will be rewarded and the latter will be rejected as unmasculine. This schema is first rewarded by social peers and adults and then operates independently through a self-evaluation process in which a child says to himself, "this is a good [i.e., strong and masculine] way for me to behave."

2. Masculine schema are then employed by men, in varying degrees, to appraise threats and challenges from the environment as well as to evaluate and guide their choice of coping strategies. Masculine schema are lenses that shape men's appraisals of threat along the lines of traditional masculine gender ideology and also guide the selection of a response from a restricted repertoire of masculine coping behaviors. From this perspective, men are more likely to display aggression when challenged than to employ cooperative or conciliatory responses.

3. Based on their disparate experiences, there are important differences among men as to how *committed* they are to culturally accepted models of masculinity. For a variety of temperamental, psychological, and cultural reasons, men differ in their level of commitment to traditional masculinity and stereotyped masculine behaviors. At one end of the continuum, men may be so committed to masculinity that they behave like certain male firefighters in New York City who, because they believed that women could not possess the skills and abilities essential to working safely with men, harassed female firefighters so that they would quit the department. At the other end of the continuum, men have relinquished their commitment to traditional masculinity by abandoning their careers to stay at home and raise their children.

4. Masculine gender role stress may arise from excessive commitment to and reliance on certain culturally approved masculine schema that limit the range of coping strategies employable in any particular situation. Some men may experience severe stress from losing in a competitive game; others who are less committed to masculine values can cope with the loss more easily, by telling themselves they played well anyway or they got healthy exercise from the competition.

5. Masculine gender role stress may also arise from the belief that one is not living up to culturally sanctioned masculine gender role behavior. Men may experience stress if they feel they have acted in an unmanly or feminine fashion. Many men are doubly stressed by experiencing fear or by feeling that they did not appear successful or tough enough in situations requiring masculine appearances of strength and invincibility.

Development of the MGRSS: Item Generation

A sentence completion task was used to elicit over 200 items from both male and female undergraduate students for both the Masculine Gender Role Stress Scale (MGRSS) for men and the Feminine Gender Role Stress Scale (FGRESS) for women. Only details regarding the gender role stress measure for men will be reported here for women. (See Gillespie & Eisler, 1992, for a description of the FGRSS.) The sentence completion task was designed to elicit sex-typed appraisals from several hundred college students by asking them to separately list what they felt would be the most difficult or most stressful things associated with being either a man or a woman. Additional items regarding the stressful aspects of being a man or woman were taken from various professional books and journals about gender issues. Based on these data, over 100 different items were written for a preliminary version of the men's MGRSS.

The preliminary items were then given to 25 male and 25 female graduate student and faculty judges in the Psychology Department at Virginia Polytechnic Institute and State University. The judges were asked to give their appraisals of how much stress the situations represented by each item would generally be expected to elicit in men and in women on seven-point intensity scales. The items retained for the initial versions of MGRSS had to meet two criteria: (1) the average intensity ratings for *both* male and female raters of men's probable stress intensity had to be assessed in the moderate to high range (4.0 or above on the 7.0 scale), and (2) the mean appraisals of *both* male and female raters had to indicate that the item was significantly *more stressful* for men than for women to be retained for the original MGRSS scale. Only 66 items passed this screen.

Validation

The 66-item version of the MGRSS was administered to another sample of 82 male and 91 female psychology undergraduates. It was deemed important to distinguish masculine gender role stress from purely sex-typed masculinity, in line with our earlier notion that not all adherence to masculine norms is stress-producing. For example, measures of sex-typed masculinity typically assess socially desirable masculine attributes, including autonomy, assertiveness, self-confidence, and so on. For this purpose, the measure of sex-typing in Spence and Helmreich's (1978) Personal Attributes Questionnaire (PAQ) was administered.

In addition, we felt it was important for this preliminary validation to determine links between masculine gender role stress, emotions frequently associated with stress—including anger and anxiety—and health risk habits. Thus, Siegel's (1986) Multidimensional Anger Inventory and the State-Trait Anxiety Inventory (Spielberger, Gorsuch, Lushene, Vagg, & Jacobs, 1983) were also included in the battery, as were items adapted from the National Health Information Clearinghouse (1984) instrument, which asks subjects about their health habits, including diet, exercise, smoking, drinking, and seat belt use. The results from administering the MGRSS with the above measures follow.

I have to caution our readers at this point that most of the items for our research MGRSS were generated by a young group of predominantly white college males and females who may have differed in their views about gender from other, more diverse educational, ethnic, and cultural groups. Additional validation studies will be needed to compare these results with those of other cultural groups.

Gender, the MGRSS, and Masculinity. Since the MGRSS items were constructed to assess experiences that were more likely to be appraised as stressful for men than for women, it was expected that in a population of "normal" men and women, men would score higher on the preliminary MGRSS than women (Eisler & Skidmore, 1987). This was confirmed in that, on average, men achieved higher MGRSS scores (mean = 265) than women (mean = 240) (p<.01).

Previous research had shown that some aspects of culturally sanctioned masculinity (e.g., assertiveness) play a positive role in the healthy adjustment of both men and women, whereas we were selecting MGRSS items to reflect the appraisal of the stress-inducing aspects of masculinity for men. Thus, we were expecting that the MGRSS would have weak associations with measures of sex-typed masculinity. The results confirmed our hope for the MGRSS in that it failed to correlate significantly with the PAQ measure of stereotypic positive masculine traits (r = .08).

The MGRSS, Anger, and Anxiety. As expected, the MGRSS had significant correlations with anger and anxiety. In this sample, the MGRSS correlated moderately highly with the Siegel anger inventory (.54), and to a lesser degree with state anxiety (.23) and trait anxiety (.22) scores. Just the opposite pattern was found for women. Their scores on the MGRSS correlated more highly with state anxiety (.40) than with anger (.17). Thus, as expected, men who scored high on appraisal of masculine stress were more prone to anger, while women who indicated such stress manifested their stress responses with elevated state anxiety (Eisler, Skidmore, & Ward, 1988). Additionally, in a recent study, Arrindell, Kolk, Pickersgill, and Hageman (1993) found a very strong relationship between MGRSS scores and the self-reported experience of irrational fears, particularly social fears in men.

Masculinity, the MGRSS, and Health Behaviors. Finally, it was predicted that sex-typed masculinity would have a positive association with psychosocial health and adjustment in men, whereas our MGRSS measure would predict high-risk health habits (smoking and high alcohol consumption) in these same men. Multiple regression and correlation analysis showed that, as expected, the PAQ measure of masculinity was negatively associated with anxiety (r =-.42) and anger (r = -.18), but positively associated with good health habits (r = .29) (Eisler, Skidmore, & Ward, 1988). On the other hand, the MGRSS, as previously indicated, was positively associated with anger and anxiety, but also positively associated, albeit weakly, with high-risk health habits.

Thus, our initial investigations with the preliminary version of the MGRSS indicate that masculine gender role stress is a viable construct conceptually and operationally distinct from sex-typed masculinity per se. For this population, MGRSS scores were higher for men than for women, whereas previous research has shown that more typically women admit to greater distress than do men. Additionally, MGRSS scores, but not masculinity, were associated with higher levels of anger and anxiety in the male samples. This is consistent with research on Type A behavior patterns, which has shown that negative emotional traits, such as impatience and hostility are associated with higher Type A health risk (Price, 1982). Finally, these results suggest that while subjects who score high in socially acceptable masculine traits may not be at especially high risk for health problems, those who score high on the MGRSS are more prone to engage in high-risk health behaviors.

The MGRSS *and Health Problems.* An additional study with employees of a telephone company was undertaken at Washington University Medical Center to determine the association between MGRSS scores and various health practices of employed adults (Watkins, Eisler, Carpenter, Schectman, & Fisher, 1991). The results indicated that high MGRSS scores were moderately associated with Type A coronary-prone behavior, hostility, and elevated blood pressure in both men and women. Also, high-scoring MGRSS participants reported less satisfaction with their lives than low-scoring MGRSS participants. Thus, there was a correlation between masculine gender role stress and cardiovascular health in a population of working adults. . . .

Discussion

The lack of association between MGRSS scores and the PAQ measure of masculinity and the different pattern of these two instruments' associations with indicators of stress, hostility, anxiety, and health risk behaviors were viewed as supportive of the masculine gender role stress construct. First, it appears that men who score high on socially desirable masculine traits are not necessarily at high risk for psychological difficulties or health problems. Being assertive, being decisive, and having the ability to act

independently contribute to positive personal adjustment for both genders. It is therefore a mistake to implicate all dimensions of traditional masculinity as the source of the host of stress and personality disorders that occur in men. However, the findings did support the notion that men's commitment or adherence to some aspects of "culturally approved masculinity" may be unhealthy and stress-producing. This was demonstrated in the associations between MGRSS scores and high levels of anger, greater fears, and a propensity for engaging in higher-risk behaviors. . . .

The MGRSS and Emotional Expressiveness

[W]e conducted a study looking at the relationship between MGRSS scores and emotional expression in college males who role-played scenes requiring expressions of anger and irritability, on the one hand, and expressions of fear and vulnerability, on the other. Verbal emotional expressions and nonverbal facial expressions were videotaped during the role-plays. Mehrabian's (1972) criteria coding "movements of facial muscles to non-neutral expressions" (p.195) were used to rate changes in facial expressions.

The results indicated that all males, irrespective of MGRSS scores, showed less facial expressiveness when they were expected to express fear or tenderness than when they were expected to express anger. Second, the high-scoring MGRSS men were less verbally expressive than the low-scorers in situations that required the expression of tender emotions. There were no differences between the high- and low-scoring MGRSS men in the verbal expression of anger. Taken as a whole, these results supported the notion that masculine gender role fears are related to the suppression of emotional expression.

Whether men's socialized tendency to inhibit emotional expression has deleterious health consequences for them has been debated in the popular literature. Recently, Pennebaker and his associates (Pennebaker, Hughes, & O'Heeron, 1987; Pennebaker, Kiecolt-Glaser, & Glaser, 1988) have shown that individuals who do not disclose unpleasant emotions have chronic physiological arousal and poorer immune system functioning. Thus, there is some support for the notion that men, with their greater tendency than women to inhibit feelings of fear or sadness, may be more vulnerable to disorders related to physiological arousal. Should future research with the MGRSS substantiate these findings, it would mean that men highly committed to suppressing their feelings of vulnerability are at greater risk for stress-induced disorders.

The MGRSS and Cardiovascular Reactivity

The previously described research on the development and measurement of masculine gender role stress has provided tentative confirmation of our belief that strong commitment to some aspects of masculinity as prescribed by Western cultures may be unhealthy for men.

The positive associations obtained between MGRSS scores and measures of anger arousal and blood pressure have led us to hypothesize that high MGRSS scores may be associated with the cardiovascular disease process, which has been a leading cause of premature death in male, as compared with female, populations. In this section, I focus on a series of laboratory studies conducted with my student colleagues that have attempted to link gender-related appraisal of stress to the increased incidence of cardiovascular disease in men. . . .

Cardiovascular Reactivity

Cardiovascular reactivity has received much attention as a potential mechanism for the development of coronary artery disease (Krantz & Manuck, 1984; Manuck, Kaplan, & Clarkson, 1985). According to the cardiovascular reactivity model, chronic and sustained increases in heart rate and blood pressure, activated by high levels of stress through endocrine responses, cause injury to the arterial walls over time. Reviews of the literature on gender differences in cardiovascular reactivity have found that men generally show greater blood pressure reactivity than do women, although the sexes typically do not differ in heart rate responses (Polefrone & Manuck, 1987).

There has been much conjecture that greater cardiovascular reactivity, and hence heart disease, in men as compared with women, is primarily a function of gender-based biological differences, including hormonal differences. However, additional studies (e.g., Van Egeren, 1979) have shown that when women are placed in some kinds of stressful situations, they exhibit similar or even more reactivity than men. Thus, researchers have speculated that gender differences in reactivity to particular situations may sometimes be a function of gender differences in the "cognitive appraisal of these situations as stressful" (Jorgenson & Houston, 1981; Polefrone & Manuck, 1987).

From this perspective, the heightened cardiovascular responses in males to the laboratory stressors of pain or competition measured in previous research may be understood as men's cognitive appraisal of these challenges as particularly threatening to their masculine self-image, whereas women are less threatened because femininity does not demand that women withstand pain or be as competitive as men.

The next section reports on a series of laboratory studies designed to explore the relationship between MGRSS scores and cardiovascular reactivity, and hence the risk of cardiovascular disease. Also, these studies were designed to determine how men's cognitive appraisals of situations containing masculine challenge situations may produce measurable differences from gender-neutral or feminine stressors.

The MGRSS, Stress, and Reactivity

The first in a series of laboratory studies was designed to evaluate the association between masculine gender role stress appraisal and cardiovascular reactivity. It was conducted by exposing college men with high, medium, or low MGRSS scores to two types of stressors. The first was a standard laboratory induction of "pain" known as the Cold Pressor Stress Test. The subject was required to place his hand in ice water for a period of several minutes. Physiological measures of cardiovascular response were measured before, during, and after the hand was immersed in the cold water. The magnitude of the increases in blood pressure and heart rate response were employed as measures of the men's reactivity to this painful stressor.

The addition to the physical stress of the cold pressor test, high-, medium-, and low-scoring MGRSS, subjects were also subjected to the Masculine Threat Interview, a psychologically stressful interview by a female confederate, who frequently challenged the subject's masculinity. The interviewer asked pointed questions based on . . . the MGRSS. For example, subjects were challenged to talk about topics such as their academic performance, problems in dating, and ability to express themselves emotionally.

The results, analyzed by multiple regression, indicated that there was a linear relationship between MGRSS scores and systolic blood pressure reactivity to both the Cold Pressor Stress Test and the Masculine Threat Interview. That is, there was a progressive increase in blood pressure reactivity associated with an increasing MGRSS score. The results for the cold Pressor Stress Test and the Masculine Threat Interview were virtually indistinguishable. The stress of both pain and psychological threat to self-esteem had very similar effects in producing greatly increased reactivity for the high-scoring MGRSS men compared with low-scorers. Thus, the nature of the challenge, pain, or psychological threat was found to be less important than the subject's tendency to appraise the situation as a threat to his masculine gender role competence as reflected in his MGRSS score.

The MGRSS, Stress, Reactivity, and Masculine Challenge

The previous study suggested that cardiovascular reactivity in men is in part a function of differences in their cognitive appraisals of threats to their masculinity. That is, high-scoring MGRSS men tend to appraise certain situations involving masculine challenge as more stressful and therefore show greater reactivity than their low-scoring counterparts. In the absence of cognitive threats to masculinity, there should be no differences in the stress responses, and hence in the reactivity of high- and low-scoring MGRSS men. However, when presented with clear evidence of masculine challenge, we expected the high-scoring MGRSS men to be more reactive than the low-scorers.

To test these predictions, we exposed both high and low-scoring MGRSS men to the previously described cold pressor test under different gender-relevant instructions, to either enhance or reduce the "masculine challenge" of the task (Lash, Eisler, & Schulman, 1990). We wanted to determine whether the greater reactivity of the high-scoring MGRSS men was a function of the pain of the cold water immersion itself or of the particular way these men assessed the implied masculine demand characteristics of the situation, as compared with the low-scoring MGRSS men.

To ensure that high- and low-scoring MGRSS men would assess the stressor differently, male groups were exposed to either a high or low masculine challenge cold pressor test that differed only in that we provided a different rationale for performing the task. In the low masculine challenge test, prior to immersion, the men were told that we simply wanted to obtain physiological measures on people who had their hands in cold water. In the high masculine challenge test, prior to immersion, we emphasized that this was a test of endurance, strength, and ability to withstand pain. The results, as expected, indicated that for the low masculine challenge test, there were no differences in the cardiovascular responses of high-scoring as compared with low-scoring MGRSS men. However, for men in the high masculine challenge groups, large differences in reactivity occurred, with high-scoring MGRSS men showing much more blood pressure reactivity both prior to and during immersion in the cold water. That is, high-scoring MGRSS men were more reactive than the low-scores during both the anticipation of the masculine challenge as well as during exposure to the stressor itself.

Further evidence that gender-determined appraisal plays a role in cardiovascular reactivity was gathered from additional studies we conducted using both male and female subjects exposed to masculine and feminine challenges (Lash, 1991; Lash, Gillespie, Eisler, & Southard, 1991). In these subsequent investigations, it was found that women were more reactive than men if the situation threatened their adequacy in areas in which females are expected to excel, such as nurturance and child-rearing ability. On the other hand, it was found that men were more reactive than women if the situations contained masculine challenges such as competitiveness or ability to withstand pain.

Discussion

It must be recognized that our studies showing relationships between the MGRSS and masculine challenge and cardiovascular reactivity have uncovered far from conclusive evidence linking masculine gender role behavior patterns with the development of coronary artery disease in men. However, I think we have been able to show that some stresses in men are gender-specific, and that by increasing the masculine relevance of tasks, we can increase arousal in susceptible high-scoring MGRSS men. Second, we have shown that in understanding how masculinity predisposes men to appraise and struggle with the environment in certain gender-stereotypic ways, we may better understand the connection between masculine constructions of the self and men's vulnerability to gender-induced health problems.

Conclusions

Our research with the MGRSS has shown that men tend to experience stress arousal when attempting to deal with emotions they feel are more appropriate for women, or when fearing that women may best them in an activity at which men are expected to excel. Men are also likely to experience stress if they appraise themselves as not performing up to manly standards of achievement in the masculine spheres of work and sexual performance. These appraisals result from pressures men tend to place on themselves to conform to outmoded stereotypes, that is, caricatures of traditional masculine roles.

Overall, the studies we have done with the MGRSS, laboratory stressors, and measures of cardiovascular reactivity have supported a cognitively mediated view of stress based on men's diverse commitments to traditional masculine ideology. High-scoring MGRSS men who were highly committed to traditional masculinity were more likely than others to become excessively emotionally aroused, as measured by their blood pressure, when asked to perform tasks at which men are expected to excel, such as the ability to withstand pain.

When the same tasks were presented without the stereotypic expectation that a man would suppress feelings of pain, there were no differences in stress arousal between high- and low-scoring MGRSS men. Additionally, when men were presented with tasks at which females were expected to excel (Lash, 1991), men did not show as much reactivity as the women. These results suggest that men and women are socialized to follow gender-segregated patterns of response based on perceived masculine- and feminine-relevant challenges. Men, for example, are more likely to be stressed by perceived inadequacies in the work environment or deficiencies in strength or mental toughness. Women, on the other hand, may be more stressed by feelings of inadequacy in such areas as the family and relationships (Gillespie & Eisler, 1992).

Future researchers into the health and adjustment problems of men, such as heart disease, hypertension, alcoholism, spouse abuse, and sexual harassment, must become more informed about the pressures and influences of socialized masculine gender roles, which promote unhealthy coping behavior. New programs for men might develop, promote, and evaluate psycho-educational programs on alternative roles and decision-making strategies for men that would expand their range of healthy behaviors.

Finally, it must be recognized that most of the research reported on here was done with relatively young, well-educated, predominantly white men. Nevertheless, there is reason to suspect that there are dysfunctional aspects to the masculinities created by men of other ages, races, and cultural groups as well. Much additional work is needed to generalize the suitability of these findings to men of other ages, races, and cultural backgrounds.

References

Arrindell, W. A., Kolk, A. M., Pickersgill, M. J., & Hageman, W. J. (1993). Biological sex, sex role orientation, masculine sex role stress, dissimulation and self-reported fears. *Advances in Behaviour Research and Therapy, 15,* 103-146.

Bem S. (1974). The measurement of psychological androgyny. *Journal of Consulting and Clinical Psychology, 42,* 155-162.

Bem S. (1981). Gender schema theory: A cognitive account of sex-typing. *Psychological Review, 88,* 354-364.

Cleary, P. D. (1987). Gender differences in stress related disorders. In R. C. Barnett, L. Biener, & G. K. Baruch (Eds.), *Gender and stress* (pp. 39-72). New York: Free Press.

Cook, E. P. (1985). *Psychological androgyny*. New York: Pergamon.

Doyle, J. A. (1989). *The male experience*. Dubuque, IA: William C. Brown.

Eisler, R. M., & Skidmore, J. R. (1987). Masculine gender role stress: Scale development and component factors in the appraisal of stressful situations. *Behavior Modification, 11,* 123-136.

Eisler, R. M., Skidmore, J. R., & Ward C. H. (1988). Masculine gender-role stress: Predictor of anger, anxiety, and health-risk behaviors. *Journal of Personality Assessment, 52,* 133-141.

Fasteau, M. F. (1975). *The male machine*. New York: Dell.

Franklin, C. W. (1988). *Men and society*. Chicago: Nelson-Hall.

Friedman, M., & Rosenman, R. (1974). *Type A behavior and your heart*. Greenwich, CT: Fawcett.

Gillespie, B. L., & Eisler, R. M. (1992). Development of the Feminine Gender Role Stress Scale: A cognitive behavioral measure of stress, appraisal and coping for women. *Behavior Modification, 16,* 426-438.

Goldberg, H. (1976). *The hazards of being male*. New York: Nash.

Goldberger, L., & Breznitz, S. (Eds). (1982). *Handbook of stress: Theoretical and clinical aspects*. New York: Free Press.

Harrison, J., Chin, J., & Ficarrotto, T. (1989). Warning: Masculinity may be dangerous to your health. In M. S. Kimmel & M. A. Messner (Eds.), *Men's lives* (pp. 296-309). New York: Macmillan.

Jorgensen, R. S., & Houston, B. K. (1981). Type A behavior patterns, sex differences, and cardiovascular responses to recovery from stress. *Motivation and Emotion, 5,* 201-214.

Krantz, D. S., & Manuck, S. B. (1984). Acute physiologic reactivity and risk of cardiovascular disease: A review and methodologic critique. *Psychological Bulletin, 96,* 435-464.

Lash, S. J. (1991). *Gender differences in cardiovascular reactivity: Effects of gender relevance of the stressor*. Unpublished doctoral dissertation, Virginia Polytechnic Institute and State University, Blaksburg, VA.

Lash, S. J., Eisler, R. M., & Schulman, R. S. (1990). Cardiovascular reactivity to stress in men. *Behavior Modification, 14,* 3-20.

Lash, S. J., Gillespie, B. L., Eisler, R. M., & Southard, D. R. (1991). Sex differences in cardiovascular reactivity: Effects of the gender relevance of the stressor. *Health Psychology, 6,* 392-398.

Lazarus, R. S. (1990). Theory-based stress measurement. *Psychological Inquiry, 1,* 2-13.

Lazarus, R. S., & Folkman, S. (1984). *Stress, appraisal, and coping*. New York: Springer.

Manuck, S. B., Kaplan, J. R., & Clarkson, T. B. (1985). Stress-induced heart rate reactivity and atherosclerosis in female macaques. *Psychosomatic Medicine, 47,* 90.

Mehrabian, A. (1972). *Nonverbal communication*. Chicago: Aldine.

National Health Information Clearinghouse. (1984). *Health style: A self test*. Washington, DC: U.S. Public Health Service.

Neufeld, R. W. (Ed.). (1989). *Advances in the investigation of psychological stress*. New York: Wiley.

O'Neil, J. M. (1982). Gender role conflict and strain in men's lives: Implications for psychiatrists, psychologists, and other human service providers. In K. Solomon & N. B. Levy (Eds.), *Men in transition: Theory and therapy* (pp. 5-44). New York: Plenum.

Pennebaker, J. W., Hughes, C. F., & O'Heeron, R. C. (1987). The psychophysiology of confession: Linking inhibitory and psychosomatic processes. *Journal of Personality and Social Psychology, 52,* 781-793).

Pennebaker, J. W., Kiecolt-Glaser, J. K., & Glaser, R. (1988). Disclosure of traumas and immune function: Health implications for psychotherapy. *Journal of Consulting and Clinical Psychology, 56,* 239-245.

Pleck, J. (1981). *The myth of masculinity*. Cambridge, MA: MIT Press.

Polefrone, J. M., & Manuck, S. B. (1987). Gender differences in cardiovascular and neuroendocrine responses to stressors. In R. Barnett, L. Biener, & G. Baruch (Eds.), *Gender and stress* (pp. 13-38). New York: Free Press.

Price, V. A. (1982) *Type A behavior pattern: A model for research and practice*. New York: Academic Press.

Robins, L. N., Helzer, J. E., Wiessman, M. M., Orvaschel, H., Gruenberg, E., Burke, J. D., & Regier, D. A. (1984). Lifetime prevalence of specific psychiatric disorders in three sites. *Archives of General Psychiatry, 41,* 949-958.

Selye, H. (1978). *The stress of life*. New York: McGraw-Hill.

Siegel, J. N. (1986). The Multidimensional Anger Inventory. *Journal of Personality and Social Psychology, 51,* 191-200.

Spence, J. T., & Helmreich, R. L. (1978). *Masculinity and femininity: Their psychological dimensions, correlates, and antecedents*. Austin: University of Texas Press.

Spielberger, C. D., Gorsuch, R. L., Lushene, R., Vagg, P. R., & Jacobs, G. A. (1983). *Manual for the State-Trait Anxiety Inventory (Form Y)*. Palo Alto, CA: Consulting Psychologists Press.

Van Egeren, L. F. (1979). Cardiovascular changes during social competition in a mixed motive game. *Journal of Personality and Social Psychology, 37,* 858-864.

Cross-Cultural Views Of Women And Men

John E. Williams and Deborah L. Best

> **Editors' Note:** Are the traits associated with being female or male consistent across cultures? Would your view of yourself as a woman be the same if you where from India as it would be if you were from France? The following article by John Williams and Deborah Best discusses the way men and women are viewed, the self-views they hold, and the roles they carry out in different cultures, as well as the factors that contribute to the development of these views and roles. To understand gender roles, we must also acknowledge the contribution of culture, and this work illustrates the contribution.

Imagine that you are on an extended trip around the world and you have visited a number of different countries on every continent. On your final airplane ride home, you decide to thumb back through the diary you have kept while on your trip—to reminisce a bit before you have to face the many tasks that will require your attention when you get home. while looking back through your diary you note that during your stay in Pakistan, you observed that men were highly visible in day-to-day activities and seemed to be "in charge" in most situations. Women were rarely seen in public places and, when they were, they appeared to be on specific errands and were often dressed in a manner that made it difficult to tell much about them. You rarely saw young men and women walking together as couples, enjoying what would be called a date in the United States. Moving a few pages ahead in your diary you see an entry that indicated that during your stay in Finland, you noticed that men and women seemed to participate equally in many daily activities. Heterosexual couples were everywhere and many young women and men were dressed in a similar unisex style.

Reflecting on the various experiences you had in Pakistan, Finland, and the other countries you visited, you conclude that there are important differences in the way that men and women behave in different countries. It is obvious that the customs governing appropriate relations between men and women differ from country to country, but you wonder if there are differences in the way that people of the same gender in different countries view themselves. Are the self concepts of men different in Pakistan and Finland? Do women in Pakistan view themselves as more feminine than women in Finland? Are the self-perceptions of men and women more similar in Finland than in Pakistan? What are the cultural perceptions and accepted behaviors of men and women in Pakistan and Finland?

These questions address the three distinct but related aspects of the way that women and men are viewed in different cultures, and these are the focus of this chapter. The first aspect concerns *gender stereotypes* which are the popular views of how men and women differ in their psychological makeup. For example, men are often said to be more aggressive than women while women are said to be more emotional than men. The second aspect addresses the manner in which women and men view themselves, that is, the degree to which the gender stereotypes are incorporated into the *self-perceptions* of the two gender groups. To what degree do men have more "masculine" self-descriptions and do women have more "feminine" self-descriptions? The third aspect to be discussed is *sex-role ideology* which pertains to beliefs about the proper role relationships between men and women in different cultures. For example, is it appropriate for men to be dominant over women or should the two gender groups relate to one another in a more equal manner? We will consider some cross-cultural research findings bearing upon each of these three matters, in turn.

Cross-cultural research can be valuable when looking at gender differences because it provides a greater range of beliefs and roles than do single-cultural studies. With greater variation comes the opportunity to look for possible causes of gender differences.

Gender Stereotypes

We will begin our discussion with gender stereotypes because they serve as the foundation for gender differences in self perceptions and roles. First, let's look at how gender stereotypes are related to gender roles. In all societies, men and women generally carry out different occupational, homemaking, and leisure roles. For example, in the United States more men than women are construction workers and more women than men care for young children. These role assignments are supported by assumptions that men are stronger, more robust, and more rational than women, and are therefore more suited to be construction workers. Women, on the other hand, are gentle, kind, patient, and understanding, and as a consequence working with children is more suited to what women are like. Cultural assumptions or stereotypes about what men and women are like may also be reflected in self perceptions and influence the way that men and women interact with one another.

Over the past 15 years, we have conducted gender stereotype studies in more than 30 countries around the world. In each country university students were asked to consider a list of 300 adjectives (e.g., aggressive, emotional) and to indicate whether, in their culture, each adjective is more frequently associated with men, with women, or equally associated with both genders. The responses of the individual subjects in each country were then tallied to determine, for each adjective, the frequency with which it was associated with men and with women. In this manner, we identified the characteristics that are most highly associated with each gender group in each country.

When these data were analyzed, we found a high degree of pancultural agreement across all the countries studied in the characteristics differentially associated with women and men. This agreement is evident in Table 1 which shows the psychological characteristics that were generally associated with men and women across the 30 countries.

Looking at the table, it is clear that very different qualities are associated with men and with women, but with so many items, it is difficult to summarize what the major differences are. To solve this problem, we scored the male-and female-associated adjectives in each country in terms of affective meaning, the *favorability, strength,* and *activity* of the adjectives. Other researchers have shown that affective meanings are important in understanding more than just the dictionary definition of words. Our analysis produced an interesting pattern. In all countries, without exception, the characteristics associated with men were *stronger* and *more active* than those associated with women, but there was no general pancultural pattern for the favorability scores. Taken as a group, the male stereotype characteristics were more favorable than the female characteristics in certain countries (Japan, South Africa, and Nigeria) and the female stereotype characteristics were more favorable in other countries (Italy, Peru, Australia). Across cultures, the stereotypes of women and men are equally favorable, but stereotypes of men are generally stronger and more active than those of women.

Despite the high degree of similarity in the gender stereotypes across the various cultural groups studied, there was also some evidence of systematic cultural variation. For example, male and female gender stereotypes were more differentiated in Protestant countries than in Catholic countries. Perhaps these differences reflect the varying place of women in both the theology and religious practices of these two religious groups.

Having found that adults hold stereotypic beliefs about characteristics associated with men and women, we naturally wondered how early in life young children begin to associate different characteristics with the two gender groups. We explored this question in a study of five-year-old and eight-year-old middle-class children in 25 countries. In this study, children were shown silhouettes of a man and a woman and were asked to select between the ones described in a brief story. The stories were written to reflect the more important features of the adult sex stereotype characteristics. For example, in one story the child would be asked to select "the person who gets into fights" (aggressive) or in another story "the person who cries a lot" (emotional).

The results indicated that the five year-old children in all countries showed at least a beginning knowledge of the adult stereotypes.

TABLE 1: The 100 items of the pancultural adjective checklist

Male-Associated		Female-Associated	
Active	Loud	Affected	Modest
Adventurous	Obnoxious	Affectionate	Nervous
Aggressive	Opinionated	Appreciative	Patient
Arrogant	Opportunistic	Cautious	Pleasant
Autocratic	Pleasure-seeking	Changeable	Prudish
Bossy	Precise	Charming	Self-pitying
Capable	Progressive	Complaining	Sensitive
Coarse	Quick	Complicated	Sentimental
Conceited	Rational	Confused	Sexy
Confident	Realistic	Curious	Shy
Courageous	Reckless	Dependent	Softhearted
Cruel	Resourceful	Dreamy	Sophisticated
Cynical	Rigid	Emotional	Submissive
Determined	Robust	Excitable	Suggestible
Disorderly	Serious	Fault-finding	Talkative
Enterprising	Sharp-witted	Fearful	Timid
Greedy	Show-off	Fickle	Touchy
Hardheaded	Steady	Foolish	Unambitious
Humorous	Stern	Forgiving	Unintelligent
Indifferent	Stingy	Frivolous	Unstable
Individualistic	Stolid	Fussy	Warm
Initiative	Tough	Gentle	Weak
Interests wide	Unfriendly	Imaginative	Worrying
Inventive	Unscrupulous	Kind	Understanding
Lazy	Witty	Mild	Superstitious

The stories most frequently associated with the male figures were those involving the characteristics strong, aggressive, and cruel while those most frequently associated with the female figures were emotional, softhearted, and weak. There were also some interesting variations among the five-year-olds from different countries in their knowledge of the adult stereotypes. For example, Pakistani children showed the greatest knowledge of gender stereotypes while Brazilian children showed relatively little knowledge.

In all countries, there was an increase in sex stereotype knowledge from age five to age eight and, based on the few countries where older children were studied, it appears that stereotype knowledge increases regularly through the teenage years and into young adulthood. In comparing the performance of the children across countries, it is interesting to note that the stereotype knowledge of the eight-year-olds was more similar than that of the five-year-olds. In other words, three additional years of exposure to their individual cultures did not lead to increased diversity but to increased similarity Presumably, this similarity is another reflection of the generality of the adult gender stereotype model which is learned by children in all cultures studied.

The children in the study just described were all from the middle classes in their respective countries, so we could not tell whether sex stereotype knowledge differs as a function of social class. In a later study, however, this question was addressed in a few countries. Children from the higher social classes learned gender stereotypes earlier than children from the lower classes, perhaps due to differences in exposure to stereotypic presentations of women and men in children's stories, in the mass media, etc. Moreover, it may be a reflection of the fact that children from higher class groups tend to be somewhat brighter than children from lower class groups and, as a result, they may learn many things more rapidly, including sex stereotypes.

Self Concepts of Women and Men

We have seen that there is a widespread belief that men and women differ significantly in their psychological makeup and that children begin to learn these beliefs at an early age. In view of these findings, a related question concerns whether these stereotypic characteristics are reflected in the self concepts of men and women.

We addressed this question in a 14-country study in which university students were asked to consider each of the 300 adjectives that we had used in the earlier gender stereotype studies and to indicate those adjectives that were descriptive of self or ideal self. These self and ideal self descriptions were then scored in two different ways. First each description was scored in terms of "masculinity/femininity" by examining the adjectives that were male-associated and female-associated in the earlier sex stereotype study in their country. For example, the self descriptions of subjects in India were examined for the items that had been identified by the earlier group of Indian students to be male-associated and female-associated. Because we used these culture-specific sex stereotype data in scoring, we were able to obtain a culture-specific definition of masculinity/femininity. Hence, a subject's self and ideal self descriptions were considered to be relatively masculine or relatively feminine depending upon how many culture-specific male-associated or female-associated adjectives the subject used in the descriptions.

Looking at masculinity/femininity, there were some interesting pancultural findings. In all countries, as expected, both the self and ideal self concepts of men were more masculine than women's while those of the women were more feminine than men's. Comparisons of the self and ideal self concepts are more informative. One might have expected that in moving from self to ideal

self, men would like to be more masculine and women would like to be more feminine. However, in all countries both genders described the person they wanted to be, the ideal self as more masculine than their actual self. What might this mean? Think about the earlier finding that, in all countries, the male stereotype is stronger and more active than the female stereotype. Perhaps in saying that they wanted to be "more masculine" subjects were, in effect, saying that they wanted to be stronger and more active than they saw themselves to be.

When the masculinity/femininity data were examined for cross-cultural differences, some variations were observed but these variations were not systematically related to cultural differences. So, the intriguing idea that there are important cultural differences in masculinity/femininity was not supported in this study.

A different picture emerged when the self and ideal self concepts were scored in terms of favorability, strength, and activity First, there was a modest tendency in most countries for the men's and women's self descriptions to parallel the strength and activity of the sex stereotypes—the self concepts of men were somewhat stronger and more active than those of women. More interesting findings were obtained when the differences between men's and women's self concepts in each country were compared using a combination of all three affective meaning scores. In some countries the men's and women's self descriptions were more similar and in other countries more differentiated.

The degree of *differentiation* of the men's and women's self concepts was related to a large number of cultural variables. Men's and women's self concepts were more differentiated in countries that were low in socioeconomic development, low in the percentage of women employed outside the home and attending the university, low in the percentage of the population identified as Christian, and relatively rural. In contrast, the countries where the self concepts of men and women were more similar tended to be more developed and more highly Christian, with higher percentages of women employed outside the home and in the university population, and relatively more urban in population distribution. One of the more intriguing relationships found was the tendency for the self concepts of men and women to become more similar as one moves north from the equator into the higher latitudes. what might account for this finding?

In summary, our cross-cultural study of self concepts of men and women suggests that there may be some interesting but relatively minor differences related to cultural factors. On the other hand, the results suggest that looking at these differences in terms of "masculinity/femininity" is not a very profitable approach.

Sex Role Ideology

We turn now to sex role ideology, beliefs concerning the proper role relationships between women and men. The same university students from 14 countries who participated in the self concept study completed a questionnaire expressing agreement or disagreement with statements concerning relationships between women and men. For example: "The husband should be regarded as the legal representative of the family group in all matters of law."; "A woman should have exactly the same freedom of action as a man." The questionnaires were scored so that high scores indicated a relatively egalitarian or "modern" ideology while low scores indicated a male dominant or "traditional" ideology. In each country the ideology scores were examined separately for the men and women subjects. The most modern or egalitarian sex role ideologies were found in the Netherlands, Germany, and Finland while the most male dominant or traditional ideologies were found in Nigeria, Pakistan, and India. The United States fell toward the middle of the distribution of countries.

Perhaps not surprisingly, in the great majority of countries the women subjects tended to have more modern views than did the men, but the differences were relatively small. Indeed, culture seems to contribute more to variations in sex role ideology than does gender, with more agreement between men and women in the same cultural group than among women or among men from different cultural groups.

The sex role ideology differences among the countries seen in the figure were related to a large number of cultural comparison variables. Sex role ideology tended to be more modern or egalitarian in countries that were more developed, more highly Christian, more urban, and, once again, from the higher northern latitudes. Stated the other way, sex role ideology tended to be more traditional and male dominant in countries that were lower in socioeconomic development, lower in the percent of Christians, more rural, and closer to the equator. These findings suggest substantial cross-cultural variations in beliefs about the proper role relationships between men and women.

Summary

Across countries as different as Finland, Pakistan, New Zealand, Nigeria, Canada, and Venezuela, there appears to be widespread cross-cultural agreement in the psychological characteristics believed to differentiate women and men. In each of the countries studied, children's learning of gender stereotypes generally begins before age five and continues through childhood and adolescence. Despite the powerful model provided by the general gender stereotypes, the self concepts of young men and women reveal only a slight echo of these stereotype characteristics. Moreover, there is substantial cross-cultural variation in beliefs concerning proper role relationships between men and women, and in most countries women have somewhat more modern or egalitarian views than do men.

Suggested Readings

Richmond-Abbott, M. (1992). *Masculine & feminine: Gender roles over the life cycle.* New York: McGraw-Hill.

Williams, J. E., & Best, D. L. (1990). *Measuring sex stereotypes: A multi-national study.* Newbury Park, CA: Sage Publications.

Williams, J. E., & Best, D. L. (1990). *Sex and psyche: Gender and self viewed cross-culturally.* Newbury Park, CA: Sage Publications.

Typical Script For A First Date

Do gender roles influence your behavior? Students often answer "no" to this question when first asked, but after giving it more thought, they realize that gender roles are pervasive in their lives. One example of the power of gender roles in determining behavior is in a heterosexual dating situation. In spite of their frequent attempts to break free from traditional gender roles, young heterosexual couples often fall back into social roles when dating. The example below of a common script for a heterosexual dating encounter illustrates just how pervasive gender roles are in American society.

The Woman's Role	The Man's Role
Tell friends and family	Ask for a date*
	Decide what to do*
Groom and dress	Groom and dress
Be nervous	Be nervous
Worry about or change appearance	Worry about or change appearance
Wait for date	Prepare car, apartment
	Check money*
Welcome date to home	Go to date's house
Introduce parents or roommates	Meet parents or roommates
Leave	Leave
	Open car door for date*
Confirm plans	Confirm plans
Get to know date	Get to know date
Compliment date	Compliment date
Joke, laugh, and talk	Joke, laugh, and talk
Try to impress date	Try to impress date
Go to movies, show, or party	Go to movies, show, or party
Eat	Eat
	Pay*
	Initiate physical contact*
	Take date home
Tell date she had a good time	Tell date he had a good time
	Ask for another date*
	Tell date will be in touch*
Kiss goodnight	Kiss goodnight
	Go home

Note: The man's script has more elements than the woman's. The man typically takes the leadership role, indicated by the asterisks next to specific activities.
From: Taylor, Peplau, and Sears (1997)

✓ PROJECT 5.1
Who Sells What? Race And Ethnicity In Advertising

I.   Social roles are portrayed in advertising everywhere and everyday. For example, in the first section of the *New York Times* (June 13, 1998), one ad calls for a stop to child abuse, and it portrays a man with a baby; another announces a change in leadership from "one great leader to another" at a university, and it depicts two older white men in suits walking down the stairs of a brick building; a woman is pictured as a real estate agent; the only Asian depicted in any of the ads is a small child looking forlorn with the words "Human Rights. . ." across her face; all of the line drawings for men's clothing are of white males; and, the only African American portrayed in any of the ads in the first section is a black male playing basketball.

II.   Just one section of a major newspaper reveals how strongly social roles are conveyed in advertising. In this project, you will investigate the social roles that are portrayed currently in advertising and in advertising from 40 years ago.

III.   To do this, choose one magazine and one newspaper. Make sure your library has editions from both today and 40 years ago (from the 1950s). You will most likely need to look at microfiche versions of the newspaper. Your periodicals librarian can help you with this.

IV.   After you choose your magazine and newspaper, please answer the following questions:

Indicate the title and date of the magazine and newspaper you chose.

Current Magazine: _____   Current Newspaper: _____

1950s Magazine: _____   1950s Newspaper: _____

How many advertisements are in the magazine and the newspaper (not including classified ads)?

      Current Magazine: _____   Current Newspaper: _____

      1950s Magazine: _____   1950s Newspaper: _____

How many of these advertisements portray people?

      Current Magazine: _____   Current Newspaper: _____

      1950s Magazine: _____   1950s Newspaper: _____

[Note: Project based on a similar project by Rickabaugh (1998).]

List the roles that are portrayed by the people in each of the ads in the magazines and newspapers (use another sheet if necessary). Then, indicate the gender and race or ethnicity of the person portrayed in each of the ads.

Current Magazine Role	Current Magazine Gender and Race/Ethnicity	1950s Magazine Role	1950s Magazine Gender and Race/Ethnicity

Current Newspaper Role	Current Newspaper Gender and Race/Ethnicity	1950s Newspaper Role	1950s Newspaper Gender and Race/Ethnicity

Are males and females represented with equal frequency in the advertisements? Are people of different races and ethnicities represented equally?

_____

_____

_____

_____

_____

_____

_____

_____

In what roles are females most likely to be portrayed? What attributes do these roles have in common?

_____

_____

_____

_____

_____

_____

_____

_____

In what roles are males most likely to be portrayed? What attributes do these roles have in common?

_____

_____

_____

_____

_____

_____

_____

In what roles are people from traditionally stigmatized groups portrayed? What attributes do these roles have in common?

_____

_____

_____

_____

_____

_____

_____

_____

Did the roles portrayed and the people portraying them change or stay the same over the 40-year period?

_____

_____

_____

_____

_____

_____

_____

_____

_____

How do you think your results were affected by the magazine and newspaper you chose?

_____

_____

_____

_____

_____

_____

_____

_____

What messages do these ads send to our culture?

_____

_____

_____

_____

_____

_____

_____

What conclusions can you draw about the prevalence of roles in advertising?

_____

_____

_____

_____

_____

_____

_____

If you were an advertising executive, what changes would you recommend, if any?

_____

_____

_____

_____

_____

_____

✓ PROJECT 5.2
Cultural Messages About
Roles In Children's Media?

I.   As mentioned in Project 5.1, advertising depicts different groups in different roles. The same phenomenon is also present in children's media. For example, children's books, television shows, toys, and magazines all portray men and women and people of different races and ethnicities in different roles. These portrayals often conform to traditional stereotypes about these groups. It is especially important to examine the children's media for the roles it portrays. Children partly learn about social roles through their exposure to the media. Examining children's television can also shed light onto the ways in which children are socialized; for example, it can reveal how little girls are socialized to believe that certain careers are for only men and not for women. This type of examination is critical because children spend a large proportion of their day watching television.

II.   While this project is structured in a format similar to Project 5.1, it focuses on the roles that are portrayed in children's television programming. For this project, read over the questions below, watch 1 hour of children's programming, and record the information that will allow you to answer the following questions:

When viewing the commercials, count and then compute the percentage of male and female narrators and voice-over narrators. What were the percentages?

   Males: _____   Females: _____

When viewing the programs, count and then compute the percentage of female and male characters. If gender is unclear (as it might be with animal characters), make your best guess based on clothing, voice, or other relevant factors.

   Males: _____   Females: _____

For the programs, also count and then compute the percentage of characters who are from traditionally stigmatized groups. For this, focus only on human characters.

   White: _____   Other race or ethnicity: _____

[Note: Project based on a similar project by Rickabaugh (1998).]

Indicate the number of male and female and white and non-white characters that engage in the role behaviors listed on the following page. Indicate the frequency with which each type of character engages in these behaviors with a hatch mark. Then, summarize your findings.

Roles	Male	Female	White	Other Race or Ethnicity
Aggressive				
Rescuing Others				
Submissive				
Passive				
Being Rescued				
Comic Roles				
Domestic Roles				
Positions of Authority				
Emotional				
Concerned with Physical Appearance				
Physically Fit				
Overweight				
Professional Occupation				
Engaging in Sporting Event				
Service Occupation				
Other (Describe)				

Are males and females represented with equal frequency in the commercials? In the programs? Are people of different races and ethnicities represented equally?

_____

_____

_____

_____

_____

_____

_____

_____

In what roles are females most likely to be portrayed? What attributes do these roles have in common?

_____

_____

_____

_____

_____

_____

_____

_____

_____

In what roles are males most likely to be portrayed? What attributes do these roles have in common?

_____

_____

_____

_____

_____

_____

_____

In what roles are people who are white portrayed? In what roles are those who are of a different race or ethnicity portrayed? What attributes do these roles have in common?

_____

_____

_____

_____

_____

_____

_____

_____

How do you think your results were affected by the program you chose?

_____

_____

_____

_____

_____

_____

_____

_____

What messages do these programs send to children?

_____

_____

_____

_____

_____

_____

_____

What conclusions can you draw about the prevalence of roles in children's programming?

_____

_____

_____

_____

_____

_____

_____

_____

If you were a television executive, what changes would you recommend, if any?

_____

_____

_____

_____

_____

_____

_____

_____

✓ PROJECT 5.3
Violating Gender Roles

I.   Gender roles are a set of behavioral expectations for males and females. In this project, you will identify some of the roles that are associated with your gender and then violate these roles by behaving in a manner that deviates from the expected behavior. Then, you will evaluate the results of this role violation by answering the following questions.

II.   A word of warning: Please do not engage in any illegal or dangerous behavior or any behaviors that will cause you and others harm or embarrassment.

First, generate a short list of behaviors that are more or less acceptable for each sex. This might include behaviors such as opening a door for the other person, wearing make-up, a skirt, or barrettes, comforting a child, or wearing a football uniform.

_____

_____

_____

_____

_____

_____

_____

_____

_____

_____

_____

_____

_____

_____

[Note: Project based on a similar project by Rickabaugh (1998).]

What are the behaviors associated with the role you chose to violate? Why do you think this role is tied to gender?

_____

_____

_____

_____

_____

_____

_____

_____

What exactly did you do to violate the role?

_____

_____

_____

_____

_____

_____

_____

_____

_____

How did violating the role make you feel?

_____

_____

_____

_____

_____

_____

_____

_____

How did other people react to you when you violated the role?

_____

_____

_____

_____

_____

_____

_____

_____

How did you respond to the reactions of others?

_____

_____

_____

_____

_____

_____

_____

_____

C h a p t e r   6

Categorizing + Evaluating = Stereotyping

The previous chapter explored the influence that gender, race, and ethnicity have on social roles. The articles and projects in it focused on a number of issues ranging from how these roles impact our level of achievement, personal and social, to their influence on our attitudes and behavior as well as on our health.

Chapter Six addresses the psychological processes involved in stereotyping. In an effort to do a task more quickly or efficiently we often categorize people or objects. For instance, we may use their size or color as a criteria for placing them in a category. This process can often lead us to create fairly fixed representations of people and objects. We can come to see people primarily as being tall or short, black or white. This relatively fixed nature of our categories can, in turn, make it more likely that we will make judgments about an individual based on the category in which they have been placed.

The articles and projects in this chapter deal with several important cognitive, interpersonal, and cultural aspects of the stereotyping process. The article by Robert Heilbroner gives a general overview of stereotyping along with a discussion of how to reduce our over-reliance on stereotypes. In the next article, Mark Snyder presents research exploring the relationship between the expectations that teachers have for their students based on stereotypes that the teachers have of them and how these influence the students' subsequent behavior. Nancy Signorielli and her colleagues describe a research study that examined the gender stereotypes that are depicted in MTV commercials. This work again demonstrates that even though our views of men and women have changed over time, we still have strong and sometimes negative stereotypes about males and females. Hilary Lips examines how gender, racial, and ethnic stereotypes can interact with one another to create new stereotypes. Finally, a newspaper article originally published in the *Washington Post* highlights the idea that the categories that serve as the basis of many stereotypes have distinctive meanings in one culture that are not shared by other cultures.

While these articles illustrate the pervasiveness of stereotypes, they also suggest that being aware of and decreasing our use of stereotypes can lead to many positive outcomes.

Don't Let Stereotypes Warp Your Judgments

Robert L. Heilbroner

Editors' Note: Stereotypes affect us all by influencing our daily interactions with others, and they even affect us when we are thinking about others. In the following article, Robert Heilbroner gives an overview of stereotypes—what they are, how they affect us, and the dangers of relying on them too much. In addition to describing the negative aspects of stereotypes, he also discusses ways to decrease our reliance on them.

Is a girl called Gloria apt to he better-looking than one called Bertha? Are criminals more likely to be dark than blond? Can you tell a good deal about someone's personality from hearing his voice briefly over the phone? Can a person's nationality be pretty accurately guessed from his photograph? Does the fact that someone wears glasses imply that he is intelligent?

The answer to all these questions is obviously, "No."

Yet, from all the evidence at hand, most of us believe these things. Ask any college boy if he'd rather take his chances with a Gloria or a Bertha, or ask a college girl if she'd rather blind-date a Richard or a Cuthbert. In fact, you don't have to ask: college students in questionnaires have revealed that names conjure up the same images in their minds as they do in yours—and for as little reason.

Look into the favorite suspects of persons who report "suspicious characters" and you will find a large percentage of them to be "swarthy" or "dark and foreign-looking"—despite the testimony of criminologists that criminals do not tend to be dark, foreign or "wild-eyed." Delve into the main asset of a telephone stock swindler and you will find it to be a marvelously confidence-inspiring telephone "personality." And whereas we all think we know what an Italian or a Swede looks like, it is the sad fact that when a group of Nebraska students sought to match faces and nationalities of 15 European countries, they were scored wrong in 93 percent of their identifications. Finally, for all the fact that horn-rimmed glasses have now become the standard television sign of an "intellectual," optometrists know that the main thing that distinguishes people with glasses is just bad eyes.

Stereotypes are a kind of gossip about the world, a gossip that makes us prejudge people before we ever lay eyes on them. Hence it is not surprising that stereotypes have something to do with the dark world of prejudice. Explore most prejudices (note that the word means prejudgment) and you will find a cruel stereotype at the core of each one.

For it is the extraordinary fact that once we have type-cast the world, we tend to see people in terms of our standardized pictures. In another demonstration of the power of stereotypes to affect our vision, a number of Columbia and Barnard students were shown 30 photographs of pretty but unidentified girls, and asked to rate each in terms of "general liking," "intelligence," "beauty" and so on. Two months later, the same group were shown the same photographs, this time with fictitious Irish, Italian, Jewish and "American" names attached to the pictures. Right away the ratings changed. Faces which were now seen as representing a national group went down in looks and still farther down in likability, while the "American" girls suddenly looked decidedly prettier and nicer.

Why is it that we stereotype the world in such irrational and harmful fashion? In part, we begin to type-cast people in our childhood years. Early in life, as every parent whose child has watched a TV Western knows, we learn to spot the Good Guys from the Bad Guys. Some years ago, a social psychologist showed very clearly how powerful these stereotypes of childhood vision are. He secretly asked the most popular youngsters in an elementary school to make errors in their morning gym exercises. Afterwards, he asked the class if anyone had noticed any mistakes during gym period. Oh, yes, said the children. But it was the *unpopular* members of the class—the "bad guys"—they remembered as being out of step.

We not only grow up with standardized pictures forming inside of us, but as grown-ups we are constantly having them thrust upon us. Some of them, like the half-joking, half-serious stereotypes of mothers-in-law, or country yokels, or psychiatrists, are dinned into us by the stock jokes we hear and repeat. In fact, without such stereotypes, there would be a lot fewer jokes. Still other stereotypes are perpetuated by the advertisements we read, the movies we see, the books we read.

And finally, we tend to stereotype because it helps us make sense out of a highly confusing world, a world which William James once described as "one great, blooming, buzzing confusion." It is a curious fact that if we don't *know* what we're looking at, we are often quite literally unable to *see* what we're looking at. People who recover their sight after a lifetime of blindness actually cannot at first tell a triangle from a square. A visitor to a factory sees only noisy chaos where the superintendent sees a perfectly synchronized flow of work. As Walter Lippmann has said, "For the most part we do not first see, and then define; we define first, and then we see."

Stereotypes are one way in which we "define" the world in order to see it. They classify the infinite variety of human beings into a convenient handful of "types" towards whom we learn to act in stereotyped fashion. Life would be a wearing process if we had to start from scratch with each and every human contact. Stereotypes economize on our mental effort by covering up the blooming, buzzing confusion with big recognizable cut-outs. They save us the "trouble" of finding out what the world is like—they give it its accustomed look.

Thus the trouble is that stereotypes make us mentally lazy. As S. I. Hayakawa, the authority on semantics, has written: "The danger of stereotypes lies not in their existence, but in the fact that they become for all people some of the time, and for some people all the time, *substitutes for observation*." Worse yet, stereotypes get in the way of our judgment, even when we do observe the world. Someone who has formed rigid preconceptions of all Latins as "excitable," or all teenagers as "wild," doesn't alter his point of view when he meets a calm and deliberate Genoese, or a serious-minded high school student. He brushes them aside as "exceptions that prove the rule." And, of course, if he meets someone true to type, he stands triumphantly vindicated. "They're all

like that," he proclaims, having encountered an excited Latin, an ill-behaved adolescent.

Hence, quite aside from the injustice which stereotypes do to others, they impoverish ourselves. A person who lumps the world into simple categories, who type-casts all labor leaders as "racketeers," all businessmen as "reactionaries," all Harvard men as "snobs," and all Frenchmen as "sexy," is in danger of becoming a stereotype himself. He loses his capacity to be himself—which is to say, to see the world in his own absolutely unique, inimitable and independent fashion.

Instead, he votes for the man who fits his standardized picture of what a candidate "should" look like or sound like, buys the goods that someone in his "situation" in life "should" own, lives the life that others define for him. The mark of the stereotype person is that he never surprises us, that we do indeed have him "typed." And no one fits this straitjacket so perfectly as someone whose opinions about *other* people are fixed and inflexible.

Impoverishing as they are, stereotypes are not easy to get rid of. The world we type-cast may be no better than a Grade B movie, but at least we know what to expect of our stock characters. When we let them act for themselves in the strangely unpredictable way that people do act, who knows but that many of our fondest convictions will be proved wrong?

Nor do we suddenly drop our standardized pictures for a blinding vision of the Truth. Sharp swings of ideas about people often just substitute one stereotype for another. The true process of change is a slow one that adds bits and pieces of reality to the pictures in our heads, until gradually they take on some of the blurriness of life itself. Little by little, we learn not that Jews and Negroes and Catholics and Puerto Ricans are "just like everybody else"—for that, too, is a stereotype—but that each and every one of them is unique, special, different and individual. Often we do not even know that we have let a stereotype lapse until we hear someone saying, "all so-and-so's are like such-and-such," and we hear ourselves saying, "Well—maybe."

Can we speed the process along? Of course we can.

First, we can become *aware* of the standardized pictures in our heads, in other peoples' heads, in the world around us.

Second, we can become suspicious of all judgments that we allow exceptions to "prove." There is no more chastening thought than that in the vast intellectual adventure of science, it takes but one tiny exception to topple a whole edifice of ideas.

Third, we can learn to be wary of generalizations about people. As F. Scott Fitzgerald once wrote: "Begin with an individual, and before you know it you have created a type; begin with a type, and you find you have created—nothing."

Most of the time, when we type-cast the world, we are not in fact generalizing about people at all. We are only revealing the embarrassing facts about the pictures that hang in the gallery of stereotypes in our own heads.

Self-Fulfilling Stereotypes

Mark Snyder

Editors' Note: Imagine the following situation: Early into the new school year, you find out that your new teacher has very negative impressions of people from your gender or ethnic group. Do you think this knowledge will affect your performance and interactions with the teacher? Is it possible that you could "live up" to some of your teacher's negative impressions? Mark Snyder discusses his research on the insidious nature of stereotypes. In it he discovered that people will sometimes fulfill the expectations that others have of them, and in the process unintentionally perpetuate stereotypes about their group.

Gordon Allport, the Harvard psychologist who wrote a classic work on the nature of prejudice, told a story about a child who had come to believe that people who lived in Minneapolis were called monopolists. From his father, moreover, he had learned that monopolists were evil folk. It wasn't until many years later, when he discovered his confusion, that his dislike of residents of Minneapolis vanished.

Allport knew, of course, that it was not so easy to wipe out prejudice and erroneous stereotypes. Real prejudice, psychologists like Allport argued, was buried deep in human character, and only a restructuring of education could begin to root it out. Yet many people whom I meet while lecturing seem to believe that stereotypes are simply beliefs or attitudes that change easily with experience. Why do some people express the view that Italians are passionate, blacks are lazy, Jews materialistic, and lesbians mannish in their demeanor? In the popular view, it is because they have not learned enough about the diversity among these groups and have not had enough contact with members of the groups for their stereotypes to be challenged by reality. With more experience, it is presumed, most people of good will are likely to revise their stereotypes.

My research over the past decade convinces me that there is little justification for such optimism—and not only for the reasons given by Allport. While it is true that deep prejudice is often based on the needs of pathological character structure, stereotypes are obviously quite common even among fairly normal individuals. When people first meet others, they cannot help noticing certain highly visible and distinctive characteristics: sex, race, physical appearance, and the like.

Despite people's best intentions, their initial impressions of others are shaped by their assumptions about such characteristics.

What is critical, however, is that these assumptions are not merely beliefs or attitudes that exist in a vacuum; they are reinforced by the behavior of both prejudiced people and the targets of their prejudice. In recent years, psychologists have collected considerable laboratory evidence about the processes that strengthen stereotypes and put them beyond the reach of reason and good will.

My own studies initially focused on first encounters between strangers. It did not take long to discover, for example, that people have very different ways of treating those whom they regard as physically attractive and those whom they consider physically unattractive, and that these differences tend to bring out precisely those kinds of behavior that fit with stereotypes about attractiveness.

In an experiment that I conducted with my colleagues Elizabeth Decker Tanke and Ellen Berscheid, pairs of college-age men and women met and became acquainted in telephone conversations. Before the conversations began, each man received a Polaroid snapshot, presumably taken just moments before, of the woman he would soon meet. The photograph, which had actually been prepared before the experiment began, showed either a physically attractive woman or a physically unattractive one. By randomly choosing which picture to use for each conversation, we insured that there was no consistent relationship between the attractiveness of the woman in the picture and the attractiveness of the woman in the conversation.

By questioning the men, we learned that even before the conversations began, stereotypes about physical attractiveness came into play. Men who looked forward to talking with physically attractive women said that they expected to meet decidedly sociable, poised, humorous, and socially adept people, while men who thought that they were about to get acquainted with unattractive women fashioned images of rather unsociable, awkward, serious, and socially inept creatures. Moreover, the men proved to have very different styles of getting acquainted with women whom they thought to be attractive and those whom they believed to be unattractive. Shown a photograph of an attractive woman, they behaved with warmth, friendliness, humor, and animation. However, when the woman in the picture was unattractive, the men were cold, uninteresting, and reserved.

These differences in the men's behavior elicited behavior in the women that was consistent with the men's stereotyped assumptions. Women who were believed (unbeknown to them) to be physically attractive behaved in a friendly, likeable, and sociable manner. In sharp contrast, women who were perceived as physically unattractive adopted a cool, aloof, and distant manner. So striking were the differences in the women's behavior that they could be discerned simply by listening to tape recordings of the woman's side of the conversations. Clearly, by acting upon their stereotyped beliefs about the women whom they would be meeting, the men had initiated a chain of events that produced *behavioral confirmation* for their beliefs.

Similarly, Susan Anderson and Sandra Bem have shown in an experiment at Stanford University that when the tables are turned—when it is women who have pictures of men they are to meet on the telephone—many women treat the men according to their presumed physical attractiveness, and by so doing encourage the men to confirm their stereotypes. Little wonder, then, that so many people remain convinced that good looks and appealing personalities go hand in hand.

Sex and Race

It is experiments such as these that point to a frequently unnoticed power of stereotypes: the power to influence social relationships in ways that create the illusion of reality. In one study, Berna Skrypnek and I arranged for pairs of previously unacquainted students to interact in a situation that permitted us to control the information that each one received about the apparent sex of the other. The two people were seated in separate rooms so that they could neither see nor hear each other. Using a system of signal lights that they operated with switches, they negotiated a division of labor, deciding which member of the pair would perform each of several tasks that differed in sex-role connotations. The tasks varied along the dimensions of masculinity and femininity: sharpen a hunting knife (masculine), polish a pair of shoes (neutral), iron a shirt (feminine).

One member of the team was led to believe that the other was, in one condition of the experiment, male; in the other, female. As we had predicted, the first member's belief about the sex of the partner influenced the outcome of the pair's negotiations. Women whose partners believed them to be men generally chose stereotypically masculine tasks; in contrast, women whose partners believed that they were women usually chose stereotypically feminine tasks. The experiment thus suggests that much sex-role behavior may be the product of other people's stereotyped and often erroneous beliefs.

In a related study at the University of Waterloo, Carl von Baeyer, Debbie Sherk, and Mark Zanna have shown how stereotypes about sex roles operate in job interviews. The researchers arranged to have men conduct simulated job interviews with women supposedly seeking positions as research assistants. The investigators informed half of the women that the men who would interview them held traditional views about the ideal woman, believing her to be very emotional, deferential to her husband, home-oriented, and passive. The rest of the women were told that their interviewer saw the ideal woman as independent, competitive, ambitious, and dominant. When the woman arrived for their interviews, the researchers noticed that most of them had dressed to meet the stereotyped expectations of their prospective interviewers. Women who expected to see a traditional interviewer had chosen very feminine-looking makeup, clothes, and accessories. During the interviews (videotaped through a one-way mirror) these women behaved in traditionally feminine ways and gave traditionally feminine answers to questions such as "Do you have plans to include children and marriage with your career plans?"

Once more, then, we see the self-fulfilling nature of stereotypes. Many sex differences, it appears, may result from the images that people create in their attempts to act out accepted sex roles. The implication is that if stereotyped expectations about sex roles shift, behavior may change, too. In fact, statements by people who have undergone sex-change operations have highlighted the power of such expectations in easing adjustment to a new life. As the writer Jan Morris said in recounting the story of her transition from James to Jan: "The more I was treated as a woman, the more woman I became."

The power of stereotypes to cause people to confirm stereotyped expectations can also be seen in interracial relationships. In the first of two investigations done at Princeton University by Carl Word, Mark Zanna, and Joel Cooper, white undergraduates interviewed both white and black job applicants. The applicants were actually confederates of the experimenters, trained to behave consistently from interview to interview, no matter how the interviewers acted toward them.

To find out whether or not the white interviewers would behave differently toward white and black job applicants, the researchers secretly videotaped each interview and then studied the tapes. From these, it was apparent that there were substantial differences in the treatment accorded blacks and whites. For one thing, the interviewers speech deteriorated when they talked to blacks, displaying more errors in grammar and pronunciation. For another, the interviewers spent less time with blacks than with whites and showed less "immediacy," as the researchers called it, in their manner. That is, they were less friendly, less outgoing, and more reserved with blacks.

In the second investigation, white confederates were trained to approximate the immediate or the nonimmediate interview styles that had been observed in the first investigation as they interviewed white job applicants. A panel of judges who evaluated the tapes agreed that applicants subjected to the nonimmediate styles performed less adequately and were more nervous than job applicants treated in the immediate style. Apparently, then, the blacks in the first study did not have a chance to display their qualifications to the best advantage. Considered together, the two investigations suggest that in interracial encounters, racial stereotypes may constrain behavior in ways to cause both blacks and whites to behave in accordance with those stereotypes.

Rewriting Biography

Having adopted stereotyped ways of thinking about another person, people tend to notice and remember the ways in which that person seems to fit the stereotype, while resisting evidence that contradicts the stereotype. In one investigation that I conducted with Seymour Uranowitz, student subjects read a biography of a fictitious woman named Betty K. We constructed the story of her life so that it would fit the stereotyped images of both lesbians and heterosexuals. Betty, we wrote, never had a steady boyfriend in high school, but did go out on dates. And although we gave her a steady boyfriend in college, we specified that he was more of a close friend than anything else. A week after we had distributed this biography, we gave our subjects some new information about Betty. We told some students that she was now living with another woman in a lesbian relationship; we told others that she was living with her husband.

To see what impact stereotypes about sexuality would have on how people remembered the facts of Betty's life, we asked each student to answer a series of questions about her life history. When we examined their answers, we found that the students had reconstructed the events of Betty's past in ways that supported their own stereotyped beliefs about her sexual orientation. Those who believed that Betty was a lesbian remembered that Betty had never had a steady boyfriend in high school, but tended to neglect the fact that she had gone out on many dates in college. Those who believed that Betty was now a heterosexual tended to remember that she had formed a steady relationship with a man in college, but tended to ignore the fact that this relationship was more of a friendship than a romance.

The students showed not only selective memories but also a striking facility for interpreting what they remembered in ways that added fresh support for their stereotypes. One student who accurately remembered that a supposedly lesbian Betty never had a steady boyfriend in high school confidently pointed to the fact as an early sign of her lack of romantic or sexual interest in men. A student who correctly remembered that a purportedly lesbian Beth often went out on dates in college was sure that these dates were signs of Betty's early attempts to mask her lesbian interests.

Clearly, the students had allowed their preconceptions about lesbians and heterosexuals to dictate the way in which they interpreted and reinterpreted the facts of Betty's life. As long as stereotypes make it easy to bring to mind evidence that supports them and difficult to bring to mind evidence that undermines them, people will cling to erroneous beliefs.

Stereotypes in the Classroom and Work Place

The power of one person's beliefs to make other people conform to them has been well demonstrated in real life. Back in the 1960s, as most people well remember, Harvard psychologist Robert Rosenthal and his colleague Lenore Jacobson entered elementary-school classrooms and identified one out of every five pupils in each room as a child who could be expected to show dramatic improvement in intellectual achievement during the school year. What the teachers did not know was that the children had been chosen on a random basis. Nevertheless, something happened in the relationships between teachers and their supposedly gifted pupils that led the children to make clear gains in test performance.

It can also do so on the job. Albert King, now a professor of management at Northern Illinois University, told a welding instructor in a vocational training center that five men in his training program had unusually high aptitude. Although these five had been chosen at random   and knew nothing of their designation as high-aptitude workers, they showed substantial changes in performance. They were absent less often than were other

workers, learned the basics of the welder's trade in about half the usual time, and scored a full 10 points higher than other trainees on a welding test. Their gains were noticed not only by the researcher and by the welding instructor, but also by other trainees, who singled out the five as their preferred coworkers.

Might not other expectations influence the relationships between supervisors and workers? For example, supervisors who believe that men are better suited to some jobs and women to others may treat their workers (wittingly or unwittingly) in ways that encourage them to perform their jobs in accordance with stereotypes about differences between men and women. These same stereotypes may determine who gets which job in the first place. Perhaps some personnel managers allow stereotypes to influence, subtly or not so subtly, the way in which they interview job candidates, making it likely that candidates who fit the stereotypes show up better than job-seekers who do not fit them.

Unfortunately, problems of this kind are compounded by the fact that members of stigmatized groups often subscribe to stereotypes about themselves. That is what Amerigo Farina and his colleagues at the University of Connecticut found when they measured the impact upon mental patients of believing that others knew their psychiatric history. In Farina's study, each mental patient cooperated with another person in a game requiring teamwork. Half of the patients believed that their partners knew they were patients, the other half believed that their partners thought they were nonpatients. In reality, the nonpatients never knew a thing about anyone's psychiatric history. Nevertheless, simply believing that others were aware of their history led the patients to feel less appreciated, to find the task more difficult, and to perform poorly. In addition, objective observers saw them as more tense, more anxious, and more poorly adjusted than patients who believed that their status was not known. Seemingly, the belief that others perceived them as stigmatized caused them to play the role of stigmatized patients.

Consequences for Society

Apparently, good will and education are not sufficient to subvert the power of stereotypes. If people treat others in such a way as to bring out behavior that supports stereotypes, they may never have an opportunity to discover which of their stereotypes are wrong.

I suspect that even if people were to develop doubts about the accuracy of their stereotypes, chances are they would proceed to test them by gathering precisely the evidence that would appear to confirm them.

The experiments I have described help to explain the persistence of stereotypes. But, as is so often the case, solving one puzzle only creates another. If by acting as if false stereotypes were true, people lead others, too, to act as if they were true, why do the stereotypes not come to *be* true? Why, for example, have researchers found so little evidence that attractive people are generally friendly, sociable, and outgoing and that unattractive people are generally shy and aloof?

I think that the explanation goes something like this: Very few among us have the kind of looks that virtually everyone considers either very attractive or very unattractive. Our looks make us rather attractive to some people but somewhat less attractive to other people. When we spend time with those who find us attractive, they will tend to bring out our more sociable sides, but when we are with those who find us less attractive, they will bring out our less sociable sides. Although our actual physical appearance does not change, we present ourselves quite differently to our admirers and to our detractors. For our admirers we become attractive people, and for our detractors we become unattractive. This mixed pattern of behavior will prevent the development of any consistent relationship between physical attractiveness and personality.

Now that I understand some of the powerful forces that work to perpetuate social stereotypes, I can see a new mission for my research. I hope, on the one hand, to find out how to help people see the flaws in their stereotypes. On the other hand, I would like to help the victims of false stereotypes find ways of liberating themselves from the constraints imposed on them by other members of society.

Gender Stereotypes In
MTV Commercials: The Beat Goes On

Nancy Signorielli, Douglas McLeod, And Elaine Healy

Editors' Note: Over time we have experienced an increasing level of technical sophistication in the media. In this article the authors discuss how this growing technical sophistication has not necessarily led to an increase in gender equality as portrayed in the media. This study illustrates the negative media depictions of males and females. Our questions for you are: What are the consequences of these depictions? How do they impact the people who watch MTV?

This study examines gender portrayals and stereotyping in a sample of commercials on MTV. The findings revealed that characters in MTV commercials, like those in music videos, are stereotyped. Female characters appeared less frequently, had more beautiful bodies, were more physically attractive, wore more sexy and skimpy clothing, and were more often the object of another's gaze than their male counterparts.

Over the past 20 years, content analyses of television and its advertising have found that women are underrepresented and portrayed in stereotypical ways (Signorielli, 1985a). This study examines gender stereotyping in a genre not previously investigated: MTV commercials.

MTV commercials have been proclaimed as trendsetters in commercial advertising (Dalton, 1985; Gershon & Gantz, 1992). Despite their innovative contributions to advertising style, MTV commercials may have patterns of gender stereotyping found in other commercials. MTV has immense appeal for adolescents and young adults and has joined the other mass media as an influential agent of socialization. Advertisers have been drawn to MTV in order to associate their products with a medium on the cutting edge of the youth culture.

Gender Roles and Television Content

Studies have consistently found that commercials are stereotyped by gender (Courtney & Whipple, 1983; Signorielli, 1985a). Research conducted over the past 25 years has revealed that commercials in prime-time and weekend daytime children's programs rarely use a woman's voice as a voice-over.

Moreover, men are presented as authoritative, even for products used primarily by women (Bretl & Cantor, 1988; Dominick & Rauch, 1972; Lovdal, 1989; O'Donnell & O'Donnell, 1978). While men and women are more equally represented (in terms of numbers) in prime-time commercials, women are very underrepresented in commercials aired during children's programs (Doolittle & Pepper, 1975; Riffe, Goldson, Saxton, & Yu, 1989).

Some recent studies (Bretl & Cantor, 1988; Ferrante, Haynes, & Kingsley, 1988; Lovdal, 1989) have examined voice-overs, occupation of major characters, product spokespersons, and general product categories, comparing findings from recent samples of commercials with those of studies conducted in the 1970s. In short, these analyses found little overall change in the presentation of men and women in commercials aired during the prime-time hours.

Standards for attractiveness, particularly in commercials, also appear to be sexually stereotyped. For example, a content analysis of 4,294 commercials found some form of attractiveness message once every 3.8 commercials and that "attractiveness is more associated with women than with men and that men (via authoritative voice-overs) are forging this attractiveness-women link" (Downs & Harrison, 1985, p.17).

MTV, It's Audience, and Content

Almost 6 out of 10 television households receive MTV as part of their basic cable service (MTV Research, 1991). As MTV grew in popularity and its audience increased in size, companies who wanted to reach young people found that MTV was an important outlet for their commercial messages. In 1991, 80% of

MTV's audience was between the ages of 12 and 34. Moreover, one quarter of the audience was between the ages of 12 and 17, an adolescent audience much larger than that reported for other television networks (MTV Research, 1991). In addition, adolescent viewers spend an average of over two hours a day watching MTV (Sun & Lull, 1986).

Whereas research has not yet examined gender stereotyping in MTV commercials, several studies have analyzed the characters in music videos. For example, Brown and Campbell (1986), using a sample of music videos from MTV and BET (Black Entertainment Television), found that women and blacks were in the minority on MTV. White men were seen most often and usually were the center of attention, while women and blacks remained in the background. Similarly, Sherman and Dominick (1986) found that women and minorities were underrepresented in samples of music videos on MTV and on network television.

Vincent, Davis, and Boruszkowski (1987), using the consciousness scale developed by Pingree, Hawkins, Butler, and Paisley (1976), found that 56.9% of the portrayals of women in concept music videos (videos that told a story) were condescending. Overall, the depiction of gender roles was traditional, and sexism was high. In a follow-up study using samples of concept videos taken 18 months apart (Vincent, 1989), most of the videos had all male performers and portrayed women condescendingly. There was, however, a significant rise in the number of videos that presented women as "fully equal" to men between the videos taped during the summer of 1985 and those taped during the winter of 1986-1987, from 15.5% to 38.5%. Conversely, there were also small but significant increases in the amount of sexy or alluring clothing (lingerie, bathing suits) and nudity in the later sample as compared to the earlier one. Similarly, Seidman (1992) found that females were more likely than males to wear sexually revealing clothing. Finally, both males and females were portrayed in sex-typed occupations.

These findings to date focus only on the content in music videos themselves, not in the ads inserted into the programs. The study will extend the literature by examining gender portrayals in the ads on MTV The focus of this study is on the frequency and type of portrayals of females compared to males in the ads.

Two broad research questions guided the study. The first asks how men and women are portrayed in MTV commercials and hypothesizes that both men and women will be portrayed in stereotypical ways. Five specific hypotheses relating to gender images in MTV commercials were tested:

> Female characters will appear less frequently than male characters in MTV commercials.
>
> Female characters will be more likely than male characters to be portrayed as having very fit bodies.
>
> Female characters will be rated as more attractive than male characters.
>
> Female characters will be more likely than male characters to wear skimpy or sexy clothing.
>
> Female characters will be more likely than male characters to be the object of another's gaze.

The second research question focuses on whether commercials for different types of products have a male or female gender orientation. In short, are there recognizable differences in terms of the types of products that are associated with men and women?

Method

A sample of MTV commercials was recorded on videotape during five weekdays in mid-November 1991.[1] Six hours of MTV programming were recorded each day, half between the hours of 3:00 and 6:00 P.M. and half between the hours of 9:00 P.M. and midnight, the hours (after school and late evening) when adolescents are most likely to watch MTV.

In total, 550 commercials were recorded. Eliminating repeat commercials, the final sample consisted of 119 individual commercials. These commercials were equally likely to be found in the after-school and late evening hours. The high rate of repetition, both within and across the time parameters, implies that there is a greater likelihood that the images in these commercials will be seen (and perhaps remembered) by viewers. In order to reflect the actual content of the time frame in which the commercials were sampled, the data for each commercial were weighted by the number of times it appeared in the entire sample of 550 commercials.[2]

The recording instrument consisted of two separate units of analysis, the commercial and the major characters. A commercial was operationalized as an advertisement with the intent to sell or promote a product, service, event, etc. This operationalization excluded promotions relating to MTV itself, such as contests, surveys, and MTV programming. PSAs and other informational spots were also excluded.

The type of product (or service) advertised was coded using a 32-product coding scheme that was collapsed into six categories:

Personal products: appearance, hygiene, and health-related products *(n = 31 unweighted; 136 weighted).*

Entertainment: games, toys, musical equipment and accessories, and video game paraphernalia *(n = 26 unweighted; 121 weighted).*

Clothing & Accessories: clothes, shoes, handbags, jewelry, and like products *(n = 16 unweighted; 97 weighted).*

Media Products: books, magazines, movies, television shows, and like products *(n = 16 unweighted; 84 weighted).*

Food & Drink: both nutritious and non-nutritious foods, all restaurants, and alcoholic and non-alcoholic beverages *(n = 18 unweighted; 68 weighted).*

Other: cars, services, household products, and like products *(n = 12 unweighted; 35 weighted).*

Two separate measures of gender orientation were used. The first, visual gender makeup, was operationalized as the physical presence of males and/or females in the commercial. A commercial with a male gender makeup had only males present. A commercial with a female gender makeup had only females present. A neutral gender makeup commercial contained both males and females. Categorizing a commercial as "cannot code" meant that there were no characters. The second measure of gender orientation was the gender of the user of the product. A product user was operationalized as someone who held, demonstrated, touched, or was in any way physically associated with the product. These two measures isolated only male and only female orientations to focus on the most pure cases of gender orientation.[3]

The second unit of analysis was the major character (or characters) within a commercial. Major characters were operationalized as humans who were central to the action of the commercial; in short, a commercial's basic nature and selling intent would be changed if this character did not appear. Announcers were not considered characters unless they appeared visually in the commercial. Basic demographic information about the major characters was coded, including gender, race or ethnicity, and social age (stages of the life cycle, ranging from infancy to old age).

Physical attractiveness was assessed by four codings. The first item measured the body type or level of fitness and muscularity of the character. It had three values: (1) out of shape (poor posture, flabby, soft, weak), (2) average fitness (little or no focus on muscularity or the body), or (3) very fit (muscular). Second, the character was rated on a 5-point attractiveness scale, ranging from (1) repulsive/ugly to (5) very attractive (stunning, above average appeal). Attractiveness was defined as the apparent physical attractiveness of the character (as opposed to the actor/actress) as s/he was portrayed within the commercial. Coders relied on the commercial context in making attractiveness judgments focusing on how the producers framed the character in order to eliminate their own subjective assessments of physical attractiveness. Third, coders also judged whether the character wore skimpy or sexy clothing, using a 4-point scale ranging from (1) neutral (non-sexy) clothing to (4) outright nudity. The final attractiveness item assessed whether the character was set up as the object of other characters' attention or admiring gazes.

Fifty commercials (42% of the individual commercials) were selected and independently coded by two separate coders[4] in order to provide data for the reliability analysis. Intercoder agreement was estimated using Krippendorff's (1980) alpha. The following reliability coefficients were calculated: product type (.98); visual gender orientation (.94); gender orientation of the user (.89); gender (.96); race (.88); body type (.75); attractiveness (.91); sexy clothing (.86); and object of gaze (.75). All of these variables were nominal in nature except for two ordinal measures—body type and attractiveness.

Findings

The demographic makeup of the characters in MTV commercials parallels the distribution of characters in music videos (see, for example, Sherman & Dominick, 1986). Almost half of the characters (48.5%) were young adults (about 18 to 25 years), and a little more than a quarter (27.4%) were adults (about 26 to 60 years). Relatively few characters were portrayed as adolescents (11.1%) or as elderly (12.1%). Children (1.0%) were almost invisible in this sample. More than 9 out of 10 characters (95%) were white. The remaining 5% included all other racial/ethnic groups (black, 2.3%; Asian, 2.1%; Hispanic, 0.6%).

There was support for hypothesis 1. Males appeared slightly more often (54.4%) than females (45.6%) in the sampled MTV commercials ("goodness of fit" X^2 based on a 50/50 distribution was 4.1, df = 1, $p < .05$). There was also support for hypothesis 2. Women were more likely than men to be portrayed as having very fit or beautiful bodies, X^2 (2, N = 489) = 96.3, $p < .001$. Almost three quarters of the men were rated as having average bodies, while more than three quarters of female characters (77.4%) were rated as having very fit or beautiful bodies.

There was also support for hypothesis 3. Females were rated as more attractive than males, X^2 (3, N = 517) = 206.6, $p < .001$. More than half of male characters were placed in the middle category of the attractiveness scale, with slightly more than one third rated

as attractive. Hardly any male characters (2.2%) were rated as extremely attractive or beautiful. Conversely, more than half of female characters were rated as extremely attractive or beautiful, and almost one quarter were rated as attractive. Few female characters were rated as neutral in attractiveness (15.1%) or unattractive (8.0%).

Hypothesis 4 was also supported. Female characters were more likely than male characters to be portrayed wearing skimpy or sexy clothing, X^2 (2, N = 513) = 148.0, $p < .001$. The clothing worn by almost all (93.5%) male characters was rated as neutral. A small percentage of male characters (6.5%) were coded as wearing clothing that was somewhat sexy. While slightly less than half the women in the sample (46.2%) were coded as wearing neutral clothing, comparatively large percentages of women were coded as wearing somewhat sexy (24.4%) or very sexy (29.4%) clothing.

Finally, there was support for hypothesis 5. Female characters were more likely than male characters to be the object of another character's gaze, X^2 (1, N = 522) 94.7, $p < .001$. One out of five male characters (19.0%) was the object of another character's admiring gaze. In contrast 6 out of 10 female characters were the object of another's gaze. When one character directed his or her gaze upon another character the object of the gaze was a female almost three quarters of the time.

The second focus of the study examined the gender orientation of the commercials. The analysis revealed that a majority of the commercials were oriented toward both men and women in regard to the visual presentation of the sexes and the user of the product. When focusing, however, on those commercials that included only men or only women more commercials were oriented towards men than women. The measure of visual gender makeup indicated that 23.7% of the commercials had only males while 9.6% had only females. The measure of the gender of the user of the product revealed that in 4 out of 10 commercials only men touched, demonstrated, or were physically associated with the product. Women, on the other hand, were primary product users in 2 out of 10 commercials. For both measures purely male orientations were found over twice as many times as purely female orientations.

The relationship between gender roles and the type of product advertised in MTV commercials was examined by looking at the crosstabulations of the type of product advertised with two measures of gender orientation—(1) the visual gender orientation of the commercial and (2) the gender orientation of the user of the product.

For the relationship between the type of product advertised and the visual gender orientation of the commercial, most of the commercials had visual representations of both men and women (85.7% of media products; 62.5% of personal products; 57.4% of food products; 42.3% of clothing; and 31.4% of entertainment products).

When only one gender was represented, the gender was more likely to be a male than a female, except for commercials for personal products. For example, 38.1% of the commercials for clothing featured only men while only 15.5% of these commercials featured only women. Only males were seen in 32.3% of the commercials for entertainment products while 4.1% of these only featured women.

More than one tenth of the commercials showing only males were for food and drink, 7.0% were for media products, 28.9% for clothing, 30.5% for entertainment, and 17.2% for personal products. On the other hand, there was a somewhat different product distribution for commercials with only females. More than three quarters of these commercials were for personal products (55.8%) and clothing (28.8%) and one tenth were for entertainment products. Only 5% of the commercials showing only women advertised media or food-related products.

Commercials with only male product users were somewhat equally divided among the four categories, but with females almost three quarters of the commercials with only female product users were for personal products.

Personal products were the only type of commercials more likely to have female rather than male users (55.1% vs. 41.2%). More than half of entertainment commercials had male users and one third (33.1%) had no specific user. Clothing commercials usually had male (39.2%) or both male and female users (30.9%). Similarly almost half of the commercials for food or drinks were classified as having both male and female users. Finally, more than 6 out of 10 commercials for media products could not be classified by the specific gender of the user.

Discussion

Commercials on MTV are gender-stereotyped. Even though a large percentage of commercials were geared toward both men and women, the data consistently revealed that when one gender was the target of a commercial, the target was typically male. The visual gender makeup of the commercial and the gender of the user had more than twice as many only male commercials as only female commercials. It is particularly interesting to note that males were far more likely than females to handle or control the object being advertised. This may reveal a bias on the part of advertisers that males are more effectively associated with the strengths of a particular product than females.

The types of products classified as male and female also revealed a gender bias. The product type most often oriented toward males was entertainment-related. In contrast, the product type most often oriented toward females was personal products—products with the primary purpose of improving or enhancing the physical attractiveness of the buyer. While commercials with only male characters included products reflecting fun and action, commercials with only female characters focused on products related to looking good. These gender associations with particular product types reveal that in regard to the specific users of the products and the visual nature of the commercials there were stereotypical designations of women's and men's roles.

The analyses of character attributes also revealed that commercials on MTV were filled with stereotypical information about gender roles. Female characters in these commercials appeared less frequently, had more beautiful bodies, were more physically attractive, wore more sexy and skimpy clothing, and were more often the object of another's gaze than male characters. All of these findings supported the idea that visual attention was highly emphasized for female characters. The portrayals in these commercials reveal a disturbing message: The primary purpose of women's effort is to "look good" and to be the object of the visual attention of others.

This study revealed that despite MTV's status as a "cutting edge" genre of television, MTV's advertisers continue to utilize stereotyped images and appeals in their commercials. Consequently, the messages about gender roles that adolescents might learn from MTV commercials uphold traditional restrictive views of men and women. On the whole the findings of this study, while examining somewhat different variables, corroborate findings from recent content analyses of commercials in prime-time programs illustrating the persistence of sex-role stereotypes (Bretl & Cantor, 1988; Ferrante et al., 1988; Lovdal, 1989).

This study indicated that MTV commercials preserve and perpetuate stereotypes about women. If adolescents, as is likely, utilize MTV as a source of social learning about gender roles, then they receive warped views of the roles and responsibilities of women in society. While we cannot say there is a causal relationship between commercial content and social problems like rape, eating disorders, and discrimination in the workplace, MTV commercials in no way contribute to a reduction of misconceptions about women and women's roles in society. As a popular maxim states, "If you're not part of the solution, you're part of the problem."

Notes

1. The choice of a week-long sample may be a limitation of the study. This decision, however, was based upon the methodology of previous content analyses of television content, many of which have used week-long samples (see, for example, Bretl & Cantor, 1988; Downs & Harrison, 1985; O'Donnell & O'Donnell, 1978; Signorielli, 1985b).
2. Analyses conducted on the weighted and unweighted data sets yielded similar findings. The weighted data are reported because they represent a more realistic approximation of the imagery seen during a week of viewing.
3. Commercials with mixed genders and those without characters were not included in the product user coding schemes.
4. All of the commercials were coded by the third author; the second coding for the reliability analysis was completed by two other (one male and one female) master's students at the University of Delaware.

References

Bretl, D. J., & Cantor, J. (1988). The portrayal of men and women in U.S. television commercials: A recent content analysis and trends over 15 years. *Sex Roles, 18*, 595-609.

Brown, J. D., & Campbell, K. (1986). Race and gender in music videos: The same beat but a different drummer. *Journal of Communication, 36*(1), 94-106.

Courtney, A. E., & Whipple, T. W. (1983). *Sex stereotyping in advertising,* Lexington, MA: Lexington Books.

Dalton, J. (1985, December). The televisionary. *Esquire*, pp. 380-387.

Dominick, J. R., & Rauch, G. E. (1972). The image of women in network TV commercials. *Journal of Broadcasting, 16*, 259-265.

Doolittle, J., & Pepper, R. (1975). Children's TV ad content: 1974. *Journal of Broadcasting, 19*, 131-142.

Downs, A. C., & Harrison, S. K. (1985). Embarrassing age spots or just plain ugly? Physical attractiveness stereotyping as an instrument of sexism on American television commercials. *Sex Roles, 13*, 9-19.

Ferrante, C. L., Haynes, A. M., & Kingsley, S. M. (1988). Image of women in television advertising. *Journal of Broadcasting & Electronic Media, 32*, 231-237.

Gershon, P. R., & Gantz, W. (1992, May). Music videos and television commercials: A comparison of production styles. Paper presented to the annual conference of the International Communication Association, Miami, FL.

Krippendorff, K. (1980). *Content analysis: An introduction to its methodology*. Beverly Hills, CA:Sage.

Lovdal, L. T. (1989). Sex role messages in television commercials: An update. *Sex Roles, 21*, 715-724.

MTV Research. (1991). *Marketing report*. New York: Time Warner.

O'Donnell, W. J., & O'Donnell, K. J. (1978). Update: Sex-role messages in TV commercials. *Journal of Communication, 28*(1), 156-158.

Pingree, S., Hawkins, R. P., Butler, M., & Paisley, W. (1976). A scale for sexism. *Journal of Communication, 26*(4), 193-200.

Riffe, D., Goldson, H., Saxton, K., & Yu, Y. C. (1989). Females and minorities in TV ads in 1987 Saturday children's programs. *Journalism Quarterly, 66*, 129-136.

Seidman, S. A. (1992). An investigation of sex-role stereotyping in music videos. *Journal of Broadcasting & Electronic Media, 36*, 209-216.

Sherman, B. L., & Dominick, J. R. (1986). Violence and sex in music videos: TV and rock 'n' roll. *Journal of Communication, 36*(1), 79-93.

Signorielli, N. (1985a). *Role portrayal and stereotyping on television: An annotated bibliography of studies relating to women, minorities, aging, sexual behavior, health, and handicaps*. Westport, CT: Greenwood.

Signorielli, N. (1985b). The measurement of violence in television programming: Violence indices. In J. R.

Dominick & J. E. Fletcher (Eds.), *Broadcasting research methods* (pp. 235-251). Boston: Allyn & Bacon.

Sun, S. W., & Lull, J. (1986). The adolescent audience for music videos and why they watch. *Journal of Communication, 36*(1), 115-125.

Vincent, R. C. (1989). Clio's consciousness raised? Portrayal of women in rock videos, re-examined. *Journalism Quarterly, 66*, 155-160.

Vincent, R. C., Davis, D. K., & Boruszkowski, L.A. (1987). Sexism on MTV: The portrayal of women in rock videos. *Journalism Quarterly, 64*, 750-755, 941.

Gender, And Other Stereotypes:
Race, Age, Appearance, Disability
Hilary M. Lips

Editors' Note: What image comes to mind when you are asked to imagine a "typical" woman? Most of us do not think of a woman who is elderly, disabled, or who is not white. Research examining the interplay between gender, racial, and ethnic stereotypes (as well as stereotypes about the elderly and disabled) suggests that stereotypes are not applied in the same way for men and women within an ethnic group. Lips describes several of these interactions between stereotypes, suggesting that social psychological research must take a broader view of stereotypes in order to account for these interactions.

When an individual completing a questionnaire to measure male-female stereotyping is asked about the "typical" woman or man, what kind of person comes to mind? An elderly black woman? A middle-aged Native American man confined to a wheelchair? A young woman who has trouble finding stylish clothing because she weighs 200 pounds? Most likely, the image is influenced by the persons tendency to define "typical" with reference to the self and the people most visible in the environment. Probably, as [H.] Landrine suggests, research participants cannot imagine a woman (or man) "without attributing a race, a social class, an age, and even a degree of physical attractiveness to the stimulus." The image, at least in North America, is likely to be of someone who is relatively young, white, able-bodied, neither too fat nor too thin, neither too short nor too tall, of average physical attractiveness. Thus, it is more than likely that our studies of the stereotypes that accompany gender are based on generalizations that systematically exclude middle-aged and old people, Asians, blacks, Chicanos, native peoples, disabled people, fat people, and people whose appearance diverges markedly from the norm. It is also likely that in holding to gender stereotypes based on the so-called typical man or woman, our society creates added difficulties for individuals already victimized by racism, ageism, an intolerance of disability, or society's obsession with attractiveness and thinness.

Gender Stereotypes and Racism

It is only in recent years that researchers have tried to understand the workings of racism and sexism by comparing the experiences of different gender-race groups. It has been noted, for example, that the forms of racism directed at black women and black men may differ, and that sexism may be expressed toward and experienced by a woman differently as a function of her race.

According to the stereotypes held by the larger society, black women may be judged as less "feminine" than white women. Indeed, there appears to be a persistent stereotype of black women in the social science literature that encompasses strength, self-reliance, and a strong achievement orientation and [J.] Fleming has documented the existence of a "black matriarchy" theory among social scientists suggesting that black women are more dominant, assertive, and self-reliant than black males. While such a stereotype may appear positive at first glance, the narrow labeling of black women's strengths as "matriarchal" represents a refusal to conceptualize strong women in anything but a family context. Moreover, there has been a tendency to blame black women's strong, assertive behavior for some of the problems experienced by black men—a tendency that surely reflects stereotypic notions about what kinds of behavior are "proper" for women. Fleming's own investigations indicate that the black matriarchy theory is based largely on flawed or misleading evidence. She suggests that this particular stereotype may have arisen from the fact that "their long history of instrumentality in the service of family functioning may well have built in black women an air of self-reliance that arouses further stereotyping among those (largely white) social scientists more accustomed to white traditional norms for women."

Studies of gender stereotyping within racial groups other than whites are fairly rare. [V.E.] O'Leary and [A.0.] Harrison, comparing the gender stereotypes of black and white women and men, found that blacks endorsed fewer items that discriminated between the sexes than whites did, and that black respondents were less likely than whites to devalue females on stereotypic grounds. White subjects of both sexes rated the white woman more negatively than the black woman was rated by black subjects.

In an attempt to determine whether the often reported stereotype of women is actually just a stereotype of middle-class white women, Landrine asked undergraduates to use a list of 23 adjectives to describe the stereotype of each of four groups of women: black and white middle-class women and black and white working-class women. She found that while the stereotypes differed significantly by both race, and social class, with white women and middle-class women being described in ways most similar to traditional stereotypes of women, all four groups were rated in ways consistent with the feminine stereotype. White women were described as higher than black women on the most traditional of stereotypical terms: dependent, emotional, and passive. However, both groups were rated similar on many other adjectives: ambitious, competent, intelligent, self-confident, and hostile, for example. The findings suggest that race and social class are implicit in what have been described as gender stereotypes, but that to some extent, there is a set of expectations for women that transcends these variables.

Gender Stereotypes and Age

The stereotypes of femininity and masculinity seem to apply most strongly to the young. As they age, both women and men describe themselves in less stereotypic terms, and older men rate older women as more active, involved, hardy, and stable than themselves.

Perhaps the reason why gender stereotypes become less pronounced for older people is that age stereotypes replace them. One of the widely accepted stereotypes about the elderly is that they are no longer interested in sexuality. But sexuality is one of the major underpinnings of social expectations about gender. One of the main reasons for a man to be masculine is to be sexually attractive to women, and vice versa. If sexuality becomes irrelevant, so, in a sense, do masculinity and femininity. While studies show that sexuality is *not;* in fact, irrelevant to older people, perhaps one accidentally beneficial consequence of this myth is that it is a partial release from the restrictions of gender stereotypes.

On the other hand, many writers have noted that there is a "double standard" of aging that places older women at a disadvantage with respect to older men. Since in contemporary North American society so much of a woman's worth tends to be defined in terms of her physical attractiveness to men, the aging woman may find that along with her "femininity" she is losing her value as a person. The changes in physical appearance that accompany aging, while often considered acceptable or even "distinguished" in men, move women farther and farther from current definitions of female beauty. For women, who often have few other sources of power and prestige than their attractiveness, these changes can signify a slide into decreasing social worth. Older men, who are less likely to have to rely on their appearance for power and prestige, may have wider access to sources of social worth through occupational achievement, money, and even relationships with younger women.

Research suggests that women who abandon the strict constraints of gender stereotypes to make nontraditional choices while they are young may find themselves better equipped than their more traditional counterparts to handle old age. Among 70-year-old women, work-centered mothers showed higher life satisfaction than women who were more exclusively family focused, and among women in their sixties, the most feminine women were the most critical of themselves.

Appearance

Psychologists have become increasingly aware that physical appearance is a critical aspect of stereotyping. In terms of gender stereotypes, physical appearance may have strong implications for how masculine or feminine a person is thought to be. Many a tall, broad-shouldered woman has slouched and crouched through life in a vain effort to appear petite and thus "feminine," and many a short man has quietly cursed his diminutive stature because it seemed to detract from his ability to project a "masculine" image.

While physical appearance is important to both males and females, beauty is generally defined as a peculiarly feminine attribute, and preoccupation with one's appearance is seen as part of the feminine stereotype. In a recent exploration of the concept of femininity, Susan Brown-Miller illustrates the powerful role played by physical appearance in cultural definitions of femininity. In various times and places, aspects of the female anatomy have become supposed signals of how feminine and how sexual a woman is. For example, she notes the way that others react to a young woman's breast development:

"Parents and relatives mark their appearance as a landmark event, schoolmates take notice, girl-friends compare, boys zero in; later a husband, a lover, a baby expect a proprietary share. No other part of the human anatomy has such semi-public, intensely private status. . . ." Why all the fuss? Brown-Miller argues that breasts are used as a prime cue to a woman's sexuality. She notes the myth that a flat-chested woman is nonsexual and that a woman with large breasts is flaunting her sexuality and seeking attention. Small wonder that women sometimes become intensely self-conscious about this part of their anatomy!

Perhaps no aspect of appearance is the cause of more grief in our own society right now than weight. Dieting has become a North American obsession, with an estimated 52 million adults in the United States either dieting or contemplating a diet at any one time. Being fat is a subject of special concern to women. Thinness is a major aspect of the definition of attractiveness, and attractiveness increases perceived femininity. When female university students were asked what kinds of activities or situations would make them feel less feminine, by far the most frequently checked item was "being overweight," endorsed by more than 50% of the sample. So highly charged is the issue of weight for women that according to [E.] Hatfield and [S.]

Sprecher women respondents in the early Kinsey surveys of sexual practices were more embarrassed when asked their weight than when asked "How often do you masturbate?" or "Have you ever had a homosexual affair?"

Research shows that physical attractiveness is a more central part of the self-concept for women than for men. Moreover, a test of a sample of college undergraduates indicated that weight and body shape, while important to men, were the *central* determinants of women's perception of their physical attractiveness. Women are less satisfied with their bodies than are men: College women report a greater discrepancy between their actual and ideal body image than men do. And women have good reason to be concerned about their weight and shape: Obesity seems to trigger more negative evaluations for women than for men. Researchers who showed silhouettes of fat and thin women and men to hundreds of passersby at a summer fair found that fat men were rated significantly less negatively than were fat women, while thin women were rated less negatively than their male counterparts.

There is some evidence that even among women who have rejected many of the traditional norms of femininity, the obsession with slenderness continues to exert a powerful force. Women who value nontraditional roles for women prefer a smaller, thinner female body shape and associate a larger, rounder form with the "wife and mother" stereotype.

Gender and Disability

While the general stereotype of persons with disabilities involves helplessness, dependence, social isolation, and suffering, this stereotype seems to be moderated by the gender of the person with the disability. For women, who are already stereotyped as more passive and dependent than men, the disability stereotype can act to reinforce the image of dependence. Indeed, newly disabled women are far more likely than their male counterparts to be advised by their physicians to retire from paid employment. For men, on the other hand, the dependence on others that many disabilities enforce is perceived as a threat to their masculine image.

Physical attractiveness is another area in which gender and disability stereotypes interact. We have already noted that physical attractiveness is more central to femininity than to masculinity; it is also apparent that a woman who is visibly disabled, even if not disfigured in any way, falls short of the cultural ideal of beauty. Here, for example, is the reaction of a former executive of the Miss Universe contest to the notion of a paraplegic woman as a contestant: "Her participation in a beauty contest would be like having a blind man compete in a shooting match." However, 1987 saw the first entry of a wheelchair-bound woman, Maria Serrao, in a major American beauty contest.

Like the elderly, persons with disabilities are often stereotyped as asexual. However, even the slowly growing public awareness that disability does not imply a lack of sexual needs or interest has been channeled by gender stereotypes that say that sex is more important to men than to women. Much more has been studied and written on the subject of sexuality among disabled men than disabled women. However, statistics indicate that the popular presumption that disabled women are asexual does not protect them from sexual assault. In fact, disabled women may be more likely than other women to be sexually assaulted. Children of both sexes are at high risk for sexual abuse if they are disabled, because they are often less able to get away from an abuser and/or unable to communicate to others about what is happening. During both childhood and adulthood, females with disabilities are more likely than their nondisabled counterparts to experience sexual or physical abuse. In one small-scale study, 67% of disabled women, as compared to 34% of nondisabled women, reported that they had been physically abused or battered as children.

Gender stereotypes are pervasive, interacting with other stereotypes to shape social perceptions of persons of various races, ages, abilities, and appearances. Gender stereotyping both grows out of and reinforces the social relations between women and men, [and] the way it works is both complete and subtle.

Stereotypes Of Women And Men From Different Ethnic Groups

Shelley E. Taylor, Letitia A. Peplau, and David O. Sears

> **Editors' Note:** As Lips notes, stereotypes can interact so that males and females from the same ethnic group may not be viewed in the same way. One way researchers tap into these effects is to have people list characteristics of different groups. The data in this table illustrate the different stereotypes that are held for males and females from various ethnic groups. These data also show that we cannot assume that all women or all Mexican Americans, for example, are viewed the same way.

Table 6-1

WOMEN	MEN
AFRICAN AMERICAN	**AFRICAN AMERICAN**
Speak loudly	Athletic
Dark skin	Antagonistic
Antagonistic	Dark skin
Athletic	Muscular appearance
Pleasant/friendly	Criminal activities
ANGLO AMERICAN	**ANGLO AMERICAN**
Attractive	Intelligent
Intelligent	Egotistical
Egotistical	Upper class
Pleasant/friendly	Pleasant/friendly
Blond/light hair	Racist
ASIAN AMERICAN	**ASIAN AMERICAN**
Intelligent	Intelligent
Speak softly	Short
Pleasant/friendly	Achievement oriented
Short	Speak softly
	Hard workers
MEXICAN AMERICAN	**MEXICAN AMERICAN**
Black/brown/dark hair	Lower class
Attractive	Hard workers
Pleasant/friendly	Antagonistic
Dark skin	Dark skin
Lower class	Non-college education

Note: The table presents the most common terms (or synonyms) used by college students to describe members of each group.

Source: Data are from Niemann, Jennings, Rozelle, Baxter, and Sullivan (1994), p. 20.

In Japan, Blood Type Can Be Key To Success — Or Failure

Kevin Sullivan

Editors' Note: Many of us are quite familiar with the stereotypes that are pervasive in American culture. This article examines a common group of stereotypes that many in Japan hold about people. These are stereotypes based not on gender, race, or ethnicity but on a person's blood type. This article also demonstrates how unchangeable biological characteristics can be given a meaning in one culture that they do not have in another, and how through the meaning they are given, they can become the basis of stereotypes. What are some biological characteristics that form the basis of stereotypes in the United States?

TOKYO—Mika Matsui finds out on the first date. First two hours, max. There's no sense getting your hopes up if Mr. Wonderful is the wrong blood type.

Her last boyfriend was type O. Never again. O's are way too needy. Type A's are too boring. B's are sweet, but they don't like her. So it's the AB man she's looking for because "he's interesting to talk to, very kind and very nice."

"I don't believe in horoscopes, but I think blood type describes character most accurately," said Matsui, 29, a clerical worker for a large Tokyo company "Check it out yourself."

Japan has an obsession with blood types. The blood in your veins is supposed to determine how well you live and love, how well you manage money, whether you will succeed at marriage or sumo wrestling. Great marriages or lousy careers are attributed to blood type.

Newspaper and magazine profiles of major political candidates always include their blood type. Job applications often ask for blood type. During World War II, Japan's imperial army and navy are said to have formed battle groups by blood type. The manager of a Japanese major league baseball team studies his players' blood types. Japanese television this year carried a sitcom about the life of a businessman called *I Am Type O.*

The Japanese buy almost 2-million blood type condoms every year.

"This is a little farfetched, but according to the survey we conducted, it was reported that the type A tends to have a very simple attitude toward sex, so we took a clue from that," said Katsuyoshi Yatsunagi, spokesman for Jex, the company that manufactures the condoms. Thus, type A condoms are standard shape, come in pink only and are 0.03 millimeters thick. Condoms for type B are slightly narrower, thicker and ribbed. For type O, the condoms are covered with a diamond-shaped pattern. Yatsunagi said he wasn't sure how colors figured into the blood type theory.

Estelle Viskovich, a stylist at the Sin Den, a popular Tokyo beauty salon, said all new customers are asked to fill out a questionnaire that includes blood type. "We thought it was cute to ask," said Viskovich, an Australian. "We think it's weird if you don't know your star sign; the Japanese think it's weird if you don't know your blood type."

Telling a Japanese person you don't know your blood type invites suspicion, Viskovich said: "It's like you're withholding information."

A Japanese company, Pokka Corp., marketed soft drinks by blood type a couple of years ago. Company spokesman Toshihiko Tarutani said the soda was intended to be little more than a "fun" marketing gimmick, but it sold more than 1.4 million cases a year in 1993 and 1994.

There are key chains and chewing gum, calendars, magazines and books, all geared toward the blood type phenomenon. While schoolgirls are the chief consumers of most products categorized by blood type, some of Japan's biggest corporations have looked into increasing their productivity by creating single-type work groups. One of the most influential companies in the country, Mitsubishi Electric Corp., created a project development team of five ABs who were supposed to be creative and enterprising. The team was called the "Fantastic Project" and

What Type Are You?

Selected supposed traits of the blood type:

TYPE A
Positive traits: Orderly law-abiding, fastidious, soft-spoken, fashionable, calm.
Negative traits: Picky, selfish, secretive, pessimistic, inflexible, reckless when drunk.
Suitable careers: Accountant, librarian, economist, novelist, computer programmer, gossip columnist.

TYPE B
Positive: Independent, flexible, candid, sensitive, passionate, persuasive.
Negative: Unpredictable, indiscreet, lazy, impatient, overbearing, can't wake up.
Suitable careers: Cook, hairdresser, military leader, talk show host, journalist, golfer.

Type AB
Positive: Rational, calculating, honest, diplomatic, organized, strong ESP.
Negative: Unforgiving, playboy, easily offended, too conservative, nitpicker, hard to know.
Suitable careers: Bartender, attorney, teacher, sales representative, social worker, witch.

TYPE O
Positive: Healthy, idealistic, goal-oriented, clear-sighted, good at sports, sexy.
Negative: Status-seeking, jealous, greedy, unreliable, obsessive lover, can't shut up.
Suitable careers: Banker, politician, gambler, minister, investment broker, baseball player.

Source: "You Are Your Blood Type," by Toshitaka Nomi and Alexander Besher.

was eventually disbanded without producing much more than publicity. Toshitaka Nomi, whose 30 books on blood types have sold more than 6 million copies in Japan, has been asked to give more than 1,000 speeches at some of Japan's biggest corporations, including Hitachi, Toyota, Nissan and several major banks. Nomi gave many of the speeches at training seminars where his theories were being studied as a potential management tool.

A person's blood type is determined by what kind of antigen, a type of protein, he has on the surface of his red blood cells. If a person has an A antigen, his blood is type A; if he has a B antigen, he's type B. People with both are type AB, and those with neither are type O. The most common type is O, followed by A, B and AB.

There is not one molecule of solid scientific evidence that blood type is related to character. Scientists say blood type is about as relevant to personality as hair color is to snorkeling ability. Of course, that's what they say about horoscopes, too—but it didn't stop Nancy Reagan from planning the president's schedule around his stars. And it hasn't stopped the Japanese from believing in blood types.

"All culture is not based upon Western science," said Marc Micozzi, a physician and director of the National Museum of Health and Medicine at Walter Reed Army Medical Center in Washington. John Stone, a cardiologist at the Emory University School of Medicine who also writes poetry said he "would not go to the mat" for the Japanese blood type theories. But the artist in him likes it: "It's a straw; we're all clutching at straws to try to explain ourselves."

According to Nomi's book *You Are Your Blood Type,* type O's are powerful leaders, goal-oriented, enthusiastic, optimistic and good at business. Famous O's include Ronald Reagan, Queen Elizabeth, Prince Charles and Al Capone.

Type A's, according to Nomi, are perfectionist, orderly, detail-oriented industrious, idealistic, soft-spoken and careful. Former presidents Jimmy Carter, Lyndon Johnson and Richard Nixon shared A blood, if not much else. Despite much that separates them, Adolf Hitler was and Pope John Paul II is type A. And some of the most famous blood in recent history was type A: that of O.J. Simpson and his late ex-wife, Nicole Brown Simpson.

Nomi says type B's are flexible, passionate, creative, unconventional and have excellent concentration, like golfer Jack Nicklaus. Type ABs are supposed to be natural leaders, great organizers, diplomatic, rational and imaginative. John Kennedy and Marilyn Monroe shared AB blood.

"For the moment, we don't know why this is happening," Nomi said. "But we have so much evidence that links blood type to character, the next step is for the scientists to find out what causes this."

Japanese psychologists and social scientists have been proposing and exploring blood type theories since the 1920s. The Japanese public has always been receptive, but it wasn't until Nomi's father came along that blood types became a national obsession.

In 1971, Masahiko Nomi published a book on the subject based on 25 years of personal observations about blood type and character. When the book sold 1.2 million copies, the Nomi family got into the blood type business for good.

They started sending out questionnaires, asking blood type and a series of questions designed to reveal personality traits. Since 1971 they have sent seven major questionnaires and elicited responses from nearly 250,000 people; those responses are the bricks and mortar of Toshitaka Nomi's writings. About 15 years ago, he said, he sent a questionnaire to every member of Japan's Parliament and received responses from 98 percent of them. (The members were disproportionately type O, the classic leadership type.)

"I would say more than half the Japanese people are very interested in blood types," Nomi said, "see some truth in it and are prepared to use it in their daily life."

✓ PROJECT 6.1
Laurie Or Larry? Gender Stereotypes Of Babies

I.   "Is it a boy or a girl?" People make judgments about babies immediately after they learn its sex. These judgments are based on stereotypes about males and females, and they are an example of how quickly we can form and use stereotypes. In this project, have four different people look at the pictures of the baby. Then, each will complete the rating sheet about the baby. Have two of the people complete the rating sheets where the baby is identified as Laurie, and the other two people complete those sheets where the baby's name is Larry.

II.   Add up the responses for the two people who rated Laurie and then add up the responses for the two who rated Larry. Once you have done this, answer the following questions:

Did you find any differences between the ratings? _____

If you did find differences, what was the nature of these differences?

_____

_____

_____

_____

Did you find anything that could be used to illustrate the nature of gender stereotypes as they are applied to babies? If yes, how?

_____

_____

_____

_____

How do you think these gender steretypes influence a child's development?

_____

_____

_____

_____

*This project is adapted from the research of Broverman et al. (1970) and is based on a similar project by Bolt and Myers (1994).

Detecting Infant Traits

Can infant traits be detected from their physical appearance and nonverbal behavior? After looking at the pictures on page 214, what impressions do you get of Laurie, who is shown at the ages of two months (left) and five months (right)?

Please look at the pictures, and then rate Laurie on each of the following characteristics.

1	2	3	4	5	6	7	8	9
firm								soft

1	2	3	4	5	6	7	8	9
big								little

1	2	3	4	5	6	7	8	9
strong								weak

1	2	3	4	5	6	7	8	9
hardy								delicate

1	2	3	4	5	6	7	8	9
well-coordinated								awkward

1	2	3	4	5	6	7	8	9
beautiful								plain

Detecting Infant Traits

Can infant traits be detected from their physical appearance and nonverbal behavior? After looking at the pictures on page 214, what impressions do you get of Larry, who is shown at the ages of two months (left) and five months (right)?

Please look at the pictures, and then rate Larry on each of the following characteristics.

| 1 | 2 | 3 | 4 | 5 | 6 | 7 | 8 | 9 |
| firm | | | | | | | | soft |

| 1 | 2 | 3 | 4 | 5 | 6 | 7 | 8 | 9 |
| big | | | | | | | | little |

| 1 | 2 | 3 | 4 | 5 | 6 | 7 | 8 | 9 |
| strong | | | | | | | | weak |

| 1 | 2 | 3 | 4 | 5 | 6 | 7 | 8 | 9 |
| hardy | | | | | | | | delicate |

| 1 | 2 | 3 | 4 | 5 | 6 | 7 | 8 | 9 |
| well-coordinated | | | | | | | | awkward |

| 1 | 2 | 3 | 4 | 5 | 6 | 7 | 8 | 9 |
| beautiful | | | | | | | | plain |

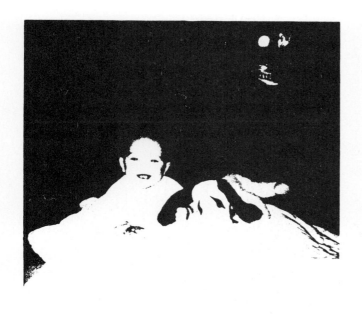

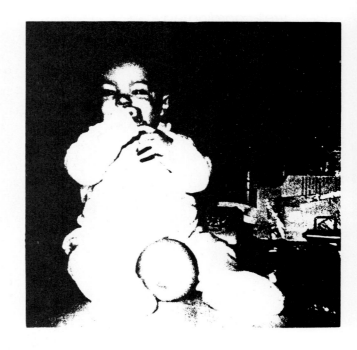

✓ PROJECT 6.2
Measuring Stereotypes

I.   In this project, you will develop a measure of stereotypes. Begin by choosing two or more groups of people for which stereotypes may be held, focusing on owners of various types of cars (e.g., sports cars versus minivan owners).

II. Next, make a list of terms that might be used to characterize the groups you have chosen. Whether you disagree with these generalizations or not, you might want to use them to study stereotypes of car owners. Select characteristics that you, other students, and the mass media have used to typify your groups. A representative list should include at least 30 characteristics, half positive and half negative. If the characteristics presented to participants in a study are predominantly negative, a negative stereotype will be more likely to result, possibly leading you to an incorrect view of the stereotypes you are studying.

III. For the third step, construct materials for collecting data. These include (1) a list of characteristics you have chosen, with positive and negative terms interspersed, and (2) instructions for subjects, explaining the several tasks to be performed with your list. Use the instructions on the next page, adapting them to fit your groups.

IV. Fourth, give your stereotype questionnaire to 6 different people (preferably people who own different types of cars).

V.   Finally, analyze the responses to the data you have collected. Write a one-page report of your findings, describing whether or not there was consistency in the words circled, the percentages given, and the confidence with which people made their ratings. Were any of your findings affected by which type of car your participants owned? Discuss the advantages and limitations of creating and using this type of stereotype questionnaire.

*This project is adapted from King and Ziegler (1975).

Stereotype Questionnaire

Part I. Below the name of each group you will find a list of words. Read through the list of words and select those which seem to you to be typical of the particular group written at the top of the list.

Circle as many of these words as you think are necessary to describe these people adequately. If you do not find adequate words on the list you may add those you think are necessary for adequate description.

Group I Name

_____   _____   _____

_____   _____

_____   _____

_____   _____

_____   _____

_____   _____

_____   _____

_____   _____

Group II Name

_____   _____   _____

_____   _____

_____   _____

_____   _____

_____   _____

_____   _____

_____   _____

_____   _____

Part II. Now, for each group, go back to the words you have circled. Place a check after the five terms you feel are the most typical of the group.

Part III. Do you own either of the two types of cars? If you do, write on the questionnaire page which type of car you own.

✓ PROJECT 6.3
America's History As Reflected In Memorabilia

I. Kenneth Goings (1990) has described how memorabilia has perpetuated stereotypes about African Americans. He points out that everyday objects and memorabilia are a window into American history, revealing dreams, achievements, and stereotypes. As an example, he describes how after World War I, black women were portrayed in the "Jemima/mammy motif: fat, silent, nurturing and taking care of the masses." In other examples, many souvenirs for the state of Texas portray white men in cowboy hats, and songs about California give the impression that everyone lives on the beach.

II. For this project, please find three artifacts—they can be memorabilia, souvenirs, pictures, books, songs, etc. For each piece, answer the following questions:

ARTIFACT 1:
What is the artifact?

_____

What period in history is it portraying (current items are acceptable)?

_____

_____

What group(s) is portrayed in the artifact?

_____

_____

What stereotypes about the group are being presented?

_____

_____

How do you think this stereotype reflected the stereotypes present at that time in American culture?

_____

_____

_____

ARTIFACT 2:
What is the artifact?

_____

What period in history is it portraying (current items are acceptable)?

_____

_____

What group(s) is portrayed in the artifact?

_____

_____

What stereotypes about the group are being presented?

_____

_____

How do you think this stereotype reflected the stereotypes present at that time in American culture?

_____

_____

_____

ARTIFACT 3:
What is the artifact?

_____

What period in history is it portraying (current items are acceptable)?

_____

_____

What group(s) is portrayed in the artifact?

_____

_____

What stereotypes about the group are being presented?

_____

_____

How do you think this stereotype reflected the stereotypes present at that time in American culture?

_____

_____

_____

C h a p t e r 7

The Prejudiced Mind: Biased Attitudes And Gender, Race, And Ethnicity

In the last chapter, we examined stereotyping, the factors that impact us when we use stereotypes, how effective we are in reducing our use of them, and how stereotypes are culturally constructed. A consistent theme in these articles was that stereotypes can dramatically affect our thoughts and behavior. In this chapter, focusing on prejudice, we more closely examine the biased thoughts that we have about people from different gender, racial, and ethnic groups.

A student recently asked, "Why study prejudice? People are not nearly as prejudiced as they used to be." The question is a good one for clearly some of the most overt and obvious forms of prejudice have lessened in the United States compared to its recent past. However, current social psychological research tells us that even though prejudice may be less obvious now than in the past, people still hold negative attitudes toward people in other groups. These beliefs are less likely to be communicated directly.

The articles in this chapter examine the causes of prejudice, highlighting the contributions of cognitive categorization processes, along with socialization and motivational forces. The first reading by Elliot Aronson and his colleagues describes a classic demonstration in which seemingly arbitrary characteristics became the basis of stereotypes and prejudice. Next, a chapter from Gordon Allport's classic book *On the Nature of Prejudice* presents an extremely influential definition of prejudice. The reading that follows, by Patricia Devine, is an example of recent research exploring how cognitive processes can influence our use of stereotypes. She discusses how our response to a person in a stereotyped group may be more positive and may actually be unrelated to our more negative attitude about that group. A brief reading next grapples with the role of culture in prejudice. The final reading examines prejudice from a more personal angle. In it, Brent Staples eloquently describes how prejudice can impact such simple behaviors as walking down a street.

Though overt prejudice may be declining, we must understand prejudice's more subtle forms and their impact on those who are targets of it. Failing to do so may hinder our ability to stop this insidious type of prejudice from harming the targets of prejudice and as a consequence, the whole society.

What Causes Prejudice?

Elliot Aronson, Timothy D. Wilson, and Robin M. Akert

> **Editors' Note:** In the last chapter, we read an article describing the stereotypes that exist in Japan based on people's blood types. The current authors raise the question—can seemingly arbitrary characteristics become the basis of stereotypes and prejudice? They describe a class exercise conducted in the 1960s in which a school teacher divided children into groups based on their eye color. The results were dramatic. The authors describe the project, but for a more in-depth look at this demonstration, we highly recommend the film *Eye of the Storm*, which is described in Project 7.1.

What makes people prejudiced? Is it part of our biological survival mechanism to favor our own family, tribe, and race and to express hostility to outsiders? ... [S]ociobiologists have suggested that all organisms have a tendency to feel more favorably toward genetically similar others and to express fear and loathing toward genetically dissimilar organisms, even if the latter have never done them any harm (Rushton, 1989; Trivers, 1985). Conversely, are we taught by our culture (i.e., by our parents, peers, the local community, and the media) to assign negative qualities and attributes to people who are different from us? Psychologists and sociologists know that prejudice is easy to learn and that young children tend to hold the same prejudiced attitudes as their parents. While we human beings might have inherited biological tendencies that predispose us toward prejudicial behavior; no one knows for sure whether or not prejudice is a part of our biological makeup. We do know that prejudice is not confined to such biologically obvious aspects of human difference as race and gender; it also exists among biologically similar people who happen to hold slightly different beliefs—for example, in religion, as with Protestant and Catholic Northern Irish. Indeed, prejudice can even be fostered in schoolchildren over such trivial differences as eye color, length of hair, and style of dress. Let's take a close look at some of the known causes of prejudice.

In the late 1960s, a third-grade teacher in Riceville, Iowa, Jane Elliot, grew concerned that her young students had no real idea of what racism or prejudice was. The children all lived in rural Iowa, they were all white, and they were all Christian. How could Elliot teach them what stereotyping and discrimination felt like?

One day, Elliot divided her class by eye color. She told her students that blue-eyed people were better than brown-eyed people—smarter, nicer, more trustworthy, and so on. The brown-eyed kids had to wear cloth collars around their necks so that they would be instantly recognizable as one of the inferior group. The blue-eyed kids got to play longer at recess, could have second helpings at the cafeteria, were praised in the classroom, and so on. How did the children respond?

In less than a half-hour; Elliot had created a microcosm of society in her classroom: a prejudiced society. While before, the children had been a cooperative, cohesive group, now they were indeed divided. The superior kids, the blue-eyed ones, made fun of the brown-eyed kids, refused to play with them, tattled on them to the teacher; thought up new restrictions and punishments for them, and even started a fistfight with them in the school yard. The inferior kids, the brown-eyed ones, were depressed and demoralized. They did significantly less well on classroom tests that day. They became shadows of their formerly happy selves.

The next day, Elliot switched the stereotypes about eye color. She said she'd made a mistake—that brown-eyed people were really the better ones. She told the brown-eyed kids to put their collars on the blue-eyed kids. They gleefully did so. The tables had turned—and the brown-eyed kids exacted their revenge.

On the morning of the third day, Elliot explained to her students that they had been learning about prejudice and discrimination and how it feels to be a person of color in this society. The children discussed the two-day experience and clearly understood its message.

In a follow-up, Elliot met with these students at a class reunion, when they were in their midtwenties. Their memories of the exercise were startlingly clear—they each said it had had an amazing effect on their lives. They felt that they were less prejudiced and more aware of discrimination against others because of this childhood experience. They said they thought every child in America should experience the eye-color exercise.

References

Rushton, J. P. (1989).   Genetic similarity, human altruism, and group selection.   *Behavioral and Brain Science, 12*, 503-559.
Trivers, R. (1985). *Social evolution.* Menlo Park, CA: Benjamin-Cummings.

What Is The Problem?

Gordon W. Allport

Editors' Note: In this chapter from his seminal work, "On the nature of prejudice, " Gordon Allport discusses and defines prejudice. As we read in Chapter 1, the definitions of terms can affect how a topic is studied, and the area of prejudice is no different. Allport's chapter is a discussion that has had a profound effect on how prejudice and discrimination have been studied since its publication. It also sheds some insight into the causes and outcomes of prejudice, and it provides an excellent background for the study of prejudice.

For myself, earthbound and fettered to the scene of my activities, I confess that I do feel the differences of mankind, national and individual. . . . I am, in plainer words, a bundle of prejudices—made up of likings and dislikings—the veriest thrall to sympathies, apathies, antipathies.

CHARLES LAMB

In Rhodesia a white truck driver passed a group of idle natives and muttered, "They're lazy brutes." A few hours later he saw natives heaving two-hundred pound sacks of grain onto a truck, singing in rhythm to their work. "Savages," he grumbled. "What do you expect?" . . .

In Boston, a dignitary of the Roman Catholic Church was driving along a lonesome road on the outskirts of the city. Seeing a small Negro boy trudging along, the dignitary told his chauffeur to stop and give the boy a lift. Seated together in the back of the limousine, the cleric, to make conversation, asked, "Little Boy, are you a Catholic?" Wide-eyed with alarm, the boy replied, "No sir, it's bad enough being colored without being one of those things." . . .

In Hungary, the saying is, "An anti-Semite is a person who hates the Jews more than is absolutely necessary."

No corner of the world is free from group scorn. Being fettered to our respective cultures, we, like Charles Lamb, are bundles of prejudice.

Two Cases

An anthropologist in his middle thirties had two young children, Susan and Tom. His work required him to live for a year with a tribe of American Indians in the home of a hospitable Indian family. He insisted, however, that his own family live in a community of white people several miles distant from the Indian reservation. Seldom would he allow Tom and Susan to come to the tribal village, though they pleaded for the privilege. And on rare occasions when they made the visit, he sternly refused to allow them to play with the friendly Indian children.

Some people, including a few of the Indians, complained that the anthropologist was untrue to the code of his profession—that he was displaying race prejudice.

The truth is otherwise. This scientist knew that tuberculosis was rife in the tribal village, and that four of the children in the household where he lived had already died of the disease. The probability of infection for his own children, if they came much in contact with the natives, was high. His better judgment told him that he should not take the risk. In this case, his ethnic avoidance was based on rational and realistic grounds. There was no feeling of antagonism involved. The anthropologist had no generally negative attitude toward the Indians. In fact he liked them very much.

Since this case fails to illustrate what we mean by racial or ethnic prejudice, let us turn to another.

In the early summer season two Toronto newspapers carried between them holiday advertisements from approximately 100 different resorts. A Canadian social scientist, S. L. Wax, undertook an interesting experiment.[1] To each of these hotels and resorts he wrote two letters, mailing them at the same time, and asking for room reservations for exactly the same dates. One letter he signed with the name "Mr. Greenberg," the other with the name "Mr. Lockwood." Here are the results:

To "Mr. Greenberg":
   52 percent of the resorts replied;
   36 percent offered him accommodations.
To "Mr. Lockwood":
   95 percent of the resorts replied;
   93 percent offered him accommodations.

Thus, nearly all of the resorts in question welcomed Mr. Lockwood as a correspondent and as a guest; but nearly half of them failed to give Mr. Greenberg the courtesy of a reply, and only slightly more than a third were willing to receive him as a guest.

None of the hotels knew "Mr. Lockwood" or "Mr. Greenberg." For all they knew "Mr. Greenberg" might be a quiet, orderly gentleman, and "Mr. Lockwood" rowdy and drunk. The decision was obviously made not on the merits of the individual, but on "Mr. Greenberg's" supposed membership in a group. He suffered discourtesy and exclusion *solely* because of his name, which aroused a prejudgment of his desirability in the eyes of the hotel managers.

Unlike our first case, this incident contains the two essential ingredients of ethnic prejudice. (1) There is definite hostility and rejection. The majority of the hotels wanted nothing to do with "Mr. Greenberg." (2) The basis of the rejection was categorical. "Mr. Greenberg" was not evaluated as an individual. Rather, he was condemned on the basis of his presumed group membership.

A close reasoner might at this point ask the question: What basic difference exists between the cases of the anthropologist and the hotels in the matter of "categorical rejection"? Did not the anthropologist reason from the high probability of infection that it would be safer not to risk contact between his children and the Indians? And did not the hotelkeepers reason from a high probability that Mr. Greenberg's ethnic membership would in fact bring them an undesirable guest? The anthropologist knew that tubercular contagion was rampant; did not the innkeepers know that "Jewish vices" were rampant and not to be risked?

This question is legitimate. If the innkeepers were basing their rejection on facts (more accurately, on a high probability that a given Jew will have undesirable traits), their action would be as rational and defensible as the anthropologist's. But we can be sure that such is not the case.

Some managers may never have had any unpleasant experiences with Jewish guests—a situation that seems likely in view the fact that in many cases Jewish guests had never been admitted to the hotels. Or, if they have had such experiences, they have not kept a record of their frequency in comparison with objectionable non-Jewish guests. Certainly they have not consulted scientific studies concerning the relative frequency of desirable an undesirable traits in Jews and non-Jews. If they sought such evidence, they would . . . find no support for their policy of rejection.

It is, of course, possible that the manager himself was free from personal prejudice, but, if so, he was reflecting the anti-Semitism of his gentile guests. In either event our point is made.

Definition

The word *prejudice,* derived from the Latin noun *praejudicium* has, like most words, undergone a change of meaning since classical times. There are three stages in the transformation.[2]

(1) To the ancients, *praejudicium* meant a *precedent*—a judgment based on previous decisions and experiences.
(2) Later, the term, in English, acquired the meaning of a judgment formed before due examination and consideration of the facts—a premature or hasty judgment.
(3) Finally the term acquired also its present emotional flavor of favorableness or unfavorableness that accompanies such a prior and unsupported judgment.

Perhaps the briefest of all definitions of prejudice is: *thinking ill of others without sufficient warrant.*[3] This crisp phrasing contains the two essential ingredients of all definitions—reference to unfounded judgment and to a feeling-tone. It is, however, too brief for complete clarity.

In the first place, it refers only to *negative* prejudice. People may be prejudiced in favor of others; they may think *well* of them without sufficient warrant. The wording offered by the *New English Dictionary* recognizes positive as well as negative prejudice:

A feeling, favorable or unfavorable, toward a person or thing, prior to, or not based on, actual experience.

While it is important to bear in mind that biases may be *pro* as well as *con*, it is none the less true that *ethnic* prejudice is mostly negative. A group of students was asked to describe their attitudes toward ethnic groups. No suggestion was made that might lead them toward negative reports. Even so, they reported eight times as many antagonistic attitudes as favorable attitudes. In this volume, accordingly, we shall be concerned chiefly with prejudice *against*, not with prejudice *in favor of*, ethnic groups.

The phrase "thinking ill of others" is obviously an elliptical expression that must be understood to include feelings of scorn or dislike, of fear and aversion, as well as various forms of antipathetic conduct: such as talking against people, discriminating against them, or attacking them with violence.

Similarly, we need to expand the phrase "without sufficient warrant." A judgment is unwarranted whenever it lacks basis in fact. A wit defined prejudice as "being down on something you're not up on."

It is not easy to say how much fact is required in order to justify a judgment. A prejudiced person will almost certainly claim that he has sufficient warrant for his views. He will tell of bitter experiences he has had with refugees, Catholics, or Orientals. But, in most cases, it is evident that his facts are scanty and strained. He resorts to a selective sorting of his own few memories, mixes them up with hearsay, and overgeneralizes. No one can possibly know *all* refugees, Catholics, or Orientals. Hence any negative judgment of these groups *as a whole* is, strictly speaking, an instance of thinking ill without sufficient warrant. . . .

Ordinarily, prejudice manifests itself in dealing with individual members of rejected groups. But in avoiding a Negro neighbor, or in answering "Mr. Greenberg's" application for a room, we frame our action to accord with our categorical generalization of the group as a whole. We pay little or no attention to individual differences, and overlook the important fact that Negro X, our neighbor, is not Negro Y, whom we dislike for good and sufficient reason; that Mr. Greenberg, who may be a fine gentleman, is not Mr. Bloom, whom we have good reason to dislike.

So common is this process that we might define prejudice as:

an avertive or hostile attitude toward a person who belongs to a group, simply because he belongs to that group, and is therefore presumed to have the objectionable qualities ascribed to the group.

This definition stresses the fact that while ethnic prejudice in daily life is ordinarily a matter of dealing with individual people it also entails an unwarranted idea concerning a group as a whole.

Returning to the question of "sufficient warrant," we must grant that few if any human judgments are based on absolute certainty. We can be reasonably, but not absolutely, sure that the sun will rise tomorrow, and that death and taxes will finally overtake us. The sufficient warrant for any judgment is always a matter of probabilities. Ordinarily our judgments of natural happenings are based on firmer and higher probabilities than our judgments of people. Only rarely do our categorical judgments of nations or ethnic groups have a foundation in high probability.

Take the hostile view of Nazi leaders held by most Americans during World War II. Was it prejudiced? The answer is No, because there was abundant available evidence regarding the evil policies and practices accepted as the official code of the party. True, there may have been good individuals in the party who at heart rejected the abominable program; but the probability was so high that the Nazi group constituted an actual menace to world peace and to humane values that a realistic and justified conflict resulted. The high probability of danger removes an antagonism from the domain of prejudice into that of realistic social conflict. . . .

We can never hope to draw a hard and fast line between "sufficient" and "insufficient" warrant. For this reason we cannot always be sure whether we are dealing with a case of prejudice or nonprejudice. Yet no one will deny that often we form judgments on the basis of scant, even nonexistent, probabilities.

Overcategorization is perhaps the commonest trick of the human mind. Given a thimbleful of facts we rush to make generalizations as large as a tub. . . .

There is a natural basis for this tendency. Life is so short, and the demands upon us for practical adjustments so great, that we cannot let our ignorance detain us in our daily transactions. . . .

Not every overblown generalization is a prejudice. Some are simply *misconceptions,* wherein we organize wrong information. One child had the idea that all people living in Minneapolis were "monopolists." And from his father he had learned that monopolists were evil folk. When in later years he discovered the confusion, his dislike of dwellers in Minneapolis vanished.

Here we have the test to help us distinguish between ordinary errors of prejudgment and prejudice. If a person is capable of rectifying his erroneous judgments in the light of new evidence he is not prejudiced. *Prejudgments become prejudices only if they are not reversible when exposed to new knowledge.* A prejudice, unlike a simple misconception, is actively resistant to all evidence that would unseat it. We tend to grow emotional when a prejudice is threatened with contradiction. Thus the difference between ordinary prejudgments and prejudice is that one can discuss and rectify a prejudgment without emotional resistance.

Taking these various considerations into account, we may now attempt a final definition of negative ethnic prejudice—one that will serve us throughout this book. Each phrase in the definition represents a considerable condensation of the points we have been discussing:

> Ethnic prejudice is an antipathy based upon a faulty and inflexible generalization. It may be felt or expressed. It may be directed toward a group as a whole, or toward an individual because he is a member of that group.

The net effect of prejudice, thus defined, is to place the object of prejudice at some disadvantage not merited by his own misconduct.

Is Prejudice a Value Concept?

Some authors have introduced an additional ingredient into their definitions of prejudice. They claim that attitudes are prejudiced only if they violate some important norms or values accepted in a culture.[4] They insist that prejudice is only that type of prejudgment that is ethically disapproved in a society.

One experiment shows that common usage of the term has this flavor. Several adult judges were asked to take statements made by ninth-grade children and sort them into piles according to the degree of "prejudice" represented. It turned out that whatever a boy may have said against girls as a group was not judged to be prejudice, for it is regarded as normal for an early adolescent to heap scorn on the opposite sex. Nor were statements made against teachers considered examples of prejudice. This antagonism, too, seemed natural to this age, and socially unimportant. But when the children expressed animosity toward labor unions, toward social classes, races or nationalities, more judgments of "prejudice" were given.[5]

In brief, the social importance of an unfair attitude entered into the judges' view of its prejudiced character. A fifteen-year-old boy who is "off" girls is not considered as biased as one who is "off" nationalities other than his own.

If we use the term in this sense we should have to say that the older caste system in India—which is now breaking down—involved no prejudice. It was simply a convenient stratification in the social structure, acceptable to nearly all citizens because it clarified the division of labor and defined social prerogatives. It was for centuries acceptable even to the untouchables because the religious doctrine of reincarnation made the arrangement seem entirely just. An untouchable was ostracized because in previous existences he failed to merit promotions to a higher caste or to a supermortal existence. He now has his just desserts and likewise an opportunity through an obedient and spiritually directed life to win advancement in future reincarnations. Assuming that this account of a happy caste system really marked

Hindu society at one time, was there then no question of prejudice?

Or take the Ghetto system. Through long stretches of history Jews have been segregated in certain residential zones, sometimes with a chain around the region. Only inside were they allowed to move freely. The method had the merit of preventing unpleasant conflict, and the Jew, knowing his place, could plan his life with a certain definiteness and comfort. It could be argued that his lot was much more secure and predictable than in the modern world. There were periods in history when neither the Jew nor gentile felt particularly outraged by the system. Was prejudice then absent?

Were the ancient Greeks (or early American plantation owners) prejudiced against their hereditary class of slaves? To be sure they looked down upon them, and undoubtedly held fallacious theories concerning their inherent inferiority and "animal-like" mentality; but so natural did it all seem, so good, so proper, that there was no moral dilemma. . . .

What shall we say about this line of argument? It has impressed some critics so much that they hold the whole problem of prejudice to be nothing more than a value-judgment invented by "liberal intellectuals." When liberals do not approve of a folkway *they* arbitrarily call it prejudice. What they should do is to follow not their own sense of moral outrage, but consult the ethos of a culture. If the culture itself is in conflict, holding up a higher standard of conduct than many of its members practice, then we may speak of prejudice existing within the culture. Prejudice is the *moral evaluation* placed by a culture on some of its own practices. It is a designation of attitudes that are disapproved.

These critics, it would seem, confuse two separate and distinct problems. Prejudice in the simple psychological sense of negative, overgeneralized judgment exists just as surely in caste societies, slave societies, or countries believing in witchcraft as in ethically more sensitive societies. The second problem— whether prejudice is or is not attended by a sense of moral outrage—is a separate issue altogether. . . .

Some cultures, like our own, abjure prejudice; some do not; but the fundamental psychological analysis of prejudice is the same whether we are talking about Hindus, Navahos, the Greeks of antiquity, or Middletown, U.S.A. Whenever a negative attitude toward persons is sustained by a spurious overgeneralization we encounter the syndrome of prejudice. It is not essential that people deplore this syndrome. It has existed in all ages in every country. It constitutes a bona fide psychological problem. The degree of moral indignation engendered is irrelevant.

Functional Significance

Certain definitions of prejudice include one additional ingredient. The following is an example:

> Prejudice is a pattern of hostility in interpersonal relations which is directed against an entire group, or against its individual members; it fulfills a specific irrational function for its bearer.[7]

The final phrase of this definition implies that negative attitudes are not prejudices unless they serve a private, self-gratifying purpose for the person who has them.

It will become abundantly clear in later chapters that much prejudice is indeed fashioned and sustained by self-gratifying considerations. In most cases prejudice seems to have some "functional significance" for the bearer. Yet this is not always the case. Much prejudice is a matter of blind conformity with prevailing folkways. Some of it has no important relation to the life-economy of the individual. For this reason it seems unwise to insist that the "irrational function" of prejudice be included in our basic definition. For this reason it seems unwise to insist that the "irrational function" of prejudice be included in our basic definition.

Attitudes and Beliefs

We have said that an adequate definition of prejudice contains two essential ingredients. There must be an *attitude* of favor or disfavor; and it must be related to an overgeneralized (and therefore erroneous) *belief*. Prejudiced statements sometimes express the attitudinal factor, sometimes the belief factor. In the following series the first item expresses attitude, the second, belief:

> I can't abide Negroes.
> Negroes are smelly.
>
> I wouldn't live in an apartment house with Jews.
> There are a few exceptions, but in general all Jews are pretty much alike.
>
> I don't want Japanese-Americans in my town.
> Japanese-Americans are sly and tricky.

Is it important to distinguish between the attitudinal and belief aspects of prejudice? For some purposes, no. When we find one, we usually find the other. Without some generalized beliefs concerning a group as a whole, a hostile attitude could not long be sustained. In modern researches it turns out that people who express a high degree of antagonistic attitudes on a test for prejudice, also show that they believe to a high degree that the groups they are prejudiced against have a large number of objectionable qualities.[8]

But for some purposes it is useful to distinguish attitude from belief. For example, certain programs designed to reduce prejudice succeed in altering beliefs but not in changing attitudes. Beliefs, to some extent, can be rationally attacked and altered. Usually, however, they have the slippery propensity of accommodating themselves somehow to the negative attitude which is much harder to change. The following dialogue illustrates the point:

> Mr. X: The trouble with the Jews is that they only take care of their own group.
> Mr. Y: But the record of the Community Chest campaign shows that they give more generously, in proportion to their numbers, to the general charities of the community, than do non-Jews.
> Mr. X: That shows they are always trying to buy favor and intrude into Christian affairs. They think of nothing but money; that is why there are so many Jewish bankers.
> Mr. Y: But a recent study shows that the percentage of Jews in the banking business is negligible, far smaller than the percentage of non-Jews.
> Mr. X: That's just it; they don't go in for respectable business; they are only in the movie business or run night clubs.

Thus the belief system has a way of slithering around to justify the more permanent attitude. The process is one of *rationalization*—of the accommodation of beliefs to attitudes.

Acting out Prejudice

What people actually do in relation to groups they dislike is not always directly related to what they think or feel about them. Two employers, for example, may dislike Jews to an equal degree. One may keep his feelings to himself and may hire Jews on the same basis as any workers—perhaps because he wants to gain goodwill for his factory or store in the Jewish community. The other may translate his dislike into his employment policy, and refuse to hire Jews. Both men are prejudiced, but only one of them practices *discrimination*. As a rule discrimination has more immediate and serious social consequences than has prejudice.

It is true that any negative attitude tends somehow, somewhere, to express itself in action. Few people keep their antipathies entirely to themselves. The more intense the attitude, the more likely it is to result in vigorously hostile action.

We may venture to distinguish certain degrees of negative action from the least energetic to the most.

1. *Antilocution.* Most people who have prejudices talk about them. With like-minded friends, occasionally with strangers, they may express their antagonism freely. But many people never go beyond this mild degree of antipathetic action.
2. *Avoidance.* If the prejudice is more intense, it leads the individual to avoid members of the disliked group, even perhaps at the cost of considerable

inconvenience. In this case, the bearer of prejudice does not directly inflict harm upon the group he dislikes. He takes the burden of accommodation and withdrawal entirely upon himself.

3. *Discrimination.* Here the prejudiced person makes detrimental distinctions of an active sort. He undertakes to exclude all members of the group in question from certain types of employment, from residential housing, political rights, educational or recreational opportunities, churches, hospitals, or from some other social privileges. Segregation is an institutionalized form of discrimination, enforced legally or by common custom. [9]

4. *Physical attack.* Under conditions of heightened emotion prejudice may lead to acts of violence or semiviolence. An unwanted Negro family may be forcibly ejected from a neighborhood, or so severely threatened that it leaves, in fear. Gravestones in Jewish cemeteries may be desecrated. The Northside's Italian gang may lie in wait for the Southside's Irish gang.

5. *Extermination.* Lynchings, pogroms, massacres, and the Hitlerian program of genocide mark the ultimate degree of violent expression of prejudice.

This five-point scale is not mathematically constructed, but it serves to call attention to the enormous range of activities that may issue from prejudiced attitudes and beliefs. While many people would never move from antilocution to avoidance; or from avoidance to active discrimination, or higher on the scale, still it is true that activity on one level makes transition to a more intense level easier. It was Hitler's antilocution that led Germans to avoid their Jewish neighbors and erstwhile friends. This preparation made it easier to enact the Nürnberg laws of discrimination which, in turn,

made the subsequent burning of synagogues and street attacks upon Jews seem natural. The final step in the macabre progression was the ovens at Auschwitz.

Notes and References

1. S. L. Wax. A survey of restrictive advertising and discrimination by summer resorts in the Province of Ontario. Canadian Jewish Congress: *Information and comment,* 1948, **7**, 10-13.

2. Cf. *A New English Dictionary.* (Sir James A. H. Murray, Ed.) Oxford: Clarendon Press, 1909, Vol. VII, Pt. II, 1275.

3. This definition is derived from the Thomistic moralists who regard prejudice as "rash judgment." The author is indebted to the Rev. J. H. Fichter, S. J., for calling this treatment to his attention. The definition is more fully discussed by the Rev. John LaFarge, S. J., in *The Race Question and the Negro,* New York: Longmans, Green, 1945, 174 ff.

4. Cf. R. M. Williams, Jr. The reduction of intergroup tensions. New York: *Social Science Research Council,* 1947, Bulletin 57, 37.

5. H. S. Dyer. The usability of the concept of "Prejudice." *Psychometrika,* 1945, **10**, 219-224.

6. The following definition is written from this relativistic point of view: "A prejudice is a generalized anti-attitude, and/or an anti-action toward any distinct category or group of people, when either the attitude or the action or both are judged by the community in which they are found to be less favorable to the given people than the normally accepted standard of that community." P. Black and R. D. Atkins. Conformity versus prejudice as exemplified in white-Negro relations in the South: some methodological considerations. *Journal of Psychology,* 1950, **30**, 109-121.

7. N. W. Ackerman and Marie Jahoda. *Anti-Semitism and emotional disorder.* New York: Harper, 1950, 4.

8. Not all scales for measuring prejudice include items that reflect both attitudes and beliefs. Those that do so report correlations between the two types of items of the order of .80. Cf. Babette Samelson. *The patterning of attitudes and beliefs regarding the American Negro.* (Unpublished.) Radcliffe College Library, 1945. Also, A. Rose, *Studies in reduction of prejudice.* (Mimeograph.) Chicago: American Council on Race Relations, 1947, 11-14.

9. Aware of the world-wide problem of discrimination, the Commission on Human Rights of the United Nations has prepared a thorough analysis of *The main types and causes of discrimination.* United Nations Publications, 1949, XIV, 3.

Breaking The Prejudice Habit

Patricia G. Devine

Editors' Note: You approach a person from a different racial group, and find yourself thinking negative and stereotypic thoughts about the person, even though you consider yourself to be unbiased toward this racial group. Why does this happen, and how can we stop it from happening? Patricia Devine has sought to answer these two questions in her research on automatic and controlled processes in prejudice. Through this work, she has also uncovered some of the underlying cognitive mechanisms that feed into prejudice. Additionally, she presents a hopeful conclusion that people can control whether or not they display prejudice.

Legal scholars, politicians, legislators, social scientists, and lay people alike have puzzled over the paradox of racism in a nation founded on the fundamental principle of human equality. Legislators responded with landmark legal decisions (e.g., Supreme Court ruling on school desegregation and the Civil Rights laws) that made overt discrimination based on race illegal. In the wake of the legislative changes, social scientists examined the extent to which shifts in whites' attitudes kept pace with the legal changes. The literature, however, reveals conflicting findings. Whereas overt expressions of prejudice on surveys declined (i.e., verbal reports), more subtle indicators (i.e., nonverbal measures) continue to reveal prejudice even among those who say they renounced prejudice. A central challenge presented to contemporary prejudice researchers is to explain the disparity between verbal reports and the more subtle measures.

Some reject the optimistic conclusion suggested by survey research and argue that prejudice in America is not declining; it is only changing form—becoming more subtle and disguised. By this argument, most (if not all) Americans are assumed to be racist, with only the *type* of racism differing between people. Such conclusions are based on the belief that *any* response that results in differential treatment between groups is taken as evidence of prejudice. However, this definition fails to consider *intent* or motive and is based on the assumption that nonthoughtful (e.g., nonverbal) responses are, by definition, more trustworthy than thoughtful responses. Indeed, nonverbal measures are assumed to be good indicators of prejudice precisely because they do not typically involve careful thought and people do not control them in the same way that they can control their verbally reported attitudes.

Rather than dismiss either response as necessarily untrustworthy, my colleagues and I have tried to understand the origin of both thoughtful and nonthoughtful responses. By directly addressing the disparity between thoughtful and nonthoughtful responses, our approach offers a more optimistic analysis regarding prospects for prejudice reduction than the extant formulations. To foreshadow, our program of research has been devoted to understanding (a) how and why those who truly renounce prejudice may continue to experience prejudice-like thoughts and feelings and (b) the nature of the rather formidable challenges and obstacles that must be overcome before one can succeed in reducing the disparity between thoughtful and nonthoughtful responses.

Automatic and Controlled Processes in Prejudice

The distinction between automatic and controlled cognitive processes has been central to our analysis in prejudice reduction. Automatic processes occur unintentionally, spontaneously, and unconsciously. We have evidence that both low- and high-prejudiced people are vulnerable to automatic stereotype activation. Once the stereotype is well-learned, its influence is hard to avoid because it so easily comes to mind. Controlled processes, in contrast, are under the intentional control of the individual. An important aspect of such processes is that their initiation and use requires time and sufficient cognitive *capacity*. Nonprejudiced responses require inhibiting the spontaneously activated stereotypes and deliberately activating personal beliefs to serve as the basis for responses. Without sufficient time or cognitive capacity, responses may well be stereotype-based and, therefore, appear prejudiced.

The important implication of the automatic/controlled process distinction is that if one looks only at nonthoughtful, automatic responses, one may well conclude that all white Americans are prejudiced. We have found important differences between low- and high-prejudiced people based on the personal beliefs that each hold, despite similar knowledge of and vulnerability to the activation of cultural stereotypes. Furthermore, low-prejudiced people have established and internalized nonprejudiced personal standards for how to treat members of stereotyped groups. When given sufficient time, low-prejudiced people censor responses based on the stereotype and, instead, respond based on their beliefs. High-prejudiced people, in contrast, do not reject the stereotype and are not personally motivated to overcome its effect on their behavior.

A strength of this approach is that it delineates the role of both thoughtful and nonthoughtful processes in response to stereotyped group members. Eliminating prejudice requires overcoming a lifetime of socialization experiences, which, unfortunately, promote prejudice. We have likened reducing prejudice to the breaking of a habit in that people must first make a decision to eliminate the habit and then *learn* to inhibit the habitual (prejudiced) responses. Thus, the change from being prejudiced to nonprejudiced is not viewed as an all or none event, but as a process during which the low-prejudiced person is especially vulnerable to conflict between his or her enduring negative responses and endorsed nonprejudiced beliefs. For those who renounce prejudice, overcoming the "prejudice habit" presents a formidable task that is likely to entail a great deal of internal conflict over a protracted period of time.

Prejudice With and Without Compunction

In subsequent work, we examined the nature and consequences of the internal conflict associated with prejudice reduction. Specifically, we have focused on the challenges faced by those individuals who have internalized nonprejudiced personal standards and are trying to control their prejudiced responses, but sometimes fail. We have shown that people high and low in prejudice (as assessed by a self-report technique) have qualitatively different affective reactions to the conflict between their verbal reports concerning how they *should* respond in situations involving contact with members of stereotyped groups and how they say they actually *would* respond. Low-prejudiced people, for example, believe that they should not feel uncomfortable sitting next to an African American on a bus. High-prejudiced people disagree, indicating that it's acceptable to feel uncomfortable in this situation. When actual responses violate personal standards, low-prejudiced people experience guilt or "prejudice with compunction," but high-prejudiced individuals do not. For low-prejudiced people, the coexistence of such conflicting reactions threatens their nonprejudiced self-concepts. Moreover, these guilt feelings play a functional role in helping people to "break the prejudice habit." That is, violations combined with guilt have been shown to help low-prejudiced people to use controlled processes to inhibit the prejudiced responses and to replace them with responses that are based on their personal beliefs.

Interpersonal Dynamics of Intergroup Contact

Until recently, our research has focused rather exclusively on the nature of internal conflict associated with prejudice reduction efforts. However, many of the challenges associated with prejudice reduction are played out in the interpersonal arena, and we believe it's important to explore the relevance of our work to issues of intergroup tension. Thus, one of our current lines of research is devoted to exploring the nature of the challenges created by the intergroup contact when people's standards are "put on the line."

In interpersonal intergroup contact situations, we have found that although low-prejudiced people are highly motivated to respond without prejudice, there are few guidelines for "how to do the intergroup thing well." As a result, many experience doubt and uncertainty about how to express their nonprejudiced attitudes in intergroup situations. Thus, for low-prejudiced people, their high motivation to respond without prejudice may actually interfere with their efforts to convey accurately their nonprejudiced intentions. Under these circumstances, they become socially anxious; this anxiety disrupts the typically smooth and coordinated aspects of social interaction. Their interaction styles become awkward and strained resulting in nonverbal behaviors such as decreased eye contact and awkward speech patterns. These are exactly the types of subtle responses that have typically been interpreted as signs of prejudice or antipathy. Indeed, it is not possible to distinguish between the type of tension that arises out of antipathy toward the group or social anxiety based on these signs alone.

We argue that it may be important to acknowledge that there are qualitatively distinct forms of intergroup tension experienced by majority group members, which are systematically related to their self-reported level of prejudice. For some, the tension can arise out of antipathy, as was always thought in the prejudice literature, but for others, the tension arises out of anxiety over trying to do the intergroup thing well. Functionally then, we have different starting points for trying to reduce intergroup tension. Strategies for attempting to reduce intergroup tension differ when the problem is conceived as one of improving skills rather than one of changing negative attitudes.

Conclusion

To sum up, although it is not easy and clearly requires effort, time, and practice, prejudice appears to be a habit that can be broken. In contrast to the prevailing, pessimistic opinion that little progress is being made toward the alleviation of prejudice, our program of research suggests that many people appear to be embroiled in the difficult or arduous process of overcoming their prejudices. During this process, low-prejudiced people are confronted with rather formidable challenges from within, as people battle their spontaneous reactions, and from the interpersonal settings in which people's standards are put on the line. We are sanguine that by developing a realistic analysis of the practical challenges faced by those who renounce prejudice, we may be able to identify strategies that may facilitate their prejudice reduction efforts.

It is important to recognize that we are not claiming to have solved the problem of intergroup prejudice, nor are we suggesting that prejudice has disappeared. The past several years have witnessed a disturbing increase in the incidence of hate crimes against minorities. And a sizable proportion of white Americans continue to embrace old-fashioned forms of bigotry. Nevertheless, we hope that by developing an understanding of the challenges associated with breaking the prejudice habit, we may gain insight into the reasons low-prejudiced people establish and internalize nonprejudiced standards. Armed with this knowledge, we may be able to encourage high-prejudiced people to renounce prejudice. And when they do, we will be in a better position to understand their challenges and, perhaps, to assist them in their efforts.

Culture And Prejudice

Shelley E. Taylor, Letitia A. Peplau, And David O. Sears

𝓔ditors' Note: Are people all over the world prejudiced? Is there some way to understand why some cultures appear to be less prejudiced than others? The research discussed by Shelley Taylor and her colleagues shed some light onto these questions by examining the role of culture in prejudice. This research, on the whole, illustrates that prejudice is a learned response that is greatly affected by culture. Whether or not we are prejudiced and who is the target of our prejudice often has its basis in our culture.

. . . Harry Triandis (1995) has argued that the private self is especially emphasized in individualistic cultures such as those found in North America and Europe, while in collectivistic cultures such as those of East Asia, Africa, and Latin America there is more emphasis on the needs of the ingroup than on the individuals needs, more on duty to the ingroup than on pleasure for the self, more on shared beliefs than on distinctive beliefs, and more on intense emotional attachment to the ingroup.

Triandis's research found that people from collectivistic cultures perceive their ingroups to be more homogeneous. Ingroup members are perceived as behaving more intimately and subordinately toward other ingroup members, and they tend to emphasize values that promote the welfare of their group (Triandis, McCusker, & Hui, 1990). Wheeler and colleagues (1989) found that students in Hong Kong had longer but fewer interactions with fewer people than did students from the United States, more group interaction, and greater self-disclosure.

What might be the implications of this distinction in the study of prejudice? Several lines of research have suggested that in North America, individualism is associated with higher levels of prejudice. "Ambivalent racism" can be stimulated when individualistic values are made more salient (Katz & Hass, 1988). Making internal, individualistic attributions for African American socioeconomic disadvantage is associated both with higher levels of prejudice and with opposition to policies intended to remedy those disadvantages. On the other hand, a more collectivist orientation is associated with less prejudice and more racial tolerance (Kluegel, 1990). Egalitarian values, in the research on symbolic racism, contribute to more support for policies intended to eliminate racial inequality and for minority political candidates (Sears, 1988); also, making egalitarianism salient reduces prejudice (Katz & Hass, 1988).

The individualistic-collectivist distinction has not been explicitly extended to the research on prejudice to date, but social identity theory might, lead us to speculate as follows. Collectivist cultures place more emphasis on the "collective self" than on the "private self" (Triandis, 1995). The implication is that prejudice against other ingroup members might be lessened in cultures that emphasize more collectivist orientations, with perceptions of the self as interdependent with other group members. For example, a fellow group member might not be stigmatized to the same degree for physical deformities or a lack of certain skills. On the other hand, prejudice against outgroups might be intensified in a culture with a dominant "collective self," because it would lead to a stronger sense of social identity, and "collective self-esteem" might be more of a culture priority. This in turn might intensify outgroup homogeneity and ingroup favoritism effects.

Although there is not much research on this topic yet, one study (Oyserman, 1993) has focused on Israel, with its two major ethnic groups, Israeli and Arab. Both groups have roots in East and West, and both worldviews are salient. The study shows that there, collective orientation appeared to be more closely related to perceiving intense intergroup conflict.

References

Katz, I., & Hass, R. G. (1988). Racial ambivalence and American value conflict: Correlational and prime studies of dual cognitive structures. *Journal of Personality and Social Psychology, 55,* 893-905.

Kluegel, J. R. (1990). Trends in whites' explanations of the black-white gap in socioeconomic status, 1977-1989. *American Sociological Review, 55,* 512-525.

Oyserman, D. (1993). The lens of personhood: Viewing the self and others in a multicultural society. *Journal of Personality and Social Psychology, 65,* 993-1009.

Sears, D. O. (1988). Symbolic racism. In P. Katz & D. Taylor (Eds.), *Eliminating racism: Profiles in controversy* (pp. 53-84). New York: Plenum Press.

Triandis, H. C. (1995). *Individualism and collectivism.* Boulder, CO: Westview Press.

Triandis, H. C., McCusker, C., & Hui, C. H. (1990). Multimethod probes of individualism and collectivism. *Journal of Personality and Social Psychology, 59,* 1006-1020.

Wheeler, L., Reis, H. T., & Bond, M. H. (1989). The Middle Kingdom and the melting pot. *Journal of Personality and Social Psychology, 57,* 79-86.

Just Walk On By

Brent Staples

Editors' Note: Social psychologists study those who are prejudiced as well as those who are their victims. Being the victim of prejudice is a powerful and negative psychological experience, because most of us are very sensitive to how others are perceiving us. These perceptions can have a profound impact on how we feel about ourselves and others. In this essay, Brent Staples talks about how it feels to be in an environment where you have to continually cope with the negative perceptions that others hold about you based on your gender and color. He also relates some of the behaviors that can follow from being the target of such negative perceptions.

My first victim was a woman—white, well dressed, probably in her early twenties. I came upon her late one evening on a deserted street in Hyde Park, a relatively affluent neighborhood in an otherwise mean, impoverished section of Chicago. As I swung onto the avenue behind her, there seemed to be a discreet, uninflammatory distance between us. Not so. She cast back a worried glance. To her, the youngish black man—a broad six feet two inches with a beard and billowing hair, both hands shoved into the pockets of a bulky military jacket—seemed menacingly close. After a few more quick glimpses, she picked up her pace and was soon running in earnest. Within seconds she disappeared into a cross street.

That was more than a decade ago. I was 22 years old, a graduate student newly arrived at the University of Chicago. It was in the echo of that terrified woman's footfalls that I first began to know the unwieldy inheritance I'd come into—the ability to alter public space in ugly ways. It was clear that she thought herself the quarry of a mugger, a rapist, or worse. Suffering a bout of insomnia, however, I was stalking sleep, not defenseless wayfarers. As a softy who is scarcely able to take a knife to a raw chicken—let alone hold it to a person's throat—I was surprised, embarrassed, and dismayed all at once. Her flight made me feel like an accomplice in tyranny. It also made it clear that I was indistinguishable from the muggers who occasionally seeped into the area from the surrounding ghetto. That first encounter, and those that followed, signified that a vast, unnerving gulf lay between nighttime pedestrians—particularly women— and me. And I soon gathered that being perceived as dangerous is a hazard in itself. I only needed to turn a corner into a dicey situation, or crowd some frightened, armed person in a foyer somewhere, or make an errant move after being pulled over by a policeman. Where fear and weapons meet— and they often do in urban America—there is always the possibility of death.

In that first year, my first away from my hometown, I was to become thoroughly familiar with the language of fear. At dark, shadowy intersections in Chicago, I could cross in front of a car stopped at a traffic light and elicit the *thunk, thunk, thunk, thunk* of the driver—black, white, male, or female— hammering down the door locks. On less traveled streets after dark, I grew accustomed to but never comfortable with people who crossed to the other side of the street rather than pass me. Then there were the standard unpleasantries with police, doormen, bouncers, cab drivers, and others whose business it is to screen out troublesome individuals *before* there is any nastiness.

I moved to New York nearly two years ago and I have remained an avid night walker. In central Manhattan, the near-constant crowd cover minimizes tense one-on-one street encounters. Elsewhere—visiting friends in SoHo, where sidewalks are narrow and tightly spaced buildings shut out the sky— things can get very taut indeed.

Black men have a firm place in New York mugging literature. Norman Podhoretz in his famed (or infamous) 1963 essay, "My Negro Problem—And Ours," recalls growing up in terror of black males; they "were tougher than we were, more ruthless," he writes—and as an adult on the Upper West Side of Manhattan, he continues, he cannot constrain his nervousness when he meets black men on certain streets. Similarly, a decade later, the essayist and novelist Edward Hoagland extols a New York where once "Negro bitterness bore down mainly on other Negroes." Where some see mere panhandlers, Hoagland sees "a mugger who is clearly screwing up his nerve to do more than just *ask* for money." But Hoagland has "the New Yorker's quick-hunch posture for broken-field maneuvering," and the bad guy swerves away.

I often witness that "hunch posture," from women after dark on the warrenlike streets of Brooklyn where I live. They seem to set their faces on neutral and, with their purse straps strung across their chests bandolier style, they forge ahead as though bracing themselves against being tackled. I understand, of course, that the danger they perceive is not a hallucination. Women are particularly vulnerable to street violence, and young black males are drastically overrepresented among the perpetrators of that violence. Yet these truths are no solace against the kind of alienation that comes of being ever the suspect, against being set apart, a fearsome entity with whom pedestrians avoid making eye contact.

It is not altogether clear to me how I reached the ripe old age of 22 without being conscious of the lethality nighttime pedestrians attributed to me. Perhaps it was because in Chester, Pennsylvania, the small, angry industrial town where I came of age in the 1960s, I was scarcely noticeable against a backdrop of gang warfare, street knifings, and murders. I grew up one of the good boys, had perhaps a half-dozen fist fights. In retrospect, my shyness of combat has clear sources.

Many things go into the making of a young thug. One of those things is the consummation of the male romance with the power to intimidate. An infant discovers that random flailings send the baby bottle flying out of the crib and crashing to the floor. Delighted, the joyful babe repeats those motions again and again, seeking to duplicate the feat. Just so, I recall the points at which some of my boyhood friends were finally seduced by the perception of themselves as tough guys. When a mark cowered and surrendered his money without resistance, myth and reality merged—and paid *off*. It is, after all, only manly to embrace the power to frighten and intimidate. We, as men, are not

supposed to give an inch of our lane on the highway; we are to seize the fighter's edge in work and in play and even in love; we are to be valiant in the face of hostile forces.

Unfortunately, poor and powerless young men seem to take all this nonsense literally. As a boy, I saw countless tough guys locked away; I have since buried several, too. They were babies, really—a teenage cousin, a brother of 22, a childhood friend in his mid-twenties—all gone down in episodes of bravado played out in the streets. I came to doubt the virtues of intimidation early on. I chose, perhaps even unconsciously, to remain a shadow—timid, but a survivor.

The fearsomeness mistakenly attributed to me in public places often has a perilous flavor. The most frightening of these confusions occurred in the late 1970s and early 1980s when I worked as a journalist in Chicago. One day, rushing into the office of a magazine I was writing for with a deadline story in hand, I was mistaken for a burglar. The office manager called security and, with an ad hoc posse, pursued me through the labyrinthine halls, nearly to my editor's door. I had no way of proving who I was. I could only move briskly toward the company of someone who knew me.

Another time I was on assignment for a local paper and killing time before an interview. I entered a jewelry store on the city's affluent Near North Side. The proprietor excused herself and returned with an enormous red Doberman pinscher straining at the end of a leash. She stood, the dog extended toward me, silent to my questions, her eyes bulging nearly out of her head. I took a cursory look around, nodded, and bade her good night. Relatively speaking, however, I never fared as badly as another black male journalist. He went to nearby Waukegan, Illinois, a couple of summers ago to work on a story about a murderer who was born there. Mistaking the reporter for the killer, police hauled him from his car at gunpoint and but for his press credentials would probably have tried to book him. Such episodes are not uncommon. Black men trade tales like this all the time.

In "My Negro Problem—And Ours," Podhoretz writes that the hatred he feels for blacks makes itself known to him through a variety of avenues—one being his discomfort with that "special brand of paranoid touchiness" to which he says blacks are prone. No doubt he is speaking here of black men. In time, I learned to smother the rage I felt at so often being taken for a criminal. Not to do so would surely have led to madness—via that special "paranoid touchiness" that so annoyed Podhoretz at the time he wrote the essay.

I began to take precautions to make myself less threatening. I move about with care, particularly late in the evening. I give a wide berth to nervous people on subway platforms during the wee hours, particularly when I have exchanged business clothes for jeans. If I happen to be entering a building behind some people who appear skittish, I may walk by, letting them clear the lobby before I return, so as not to seem to be following them. I have been calm and extremely congenial on those rare occasions when I've been pulled over by the police.

And on late-evening constitutionals along streets less traveled by, I employ what has proved to be an excellent tension-reducing measure: I whistle melodies from Beethoven and Vivaldi and the more popular classical composers. Even steely New Yorkers hunching toward nighttime destinations seem to relax, and occasionally they even join in the tune. Virtually everybody seems to sense that a mugger wouldn't be warbling bright, sunny selections from Vivaldi's *Four Seasons*. It is my equivalent of the cowbell that hikers wear when they know they are in bear country.

Note: Staples writes editorials for the *New York Times* and is author of the memoir, "Parallel Time."

✓ PROJECT 7.1
Brown Eyes, Blue Eyes

I.   In this project, you will watch the program *Eye of the Storm*, which is also available from the Public Broadcasting System as the *Frontline* episode "A Class Divided." As described in an earlier article in this Workbook, Jane Elliot, after dividing her class into those with blue eyes and those with brown eyes, created stereotypes about each group as a way of teaching her students about prejudice and discrimination.

II.   After watching it, please write a one-page report of the film, analyzing the processes that Mrs. Elliot used to create and maintain prejudice—negative attitudes toward others—in her students. How was she able to get the students to move from holding simple stereotypes about people with different eye colors to being prejudiced against each other? And, what happened to the targets of the prejudice? What are the larger societal implications of this demonstration?

✓ PROJECT 7.2
Subtle And Overt Prejudice

I.   A number of social psychological investigations, including the research by Patricia Devine which you read in this chapter, discuss the distinction between subtle and overt forms of prejudice. In this project, you are asked to imagine how you would subtly communicate a bias against a group of people about whom you hold a negative attitude.

II.   *Imagine this scenario:* You are in the process of buying a new car, and you are discussing the different types of cars you are considering with a close friend or your roommate. Your roommate suggests that you look at a type of car he or she views very positively and about which you hold a strong, negative bias. How do you tell your roommate that you would never consider such a car because you think that only certain kinds of people have that car?

Answer the following questions:

What is the group about whom you are communicating?

_____

_____

If you were to overtly communicate your bias, what would you say?

_____

_____

_____

_____

If you were to subtly communicate your bias, what would you say?

_____

_____

_____

What factors influenced the difference between your overt and subtle communications?

_____

_____

_____

_____

In what circumstances would you want to subtly communicate your bias? In what circumstances would you want to overtly communicate your bias?

_____

_____

_____

_____

✓ PROJECT 7.3
Are Salads Just For Women?

I.   In this project, you will serve in the role of a consultant who has been hired to change a belief that a certain product is just for women.

II.   *The Situation:* A restaurant that specializes in gourmet salads has realized through market research that its clientele is primarily made up of females. The owners of the restaurant want to attract men to their restaurant in addition to women, but from the market research, they have learned that people have the belief that "salads are food for women."

III.   *Your Job:* The restaurant owner would like to change the way people perceive salads, making them more attractive to men. You have been hired to change people's attitudes linking salads to one gender. How do you do this?

IV.   In a one-page report, specify the attitudes you would want to change, how you would attempt to change these attitudes, and then, how you would measure that people's attitudes have changed (measuring both attitudes and the percentage of the clientele who are male). What barriers would you face in changing attitudes?

C h a p t e r   8

The Problem Of Discrimination

In Chapter 7, we discussed prejudice, the negative attitudes people may hold toward individuals from other groups. The articles underscored how, in addition to overt prejudice, we must also study more subtle forms of prejudice which exist in our society.

In some cases, both overt and subtle forms of prejudice can be manifested in discriminatory behaviors, at the individual, institutional, or societal levels. The articles in this chapter look at the situations which can give rise to discrimination and the sometimes surprising lack of consistency between prejudiced attitudes and behavior. A common theme that runs throughout the chapter is that discrimination is pervasive in our society — affecting nearly every aspect of it.

A report by the U.S. Civil Rights Commission sets the stage for studying discrimination by presenting a broad definition of discrimination. LaPiere, in the next article, describes a classic study investigating the sometimes tenuous link between prejudice and discrimination — that is, between an attitude and a behavior. He reports a finding that is often replicated in social psychological research that attitudes do not always predict behavior.

The next three articles discuss the outcomes of discrimination. Hyde finds that our everyday language can be sexist and can impact the perceptions children have of males and females. Landry describes findings that have linked racism to poor health outcomes, and Swallow poignantly describes the impact of discrimination on one's personal identity.

The articles and projects in this chapter all point to ways of dealing with discrimination. As a whole, they suggest that the first step in stopping it from happening and to curb its destructive force when it does occur, is gaining an awareness of its effects. The next step is to identify measures that will help eliminate it. While reading these articles and doing the projects in this chapter, challenge yourself to think of ways to stop the discrimination that occurs in your life and in the lives of those around you. Reviewing some of the articles from earlier sections of the Workbook may aid you in this process. For example, the articles on group processes in Chapters 2 and 3 may help you understand negative behaviors toward those in the outgroup, and may help suggest strategies for using group processes to decrease discrimination.

The Problem: Discrimination

U.S. Commission on Civil Rights

> **Editors' Note:** What qualifies as discrimination? The following selection by the United States Civil Rights Commission provides a number of examples of discrimination by individuals, organizations, and larger structural entities. Many of these examples are not often thought of as discrimination, but the outcomes can be just as destructive as more obvious forms of discrimination. This suggests that in order to counter discrimination, we must broaden our definitions of it.

Making choices is an essential part of everyday life for individuals and organizations. These choices are shaped in part by social structures that set standards and influence conduct in such areas as education, employment, housing, and government. When these choices limit the opportunities available to people because of their race, sex, or national origin, the problem of discrimination arises.

Historically, discrimination against minorities and women was not only accepted but it was also governmentally required. The doctrine of white supremacy used to support the institution of slavery was so much a part of American custom and policy that the Supreme Court in 1857 approvingly concluded that both the North and the South regarded slaves "as beings of an inferior order, and altogether unfit to associate with the white race, either in social or political relations; and so far inferior, that they had no rights which the white man was bound to respect." White supremacy survived the passage of the Civil War amendments to the Constitution and continued to dominate legal and social institutions in the North as well as the South to disadvantage not only blacks,[2] but other racial and ethnic groups as well—American Indians, Alaskan Natives, Asian and Pacific Islanders and Hispanics.[3]

While minorities were suffering from white supremacy women were suffering from male supremacy. Mr. Justice Brennan has summed up the legal disabilities imposed on women this way:

> [T]hroughout much of the 19th century the position of women in our society was, in many respects, comparable to that of blacks under the pre-Civil War slave codes. Neither slaves nor "omen could hold office, serve on juries, or bring suit in their own names, and married women traditionally were

denied the legal capacity to hold or convey property or to serve as legal guardians of their own children.[4]

In 1873 a member of the Supreme Court proclaimed, "Man is, or should be, woman's protector and defender. The natural and proper timidity and delicacy which belongs to the female sex evidently unfits it for many of the occupations of civil life.[5] Such romantic paternalism has alternated with fixed notions of male superiority to deny women in law and in practice the most fundamental of rights, including the right to vote, which was not granted until 1920; the Equal Rights Amendment has yet to be ratified.[7]

White and male supremacy are no longer popularly; accepted American values. The blatant racial and sexual discrimination that originated in our conveniently forgotten past, however, continues to manifest itself today in a complex interaction of attitudes and actions of individuals, organizations, and the network of social structures that make up our society.

Individual Discrimination

The most common understanding of discrimination rests at the level of prejudiced individual attitudes and behavior. Although open and intentional prejudice persists, individual discriminatory conduct is often hidden and sometimes unintentional.[8] Some of the following are examples of deliberately discriminatory actions by consciously prejudiced individuals. Some are examples of unintentionally discriminatory actions taken by persons who may not believe themselves to be prejudiced but whose decisions continue to be guided by deeply ingrained discriminatory customs.

•Personnel officers whose stereotyped beliefs about women and minorities testify hiring them for low level and low paying jobs exclusively, regardless of their potential experience or qualifications for higher level jobs.[9]

•Administrators, historically white males, who rely on "word-of-mouth" recruiting among their friends and colleagues, so that only their friends and protégés of the same race and sex learn of potential job openings.[10]

•Employers who hire women for their sexual attractiveness or potential sexual availability rather than their competence, and employers who engage in sexual harassment of their female employees.[11]

•Teachers who interpret linguistic and cultural differences as indications of low potential or lack of academic interest on the part of minority students.[12]

•Guidance counselors and teachers whose low expectations lead them to steer female and minority students away from "hard" subjects, such as mathematics and science, toward subjects that do not prepare them for higher paying jobs.[13]

•Real estate agents who show fewer homes to minority buyers and steer them to minority or mixed neighborhoods because they believe white residents would oppose the presence of black neighbors.[14]

•Families who assume that property values inevitably decrease when minorities move in and therefore move out of their neighborhoods if minorities do move in.[15]

•Parole boards that assume minority offenders to be more dangerous or more unreliable than white offenders and consequently more frequently deny parole to minorities than to whites convicted of equally serious crimes.[16]

These contemporary examples of discrimination may not be motivated by conscious prejudice. The personnel manager is likely to deny believing that minorities and women can only perform satisfactorily in low level jobs and at the same time allege that other executives and decision makers would not consider them for higher level positions. In some cases, the minority or female applicants may not be aware that they have been discriminated against—the personnel manager may inform them that they are deficient in experience while rejecting their applications because of prejudice; the white male administrator who recruits by word-of-

mouth from his friends or white male work force excludes minorities and women who never learn of the available positions. The discriminatory results these activities cause may not even be desired. The guidance counselor may honestly believe there are no other realistic alternatives for minority and female students.

Whether conscious or not, open or hidden, desired or undesired, these acts build on and support prejudicial stereotypes, deny their victims opportunities provided to others, and perpetuate discrimination, regardless of intent.

Organizational Discrimination

Discrimination, though practiced by individuals, is often reinforced by the well-established rules, policies, and practices of organizations. These actions are often regarded simply as part of the organization's way of doing business and are carried out by individuals as just part of their day's work.

Discrimination at the organizational level takes forms that are similar to those on the individual level. For example:

•Height and weight requirements that are unnecessarily geared to the physical proportions of white males and, therefore, exclude females and some minorities from certain jobs.[17]

•Seniority rules, when applied to jobs historically held only by white males, make more recently hired minorities and females more subject to layoff—the "last hired, first fired" employee—and less eligible for advancement.[18]

•Nepotistic membership policies of some referral unions that exclude those who are not relatives of members who, because of past employment practices, are usually white.[19]

•Restrictive employment leave policies, coupled with prohibitions on part-time work or denials of fringe benefits to part-time workers, that make it difficult for the heads of single parent families, most of whom are women, to get and keep jobs and meet the needs of their families.[20]

•The use of standardized academic tests or criteria, geared to the cultural and educational norms of the middle-class or white males, that are not relevant indicators of successful job performance.[21]

•Preferences shown by many law and medical schools in the admission of children of wealthy and influential alumni, nearly all of whom are white.[22]

•Credit policies of banks and lending institutions that prevent the granting of mortgage monies and loans in minority neighborhoods, or prevent the granting of credit to married women and others who have previously been denied the opportunity to build good credit histories in their own names.[23]

Superficially "color blind" or "gender neutral," these organizational practices have an adverse effect on minorities and women. As with individual actions, these organizational actions favor white males, even when taken with no conscious intent to affect minorities and women adversely, by protecting and promoting the status quo arising from the racism and sexism of the past. If, for example, the jobs now protected by "last hired, first fired" provisions had always been integrated, seniority would not operate to disadvantage minorities and women. If educational systems from kindergarten through college had not historically favored white males, many more minorities and women would hold advanced degrees and thereby be included among those involved in deciding what academic tests should test for. If minorities had lived in the same neighborhoods as whites, there would be no minority neighborhoods to which mortgage money could be denied on the basis of their being minority neighborhoods.

In addition, these barriers to minorities and women too often do not fulfill legitimate needs of the organization, or these needs can be met through other means that adequately maintain the organization without discriminating. Instead of excluding all women on the assumption that they are too weak or should be protected from strenuous work, the organization can implement a reasonable test that measures the strength actually needed to perform the job or, where possible, develop ways of doing the work that require less physical effort. Admissions to academic and professional schools can be decided not only on the basis of grades, standardized test scores, and the prestige of the high school or college

from which the applicant graduated, but also on the basis of community service, work experience, and letters of recommendation. Lending institutions can look at the individual and his or her financial ability rather than the neighborhood or marital status of the prospective borrower.

Some practices that disadvantage minorities and women are readily accepted aspects of everyday behavior. Consider the "old boy" network in business and education built on years of friendship and social contact among white males, or the exchanges of information and corporate strategies by business acquaintances in racially or sexually exclusive country clubs and locker rooms paid for by the employer.[24] These actions, all of which have a discriminatory impact on minorities and women, are not necessarily acts of conscious prejudice. Because such actions are so often considered part of the "normal" way of doing things, people have difficulty recognizing that they are discriminating and therefore resist abandoning these practices despite the clearly discriminatory results. Consequently, many decision-makers have difficulty considering, much less accepting, nondiscriminatory alternatives that may work just as well or better to advance legitimate organizational interests but without systematically disadvantaging minorities and women.

This is not to suggest that all such discriminatory organizational actions are spurious or arbitrary. Many may serve the actual needs of the organization. Physical size or strength at times may be a legitimate job requirement; sick leave and insurance policies must be reasonably restricted; educational qualifications are needed for many jobs; lending institutions cannot lend to people who cannot reasonably demonstrate an ability to repay loans. Unless carefully examined and then modified or eliminated, however, these apparently neutral rules, policies, and practices will continue to perpetuate age-old discriminatory patterns into the structure of today's society.

Whatever the motivation behind such organizational acts, a process is occurring, the common denominator of which is unequal results on a very large scale. When unequal outcomes are repeated over time and in numerous societal and geographical areas, it is a clear signal that a discriminatory process is at work.

Such discrimination is not a static, one-time phenomenon that has a clearly limited effect. Discrimination can feed on discrimination in self-perpetuating cycles.[25]

•The employer who recruits job applicants by word-of-mouth within a predominantly white male work force reduces the chances of receiving applications from minorities and females for open positions. Since they do not apply, they are not hired. Since they are not hired, they are not present when new jobs become available. Since they are not aware of new jobs, they cannot recruit other minority or female applicants. Because there are no minority or female employees to recruit others, the employer is left to recruit on his own from among his predominantly white and male work force.[26]

•The teacher who expects poor academic performance from minority and female students may not become greatly concerned when their grades are low. The acceptance of their low grades removes incentives to improve. Without incentives to improve, their grades remain low. Their low grades reduce their expectations, and the teacher has no basis for expecting more of them.[27]

•The realtor who assumes that white home owners do not want minority neighbors "steers" minorities to minority neighborhoods. Those steered to minority neighborhoods tend to live in minority neighborhoods. White neighborhoods then remain white and realtors tend to assume that whites do not want minority neighbors.[28]

•Elected officials appoint voting registrars who impose linguistic, geographic, and other barriers to minority voter registration. Lack of minority registration leads to low voting rates. Lower minority voting rates lead to the election of fewer minorities. Fewer elected minorities leads to the appointment of voting registrars who maintain the same barriers.[29]

Structural Discrimination

Such self-sustaining discriminatory processes occur not only within the fields of employment, education, housing, and government but also between these structural areas. There is a classic cycle of structural discrimination that reproduces itself. Discrimination in education denies the credentials to get good jobs. Discrimination in employment denies the economic resources to buy good housing. Discrimination in housing confines minorities to school districts providing inferior education, closing the cycle in a classic form.[30]

With regard to white women, the cycle is not as tightly closed. To the extent they are raised in families headed by white males, and are married to or live with white males, white women will enjoy the advantages in housing and other areas that such relationships to white men can confer. White women lacking the sponsorship of white men, however, will be unable to avoid gender-based discrimination in housing, education, and employment. White women can thus be the victims of discrimination produced by social structures that is comparable in form to that experienced by minorities.

This perspective is not intended to imply that either the dynamics of discrimination or its nature and degree are identical for women and minorities. But when a woman of any background seeks to compete with men of any group, she finds herself the victim of a discriminatory process. Regarding the similarities and differences between the discrimination experienced by women and minorities, one author has aptly stated:

> [W]hen five groups exist in a situation of inequality it may be self-defeating to become embroiled in a quarrel over which is more unequal or the victim of greater oppression. The more salient question is how a condition of inequality for both is maintained and perpetuated—through what means is it reinforced?[31]

The following are additional examples of the interaction between social structures that affect minorities and women:

•The absence of minorities and women from executive, writing, directing, news reporting, and acting positions in television contributes to unfavorable stereotyping on the screen, which in turn reinforces existing stereotypes among the public and creates psychological roadblocks to progress in employment, education, and housing.[32]

•Living in inner-city high crime areas in disproportionate numbers, minorities, particularly minority youth, are more likely to be arrested and are more likely to go to jail than whites accused of similar offenses, and their arrest and conviction records are then often used as bars to employment.[33]

•Because of past discrimination against minorities and women, female and minority-headed businesses are often small and relatively new. Further disadvantaged by contemporary credit and lending practices, they are more likely than white male-owned businesses to remain small and be less able to employ full-time specialists in applying for government contracts. Because they cannot monitor the availability of government contracts, they do not receive such contracts. Because they cannot demonstrate success with government contracts, contracting officers tend to favor other firms that have more experience with government contracts.[34]

Discriminatory actions by individuals and organizations are not only pervasive, occurring in every sector of society, but also cumulative with effects limited neither to the time nor the particular structural area in which they occur. This process of discrimination, therefore, extends across generations, across organizations, and across social structures in self-reinforcing cycles, passing the disadvantages incurred by one generation in one area to future generations in many related areas.[35]

These interrelated components of the discriminatory process share one basic result: the persistent gaps seen in the status of women and minorities relative to that of white males These unequal results themselves have real consequences. The employer who wishes to hire more minorities and women may be bewildered by charges of racism and sexism when confronted by what appears to be a genuine shortage of qualified minority and female applicants. The guidance counselor who sees one promising minority student after another drop out of school or give up in despair may be resentful of allegations of racism when there is little he or she alone can do for the student. The banker who denies a loan to a female single parent may wish to do

differently, but believes that prudent fiscal judgment requires taking into account her lack of financial history and inability to prove that she is a good credit risk. These and other decision makers see the results of a discriminatory process repeated over and over again, and those results provide a basis for rationalizing their own actions, which then feed into that same process.

When seen outside the context of the interlocking and intertwined effects of discrimination, complaints that many women and minorities are absent from the ranks of qualified job applicants, academically inferior and unmotivated, poor credit risks, and so forth, may appear to be justified. Decision makers like those described above are reacting to real social problems stemming from the process of discrimination. But many too easily fall prey to stereotyping and consequently disregard those minorities and women who have the necessary skills or qualifications. And they erroneously "blame the victims" of discrimination,[36] instead of examining the past and present context in which their own actions are taken and the multiple consequences of these actions on the lives of minorities and women.

The Process of Discrimination

Although discrimination is maintained through individual actions, neither individual prejudices nor random chance can fully explain the persistent national patterns of inequality and underrepresentation. Nor can these patterns be blamed on the persons who are at the bottom of our economic, political, and social order. Overt racism and sexism as embodied in popular notions of white and male supremacy have been widely repudiated, but our history of discrimination based on race, sex, and national origin has not been readily put aside. Past discrimination continues to have present effects. The task today is to identify those effects and the forms and dynamics of the discrimination that produced them.

Discrimination against minorities and women must now be viewed as an interlocking process involving the attitudes and actions of individuals and the organizations and social structures that guide individual behavior. That process, started by past events, now routinely bestows privileges, favors, and advantages on white males and imposes disadvantages and penalties on minorities and women. This process is also self-perpetuating. Many normal, seemingly neutral, operations of our society create stereotyped expectations that justify unequal results; unequal results in one area foster inequalities in opportunity and accomplishment in others; the lack of opportunity and accomplishment confirm the original prejudices or engender new ones that fuel the normal operations generating unequal results.

As we have shown, the process of discrimination involves many aspects of our society. No single factor sufficiently explains it, and no single means will suffice to eliminate it. Such elements of our society as our history of *de lure* discrimination, deeply ingrained prejudices,[37] inequities based on economic and social class,[38] and the structure and function of all our economic, social, and political institutions[39] must be continually examined in order to understand their part in shaping today's decisions that will either maintain or counter the current process of discrimination.

It may be difficult to identify precisely all aspects of the discriminatory process and assign those parts their appropriate importance. But understanding discrimination starts with an awareness that such a process exists and that to avoid perpetuating it, we must carefully assess the context and consequences of our everyday actions.

Notes

1. Dred Scott *v.* Sanford, 60 U.S. (19 How.) 393, 408 (1857).
2. For a concise summary of this history; see U.S. Commission on Civil Rights, *Twenty Years After Brown,* pp. 4-29 (1975); *Freedom to the Free: 1863, Century of Emancipation* (1963).
3. The discriminatory conditions experienced by these minority groups have been documented in the following publications by the U.S. Commission on Civil Rights: *The Navajo Nation: An American Colony* (1975); *The Southwest Indian Report* (1973); *The Forgotten Minority: Asian Americans in New York City* (State Advisory Committee Report 1977); *Success of Asian Americans: Fact or Fiction?* (1980); *Stranger in One's Land* (1970); *Toward Quality Education for Mexican Americans* (1974); *Puerto Ricans in the Continental United States: An Uncertain Future* (1976).

4. Frontiero v. Richardson, 411 U.S. 677, 684-86(1973), citing L. Kanowitz, *Women and the Law: The Unfinished* Revolution, pp. 5-6 (1970), and G. Myrdal, *An American Dilemma* 1073 (20th Anniversary Ed., 1962). Justice Brennan wrote the opinion of the Court, joined by Justices Douglas, White, and Marshall. Justice Stewart concurred in the judgment. Justice Powell, joined by Chief Justice Burger and Justice Blackmun, wrote a separate concurring opinion. Justice Rehnquist dissented. See also H. M. Hacker, "Women as a Minority Group," *Social Forces,* vol.30 (1951), pp. 60-69; W. Chafe, W*omen and Equality: Changing Patterns in American Culture* (New York: Oxford University Press, 1977).
5. Bradwell v. State, 83 U.S. (16 Wall) 130, 141(1873) (Bradley, J., concurring), quoted in *Frontiero, supra* note 4.
6. U.S. Const. amend. XIX.
7. See U.S. Commission on Civil Rights, *Statement on the Equal Rights Amendment* (December 1978).
8. See, e.g., R. K. Merton, "Discrimination and the American Creed," in R. K. Merton, *Sociological Ambivalence and Other Essays* (New York: The Free Press, 1976), pp. 189-216. In this essay on racism, published for the first time more than 30 years ago, Merton presented a typology which introduced the notion that discriminatory actions are not always directly related to individual attitudes of prejudice. Merton's typology consisted of the following: Type I—the unprejudiced nondiscriminator; Type II—the unprejudiced discriminator; Type III—the prejudiced nondiscriminator; Type IV—the prejudiced discriminator. In the present context, Type II is crucial in its observation that discrimination is often practiced by persons who are not themselves prejudiced, but who respond to, or do not oppose, the actions of those who discriminate because of prejudiced attitudes (Type IV). See also D. C. Reitzes, "Prejudice and Discrimination: A Study in Contradictions," in *Racial and Ethnic Relations,* ed. H. M. Hughes (Boston: Allyn and Bacon, 1970), pp. 56-65.
9. See R. M. Kanter and B. A. Stein, "Making a Life at the Bottom," in *Life in Organizations, Workplaces as People Experience Them,* ed. Kanter and Stein (New York: Basic Books, 1976), pp. 176-90; also L. K. Howe, "Retail Sales Worker," ibid., pp. 248-51; also R. M. Kanter, *Men and Women of the Corporation* (New York: Basic Books, 1977).
10. See M. S. Granovetter, *Getting a Job: A Study of Contract and Careers* (Cambridge: Harvard University Press, 1974), pp. 6-11; also A. W. Blumrosen, *Black Employment and the Law* (New Brunswick, N.J.: Rutgers University Press, 1971), p. 232.
11. See U.S. Equal Employment Opportunity Commission, "Guidelines on Discrimination Because of Sex," 29 C.F.R. s1604.4 (1979); L. Farley, *Sexual Shakedown: The Sexual Harassment of Women on the Job* (New York: McGraw-Hill, 1978), pp. 92-96, 176-79; C. A. Mackinnon,

Sexual Harassment of Working Women (New Haven: Yale University Press, 1979), pp. 25-55.

12. See R. Rosenthal and L. F. Jacobson, "Teacher Expectations for the Disadvantaged," *Scientific American,* 1968 (b) 218, 219-23; also D. Bar Tal, "Interactions of Teachers and Pupils," in *New Approaches to Social Problems,* ed. I. H. Frieze, D. Bar Tal, and J. S. Carrol (San Francisco: Jossey Bass, 1979), pp. 337-58; also *U.S. Commission on Civil Rights, Teachers and Students, Report V: Mexican American Education Study. Differences in Teacher Interaction with Mexican American and Anglo Students* (1973), pp. 22-23.

13. Ibid.

14. U.S. Department of Housing and Urban Development, "Measuring Racial Discrimination in American Housing Markets: The Housing Market Practices Survey" (1979); D. M. Pearce, "Gatekeepers and Home Seekers Institutional Patterns in Racial Steering," *Social Problems,* vol. 26 (1979) pp. 325-42; "Benign Steering and Benign Quotas: The Validity of Race Conscious Government Policies to Promote Residential Integration," 93 *Harv.* L. Rev. 938, 944(1980).

15. See M. N. Danielson, *The Politics of Exclusion* (New York: Columbia University Press, 1976), pp. 11-12; U.S. Commission on Civil Rights, *Equal Opportunity in Suburbia* (1974).

16. See L. L. Knowles and K. Prewitt, eds., *Institutional Racism in America* (Englewood Cliffs, N.J.: Prentice Hall, 1969) pp. 58-77, and E. D. Wright, *The Politics of Punishment* (New York: Harper and Row, 1973). Also, S. V. Brown, "Race and Parole Hearing Outcomes," in *Discrimination in Organizations,* ed. R. Alvarez and K. C. Lutterman (San Francisco: Jossey Bass, 1979), pp. 355-74.

17. Height and weight minimums that disproportionately exclude women without a showing of legitimate job requirement constitute unlawful sex discrimination. *See* Dothard v. Rawlinson, 433 U.S. 321(1977); Bowe v. Colgate Palmolive Co., 416 F.2d 711(7th Cir. 1969). Minimum height requirements used in screening applicants for employment have also been held to be unlawful where such a requirement excludes a significantly higher percentage of Hispanics than other national origin groups in the labor market and no job relatedness is shown. See Smith v. City of East Cleveland, 520 F.2d 492 (6th Cir. 1975).

18. U.S. Commission on Civil Rights, *Last Hired, First Fired* (1976); Tangren v. Wackenhut Servs., Inc., 480 F. Supp. 539 (D. Nev. 1979).

19. U.S. Commission on Civil Rights, *The Challenge Ahead, Equal Opportunity in Referral Unions* (1977), pp. 84-89.

20. A. Pifer, "Women Working: Toward a New Society," pp. 13-34, and D. Pearce, "Women, Work and Welfare: The Feminization of Poverty," pp. 103-24, both in K. A. Fernstein, ed., *Working Women and Families* (Beverly Hills: Sage Publications, 1979). Disproportionate numbers of single-parent families are minorities.

21. See Griggs v. Duke Power Company, 401 U.S. 424 (1971); U.S. Commission on Civil Rights, *Toward Equal Educational Opportunity: Affirmative Admissions Programs at Law and Medical Schools* (1978), pp. 10-12; I. Berg, *Education and Jobs: The Great Training Robbery* (Boston: Beacon Press, 1971), pp. 58-60.

22. See U.S. Commission on Civil Rights, *Toward Equal Educational Opportunity: Affirmative Admissions Programs at Law and Medical Schools* (1978), pp. 14-15.

23. See U.S. Commission on Civil Rights, *Mortgage Money: Who Gets It? A Case Study in Mortgage Lending Discrimination in Hartford, Conn.* (1974); J. Feagin and C. B. Feagin, *Discrimination American Style, Institutional Racism and Sexism* (Englewood Cliffs, N.J.: Prentice Hall, 1976), pp. 78-79.

24. See *Club Membership Practices by Financial Institutions: Hearing before the Comm. on Banking, Housing and Urban Affairs, United States Senate,* 96th Cong., 1st Sess. (1979). The Office of Federal Contract Compliance Programs of the Department of Labor has proposed a rule that would make the payment or reimbursement of membership fees in a private club that accepts or rejects persons on the basis of race, color, sex, religion, or national origin a prohibited discriminatory practice. 45 Fed. Reg. 4954 (1980) (to be codified cn41 C.F.R. s60-l.11).

25. See U.S. Commission on Civil Rights, *For All The People . . By All the People* (1969), pp. 122-23.

26. See note 10.

27. See note 12.

28. See notes 14 and 15.

29. See Statement of Arthur S. Flemming, Chairman, U.S. Commission on Civil Rights, before the Subcommittee on Constitutional Rights of the Committee on the Judiciary of the U.S. Senate on S.407, S.903, and S.1279, Apr. 9,1975, pp. 15-18, based on U.S. Commission on Civil Rights, *The Voting Rights Act: Ten Years After* (January 1975).

30. See, e.g., U.S. Commission on Civil Rights, *Equal Opportunity in Suburbia* (1974).

31. Chafe, *Women and Equality,* p. 78.

32. U.S. Commission on Civil Rights, *Window Dressing on the Set* (1977).

33. See note 16; Gregory v. Litton Systems, Inc., 472 F.2d 631(9th Cir. 1972); Green v. Mo.-Pac. R.R., 523 F.2d 1290 (8th Cir. 1975).

34. See U.S. Commission on Civil Rights, *Minorities and Women as Government Contractors,* pp. 20, 27, 125(1975).

35. See, e.g., A. Downs, *Racism in America and How to Combat It* (U.S. Commission on Civil Rights, 1970); "The Web of Urban Racism," in *Institutional Racism in America,* ed. Knowles and Prewitt (Englewood Cliffs, N.J.: Prentice Hall, 1969) pp. 134-76. Other factors in addition to race, sex, and national origin may contribute to these interlocking institutional patterns. In *Equal Opportunity in Suburbia* (1974), this Commission documented what it termed "the cycle of urban poverty" that confines minorities in central cities with declining tax bases, soaring educational and other public needs, and dwindling employment

opportunities, surrounded by largely white, affluent suburbs. This cycle of poverty, however, started with and is fueled by discrimination against minorities. *See also* W. Taylor, *Hanging Together, Equality in an Urban Nation* (New York: Simon & Schuster, 1971).

36. The "self-fulfilling prophecy" is a well known phenomenon. "Blaming the victim" occurs when responses to discrimination are treated as though they were the causes rather than the results of discrimination. *See* Chafe, *Women and Equality* (New York: Oxford University Press, 1977) pp. 76-78; W. Ryan, *Blaming the Victim* (New York: Pantheon Books, 1971).

37. See, e.g., J. E. Simpson and J. M. Yinger, *Racial and Cultural Minorities* (New York: Harper and Row, 1965) pp. 49-79; J. M. Jones, *Prejudice and Racism* (Reading, Mass.: Addison Wesley, 1972) pp. 60-111; M. M. Tumin, "Who Is Against Desegregation?" in *Racial and Ethnic Relations,* ed. H. Hughes (Boston: Allyn and Bacon, 1970) pp. 76-85; D. M. Wellman, *Portraits of White Racism* (Cambridge: Cambridge University Press, 1977).

38. See, e.g., D. C. Cox, *Caste, Class and Race: A Study in Social Dynamics* (Garden City, N.Y.: Doubleday, 1948); W. J. Wilsoce, *Power, Racism and Privilege* (New York: Macmillan, 1973).

39. H. Hacker, "Women as a Minority Group," *Social Forces,* vol. 30 (1951) pp. 60-69; J. Feagin and C. B. Feagin, *Discrimination American Style;* Chafe, *Women and Equality;* J. Feagin, "Indirect Institutionalized Discrimination," *American Politics Quarterly,* vol. 5 (1977) pp. 177-200; M. A. Chesler, "Contemporary Sociological Theories of Racism," in *Towards the Elimination of Racism,* ed. P. Katz (New York: Pergamon Press, 1976); P. Van den Berghe, *Race and Racism: A Comparative Perspective* (New York: Wiley, 1967); P. Carmichael and C. Hamilton, *Black Power* (New York: Random House, 1967); Knowles and Prewitt, *Institutional Racism in America;* Downs, *Racism* in *America and How to Combat It* (1970).

Attitudes vs. Actions

Richard T. LaPiere

Editors' Note: We often assume that we will discriminate against people toward whom we are prejudiced. In this classic article, Richard LaPiere tests how consistent people's behavior is with their previously stated attitude. Surprisingly, he finds very little consistency, raising the question of whether we should study attitudes or behaviors. This work also suggests that even if people hold negative beliefs, they may not act on them—which is a positive note in the often negative research on discrimination.

. . . Some years ago I endeavored to obtain comparative data on the degree of French and English antipathy towards dark-skinned peoples. The informal questionnaire technique was used, but, although the responses so obtained were exceedingly consistent, I supplemented them with what I then considered an index to overt behavior. The hypothesis as then stated *seemed* entirely logical. "Whatever our attitude on the validity of 'verbalization' may be, it must be recognized that any study of attitudes through direct questioning is open to serious objection, both because of the limitations of the sampling method and because in classifying attitudes the inaccuracy of human judgment is an inevitable variable. In this study, however, there is corroborating evidence on these attitudes in the policies adopted by hotel proprietors. Nothing could be used as a more accurate index of color prejudice than the admission or non-admission of colored people to hotels, for the proprietor must reflect the group attitude in his policy regardless of his own feelings in the matter.   Since he determines what the group attitude is towards Negroes through the expression of that attitude in overt behavior and over a long period of actual experience, the results will be exceptionally free from those disturbing factors which inevitably affect the effort to study attitudes by direct questioning."

But at that time I overlooked the fact that what I was obtaining from the hotel proprietors was still a "verbalized" reaction to a symbolic situation.   The response to a Negro's request for lodgings might have been an excellent index of the attitude of hotel patrons towards living in the same hotel as a Negro. Yet to ask the proprietor "Do you permit members of the Negro race to stay here?" does not, it appears, measure his potential response to an actual Negro.

All measurement of attitudes by the questionnaire technique proceeds on the assumption that there is a mechanical relationship between symbolic and nonsymbolic behavior. It is simple enough to prove that there is no *necessary* correlation between speech and action, between response to words and to the realities they symbolize. A parrot can be taught to swear, a child to sing "Frankie and Johnny" in the Mae West manner. The words will have no meaning to either child or parrot. But to prove that there is no *necessary* relationship does not prove that such a relationship **may** not exist. There need be no relationship between what the hotel proprietor says he will do and what he actually does when confronted with a colored patron. Yet there may be. Certainly we are justified in assuming that the verbal response of the hotel proprietor would be more likely to indicate what he would actually do than would the verbal response of people whose personal feelings are less subordinated to economic expediency. However, the following study indicates that the reliability of even such responses is very small indeed.

Beginning in 1930 and continuing for two years thereafter, I had the good fortune to travel rather extensively with a young Chinese student and his wife. Both were personable, charming, and quick to win the admiration and respect of those they had the opportunity to become intimate with. But they were foreign-born Chinese, a fact that could not be disguised. Knowing the general "attitude" of Americans towards the Chinese as indicated by the "social distance" studies which have been made, it was with considerable trepidation that I first approached a hotel clerk in their company. Perhaps that clerk's eyebrows lifted slightly, but he accommodated us without a show of hesitation. And this in the "best" hotel in a small town noted for its narrow and bigoted "attitude" towards Orientals. . . .

In something like ten thousand miles of motor travel, twice across the United States, up and down the Pacific Coast, we met definite rejection from those asked to serve us just once. We were received at 66 hotels, auto camps, and "Tourist Homes," refused at one. We were served in 184 restaurants and cafes scattered throughout the country and treated with what I judged to be more than ordinary consideration in 7 of them. Accurate and detailed records were kept of all these instances. . . .

[I]n only one out of 251 instances in which we purchased goods or services necessitating intimate human relationships did the fact that my companions were Chinese adversely affect us. Factors entirely unassociated with race were, in the main, the determinant of significant variations in our reception. It would appear reasonable to conclude that the "attitude" of the American people, as reflected in the behavior of those who are for pecuniary reasons presumably most sensitive to the antipathies of their white clientele, is anything but negative towards the Chinese. In terms of "social distance" we might conclude that native Caucasians are not averse to residing in the same hotels, auto-camps, and "Tourist Homes" as Chinese and will with complacency accept the presence of Chinese at an adjoining table in restaurant or cafe. It does not follow that there is revealed a distinctly "positive" attitude towards the Chinese, that whites prefer the Chinese to other whites. But the facts as gathered certainly preclude the conclusion that there is an intense prejudice towards the Chinese.

Yet the existence of this prejudice, very intense, is proven by a conventional "attitude" study. To provide a comparison of symbolic reaction to symbolic social situations with actual reaction to real social situations, I "questionnaired" the establishments which we patronized during the two year period. Six months were permitted to lapse between the time I obtained the overt reaction and the symbolic. It was hoped that the effects of the actual experience with Chinese guests,

adverse or otherwise, would have faded during the intervening time. To the hotel or restaurant a questionnaire was mailed with an accompanying letter purporting to be a special and personal plea for response. The questionnaires all asked the same question, "Will you accept members of the Chinese race as guests in your establishment?" Two types of questionnaire were used. In one this question was inserted among similar queues concerning Germans, French, Japanese, Russians, Armenians, Jews, Negroes, Italians, and Indians. In the other the pertinent question was unencumbered. With persistence, completed replies were obtained from 128 of the establishments we had visited; 81 restaurants and cafes and 47 hotels, auto-camps, and "Tourist Homes." In response to the relevant question 92 per cent of the former and 91 per cent of the latter replied "No." The remainder replied "Uncertain; depend upon circumstances." From the woman proprietor of a small auto-camp I received the only "Yes," accompanied by a chatty letter describing the nice visit she had had with a Chinese gentleman and his sweet wife during the previous summer.

A rather unflattering interpretation might be put upon the fact that those establishments who had provided for our needs so graciously were, some months later, verbally antagonistic towards hypothetical Chinese. To factor this experience out responses were secured from 32 hotels and 96 restaurants located in approximately the same regions, but uninfluenced by this particular experience with Oriental clients. In this, as in the former case, both types of questionnaires were used. The results indicate that neither the type of questionnaire nor the fact of previous experience had important bearing upon the symbolic response to symbolic social situations.

It is impossible to make direct comparison between the reactions secured through questionnaires and from actual experience. On the basis of the above data it would appear foolhardy for Chinese to attempt to travel in the United States. And yet, as I have shown, actual experience indicates that the American people, as represented by the personnel of hotels, restaurants, etc., are not at all averse to fraternizing with Chinese within the

252 The Problem of Discrimination

limitations which apply to social relationships between Americans themselves. . . .

No doubt a considerable part of the data which the social scientist deals with can be obtained by the questionnaire method. The census reports are based upon verbal questionnaires and I do not doubt their basic integrity. If we wish to know how many children a man has, his income, the size of his home, his age and the condition of his parents, we can reasonably ask him. These things he has frequently and conventionally converted into verbal responses. He is competent to report upon them, and will do so accurately, unless indeed he wishes to do otherwise. A careful investigator could no doubt even find out by verbal means whether the man fights with his wife (frequently, infrequently, or not at all) though the neighbors would be a more reliable source. But we should not expect to obtain by the questionnaire method his "anticipatory set or tendency" to action should his wife pack up and go home to Mother, should Elder Son get into trouble with the neighbor's daughter, the President assume the status of dictator, the Japanese take over the rest of China, or a Chinese gentleman come to pay a social call.

Only a verbal reaction to an entirely symbolic situation can be secured by the questionnaire. It may indicate what responder would actually do when confronted with the situation symbolized in the question, but there is no assurance that it will. And so to call the response a reflection of a "social attitude" is to entirely disregard the definition commonly given for the phrase "attitude." If social attitudes are to be conceptualized as partially integrated habit sets which will become operative under specific circumstances and lead to a particular pattern of adjustment they must, in the main, be derived from a study of humans behaving in actual social situations. They must not be imputed on the basis of questionnaire data.

The questionnaire is cheap, easy, and mechanical. The study of human behavior is time consuming, intellectually fatiguing, and depends for its success upon the ability of the investigator. The former method gives quantitative results, the latter mainly qualitative. Quantitative measurements are quantitatively accurate; qualitative evaluations are always subject to the errors of human judgment. Yet it would seem far more worth while to make a shrewd guess regarding that which is essential than to accurately measure that which is likely to prove quite irrelevant.

Children's Understanding Of Sexist Language

Janet Shibley Hyde

Editors' Note: Who do you think of when you hear the following sentences: "When a kid goes to school, he often feels excited on the first day." versus hearing the sentence: "When a kid goes to school, he or she often feels excited on the first day." Discrimination, sexism, and racism exist in many forms, many of which are not always obvious. Even our language is sprinkled with ways of speaking that can lead to sexism. In the research presented in this article, Janet Hyde discovers that the language we use can impact children's perceptions of men and women, and even the jobs for which they think men and women are qualified. This work also suggests that the language we use can affect the roles which we think are appropriate for males and females, and that modifying the language we use is a step toward eliminating discrimination.

This article explores the role of language in the sex-typing process, focusing specifically on the "gender neutral" use of "he" and "his." In Experiment 1 first, third, and filth graders and college students were tested using a modified version of the task developed by Moulton et al. (1978), in which subjects told stories in response to a cue sentence containing "he;" "he or she;" or "they." Subjects also supplied pronouns in a fill-in task and were explicitly questioned about their knowledge of the gender-neutral use of "he." The results indicated that 12%, 18%, and 42% of the stories were about females when "he;" "they;" and "he or she" were used, respectively. There was a significant interaction of grade level, sex of subject, and pronoun. Children, even first graders, supplied "he" in gender-neutral fill-in sentences. Only 28% of first graders, but 84% of college students appear to understand the grammatical rule for the gender neutral use of "he." Experiment 2 replicated some aspects of Experiment 1 and extended the design with third and fifth graders. "She" was included as a fourth pronoun condition in the storytelling and produced 77% female stories. A description of a fictitious, gender-neutral occupation, wudgemaker, was read to children, with repeated references either to "he," "they," "he or she," or "she." Subjects' ratings of how well women could do the job were significantly affected by pronoun, ratings being lowest for "he," intermediate for "they" and "he or she," and highest for "she." The wudgemaker data demonstrate that the use of gender-neutral "he," compared with other pronouns, affects the formation of gender schemas in children. It is argued that the role of language in gender-role development should receive more attention, both theoretically and empirically.

Beginning a little more than a decade ago, the feminist movement raised a number of issues, including equal pay for equal work and availability of day care. One of those issues was sexism in language—the notion that the English language contains sex bias, particularly in usages such as "he" and "man" to refer to everyone (e.g., Martyna, 1980).

Concern over sexism in language raises a number of interesting questions for which the psychologist can provide empirical answers. How do people process gender-neutral uses of "her"? How do they interpret that pronoun when they hear or read it? And how does that processing affect other factors such as memory, stereotyping or attitudes?

Moulton, Robinson, and Elias (1978) conducted an important first empirical study on sex bias in language use. College students were asked to make up a story about a fictional character who fit the following theme: "In a large coeducational institution the average student will feel isolated in introductory courses." One third of the students received the pronoun "his" in the blank, one third received "his or her," and one third received "their." (Some students instead received a sentence concerning personal appearance, but the coeducational-institution cue is most relevant to the present study because it is explicitly gender neutral.) There was a strong tendency for male subjects to write stories about male characters and for female subjects to write about female characters. But strikingly, over all conditions, when the pronoun "his" was used, 35% of the stories were about females, compared with 46% for "their" and 56% female stories for "his or her." Thus, this study demonstrated that, although "his" may be gender-neutral in a grammatical sense, it is not gender neutral in a psychological sense. Even when the rest of the sentence explicitly provides a gender-neutral context, subjects more often think of a male when the pronoun is "his."

Other studies have yielded similar results. For example, Mackay (1980; Mackay & Fulkerson, 1979), using somewhat different methods, has also demonstrated that subjects respond to gender-neutral uses of "he" not as being neutral, but as being masculine. College students read paragraphs about a neutral person (e.g., student) in which the pronoun was either "he" consistently or "E," "e," or "tey." Subjects receiving "he" had a high rate —50%—of comprehension errors, responding that the paragraph was about a male, compared with a 13% error rate for those receiving a neologism.

In theoretical accounts and empirical investigations of gender-role development, the roles of imitation and reinforcements (Bandura & Walters, 1963; Mischel, 1966) and level of cognitive development (Kohlberg, 1966) have received great attention. In contrast, the role of language in gender-role development has been virtually ignored. The foregoing studies of adults raise some important questions for the developmental psychologist. How do children process sexist language, specifically gender-neutral "he"? Does their processing change with age, and does it differ from adults' processing? Is language a contributor to gender-role development, and can it be integrated into theories of gender-role development? . . .

A more complete statement of the cognitive approach is Bem's Gender Schema Theory (1981; see also Martin & Halverson, 1981). Bem argued that children learn a gender schema, a set of associations linked with maleness and femaleness in our society. This schema in turn organizes perception and affects the processing of information. Sex typing occurs because the self-concept becomes assimilated to the gender schema. Her studies with college students provided evidence consistent with the processing of information according to a gender schema, based on measures of clustering in free-recall and reaction times. Although she provided no data for children she cited two studies, the results of which are consistent with the existence of gender schematic processing in children as early as 6 years of age (Kail & Levine, 1976; Liben & Signorella, 1980). Martin and Halverson (1983) have also demonstrated, with 5- and 6-year-olds, that children distort information in sex-inconsistent pictures to make them sex consistent, a result that is congruent with the Gender Schema Theory. According to Bem, there are numerous inputs into the formation of the gender schema, and one of these is language, although she did not pursue this point empirically.

Two lines of thought, then—concern over sexist language as a social issue and a concern for a theoretical understanding of inputs into gender-role development—combine to raise a number of questions. How do children, compared with adults, process sexist language, specifically gender-neutral "he"? What is the effect on children of the use of gender-neutral "he"—does it contribute to the sex-typing process? Does it contribute to stereotyping, for example, stereotyping of occupations? Does it affect the formation of the gender schema? If so, what specific aspects of the gender schema might be affected— stereotyping of occupations, or perhaps more diffuse aspects, such as the relative status attached to the male and female roles, or the relative status of the self as a male or female?

The purpose of Experiment 1 was to replicate the Moulton et al. study with college students, and to extend it to first, third, and fifth graders, to assess age differences in responses to gender-neutral "he." Several other tasks were included in order to gain a more complete understanding of the nature of the responses. A fill-in task was used, and subjects were questioned for their understanding of the grammatical rule underlying the use of gender neutral "he."

EXPERIMENT I

Method

Subjects

A total of 310 subjects participated: 60 first graders (23 boys, 37 girls, 5-8 to 7-8, M = 6-7), 67 third graders (34 boys, 33 girls, 7-8 to 10-2, M = 8-11), 59 fifth graders (26 boys, 33 girls, 9-8 to 12-0, M = 10-10), and 124 college students (57 men, 67 women, 17-11 to 21-9, *M* = 19-3). College students participated in order to fulfill the requirements for introductory psychology. The parents of all elementary school subjects had returned signed consent forms for their children to participate. The elementary school children were drawn from three elementary schools, two middle-class, the other working-class to lower class.

Procedure

All elementary school children were interviewed individually, half by a male interviewer, half by a female.

Stories. After a brief warm up, the interviewer said "I'm going to tell you a little bit about a kid, and then I want you to make up a story about that child and tell it to me, and I'll write it down. When a kid goes to school, __ often feels excited on the first day." One third of the subjects received "he" for the blank, one third "they" and one third "he or she." The cue sentence was designed as an age-appropriate parallel to the neutral sentence used by Moulton et al. The interviewers recorded the basic content of the story, including the character's name. Later in the interview (at the end of the correct-sentences task), subjects were explicitly asked "Is (name of their character) a boy or a girl? Why did you make up your story about a __ ?"

Fill-in sentences. Next, children were questioned in several ways to determine their understanding of gender-neutral masculine pronoun use. First they were asked to complete a fill-in-the-blank task. In each case, the interviewer read the following sentences (or allowed the child to read it if he or she wanted to and was able):

1. If a kid likes candy, __ might eat too much.

2. Most parents want __ kids to get good grades.

3. When a kid plays football, __ likes to play with friends.

4. When a kid learns to read, __ can do more at school.

Correct sentences. Children were then asked to correct sentences with pronouns. They were told, "Now I'm going to read you some sentences and I want you to tell me if they're right or wrong, and if they're wrong, what's wrong with them. For example, if I say 'he goed to the store,' would that be right or wrong? Why?"

1. When a baby starts to walk __ often falls down. Right or wrong? Why?

2. Usually a kid wants to be just like __ own parents. Right or wrong? Why?

3. The average kid learns to read before __ can write. Right or wrong? Why?

4. The average kid likes to play football with __ friends. Right or wrong? Why?

Each child randomly received one of the following four pronouns replacing the blank: his (or he), they (or their), he or she (or his or her), or her (she).

Rule knowledge. Subjects were asked "When you use 'he' in a sentence, does it always mean it's a boy? For example, when I say 'When a kid goes to school, he often feels excited on the first day, does that mean the kid is a boy?" If the child answered no, then he or she was asked what it did mean.

College students. College students were tested in groups using a printed form. The form said

> Your task is to make up a story creating a fictional character who fits the following theme. Please do not write about yourself.
> In a large coeducational institution the average student will feel isolated in __ introductory courses.

One third received "his" for the blank, one third "his or her" and one third "their."

When subjects had completed the task, they were told to turn the papers over and answer the following questions briefly:

> When a person uses "he" or "his" in a sentence, does it always mean it's a male? For example, if I say "In a large coeducational institution the average student

will feel isolated in his introductory courses, does that mean that the student is a male? If your answer is no, then what does the "he" or "his" mean?

Results

Sex of Character in Story

... The data were analyzed using a four-way chi-square (Sex of Subject x Sex of Character in Story X Pronoun X Grade).... The results were highly significant, $x^2(40, N = 310) = 95.36$, p <.001. Once this test was significant, other specific hypotheses of interest could be tested (Everitt, 1977). In particular, the main effect for sex of subject was significant, $x^2(1, N = 310) = 35.54$, p < .001, with males overall telling 8% of their stories about females and females telling 38% female stories. The main effect for pronoun was also significant, $x^2(2, N = 310) = 28.81$, p < .001. When the pronoun was "he" or "his," overall 12% of the stories were about females; when it was "they" or "their," 18% were female, and when the pronoun was "his" or "her" ("he" or "she"), 42% of the stories were about females. The main effect of grade level was not significant, $x^2(3, N = 310) = 5.34$, although it must be remembered that grade level interacted significantly with sex of subject and pronoun as noted above. Note that not a single first-grade boy told a story about a female. Third-grade boys produced no female stories when the pronoun was "he" or "they," but nearly 30% of their stories were about females in response to "his" or "her."

Correct Sentences

Overall, children (the correct-sentences task was not given to college students) judged most sentences to be correct (76%). Sentences with "he" inserted were judged wrong 19% of the time, whereas sentences with "she" were judged wrong 28% of the time. The children's judgments interacted with the sex typing of the sentence. For example, in the sentence about football, "he" was judged wrong 6% of the time, but "she" was judged wrong 39% of the time. This effect in turn showed age trends. "She" in the football sentence was judged wrong by 18% of the first graders and by 67% of the fifth graders. ...

Fill-In Sentences

... At all grade levels, the great majority of children supplied "he" or "his" in the sentences, with the exception of Sentence 2, in which "their" was correct, and was correctly supplied. In the remaining three singular sentences, the sex typing of the sentence was varied, "candy" being gender-neutral, "football" masculine, and "read" feminine. In fact, "he" was supplied so uniformly and frequently that the sex typing of the sentence had little impact. The most important sentence is the first, in which the cue is explicitly gender neutral (referring to candy), yet 72% of first graders, 88% of third graders, and 76% of fifth graders provided the pronoun "he" for the blank.

Rule Knowledge

Knowledge of the rule that, in gender-neutral contexts, "he" refers to both males and females was tested by asking "when you use 'he' in a sentence, does it always mean it's a boy? For example, when I say 'when a kid goes to school, he often feels excited on the first day,' does that mean the kid is a boy?" If the subject responded "no" and indicated that it could be a boy or girl, the subject was scored as knowing the rule. Knowledge of the rule increased with age: 28% of first graders, 32% of third graders, 42% of fifth graders, and 84% of college students gave responses indicating they knew the rule. An additional 6% of college students gave "feminist" responses indicating that they knew the rule but disagreed with it—for example, "Yes, he refers to males, so one should use 'he or she' to be clear that everyone is included."

EXPERIMENT 2

This study replicated and extended Experiment 1. The pronoun "she" was included for a fourth comparison group in the story-telling task. The protocol for questioning children about rule knowledge was expanded in order to correct for possible response bias. Finally, an attempt was made to test directly for possible effects of gender-related pronoun use on stereotyping and cognition with the Wudgemaker task, described below. Only third and fifth graders were used as subjects, because so few first graders had demonstrated rule knowledge in Experiment 1.

Method

Subjects

A total of 132 children participated: 59 third graders (28 boys, 31 girls, 8-7 to 10-0, mean 9-4) and 73 fifth graders (36 boys, 37 girls, 10-8 to 12-7, mean 11-3).

Procedure

The story-telling task was identical to that in Experiment I, except that a fourth condition, with the pronoun "she," was added. The fill-in task was identical to Experiment 1. Children were next asked to rate on a 3-point scale *(very well. just OK. not very well)* how well women and men could do each of several jobs. The first was teacher and the second was doctor. The next was fireman or firefighter, half of the subjects receiving each alternative. The final occupation was wudgemaker. It was a fictitious, gender-neutral occupation; the description read to subjects was as follows:

Few people have heard of a job in factories, being a wudgemaker. Wudges are made of plastic, oddly shaped, and are an important part of video games. The wudgemaker works from a plan or pattern posted at eye level as *he or she* puts together the pieces at a table while *he or she* is sitting down. Eleven plastic pieces must be snapped together. Some of the pieces are tiny, so that *he or she* must have good coordination in *his or her* fingers. Once all eleven pieces are put together, *he or she* must test out the wudge to make sure that all of the moving pieces move properly. The wudgemaker is well paid, and must be a high school graduate, but *he or she* does not have to have gone to college to get the job.

One quarter of the subjects received "he" for the pronoun, one quarter received "they;" one quarter received "he or she," and one quarter received "she." They were asked to rate how well women could do the job on the 3-point scale and how well men could do the job.

Finally, a series of questions was asked to ascertain the subject's knowledge of the grammatical rule for gender-neutral "he" as follows:

When you use "he" in a sentence, what does it mean? For example, if I say "When a kid goes to school, he often feels excited on the first day;" does that mean the kid is a boy, or does it mean it's a girl, or could it be either a boy or a girl?

Following the response, the subject was asked "Why?" The question was then repeated, substituting "she" and then "they." Subjects were scored as knowing the rule if they responded boy or girl to the first question, gave a reason indicating understanding (e.g., it's like when they use man-kind to mean everyone) and answered the questions on the other pronouns correctly.

Results

Stories

There was a significant effect of pronoun on sex of story character, $x^2(^6 N = 132) = 36.86$, p <.0001, with 17% female stories when the pronoun was "he," 31% for "they," 18% for "he or she," and 77% for "she," The four-way chi-square (Sex of Subject X Pronoun X Grade X Sex of Story Character) yielded a significant three-way interaction effect on sex of story character; $X^2(26, N = 132) = 70.53$, p <.001. The results of these significance tests are thus the same as the similar tests in Experiment 1.

Fill-Ins

The data were so similar to those of Experiment 1 that they will not be reported in detail here; for example, 73% of subjects supplied "he" in the gender-neutral fill-in (candy).

Occupations and Wudgemaker

. . . The gender neutrality of the description of the wudgemaker was verified in two ways. First, 63 college students read the description with "they" as the pronoun. They then rated how well women could do the job, on a 5-point scale, how well men could do the job, and the percentage of people in the job who were men and the percentage who were women. The average ratings of males and females in the job were indeed quite close (females M = 4.24, males = 4.02), and the average percentages were close to even (58.5% males, 41.5% females). . . .Second, an analysis of data from those third and fifth graders who had received the most neutral pronouns, "they" and "he and she," was done for the ratings of women compared with their ratings of men. If the occupation is truly gender neutral, then when it is described with those pronouns there should be no significant differences between ratings of men and women on the job. A matched-group *t* test for ratings of women versus men was done, and did prove to be nonsignificant, both for "they," $t(32)$ = -.40, *ns,* and for "he or she" $t(31)$ = 1.09, *ns.*

A three-way ANOVA (Pronoun X Grade X Subject Sex) of ratings of women as wudgemakers produced a significant effect for pronoun, $F(3, 116)$ 7.77, p <.0001. All other main effects, two-way interactions, and three-way interactions were nonsignificant. . . . Ratings of women were lowest when the pronoun was he, (M = 2.00, on a scale from 1 to 3), intermediate for they and he or she, and highest for she (M = 2.72). . . .

Discussion

In general, the results from the college students in Experiment 1 replicate those of Moulton et al. (1978), although with even lower percentages of female stories (39% in Moulton et al.'s study vs. 30% in the present study). As Moulton et al. found, females are more likely to write stories about female characters than males are. The pronoun "his" yielded the lowest percentage of female stories, and "his or her" yielded the highest percentage. If "his" were gender neutral in a psychological sense, then approximately 56% of stories would be about females, yet college students created only 21% of their stories about females in response to "his." Thus the conclusion from the present data is the same as the conclusion of Moulton et al. (1978): "His" is not gender neutral in a psychological sense.

The data for the children are equally striking. The tendency for first, third, and fifth graders to create male characters when the pronoun is "he" is even stronger than it is for college students. Only 7% of elementary school children's stories were about females when the pronoun was "he." The data from Experiment 2 indicate that children are capable of creating a substantial number (77%) of female stories, but only when the pronoun is "she."

The strong tendency for children to tell stories about male characters in response to the "he" cue becomes more understandable when one looks at the data on the children's knowledge of the grammatical rule. Few know the rule and the majority apparently believe that "he" always means the person is a male.

The data from the fill-in task indicate that elementary school children, and particularly third and fifth graders, have already learned to supply "he" in a singular, gender-neutral context, although the correct-sentences task indicates that they cannot articulate why they do so. The results of the fill-in task are quite similar to those of Martyna (1978) with college students completing sentences.

The following phenomena were replicated from Experiment 1 to Experiment 2: The low percentage of female stories in response to "he"; the low percentage of children knowing the grammatical rule; and the supplying of "he" in gender-neutral all-ins. Thus these three phenomena appear to be reliable.

Therefore, it seems reasonable to conclude that (a) the majority of elementary school children have learned to supply "he" in gender-neutral contexts, and (b) the majority of elementary school children do not know the rule that "he" in gender-neutral contexts refers to both males and females, and have a strong tendency to think of males in creating stories from "he" cues. The chain of concepts for them, then, is that (a) the typical person is a "he;" and (b) "he" refers only to males. Logically then, might they not conclude (c) the typical person is a male?

We know that by first grade, girls have less self-confidence and lower expectations for success than do boys (Block, 1976; Crandall, 1969, 1978). A speculation as to one of the causes of that phenomenon arises from the present studies, namely that language may be a contributor. That is, if first graders routinely use "he" to refer to everyone without knowing the grammatical rule behind the use, might they not begin to attach greater status and normativeness to the male, and correspondingly devalue the female? If Bem (1981) is correct that self-concept is assimilated to the gender schema, could low self-confidence in females be related to aspects of the gender schema that have been shaped by sexist language? These are important questions deserving research. . . .

[T]he wudgemaker data (Experiment 2) showed strong effects due to pronoun Women were rated as least able at the job when the description used "he," intermediate for "they" and "he or she," and most able when "she" was used. It should be emphasized that the effect is a large one, with ratings of women moving from the middle of the 1 to 3 scale when the pronoun is "he" (M = 2.00) to close to the top of the scale when the pronoun is "she" (M = 2.72). These data permit the important conclusion that the use of gender-neutral "he," compared with other pronouns, does indeed affect the formation of gender-related schemas in children.

We know that, by first grade, children hold many stereotyped ideas, including stereotypes about adult occupations (O'Keefe & Hyde, 1983). The wudgemaker data permit the more general conclusion that one likely input into the formation of these stereotyped ideas has been the language the children have learned, and specifically the pronouns used in referring to people in the occupation—for example, "he" for firefighters and doctors, and "she" for nurses and teachers. Depending on the terminology one prefers, it can be concluded that the use of "he" affects the stereotyping of occupations, or the schema of an occupation that children form. . . .

In summary, it is clear that the tendency for subjects to think of males when they hear "he" in a gender-neutral context (storytelling data) is present from first grade through the college years. The wudgemaker data demonstrate that the use of gender-related pronouns affects the concepts children form of an occupation, and particularly their idea of how well women would do at the occupation. The contributions of language to sex role development are deserving of considerably more attention, both theoretical and empirically. We must find out how children think about sexist language and other gender-related features of language, and how these features influence the developing gender schema.

References

Bandura. A., & Walters, R. H. (1963). *Social learning and personality development.* New York: Holt, Rinehart & Winston.

Bem, S. L. (1981). Gender schema theory: A cognitive account of sex typing. *Psychological Review, 88,* 354-364.

Block, J. H. (1976). Issues, problems, and pitfalls in assessing sex differences: A critical review of *The Psychology of Sex Differences. Merrill-Palmer Quarterly 22,* 283-308.

Crandall, V. C. (1978, August). *Expecting sex differences and sex differences in expectancies: A developmental analysis.* Paper presented at the meeting of the American Psychological Association, Toronto.

Everitt, B. S. (1977). *The analysis of contingency tables.* London: Chapman and Hall.

Kail, R. V., & Levine, L. E. (1976). Encoding processes and sex-role preferences. *Journal of Experimental Child Psychology 21,* 256-263.

Kohlberg, L. (1966). A cognitive-developmental analysis of children's sex-role concepts and attitudes. In E. E. Maccoby (Ed.), *The development of sex differences* (pp. 82-172). Stanford, CA: Stanford University Press.

Liben, L. S., & Signorella, M. L. (1980). Gender-related schemata and constructive memory in children. *Child Development. 51,* 11-18.

MacKay, D. G. (1980). Psychology, prescriptive grammar, and the pronoun problem. *American Psychologist, 35,* 444-449.

MacKay, D. G., & Fulkerson, D. (1979). On the comprehension and production of pronouns. *Journal of Verbal Learning* and *Verbal Behavior 18,* 661-673.

Martin, C. L., & Halverson, C. F. (1981). A schematic processing model of sex-typing and stereotyping in children. *Child Development. 52,* 1119-1134.

Martin, C. L., & Halverson, C. F. (1983). The effects of sex-typing schemas on young children's memory. *Child Development, 54,* 563-574.

Martyna, W. (1978, Winter). What does "he" mean? Use of the generic masculine. *Journal of Communication, 28,* 131-138.

Martyna, W. (1980). Beyond the "he/man" approach: The case for nonsexist language. *Signs. 5,* 482-493.

Mischel, W. (1966). A social learning view of sex differences in behavior. In E. E. Maccoby (Ed.), *The development of sex differences.* Stanford, CA: Stanford University Press.

Moulton, J., Robinson, G. M., & Elias, C. (1978). Psychology in action: Sex bias in language use: "Neutral" pronouns that aren't. *American Psychologist, 33,* 1032-1036.

O'Keefe, E. S. C., & Hyde, J. S. (1983). The effects of gender stability and age on children's occupational sex-role stereotypes. *Sex Roles, 9,* 481-492.

Study: Racism Is Health Risk To Black Americans

Sue Landry

---

*E***ditors' Note:** In the following article, Sue Landry reports on research investigating the effects of chronic racism on health outcomes. More generally, the article highlights an often overlooked yet important negative aspect of racism. Many researchers examine people's thoughts and behaviors when they are targets of prejudice. This research goes a step further to examine poor health as a consequence of being discriminated against. It suggests that the effects of racism are even more pervasive than is often assumed.

Warning: Racism can be dangerous to your health.

That's what a Duke University researcher found when she set up confrontations between black people and white people.

Faced with racist provocation, the heart rate and blood pressure of African-American volunteers shot up and stayed elevated after the debate ended.

The study represents the first time a researcher has directly measured the potential health effects of face-to-face racism. The research supports previous theories that chronic racism might be one factor contributing to higher rates of hypertension and heart disease among African-Americans.

"It is well-documented that racism has negative social, economic and political consequences on African-Americans, but the direct effects of racism on physical and emotional health have only begun to be explored," said Duke psychologist Maya McNeilly, whose study was published in the July issue of the *International Journal of Behavioral Medicine*.

Measuring the health effects of racism could help boost societal change, McNeilly said. But it also can help identify methods of coping that help individuals combat the negative effects of racism.

In the past, researchers have tried to determine whether racism affects health by having volunteers view videos of racially charged incidents or by asking volunteers to imagine a racially charged experience. In those studies, volunteers view videos of racially charged incidents or by asking volunteers to imagine a racially charged experience. In those studies, volunteers exhibited a slight increase in blood pressure and heart rate.

McNeilly wanted to investigate a more realistic situation.

In her study, 30 African-American women participated in two debates with a white person. One debate was about a racial topic while the other debates were about controversial, but non-racial, topics. A second African-American sat nearby in some cases offering supportive comments and gestures, and, in others, sifting quietly.

During each debate, researchers measured the heart rate and blood pressure of the black participants. They also were rated on emotions such as anger, resentment, cynicism and anxiety.

"We thought that this interactive confrontation with provocation would be a lot more lifelike, McNeilly said. "We did, in fact, find that the increases (in blood pressure and heart rate) were much greater?

Participants exhibited blood pressure as much as 40 percent higher during the racial debates than during the non-racial debates. Heart rates among participants were as much as 61 percent higher during the racist confrontations.

Emotions ran at least twice as high, and, in some cases, as much as seven-times higher during the racial confrontations.

The emotions reported by participants could have as significant an effect on health as blood pressure and heart rate. Emotions such as anger and resentment can cause the body to release increased amounts of hormones such as adrenaline and cortisol, which also can damage the heart

While a single incident of stress wouldn't cause much damage, the physical effects can take a serious toll if the stress is chronic.

During the debates in which the black participant received support from another black person, the participant reported less anger. But the social support didn't change the effect on blood pressure and heart rate.

McNeilly plans to further investigate factors that might buffer the negative effects of racism. Preliminary results of another study indicate that black people who feel hopeless and powerless in the face of racism have higher blood pressures than those who don't have those feelings.

A psychologist at Florida A & M University, John Chambers, has found evidence that African-Americans with a strong sense of identity and a strong awareness of their culture are less likely to have high blood pressure.

McNeilly's studies on racism build on a large body of research at Duke on the effects of mental stress on physical health. That research has documented that family and work-related stress can increase the risk of heart disease by releasing stress hormones and raising blood pressure and heart rate.

Identifying racism as another stress factor with health effects is important because hypertension strikes African-Americans ages 25 to 44 at 20 times the rate it affects Caucasians of the same age. Researchers hypothesize that other factors include genetics, diet and exercise.

McNeilly said her study opens the door to further research. She plans to study the effects of gender discrimination, discrimination within the same race, and the effects of racism on other ethnic groups.

"It has opened up a host of areas that really are in desperate need of exploration," McNeilly said. "There has not been a single study that has looked at the effects of gender discrimination on the heart and blood vessels."

A White Man's Word

Debra Swallow

> **Editors' Note:** In this brief autobiographical recollection, Debra Swallow, who is of mixed racial heritage, relates a disturbing early encounter with racism. Her experience illustrates the emotional impact racism can have on its targets, as well as its lasting impact on their identity.

The screen door slammed shut, and I just knew eighty flies came in. Then I heard wailing and gibberish and ran to see who it was. My nine-year-old son was running toward me with blood, tears and dirty sweat trickling off his chin, making my knees go weak.

"What happened? Who did this to you?" I asked, kneeling to wipe his round face with a cool, damp cloth.

"I got in a fight, Mom. Mom, what's a half-breed?"

I felt like my blood stopped running, and I closed my eyes to kill my tears, my mind opening up a day I'd almost forgotten.

I opened my eyes to see how under-water looked, and a sting like cactus tips closed them fast. Surfacing, I looked across the pool for my friend. The water shimmered turquoise blue, reflecting nothing but the painted concrete bottom and rectangles of green light from the roof. Forty or fifty pale faces and arms bobbed and floated above the water, but no sign of my friend's brown, familiar face.

"Maybe it's time to go," I thought and swam to the closest edge. Feeling the rough, slimy cement on the palms of my hands, I hauled myself out of the water. Unsure of my footing, I walked slowly toward the shower rooms.

Screams, giggles and little-girl conversation filled the room, along with spraying, splashing and draining water. Stooping to peek under the first shower stall, I saw two white feet and moved on to the second door. Also two white feet. Next door, four white feet. I could feel myself starting to shiver now and my breath felt trapped in my chest. "What if they left me? I don't know anybody here," I thought.

My friend and her mom took me with them to Rushville to swim. My first time alone away from my family, and here I was, scared among white people—the only Indian in sight.

I decided to just kind of stand around in the shower room. I knew she wasn't in the pool, so she had to come here, where our clothes were. Trying to be as unnoticeable as possible, I leaned against a cool, wet wall and watched the white girls in the room, curious because I'd never been around any before.

"My dad bought me a brand-new bike and it has a blue daisy basket on the handlebars," one girl whined to her friend. "Well, I already knew that, but did you know my dad bought me a new bed and it has a canopy on it!" she whined back in a sing-song voice. The two girls were probably eight years old like me, but both were chubby with blonde ringlets and painted toenails.

Spacing out their words, I was thinking about the bike Dad made my sister and me. He made it from all different parts he found at the trash pile, and it looked funny and rusty, but it worked real well. Daddy also made us a pair of stilts, a playhouse and a pogo stick, which all our friends wanted to play with. I knew my dad was better than theirs, he BUILT stuff for us.

I noticed the first girl was dressed now, and while waiting for her friend to finish, she pulled out a whole handful of red licorice and chewed on one while her friend jabbered, every once in a while glancing at me, not knowing my tongue ached to taste just one mouthful of her licorice. Every time she looked at me, I wanted to evaporate. I had on a borrowed swimsuit a size too big, dull and old-fashioned compared to the bright-colored flower or print-covered two-pieces all the other girls wore. My hair hung down my back, straight and thick and dark.

The first girl said, "Look, this Indian is staring at us," glared at me with icy blue eyes, her nose pointing to the ceiling. The second girl said, "Oh, she don't know what we're saying anyhow. Dirty Indians don't know anything." Her friend said, "I don't think she's really a real Indian. My dad says some of them are half-breeds. So she's not *all* dirty."

"Only half-dirty," her friend said, and they giggled together and laughed at me.

My face felt hot and my arms were heavy as I walked carefully across the wet, slippery floor towards them. I noticed from far away that the room's noises started to fade.

I grabbed one of them by her hair and threw her away, wrapped my arm around the other one's neck and wrestled her down, and sitting on her, I kept punching her till her friend grabbed me. I stood up, and jerking away, I tripped her, landing her by her friend. They were both still crying and screaming on the floor when I walked out, carrying my bundle of clothes under my arm.

Standing outside in the shade of the pool building, I was really scared. There was someone yelling, "Debi! Debi!" but I wouldn't look. Somehow I thought they found out my name and were going to do something to me. But it was my friend's mom; she and my friend went for popsicles and just got back. I ran to their car and told them what I did, so my friend's mom went in after the clothes my friend left in the shower room and we headed back for home.

Safe once again with my family, I told Mom and Dad I got in a fight.

"Daddy, what's a half-breed?" I asked him.

The house got quiet, the only sound was the wind. Daddy looked at me and his eyes were sad.

"My girl, you're an Indian. The way of living is Indian. Lakota."

I said, "Yes, but what is a half-breed?"

"A white man's word," is what he said. "It's just a white man's word."

Now, eighteen years later, I was wiping blood from my son's face, and his question made my body shake with anger, sadness, frustration and hatred. Opening my eyes, I answered, "You're Lakota son. The way of living is Indian. You're Lakota. He looked at me with black eyes shining with tears he now refused to shed, and asked me again what a half-breed was.

"A white man's word," is what I said. "It's just a white man's word."

✓ PROJECT 8.1
Language And Academic Textbooks

I.   Picking up on the themes discussed in Janet Hyde's article on gender and language, this project focuses on the way that gender-related language is used in academic textbooks.

II.   For this project, go to your library and find a recent edition of an introductory psychology textbook and an older edition of that same textbook that was published in the 1960s or 1970s. If you cannot find two editions of the same textbook, pick a text published recently and a similar text published in the 1960s or 1970s. Choose a chapter that is common to both texts, preferably focusing on the social psychology chapter. Count the number of male and female pronouns or names and the number of pictures of males and females used in the chapter. Count the number of references to or pictures of people who are not white or Caucasian. Then, answer the following questions:

How many references to males did you find?

Older Text _____   Current Text _____

How many references to females did you find?

Older Text _____   Current Text _____

How many references to people who are not white did you find?

Older Text _____   Current Text _____

How many pictures of males did you find?

Older Text _____   Current Text _____

How many pictures of females did you find?

Older Text _____   Current Text _____

How many pictures of people who are not white did you find?

Older Text _____   Current Text _____

Were there any changes in the number of references to or pictures of males and females and people from different races and ethnicities from the older text to the newer text?

_____

_____

_____

_____

_____

Regardless of whether or not there were changes in the numbers of references, were there any changes in the roles in which males and females were portrayed?

_____

_____

_____

_____

_____

_____

_____

_____

Were people of different racial or ethnic groups depicted differently in the older text compared to the newer text? For example, did the roles or the status of people of different ethnicities or races change over time?

_____

_____

_____

_____

_____

_____

_____

What are your conclusions? Are males and females and people of different ethnicities represented in the text equally? Did this representation change over time? What message do the texts send to students regarding males and females and people of different ethnicities?

_____

_____

_____

_____

_____

_____

_____

_____

_____

✓ PROJECT 8.2
Discriminatory Policies

I.   The article written by the U.S. Civil Rights Commission gave a number of examples of policies or procedures that can be classified as discrimination. These policies and procedures were initially created to achieve a purpose, and they were not necessarily intended to be discriminatory by their creators. However, the policy as implemented may have had an unintentional discriminatory effect.

II.   For this project, choose three examples of the discriminatory policies or procedures given in the article. For each example, please answer the following questions:

EXAMPLE 1: _____

Who, if anyone, could be discriminated against in this example?

_____

_____

What was the creator's intended purpose of this policy or procedure?

_____

_____

_____

_____

_____

_____

_____

_____

Why could this policy or procedure be considered discrimination?

_____

_____

_____

_____

_____

_____

How could you achieve the purpose of the policy or procedure without being discriminatory?

_____

_____

_____

_____

_____

_____

_____

_____

EXAMPLE 2: _____

Who, if anyone, could be discriminated against in this example?

_____

_____

_____

_____

_____

_____

_____

What was the creator's intended purpose of this policy or procedure?

_____

_____

_____

_____

_____

_____

_____

_____

Why could this policy or procedure be considered discrimination?

_____

_____

_____

_____

_____

_____

_____

_____

How could you achieve the purpose of the policy or procedure without being discriminatory?

_____

_____

_____

_____

_____

_____

_____

_____

_____

EXAMPLE 3: _____

Who, if anyone, could be discriminated against in this example?

_____

_____

_____

_____

_____

_____

_____

_____

What was the creator's intended purpose of this policy or procedure?

_____

_____

_____

_____

_____

_____

_____

_____

Why could this policy or procedure be considered discrimination?

_____

_____

_____

_____

_____

_____

_____

_____

_____

How could you achieve the purpose of the policy or procedure without being discriminatory?

_____

_____

_____

_____

_____

_____

_____

_____

_____

✓ PROJECT 8.3
Discrimination And The Mall

I.   Most of the articles in this chapter of the Workbook describe discrimination targeted at members of gender, racial, or ethnic groups. In addition to these types, other types of discrimination exist. In this project, we will focus on discrimination against those of different socio-economic status.

II.   For this project, you will go into a very nice department store in your city or town on two different occasions. On one occasion you will dress in your nicest clothes. On another, you will dress in very shabby clothes. Please do not do any behaviors that will negatively impact the store, the store personnel, or yourself.

III. After these experiences, write a report describing the store in which you conducted your test, the clothes that you wore on each occasion, the reactions you received when you dressed poorly, the reactions you received when you dressed nicely, and any differences or similarities between these reactions. For example, how much attention did they pay to you? How did they treat you? Did they answer your questions about a very expensive item? Did you suffer any other form of discrimination, such as age discrimination? Turn in your report to your instructor.

C h a p t e r   9

Applying Research On Gender, Race, And Ethnicity: Education And The Intelligence Debate

An aim of the articles and projects in Chapter 8 was to increase your understanding of how pervasive discrimination is in society. The articles and projects in that chapter explored, among other things, how critical factors such as everyday language use, institutional structure, and the relationship between a person's attitudes and behaviors can affect how we treat one another.

Chapter 9 applies many of the concepts and problems discussed in early chapters to the important social domain of education, and to a critical issue in it, the debate surrounding the concept of intelligence. The articles that follow explore the concept of intelligence, particularly as it relates to educational performance. They also describe interventions or programs designed to address problems in education that are related to gender, race, and ethnicity.

In the initial article in this section, Serpell addresses the issue of what "intelligence" is by discussing its culturally constructed nature. This point is also taken up in Stephen Jay Gould's article. In it he discusses how overarching social values have influenced how intelligence is conceptualized, what we accepted as being true about it, and how we should measure it.

The remaining articles directly address the area of academic performance. Steele's work focuses on the impact that negative stereotypes can have on academic performance. Gup goes on to examine the surprisingly negative consequences that can arise from being a member of a group that is viewed positively in the academic domain.

Overall, the articles and projects in this chapter not only address the problems related to discrimination in educational settings, but they raise our awareness of them. In addition, they offer suggestions for how to begin to overcome these problems.

The Cultural Construction Of Intelligence

Robert Serpell

Editors' Note: What does it mean to be "intelligent"? How intelligent do you think you are? Does your answer depend on your definition of intelligent? Robert Serpell discusses how definitions of intelligence vary by culture and that who is characterized as intelligent also varies according to these different culturally-constructed definitions. This work challenges conceptions of intelligence that view intelligence as fixed, biologically determined, and consistent across cultures, instead arguing that intelligence is a socially constructed concept.

Why do psychologists assess intelligence? Since you are reading this chapter, you have probably been described by someone as an intelligent person. Whatever your immediate reasons for picking up this book and for turning to this chapter, it is likely that you are involved in a course or a program of higher education. A series of decisions led to your participation in those studies, some of which depended on estimates by other people of how well you were likely to understand such topics as psychology and culture. Those estimates almost certainly involved some elements of what is called the assessment of intelligence.

Some estimates may have been based in part on scores assigned to your performance on a standardized test. For instance, a college admissions committee may have selected you because your *S.A.T.* scores fell above a certain criterion. In other cases, the estimate may have involved a more informal, impressionistic synthesis from observations across a number of different settings, in which your behavior was compared to that of other people engaged in the same activities as you. For instance, a letter of recommendation to the college by one of your high-school teachers might include such statements as "This is one of the *brightest* students in my class" ... in Chemistry, in Literature, or in World History.

Each of these forms of assessment—by a committee looking at your test scores, or by a teacher reminiscing about your behavior in class is—derived indirectly from judgments of the quality of your responses to particular tasks. Consider a task of special interest to many school teachers: the student is asked to propose an explanation to the rest of the class for a surprising event you have all recently witnessed. In chemistry, the event might be a sudden change in color of the contents of a test-tube during an experiment, in literature it might be a betrayal of trust by the hero of a novel you are studying, in history it might be a news item announced last night on television or radio. Depending on the context and on her philosophy of education, the teacher might assess the quality of your response to such a challenge on only one or more of the following dimensions: How appropriate was the evidence you cited? How logically coherent was your reasoning? How much insight did you show into the nature of the problem? How precisely did you make your case? How subtle was your interpretation? How eloquently did you phrase your idea? And so on.

The tasks used for professional psychological assessment are usually more strictly controlled than this, and the best performance is defined as choosing the correct one among four or five alternatives. Critics of such tests often complain that the way in which their tasks are posed is unnatural, and their definition of a correct response is narrow and arbitrary, Both of these prevalent features of psychological tests arise from the attempt to control and standardize the task presented to the respondent. The construction of a multiple-choice test begins with an intuitive phase involving similar criteria to those used by the teacher in her classroom assessment, but is then followed by a systematic, empirical process known in the field of mental measurement as standardization. The idea is to reduce the chances that the personal opinions of the tester could bias his or her assessment of the subject's intelligence. Rather than following her intuitive judgment, the psychologist is trained to follow with great precision a standard set of procedures that have been tried out with many people before, and to interpret the subject's responses in accordance with a set of guidelines derived from the experience gained when the procedures were being standardized on other people with comparable experience. The quality of the subject's performance is thus compared with the performance of other subjects under very similar conditions.

This particular format of psychological assessment, grounded in systematic research and protected by professional regulations, has acquired a privileged status in the culture of the modern world, especially in the fields of education and mental health. Yet the evaluation of how intelligently a person has behaved is also regarded as transparent, in the sense that everyone is expected to agree at least about the most extreme cases. Professional psychology depends on this assumption to guarantee its cultural validity.

However, when the performance of people from different cultural backgrounds is compared on a single, isolated intelligence test, considerable differences are often observed. One interpretation of such findings has been that some cultures have greater potential than others for the cultivation of intelligence. An alternative view has been that the test is less appropriate for the assessment of intelligence in one culture than in another. Psychologists have debated these and other alternatives intensively, seeking to establish how psychological assessment can best contribute to educational practice.

In this paper, I will describe three different ways in which culture may be said to construct intelligence. We may think of culture: (1) as a nurturant environment from which the developing mind derives its nourishment; (2) as a system of meanings in terms of which the nature of intelligence is formulated; or (3) as a forum in which alternative approaches to the definition and measurement of intelligence are debated. I do not intend to argue that one of these versions is radically superior to the others. But their emergence in my own thinking has been sequential, with each newer version arising in reaction to a limitation of its predecessor.

Culture as a Nurturant Environment

At the beginning of my research program at the University of Zambia, I thought of

culture as achieving its constructive influence on the course of cognitive development in much the same way that evolutionary pressures over a much longer period of time have shaped the behavioral repertoire of different biological species to fit the ecological niche they inhabit. Examples of such ecological adaptation in biology include the capacity of mammals that live in trees to climb, and of those that live in water to swim. Human cultures add a further dimension of structure to the habitat, with technological artifacts and recurrent practices. Children are enculturated in the course of their development into a facility with the machines, the language, and the rituals of their society.

A distinctive feature of children's behavior all over the world is their playfulness. In addition to physical exercise and social interaction, children's play affords opportunities for the exercise of cognitive skills. Many of the games played by children in Western societies involve the solution of puzzles similar in design to those that are featured in the school curriculum, and psychological tests have often been designed to capitalize on children's familiarity with and interest in this type of game.

To a cross-cultural voyager to Zambia from Britain in the 1960s, certain differences in the types of games children played were immediately apparent. During the course of my visits to the homes of school children in the capital city of Lusaka, I very rarely saw any commercially manufactured toys, children's books, or crayons. Yet, in almost every neighborhood, I would meet a group of boys "driving" along the gravel road in front of them skeletal model cars built from scraps of wire. These wire cars are popular all over central and southern Africa. They are constructed by boys between the ages of about six and fourteen, without any instruction manuals or any guidance from adults. The models vary in many points of detail, and most of the young craftsmen will gladly explain to a curious researcher how the axles are connected to the chassis, how the steering works, how the doors are hinged, etc., as well as telling what make of car the model represents.

The conspicuous skill and ingenuity displayed in this context impressed me as evidence of a high degree of competence in a cognitive domain very similar to that sampled by several Western psychological tests, such as the Block Design assembly test, the Bender-Gestalt test, and the Draw-a-Person test. Yet, I soon discovered in my research laboratory at the university; that these were among the most difficult tests for Lusaka school children, and were even more difficult for children living in rural areas of the country. After reviewing and adding to an inconclusive literature on the nature of those difficulties, I designed a study to bridge the gap between Zambian children's skillful toy-making and their poor performance on Western tests.

The guiding hypothesis of the study (Serpell, 1979) was that the abstract psychological function of pattern reproduction can manifest itself in different ways according to the demands of the eco-cultural niche to which the subject's behavior is adapted. In an environment abundant with paper and pencils, children would be likely to acquire greater pattern reproduction skills in the medium of drawing than in an environment where the relevant materials were scarce. Conversely, in an environment where modeling in wire was a recurrent play activity, children would be likely to acquire greater pattern reproduction skills in the medium of wire-modelling than in an environment where the activity was unknown.

We sampled two contrasting, low-income neighborhoods to test the hypothesis, one in Lusaka, the other in Manchester, England. Eight-year-old boys and girls were asked to reproduce a standard pattern, such as a square with diagonals, a human figure, or a flower. In the drawing version of the task the child was given a blank sheet of paper and a pencil and asked to copy a printed standard. In the wire-modelling task, the child was handed a strip of wire and asked to make a model just like a standard wire model. We also administered a clay-modelling version of the same task, which we predicted would be of equal difficulty for both samples, since many Zambian children make models from natural clay during the rainy season, and many English children play with industrially produced modelling clay. As we had predicted, the English children performed significantly better on the drawing task, while the Zambian children performed much better on the wire-modelling task, and

there was no group difference on the clay-modelling task

A similar pattern of results was obtained by Irwin, Schafer, and Feiden (1974) in a study that compared the performance of two groups of adult men with different cultural experience on two versions of another cognitive task often regarded in Western psychology as an index of intelligence. Mano rice-farmers in Liberia were able to sort bowls of rice according to three alternative dimensions significantly more often than psychology undergraduates in the United States, whereas the same Americans were able to perform significantly more sorts than the Liberians when the materials were cards displaying colored geometrical shapes. Thus cognitive flexibility in classification was found to depend on the cultural familiarity of the medium in which it was assessed.

In both of these studies, the focus is on culture as a source of structure in the external, material environment which the developing child explores and incorporates. The significance of culture for development is likened to that of a womb, enclosing and feeding the growing mind. However, the constructive cultural context of human development is not only material but also social: adults and older children provide guidance and feedback to the child's activity and interpret these interactions in terms of a shared system of meanings, which the developing child gradually appropriates as his or her own.

Culture as a System of Meanings

While we admire the ingenuity of expert toymakers, farmers, and scholars, these are not the only qualities of mind that are valued by humans. Fairness and the capacity to appreciate another person's point of view often carry great weight in our choice of advisors in moments of crisis. These are qualities of mental depth rather than speed, and they feature prominently among the goals of child-rearing and education cited in studies of indigenous African cultures (Serpell, in press). The ideal endpoint of personal development in these societies is construed as someone who can preside effectively over the settlement of a dispute, whose judgment can be trusted in questions of character, who can and will take on social responsibility

This broader range of applications for human intelligence came to my attention in the 1970s while reflecting on a professional problem raised by many clinicians in African mental health services. How should one approach the assessment of intelligence in the case of an adult patient referred for treatment because of socially deviant behavior in a rural community? Modern psychiatry takes account of a patient's intelligence in determining the diagnosis of psychological problems and in planning a course of treatment. But none of the tests standardized for the schoolgoing population seem at all appropriate for the assessment of intelligence in an adult who has never been to school, has not learned to read and write, and has lived all her or his life within a subsistence agricultural community

The problem here is more fundamental than how to measure a particular cognitive process such as pattern reproduction. We need to know what qualities of mind are adaptive within such a sociocultural setting. I therefore sought an introduction through students enrolled at the University of Zambia to a remote rural community where we could invite some of the village elders to share their views with us. We decided to retain a focus on children, since adults in every society tend to hold definite views about how they wish their children to grow up. Our goal was to learn from elders about the qualities of child behavior they valued most, in contexts where it matters within the framework of the community's way of life (Serpell, 1982). A group of friends and colleagues who had grown up and lived in Zambian villages helped me to brainstorm a set of vignettes, including the following:

"If a house caught fire and there were just these children there, whom would you send to call others for help?"

"Suppose you go to a house early in the morning . . . and you find all the adults are away at work. Then these children come to you shouting to you 'knife,' 'he's run away.' The things the children are saying are not clear at all. Which child would you ask to explain clearly what had happened?"

"Suppose you are washing your clothes and you see that the place where you usually spread them out to dry is muddy, which of these girls would you send to search for another good place to spread your clothes?"

Before posing these questions, we identified for the respondent a set of between four and seven children of the same gender and similar age, all resident within the same village, and all well-known to him or her in the course of everyday life. After she had chosen one child for each hypothetical task, we asked the elder to explain her choice.

We sampled six small villages (with 60-170 inhabitants) within a small radius in Zambia's Katete District. The reasons cited by our informants for their choices provided a rich collection of words and phrases in common usage in this rural Chewa community for evaluating the behavior of children. We were also able to count the frequency with which a given child was cited as the best choice, within the village, for each task. We also administered several cognitive tests including a clay or wire modelling adaptation of the Draw-a-Person test and other tests based on recurrent local children's activities. Adults who were reinterviewed after an interval of several months were quite consistent, but the level of consensus among different informants was quite low. We therefore computed for each child an aggregated index of her ratings by four or five adults.

This index showed little or no correlation with our independent assessments of individual differences on the behavioral tests. Although some doubts can be raised about the reliability and validity of each of these two sets of estimates of intelligence, I regard their lack of convergence as a valid and significant finding. The indigenous Chewa point of view for conceptualizing children's intellectual development was articulated by our informants in terms of an overarching, superordinate concept, *nzelu,* which encompasses the notions of wisdom and intelligence, as well as two subordinate dimensions, cognitive alacrity *(ku-chenjela),* and cooperative social responsibility *(ku-tumikila).* These elders, and indeed the young people themselves when we interviewed them many years later as young adults, indicated that *ku-chenjela* in the absence of *ku-tumikila* is a negative social force that runs contrary to the objectives of the indigenous educational philosophy (Serpell, in press). Despite the rarity with which its dimensions are explicitly articulated or affirmed in public discourse, and despite its low prestige in the arena of national and international debate about education, this system of constructs and the associated practices encoded in Chewa culture constitutes a coherent alternative to those represented by the system of formal schooling. Moreover the point of view represented by this indigenous system derives great strength from the facts of its familiarity and its continuity with many other aspects of contemporary life in the community

Even in the United States, where the practice of intelligence testing, and the theoretical rationale for the tests have been widely promoted through the schools and the media for many decades, members of the general public have retained some skepticism about the psychological establishment's approach to the definition of intelligence. Sternberg, Conway, Ketron, and Bernstein (1981) asked two large samples of Americans, a group of specialists engaged in research on intelligence and a group of "laypeople" residents, in a middleclass suburb on the East Coast, to rate each of a set of behaviors in terms of how characteristic they were of "an ideally intelligent person." Factor analysis of the responses revealed two main factors among the ratings by the specialists, centering on verbal ability and problem-solving ability. Ratings by members of the general public yielded these same two factors, but in addition a third factor that centered on social sensitivity and responsibility.

Now the specifics of how social competence is manifested will likely differ considerably from one culture to another. For instance, the item "is on time for appointments" (see Table 1) would have little meaning in the life of a Chewa village. Nevertheless, the research evidence points to a comparable challenge for educational psychology in both North America and Africa. Technical definitions and tests of intelligence cannot afford to become too far alienated from the wider culture's concerns about children's development, if they are to contribute to the task of optimizing the match between educational provision and the developmental needs of individual children.

TABLE 1: Behaviors rated characteristic of an ideally intelligent person by members of the general public in Connecticut

The social competence factor	Factor loading
Accepts others for what they are.	.88
Admits mistakes.	.74
Displays interest in the world at large.	.72
Is on tine for appointments.	.71
Has a social conscience.	.70
Thinks before speaking and doing.	.70
Displays curiosity.	.68
Makes fair judgments.	.68
Does not make snap judgments.	.66
Assesses well the relevance of information to the problem at hand.	.66
Is sensitive to other people's needs and desires.	.65
Is frank and honest with self and others.	.64
Displays interest in the immediate environment.	.64

Excerpted from Sternberg et al., 1981, Table 4, p. 45.

Culture as a Forum

If a parent's conceptions of intelligence and cognitive development differ from those implicit in the school curriculum, the parent has a number of choices. She or he can treat school and home as complementary environments, each with its own agenda for the child's socialization. Many immigrant families opt for this strategy and strive to ensure that their children become bicultural—competent in both the "mainstream" culture of the host society and also in the minority culture of their ancestors abroad. A more radical option is not to enroll one's children in school at all. In some societies, this option is prohibited by law. But various compromise formulas have been devised, such as establishing an alternative school designed to reflect the values of a particular minority culture.

Perhaps the most demanding strategy is to confront the dissonance between the parents' cultural agenda and that of the school, seeking through negotiation to work out a new curriculum that will respond to both sets of goals. One organization that has pursued this approach vigorously in recent decades is composed of parents with a child whose intelligence was seriously impaired early in life by a biological accident. Rather than accepting the provision of separate, protective services, parents of children with intellectual disability (or mental handicap) in many of the affluent industrialized nations have pressed for their children's right to participate in mainstream schooling and to receive special educational support within that setting (Mittler and Serpell 1985).

In the rural Zambian community described above, the dissatisfaction of families with their local primary school was expressed in a variety of ways (Serpell, in press). Unlike the city schools, which every year experience long queues of eager parents clamoring to enroll their child in the first grade, at this school, the teachers felt the need to mount a door-to-door recruitment drive each year to fill the vacancies. Moreover, many pupils dropped out of school after two or three years, and only a small minority completed the full seven-year primary curriculum.

When we interviewed young men and women in this community about their reasons for dropping out, a few justified their decision with reference to immediate social or economic opportunities, such as getting married or herding cattle. But most of them stated that the curriculum had been too difficult, and described themselves as school failures. Many used the expression *ndinalibe nzelu,* meaning I lacked the necessary nzelu— the quality of mind that we had found so highly valued by their elders in the context of village life. Yet these voting people were coping resourcefully with the demands of a challenging environment. Some were growing cash crops and commuting with rides on long-haul trucks to sell their produce in the city; others had migrated to the city where they were scraping a living from marginal, poorly paid jobs. Many were raising young children with meager resources, and all of them planned to enroll their own children in school when they grew up.

A salient feature of the school system that most of these young people had abandoned is its rigid hierarchy of grade levels, segmented by competitive selection examinations. Less than 20 percent of more than 100,000 candidates who take the grade 7 exam each year are offered places in grade 8, and of the 20,000 or so who take the Grade 9 exam less than half are offered places in Grade 10. Locally constructed tests of verbal and nonverbal reasoning, modeled on Western intelligence tests play an important part in the national competition for places in Grade 8. The cut-off points on the scales of performance are arbitrary, simply reflecting the number of vacancies in the next grade. The stringency of this selection process is well-known to rural communities. They also know that formal schooling only conveys a reliable advantage in the national labor market if the student completes Grade 12. Yet, rather than challenging the validity of a school system that denies real opportunities for educational success to all but a small minority, most of our cohort of young people blamed themselves as insufficiently intelligent.

Searching for ways to communicate the implications of our research to this community, we eventually found a fertile medium in popular participatory theater. A drama was composed with the active participation of young men and women from the community, portraying a variety of life journeys. At one extreme, explicit opposition to the culture of the school was represented by a young man enrolled in an indigenous secret society, while at the other was a young man whose success up to the level of Grade 9 had led him to seek his fortune in the city. Other characters in the play had left school either before or after completing the primary curriculum. Teachers and students as well as adult school-leavers role-played characters on stage very different from their actual lives, and the audience reacted with enthusiasm to the dilemmas portrayed. At the end of the drama, attention was drawn to the positive contributions made to the local community by those who had "failed" to qualify for further schooling, but had made a success of their life in other ways. Different constituencies within the community interpreted the significance of the drama in different ways (Serpell, in press). The drama thus became a forum for the articulation and debate of different perspectives on the significance of schooling as a resource for enhancement or frustration in the lives of local people.

Popular theater is one of several cultural modes of collaborative construction of shared meanings. Others are differently constituted. For example, when a psychologist seeks to share with the family of an intellectually disabled child some of the principles of task analysis and behavior modification, she or he may improve the demonstration of a specialized technique by inviting a parent or sibling to model a planned intervention with the child. In the course of such interaction, the caregiver is more likely to appropriate the new technology if her preexisting, indigenous ideas about disability and learning are acknowledged. Moreover, in any culture, the child's prospects of benefitting from planned intervention will be enhanced if the relationship between caregiver and professional is based on mutual respect for each other's complementary domains of expertise (Mittler & Serpell, 1985).

Conclusion

I have suggested three different metaphors for the function of culture in the construction of intelligence: the nurturant environment of a womb, the vocabulary of a language, and the exchange of ideas in a forum. Each of these metaphors of cultural construction is complementary to the others. Culture structures the effective opportunities for intellectual development, defines the goals of socialization, and constitutes the context within which the definition of goals and opportunities for attaining them is debated among the people who collectively own, belong to, and construct that culture.

The social problem of alienation between technical psychology and the mainstream of cultural understanding cannot be resolved by merely selling the ideas of science to the general public. Because intelligence is itself a culturally constructed aspect of the human mind, scientific theories of intelligence need to incorporate the common-sense intuitions of the society at large. Professional psychologists need to adapt their definitions, their assessment methods, and their interventions in the light of open and constructive discourse with other participants of the culture.

References

Irwin, M. H., Schafer, G. N., & Feiden, C. P (1974). Emic and unfamiliar category sorting of Mano farmers and U.S. undergraduates. *Journal of Cross-cultural Psychology, 5,* 407-423.

Mittler, P., & Serpell, R. (1985). Services: An international perspective. In A. M. Clarke, A. D. B. Clarke, & J. M. Berg (Eds.), *Mental deficiency: The changing outlook* (4th edition), pp. 715-787. New York: Free Press.

Serpell, R. (1979). How specific are perceptual skills? A cross-cultural study of pattern reproduction. *British Journal of Psychology, 70,* 365-380.

Serpell, R. (in press). *The significance of schooling: Life journeys in an African society.* Cambridge: Cambridge University Press.

Sternberg, R., Conway, B., Ketron, J., and Bernstein, M. (1981). People's conceptions of intelligence. *Journal of Personality and Social Psychology, 4,* 37-55.

Racist Arguments And IQ

Stephen Jay Gould

ℰditors' Note: The previous reading by Robert Serpell argues that "intelligence" is a culturally constructed concept, and is dramatically influenced by the environment in which we live. Some researchers argue that intelligence is determined by the environment ("nurture") while others argue it is determined by biology ("nature"). Still others argue that both nurture and nature impact intelligence. The nature versus nurture debate and its implications for how we view intelligence has engaged psychology for much of its history. In this short piece Stephen Jay Gould, a biologist, writes about how the nature versus nurture debate in intelligence research has not always been free of the influences of the larger society which has often been invested in perpetuating the "objective" differences between gender, racial, and ethnic groups.

Louis Agassiz, the greatest biologist of mid-nineteenth century America, argued that God had created blacks and whites as separate species. The defenders of slavery took much comfort from this assertion, for biblical proscriptions of charity and equality did not have to extend across a species boundary. What could an abolitionist say? Science had shone its cold and dispassionate light upon the subject; Christian hope and sentimentality could not refute it.

Similar arguments, carrying the apparent sanction of science, have been continually invoked in attempts to equate egalitarianism with sentimental hope and emotional blindness. People who are unaware of this historical pattern tend to accept each recurrence at face value; that is, they assume that each statement arises from the "data" actually presented, rather than from the social conditions that truly inspire it.

The racist arguments of the nineteenth century were based primarily on craniometry, the measurement of human skulls. Today, these contentions stand totally discredited. What craniometry was to the nineteenth century, intelligence testing has been to the twentieth. The victory of the eugenics movement in the Immigration Restriction Act of 1924 signaled its first unfortunate effect— for the severe restrictions upon non-Europeans and upon southern and eastern Europeans gained much support from results of the first extensive and uniform application of intelligence tests in America—the Army Mental Tests of World War I. These tests were engineered and administered by psychologist Robert M. Yerkes, who concluded that "education alone will not place the negro

[sic] race on a par with its Caucasian competitors." It is now clear that Yerkes and his colleagues knew no way to separate genetic from environmental components in postulating causes for different performances on the tests.

The latest episode of this recurrent drama began in 1969, when Arthur Jensen published an article entitled, "How Much Can We Boost IQ and Scholastic Achievement?" in the *Harvard Educational Review*. Again, the claim went forward that new and uncomfortable information had come to light, and that science had to speak the "truth" even if it refuted some cherished notions of a liberal philosophy. But again, I shall argue, Jensen had no new data; and what he did present was flawed beyond repair by inconsistencies and illogical claims.

Jensen assumes that IQ tests adequately measure something we may call "intelligence." He then attempts to tease apart the genetic and environmental factors causing differences in performance. He does this primarily by relying upon the one natural experiment we possess: identical twins reared apart—for differences in IQ between genetically identical people can only be environmental. The average difference in IQ for identical twins is less than the difference for two unrelated individuals raised in similarly varied environments. From the data on twins, Jensen obtains an estimate of environmental influence. He concludes that IQ has a heritability of about 0.8 (or 80 percent) *within* the population of American and European whites. The average difference between American whites and blacks is 15 IQ points (one standard deviation). He asserts that this difference is too large to attribute to environment, given the high heritability of IQ. Lest anyone think that Jensen writes in the tradition of abstract scholarship, I merely quote the first line of his famous work: "Compensatory education has been tried, and it apparently has failed."

I believe that this argument can be refuted in a "hierarchical" fashion—that is, we can discredit it at one level and then show that it fails at a more inclusive level even if we allow Jensen's argument for the first two levels:

Level 1: The equation of IQ with intelligence. Who knows what IQ measures? It is a good predictor of "success" in school, but is such success a result of intelligence, apple polishing, or the assimilation of values that the leaders of society prefer? Some psychologists get around this argument by defining intelligence operationally as the scores attained on "intelligence" tests. A neat trick. But at this point, the technical definition of intelligence has strayed so far from the vernacular that we can no longer define the issue. But let me allow (although I don't believe it), for the sake of argument, that IQ measures some meaningful aspect of intelligence in its vernacular sense.

Level 2: The heritability of IQ. Here again, we encounter a confusion between vernacular and technical meanings of the same word. "Inherited," to a layman, means "fixed," "inexorable," or "unchangeable." To a geneticist, "Inherited" refers to an estimate of similarity between related individuals based on genes held in common. It carries no implications of inevitability or of immutable entities beyond the reach of environmental influence. Eyeglasses correct a variety of inherited problems in vision; insulin can check diabetes.

Jensen insists that IQ is 80 percent heritable. Princeton psychologist Leon J. Kamin has done the dog-work of meticulously checking through details of the twin studies that form the basis of this estimate. He has found an astonishing number of inconsistencies and downright inaccuracies. For example, the late Sir Cyril Burt, who generated the largest body of data on identical twins reared apart, pursued his studies of intelligence for more than forty years. Although he increased his sample sizes in a variety of "improved" versions, some of his

correlation coefficients remain unchanged to the third decimal place—a statistically impossible situation. IQ depends in part upon sex and age; and other studies did not standardize properly for them. An improper correction may produce higher values between twins not because they hold genes for intelligence in common, but simply because they share the same sex and age. The data are so flawed that no valid estimate for the heritability of IQ can be drawn at all. But let me assume (although no data support it), for the sake of argument, that the heritability of IQ is as high as 0.8.

Level 3: The confusion of within- and between-group variation. Jensen draws a causal connection between his two major assertions—that the within-group heritability of IQ is 0.8 for American whites, and that the mean difference in IQ between American blacks and whites is 15 points. He assumes that the black "deficit" is largely genetic in origin because IQ is so highly heritable. This is a *non sequitur of* the worst possible kind—for there is no necessary relationship between heritability within a group and differences in mean values of two separate groups.

A simple example will suffice to illustrate this flaw in Jensen's argument. Height has a much higher heritability within groups than anyone has ever claimed for IQ. Suppose that height has a mean value of five feet two inches and a heritability of 0.9 (a realistic value) within a group of nutritionally deprived Indian farmers. High heritability simply means that short farmers will tend to have short offspring, and tall farmers tall offspring. It says nothing whatever against the possibility that proper nutrition could raise the mean height to six feet (taller than average white Americans). It only means that, in this improved status, farmers shorter than average (they may now be five feet ten inches) would still tend to have shorter than average children.

I do not claim that intelligence, however defined, has no genetic basis—I regard it as trivially true, uninteresting, and unimportant that it does. The expression of any trait represents a complex interaction of heredity and environment. Our job is simply to provide the best environmental situation for the realization of valued potential in all individuals. I merely point out that a specific claim purporting to demonstrate a mean genetic deficiency in the intelligence of American blacks rests upon no new facts whatever and can cite no valid data in its support. It is just as likely that blacks have a genetic advantage over whites. And, either way, it doesn't matter a damn. An individual can't be judged by his group mean.

If current biological determinism in the study of human intelligence rests upon no new facts (actually, no facts at all), then why has it become so popular of late? The answer must be social and political. The 1960s were good years for liberalism; a fair amount of money was spent on poverty programs and relatively little happened. Enter new leaders and new priorities. Why didn't the earlier programs work? Two possibilities are open: (1) we didn't spend enough money, we didn't make sufficiently creative efforts, or (and this makes any established leader jittery) we can-

not solve these problems without a fundamental social and economic transformation of society; or (2) the programs failed because their recipients are inherently what they are—blaming the victims. Now, which alternative will be chosen by men in power in an age of retrenchment?

I have shown, I hope, that biological determinism is not simply an amusing matter for clever cocktail party comments about the human animal. It is a general notion with important philosophical implications and major political consequences. As John Stuart Mill wrote, in a statement that should be the motto of the opposition: "Of all the vulgar modes of escaping from the consideration of the effect of social and moral influences upon the human mind, the most vulgar is that of attributing the diversities of conduct and character to inherent natural differences."

A Threat In The Air: How Stereotypes Shape Intellectual Identity And Performance

Claude M. Steele

Editors' Note: Psychology has consistently debated the causes of differences on standardized measures of intelligence between racial and ethnic groups, and between the genders in the domain of math. Some argue that biological differences cause performance differences, others argue the environment is a cause of these differences, and others examine both biology and the environment. Claude Steele, in the following article, presents research in which he and his colleagues examine a phenomenon called "stereotype threat" as an explanation for these performance differences between groups. In its most general form, stereotype threat is the belief that your intellectual performance, if poor, could be used by others to validate a negative view that they have of your group. He also discusses an alternative conception of education, which he calls "wise schooling." This concept's aim is to improve the educational environment and outcomes in it for all students, whether or not they are vulnerable to stereotype threat.

A general theory of domain identification is used to describe achievement barriers still faced by women in advanced quantitative areas and by African Americans in school. The theory assumes that sustained school success requires identification with school and its subdomains; that societal pressures on these groups (e.g., economic disadvantage, gender roles) can frustrate this identification; and that in school domains where these groups are negatively stereotyped, those who have become domain identified face the further barrier of stereotype threat, the threat that others' judgments or their own actions will negatively stereotype them in the domain. Research shows that this threat dramatically depresses the standardized test performance of women and African Americans who are in the academic vanguard of their groups (offering a new interpretation of group differences in standardized test performance), that it causes disidentification with school, and that practices that reduce this threat can reduce these negative effects.

From an observer's standpoint, the situations of a boy and a girl in a math classroom or of a Black student and a White student in any classroom are essentially the same. The teacher is the same; the text-books are the same; and in better classrooms, these students are treated the same. Is it possible, then, that they could still experience the classroom differently, so differently in fact as to significantly affect their performance and achievement there? This is the central question of this article, and in seeking an answer, it has both a practical and a theoretical focus. The practical focus is on the perhaps obvious need to better understand the processes that can hamper a group's school performance and on what can be done to improve that performance. The theoretical focus is on how societal stereotypes about groups can influence the intellectual functioning and identity development of individual group members. To show the generality of these processes and their relevance to important outcomes, this theory is applied to two groups: African Americans, who must contend with negative stereotypes about their abilities in many scholastic domains, and women, who must do so primarily in math and the physical sciences. In trying to understand the schooling outcomes of these two groups, the theory has a distinct perspective, that of viewing people, in Sartre's (1946/1965) words, as "first of all beings in a situation" such that if one wants to understand them, one "must inquire first into the situation surrounding [them]" (p.60).

The theory begins with an assumption: that to sustain school success one must be identified with school achievement in the sense of its being a part of one's self-definition, a personal identity to which one is self-evaluatively accountable. This account-ability—that good self-feelings depend in some part on good achievement—translates into sustained achievement motivation. For such an identification to form, this reasoning continues, one must perceive good prospects in the domain, that is, that one has the interests, skills, resources, and opportunities to prosper there, as well as that one belongs there, in the sense of being accepted and valued in the domain. If this relationship to schooling does not form or gets broken, achievement may suffer. Thus, in trying to understand what imperils achievement among women and African Americans, this logic points to a basic question: What in the experience of these groups might frustrate their identification with all or certain aspects of school achievement?

One must surely turn first to social structure: limits on educational access that have been imposed on these groups by socioeconomic disadvantage, segregating social practices, and restrictive cultural orientations, limits of both historical and ongoing effect. By diminishing one's educational prospects, these limitations (e.g., inadequate resources, few role models, preparational disadvantages) should make it more difficult to identify with academic domains. To continue in math, for example, a woman might have to buck the low expectations of teachers, family, and societal gender roles in which math is seen as unfeminine as well as anticipate spending her entire professional life in a male-dominated world. These realities, imposed on her by societal structure, could so reduce her sense of good prospects in math as to make identifying with it difficult.

But this article focuses on a further barrier, one that has its effect on the already identified, those members of these groups who, having survived structural obstacles, have achieved identification with the domain (of the present groups, school-identified African Americans and math-identified women). It is the social-psychological threat that arises when one is in a situation or doing something for which a negative stereotype about one's group applies. This predicament threatens one with being negatively stereotyped, with being judged or treated stereotypically, or with the prospect of conforming to the stereotype. Called *stereotype threat*, it is a situational threat—a threat in the air—that, in general form, can affect the members of any group about whom a negative stereotype exists (e.g., skateboarders, older adults, white men, gang members). Where bad stereotypes about these groups apply, members of these groups can

fear being reduced to that stereotype. And for those who identify with the domain to which the stereotype is relevant, this predicament can be self-threatening.

Negative stereotypes about women and African Americans bear on important academic abilities. Thus, for members of these groups who are identified with domains in which these stereotypes apply, the threat of these stereotypes can be sharply felt and, in several ways, hampers their achievement.

First, if the threat is experienced in the midst of a domain performance—classroom presentation or test-taking for example—the emotional reaction it causes could directly interfere with performance. My colleagues and I (Spencer, Steele, & Quinn, 1997; C. M. Steele & Aronson, 1995) have tested this possibility with women taking standardized math tests and African Americans taking standardized verbal tests. Second, when this threat becomes chronic in a situation, as for the woman who spends considerable time in a competitive, male-oriented math environment, it can pressure *disidentfication,* a reconceptualization of the self and of one's values so as to remove the domain as a self-identity, as a basis of self-evaluation. Disidentification offers the retreat of not caring about the domain in relation to the self. But as it protects in this way, it can undermine sustained motivation in the domain, an adaptation that can be costly when the domain is as important as schooling.

Stereotype threat is especially frustrating because, at each level of schooling, it affects the vanguard of these groups, those with the skills and self-confidence to have identified with the domain. Ironically, their susceptibility to this threat derives not from internal doubts about their ability (e.g., their internalization of the stereotype) but from their identification with the domain and the resulting concern they have about being stereotyped in it. (This argument has the hopeful implication that to improve the domain performance of these students, one should focus on the feasible task of lifting this situational threat rather than on altering their internal psychology.) Yet, as schooling progresses and the obstacles of structure and stereotype threat take their cumulative toll, more of this vanguard will likely be pressured into the ranks of the unidentified. These students, by not caring about the domain vis-à-vis the self, are likely to underperform in it regardless of whether they are stereotype threatened there. Thus, although the identified among these groups are likely to underperform only under stereotype threat, the unidentified (casualties of sociocultural disadvantage or prior internalization of stereotype threat) are likely to underperform and not persist in the domain even when stereotype threat has been removed.

In these ways, then, the present analysis sees social structure and stereotypes as shaping the academic identities and performance outcomes of large segments of society. But first, for the two groups under consideration, what are these outcomes?

As is much discussed, these outcomes are in a crisis state for African Americans. Although Black students begin school with standardized test scores that are not too far behind those of their White counterparts, almost immediately a gap begins to appear (e.g., Alexander & Entwistle, 1988; Burton & Jones, 1982; Coleman et al., 1966) that, by the sixth grade in most school districts, is two full grade levels (Gerard, 1983). . . . Perhaps most discouraging has been the high dropout rate for African American college students: Those who do not finish college within six years is 62%, compared with a national dropout rate of 41% (American Council on Education, 1995-1996). And there is evidence of lower grade performance among those who do graduate of, on average, two thirds of a letter grade lower than those of other graduating students (Nettles, 1988). . . .

Women clearly thrive in many areas of schooling. But in math, engineering, and the physical sciences, they often endure lesser outcomes than men. In a meta-analysis involving over 3 million participants, Hyde, Fennema, and Lamon (1990), for example, found that through elementary and middle school, there are virtually no differences between boys and girls in performance on standardized math tests but that a trend toward men doing better steadily increases from high school *(SD = .29)* through college *(SD = .41)* and into adulthood *(SD = .59)*. And, as their college careers begin, women leave these fields at a rate two and a half times that of men (Hewitt & Seymour, 1991). . . .

Social and Stereotype Structure as Obstacles to Achievement Identification

Academic Identification

As noted, this analysis assumes that sustained school achievement depends, most centrally, on identifying with school, that is, forming a relationship between oneself and the domains of schooling such that one's self-regard significantly depends on achievement in those domains. Extrinsic rewards such as better career outcomes, personal security, parental exhortation, and so on, can also motivate school achievement. But it is presumed that sustaining motivation through the ebb and flow of these other rewards requires school identification. How, then, is this identification formed?

Not a great deal is known about the process. . . . [T]he argument goes, identification with a given domain of life depends, in large part, on the self-evaluative prospects it offers. . . . This choice and the assessment of prospects that goes into it are, of course, multifaceted: Are the rewards of the domain attractive or important? Is an adequate opportunity structure available? Do I have the requisite skills, talents, and interests? Have others like me succeeded in the domain? Will I be seen as belonging in the domain? Will I be prejudiced against in the domain? Can I envision wanting what this domain has to offer? and so on. Some of these assessments undergird a sense of efficacy in the domain (e.g., Bandura, 1977, 1986). Others have to do with the rewards, importance, and attractiveness of the domain itself. And still others have to do with the feasibility and receptiveness of the domain. The point here is that students tacitly assess their prospects in school and its subdomains, and, roughly speaking, their identifications follow these assessments: increasing when they are favorable and decreasing when they are unfavorable. . . .

Threats to Academic Identification

Structural and cultural threats. Both groups have endured and continue to endure sociocultural influences that could have such effects. Among the most replicable facts in the schooling literature is that SES is strongly related to school success and cognitive performance (e.g., Coleman et al., 1966; Miller, 1996). And because African Americans have long been disproportionately represented in lower socioeconomic classes, this factor surely contributes to their achievement patterns in school, both through the material limitations associated with lower SES (poor schools, lack of resources for school persistence, etc.) and through the ability of these limitations, by downgrading school-related prospects, to undermine identification with school. . . .

Stereotype threat. Beyond these threats, waiting for those in these groups who have identified with school, is yet another threat to their identification, more subtle perhaps but nonetheless profound: that of stereotype threat. I define it as follows: the event of a negative stereotype about a group to which one belongs becoming self-relevant, usually as a plausible interpretation for something one is doing, for an experience one is having, or for a situation one is in, that has relevance to one's self-definition. It happens when one is in the *field* of the stereotype, what Cross (1991) called a "spotlight anxiety" (p. 195), such that one can be judged or treated in terms of a racial stereotype. Many analysts have referred to this predicament and the pressure it causes (e.g., Allport, 1954; Carter, 1991; Cose, 1993; Goffman, 1963; Howard & Hammond, 1985; E. E. Jones et al., 1984; Sartre, 1946/1965; C. M. Steele, 1975; C. M. & Aronson, 1995; S. Steele, 1990). The present definition stresses that for a negative stereotype to be threatening, it must be self-relevant. Then, the situational contingency it establishes—the possibility of conforming to the stereotype or of being treated and judged in terms of it—becomes self-threatening. . . .

Stereotype threat . . . refers to the strictly situational threat of negative stereotypes, the threat that does not depend on cuing an internalized anxiety or expectancy. It is cued by the mere recognition that a negative group stereotype could apply to oneself in a given situation. How threatening this recognition becomes depends on the person's identification with the stereotype-relevant domain. For the domain identified, the situational relevance of the stereotype is threatening because it threatens diminishment in a domain that is self-definitional. For the less domain identified, this recognition is less threatening or not threatening at all, because it threatens something that is less self-definitional.

Stereotype threat, then, as a situational pressure "in the air" so to speak, affects only a subportion of the stereotyped group and, in the area of schooling, probably affects confident students more than unconfident ones. Recall that to be identified with schooling in general, or math in particular, one must have confidence in one's domain-related abilities, enough to perceive good prospects in the domain. This means that stereotype threat should have its greatest effect on the better, more confident students in stereotyped groups, those who have not internalized the group stereotype to the point of doubting their own ability and have thus remained identified with the domain—those who are in the academic vanguard of their group.[1]

Several general features of stereotype threat follow:

1. Stereotype threat is a general threat not tied to the psychology of particular stigmatized groups. It affects the members of any group about whom there exists some generally known negative stereotype (e.g., a grandfather who fears that any faltering of memory will confirm or expose him to stereotypes about the aged). . . .

2. That which turns stereotype threat on and off, the controlling "mechanism" so to speak, is a particular concurrence: whether a negative stereotype about one's group becomes relevant to interpreting oneself or one's behavior in an identified-with setting. When such a setting integrates stereotyped and nonstereotyped people, it may make the stereotype, as a dimension of difference, more salient and thus more strongly felt (e.g., Frable, Blackstone, & Sherbaum, 1990; Goffman, 1963; Kleck & Strenta, 1980; Sartre, 1946/1965; S. Steele, 1990). But such integration is neither necessary nor sufficient for this threat to occur. It can occur even when the person is alone, as for a woman taking an important math test alone in a cubicle but under the threat of confirming a stereotyped limitation of ability. And, in integrated settings, it need not occur. Reducing the interpretive relevance of a stereotype in

the setting, say in a classroom or on a standardized test, may reduce this threat and its detrimental effects even when the setting is integrated.[2]

3. This mechanism also explains the variabilities of stereotype threat: the fact that the type and degree of this threat vary from group to group and, for any group, across settings. For example, the type and degree of stereotype threat experienced by white men, Black people, and people who are overweight differ considerably, bearing on sensitivity and fairness in the first group, on school performance in the second, and on self-control in the third. Moreover, for any of these groups, this threat will vary across settings (e.g., Goffman, 1963; S. Steele, 1990). . . .

4. To experience stereotype threat, one need not believe the stereotype nor even be worried that it is true of oneself. . . .

5. The effort to overcome stereotype threat by disproving the stereotype—for example, by outperforming it in the case of academic work—can be daunting. . . .

Empirical Support for a Theory of Stereotype Threat and Disidentification

In testing these ideas, the research of my colleagues and I has had two foci: The first is on intellectual performance in the domain in which negative group stereotypes apply. Here, the analysis has two testable implications. One is that for domain-identified students, stereotype threat may interfere with their domain-related intellectual performance. . . . The other testable implication is that reducing this threat in the performance setting, by reducing its interfering pressure, should improve the performance of otherwise stereotype-threatened students.

The second research focus is the model's implication that stereotype threat, and the anticipation of having to contend with it unceasingly in school or some domain of schooling, should deter members of these groups from identifying with these domains, and, for group members already identified, it should pressure their disidentification.[3]

Stereotype Threat and Intellectual Performance

Steven Spencer, Diane Quinn, and I (Spencer et al., 1997) first tested the effect of stereotype threat on intellectual performance by testing its effect on the standardized math test performance of women who were strong in math.

The stereotype threat of women performing math. At base, of course, the stereotype threat that women experience in math-performance settings derives from a negative stereotype about their math ability that is disseminated throughout society. But whether this threat impaired their performance, we reasoned, would depend on two things. First, the performance would have to be construed so that any faltering would imply the limitation of ability alleged in the stereotype. This means that the performance would have to be difficult enough so that faltering at it would imply having reached an ability limit but not so difficult as to be nondiagnostic of ability. And second, as has been much emphasized, the women in question would have to be identified with math, so that faltering and its stereotype-confirming implication would threaten something they care about, their belongingness and acceptance in a domain they identify with. Of course, men too (at least those of equal skill and identification with math) could be threatened in this situation; faltering would reflect on their ability too. But their faltering would not carry the extra threat of confirming a stereotyped limitation in math ability or of causing them to be seen that way. Thus, the threat that women experience, through the interfering pressure it causes, should worsen their performance in comparison to equally qualified men. Interestingly, though, these otherwise confident women should perform equally as well as equally qualified men when this situational threat is lessened. . . .

In dramatic support of our reasoning, women performed worse than men when they were told that the test produced gender differences, which replicated women's underperformance observed in the earlier experiments, but they performed equal to men when the test was represented as insensitive to gender differences, even though, of course, the same difficult "ability" test was used in both conditions. Genetic limitation did not cap the performance of women in these experiments. . . . [And], the disruptive effect of stereotype threat was mediated more by the self-evaluative anxiety it caused than by its lowering of performance expectations or self-efficacy. . . .

The stereotype threat of African Americans on standardized tests. Joshua Aronson and I (C. M. Steele & Aronson, 1995) examined these processes among African American students. In these studies, Black and White Stanford University students took a test composed of the most difficult items on the verbal GRE exam. Because the participants were students admitted to a highly selective university, we assumed that they were identified with the verbal skills represented on standardized tests. The first study varied whether or not the stereotype about Black persons' intellectual ability was relevant to their performance by varying whether the test was presented as *ability-diagnostic,* that is, as a test of intellectual ability, or as *ability-nondiagnostic,* that is, as a laboratory problem-solving task unrelated to ability and thus to the stereotype about ability. Analysis of covariance was used to remove the influence of participants' initial skills, measured by their verbal SAT scores, on their test performance. This done, the results showed strong evidence of stereotype threat: Black participants greatly underperformed White participants in the diagnostic condition but equaled them in the nondiagnostic condition. A second experiment produced the same pattern of results with an even more slight manipulation of stereotype threat: whether or not participants recorded their race on a demographic questionnaire just before taking the test (described as nondiagnostic in all conditions). Salience of the racial stereotype alone was enough to depress the performance of identified Black students. . . .

Stereotype threat and the interpretation of group differences in standardized test performance. Inherent to the science of quantifying human intelligence is the unsavory possibility of ranking societal groups as to their aggregated intelligence. It is from this corner of psychology that the greatest controversy has arisen, a controversy that has lasted throughout this century and that is less about the fact of these group differences than about

their interpretation (cf. Herrnstein & Murray, 1994; Kamin, 1974). To the set of possible causes for these group differences, our (C. M. Steele & Aronson, 1995) findings add a new one: the differential impact of stereotype threat on groups in the testing situation itself. Thus, stereotype threat may be a possible source of bias in standardized tests, a bias that arises not from item content but from group differences in the threat that societal stereotypes attach to test performance. . . .

Reaction of Disidentification

Stereotype threat is assumed to have an abiding effect on school achievement—an effect beyond its impairment of immediate performance—by preventing or breaking a person's identification with school, in particular, those domains of schooling in which the stereotype applies. This reasoning has several implications for which empirical evidence can be brought to bear: the resilience of self-esteem to stigmatization; the relationship between stigmatized status and school achievement; and, among ability-stigmatized people, the relationship between their school performance and self-esteem.

Self-esteem's resilience to stigmatization. In a recent review, Crocker and Major (1989) were able to make a strong case for the lack of something that common sense suggests should exist: a negative effect of stigmatization on self-esteem. Following the logic of the internalization models described above and viewing stigmatization as, among other things, an assault to self-esteem, one might expect that people who are stigmatized would have lower self-esteem than people who are not. Yet, as Crocker and Major reported, when the self-esteem of stigmatized groups (e.g., Blacks, Chicanos, the facially disfigured, obese people, etc.) is actually measured, one finds that their self-esteem is as high as that of the nonstigmatized.

Crocker and Major (1989) offered the intriguing argument that stigma itself offers esteem-protective strategies. For example, the stigmatized can blame their failures on the prejudice of out-group members, they can limit their self-valuative social comparisons to the in-group of other stigmatized people, and they can devalue the domains in which they feel devalued. . . . In the present reasoning, stigmatization stems from stereotype threat in specific domains. Thus, it adds to the list of stigma adaptations the possibility of simple domain disidentification, the rescuing of self-esteem by rendering as self-evaluatively irrelevant the domain in which the stereotype applies. . . .

A universal connection between stigmatization and poor school achievement. If disidentification with school, and the resulting underachievement, can be a reaction to ability-stigmatizing stereotypes in society, then it might be expected that ability stigmatization would be associated with poor school performance wherever it occurs in the world. Finding such a relationship would not definitively prove the present theory; the direction of causality could be quarreled with, as could the mediation of such a relationship. . . .

The disassociation of self-esteem and school achievement. If the poor school achievement of ability-stigmatized groups is mediated by disidentification, then it might be expected that among the ability stigmatized, there would be a disassociation between school outcomes and overall self-esteem. Several kinds of evidence suggest this process among African Americans. First, there is the persistent finding that although Black students underperform in relation to White students on school outcomes from grades to standardized tests (e.g., Demo & Parker, 1987; Simmons, Brown, Bush, & Blyth, 1978; C. M. Steele, 1992), their global self-esteem is as high or higher than that of White students (e.g., Porter & Washington, 1979; Rosenberg, 1979; Wylie, 1979). For both of these facts to be true, some portion of Black students must have acquired an imperviousness to poor school performance. . . .

Can stereotype threat directly cause this disconnect? To test this question, Kirsten Stoutemeyer and I varied the strength of stereotype threat that female test takers (Stanford students) were under by varying whether societal differences between women and men in math performance were attributed to small but stable differences in innate ability (suggesting an inherent, gender-based limit in math ability) or to social causes such as sex-role prescriptions and discrimination (suggesting no inherent, gender-based limit in math ability). We then measured their

identificaion with math and math-related careers, either before or after they took a difficult math test. Regardless of when identification was measured, women under stronger stereotype threat disidentified with math and math-related careers more than women under weaker stereotype threat. Although domain identification has several determinants, these findings suggest that stereotype threat is an important one of them.

"Wise" Schooling: Practice and Policy

As a different diagnosis, the present analysis comes to a different prescription: The schooling of stereotype-threatened groups may be improved through situational changes (analogous to those manipulated in our experiments) that reduce the stereotype threat these students might otherwise be under. As noted, psychological diagnoses have more typically ascribed the problems of these students to internal processes ranging from genes to internalized stereotypes. On the face of it, at least, internal states are more difficult to modify than situational factors. Thus, the hope of the present analysis, encouraged by our research, is that these problems might be more tractable through the situational design of schooling, in particular, design that secures these students in the belief that they will not be held under the suspicion of negative stereotypes about their group. Schooling that does this, I have called *wise,* a term borrowed from Irving Goffman (1963), who borrowed it from gay men and lesbians of the 1950s. They used it to designate heterosexuals who understood their full humanity despite the stigma attached to their sexual orientation: family and friends, usually, who knew the person beneath the stigma. So it must be, I argue, for the effective schooling of stereotype-threatened groups.

Although "wisedom" may be necessary for the effective schooling of such students, it may not always be sufficient. The chief distinction made in this analysis (between those of these groups who are identified with the relevant school domain and those who are not) raises a caution. As noted, stereotype threat is not keenly felt by those who identify little with the stereotype-threatening domain. Thus, although reducing this threat in the domain may be necessary to encourage their identification, it may not be sufficient to build an identification that is not there. For this to occur, more far-reaching strategies that develop the building blocks of domain identification may be required: better skills, greater domain self-efficacy, feelings of social and cultural comfort in the domain, a lack of social pressure to disidentify, and so on. . . .

Some wise strategies, then, may work for both identified and unidentified students from these groups, but others may have to be appropriately targeted to be effective. I offer some examples of both types.

For both domain-identified and domain-unidentified students:

1. Optimistic teacher-student relationships. The prevailing stereotypes make it plausible for ability-stigmatized students to worry that people in their schooling environment will doubt their abilities. Thus, one wise strategy, seemingly suitable for all students, is to discredit this assumption through the authority of potential-affirming adult relationships. . . .

2. Challenge over remediation. Giving challenging work to students conveys respect for their potential and thus shows them that they are not regarded through the lens of an ability-demeaning stereotype. Urie Treisman (1985) used this strategy explicitly in designing his successful group-study workshops in math for college-aged women and minorities. Taking students where they are skillwise, all students can be given challenging work at a challenging, not overwhelming, pace, especially in the context of supportive adult-student relationships. . . .

3. Stressing the expandability of intelligence. The threat of negative-ability stereotypes is that one could confirm or be seen as having a fixed limitation inherent to one's group. To the extent that schooling can stress what Carol Dweck (1986) called the *incremental* nature of human intelligence—its expandability in response to experience and training—it should help to deflect this meanest implication of the stereotype. . . .

For domain-identified students:

1. Affirming domain belongingness. Negative-ability stereotypes raise the threat that one does not belong in the domain. They cast doubt on the extent of one's abilities, on how well one will be accepted, on one's social

compatibility with the domain, and so on. Thus, for students whose primary barrier to school identification is stereotype threat, direct affirmation of their belongingness in the domain may be effective. But it is important to base this affirmation on the students' intellectual potential. Affirming social belonging alone, for those under the threat of an ability stereotype, could be taken as begging the question.

2. Valuing multiple perspectives. This refers to strategies that explicitly value a variety of approaches to both academic substance and the larger academic culture in which that substance is considered. Making such a value public tells stereotype-threatened students that this is an environment in which the stereotype is less likely to be used.

3. Role models. People from the stereotype-threatened group who have been successful in the domain carry the message that stereotype threat is not an insurmountable barrier there.

For domain-unidentified students:

1. Nonjudgmental responsiveness. Research by Lepper, Woolverton, Mumme, and Gurtner (1993) has identified a distinct strategy that expert tutors use with especially poor students: little direct praise, Socratic direction of students' work, and minimal attention to right and wrong answers. . . .

2. Building self-efficacy. Based on Bandura's (1977, 1986) theory of self-efficacy, this strategy attempts to build the student's sense of competence and self-efficacy in the schooling domain. . . .

Existence Proof: A Wise Schooling Intervention

Providing a definitive test of wise schooling theory will require, of course, an extensive research program. But as a first step, something might be learned from what Urie Treisman (1985) called an existence proof, in this case, a demonstration that an intervention derived from the theory could stop or reverse a tenacious negative trajectory in the school performance of stereotype-threatened students. . . .

With this rationale, my colleagues and I (Steven Spencer, Richard Nisbett, Mary Hummel, David Schoem, Kent Harber, Ken

Carter) implemented a freshman-year program at the University of Michigan aimed at the underachievement and low retention rates of African American students. . . .

In this context, we implemented several wise strategies. The program was presented as a transition program aimed at helping students maximize the advantages of university life. We also recruited students honorifically; they were told that, as Michigan admittees, they had survived a very competitive selection process and that our program was designed to help them maximize their strong potential. These practices represented the program as nonremediational and represented the university as having acknowledged their intellectual potential and as having high expectations for them—all things that signal the irrelevance of negative group stereotypes. Once the students were in the program, these expectations were reinforced by their being offered a "challenge" workshop, modeled on those developed by Treisman (1985) for calculus, in either freshman calculus, chemistry, physics, or writing. These were taken on a voluntary basis in the dormitory. Students also participated in small weekly discussion groups, centered on brief readings, that allowed discussion of adjustment-relevant social and even personal issues. This activity has the wisdom of letting students know that they, or other members of their group, are not the only ones with concerns about adjusting to university life—an insight that can deflect the relevance of negative group stereotypes. These formal program components lasted for the first 10 weeks of the school year, and, as voluntary activities, approximately half of the students regularly participated in either one or both of them.

The first-semester grades averaged over the first two years of this ongoing project give a reliable picture of the program's initial impact. . . . Black students [in the program] showed almost no underperformance; in the top two thirds of the test distribution, they had essentially the same grades as White students. We also know from follow-up data that their higher grade performance continued at least through their sophomore year and that as long as four years later, only one of them had dropped out.

Conclusion

In social psychology, we know that as observers looking at a person or group, we tend to stress internal, dispositional causes of their behavior, whereas when we take the perspective of the actor, now facing the circumstances they face, we stress more situational causes (e.g., E. E. Jones & Nisbett, 1972; Ross, 1977). If there is a system to the present research, it is that of taking the actor's perspective in trying to understand the intellectual performance of African American and female students. It is this perspective that brings to light the broadly encompassing condition of having these groups' identification with domains of schooling threatened by societal stereotypes. This is a threat that in the short run can depress their intellectual performance and, over the long run, undermine the identity itself, a predicament of serious consequence. But it is a predicament—something in the interaction between a group's social identity and its social psychological context, rather than something essential to the group itself. Predicaments can be treated, intervened on, and it is in this respect that I hope the perspective taken in this analysis and the early evidence offer encouragement.

Footnotes

[1]The point is not that negative stereotypes are never internalized as low self-expectancies and self-doubts. It is that in such internalization, disidentification is the more primary adaptation. That is, once the stereotype-relevant domain (e.g., math) is dropped as a self-definition, the negative stereotype (e.g., that women are limited in math) can be accepted as more self-descriptive (i.e., internalized) without it much affecting one's self-regard (as for the woman who, not caring about math, says she is lousy at it). But this internalization is probably resisted (e.g., Crocker & Major, 1989) until disidentification makes it less self-threatening. Once this has happened, the person is likely to avoid the domain because of both disinterest and low confidence regardless of whether stereotype threat is present.

[2]As a process of social devaluation, stereotype threat is both a subform of stigmatization and something more general. It is that form of stigmatization that is mediated by collectively held, devaluing group stereotypes. This means that it does not include stigmatization that derives from nonstereotyped features such as a facial disfigurement or, for example, what Goffman (1963) called abominations of the body.

Stereotyped threat is a stituational predicament. It is a threat that can befall anyone about whom a negative reputation or group stereotype exists.

[3]Moreover, a protective avoidance of identification can become a group norm. In reaction to a shared sense of threat in school, for example, it can become a shared reaction that is transmitted to group members as the normative relation to school. Both research (e.g., Ogbu, 1986; Solomon, 1992) and the media have documented this reaction in minority students from inner-city high schools to Harvard University's campus. Thus, disidentification can be sustained by normative pressure from the in-group as well as by stereotype threat in the setting.

References

Alexander, K. L., & Entwistle, D. R. (1988). Achievement in the first two years of school: Patterns and processes. *Monographs of the Society for Research in Child Development, 53(2).*

Allport, G. (1954). *The nature of prejudice.* New York: Doubleday.

American Council on Education. (1995-1996). *Minorities in higher education.* Washington, DC: Office of Minority Concerns.

Bandura, A. (1977). Self-efficacy: Toward a unifying theory of behavior change. *Psychological Review 84*, 191-215.

Bandura, A. (1986). *Social foundations of action: A social-cognitive theory.* Englewood Cliffs, NJ: Prentice Hall.

Burton, N. W., & Jones, L. V. (1982). Recent trends in achievement levels of Black and White youth. *Educational Researcher: 11,* 10-17.

Carter, S. (1991). *Reflections of an affirmative action baby.* New York: Basic Books.

Clark, K. B. (1965). *Dark ghetto: Dilemmas of social power.* New York: Harper & Row.

Coleman, J. S., Campbell, E. Q., Hobson, C. J., McPartland, J., Mood, A. M., Weinfield, F. D., & York, R. L. (1966). *Equality of educational opportunity.* Washington, DC: U.S. Government Printing Office.

Cose, E. (1993). *The rage of a privileged class.* New York: Harper Collins.

Crocker, J., & Major, B. (1989). Social stigma and self-esteem: The self-protective properties of stigma. *Psychological Review, 96,* 608-630.

Cross, W. E., Jr. (1991). *Shades of black: Diversity in African-American identity.* Philadelphia: Temple University Press.

Demo, D. H., & Parker, K. D. (1987). Academic achievement and self-esteem among Black and White college students. *Journal of Social Psychology, 4,* 345-355.

Dweck, C. (1986). Motivational processes affecting learning. *American Psychologist, 41,* 1040-1048.

Frable, D., Blackstone, T., & Sherbaum, C. (1990). Marginal and mindful: Deviants in social interaction. *Journal of Personality and Social Behavior. 59,* 140-149.

Gerard, H. (1983). School desegregation: The social science role. *American Psychologist, 38,* 869-878.

Goffman. E. (1963). *Stigma: Notes on the management of spoiled identity.* New York: Touchstone.

Herrnstein, R. A., & Murray. C. (1994). *The bell curve.* New York: Grove Press.

Hewitt, N. M., & Seymour, E. (1991). *Factors contributing to high attrition rates among science and engineering undergraduate majors.* Unpublished report to the Alfred P. Sloan Foundation.

Howard, J., & Hammond, R. (1985, September 9). Rumors of inferiority. *New Republic, 72,* 18-23.

Hyde, J. S., Fennema, E., & Lamon, S. J. (1990). Gender differences in mathematics performance: A meta-analysis. *Psychological Bulletin, 107,* 139-155.

Jones, E. E., Farina, A., Hastorf, A. H., Markus, H., Miller, O. T., & Scott, R. A. (1984). *Social stigma: The psychology of marked relationships.* New York: Freeman.

Jones, E. E., & Nisbett, R. E. (1972). The actor and the observer: Divergent perceptions of the causes of behavior. In E. E. Jones; D. E. Kanouse, H. H. Kelley, R. E. Nisbett, S. Valins, & B. Weiner (Eds.), *Attribution: Perceiving the causes of behavior* (pp. 79-94). Morristown, NJ: General Learning Press.

Kamin, L. (1974). *The science and politics of I.Q,.* Hillsdale, NJ: Erlbaum.

Kleck, R. F., & Strenta, A. (1980). Perceptions of the impact of negatively valued physical characteristics on social interactions. *Journal of Personality and Social Psychology, 39,* 861-873.

Lepper, M. R., Woolverton, M., Mumme, D. L., & Gunner J. L. (1993). Motivational techniques of expert human tutors: Lessons for the design of computer-based tutors. In S. P. Lajoie & S. J. Derry (Eds.), *Computers as cognitive tools* (pp. 75-104). Hillsdale, NJ: Erlbaum.

Miller, L. S. (1996, March). *Promoting high academic achievement among non-Asian minorities.* Paper presented at the Princeton University Conference on Higher Education, Princeton, NJ.

National Coalition of Advocates for Students Report. (1988, December 12). *The Ann Arbor News,* pp. Al, A4.

Nettles, M. T. (1988). *Toward undergraduate student equality in American higher education.* New York: Greenwood.

Ogbu, J. (1986). The consequences of the American caste system. In U. Neisser (Ed.), *The school achievement of minority children: New perspectives* (pp. 19-56). Hillsdale, NJ: Eribaum.

Porter, J. R., & Washington, R. E. (1979). Black identity and self-esteem: A review of the studies of Black self-concept, 1968-1978. *Annual Review of Sociology, 5,* 53-74.

Rosenberg, M. (1979). *Conceiving self.* New York: Basic Books.

Ross, L. (1977). The intuitive psychologist and his shortcomings: Distortions in the attribution process. In L. Berkowitz (Ed.), *Advances in experimental social psychology* (Vol.10, pp. 337-384). New York: Academic Press.

Sartre, J. P. (1965). *Anti-Semite and Jew.* New York: Schocken Books. (Original work published 1946)

Simmons, R. G., Brown, L., Bush, D. M., & Blyth, D. A. (1978). Self-esteem and achievement of Black and White adolescents. *Social Problems, 26*, 86-96.

Solomon, R. P. (1992). *Forging a separatist culture.* Albany: State University of New York Press.

Spencer, S., Steele, C. M., & Quinn, D. (1997). *Under suspicion of inability: Stereotype threat and women's math performance.* Manuscript submitted for publication.

Steele, C. M. (1975). Name-calling and compliance. *Journal of Personality and Social Psychology 31,* 361-369.

Steele, C. M. (1992, April). Race and the schooling of Black Americans. *The Atlantic Monthly,* pp. 68-78.

Steele, C. M., & Aronson, J. (1995). Stereotype threat and the intellectual test performance of African Americans. *Journal of Personality and Social Psychology, 69,* 797-811.

Steele, S. (1990). *The content of our character.* New York: St Martin's Press.

Treisman, U. (1985*). A study of mathematics performance of Black students at the University of California, Berkeley.* Unpublished report.

Wylie, R. (1979). *The self-concept* (Vol.2). Lincoln: University of Nebraska Press.

Who Is A Whiz Kid?

Ted Gup

ditors' Note: Claude Steele's work on stereotype threat dramatically illustrates the negative effect stereotypes can have on the academic performance of those who are the targets of stereotypes. In the following article, Ted Gup explores the other side of the coin—what effects do positive stereotypes of a group have on academic performance? Can positive stereotypes also have a negative side? Gup points to the stereotype of Asian children being good in math as an example of the double-edged sword of positive stereotypes.

Shortly after joining a national magazine some years ago as a writer, I found myself watching in horror as the week's cover story was prepared. The story was about "Asian-American whiz kids," and it featured a series of six student portraits, each face radiating with an intellectual brilliance. Being new to the enterprise, I was at first tentative in my criticism, cautioning that such a story was inherently biased and fueled racial and ethnic stereotypes. My criticism was dismissed. "This is something good we are saying about them," one top editor remarked. I reduced my criticism to writing. "What," I asked, "would be the response if the cover were about 'Jewish whiz kids'? Would anyone really dare to produce such an obviously offensive story?" My memo was ignored Not long after, the cover appeared on the nation's newsstands, and the criticism began to fly. The editors were taken aback

As a former Fulbright Scholar to China I have long taken a strong interest in the portrayal of Asian-Americans. But my interest went well beyond the academic. Even as the cover was being prepared, I was waiting to adopt my first son from Korea. His name was to be David. He was 5 months old when he arrived. That did not stop even some otherwise sophisticated friends from volunteering that he would no doubt be a good student. Probably a mathematician, they opined, with a tone that uncomfortably straddled jest and prediction. I tried to take it all with good humor, this idea that a 5-month-old who could not yet sit up, speak a word or control his bowels was already destined for academic greatness. Even his major seemed foreordained.

Many Asian-Americans seem to walk an uneasy line between taking pride in their remarkable achievements and needing to shake off stereotypes. The jokes abound. There is the apocryphal parent who asks "where is the other point?" when his or her child scores a 99 on a test. Another similar refrain has the young Asian-American student enumerating his or her hobbies: "studying, studying and more studying."

Several months after David arrived he and I entered a small mom-and-pop convenience store in our neighborhood. The owners were Korean. I noticed that the husband, standing behind the cash register, was eying my son. "Is he Korean?" he asked. "Yes," I nodded. He reached out for him and took him into his arms. "He'll be good in math," declared the man. "My God," I muttered. Not him, too!

It was preposterous. It was funny. And it was unnerving. Embedded in such elevated expectations were real threats to my son. Suppose, I wondered, he should turn out to be only a mediocre student, or, worse yet, not a student at all. I resented the stereotypes and saw them for what they were, the other side of the coin of racism. It is easy to delude one's self into thinking it harmless to offer racial compliments, but that is an inherent contradiction in terms. Such sweeping decriptives, be they negative or positive, deny the one thing most precious to all people—individuality. These stereotypes are pernicious for two reasons. First, such attributes are relative and tend to pit one race against another. Witness the seething enmity in many inner cities between Korean store owners and their African-American patrons. Stereotypes that hint at superiority in one race implicitly suggest inferiority in another. They are ultimately divisive, and in their most virulent form, even deadly. Who can forget the costs of the Aryan myth?

Such stereotypes also place a crushing burden on Asian-Americans. Few would deny that disproportionate numberrs of Asian surnames appear each year among the winners of the Westinghouse science prizes or in the ranks of National Merit Scholars. But it might be a reflection of parental influences, personal commitment and cultural predilections, not genetic predisposition. A decade ago, as a Fulbright Lecturer in Beijing, I saw firsthand the staggering hours my Chinese students devoted to their studies. Were my students in the United States to invest similar time in their books I would have every reason to expect similar results.

I have often been told that Koreans are the "Jews of Asia," a reference to both their reported skills in business and their inherent intelligence. As a Jew, I cannot help but wince at such descriptions. I remember being one of the very few of my faith in a Midwest boarding school. There were many presumptions weighing on me, most of them grounded in my religion. My own classroom performance almost singlehandedly disabused my teachers of the myth that Jews were academically gifted. I barely made it through. Whether it was a lack of intelligence or simple rebellion against expectation, I do not know. I do know that more than once the fact that I was Jewish was raised as evidence that I could

and should be doing better. Expectations based on race, be they raised or lowered, are no less galling.

David is now in the first grade. He is already taking math with the second graders and asking me about square roots and percentiles. I think back to the Korean merchant who took him in his arms and pronounced him a math whiz. Was he right? Do Asian-Americans have it easier, endowed with some special strand of DNA? The answer is a resounding no. Especially in our house. My son David has learning disabilities to overcome and what progress he has made is individual in the purest and most heroic sense. No one can or should take that away from him, suggesting he is just another wunderkind belonging to a favored race.

A year after my first son arrived, we adopted his brother from Korea. His name is Matthew. Let it be known that Matthew couldn't care less about math. He's a bug man. Slugs and earthworms. I suspect he will never be featured on any cover stories about Asian-American whiz kids, but I will continue to resist anything and anyone who attempts to dictate either his interests or his abilities based on race or place of birth. Bugs are fine by me and should be more than fine by him.

✓ PROJECT 9.1
The Multiple Intelligences Of Forest Gump

I.   Howard Gardner, a prominent psychologist at Harvard University, has proposed that instead of limiting our view of intelligence to "an ability assessed by academic tests," intelligence should be defined, studied, and assessed as multi-faceted. He has proposed 7 different types of intelligences:

Intelligence	Description*
Logical-mathematical	Sensitivity to, and capacity to discern, logical or numerical patterns; ability to handle long chains of reasoning.
Linguistic	Sensitivity to the sounds, rhythms, and meanings of words; sensitivity to the different functions of language.
Musical	Abilities to produce and appreciate rhythm, pitch, and timbre; appreciation of the forms of musical expressiveness.
Spatial	Capacities to perceive the visual-spatial world accurately and to perform transformations on one's initial perceptions.
Bodily-kinesthetic	Abilities to control one's body movements and to handle objects skillfully.
Interpersonal	Capacities to discern and respond appropriately to the moods, temperaments, motivations, and desires of other people.
Intrapersonal	Access to one's own feelings and the ability to discriminate among them and draw upon them to guide behavior; knowledge of one's own strengths, weaknesses, desires, and intelligences.

A.   For this project, you will analyze the main character in the movie *Forest Gump*, creating an evaluation of his abilities on each of the 7 different types of intelligences. Rate Gump on the following dimensions.

Intelligence	extremely low	very low	low	somewhat below average	average	somewhat above average	high	very high	extremely high
Logical-mathematical	1	2	3	4	5	6	7	8	9
Linguistic	1	2	3	4	5	6	7	8	9
Musical	1	2	3	4	5	6	7	8	9
Spatial	1	2	3	4	5	6	7	8	9
Bodily-kinesthetic	1	2	3	4	5	6	7	8	9
Interpersonal	1	2	3	4	5	6	7	8	9
Intrapersonal	1	2	3	4	5	6	7	8	9

*Chart is taken from Zimbardo & Gerrig (1996), p. 559.

How does your evaluation compare to an evaluation of Gump on a more traditional definition of intelligence?

_____

_____

_____

_____

_____

_____

_____

_____

_____

_____

_____

_____

_____

_____

_____

_____

_____

_____

_____

_____

_____

_____

_____

_____

_____

_____

_____

_____

✓ PROJECT 9.2
How Fair Are Intelligence Tests?

I.   Intelligence tests have often been criticized for being culturally biased. The following questions are from an intelligence test published in 1974 by The Psychological Corporation.

q1: What are some reasons why we need policemen?
q2: Why is it usually better to give money to a well-known charity than to a street beggar?
q3: Who discovered America?
q4: How far is it from New York to Los Angeles?
q5: What is the thing to do if a boy (girl) much smaller than you starts to fight with you?

How fair are each of the questions? Please rate each question using the following scale:

    1   2   3   4   5   6   7   8   9
not at all fair   extremely fair

q1: _____   q4: _____
q2: _____   q5: _____
q3: _____

If they are not fair, who are they biased against?

q1: _____

q2: _____

q3: _____

q4: _____

q5: _____

How would you change each question to be culturally fair, if possible?

q1: _____

q2: _____

q3: _____

q4: _____

q5: _____

✓ PROJECT 9.3
Creating A Wise School

I.   For this project, your class will break into groups of 3–4 students in each group. You and your group will read the following scenario and complete the assigned task.

II.   *Scenario.* You and the members of your group have been hired to be educational consultants by a school district in your town. The members of the school board have read Claude Steele's article on Stereotype Threat, and now would like for you to design ways to implement the eight strategies suggested by Steele for Wise schooling (listed on page 291).

III.   *The Task.* In your group, create specific ways to implement each strategy. Then, design ways to test whether or not your implementation of the strategy has made a difference (and specify what kind of difference).

IV.   *The Presentation.* After you have created these strategies and ways to evaluate your strategies, you and your group will present these to the rest of the class. Are there common ways that the groups in your class have arrived at to implement these strategies? Are there common ways of testing their effectiveness? What characterized the seemingly most effective strategies and assessments?

C h a p t e r   1 0

Applying Research On Gender, Race, And Ethnicity: The Workplace And The Affirmative Action Debate

The articles and projects in Chapter 9 called on knowledge from previous chapters in this Workbook, applying it to the very important social domain of education. The power of the group, cognitive processes that create and sustain stereotypes and social roles, and the link between an individual's identity and her or his group membership were all touched on in this material. It also focused on the consequences that follow from how we define intelligence both for the individual and educational systems. Perhaps, most importantly, Chapter 9 is an example of how social psychologists have sought to answer the challenge issued by Dr. Martin Luther King, Jr., in his speech to social scientists, presented in Chapter 1, to engage in the struggle for a better society.

This chapter continues to apply the knowledge we have gained by focusing on the problem of discrimination, racism, and sexism in the workplace. Affirmative action policies that are intended to reduce discrimination serve as the focal point for the articles and projects in this section. The first of these, written by Robert Cherry, discusses the phenomenon of institutionalized discrimination. Cherry, a sociologist, describes the personal, social, and economic consequences that those who are the target of such discrimination suffer. Next, Madeleine Heilman and her colleagues discuss how our responses to policies designed to deal with existing inequities for women in the workplace can be influenced by how fair such policies are perceived to be. In their piece Audrey Murrell and her collaborators also examine people's perceptions of affirmative action. However, in contrast to Heilman's article, they show that the issue of fairness is not the only factor driving people's response to such policies. Who people think will benefit from the policies also matters. The following item is a brief summary of research conducted at Michigan State debunking some of the prevalent views of those who are hired under affirmative action plans.

The next article by Tori DeAngelis returns us to the important issue of the influence that social roles have in our lives. It reports research showing a link between how much people endorse central social values and the jobs they believe are appropriate for women and men. The final item in this section presents the findings of a study showing how men and women in academia are perceived and evaluated differently by their peers.

In this section we are confronted by many of the negative social outcomes related to discrimination, racism, and sexism. On the other hand, these articles, either directly, or indirectly, provide information that could help us become more aware of the presence of discrimination and suggest strategies for diminishing and eliminating this social ill.

Institutionalized Discrimination

Robert Cherry

ℰditors' Note: In Chapter 8 we examined policies that have often discriminatory outcomes. These policies result in institutionalized discrimination which is discussed in this article by Robert Cherry. Cherry explores the often unintended ways organizational structures and practices support discrimination which helps perpetuate poverty among women and members of traditionally stigmatized groups. While this article approaches the problem from a sociological perspective, it provides an overview of the problem of discrimination in the workplace, a problem affirmative action policies have attempted to rectify.

Individuals and institutions may use decision-making procedures that inadvertently discriminate and reinforce inequalities. For example, income differentials can cause unequal access to education even though the school system does not intend to discriminate; locational decisions of firms may have the unintended impact of reducing access to jobs. Similarly, when housing is segregated by income (race), all individuals do not have equal access to job information, as higher-income (white) households will tend to have greater access to job information through personal contacts than lower-income (black) households. Thus, employers will have more higher-income white applicants than if housing was distributed without regard to race or income. Also, employers attempting to reduce their screening costs might rely on group stereotypes rather than more individualized information when deciding which applicants to interview.

In none of these instances is discrimination consciously undertaken, but disadvantaged groups, having unequal access to education, job information, and the interviewing process, are nonetheless harmed. Though unintentional, these problems reinforce the "vicious cycle" of poverty.

Income Differentials and Educational Attainment

Income constraints place heavy burdens on the allocation decisions of low-income households. Often they must "choose" to do without many necessities, such as education. In addition, children from low-income households often have explicit household responsibilities that take time away from school activities. This may involve responsibility for household activities (baby-sitting, shopping, and so on) or earning income. In either case, economists would argue that on average low-income students have a greater opportunity cost on their time than high-income students. Since their opportunity costs are greater, lower-income students rationally allocate less time to studying and school-related activities than equally motivated higher-income students.

At the college level, even the availability of low-cost public institutions does not necessarily equalize the economic cost of education to all students. Just as at the elementary and secondary school level, lower-income students have a greater opportunity cost on their time than comparable higher-income students. Even if family responsibilities are negligible, students still re-quire income for their own support. This invariably requires lower-income students to work at least part-time while attending school and has often led to the sending of male but not female offspring to college.

The level of income required is influenced by whether the student can live at home while attending college. Historically, public colleges were located in rural areas. For example, none of the original campuses of the Big Ten or Big Eight colleges are located in the states' largest metropolitan areas. The original campus of the University of Illinois is not located in Chicago and the University of Missouri is not located in St. Louis or Kansas City. Thus, not only did lower-income students have to pay for room and board away from home, but it was usually difficult to find part-time employment in these rural communities. This implies that even the availability of low-cost public colleges did not necessarily place the lower-income student on an equal footing with more prosperous students.

Theoretically, low-income youths with appropriate abilities and motivation should be able to borrow money to finance their education. As long as the economic returns from schooling are greater than the interest rate, students will gain from borrowing rather than forgoing additional education. The equalizing of economic costs can occur only if all students of equal promise can borrow at the same rates. Financial institutions, however, cannot accept expectations or probabilities of future income as sufficient collateral for loans. They require bank accounts or other tradable assets, which are normally held by upper-income but not lower-income households. Thus, students from lower-income households cannot borrow readily for education without government intervention.

It also appears that schools in poorer neighborhoods tend to have larger classes and weaker teachers. John Owen found that within the same city, as the mean neighborhood income rose by 1 percent, class size decreased by 0.24 percent and the verbal ability of teachers rose by 0.11 percent. This inequality is even more glaring when comparisons are made between cities. Owen found that for each 1 percent increase in the mean income of a city, there was a rise of 0.73 percent in real expenditures per student and a 1.20 percent increase in the verbal ability of teachers. Thus, students living in poorer neighborhoods in poorer cities have a double disadvantage.

If higher opportunity costs and lower-quality education were not sufficient to discourage educational attainment, Bennett Harrison found that for black inner-city youths, incomes are hardly affected by increases in educational attainment. He notes, "[A]s their education increases, blacks move into new occupations, but their earnings are hardly affected at all by anything short of a college degree, and there is no effect whatever on their chances of finding themselves without a job over the course of the year." Thus, independent of conscious discrimination by the educational system, we should expect low-income minority youths to have lower educational attainment than white youths, even when ability and motivation are held constant.

During the 1970s, a number of policies were implemented in an attempt to compensate for the influence of family income on educational attainment. First, legislatures began funding state universities in larger urban areas. Second, court rulings forced states to change funding formulas so that per capita funding from wealthy and poor communities within each state would become more equal. Third, guaranteed student loans reduced the disadvantage low-income students faced when attempting to finance their education.

Differential Impact of Incomplete Information

In the most simplified labor models, it is assumed that workers and firms act with complete information: Workers know the jobs that are available, and firms know the productivity of job seekers. In this situation, competitive firms would hire the best applicants for the jobs available, and workers would gain the maximum wage obtainable.

Economists have recently developed models in which information has a price; it is only "purchased" up to the point at which its benefits are at least as great as its costs. Neither firms nor workers rationally attempt to gain complete information concerning the labor market opportunities available. Workers find that some additional job information is not worth its cost, while firms find that some information on the productivity of applicants is not worth the additional personnel expenses. Liberals have argued that when workers and firms rationally decide to act on the basis of optimal rather than complete information, biases are generated.

Let us begin by analyzing how firms decide the optimal productivity information they should obtain. A firm benefits from additional productivity information if it translates into hiring a more profitable work force. A firm must weigh this increased profitability against the cost involved in seeking the additional information. After some point, it is likely that the benefits from additional information are insufficient to outweigh its cost. Even though the firm realizes additional information would probably result in hiring a somewhat more productive worker than otherwise, it knows that the added screening expenses would be even greater.

When a strong profit motive and wide productivity differentials among applicants are present, extensive screening will occur. This is the case with professional sports teams, especially since television revenues have transformed ownership from a hobby to a profit-making activity. Liberals believe, however, that in the vast majority of situations, productivity differentials among applicants are quite small and benefits from extensive screening are minimal.

Liberals suggest that the initial screening of applicants is often done with very little individual productivity information available. For firms with a large number of relatively equally qualified applicants, there is no reason to spend much time determining which applicants should be interviewed. These firms simply take a few minutes (seconds) to look over applications and select a promising group to interview. The employer realizes that such a superficial procedure will undoubtedly eliminate some job applicants who are slightly more productive than those selected for interviews. Since productivity differentials are perceived to be minor, however, this loss is not sufficient to warrant a more extensive (expensive) screening procedure.

There would be no discrimination if the job applicants victimized were random, but let us see why the screening method might cause the consistent victimization of individuals from disadvantaged groups. Suppose a firm considering college graduates for trainee positions decides that it has many equally qualified candidates. Looking at resumes, the firm can quickly identify each applicant's race, sex, and college attended. If the firm has enough applicants from better colleges, it is likely to say, "All things being equal, students from these colleges are likely to be more qualified than applicants who attended weaker colleges." Thus, the firm dismisses applicants from the weaker colleges, even though it realizes that weaker schools produce some qualified applicants. The firm has nothing against qualified graduates of weaker colleges. It simply reasons that the extra effort required to identify them is not worth the expense.

However unintentional, highly qualified graduates from weaker schools are discriminated against. Discrimination occurs because this screening method determines the selection for interviews on the basis of group characteristics rather than individual information. More generally, highly qualified applicants from any group that is perceived to have below-average productivity would be discriminated against by this superficial screening method.

Suppose employers believe that black and female applicants are typically less productive than their white male counterparts. If the firm has sufficient white male applicants, it will not interview black or female applicants. The firm will decide that although there are some black and female applicants who are slightly more productive than some white male applicants, it is not worth the added expense to identify them. The process by which individuals are discriminated against when firms use group characteristics to screen individuals is usually called statistical discrimination.

Statistical discrimination can occur indirectly. A firm hiring workers for on-the-job training may be primarily interested in selecting applicants who will stay an extended period of time. The firm does not want to invest training in individuals who will leave the firm quickly. Presumably, if the firm had a sufficient number of applicants who worked more than four years with their previous employer, it would not choose to interview applicants with more unstable work experience. Again, the firm reasons that although there are likely to be some qualified applicants among those with an unstable work record, it is too costly to identify them. This method of screening is likely to discriminate because of the nature of seniority systems, which operate on a "last hired, first fired" basis. Many minorities and women have unstable work records because they are hired last and fired first. Thus, even when firms do not use racial or gender stereotypes, they discriminate, since women and minorities are more likely to come from weaker schools and have more unstable work records than equally qualified white male applicants.

Financial and Occupational Effects

Many economists believe the job market is divided between good (primary) and bad (secondary) jobs. Good jobs have characteristics such as on-the-job training and promotions through well-organized internal labor markets.

Bad jobs have little on-the-job training and minimum chance for promotions; they are dead-end jobs. Since on-the-job training is a significant aspect of primary-sector jobs, employment stability and behavioral traits are often more important than formal education and general skills. Both conservative and liberal economists agree that workers who do not possess the proper behavioral traits, such as low absenteeism and punctuality, will not be employed in the primary sector. Most liberals believe that many women and minority workers who possess the proper behavioral traits also will not find jobs in the primary sector as a result of statistical discrimination.

Facing discrimination in the primary sector, many qualified female and minority workers shift to secondary labor markets. As a result, secondary employers have a greater supply of workers and can reduce wages and standards for working conditions. Primary employers and majority workers also benefit from statistical discrimination. Since majority workers face less competition, more of them will gain primary employment than they would in the absence of statistical discrimination.

Primary employers may have to pay somewhat higher wages and employ somewhat less productive workers as a result of statistical discrimination, but the reduced screening costs more than compensate for the higher wages and productivity losses. Moreover, many primary employers also hire secondary workers. For them, the higher cost of primary employees will be offset by the resulting reduction in wages paid to secondary workers and their somewhat higher productivity.

Since primary workers, primary employers, and secondary employers benefit from statistical discrimination, there are identifiable forces opposed to change. Thus, rather than the market disciplining decision makers, statistical discrimination creates groups having a financial stake in its perpetuation.

Applicants and Their Search for Job Information

For job seekers, the cheapest source of job information is personal contacts, including neighbors and relatives and their acquaintances. Additional information can be obtained from newspaper advertisements and government employment offices. The most costly information is obtained from private employment agencies. A significant difference in the cost of job information would occur if one individual had few personal contacts and was forced to use private employment services, while another individual had extensive personal contacts. All things being equal, the individual with the lower cost of obtaining information would be better informed and hence more likely to obtain higher earnings.

The job information minorities receive from their search effort is likely to be less valuable than the job information received by their white counterparts. The fact that an individual is recommended by a personal contact might be sufficient reason to grant the person an interview. Those who obtain information from newspaper ads or government employment services do not have this advantage. This distinction is summed up in the adage "It's not what you know but who you know that counts."

Low-income (minority) individuals tend to have fewer contacts than high-income (white) individuals of equal abilities and motivation. High-income (white) individuals tend to have many neighbors or relatives who have good jobs, own businesses, or are involved in their firm's hiring decisions. Low-income (minority) individuals, having few personal contacts, are forced to spend additional time and money to obtain job information. Even if the job information is as valuable as that obtained by their white counterparts, minorities might give up searching for employment sooner because it is more costly. They do not do so because they are less able or less motivated; they simply face greater expenses.

Affirmative Action

Affirmative action legislation is the major government attempt at counteracting the discriminatory features of the hiring process. Affirmative action assumes that discrimination results from employment decisions based on incomplete information. The role of the government is simply to encourage firms to hire all qualified applicants by forcing them to gather individualized productivity information. Guidelines stipulate that all government agencies and private firms doing business with the government must publicly announce job openings at least forty-five days prior to the termination of acceptance of applications. This provision attempts to offset the information inequality disadvantaged workers face. More importantly, these employers must interview a minimum number of applicants from groups that tend to be victims of statistical discrimination.

It is important to remember the difference between affirmative action and quotas. Under affirmative action, there is no requirement to hire; employers are required only to interview female and minority applicants and make sure they have access to job information. Quotas are more drastic actions reserved for situations in which firms are not making good faith efforts to seek out and hire qualified female and minority applicants. For example, if a firm attempts to circumvent affirmative action guidelines by announcing job openings in papers that reached only the white community or, after interviewing applicants, uses discriminatory procedures to eliminate women from employment, the government can impose quotas. Thus, quotas are imposed only when it is demonstrated that the lack of female or minority employment reflects something more conscious than the unintentional effects of incomplete information.

Besides the government, some private groups have attempted to compensate for unequal access to information. Women's groups have attempted to set up networks to aid female job applicants for management positions. Female executives are encouraged to share as much information as possible with other women to offset the traditional networking done by men. In many areas, male networking is referred to as the old boy network, and entry into it has historically been critical to obtaining the most desirable jobs. Thus, the lack of personal contacts is at least partially offset by networks that direct job information to disadvantaged workers and provide low-cost productivity information to firms.

Skill and Locational Mismatches

Many individuals reject the view that groups are held back due to external pressures by noting that "when we came to America, we faced discrimination but were able to overcome it." In particular, these individuals often believe that internal inadequacies are responsible for the seemingly permanent economic problems minorities face. One response is to argue that the discrimination minorities face is more severe and their economic resources fewer than those of European immigrants at the turn of the century. Another response dominated the U.S. Riot Commission's assessment of black poverty. This presidential commission, which was created to study the causes of the urban rebellions of the late 1960s, noted,

> When the European immigrants were arriving in large numbers, America was becoming an urban-industrial society. To build its major cities and industries, America needed great pools of unskilled labor. Since World War II . . . America's urban-industrial society has matured: unskilled labor is far less essential than before, and blue-collar jobs of all kinds are decreasing in numbers and importance as sources of new employment. . . . The Negro, unlike the immigrant, found little opportunity in the city; he had arrived too late, and the unskilled labor he had to offer was no longer needed.

This commission, commonly known as the Kerner commission, avoided blaming either the victims (culture of poverty) or society (discrimination) for black economic problems; they were simply the result of technological change. To compensate for the higher skill levels required for entry-level positions, the Kerner commission recommended extensive job-training programs. Supposedly, once these skills were obtained, blacks would enter the employment mainstream and racial income disparities would diminish.

Job-training programs became the centerpiece of the liberal War on Poverty initiated during the Johnson administration. To an extent, these job-training programs complemented compensatory educational programs. Whereas the compensatory programs attempted to develop general skills, job-training programs attempted to develop specific job-related skills. Whereas the compensatory programs were attempts to increase white-collar skills, job-training programs were attempts to increase blue-collar skills.

The government's involvement in job-training programs was pragmatic; it sought upward mobility in ways that would not conflict with the interests of other groups. Thus, it did not aggressively institute training programs that would conflict with the objective; of many craft unions. This meant that in many of the construction trades, which had historically restricted membership, the government accepted union prerogatives. Job-training success also was impeded by the seeming irrelevance of many of the skills taught, and there were complaints that training programs did not use the latest equipment and the newest methods.

Many liberals discounted these complaints. They agreed with conservatives that the problems disadvantaged groups faced stemmed from their internal inadequacies. These liberals thought the actual technical skills developed were irrelevant; what was critical was the development of the proper behavioral traits of punctuality and low absenteeism. These liberals also recommended more restrictive programs that would train only the least deficient of the disadvantaged group. In contrast, those liberals who believed that external pressures, particularly discrimination, were dominant proposed costly training programs and a more aggressive approach to craft unions.

Job-training success also was impeded by the shifting of blue-collar jobs out of Northeastern and Midwestern urban areas. After World War II, technological changes decreased the viability of central city locations. First, trucking replaced the railroads as the major transportation mode. When firms delivered their output (and received their

input) on railcars, central city locations were ideal. When trucking became dominant, traffic tie-ups made those locations too costly. Indeed, recognizing these costs, the federal government built a new interstate highway system so that travelers could bypass congested central city areas.

Second, new technologies emphasized assembly-line techniques that required one-level production. No longer could manufacturing firms use factory buildings in which they operated on a number of floors. High land costs made it too expensive to build one-level plants in urban centers, so manufacturing firms began to locate in industrial parks near the new interstate highways on the outskirts of urban areas. This intensified minority employment problems, as most minorities continued to live in the inner city.

Minorities with the proper behavioral requirements, education, and skills have difficulty obtaining employment due to these locational mismatches. Inner-city residents are likely to lack the financial ability to commute to suburban jobs. They are unlikely to own a car or to earn a sufficient income to justify the extensive commuting required, even if public transportation is available. Minorities also are less likely to have access to these jobs because they have fewer personal contacts working in suburban locations.

Liberals have offered a number of recommendations to offset locational mismatches. Some economists have favored government subsidies to transportation networks that would bring inner-city workers to suburban employment locations. These subsidies would be cost-effective if the added employment generated greater income tax revenues and government spending reductions. Other economists have favored subsidizing firms to relocate in targeted inner-city zones. This approach was even endorsed by President Reagan under the catchy name "Free Enterprise Zones."

Type Of Affirmative Action Policy: A Determinant Of Reactions To Sex-Based Preferential Selection?

Madeleine E. Heilman, William S. Battle, Chris B. Keller, and R. Andrew Lee

$\mathcal{E}$ditors' Note: The United States is currently embroiled in a national debate about affirmative action. Some argue that it has greatly helped women and people from traditionally unrepresented groups, and that any costs associated with it are far outweighed by its benefits. Others argue that affirmative action discriminates against those who are not recipients of it. Still others claim that recipients of affirmative action are perceived by others and themselves as less capable than those not recipients of affirmative action. This article by Madeleine Heilman and her colleagues examines the views people have of themselves as recipients of affirmative action policies, as well as the views others have of them. Her work has important policy implications as she finds that these perceptions vary according to how the selection procedure is formulated.

In 3 studies, 150 undergraduates and 75 MBA students, men and women, were exposed to selection policies differing in the degree to which merit and group membership were weighted in selection decisions involving women. Results indicated that in self-views and self-assessments of beneficiaries (Study 1), competence perceptions on the part of others (Study 2), and work-related reactions of nonbeneficiaries (Study 3), many, but not all, negative reactions to sex-based preferential selection were alleviated when the policy made clear that merit considerations were central to the decision-making process. In the absence of information about policy type, participants acted as if merit had not been a factor in preferential selection decisions.

Public controversy abounds about affirmative action and the preferential procedures it typically spawns. There are those who see it as a necessary antidote to widespread discrimination against women and minorities and others who see it as self-defeating, creating more problems than it remedies. But the debate often rests on a particular conception of affirmative action for, increasingly, the public has come to see affirmative action as involving preferential selection of women and minorities without regard to their qualifications, often in the form of quotas in hiring (Holloway, 1989; Kravitz & Platania, 1993). In actuality, there are many variants of affirmative action policies and many different forms that affirmative action practices and initiatives can take, and distinguishing among them is crucial

if there is to be a productive debate. The research reported here is designed to examine the psychological consequences of different terms of affirmative action, forms that differ in the degree to which merit enters into the personnel decision process. The focus is on women in the workplace, and the specific question addressed is whether the empirically demonstrated adverse effects of sex-based preferential selection are dependent on the type of affirmative action policy that is being enacted.

Research on affirmative action has documented many negative consequences of preferential selection procedures in work settings. Investigations have demonstrated detrimental effects on the beneficiary's self-perceptions and reactions to work situations. Women who believe they have benefited from such initiatives have been shown to report lower job satisfaction and organizational commitment (Chacko, 1982), greater evaluation apprehension (Nacoste & Lehman, 1987) and role stress (Chacko, 1982), and, as compared with women selected on a merit basis, to devalue their leadership capability and task performance (Heilman, Simon, & Repper, 1987) and select less demanding work tasks (Heilman, Rivero, & Brett, 1991). Research also has demonstrated observers' negative judgments about those believed to have benefited from affirmative action; in fact, beneficiaries seem tainted with a stigma of incompetence. Denigration of the skills and abilities of apparent beneficiaries has been evidenced in assessment of qualifications (Garcia, Erskine, Hawn, & Casmay, 1981;

Summers, 1991), evaluations of leadership performance (Jacobson & Koch, 1977), and competence judgments (Heilman, Block, & Lucas, 1992; Northcraft & Martin, 1982), and recent research demonstrates the tenacity of the incompetence stigma even in the face of disconfirming information (Heilman, Block, & Stathatos, 1997). In addition, research has demonstrated negative consequences for the nonbeneficiaries, those who feel themselves to be bypassed by preferential selection procedures. Results of a recent investigation indicate that these individuals are unlikely to engage in citizenship behavior and, unless they feel that the beneficiary was more or at least equally worthy of the position in contention (something not typically believed in such situations), there were costs in terms of motivation, affect, and work orientation, as well as in perceptions of the beneficiary's competence Heilman, McCullough, & Gilbert, 1996).

The consistent finding of negative consequences from so many different studies clearly signals a problem; no doubt there is reason for concern. The findings suggest that affirmative action can have decidedly unfavorable consequences, impacting beneficiary and nonbeneficiary alike. But caution must be exercised. In all of the investigations cited, either it was made explicit that preferential selection was enacted without consideration of merit or, alternatively, the nature of the preferential selection procedure was ambiguous. Because, without information to the contrary, people tend to assume that affirmative action entails preferential selection without regard to merit (Holloway, 1989; Kravitz & Platania, 1993), it appears that only one form of affirmative action has been explored in research in this area. Given the important policy implications of the research, it is essential to test the robustness of the findings, asking whether the effects of preferential selection are equally pernicious whatever the policy guiding its use. . . .

What follows are three studies. . . . The first involves the self-perceptions and evaluations of beneficiaries, the second involves others' perceptions of those targeted for benefit, and the third involves reactions of non-beneficiaries to the beneficiary and to the work setting. In each of these studies, the policy said to be used for selection was varied: It was totally merit based. totally group

membership based. or one of two mixed criteria policies. In one of the mixed criteria policies, in which minimum qualifications were used as a screen before further consideration, merit played less of a role than in the other, in which equal qualifications were required for group membership to be considered in selection. It was expected that there would be different reactions depending on the selection policy enacted, with the harder policies eliciting the more negative reactions. Also included was an ambiguous condition to empirically determine whether in the absence of explicit information about affirmative action policy, the assumption is in fact made that a hard policy is in use. In all three studies, preferential selection was based on sex, and the beneficiary was always a woman.

Study 1

Study 1 focuses on the reactions of women beneficiaries to having been selected to a leadership role on a preferential basis. Earlier work on which this study is based had posited that because they typically approach male sex-typed tasks with low confidence in their abilities, women are in need of competence affirmation. When women are selected on the basis of their merit, their competence is affirmed and their confidence bolstered, but when gender-based preference is involved in their selection, information about their competence is left ambiguous and they are left vulnerable to the consequences of negative performance expectancies. Results supported these ideas by demonstrating that preferential selection as opposed to merit-based selection to a leadership role triggered negative self-regard, self-evaluations, and motivational decrements for women beneficiaries (Heilman et al., 1987). . . .

If verification of ability mitigates negative effects of preferential selection for women beneficiaries, then a policy that includes a merit criterion, because it implicitly provides such verification, should have similar consequences. Furthermore, the strength of its palliative effects should be determined by the extent to which merit is central to the decision process. Accordingly, we expected that a preferential selection policy in which merit was a more important criterion than group membership would differ less from a merit-based policy in its consequences than a preferential selection policy in which merit was not a consideration or in which it was not the primary consideration.

Method

Participants and Design

Participants were 75 female undergraduates who participated in the research for partial fulfillment of an introductory psychology course requirement at New York University. They ranged from 18 to 22 years of age. The between-subjects design consisted of five different assignment policies: *merit,* in which selection decisions were based solely on qualifications; *preferential equivalent,* in which women were selected if their qualifications were equivalent to those of men; *preferential minimum standard,* in which women were selected if their qualifications exceeded a minimum threshold; *preference absolute,* in which women were selected without regard to qualifications; and *preferential ambiguous,* in which gender had an unspecified effect on decisions. A total of 15 participants were assigned to each of the five experimental conditions.

Procedure

The procedure closely followed that of earlier studies (Heilman et al., 1987, 1990). Participants were met by a male experimenter and were informed that the research would begin as soon as the other participant arrived. When the other participant (actually a male confederate posing as another student) arrived, the experimenter escorted them into the research room, where they were guided to seats at desks on different sides of the room. They sat with their backs to one another.

The experimenter introduced the study as part of a continuing program of research concerning communication. Participants were told that they would be either a leader or a follower in a one-way communication task in which the leader would instruct the follower in the drafting of geometric figures. It was stated that the leader would have the more creative and visible position, although task performance ultimately depended on both leader and follower. Participants were then asked to complete the 18-item Spatial Communication Skills Inventory (SCSI), a bogus test that was said to reliably assess their one-way communication abilities. . . .

After completing the SCSI, participants were instructed to remain seated while the experimenter left the room briefly to have their SCSIs scored. He returned to the room to explain the one-way communication task. . . .

At this point, the assignment policy experimental manipulations were enacted, and the participant and confederate were assigned to roles. The participant was always made the leader, and the confederate, the follower. The task materials were then distributed, and the task begun. . . . The experimenter then gave two brief questionnaires to the participant and confederate to complete. The questionnaires contained both manipulation checks and dependent variable measures. . . .

Experimental Manipulations

After the experimenter finished explaining the one-way communication task and the role of leader and follower, he proceeded to say,

> Typically in situations like this, leaders are selected on the basis of both skill and ability, which basically means that they are good at the task. In our study, we also have been attempting to select individuals who have demonstrated that they have the skill and ability to perform well as leaders, as measured by the Spatial Communication Skills Inventory which you just completed.

At this point, the experimenter delivered the selection policy manipulation. In the merit condition he said, "In other words, we have adopted a policy of always giving the leadership role to the more qualified individual on the basis of scores on the SCSI." However, in the preferential conditions, he said,

> But because there have not been enough female participants signing up for this study so far, we now have adopted a policy of giving the leadership role to women if there is only a negligible difference between participants' scores on the SCSI (preferential equivalent), giving the leadership role to women if they achieve at least a minimum score on the SCSI (preferential minimum standard),

giving women the leadership role (preferential absolute), and taking gender into account when we select leaders (preferential ambiguous).

In all but the preferential absolute condition, the experimenter then left the room to see if the tests had been scored and returned with three computerized sheets that he distributed, keeping one for himself. The sheets indicated that on the basis of the policy guiding selection of participants to the leader role, the leader for the session would be Participant 1 (the participant). In the merit, preferential equivalent, and preferential minimum standard conditions, the experimenter said,

> I don't know exactly how each of you did on the SCSI but, as you can see, the computer sheet indicates that on the basis of your scores you (the participant) will get to be leader and you (the confederate) will be the follower.

In the preferential ambiguous condition, the experimenter said,

> I don't know exactly how each of you did on the SCSI. It's not very clear to me if, in this case, your scores were used at all. But, as you can see, the computer sheet indicates that you (the participant) will get to be the leader and you (the confederate) will be the follower.

In the preferential absolute condition, the experimenter never left the room to get the computer sheets. He simply said, "So, regardless of your scores on the SCSI, you (the participant) will get to be the leader and you (the confederate) will be the follower."

Dependent Measures

The dependent measures obtained here were identical to those obtained in earlier studies (Heilman et al., 1987, 1990). Three of them were of primary interest: self-evaluation of performance, self-perception of competence, and desire to remain in the leadership position. . . .

Results

Dependent Measures

Self-evaluation of performance. . . . [I]ntercell comparisons supported our hypothesis: they indicated that preferentially selected participants evaluated their performance significantly less favorably than those selected on a merit basis when scores were not used at all, when a minimum score was said to be set, or when the way in which scores entered into the decision was left ambiguous. However, preferentially selected participants who were selected under an equivalent qualifications policy did not evaluate their performance more negatively than did those participants selected on the basis of merit and, in fact, were significantly more favorable in their performance evaluations than preferentially selected participants who were selected under a minimum standards or a no-score-considered policy.

Perception of leadership ability. Intercell contrasts revealed the same pattern of results as for performance evaluations: Preferentially selected participants were more negative in their self-perceptions than participants selected on a merit basis in absolute, minimum standard, and ambiguous preferential conditions, but not in the equivalent condition. Furthermore, responses of those in the equivalent condition were more favorable than those in each of the other preferential selection conditions.

Desire to persist in the leadership position. Intercell contrasts once again revealed significant differences in responses of those in the preferential absolute, the preferential minimum standard, and the preferential ambiguous conditions from those in merit conditions. However, in this case, there also was a significant difference between responses of those in the preferential equivalent and the merit conditions, indicating greater reported reluctance to remain leader on the part of participants in all preferential selection conditions, as compared with those selected in the merit condition. There were no significant

Table 1
Means and Standard Deviations of Dependent Variables in Each Experimental Condition: Study 1

Variable	Merit	Preferential selection condition			
		Preferential equivalent	Preferential minimum standard	Preferential absolute	Preferential ambiguous
Self-evaluation of performance					
M	5.89_a	$5.15_{a,b}$	4.15_c	4.01_c	$4.64_{b,c}$
SD	.64	1.74	1.34	1.00	1.22
Perception of leadership ability					
M	6.93_a	6.60_a	5.27_b	5.07_b	5.33_b
SD	1.10	1.64	2.02	1.10	.98
Desire to remain leader					
M	7.13_a	5.27_b	4.27_b	3.67_b	4.40_b
SD	.99	1.89	2.09	1.91	1.45
Stress					
M	4.76_a	5.00_a	3.29_b	3.54_b	$3.96_{a,b}$
SD	1.46	2.01	1.70	1.18	1.80
Perceived fairness					
M	7.53_a	6.67_a	4.80_b	3.40_c	4.60_b
SD	1.19	2.02	1.26	1.80	1.30

Note: The higher the mean, the more favorable the rating. $n = 15$ in each condition. Different subscripts within a row indicate significant differences at the $p = .05$ level using the Fisher least square difference procedure. The minimum significant difference between the means was 0.90 for performance evaluation, 1.04 for perception of leadership ability, 1.44 for desire top remain leader, 1.20 for stress, and 1.113 for perceived fairness.

differences among responses of those in the four preferential selection conditions.

Additional Findings

As in the earlier studies on which this one is based, several additional measures were obtained. Means, standard deviations, and results of intercell contrasts of these additional measures appear in Table 1.

Stress. . . . [I]ntercell comparisons indicated that those in the merit condition reported themselves to be significantly less stressed than those in either the minimum standard or the absolute preferential selection conditions but no different in level of stress from those in the preferential equivalent condition. Those in the ambiguous preferential selection condition did not differ from any of the others in the degree of stress reported.

Reactions to the task. An ANOVA of reactions to the task revealed no significant effect of selection policy, F(4, 70) 2. 16. *n s.* In general, reactions to the task were favorable *(M* 6.09).

Perceived fairness of the leader selection process. Intercell contrasts indicated a significant difference between ratings of those in merit conditions and those in each of the preferential selection conditions, except for the one entailing an equivalent qualifications criterion. It is also of note that preferential selection guided by a policy in which qualifications are not considered (preferential absolute condition) was perceived to be the least fair of all.

Discussion

These results replicate earlier ones demonstrating the negative consequences of hard preferential selection policies for women beneficiaries; this effect was consistent across all dependent measures. But the results also supported our idea that the negative self-view's of women beneficiaries of preferential selection can be tempered by the preferential selection policy used. Specifically, when it was clear that merit played a central role in the preferential selection decision, as was the case in the equivalent qualifications condition, women's performance evaluations and assessments of their leadership ability did not differ from those of women selected on a merit basis and were decidedly more favorable than the self-view's reported by preferentially selected women for whom merit was only a perfunctory consideration (minimum standards) or no consideration at all (absolute condition). Reported stress and perceived fairness ratings were consistent with this data pattern. . . .

Finally, the fact that the minimum standard policy was not distinct from the absolute preferential policy in any of the dependent measure ratings suggests that the role of merit in the decision process must be perceived as substantial if it is to temper reactions to preferential selection; simple mention of a vague and minimal standard does little to assuage its detrimental effects. This—coupled with the data showing that when information about the policy underlying preferential selection is absent women often act as if merit was only of negligible importance in decision making—makes clear how crucial the criterion of merit is and how important that its use be made explicit, if adverse consequences for beneficiaries of preferential selection processes are to be averted.

Study 2

Study 2 focuses on how the woman beneficiary of preferential selection is regarded by others. Earlier work, on which this study is based, demonstrated that association with affirmative action stigmatizes intended beneficiaries by causing inferences of incompetence. Attributional processes, specifically *discounting* (Kelley, 1972; Kelley & Michela, 1980), has been posited to account for this. It has been shown that if someone is believed to be hired preferentially as part of an affirmative action effort, then the role of qualifications in the decision process are discounted, the individual is assumed to be hired primarily because of his or her minority status and, therefore, is not seen to be well-equipped to handle the job when hired (Heilman et al., 1992, 1997). Thus, the perception that ordinary and expected decision criteria were suspended seems to provide the impetus for inferences of incompetence.

If affirmative action leads to the assumption that qualifications, or merit, have not been key to decision making, and that is the source of incompetence inferences, then preferential selection policies that explicitly include a merit criterion should attenuate these inferences. Moreover, the more heavily weighted the merit criterion is seen to be as compared with demographic status, the more likely should be attenuation of affirmative action-based incompetence inferences.

Method

Participants and Design

A total of 75 MBA students, 37 men and 38 women, participated in the research. The mean age for the population was 24.44 with a range of 18–45. Of the population 59% were White, 19% were Asian, 12% were African American, 5% were Hispanic, and 5% rated themselves as "other." Participation took place in various business classes and in all cases was voluntary.

As in Study 1, the design included five levels of the selection policy variable. Participants were randomly assigned to experimental condition.

Procedure

Participants were told they were participating in a study investigating the decision making underlying the personnel selection and placement process. They were asked to review information about an employee being considered for promotion and then answer a number of questions about the employee, the organization, and their expectations of the employee's performance in the organization. The participants were told that their predictions (as well as the predictions of other similar groups) would be compared with the applicants' subsequent job performance.

Participants received packets that included a job description, a page from the hiring company's policies and procedures manual, a photocopy of an employment application, and a brief questionnaire. The job description was in the form of a job posting describing a position for a production supervisor for the Corporate Paper Company. Included were the job requirements (BA or BS in business management and 1 to 2 years of experience) and general work duties and responsibilities. The page from the company's policies and procedures manual described the company's hiring policy and emphasized the company's commitment to its enforcement in hiring decisions. The employment application contained information about the applicant's education, work experience, and general background. In all cases, the applicant was depicted as being a 25-year-old woman, having a BA in business from a large state university, and having graduated with honors. In addition, the applicants were said to have been involved in community service and to have held one position as an associate manager since graduation. A photograph of the applicant, who was always White, appeared in the upper right-hand corner of the application form to ensure that sex, not race, was recognized as the basis of the hiree's preferential selection. To protect against idiosyncratic reactions to a particular applicant, photos of two different women were used each equivalent in attractiveness, sociability, intellectual skills, and emotional adjustment as rated by individuals from the same population as our participants (they were rated favorably on each of these dimensions, although not extreme on any of them). The two photos, which were black and white, and approximately 4 x 6 mm, were used with equal frequency within experimental condition.

After reviewing the job description, hiring policy statement, and the candidate's application form, participants were instructed to complete the research questionnaire. They then were debriefed, the rationale for the study was explained, and any questions they had were answered.

Experimental Manipulations

A page from the company's policies and procedures manual was used to convey the selection policy manipulation. The page was made to look official, with policy numbers, dates, and so forth. The text included a general statement about the policy and the company's goals followed by a brief procedural directive. In merit conditions, it read,

> Corporate Paper Company (CPC) is a quality employer and has a merit-based employment policy. CPC is committed to promote excellence as well as to broaden the talent pool by actively seeking the most competent employees. In all cases, CPC gives primary consideration to hiring individuals with the strongest qualifications.

In preferential selection conditions, the general policy statement read,

> Corporate Paper Company (CPC) is an equal opportunity employer and has an affirmative action employment policy. CPC is committed to promote a fair distribution of employment opportunities as well as to broaden the overall talent pool by actively seeking female and minority employees.

What followed differed by preferential selection condition:

> Preferential absolute: In all cases CPC gives primary consideration to hiring women and members of minority groups.

Preferential minimum standard: When applicants are determined to have the minimum job qualifications CPC gives primary consideration to hiring women and members of minority groups.

Preferential equivalent: When applicants are determined to be equally qualified, CPC gives primary consideration to hiring women and members of minority groups.

Those in the preferential ambiguous condition were provided with only the initial general policy statement.

Dependent Measures

. . . To assess the key dependent variable in the study, perceived competence, participants were asked to respond to two questions on a 9-point scale: "How competently do you expect this individual to perform this job?" *(very competently—not at all competently)* and "How effective do you think this individual will be at doing the work?" *(very effective—not at all effective)*. The two items were combined into a scale (a = .94), and the average of the two scores was taken as the perceived competence rating.

An additional series of 9-point bipolar adjective scales was used to explore how applicants were described in terms of activity (hardworking—lazy, persistent—gives up easily, energetic—lethargic, and efficient—inefficient), potency (strong—weak, forceful—timid, and tough—soft), and interpersonal characteristics (responsible—irresponsible, helpful—not helpful, cooperative—uncooperative, trustworthy—untrustworthy, and good coworker—bad coworker). . . .

To determine projections about the applicant's career progress, participants were asked two questions, also on 9-point scales. The responses to the questions "How likely do you think it is that this individual will move up in the organization?" *(very likely—not at all likely)* and "If the individual does get a promotion, how quickly do you think it will happen?" *(very quickly—not at all quickly)*

were averaged to form a projected career progress scale (a = .82).

Results

Perceived Competence

. . . [I]ntercell contrasts indicated that in all cases the hiree was viewed as more competent in the merit policy condition than in the preferential selection condition (see Table 2). However, participants did make distinctions among the various preferential policies; the hiree was viewed as more competent in the preferential equivalent condition than in any of the other preferential policy conditions (which did not differ from one another).

Additional Findings

Adjectival characterizations. . . .[I]ntercell contrasts indicated that the hiree was rated more favorably when she reportedly was hired on a merit basis than when she was hired preferentially, and the particular nature of the preferential policy had little consequence; each was equally detrimental (see Table 2).

Projected career progress. The pattern of projected career progress ratings paralleled that for competence perceptions. Intercell comparisons made clear that those female hirees selected with a merit-based policy were expected to advance in their career far more quickly and successfully than female hirees selected preferentially, whatever the nature of the preferential selection policy. However, prognoses for career progress were significantly more sanguine in the preferential equivalent condition than in the preferential minimum, preferential ambiguous, and preferential absolute conditions (see Table 2).

Discussion

These data once again demonstrate that a stigma of incompetence is often attached to those believed to have benefited from affirmative action. This was the case whether merit considerations were thought to be absent or only minimally involved in selection

Table 2
Means and Standard Deviations of Dependent Variables in Each Experimental Condition: Study 2

Variable	Merit	Preferential selection condition			
		Preferential equivalent	Preferential minimum standard	Preferential absolute	Preferential ambiguous
Perceived competence					
M	8.30$_a$	7.47$_b$	6.67$_c$	6.07$_c$	6.00$_c$
SD	0.47	0.67	0.98	1.03	1.22
Activity					
M	7.94$_a$	7.12$_b$	6.69$_b$	6.64$_b$	6.85$_b$
SD	0.49	1.10	0.78	0.76	.85
Potency					
M	6.18$_a$	5.27$_b$	5.29$_b$	4.96$_b$	5.20$_b$
SD	1.04	1.43	0.50	1.23	1.17
Interpersonal characteristics					
M	8.43$_a$	7.37$_b$	6.93$_b$	7.32$_b$	7.23$_b$
SD	0.39	1.20	1.10	1.06	1.04
Projected career progress					
M	7.57$_a$	6.80$_b$	5.67$_c$	6.10$_c$	5.56$_c$
SD	.42	0.77	1.05	0.93	1.35

Note: The higher the mean, the more favorable the rating. $n = 15$ in each condition. Different subscripts within a row indicate significant differences at the $p = .05$ level using the Fisher least square difference procedure. The minimum significant difference between the means was 0.67 for perceived competence, 0.60 for activity, 0.81 for potency, 0.70 for projected career progress.

processes or when no information was available about the role of merit in decision making. But the data also demonstrate the mitigating effects on competence perceptions when it is made clear that although preferential selection had occurred, merit was a primary consideration in the decision. Those in preferential-equivalent conditions were rated as more competent than others selected preferentially, and prognoses for their career progress were more sanguine.

But the data also make clear that, even with merit criteria, there always was a distinction made between how women are regarded when selected on a preferential as compared with a merit basis, whether in competence assessments and career predictions or in characterizations in terms of activity, potency, or interpersonal qualities. Thus, there seemed to be a residual effect of preferential selection, one that persisted regardless of the affirmative action policy said to be in operation.

The results of this study repeat those of the first study in that the minimum standard policy was not appreciably different in effect from a policy in which merit was not a consideration at all. Also, as in Study 1, the absence of information about a merit criterion seems to lead to the assumption that it was not a major factor in decision making. These two findings underscore the fact that the contribution of merit to the selection process must be both substantial and explicit if it is to attenuate the negativity that is associated with affirmative action and taints its beneficiaries.

Study 3

Study 3 concerns the reactions of those who have been directly affected by preferential selection, those who have been bypassed in the selection decision. These are the individuals who often consider themselves to be "victims" of affirmative action (Lynch, 1992), the men who traditionally would have been selected for "male" tasks and roles. Whether correctly or not, many White male managers believe that their career advancement has been thwarted by affirmative action (Bremilow, 1992; Feiden, 1992; Henry, 1991). . . .

If feelings of inequity mediate job-related reactions to preferential selection, then policies that include a merit criterion should preclude these reactions. For, if the non-beneficiary believes the beneficiary to be deserving of the position, and the distribution of rewards is therefore consistent with their relative inputs, then feelings of having been denied what one deserves are not likely to occur. We therefore would expect that, as compared with an exclusively merit-based selection policy, preferential policies in which merit is said to have played a major role would not only promote a more favorable view of the beneficiary's competence, but would produce less negative job-related reactions than those in which merit is believed to have received only scant consideration in the selection decision. However, no differences were expected among the various preferential selection conditions in intended citizenship behavior, a reaction shown in earlier work to be mediated by procedural rather than distributive justice concerns.

Method

Participants and Design

Participants were 75 male undergraduates who participated in the research for partial fulfillment of an introductory psychology course requirement at New York University.

They ranged from 18 to 22 years of age. As in both Studies 1 and 2, the design included five levels of one independent variable, assignment policy. The 75 participants were randomly assigned to each of the five experimental conditions.

Procedure

The procedure and experimental manipulations were identical to that used in Study I. except that in this study the participant, who was always a man, was assigned to the follower role and the confederate, who was always a woman, was assigned to the leader role. The confederate leader gave task instructions to the participant using a standardized script.

Dependent Measures

A series of 9-point bipolar adjective scales were used to assess participants' task-related reactions: task evaluation (pleasant—unpleasant, involving—not involving, stimulating—dull, and enjoyable—unenjoyable), motivation while working on the task (motivated—unmotivated, interested—bored, and involved—uninvolved), and affective reactions while working on the task (angry—not angry, resentful—not resentful, frustrated—not frustrated, and annoyed—content). Reactions to the leader were obtained through ratings of the leader's competence (competent—incompetent, clear—muddled, effective—ineffective, and high-leadership-ability—low-leadership-ability) and likability (likable—unlikable, pleasant—unpleasant, and agreeable—disagreeable), all measured on 9-point scales. Each of these sets of items was combined into a separate scale, and the average of responses to items composing the scale was taken as the scale rating. . . .

A measure of citizenship intention was used to assess participants' prosocial orientation to the work setting. Participants were asked if they were willing to help collate the results of the study. They were asked to check "yes" or "no," and, if they checked yes, to indicate their phone numbers so they could be contacted subsequently.

To get a measure of experienced inequity, we used a 9-point scale anchored by *very fair* and *not at all fair* and asked participants to indicate how fair they felt the outcome of the leader selection process had been.

Table 3
Means and Standard Deviations and/or Frequencies of Dependent Variables in Each Experimental Condition: Study 3

Variable	Merit	Preferential equivalent	Preferential minimum standard	Preferential absolute	Preferential ambiguous
			Preferential selection condition		
Task evaluation					
M	7.32_a	7.00_a	5.60_b	5.45_b	5.13_b
SD	1.44	0.89	120	1.26	1.59
Motivation					
M	7.71_a	$7.47_{a,c}$	$6.18_{b,c}$	$6.29_{b,c}$	5.29_b
SD	1.39	1.21	1.29	1.63	1.45
Affect					
M	7.50_a	7.02_a	5.22_b	4.75_b	4.02_b
SD	1.57	1.29	1.06	1.22	1.47
Leader competence					
M	7.87_a	7.50_a	4.42_b	4.95_b	4.97_b
SD	1.03	0.97	0.98	0.94	1.46
Liking for leader					
M	7.87_a	7.57_a	$6.87_{a,b}$	$6.70_{a,b}$	6.07_b
SD	1.00	1.08	1.13	1.32	1.18
Citizenship intention	$66.67\%_a$	$33.13\%_a$	$20.00\%_b$	$20.00\%_b$	$26.67\%_b$
Perceived fairness					
M	6.73_a	6.80_a	3.80_b	3.60_b	4.36_b
SD	1.53	1.57	1.47	1.06	1.08

Note: The higher the mean, the more favorable the rating. $n = 15$ in each condition. Different subscripts within a row indicate significant differences at the $p = .05$ level using the least square difference procedure or chi-square procedures. The minimum significant difference between the means was 0.95 for task evaluation, 1.02 for motivation, 0.97 for affect, 0.80 for leader, and 0.99 for perceived fairness.

Results

Dependent Measures

The dependent measures were grouped into three categories: task-related ratings, reactions to the preferentially selected other and intended citizenship behavior. Condition means and standard deviations as well as condition frequencies of the citizenship measure appear in Table 3.

Task-related ratings. . . . The results of the intercell contrasts (see Table 3) indicated that for each of these scales, participants were significantly more favorable in merit conditions than in all the preferential selection conditions, except for the preferential equivalent condition. Furthermore, for each of the three measures, ratings in the preferential equivalent condition were more favorable than reactions in each of the other three preferential selection conditions, none of which differed from one another.

Responses to the leader. . . .Intercell contrasts revealed that leaders were perceived to be more competent and were found to be more likable in the merit condition than in the preferential absolute, preferential minimum standard, and preferential ambiguous conditions, but not than the preferential-equivalent condition. Furthermore. the participants in the preferential equivalent condition were significantly more favorable in their leader competence ratings than participants in any of the other preferential selection conditions (which did not differ significantly from one another), and significantly more favorable in their leader likability ratings than those in the preferential-ambiguous condition.

In tended citizenship behavior At the very end of the dependent measure instrument, participants were asked whether they would be willing to help out by collating data from the study. Their responses were considered to be affirmative only when they both indicated "yes" and also provided a telephone number where they could be reached to make scheduling arrangements. The frequency of those who offered help in each experimental condition is shown in Table 3.

An examination of these data and chi-square analyses demonstrated that there was an overall difference between citizenship intentions of those in the merit conditions and those in the preferential selection conditions, $x^2(1) = 9.375$, $p < .01$. Subsequent analyses revealed that the frequency of indicated willingness to help was higher in merit condition than in the preferential absolute, the preferential minimum standard, the preferential ambiguous, and the preferential equivalent conditions. There was no difference in the frequency of volunteering to help among any of the individual preferential selection conditions.

Additional Findings

Perceived fairness. According to our ideas, perceptions of the fairness of the outcome should be affected by the selection policy. Indeed, the data support this con-

tention. . . .[I]ntercell comparisons make clear that the selection outcome was rated as far more fair when it was said to be based on a merit-based policy than on a preferential policy that was absolute, set a minimum qualifications standard, or was ambiguous with regard to information about how qualifications were weighted in decision making, but was not rated as more fair than a preferential policy that required equivalent qualifications. Also, no distinction was made among the preferential absolute, minimum standard, and ambiguous conditions in terms of fairness ratings, but each of these prompted more negative fairness ratings than a preferential-equivalent policy (see Table 3).

Discussion

Results of Study 3 demonstrate that task-related reactions as a consequence of preferential selection differ depending on the role merit is believed to have played in the preferential selection process. When merit was thought to be a primary concern in decision making, as when equivalence of qualifications was taken as a prerequisite for gender preference, differences between preferential and merit-based selection procedures were nonexistent, but when merit was given only a little weight or no weight whatsoever, negativity abounded. The bypassed participant not only derogated the selectee's competence, but also evaluated the task more negatively, reported himself to be less motivated, experienced more negative affect, and rated the outcome of the selection process as less fair. . . .

Once again, it is important to consider the preferential ambiguous conditions. As in Studies 1 and 2, without information to the contrary, participants seem to make the most negative inferences. In the case of each and every dependent measure, those given no information about the nature of the preferential selection policy responded no differently than those who were explicitly told that merit played a negligible role or no role at all in the selection decision. Thus, once again, the importance of explicit information about the selection policy is underscored by these data.

It should be noted that the nonbeneficiaries in this study not only lost the opportunity to be selected for the leadership role but also were placed under the direction of the female beneficiary. It is possible that this had special implications for the nonbeneficiary's reactions, particularly in affect and motivation. Because nonbeneficiaries only sometimes become subordinates of the preferentially selected other (e.g., when an internal promotion decision is made), and at other times are affected in a less direct and enduring way (e.g., when competing for selection from outside the particular unit), additional research is needed to compare reactions of these different types of nonbeneficiaries.

General Discussion

Taken together, the results of these three studies attest to the importance of the merit criterion in affirmative action decision making. Not only does each study replicate earlier work in which the negative consequences of preferential selection procedures were demonstrated, but each also makes clear the importance of distinguishing among affirmative action policies in which merit has played different roles. Whether in self-views and self-assessment of beneficiaries (Study 1), competence perceptions of beneficiaries on the part of others (Study 2), or work-related reactions of nonbeneficiaries (Study 3), when merit considerations were said to take priority in selection, many negative reactions to sex-based preferential selection were alleviated.

The effects of the equivalent qualification merit criteria apparently were mediated by the assurance about the beneficiary's qualifications that it imparted. By providing affirmation of competence to the beneficiaries themselves, it staved off negative self-evaluations and performance assessments. By directly negating the assumptions that allow for the beneficiary's qualifications to be discounted by onlookers, it precluded inferences of incompetence. And, by supplying information about the deservingness of the beneficiary, it precluded perceptions of inequitable outcomes on the part of those bypassed for the target position. Thus, because it implicitly provided information about the beneficiary and

prevented the presumption of incompetence that underlies the many negative consequences of preferential selection, the inclusion of a heavily weighted merit criterion had powerful consequences.

But, it should be noted that not all of the negative consequences of sex-based preferential selection were ameliorated by including a merit criterion in selection policy. Study 1 indicated that the beneficiaries' desire to persist in the leadership role were uniformly and negatively affected by preferential selection procedures, regardless of the policy guiding such procedures. Nonbeneficiaries in Study 3 indicated weaker intentions to engage in citizenship behavior when the selection policy was preferential—whatever the nature of the merit criterion—than when it was merit based. And, this tendency was particularly evident when participants were put into the role of onlooker in Study 2. Here participants made no distinction whatsoever in attributing characteristics to beneficiaries of different types of preferential selection and, even when beneficiaries were responded to more favorably when equivalent qualifications were said to be required before consideration of demographic status (as with competence assessments and career prognoses). they still were not responded to as favorably as those reportedly selected on a merit basis. So, despite the incorporation of merit criteria in preferential selection decisions, some negative consequences apparently prevail, and others are merely tempered but not eliminated. . . .

Although the policy implications of these results are potentially wide ranging and are consistent with those voiced by Nacoste (1996), it is important to emphasize two critical points raised by each of the studies. First, the research has demonstrated that the impact of including merit criteria in affirmative action policy is regulated by the nature of the specific merit criterion. In none of the three studies reported here was the minimum requirement policy at all successful in mitigating the negativity spawned by preferential selection processes. . . . Second, the research supports earlier research indicating that in the absence of information about affirmative action policy, people act as if they had received information of a policy in which merit criteria had been totally disregarded. This result, consistent throughout the three studies, has important implications. It emphasizes the need not only for the inclusion of a strict merit criterion, but also for conveying this policy information to all who might be affected by it, if the unintended and unwanted byproducts of affirmative action initiatives are to be effectively combatted. . . .

[T]he consistency of the findings across the three studies reported here is noteworthy. It clearly focuses attention on the importance of the merit criterion in affirmative action decision making. Evidently, people do differentiate among affirmative action policies, and their reactions to preferential selection are strongly influenced by the degree to which they believe merit considerations have predominated in the decision process.

References

Bremilow, P. (1992, May 25). Spiral of silence. *Forbes*, pp. 76-77.

Chacko, T. I. (1982). Women and equal employment opportunity: Some unintended effects. *Journal of Applied Psychology, 67,* 119-123.

Feiden, D. (1992, April 13). Firms fed up with affirmative action. *Grains New York Business*, pp. 1-2.

Garcia, L. T., Erskine, N., Hawn, K., & Casmay, S. R. (1981). The effect of affirmative action on attributions about minority group members. *Journal of Personality, 49,* 427-437.

Heilman, M. E., Block, C. J., & Lucas, J. A. (1992). Presumed incompetent? Stigmatization and affirmative action efforts. *Journal of Applied Psychology, 77,* 536-544.

Heilman, M. E., Block, C., & Stathatos, P. (1997). The affirmative action stigma of incompetence: Effects of performance information. *Academy of Management Journal, 40,* 603-625.

Heilman, M. E., Lucas, J. A., & Kaplow, S. R. (1990). Self-derogating consequences of preferential selection: The moderating role of initial self-confidence. *Organizational Behavior and Human Decision Processes, 46,* 202-216.

Heilman, M. E., McCullough, W. F., & Gilbert, D. (1996). The other side of affirmative action: Reactions of nonbeneficiaries to sex-based preferential selection. *Journal of Applied Psychology, 81,* 346-357.

Heilman, M. E., Rivero, C., & Brett, J. (1991). Skirting the competence issue: The effects of sex-based preferential selection on the task choices of women and men. *Journal of Applied Psychology, 76,* 99-105.

Heilman, M. E., Simon, M. C., & Repper, D. P. (1987). Intentionally favored, unintentionally harmed? The impact of gender-based preferential selection on self-perceptions and self-evaluations. *Journal of Applied Psychology, 72,* 62-68.

Henry, W. A., III. (1991, Sept. 30). What price preference? *Time*, pp. 30-31.

Holloway, F. (1989). What is affirmative action? In F. Blanchard & F. Crosby (Eds.), *Affirmative action in perspective* (pp. 9-19). New York: Springer-Verlag.

Jacobson, M. B., & Koch, W. (1977). Women as leaders: Performance evaluation as a function of method of leader selection. *Organizational Behavior and Human Performance, 20,* 149-157.

Kelley, H. H. (1972). Attribution in social interaction. In E. E. Jones, D. E. Kanouse, H. H. Kanouse, H. H. Kelley, R. E. Nisbett, S. Valins, & B. Weiner (Eds.), *Attribution: Perceiving the causes of behavior.* Morristown, NJ: General Learning Press.

Kelley, H. H., & Michela, J. L. (1980). Attribution theory and research. In M. Rosensweig & L. Pater (Eds.). *Annual review of psychology* (Vol. 31, pp. 457-501). Palo Alto. CA: Annual Reviews.

Kravitz, D., & Platania, J. (1993). Attitudes and beliefs about affirmative action: Effects of target and/or respondent sex and ethnicity. *Journal of Applied Psychology, 78,* 928-938.

Lynch, F. R. (1992). *Invisible victims: White males and the crisis of affirmative action.* New York: Praeger.

Nacoste, R. W. (1996). Social psychology and the affirmative action debate. *Journal of Social and Counseling Psychology, 15,* 261-282.

Nacoste, R. W., & Lehman, D. (1987). Procedural stigma. *Representative Research in Social Psychology. 17(1),* 25-38.

Northcraft, G. B., & Martin, J. (1982). Double jeopardy: Resistance to affirmative action from potential beneficiaries. In B. Gutek (Ed.), *Sex role stereotyping and affirmative action policy* (pp. 81-130). Los Angeles: University of California, Institute of Industrial Relations.

Summers, R. J. (1991). The influence of affirmative action on perceptions of a beneficiary's qualifications. *Journal of Applied Social Psychology, 21,* 1265-1276.

Aversive Racism And Resistance To Affirmative Action: Perceptions Of Justice Are Not Necessarily Color Blind

Audrey J. Murrell, Beth L. Dietz-Uhler, John F. Dovidio,
Samuel L. Gaertner, and Cheryl Drout

Editors' Note: In the early 1980s, Gaertner and Dovidio found that white Americans who endorsed egalitarian values and considered themselves racially tolerant were not racist on questionnaire measures of racism. However, in more subtle and indirect ways, they expressed their negative beliefs about African Americans. This pattern of behaviors draws on the same principles examined in Chapter 7's discussion of subtle and overt forms of prejudice. Gaertner and Dovidio defined this pattern as "aversive racism." The present article extends the aversive racism research to attempt to understand resistance to affirmative action policies. Overall, this article applies our knowledge of prejudice to gain a deeper understanding of negative attitudes in the workplace.

This study utilized a factorial survey design to assess attitudes toward affirmative action as a function of targeted groups (Black, handicapped, or elderly persons), framing of the policy (with or without social justification), and institutional context (business, college, or social organization). Resistance to affirmative action was aroused more by policies specifying Blacks as the targeted group and by policies presented without justification. Supportive of the aversive racism framework, the level of resistance to the policies presented without justification for Blacks as the targeted group was higher than for all other targeted groups with or without justification. Implications for these findings for strategies to reduce negative attitudes toward affirmative action are discussed.

The process of implementing affirmative action programs to address disparities and correct injustices is an extremely volatile, complex, and widely debated issue (see Blanchard & Crosby, 1989). The paradox of the contemporary response to affirmative action is that although individuals may support the principles underlying affirmative action, they may resist the implementation of specific affirmative action policies. . . . Explanations for resistance to the implementation of affirmative action commonly focus on the perceived fairness of the policy itself (see Barnes Nacoste, 1994/this issue). Lipset and Schneider (1978), for example, suggest that many Whites will resist a specific affirmative action program "not because they oppose racial equality, but because they feel it violates their individual freedom" (p.43). We propose that policy-focused explanations do not provide a complete account of Whites' resistance to affirmative action. Our research, in particular, examined the role of a subtle, modern type of racism—aversive racism—on Whites' reactions to affirmative action. . . .

The aversive racism perspective, which guided the present work, proposes that subtle bias results from the assimilation of an egalitarian value system with prejudice and racist feelings (Gaertner & Dovidio, 1986; Kovel, 1970). Specifically, the aversive racism perspective assumes that cognitive (e.g., in-group favoritism), motivational (e.g., personal or group interest), and sociocultural processes (e.g., historical racist traditions) have led most White Americans to develop negative feelings and beliefs about Blacks. Because of traditional cultural values, however, most Whites also have sincere convictions concerning fairness, justice, and racial equality. The existence of both—almost unavoidable racial biases and the desire to appear egalitarian—forms the basis of an ambivalence that aversive racists experience.

Because aversive racists endorse egalitarian values and regard themselves as racially tolerant, their negative feelings and beliefs are expressed primarily in subtle and indirect ways that do not threaten the aversive racist's nonprejudice self-image (see Gaertner & Dovidio, 1986). Bias against Blacks is not typically expressed overtly, in ways that can be readily recognized as racial discrimination. Thus, aversive racism cannot reliably be assessed using self-report attitude measures, for which socially appropriate responses are normally identifiable (Dovidio & Fazio, 1992; cf. McConahay, 1986; Sears et al., 1979). In situations in which a negative response can be rationalized on the basis of some factor *other* than race, however, bias against Blacks is likely to occur. . . .

The Dovidio and Gaertner (1981) finding suggests that resistance to affirmative action programs designed to benefit Blacks may be moderated by how those programs are framed. We hypothesize that resistance will be greater, particularly for programs benefiting Blacks, when these programs can more readily be objected to on the basis of non-race-related factors (e.g., threats to freedom, unfairness). Our research, therefore, examined how the presentation of the program for implementing affirmative action and the targeted group combine to influence reactions to affirmative action.

Both public opinion and laboratory research demonstrate the extent to which policy procedures can influence reactions to affirmative action. For example, a popular criticism of some affirmative action policies centers on negative reactions to specific selection procedures. The protest expressed by many Whites concerning the *Regents of the University of California v. Bakke* (1978) decision illustrates this point. In the Bakke case, many people objected to the admissions procedure of the medical school because it was seen as a form of "reverse discrimination" that violated their fundamental beliefs about procedural fairness or justice (Binion, 1987). That is, the commonly articulated reason for challenging the admissions procedure that involved preferential treatment for Blacks was that this policy was discriminatory and negated individual selection, evaluation, and advancement based on merit. Thus, resistance may occur because individuals believe that category membership (e.g., race or sex) should not be a relevant criterion used in merit-based decisions.

There is indeed theoretical and empirical support for this view. According to the concept of *procedural justice* (Thibaut & Walker, 1975), the perceived fairness of a procedure influences an individual's evaluations of agents, representatives, and other persons associated with that procedure.

The fairer a procedure is perceived to be, the more positive are the evaluations of those associated with the policy (Lind, Kurtz, Musante, & Thibaut, 1980). With respect to affirmative action, the more weight given to category-based criteria, such as race or sex, the less fair the procedure is perceived to be and the more negative the reaction to the policy and the persons involved (Greenberg, 1987; Lind et al., 1980; Nacoste, 1985, 1986, 1987a, 1987b). From this perspective, perceived fairness of the specific policy is highly influential in determining a person's evaluation of an affirmative action policy.

If perceptions of fairness are a key factor in resistance to affirmative action, then how a specific policy is framed can substantially influence an individual's response (Gamson & Modigliani, 1987; Kinder & Sanders, 1990). . . .

To examine how the framing of affirmative action policies moderate Whites' resistance to programs benefiting Blacks, subjects in our study were questioned using a full-profile (factorial) survey design (Rossi & Anderson, 1982; Wittink & Cattin, 1989). This technique is particularly desirable when there are many questions that are very similar both in wording and response format that may produce contrast or carry-over effects which threaten external validity. Specifically, full-profile analysis involves presenting each subject with a subset of the total pool of items. Across all subjects, however, all possible combinations of the various independent variables are represented. Using the item as the level of analysis, main effects and interactions can be assessed. We systematically varied the groups targeted as benefiting from an affirmative action policy, policy descriptions, and the institutional context of the policy.

With respect to targeted groups, we assessed subjects reactions to affirmative action policies involving three groups that subjects were not members of: Blacks, elderly persons, and physically handicapped persons. With regard to policy descriptions, respondents were questioned about their perceptions of fairness and support for four common ways of presenting affirmative action policies. Two of these policies focused on micro-level actions varying in the degree to which the action emphasized nonmerit factors to address disparities (preferential treatment and reverse discrimination). The other two policies provided a macro-level justification in terms of achieving diversity or remediating historical injustices.... [W]e predicted that respondents would show less resistance to policy statements with explicit macro justifications than to policy statements focusing on the micro level of implementation. Furthermore, the central prediction based on the aversive racism framework was that the more negative response to policies focusing solely on the micro-level implementation, compared to those providing macro-level justifications, would be particularly pronounced when those policies were presented as benefiting Blacks relative to other targeted groups. Thus, a Targeted Group x Policy Description interaction was anticipated.

Finally, concerning institutional context, we tested for differences in response to affirmative action policies for businesses, colleges, and social organizations. Kinder and Sanders (1990) found that resistance to affirmative action was stronger for cases in which preference was given for selection in employment, which may be seen as a violation of the principles of merit and economic individualism, than for college admissions, which may be viewed as an opportunity for the development of new skills. In addition to the main effect for institutional setting, which is suggested by the Kinder and Sanders findings, our study explored whether our predicted pattern of Whites' resistance to affirmative action programs benefiting Blacks would vary across the three different institutional contexts.

Method

Subjects

A sample of 337 White (135 male, 202 female) college undergraduates (mean age = 19 years) attending two mideastern universities participated in this survey study in partial fulfillment of one alternative option of a course requirement.

Survey Design

Using the full-profile survey technique, 36 items represented factorial combinations of three independent variables: (a) targeted group, (b) policy, and (c) institutional setting. Concerning targeted group, policies were presented as benefiting Blacks, handicapped persons, or elderly persons. The two levels of policy were (a) justification and (b) no justification. Two instances of justification (framing the program in terms of addressing past discrimination or enhancing cultural diversity) and two examples of no justification (framing the programs as preferential treatment or reverse discrimination) were nested within each level of policy. Institutional context, which represented the setting in which the policy would be implemented, had three levels. Policies were presented as applying to business, college, or social organizations. Thus, items in the survey reflected a 3 (Targeted Group: Black, Handicapped, Elderly) x 2 (Policy: Justification [Past Discrimination or Cultural Diversity] vs. No Justification [Preferential Treatment or Reverse Discrimination]) x 3 (Institutional Setting: Business, College, Social Organization) experimental design. Examples of items reflecting the combinations of these independent variables are presented in Table 1.

TABLE 1: Description of Policy Frames

Policies without justification
  Preferential treatment (9 items)
    "Employers (colleges, or social organizations) should consider whether an applicant is black (elderly, or handicapped) along with other information when making selection decisions."
  Reverse discrimination (9 items)
    "Employers (colleges, or social organizations) should consider whether an applicant is black (elderly, or handicapped) as very important when making selection decisions."
Policies with macro-level justification
  Past discrimination (9 items)
    "To compensate for past discrimination, employers (colleges, or social organizations) should make an extra effort to hire a greater number of black (elderly, or handicapped) applicants."
  Increasing diversity (9 items)
    "To provide diversity within the organization, employers (colleges, or social organizations) should make a special effort to admit a greater number of black (elderly, or handicapped) applicants."

Procedure

Subjects were administered the survey instrument in small groups that varied from 5 to 15 participants during research sessions. Each subject completed the measure individually, without discussion or knowledge of the responses of other participants in the room. Subjects were asked to rate each item on 7-point bipolar scales for each of three dimensions: (a) agree-disagree, representing the extent to which the subject agreed with the proposition stated by the item; (b) fair-unfair, reflecting how fair the respondent felt the policy was to those people specifically mentioned or affected by the proposition; and (c) effective-ineffective, indicating the perceived effectiveness of the proposition for selecting competent people. In addition, information was requested concerning the respondent's race, city, sex, and age. After subjects completed the survey, they were debriefed and thanked for their participation.

Results

The primary analysis involved a 3 (Targeted Group: Blacks, Handicapped Persons, or Elderly Persons) x 2 (Policy: Justification vs. No Justification) x 2 (Subject Sex) analysis of variance. Note that higher ratings on the dependent measure indicate that the policy was perceived as less fair and effective and as more disagreeable. Consistent with target-based explanations of resistance to affirmative action (e.g., symbolic or modern racism), which predict that responses will be more negative toward specific groups (such as Blacks) independent of how a policy is framed, a main effect for targeted group was obtained, $F(2, 30) = 18.66$, $p < .001$. Response was most negative for Blacks ($M = 5.56$), next most negative for elderly persons ($M = 4.85$), and least negative for physically handicapped persons ($M = 4.61$). By Tukey's Honestly Significant Differences (HSD) post hoc procedure, response was more negative ($p < .05$) toward Blacks than toward either elderly or physically handicapped persons; there was no significant difference between the response to elderly and physically handicapped persons. Consistent with the hypothesized importance of procedural justice, a main effect for policy,

$F(1, 30) = 25.34$, $p < .001$, revealed that response was less negative to implementation policies that included explicit justifications (=4.68) than to policies without justifications ($M = 5.34$). The analysis also yielded a main effect for sex, $F(1, 30) = 4.69$, $p < .038$. Women displayed more negative responses to affirmative action policies than did men ($Ms = 5.05$ vs. 4.96).

The aversive racism framework further suggests the more subtle effect that negative reactions to affirmative actions policies benefiting Blacks would be more pronounced when these reactions could be more easily rationalized on the basis of some factor other than race (i.e., in the absence of macro-level justifications). A marginally significant Targeted Group x Policy interaction, $F(2, 30) = 3.00$, $p < .065$, was consistent with this prediction (see Table 2). The more negative response for policies with no justification, compared to those with justification, was most pronounced for Blacks, $t(30) = 3.41$, $p < .01$; next most for physically handicapped persons, $t(30) = 1.91$, $p < .10$; and least pronounced for elderly persons, $t(30) = 0.93$, $p < .20$. Post hoc comparisons (Tukey's HSD) revealed that policies without explicit justification that were targeted for Blacks were responded to more negatively ($p < .05$) than each of the other five conditions. These results suggest that resistance to affirmative action, although in part due to policy-based reactions, may also reflect subtle prejudice toward Blacks.

The analysis of variance revealed only one other significant effect, a Sex x Policy interaction, $F(1, 30) = 42.34$, $p < .001$. Women displayed a relatively stronger negative response to policies without explicit justification than to those with justification ($Ms = 5.53$ vs. 4.58) than did men ($Ms = 5.15$ vs. 4.77).

Table 2: Means for Policies and Targeted Groups

		Targeted Group	
Policy	Blacks	Handicapped	Elderly
Without justification	6.10	4.91	5.00
Preferential treatment	6.08	4.60	4.89
Reverse discrimination	6.13	5.23	5.11
With justification	5.02	4.31	4.70
Cultural diversity	5.07	4.44	4.73
Past discrimination	4.97	4.18	4.67

Note. Higher response scores indicate more negative responses toward targeted group.

Discussion

The primary focus of this study was to identify some of the unique and combined effects of factors that influence reactions to affirmative action. Although a variety of previous studies have addressed aspects of policy, target, and institution separately, this study addressed the *combined* effects of these variables. Our results underscore the importance both of the type of policy (i.e., whether it is framed at the micro or macro level of perceived fairness) and the identity of the specific groups targeted to benefit from the policy. The results revealed, however, that the institution or agent of the affirmative action policy had little impact on individual attitudes toward affirmative action (cf. Kinder & Sanders, 1990).

With respect to type of policy, programs that were framed in terms of macrojustice by remedying historical injustice (past discrimination) or increasing cultural diversity were more acceptable to respondents than were those that focused on specific implementations (i.e., preferential treatment and reverse discrimination). Overall, resistance was quite strong for the policies without justification, 5.34 on a measure that could range from 1 (low) to 7 (high); resistance was lower, but still substantial, even when framed in terms of historical or social justice (4.68). . . .

With regard to targeted groups, policies directed at benefiting Blacks were resisted more strongly than were policies for physically handicapped or elderly persons.

The idea that negative attitudes toward affirmative action are tied to the effects of racism has been suggested previously (e.g., Benokraitis & Feagin, 1978). Both Kinder and Sears (1981) and C. K. Jacobson (1985) have provided empirical support for the notion that negative attitudes toward affirmative action are predicted by modern or symbolic forms of racism. The main effect for targeted group that was obtained in our study is consistent with their conclusions.

This main effect for targeted group may alternatively be interpreted as revealing a belief that elderly and handicapped persons are especially deserving of assistance. Our respondents may have viewed the handicapped or elderly, relative to Blacks, as generally more deserving of preferential treatment because these individuals have in some way earned this treatment or are disadvantaged due to factors outside their control (e.g., age, illness). This explanation suggests the value of future research examining reactions to affirmative action programs targeted at benefiting a range of groups that systematically vary in level of stigmatization, perceived deservingness of outside assistance, qualifications, and perceived controllability of need. . . .

Specifically supportive of the aversive racism framework that guided our research, our findings revealed that among the policies that were most strongly associated with negative attitudes toward affirmative action, the presence of Blacks as the target of these policies produced the greatest level of resistance compared to the other targeted groups. The aversive racism framework asserts that resistance to the fairness of the affirmative action procedure may be used as the non-race-related rationale for evaluations that are based on subtle but negative racial attitudes (Dovidio et al., 1989). The interaction effect presented here supports this view. Although the type of policy was important in predicting attitudes toward affirmative action, these attributes did not exclusively account for individual reactions to these policies. Not only did the specific targeted groups exert a unique effect on level of individual resistance to affirmative action, but when the targeted groups and policy justification were considered together, responses were more negative when the policy was targeted for Blacks than for other groups, particularly when the policy could be perceived as violating principles of fairness without further justification.... In other words, whereas giving preference based on nonmerit factors is perceived at unfair, giving such preference to Blacks is perceived as more unfair. Thus, perceptions of fairness may be important in determining attitudes toward affirmative action, but they are not immune to the effects of aversive racism.

Although not predicted, our finding that women exhibited stronger negative reactions to policies without justification than did men (consistent with other research indicating that women are more sensitive to violations of justice than are men; Stake, 1983) suggests promising avenues for future research. Would, for example, the same pattern of data be obtained if women replaced Blacks as the targeted group? The aversive racism effect, which may operate because those in power are motivated to maintain their status, suggests that men would be more resistant than women to unjustified affirmative action programs benefiting women. However, this would put women in conflict with the ill effects of being preferentially selected, a conflict that could lead women to reject the unjust policy despite the program's benefit to them. Thus, future research on gender can help to identify gender differences more fully and to clarify whether the aversive racism framework applies only to resistance to affirmative action programs that benefit racial minorities or whether these findings demonstrate a specific case of a more general process of defending the status quo.

Two general implications can be derived from the present work. One concerns recognition of racial bias within resistance to affirmative action, and the other involves ways of reducing resistance to affirmative action based on racial bias. First, our findings suggest that future models may need to address more systematically the complex nature of individual opposition to affirmative action policies. Although concepts such as perceptions of fairness and distributive and procedural justice are useful for explaining some of the diversity in individual attitudes, these concepts alone may be insufficient. Our data indicate that not only is the question of fairness alive and well and affecting individual reactions to affirmative action, but aversive forms of racism are also alive and well and having an equal—and, in some instances, a greater—impact on these attitudes.

Models that strictly concentrate on the nature of the selection procedure or the outcomes of resource distribution may be problematic for two reasons. First, they may severely underrepresent the complexity of individual resistance to affirmative action. As a consequence, the substantial role of racial bias may be overlooked or obscured. Second, these models may minimize the impact of negative and subtle forms of racism on individual reactions to specific affirmative action candidates once these individuals have been selected for employment or admitted to college. Garcia, Erskine, Hawn, and Casmay (1981) demonstrated that successful minority candidates were judged to be less qualified when evaluators believed that the institution had an affirmative action policy. These misperceptions occurred regardless of whether that individual was specifically said to be an affirmative action hiree. Perceptions of this type, which can also involve self-perceptions, may ultimately erode an individual's self-confidence and effectiveness (Chacko, 1982; Heilman, Simon, & Repper, 1987; M. B. Jacobson & Koch, 1977; Steffy & Ledvinka, 1989; Turner, Pratkanis, & Hardaway, 1991). Clearly, these types of social perceptions are a function of a significantly more complex process than the disturbances that models of procedural fairness imply.

The second implication of our findings concerns the most effective strategies for facilitating acceptance and reducing opposition to affirmative action. Our findings support Clayton and Tangri's (1989) suggestion: Policies framed to appeal to wider, more macro-level perspectives of justice arouse less resistance compared to policies that focus more narrowly on procedures of affirmative action itself. In addition, although the articulation of the specific procedures appears to be a critical component in reducing opposition to affirmative action, we suspect that the process underlying aversive racism stems from the more generic consequences of social categorization. When individuals classify or categorize others as members of their own group (in-group) or as members of another group (out-group), a variety of cognitive, affective, and motivational processes are activated (see, e.g., Allen & Wilder, 1975; Dovidio & Gaertner, 1993; Judd & Park, 1988; Linville & Jones, 1980). Specifically concerning perceptions of justice, when people interact with an in-group member, they may be more likely to focus on the other person's needs than on narrowly defined equity rules (i.e., microjustice; Deutsch, 1975).

Also, with respect to social categorization, individuals are motivated to defend or promote the interests of the social groups to which they belong, regardless of whether these actions benefit them personally.... In the case of affirmative action, individuals may be motivated to promote their own group's interests. Thus, resistance to affirmative action policies is likely to be contingent on the extent to which these policies are seen as benefiting outgroup members at the expense of in-group members.

This conceptualization suggests that strategies that reduce the extent to which affirmative action is seen as benefiting an out-group (e.g., Blacks) relative to an in-group (e.g., Whites) should reduce opposition to affirmative action. Thus, refocusing or recategorizing social boundaries may reduce evaluations of affirmative action on the basis of racial group boundaries. One such strategy, termed *recategorization,* accomplishes this by changing individuals' cognitive representations from different groups (e.g., in-group vs. out-group; Blacks vs. Whites) to a more inclusive, common in-group identity (Gaertner, Mann, Murrell, & Dovidio, 1989). Findings from a recent survey study of a multicultural high school (Gaertner, Dovidio, Anastasio,

Bachman, & Rust, in press) demonstrate that the development of a superordinate identity does not require each group to forsake its subgroup identity to reduce intergroup bias. This finding increases our confidence that the recategorization strategy can be effective in real, complex intergroup settings in which group identities are important and would not be relinquished easily.

The salience of a common group identity reduces the need to separate evaluations and preferences across group boundaries. For example, reconceptualizing affirmative action in terms of a common group identity would focus on the need for affirmative action policies in terms of the beneficial consequences for the society as a whole in meeting the demands of the future, more diverse work force (Johnston & Packer, 1987). This speculation is supported by findings that the actions perceived as most important by Federal compliance officers in implementing affirmative action policies are the demonstrations of top management's support and the integration of the organization's identity with the goals of affirmative action (Marino, 1980). This finding, along with our results, suggests that considering affirmative action as an effective strategy for providing assistance to members of an overall superordinate social group should return the sentiment of affirmative action back to that originally articulated by its founders; that is, to ameliorate the negative effects on society of disparate treatment due to race and ultimately reduce resistance to affirmative action.

References

Allen, V. L., & Wilder, D. A. (1975). Categorization, belief similarity, and intergroup discrimination. *Journal of Personality and Social Psychology, 49,* 1621-1630.

Barnes Nacoste, R. (1994/this issue). If empowerment is the goal: Affirmative action and social interaction. *Basic and Applied Social Psychology, 15,* 87-112.

Benokraitis, N. V., & Feagin, J. R. (1978). *Affirmative action and equal opportunity: Action, inaction, reaction.* Boulder, CO: Westview.

Binion, G. (1987). Affirmative action reconsidered: Justifications, objections, myths, and misconceptions. *Women and Politics, 7,* 43-62.

Blanchard, F. A., & Crosby, F. J. (Eds.). (1989). *Affirmative action in perspective.* New York: Springer-Verlag.

Chacko, T. T. (1982). Women and equal employment opportunity: Some unintended effects. *Journal of Applied Psychology, 67,* 119-123.

Clayton, S. D., & Tangri, S. S. (1989). The justice of affirmative action. In F. A. Blanchard & F. J. Crosby (Eds.), *Affirmative action in perspective* (pp. 177-192). New York: Springer-Verlag.

Deutsch, M. (1975). Equity, equality, and need: What determines which value will be used as a basis for distributive justice? *Journal of Social Issues, 31,* 137-149.

Dovidio, J. F., & Fazio, R. H. (1992). New technologies for the direct and indirect assessment of attitudes. In J. Tanur (Ed.), *Questions about survey questions: Meaning, memory, attitudes, and social interaction* (pp. 204-237). New York: Russell Sage Foundation.

Dovidio, J. F., & Gaertner, S. L. (1981). The effects of race, status, and ability on helping behavior. *Social Psychology Quarterly, 44,* 192-203.

Dovidio, J. F., & Gaertner, S. L. (1993). Stereotypes and evaluative intergroup bias. In D. M. Mackie & D. L. Hamilton (Eds.), *Affect, cognition, and stereotyping* (pp. 167-193). Orlando, FL: Academic.

Dovidio, J. F., Mann, J. A., & Gaertner, S. L. (1989). Resistance to affirmative action: The implication of aversive racism. In F. A. Blanchard & F. J. Crosby (Eds.), *Affirmative action in perspective* (pp. 83-102). New York: Springer-Verlag.

Gaertner, S. L., & Dovidio, J. F. (1986). The aversive form of racism. In J. F. Dovidio & S. L. Gaertner (Eds.), *Prejudice, discrimination, and racism* (pp. 61-89). Orlando, FL: Academic.

Gaertner, S. L., Dovidio, J. F., Anastasio, P., Bachman, B., & Rust, M. (in press). The Common Ingroup Identity Model: Recategorization and the reduction of intergroup bias. *European Review of Social Psychology.*

Gaertner, S. L., Mann, S. A., Murrell, A. J., & Dovidio, J. F. (1989). Reducing intergroup bias: The benefits of recategorization. *Journal of Personality and Social Psychology, 57,* 239-249.

Gamson, W. A., & Modigliani, A. (1987). The changing culture of affirmative action. In R. D. Braugart (Ed.), *Research in political sociology* (Vol.3, pp. 137-177). Greenwich, CT: JAI.

Garcia, L. T., Erskine, N., Hawn, K., & Casmay, S. R. (1981). The effect of affirmative action on attributions about minority group members. *Journal of Personality, 49,* 23-30.

Greenberg, J. (1987). Reactions to procedural injustice in payment distributions: Do the means justify the ends? *Journal of Applied Psychology, 72,* 55-61.

Heilman, M. E., Simon, M. C., & Repper, D. P. (1987). Intentionally favored, unintentionally harmed? Impact of sex-based preferential selection on self-perceptions and self-evaluations. *Journal of Applied Psychology, 72,* 62-66.

Jacobson, C. K. (1985). Resistance to affirmative action: Self-interest or racism? *Journal of Conflict Resolution, 29,* 306-329.

Jacobson, M. B., & Koch, W. (1977). Women as leaders: Performance evaluation as a function of leader

selection. *Organizational Behavior and Human Performance, 20,* 149-157.

Johnston, W. B., & Packer, A. E. (1987). *Workforce 2000: Work and workers for the twenty-first century.* Washington, DC: U.S. Department of Labor.

Judd, C. M., & Park, B. (1988). Out-group homogeneity: Judgments of variability at the individual and group levels. *Journal of Personality and Social Psychology, 54,* 778-788.

Kinder, D. R., & Sanders, L. M. (1990). Mimicking political debate with survey questions: The case of white opinion on affirmative action for blacks. *Social Cognition, 8,* 73-103.

Kinder, D. R., & Sears, D. O. (1981). Symbolic racism versus threats to "the good life." *Journal of Personality and Social Psychology, 40,* 414-431.

Kovel, J. (1970). *White racism: A psychohistory.* New York: Pantheon.

Lind, E. A., Kurtz, S., Musante, L., Walker, L., & Thibaut, J. W. (1980). Procedure and outcome effects on reactions to adjudicated resolution of conflicts of interest. *Journal of Personality and Social Psychology, 39,* 643- 653.

Linville, P. W., & Jones, E. E. (1980). Polarized appraisals of out-group members. *Journal of Personality and Social Psychology, 3,* 689-703.

Lipset, S. M., & Schneider, W. (1978). The Bakke case: How would it be decided at the bar of public opinion? *Public Opinion, 1,* 38-44.

Marino, K. E. (1980). A preliminary investigation into behavioral dimensions of affirmative action compliance. *Journal of Applied Psychology, 65,* 346-350.

McConahay, J. B. (1986). Modern racism, ambivalence, and the Modern Racism Scale. In J. F. Dovidio & S. L. Gaertner (Eds.), *Prejudice, discrimination, and racism* (pp. 91-125). Orlando, FL: Academic.

Nacoste, R. W. (1985). Selection procedure and responses to affirmative action: The case of favorable treatment. *Law and Human Behavior, 9,* 225-242.

Nacoste, R. W. (1986). The effects of affirmative action on minority persons: Research in the Lewinian tradition. In E. Stivers & S. Wheelan (Eds.), *The Lewin legacy: Field, theory, and current practice* (pp. 268-281). New York: Springer-Verlag.

Nacoste, R. W. (1987a). But do they care about fairness? The dynamics of preferential and minority influence. *Basic and Applied Social Psychology, 8,* 77-171.

Nacoste, R. W. (1987b). Social psychology and affirmative action: The importance of process in policy analysis. *Journal of Social Issues, 43,* 127-132.

Regents of the University of California v. Bakke, 438 U.S. 265 (1978).

Rossi, P. H., & Anderson, A. B. (1982). The factorial survey approach: An introduction. In P. Rossi & S. Nock (Eds.), *Measuring social judgments: The factorial survey approach* (pp. 15-67). Beverly Hills, CA: Sage.

Sears, D. O., Hensler, C. P., & Speer, L. K. (1979). Whites' opposition to "busing": Self-interest or symbolic politics? *American Political Science Review, 73,* 369-384.

Stake, J. E. (1983). Factors in reward distribution: Allocator motive, gender and Protestant ethic endorsement. *Journal of Personality and Social Psychology, 44,* 412-418.

Steffy, B. D., & Ledvinka, J. (1989). The long-range impact of five definitions of "fair" employee selection on black employment and employee productivity. *Organizational Behavior and Human Decision Making, 44,* 297-324.

Thibaut, J., & Walker, L. (1975). *Procedural justice: A psychological analysis.* Hillsdale, NJ: Lawrence Erlbaum Associates, Inc.

Turner, M. E., Pratkanis, A. R., & Hardaway, T. J. (1991). Sex differences in reactions to preferential selection: Towards a model of preferential selection as help. *Journal of Social Behavior and Personality, 6,* 797-814.

Wittink, D. R., & Cattin, P. (1989). Commercial use of conjoint analysis: An update. *Journal of Marketing, 53,* 91-96.

Affirmative Action Hires Affirmed
Advancing Women In Higher Education

---

*E*ditors' Note: This brief article highlights a study conducted by two Michigan State economists which speaks directly to the current debate about the qualifications and performance of women and minorities hired under affirmative action initiatives. It builds on Heilman, et al.'s findings, showing that affirmative action policies, when framed in certain ways, do not necessarily have a negative impact on the recipients of the policies.

A prevailing myth is that affirmative action has flooded the workplace with unqualified and underperforming women and minority employees. Is this true? In a study of more than 3,200 randomly selected worksites in Detroit, Boston, Atlanta and Los Angeles, two Michigan State economists examined employees who had been identified by their employers as having been hired, in part, as a consequence of an affirmative action plan. These employees were then compared to white men in comparable jobs and the employees hired by companies without affirmative action plans.

The findings showed that, as a group, affirmative action hires appear to do just as well or better than white males on the job. Differences in qualifications between affirmative action hires and white men were small. White males were somewhat better educated than women and minorities holding similar jobs, with the differences ranging from a few months to more than a year of formal schooling.

When the researchers analyzed performance, however, there were two substantial differences: African American females generally out-performed white males according to job evaluations filled out by their supervisors, with white females, Black males, and Hispanic females performing similarly to white males in similar firms. Latino men, however, had significantly lower ratings than their Anglo counterparts

Although the research did not cover academic institutions, one might expect similar findings. The research was conducted by Harry Holzner and David Neumark at Michigan State University, East Lansing, MI 48824.

Societal Values Dictate Job Paths For Women
Tori DeAngelis

Editors' Note: As Chapter 5 demonstrated, society views certain social roles as appropriate for females and others as appropriate for males. Tori DeAngelis' report discusses research by Felicia Pratto, among others, which investigates the relationship between what jobs are open to women and the values that a society deems important. A central theme of the research is how endorsing social values that either support or lessen the social hierarchy can influence how appropriate different jobs are for women and men.

Cultures have traditionally divided the tasks of their group by gender, with women performing some roles and men others. But those duties vary from society to society. In some early tribes, for instance, women built the houses, while men helped rear the children, says Stanford University professor Felicia Pratto, Ph.D.

Today, gender divisions still pervade the workplace, with women taking on the bulk of "pink-collar" jobs like secretary and men most of the "blue-collar" ones such as construction worker. These divisions are based on our society's power structure, with employers undermining women for having values that challenge a male-dominated system, Pratto contends. In particular, Pratto says that managers make hiring decisions on the belief that women hold values that seek to fix injustices in an unfair system. And they hire men in certain jobs based on the view that men have values that aim to perpetuate the system. The findings differ from previous research in showing that employers don't just show bias based on gender, but also on their perceptions of women's values, Pratto says.

Pratto is one of several psychologists studying the gender gap in the workplace. She and others have found that while women have made great professional strides and are no longer barred from any career, employers still use subtle tactics to keep women from gaining equal treatment with men.

New York University psychologist Madeleine Heilman, Ph.D., for example, has found that some employers can't see past women's gender—that even when women possess traditionally "masculine" leadership traits such as decisiveness and strength, employers don't think women are capable of holding leadership positions.

"They see management jobs as requiring male qualities and they see women as not having those qualities, " Heilman says.

Similarly, other psychologists have found that people automatically rate a wide range of jobs as "masculine."

Social Dominance

In her work, Pratto applies the "social dominance" theory to managers' perceptions of jobs candidates value systems. The theory maintains that one group in a society shapes the direction of values in the entire system. Roles that serve the interests of elite groups are called *heirarchy-enhancing* roles, and those that serve oppressed groups are *heirarchy-attenuating* ones, the theory maintains.

Jobs can be rated in ways that reflect one dimension or the other: Corporate managers for instance, reflect hierarchy-enhancing values, while civil-rights advocates reflect hierarchy-attenuating ideals. Heirarchy-attenuating jobs tend to be lower-paid than hierarchy-enhancing jobs, and more women are likely to be interested in those jobs than men, given their place in the power structure. But that is of course not always the case, says Pratto.

Testing the Idea

In two recent studies examining how this theory may apply at work, Pratto and colleagues Jim Sidanius, Ph.D., and Bret Siers, Ph.D., of the University of California, Los Angeles, tested whether "employers" were more likely to hire men for jobs that maintain the status quo (hierarchy-enhancing jobs) and to hire women for jobs that seek to right systemic wrongs or to care for marginalized members of society (hierarchy-attenuating ones). The studies were reported in the January *Journal of Personality and Social Psychology* (Vol. 72, No. 1, p. 37-53).

The team found that employers did have biased perceptions of men's and women's values and acted on those biases, even when they received equivalent information about the job seekers.

In both studies, Pratto used the same paradigm, first with 86 college students, then with 104 business people commuting to work on a train. Participants were given four résumés, each of which reflected a prototypical male "enhancer," a prototypical female "enhancer," a prototypical male "attenuator," and a prototypical female "attenuator." They were asked to place applicants into five positions, each with different levels of heirarchy-attenuating or enhancing features.

In both studies, participants hired far more women than men into heirarchy-attenuating jobs and far more men than women into heirarchy-enhancing positions, the team found.

"The gender stereotype bias. . .was not simply to hire one gender preferentially, but rather to channel men into heirarchy-enhancing jobs and women into heirarchy-attenuating jobs," Pratto concluded.

The findings illuminate the importance of viewing workplace issues not just psychologically, but also sociologically and culturally, Pratto believes.

"Stereotypes and other social ideologies do not merely reflect a kernel of truth about group differences," says Pratto. "They [also] justify and perpetuate the social systems of inequality of which they are part."

Shameful: Women Really Do Have To Be At Least Twice As Good As Men To Succeed

The Economist

> **Editors' Note:** It is common to hear women and minorities voice the complaint that they must be twice as good as their white male colleagues in order to succeed in many domains. The following short article from *The Economist* magazine reports evidence that suggests that such views may not be too far from the truth.

Sex and connections: these are not the criteria on which science should be judged, least of all by scientists. But in the first extensive analysis of the way that fellowships in science are awarded, which is published this week in *Nature*, Christine Wenneras and Agnes Wold, microbiologists at Gothenburg University, in Sweden, found what many graduate students and postdoctoral fellow have long suspected. Namely, that these factors matter as much as, if not more than, scientific merit.

Peer review, the evaluation (often anonymous) of a piece of scientific work by other scientists in the same field, is central to the way in which science proceeds. Journals use it to help decide whether to publish papers; funding agencies use it when deciding to whom to award grants. Anecdotal accounts of abuses abound. But considering how essential it is, there is surprisingly little information on how well it works.

This is in part because the raw data are difficult to obtain. To get the data for their study, Dr. Wenneras and Dr. Wold had to go to court. The Swedish Medical Research Council (MRC), a government body that funds biomedical research, did not want to release the records of who had said what about whom in the evaluation of fellowship applications. Fortunately, the courts declared the records to be official documents—and, therefore, public under Sweden's Freedom of the Press Act.

To start with, Dr. Wenneras and Dr. Wold analyzed the review of the 114 applications that the MRC received for the 20 postdoctoral fellowships it offered in 1995. Of the applicants, 46% were women. Of the successful recipients of the awards, only 20% were women. This was not a freak year: in Sweden in the 1990s, women have received 44% of the doctorates awarded in the biomedical sciences but have been less than half as successful as men at getting postdoctoral fellowships from the MRC. In principle, of course, that might reflect their abilities. In practice, however, other factors seem to be at work.

When the council gets a grant application, it is evaluated by five reviewers, on three measures; scientific competence, the proposed methodology and the relevance of the research. Each measure is given a score of between zero and four; each reviewer's scores are multiplied together, giving a single score between zero and 64; and finally, the scores from the reviewers are averaged together, giving the total score.

Dr. Wenneras and Dr. Wold found that women received lower than average scores on all three criteria, but especially low scores for scientific competence. To see whether women really were bumbling scientists, the researchers devised three quantifiable measures of competence, and used these to assess the applicants' abilities.

The first measure is crude: how many papers have you published? This measures productivity more than competence—you might publish a lot, but in trivial journals that no one reads. More refined is something known as an "impact" factor. Calculated by an independent body, the Institute for Scientific Information, the impact of a journal is the number of times an average paper in that journal is cited elsewhere in a given year. To calculate a scientist's impact, just add up the impact factors of all of his or her papers. The third measure was the number of times that an individual's papers had actually been cited in the previous year. Moreover, each of these measures can be calculated in two ways: total productivity and first author productivity. In biomedical research, the first author listed on a paper is typically the one who contributed the most—so being one frequently is a good measure of individual competence that is independent of collaborations.

Having compiled this information for each applicant, Dr. Wenneras and Dr. Wold looked to see how well it matched the competence rating given by the MRC. They found an astonishing—and shocking—discrepancy. Women with the same impact and productivity as men were consistently given much lower competence scores. The women with the most impact—those with a total score of over 100 points—were deemed to be only as competent as those men whose total impact was less than 20.

Although these figures look like the result of sex bias, other kinds of bias could produce them too. Women might more often come from insignificant universities, or hold their Ph.D.s in subjects—such as nursing—that might be perceived as inferior.

To identify such factors, the researchers analyzed how much an applicant's competence score was affected by nine different variables, including sex and whether or not the applicant knew a member of the reviewing committee. They found that just two factors improved the score significantly: being male and knowing a reviewer. In fact, the difference was so great that in order to get the same competence score as a man, a woman would need either to know someone on the committee or to have published three more papers than the man in *Nature* or *Science*, the two journals with the highest impact—or 20 more papers in good specialist journals. It is often joked that a woman has to be twice as good as a man to do as well; Dr. Wenneras and Dr. Wold found that she would need to be, on average, 2.5 times as good on their measures to be rated as highly by reviewers.

This could partly explain why, although women receive almost half the Ph.Ds in biomedical fields, more women than men leave at all later stages. This exodus is often explained as women not having the motivation or perseverance to work in a male-dominated scientific establishment, but Drs. Wenneras and Wold reckon that their results could account entirely for the large numbers of women who have left biomedical research in Sweden. This, if true, is not only unfair, but a waste of public money.

Granted there is only one study from one country. But it is the first study of its kind, and it comes from a country in which sexual equality is formally entrenched in public life. Other similar research will have to be done, and if the same pattern is found, the peer review system will have to be overhauled. America's National Science Foundation is currently assessing its system—but in the absence of similar data. In the meantime, ambitious women would do well to return to a time-honoured but supposedly obsolete tradition, and apply under a male name.

✓ PROJECT 10.1
Personal Versus Group Discrimination

I.   Faye Crosby, in her research on gender discrimination, has uncovered a perplexing finding. When women are asked if they as a group are discriminated against, they agree. However, women are much less likely to agree when asked if they personally suffer from discrimination. In this project, you will replicate her work, applying the theory to people of different races or ethnicities.

II.   For this project, you are to ask five people who are not European-American (if possible—otherwise ask European-American women) to complete the two questions on the next page. After they complete the questions, bring your questionnaires back to class. You will create a difference score for each of your participants, subtracting each participant's response to the question about personal discrimination from their response to the question about group discrimination. Then, take the average of all of these difference scores from all of the participants your class has gathered (your instructor can help the class with this). Once your class has calculated the average of the difference scores, discuss the following questions in your class: Is there a difference between the responses or did your participants respond the same way to both questions? Were they more likely to respond with higher numbers on one of the two questions? Which one? Does it matter what order they completed the two questions (note: there are two different orders for the questions)? What do your class's results suggest about our own perceptions of discrimination? Does this pattern make it easier or harder to rally support for fighting against discrimination?

How often do you personally suffer from discrimination as a member of a gender, racial, or ethnic group?

    1   2   3   4   5   6   7   8   9
  not at all   sometimes   always

How often is your group (either gender, ethnic, or racial) discriminated against?

    1   2   3   4   5   6   7   8   9
  not at all   sometimes   always

✂──

How often is your group (either gender, ethnic, or racial) discriminated against?

    1   2   3   4   5   6   7   8   9
  not at all   sometimes   always

How often do you personally suffer from discrimination as a member of a gender, racial, or ethnic group?

    1   2   3   4   5   6   7   8   9
  not at all   sometimes   always

✂──

How often do you personally suffer from discrimination as a member of a gender, racial, or ethnic group?

    1   2   3   4   5   6   7   8   9
  not at all   sometimes   always

How often is your group (either gender, ethnic, or racial) discriminated against?

    1   2   3   4   5   6   7   8   9
  not at all   sometimes   always

✂──

How often is your group (either gender, ethnic, or racial) discriminated against?

    1   2   3   4   5   6   7   8   9
  not at all   sometimes   always

How often do you personally suffer from discrimination as a member of a gender, racial, or ethnic group?

    1   2   3   4   5   6   7   8   9
  not at all   sometimes   always

How often do you personally suffer from discrimination as a member of a gender, racial, or ethnic group?

    1   2   3   4   5   6   7   8   9
not at all   sometimes   always

How often is your group (either gender, ethnic, or racial) discriminated against?

    1   2   3   4   5   6   7   8   9
not at all   sometimes   always

✓ PROJECT 10.2
Wanted: Employees From
Traditionally Underrepresented Groups

I.   Employers, in their announcements for job openings, will often include a statement inviting members of traditionally underrepresented groups to apply. These statements vary in their openness, the groups they target, and they way in which they make the statement.

II.   For this announcement, access the World Wide Web (for information how to do this, we suggest you consult with the computer consultants at your university). Once on the web, search for job announcements in an area in which you would possibly like to work in the future. Pick three announcements for jobs that look interesting to you and that have enough information to answer the questions below.

III.   For each job announcement, please evaluate them on the following dimensions:

POSITION 1:
Describe the position.

_____

_____

_____

What were the qualifications necessary for candidates?

_____

_____

Was the announcement written in a clear and complete fashion? _____

Did the ad make the company or business appear to be a place you would like to work? _____

Was there any statement inviting members of traditionally underrepresented groups to apply? ____

If so, which groups appeared to be targeted?

_____

_____

How open did the announcement appear to hiring members of traditionally underrepresented groups?

_____

_____

How could the announcement have been phrased to be more open to members of traditionally underrepresented groups?

_____

_____

POSITION 2:
Describe the position.

_____

_____

_____

What were the qualifications necessary for candidates?

_____

_____

Was the announcement written in a clear and complete fashion? _____

Did the ad make the company or business appear to be a place you would like to work? _____

Was there any statement inviting members of traditionally underrepresented groups to apply? ____

If so, which groups appeared to be targeted?

_____

_____

How open did the announcement appear to hiring members of traditionally underrepresented groups?

_____

_____

How could the announcement have been phrased to be more open to members of traditionally underrepresented groups?

_____

_____

POSITION 3:
Describe the position.

_____

_____

_____

What were the qualifications necessary for candidates?

_____

_____

Was the announcement written in a clear and complete fashion? _____

Did the ad make the company or business appear to be a place you would like to work? _____

Was there any statement inviting members of traditionally underrepresented groups to apply? ____

If so, which groups appeared to be targeted?

_____

_____

How open did the announcement appear to hiring members of traditionally underrepresented groups?

_____

_____

How could the announcement have been phrased to be more open to members of traditionally underrepresented groups?

_____

_____

✓ PROJECT 10.3
Who Does What? An Analysis
Of Men's And Women's Magazines

I.   The media often depicts males and females in traditional gender roles. This may
      also be the case for the occupations in which males and females are pictured.
      However, does it make a difference if the media is aimed at a male or female
      audience? That is, will a magazine whose readership is primarily female depict
      women in traditional gender roles more or less than a magazine that is targeted
      at men?

II.   For this project, you will evaluate two different magazines, one that is targeted at
      women (such as *Vogue* or *Cosmopolitan*) and one that is targeted at males
      (such as *GQ* or *Men's Health*). Choose a current magazine from each category.
      Then, count the number of pictures, advertisements, or references in the text that
      depict either males or females in an occupation. Keep track of the types of
      occupations and the sex of those in the different occupations, keeping separate
      records for each magazine.

	Female Targeted Magazine	Male Targeted Magazine
Title of magazine		
Occupations and sex of person in occupations		

Answer the following questions:

Did the male and female targeted magazines differ in the occupations they depicted?

_____

_____

_____

_____

Did the two magazine types differ in the sex of the people depicted in each of the occupations?

_____

_____

_____

_____

Were your findings consistent or inconsistent with your expectations?

_____

_____

_____

_____

Were your findings consistent or inconsistent with traditional gender roles?

_____

_____

_____

_____

Were your findings consistent or inconsistent with the findings reported in DeAngelis' article?

_____

_____

_____

_____

A p p e n d i x

The Research Project

The media is constantly bombarding us with the latest scientific research findings, including those dealing with issues of gender, race, and ethnicity. One way to become an educated consumer of this scientific research, one who makes informed decisions about the issues raised by it, is to become actively engaged in scientific research.

This Appendix asks you to do two things. First, it presents a series of articles chosen to provide you with both a general overview of the experimental process and more specific information concerning the particular tasks involved in conducting and writing up an experimental study. The first of the Aronson, Ellsworth, and Gonzales articles in this section offers a clear introduction to experiments, describing the key elements and procedures involved in designing and carrying them out. Ellyson and Halberstadt discuss a critical process in experimental research in their article on how to study original research journal articles. The process of writing up an experimental study is laid out in the second Aronson, Ellsworth, and Gonzales article in this Appendix.

This Appendix also is structured to help you to design and write up a proposal for an experimental study. This multi-stage project is designed to help you investigate a topic that is of particular interest to you relating to gender, race, or ethnicity. You will design a study that will adequately test an original hypothesis and write a report of your proposed study that attempts to persuasively convince the reader that your study would contribute to social psychological research. Overall, this project will give you an opportunity to be exposed to and engage in psychological research.

This Appendix will guide you through a series of steps leading you through each stage of writing up a research proposal. First, you will decide on a topic relating to the psychology of gender, race, or ethnicity that interests you (Project A.1). For instance, you may wonder how being bi-cultural influences a person's attitudes and behavior toward a parent who is not bi-cultural, or how gender differences in leadership styles in the workplace influence people's productivity. After choosing a topic that is interesting to you, you will familiarize yourself with the existing psychological journal articles and books describing research on your topic in order to gain the necessary background and to help you focus on a specific question related to your topic.

After formalizing your question into a testable hypothesis (Project A.2) you will write the introduction to the experiment you are proposing. In the introduction, you will discuss the existing research relating to your hypothesis, describing what other researchers have found in similar studies and why your experiment is important (Project A.3). Next, you will explain the specific methods you would use to test your hypothesis (Project A.4), describe the results you expect to obtain from your study (Project A.5), and discuss the importance and limitations of these results (Project A.6).

Again, this Appendix will guide you step-by-by-step through the proposal writing process in order to provide you with the necessary information for gaining a deeper understanding of the importance of the steps involved in psychological research.

Psychological research often plays an important role in our everyday lives. Because of this, it is critical that as many of us as possible become educated to the basic elements involved in this research. This is particularly true for research concerning issues relating to gender, race, and ethnicity—the focus of this Workbook—as research concerning these topics could have a major impact on how we as a society approach and deal with these issues.

An Introduction To Experiments[*]

Elliot Aronson, Phoebe C. Ellsworth, and Marti H. Gonzales

Why Methodology? Why Experiments?

"I'm not planning to do any psychological research myself, so why should I study research methods?" This is a question students ask us from time to time, and it deserves some answers.

The first answer is that you never know when you might be called upon to carry out some "research." No matter what field you enter, you may feel a need to improve your performance or that of your subordinates. You will inevitably run up against problems, and you may have to try out different ways of solving them. People in business are constantly striving to figure out ways to improve sales or productivity; doctors test new ways to persuade patients to follow their advice; lawyers try out new strategies for successful argument or negotiation. An understanding of the logic of research design is as useful in improving the informal research questions that continually arise in our professional and personal lives as it is in designing formal research studies.

The second answer is that understanding how to do research prepares us to *evaluate* the research we read about. In this information age, we are inundated with communications from the press and television media: If parents share custody of their children after divorce, the children will be better off than if only one parent has custody; coconut oil raises cholesterol and olive oil lowers it; bottling up one's emotions leads to illness; "back to basics" education results in higher S.A.T. scores; and so on and so on. As consumers of this information, we face the task of figuring out what claims to believe, of separating reasonable journalistic conclusions or interpretations from inferences that are biased or just plain wrong. An understanding of research methods prompts the consumer to ask "How do they know?" when faced with news of a new discovery and provides the tools to answer that question. Quite often it turns out that "they" don't know.

Finally, studying the methods of social psychological research can improve people's reasoning ability more generally. Darrin Lehman and his colleagues (Lehman, Lempert & Nisbett, 1988) found that training in social psychology improved students' ability to reason about everyday problems. Because the topics studied by social psychologists are quite similar to the problems we face in everyday life, learning to think about them the way researchers do creates skills that can be transferred to real-life problems. . . .

The Nature of Experiments

A scientific investigation starts with a question. Why do people yield to group pressure? Do people like something better if they have had to work hard to get it? How does a steady diet of violent television shows affect a person's behavior? Any question can be studied scientifically, provided that it involves something that can be observed. After formulating the question, the scientist must decide exactly what to observe in order to answer it. For many questions, the scientist's next task will be to find a situation in which to observe the phenomenon. A researcher who is interested in the effects of different kinds of college curriculum on graduates' subsequent success, for example, will have to specify the types of curriculum that might make a difference. For some questions, the scientist may even have to wait for circumstances in which to make observations. Social psychologists who want to study people's responses to a natural disaster will have to wait for a flood, tornado, earthquake

---

[*] Excerpted from Aronson, E., Ellsworth, P. C., Gonzales, M. H. (1990). An introduction to experiments. (Chapter 1, pp. 8-39). In *Methods of Research in Social Psychology* (2nd ed.). New York: McGraw-Hill. Copyright ©1990 by McGraw-Hill Publishing Company. Reprinted with permission of The McGraw-Hill Companies.

or other calamity to happen. Similarly, astronomers must wait for the earth to move into a particular position before they can make specific observations.

An experiment differs from other types of scientific investigation in that rather than searching for naturally occurring situations, the experimenter *creates* the conditions necessary for observation. There are several advantages to this procedure. First, by setting up the conditions, the experimenter has a better chance of capturing exactly what was intended. For example, Solomon Asch deliberately set up his experimental group so that the subject was faced with several other people who steadily and consistently disagreed with him about an apparently obvious judgment. It is hard to imagine a natural situation which so clearly and forcefully pits the evidence of one's senses against the evidence of one's peers.

Second, the experimenter can *control*— and thus systematically *vary* conditions in order to study the same general situation with and without the crucial element. In studying the effects of group pressure, Asch arranged his experiment so that all subjects were members of a group in which the members' task was to judge the lengths of lines. In some groups the members called out their judgments so that everybody could hear them, and of course the subject had to let everybody hear his judgment, too. Since expressing his true opinion meant making a spectacle of himself by announcing the only deviant opinion in the group, there was a great deal of pressure toward conformity in these groups. In one group (the control group), the members simply wrote down their judgments, so the subject had no idea what the other members were saying and thus experienced no group pressure. If Asch had used a non-experimental procedure, he would have had to try and find naturally occurring groups working on similar tasks in similar settings but differing in that some groups were characterized by high amounts of pressure on the individual and others were pressure-free. It is often extremely difficult, if not impossible, to find natural situations which are alike in all respects except the one that interests the experimenter.

Finally, and most important, the experimenter has the power to decide which individuals will be exposed to which conditions. Outside the experiment, people who are more independent may choose groups in which less pressure is exerted; less independent people may like to have their decisions made for them and so prefer groups with obvious pressure. Thus, if the individuals in the groups with the most pressure conformed more to their groups, this finding might not be due to the group pressure but to the fact that the people who chose those groups were more conforming to begin with. In an experiment, the experimenter assigns subjects to treatments *at random.* Thus, whether a person happens to be a member of a group that exerts pressure is due to chance alone and not to any prior differences among subjects. If the subjects in the group that exerts pressure make more errors in their judgments of the lines, the experimenter *knows* that this difference was caused by the group pressure and not by any prior differences in the individuals who were members of the two types of group. Because the experimenter can assign subjects to treatments at random, the experiment, unlike other procedures, can provide a strong basis for making statements about causality. . . .

The experimenter begins with an idea, or a question, or a hypothesis. The idea may derive from a theory, from doubts about the validity of some previous experiment or theoretical formulation, from a concern with a social problem, or simply from curiosity about some kind of behavior. Asch was generally interested in the conditions of submission to group pressure, which he felt to be a problem involving important social issues. He was dissatisfied with earlier social psychological accounts, because they tended to give the phenomenon a label, such as "suggestion," which explained little, and because they paid too little attention to the processes that enable a person to *withstand* group pressure. Thus, like most experimenters, he was interested in the problem for a variety of reasons.

Independent and Dependent Variables

The next step is to translate a concern for a general problem area into a specific question. Asch's specific question was: What are "the social and personal conditions that induce individuals to resist or to yield to group pressures when the latter are perceived to be *contrary to fact?"* (Asch, 1965, p. 393), and he started out with one "social condition"—the presence of a unanimous majority. In many experiments the basic question is stated as a *hypothesis*, or prediction about the outcome of an experiment. Either way, an inquiry is made about a causal sequence. The antecedent event, or "cause," in the proposed sequence is called the independent variable, because the experimenter creates it and controls its variation; it is independent of all other causative influences. The experimenter is sometimes said to manipulate the independent variable. In the initial Asch experiment, the independent variable was group pressure-specifically, the pressure assumed to be exerted by a unanimous majority which gave false judgments. The *"effect"* in the causal sequence is called the dependent variable, because the experimenter expects its value to depend on the changes introduced in the independent variable. In the Asch experiment the dependent variable was the number of errors the subject made in the direction of the false judgments of the majority.

Technically, a variable is any attribute which can assume different values among the members of a class of subjects or events but which has only one value for any given member of that class at any given time. Thus, height is a variable within the class of human beings (and other things); within the class as a whole height can assume a large range of values, but at any given moment a given human being can be only one height. Some variables, such as height, are continuous and can assume any value within some finite range. Others . . . *are discrete* and can assume only a limited number of values. . . . In a psychology experiment the independent variable is usually a stimulus event, and the dependent variable is a response made by the subject.

The values of the independent variable (or variables) that the experimenter chooses to use define the experimental conditions. At least two values of the independent variable are necessary in order to demonstrate that the variable is having an effect, since in an "experiment" with only one value of the independent variable, it is impossible to determine whether the results (the

measurements of the dependent variable) have anything to do with the presence of the independent variable. In the Asch experiment there were two values of the independent variable: presence of group pressure (in the form of a unanimous majority) and absence of group pressure. In a study of this sort, in which there are only two conditions defined by presence *versus* absence of the independent variable, the subjects who receive the independent variable (those who had to make their judgments in the face of unanimous opposition) constitute the experimental group, and those who do not receive it constitute the control group.

Having formulated a question or hypothesis, the experimenter must decide how to turn it into a set of experimental procedures. One of the most important parts of this transformation involves translating the concepts of the hypothesis into specific, observable events. This substitution may he viewed as the empirical realization of the conceptual or abstract variables contained in the question. An abstract concept such as "group pressure" is "made real" in terms of the events actually experienced by the subjects—thus the term "empirical realization." Usually in social psychology the process of creating an empirical realization is intimately bound up with decisions about the overall staging and context of the experiment. Thus, in the Asch experiment the impact of the group pressure depended on a great many elements of the situation-the apparent simplicity of the task, the public announcements of the members' judgments, the unanimity of the judgments by the other "subjects," and the consistency of those judgments through time. Certainly, this was an extreme form of group pressure, unlikely to be encountered outside the laboratory, and Asch intended it to be so. In many real-life situations, people are able to avoid the dilemma created by a contradiction between their own beliefs and the norms of a group. For one thing, the ambiguity of some situations allows people to avoid even perceiving that there is a dilemma. Also, the fact that people typically are not required to state their opinions publicly may allow them to assume that they are not the kind of people who yield to others. In addition, it is often possible to explain away discrepancies by referring to factors outside the situation or by assuming that the majority are motivated by a desire to persuade others or to play devil's advocate and don't "really mean" what they are saying. Asch wanted to remove these extraneous defenses in his empirical realization of the concept "group pressure" in order to study it in the pure case, forcing the subject to face the dilemma and to resolve it by yielding or by standing firm. Once having determined what happens in this extreme case, he could then make the situation less extreme and compare the results with those obtained in the initial experiment.

In Asch's experiment the empirical realization of the dependent variable followed naturally from the rest of the situation; the conceptual dependent variable, yielding, was simply realized as the number of times a subject went along with the group and gave the wrong answer.

For the kind of complex variables studied by social psychologists—variables such as guilt, anxiety, self-esteem, and group pressure—there is no one "right" empirical realization. Some are better than others. . . . More than one empirical realization may capture essential features of some variable such as "group pressure," but they may emphasize different features. An experimenter interested in studying how people evade facing the dilemma posed by conflicting group and personal values, for example, might create a situation in which the pressure was less obvious or in which the subject could attribute the group's disagreement to some external factor. . . .

Random Assignment of Subjects to Treatments

In general, random assignment is one of the experimenter's most important tools for ruling out the dangers of systematic error. It is so important, in fact, that it is considered the criterial attribute for defining a study as an *experiment*. The most common variety of random assignment is the random assignment of subjects to experimental conditions. . . . The experimenter's goal is to make sure that none of the myriad extraneous factors which might affect a subject's behavior in the experiment. . .is more likely to be associated with one of the experimental conditions than with the other (or others). Since the conditions are defined by the independent-variable treatments, they must be kept free of any extraneous factors that may cause differences between them in order for the experimenter to conclude that the differences were *caused* by the independent variable alone. . . .

Assigning subjects to conditions at random means that each subject who walks in the door has an equal chance of being placed in any one of the experimental conditions. If there are two conditions, each subject has a 50:50 chance of being in either one. . . .The end result is that there will be roughly equal numbers of . . . subjects in the experimental and control groups. . . for intelligent subjects, unhappy subjects, and so on for *all* kinds of traits. By randomly assigning subjects to conditions, the experimenter can be sure that *no* subject variable is more likely to occur in one condition than in the other and thus that no subject variable is a source of systematic error.

We can look at random assignment in another way—as the "great equalizer." Because random assignment ensures that all extraneous factors that might influence the subject's behavior in the experiment are approximately equal in the two (or more) conditions, we would expect that if we *left out* the experimental treatments and ran both groups of subjects as control groups, the average scores of these two groups on the dependent-variable measure would be the same. Not every subject would have the same score, of course. Even in Asch's control group, in which there was no group pressure, 5 percent of the subjects made errors of judgment. With random assignment, we can assume that in a group of subjects exposed to group pressure, about 5 percent of them would have made mistakes even without the pressure. Since in the Asch experiment 74 percent of the subjects who were exposed to group pressure made at least one mistake, we can conclude that the independent variable had a large effect.

Factors other than subject variables can cause systematic error, if they are associated with some conditions more than with others, and these factors may also be eliminated by random assignment. For example, if there is more than one experimenter, it is important that each experimenter run about the same number of subjects in each condition. If one experimenter ran subjects only (or mostly) in the experimental group, and the other experimenter ran subjects mostly in the control group, differences between these two conditions could be due to differences in the personalities or techniques of the two experimenters. Thus, subjects should be assigned to experimenters at random.

Holding Variables Constant

Although random assignment is essential for eliminating systematic error, it cannot reduce the amount of random error, or "background noise," in the experiment. If the treatment is only one of a large number of factors influencing the subject's behavior in important ways, its influence may not be strong enough to stand out above the variability introduced by all the other extraneous factors. A common means of controlling random error is to *hold* important extraneous variable *constant* at a single level (or to reduce the possible levels to a more limited range). In his initial experiment Asch always used the same sets of lines (holding stimulus materials constant) and always used a unanimous majority of seven accomplices (holding size of group constant). . . . The principle behind the technique of holding a variable constant is that the less an extraneous variable is allowed to vary, the less it can affect the dependent variable. Of course, it is never possible to control all sources of random error; the experimenter must use judgment in deciding which extraneous factors are most likely to produce large fluctuations in the particular dependent variable being measured. . . .

Although this procedure is valuable, holding a variable constant at some level restricts the generality of the experimenter's conclusions to situations involving that particular level. . . .

Systematic Variation

Besides holding a variable constant and allowing it to vary at random, the researcher has a third choice-varying it *systematically,* adding it to the experiment as a second independent variable. In effect, the experimenter asks a direct question about the additional variable instead of hoping to pick up some relevant information indirectly, as happens when the variable is allowed to vary randomly. In the Asch experiment, this would be equivalent to having several different groups of subjects who were exposed to group pressure, some subjects being assigned to a condition in which the majority consisted of seven people, some to a majority of six people, some to a majority of eight people, and so on. By comparing the number of errors made by subjects in each of these conditions, the experimenter gains a much surer understanding of the relation between size of majority and conformity than is possible by with either of the other methods.

In fact, Asch did vary the size of the majority systematically in a later experiment. Some subjects were members of pairs—they were faced with only one other person who gave wrong answers. Other subjects had to face a majority of two; others, majorities of three, four, or eight; and finally, some subjects were members of very large groups in which the size of the majority ranged from ten to fifteen. Asch found that subjects could hold their own against a single other person who disagreed with them; no subject made more than one mistake, and most made none at all. When the majority consisted of two, conformity began to show up, subjects averaging 1.53 errors. With three people in the majority, the effect increased to its full strength, with subjects making an average of four errors. Larger majorities, even those of ten to fifteen, did not produce effects stronger that did a majority of three.

Interactions

Another advantage of varying more than one independent variable at a time is that this technique can provide information about how one independent variable *interacts* with the other. An interaction is a situation in which the independent variable has *different* effects, depending on the value of some other variable. It the other variable is also experimentally varied, the data will show the interaction. But if the other variable is either held constant or allowed to vary at random, information about the interaction may be suppressed.

To take a hypothetical example, suppose that Asch had run an experiment in which there were two independent variables—majority size and similarity of the people in the majority to the subject. To simplify things, we will imagine that only two levels of each of these variables are used; thus, the experimenter has (1) majorities of two and (2) majorities of four, and these majorities are made up either of people very similar to the subject or of people very dissimilar to the subject. Each subject is randomly assigned to one of these four types of groups.

Given this design, we can envision several possible patterns of results. If the size of the majority has a large influence on the number of errors the subject makes but the similarity of the group makes no difference.... In other words, large majorities (defined here as four people) cause people to conform more than do small majorities (defined here as two people), and they have this effect whether or not the members of the majority are similar to the subject.

We can also envision a situation in which people tend to conform to the judgments of those who are similar to them but are able to maintain their independence when they perceive the others as dissimilar, regardless of how many others there are. In other words, we can imagine a situation in which there is a *main* effect for similarity, with majority size having no effect....

Or, we can envision a situation in which both the size of the majority and its similarity to the subject make a difference. For example, subjects may tend to agree with similar people more than with dissimilar people, and they *also* tend to agree with large majorities (four people). There are then two main effects, one for similarity and one for majority size....

Artifacts

Although there are inherent difficulties in both strategies—holding variables constant and allowing them to vary at random—both are necessary techniques in any social psychological experiment, since there are so many possible variables that affect social behavior that it is impossible to vary them all systematically in a single experiment. Some random error, as well as many limitations on the generality of the findings, are inevitable. It is crucial, however, to make sure that no other variables change *with* the independent variable, always taking on one range of values in the experimental group and another in the control group. Such variables can be sources of systematic error in that they can cause differences between the two groups, differences which are mistakenly attributed to the independent variable. An extraneous variable that varies along with the treatment is said to be *confounded* with the independent variable. When the extraneous variable is a relatively trivial methodological event, the error is often called an artifact.

To take a hypothetical example, if the subjects in the experimental group undergo a complex and interesting experience during the presentation of the independent variable, but subjects in the control group simply come into the lab and sit and wait for the same amount of time, differences between the two groups could be caused by the boredom of the control subjects rather than by the effects of the independent variable on the experimental subjects. If in the Asch experiment the lines to be judged were flashed on a screen and removed before the judging started, subjects in the control group would be writing down their judgments immediately after the stimulus disappeared, but subjects in the experimental group would have to wait until all the "subjects" before them had given their answers. This longer delay between seeing the lines and giving their judgments might have caused the subjects to forget which line was really longest and thus could have operated to increase the number of errors made, even in the absence of group pressure.

Two special kinds of artifact are demand characteristics (changes in the subjects' behavior simply from the experience of being in an experiment) and experimenter bias (changes in the subjects' behavior resulting from subtle hints unintentionally given off by the experimenter which let the subjects know how they are expected to respond)....

Alternative Explanations

Sometimes, the whole experimental procedure may allow for two substantively different and theoretically interesting interpretations of the results. In other words, the variables are not well enough defined so that the expected results *necessarily* indicate the validity of the experimenter's hypothesis. Someone reading the experiment may think of an *alternative explanation* which also fits all the experimental data.

A tradition of research on the *risky shift* illustrates what we mean by the term "alternative explanations." In the 1950s, many people believed that groups were more cautious than individuals in making decisions; that is, members of a group would be more level-headed and would tend to avoid extreme behavior. James Stoner (1961) set out to test that proposition. Briefly, he had people read about fictitious characters who had to make a choice between two alternatives: to take a risk or to adopt a more conservative stance. Participants were asked to decide how much risk they would advise the character to take. After they made their decisions individually, participants met in groups to discuss the situations and to reach agreement on what the group would advise. Were group decisions after discussion more cautious than the individuals' earlier decisions? Surprisingly not. By and large, groups recommended that the characters adopt a riskier strategy than did the average individuals, hence the term "risky shift."

These unexpected results initiated a whole line of research on group decision making in many different countries and with people of all ages from all walks of life. Investigators using Stoner's choice dilemma found consistent evidence of the risky shift. It seemed to be an amazingly robust finding. Eventually, however, some researchers uncovered the existence of a *conservative shift*. That is, under some circumstances, group decisions are more conservative than the average individual decision. Given these conflicting findings, it became the task of investigators to explain them. Are groups *really* more willing to take risks than are individuals?

Careful study revealed that group decisions are not always more risky than individual decisions; neither are they always more conservative. There is one reliable characteristic of group decisions, however: They tend to be more *extreme* than the average individual decision. That is, if individuals initially tend to favor conservative solutions to choice dilemmas, they are likely to shift to an even more conservative position

when they get together as a group. Similarly, if individuals tend to favor risky solutions, group decisions are likely to shift to a more risky position. Thus, the risky shift demonstrated by Stoner and the conservative shift demonstrated by others were both examples of a more general tendency of group discussions to exaggerate individual group members' initial inclinations. This more general phenomenon has been labeled *group polarization.*

The preceding story serves as an example of a "reasonable" explanation for research findings and an even *more* reasonable alternative explanation. The story also has a moral: Researchers should try to anticipate alternative explanations and design experiments that will rule them out by adding extra control groups, by changing the design, or, if these are not feasible, by collecting additional data which may help to discriminate between two plausible explanations. For example, had Stoner and others used two kinds of choice dilemmas—yielding both conservative and risky decisions by individuals prior to group discussion or had investigators used different measures of risk taking, this interesting group phenomenon might have been understood sooner.

If some potentially interesting variables have been held constant or allowed to vary at random, the experimenter often decides to run a *replication* of the experiment, this time systematically varying one or more of these variables to find out what effect it has within the context of the experimental situation. Or, if an alternative explanation has been suggested, the experimenter may run a replication in which the conditions are changed in such a way as to rule out the alternative explanation. A replication is nothing more than a repetition of the experiment. In a direct replication the experimenter tries to make the conditions exactly the same as they were in the original experiment in order to see if the experimental effect is a stable (or reliable) one. If the replication is successful—if the results in the two experiments are the same—the experimenter will be more confident that the observed effect is a stable one that will be consistently achieved in the same conditions. We hasten to add, however, that direct replications are relatively rare in social psychological research. More often, investigators replicate and extend previous research; that is, direct replications are typically only part of a study in which additional variables are studied as well.

In a systematic replication the experimenter varies some quality of the original situation in order to resolve ambiguities or to add new information about the variables controlling the subjects' behavior. Asch's follow-up experiment with different majority sizes may be viewed as a systematic replication of the original experiment. It provided additional information about the relationship between the size of the erroneous majority and its effectiveness in inducing the subject to conform.

Nonexperimental Methods of Research

So far, we have been discussing research that falls into the category of the *experiment,* a study in which the investigator has some control over the independent variables and can assign subjects to conditions at random. By *manipulating some variable,* the experimenter creates differences in the experiences of two or more groups of subjects; and by *assigning subjects to the groups at random,* the experimenter creates groups which are equivalent in all respects except their experience with the independent variable. The experimenter can be reasonably sure that any differences in the behavior of the subjects in the groups are due to the differences in the treatments, since the random assignment of subjects to conditions has ruled out everything that might have made the two groups different to begin with. If the experiment has been conducted properly, the investigator can legitimately say that the treatments *caused* differences in behavior. Thus, Asch was justified in claiming that in his experiment, unanimous majorities *caused* many people to distort their judgment so as to correspond more closely to the majority judgment.

Only in an experiment can we *control the independent variable* and *assign subjects randomly* to conditions. For this reason, the controlled experiment is the only research method that allows us to make unequivocal cause-effect statements. The experiment is thus an extremely important method of conducting empirical research, but it is by no means the only method. It is true that in other kinds of research we invariably sacrifice the chance to make definite statements about causality, but below this rigorous standard extends a long continuum of methods, ranging from those that are simply suggestive, providing ideas in the same way as a novel or a newspaper article might, to designs that may provide a tenable scientific basis for inferring causality, designs hardly distinguishable from experiments.

Correlational Studies

Many important and interesting questions are not amenable to experimental research, because the experimenter cannot control the presumed antecedents or cannot assign subjects at random. Instead of introducing treatments, the researcher makes observations of events as they occur in nature. This does not mean that the research is "unscientific;" anyone who lacks faith in the development of a science through the exclusive use of correlational methods need only look at the history of astronomy. It does not even mean that statements of cause and effect are forever destined to be regarded as questionable. We do not raise our eyebrows and ask for experimental evidence when we read that eclipses of the moon are caused by the earth passing between the moon and the sun or that the odd footprints scattered across some outcroppings of Connecticut red sandstone were made by dinosaurs. When measurement of naturally occurring phenomena provides enough evidence that supports a theory and none that refutes it, causal statements are made and accepted, regardless of the scientist's inability to control the phenomena under investigation.

There are also many problems in psychology which cannot be studied experimentally. Every researcher faces ethical issues; for certain questions, ethical considerations may rule out the use of experimentation altogether. We do not feel free to assign subjects at random to conditions that might damage them physically or psychologically. For moral reasons, we are unwilling to tell someone that he or she is about to die, to remove people's frontal lobes, or to study the causes of psychosis by driving people crazy. Instead, we must find people who are already suffering in these situations and look to see if they are also characterized by other variables that we believe to be causes or consequences. For example, cigarette manufacturers frequently claim that there is no direct evidence showing that cigarette smoking *causes* lung cancer or heart disease in humans. They are right. This is because researchers are loath to randomly assign humans to "smoking" and "nonsmoking" conditions in order to demonstrate to skeptics that smoking cigarettes endangers life. Instead, they simply look to see if people who smoke are more frequently diagnosed with lung cancer or heart disease than people who do not smoke. Actually, in the case of research on smoking, researchers have done much more than "simply look." The simple observation was made decades ago, and hundreds of studies were conducted in attempts to separate the effects of smoking from the effects of diet, stress, personality type, and a host of other variables. The Surgeon General finally found the evidence convincing enough to declare that smoking *causes* the diseases that smokers get more often than nonsmokers. Without the experimental method, the demonstration of causal relationships generally requires a great deal of patience and effort and is often costly.

Studies in which the investigator is looking for a relationship between two variables which can be measured—but which cannot be controlled—are called correlational studies. When one variable causes another, the two will inevitably be correlated. However, the reverse is not true; discovering that two variables are correlated can never (without other evidence) provide unequivocal proof of causality. We might hypothesize, for example, that children who watch hours of violent television shows every day are more violent and aggressive than children who don't. Since we cannot assign some children at random to homes that encourage them to watch violent television shows and others to homes that prohibit them, we may decide that a correlational study is the most suitable method for studying this hypothesis. In such a study, we might observe children from 100 households, measuring the amount of violent television they watch. We might also measure the children's aggression: the frequency with

which they fight with their siblings, break toys, throw tantrums, and so on. Suppose that our hypothesis was confirmed and that on the whole, the children who watched the most violence on television were also the most aggressive (a high positive correlation). Would we be able to conclude from these data that the children's aggression was *caused* by the violent television shows? No. There are all sorts of other things that could have led to the same high positive correlation.

First, it is possible that the causal relationship is exactly the opposite of the one we have hypothesized. Perhaps children who are more aggressive *to begin with* prefer watching television characters punch, shoot, stab, or otherwise harm one another more than do children who are less aggressive. An even more common situation is that of a third-variable correlation; the two observed variable—X and Y—are correlated because both of them are highly correlated with (and maybe caused by) a third variable—Z—which we don't know about and haven't measured. Returning to our aggressive children, a third variable would exist if some other factor encouraged them both to view violent television shows and to behave aggressively. For example, it is possible that in homes where parents are frequently absent children have the opportunity to watch a lot of violent television shows and to engage in aggressive, destructive acts with no restraints. That is, the observed positive correlation may occur because parents are not at home to impose limits on television watching and aggressive behaviors. Or perhaps the relationship exists because parents who are themselves aggressive allow their children to watch violent fare on television, use corporal punishment, and condone aggressive behavior in their children. Plausible explanations for the observed positive correlation are limited only by our imaginations.

Thus, in a correlational study we can never be sure what the independent and dependent variables are. A correlational study can neither guarantee that the causal variables have been isolated nor provide the experimenter with control over the phenomena being studied. A correlational study does, however, allow the researcher to find out whether the phenomenon is *predictable* from knowledge about some other variable. Converging evidence from a large number and variety of correlational studies, all of which provide support for the same general theory, can ultimately satisfy scientists about causal relationships, as in the cases of eclipses and dinosaurs.

Basically, a correlational study consists of two sets of measurements, one of each member of a pair of variables which the scientist believes to be related: height and weight, extent of brain damage and extent of language loss, college board scores and grades in college, self-confidence and attractiveness, and so on. The degree of relationship between the two variables is tested mathematically and expressed as a correlation coefficient (symbolized as *r)*. The value of *r* ranges from +1.00 to -1.00. A perfect positive correlation, +1.00, indicates that as one variable increases a constant amount, the other does too; by knowing how much of one variable is present, one can predict the exact value of the other. An *r* of -1.00 (a perfect negative correlation) also allows one to make exact predictions, but in this case the higher the value of one variable, the lower the value of the other (e.g., the *higher* the horsepower of a car, the *lower* the amount of time necessary to reach 60 miles per hour). An *r* of 0 indicates no relationship; knowing the value of one variable does not tell us anything about the value of the other (e.g., horsepower and color of the car). As *r* moves from 0 to +1.00 through the range of positive correlations or from 0 to -1.00 through the range of negative correlations, our ability to predict improves; the variables are more strongly related.

Very seldom do correlations among variables of interest to social psychologists approach +1.00 or -1.00. To cite but two examples, the correlation between general attitudes toward birth control and use of the birth control pill is only +.08 (Davidson & Jaccard, 1979) and the correlation between environmental attitudes and recycling behaviors is +.39 (Heberlein & Black, 1976). Although the magnitude of these correlation coefficients is not impressive in an absolute sense, it is worth noting that when the implications of even a "small" relationship are important, it is often worthwhile to pursue research. For example, the correlation between watching television violence and aggressive behavior ranges from +.10 to +.20

across a wide range of studies (Freedman, 1988): a relatively "weak" relationship. However, few people would argue that violence and aggression are not serious social problems. Thus, it is of both theoretical and practical import to determine if viewing television violence actually causes aggression. Moreover, if indeed it does, it is also important to determine how to explain that causal relationship and to arrive at ways to offset the deleterious effects of televised violence on aggressive, socially destructive behavior. Complex social variables such as aggression have many causes. It is completely unreasonable and simplistic to expect any single predictor variable to have a very high correlation with aggression. Even a history of actual aggressive behavior is an important predictor. It is worthwhile, though difficult, to pursue even weak correlations if they keep turning up to find out whether a variable such as viewing televised violence is part of the reason some people are violent. The problem, of course, is to distinguish between weak-but-reliable correlations and imaginary ones.

Quasi-Experimental Designs

Of course, in the world outside the laboratory, there are phenomena that are easier to control than the movement of the planets, dinosaurs, or even what children watch on television. Social psychologists frequently design and implement interventions in government, industry, and educational settings and measure the effect of those interventions. However, despite control over the treatment or intervention, researchers are sometimes unable to assign individuals randomly to experimental and control conditions: they may be required to utilize only one group or to use intact, preexisting groups.

Studies that have independent variables and dependent variables but do not use randomization to assign subjects to groups are called quasi-experiments (Cook & Campbell, 1979). Because random assignment is not used, the groups compared are likely to differ in many ways aside from the treatment. In the absence of the "great equalizer," the groups are nonequivalent, and the researcher must determine which differences, if any, between these non-equivalent group are due to the effects of the treatment and which are due to other differences between the groups. Without random assignment, one cannot say with certainty that the independent variable is the sole cause of some outcome, so the investigator has to "play detective" and logically and/or statistically eliminate as many rival causes as possible.

There are many varieties of quasi-experiments. Sometimes researchers use only one group to measure the effects of their intervention. Measures might be taken at some time before an intervention and again at one or more points after the intervention. Participants' behaviors or characteristics *before* the treatment can then be compared to their behaviors or characteristics *after* the treatment. For example, medical researchers may measure the physical and psychological functioning of a group of patients *before* the administration of a new drug and at various times *after* the administration of the drug. This strategy allows for a comparison of the patients' functioning before and after the drug is prescribed. Should symptoms subside, the researchers can be *somewhat confident* that the drug was the cause of improvement.

Or, unable to create groups by random assignment, a researcher may use two groups that already exist, giving the treatment to one but not to the other. These two groups can then be compared on dependent variables designed to measure the effects of the treatment. For example, researchers may be interested in improving employee morale in a corporation. Two different departments within the organization can be used to assess the effects of an intervention designed to improve employee morale. Before the treatment is implemented in one department, the morale of employees in both departments is measured (e.g., attitudes toward the organization, ratings of job satisfaction, absentee rates). Thereafter, employees in one department receive the "morale-boosting" treatment, and employees in the comparison group carry on as usual. The effectiveness of the treatment is then assessed by administering the same dependent measures to employees in both departments after those in the experimental group receive the treatment. If employees exposed to the treatment show improved morale compared to employees in the comparison group, results are *suggestive* of

the efficacy of the intervention. We hasten to add, however, that such a conclusion is still open to debate, because we can't be sure that it was our intervention *alone* that caused improvement in employee morale.

Whatever form they take, quasi-experiments differ from true experiments in that subjects are not randomly assigned to treatment or control conditions. . . .

The Advantages of Experimentation

The implication that the experiment is to be preferred over other techniques has provided an undertone to much of our discussion so far. It is now time to examine this implication explicitly and to ask why one should bother to attempt an experiment in the first place. Certainly, there are disadvantages to the social psychology experiment. It is often difficult to design. Hours of critical and creative thought go into selecting the appropriate empirical realizations of the experimenter's concepts. Alternative explanations must be eliminated, and stimulus materials and dependent measures must be carefully selected or developed. It is also likely to be laboriously time-consuming. Permission to proceed must first be secured from human subjects committees; subjects must be recruited; numerous "dress rehearsals" must be conducted with pretest subjects to ensure that the instructions are understandable and that the stimuli and events are interpreted appropriately. Once the experiment is finally up and running, it is not unusual for the experimenter and one or more assistants or confederates to spend an hour or more with each subject. The experimenter frequently has to make elaborate preparations to set the stage, to motivate the subject, and (in certain kinds of experiments) to deceive the subject. After expending all this time and effort, the investigator may obtain only a single datum: perhaps something as simple as a yes or no answer to a single question. Once the data have been collected—questionnaire responses, subject ratings of stimulus materials, overt behaviors, and so on—they must be scored, coded, and prepared for statistical analysis.

Furthermore—and this is perhaps the most common criticism—the experiment is usually far removed from the real-life phenomena in which the experimenter is supposedly interested. To the layperson it may seem ludicrous for psychologists interested in the formation and change of basic attitudes and important values to study children picking out toys or eating spinach, or college students guessing the lengths of lines, deciding how much they like a group on the basis of an "interaction" consisting entirely of written messages, or using 7-point scales to rate a person who appears on a videotape. . . .

In sum, the major advantage of an experimental enquiry is that it provides us with unequivocal evidence about causation. Second, it gives us better control over extraneous variables. Finally, it allows us to explore the dimensions and parameters of a complex variable.

References

Asch, S. E. (1965). Effects of group pressure upon the modification and distortion of judgments. In H. Proshansky and B. Seidenberg (Eds.), *Basic studies in social psychology* (pp. 393-401). New York: Holt, Rhinehart, and Winston.

Cook, T. D., & Campbell, D. T. (1979). *Quasi-experimentation: Design and analysis issues for field settings.* Boston: Houghton Mifflin.

Davidson, A. R., & Jaccard, J. J. (1979). Variables that moderate the attitude-behavior relation: Results of a longitudinal survey. *Journal of Personality and Social Psychology, 37,* 1364-1376.

Freedman, J. L. (1988). Television violence and aggression: What the evidence shows. In S. Oskamp (Ed.), *Applied social psychology annual* (Vol. 8, pp. 144-162). Newbury Park, CA: Sage Publications.

Heberlein, T. A., & Black, J. S. (1976). Attitudinal specificity and the prediction of behavior in a field setting. *Journal of Personality and Social Psychology, 33,* 474-479.

Lehman, D. R., Lempert, R. O., & Nisbett, R. E. (1988). The effects of graduate training on reasoning: Formal discipline and thinking about everyday-life events. *American Psychologist, 43,* 431-442.

Stoner, J. A. F. (1961). *A comparison of individual and group decisions involving risk.* Unpublished master's thesis, Sloan School of Management, Massachusetts Institute of Technology.

On Reading The Research Literature*

Steve L. Ellyson and Amy G. Halberstadt

Why should you study original journal articles about social psychology? Good question. After all, many of the works reported in this reader will be summarized in your text. Why read further?

First, reading actual articles allows you to get a better understanding of the complexity and richness of the questions social psychologists ask and the answers that they obtain. Textbook authors must provide comprehensive coverage of many topics, so they can only briefly summarize the numerous studies that they describe. This strategy necessarily precludes an in-depth analysis of any one idea or of examples of how research studies investigate a particular topic or theory. This reader, by contrast, includes both in-depth reviews, theoretical discussions, and research studies that explore a variety of important and interesting topics. Also, the historical perspective of this reader highlights how social psychology has developed over the last 100 years.

Second, by reading the original sources you experience the research as directly as anyone can without actually being a participant in that particular study. We think that first-hand encounters with the actual foundations of social psychology enhances one's understanding of the field. Instead of reading someone else's very brief summaries, you can explore the research on your own, without anyone else mediating your analysis of the research questions or how the studies address them.

Third, because no one has predigested the material, you will find yourself organizing the material for yourself. This is an advantage! You may remember from your introductory psychology course that learning is promoted by active processing and or organizing of material. You will certainly be doing this as you read and reread these classic and contemporary articles.

A word of caution: These readings are not designed to provide you with final answers. Rather, they are intended to further engage your curiosity about social phenomena. Coming to understand social psychology is a process. It involves questioning assumptions, developing tentative ideas, analyzing those ideas and their underlying assumptions, reworking new tentative hypotheses in association with close examination of data and theory, and analyzing them all over again. Thus, these readings are designed to stimulate further questioning, to help clarify your own assumptions, and to assist you in developing careful, thoughtful models of social behavior.

We encourage you to be an active participant as you encounter the articles in this book. As you read and reread these articles, try to imagine yourself as one of the subjects who took part in the study. What do you think you would have done in this study as a subject, or even as an experimenter? Ask yourself questions. Are the results intuitively plausible? Do they fit your social reality? If so, do the authors' explanations also make sense? What other explanations are possible? If the results don't fit your social experience, can you think of reasons why both the author's results and your own experience might be right (or wrong)? Could your social reality be influenced by idiosyncratic factors or by your own hidden assumptions? Or could the population sample studied be sufficiently different to account for different results? Or are these results counter-intuitive, yet reasonable in retrospect?

Because each of the following articles addresses human social behavior, apply your own knowledge and add to it. Natural curiosity about yourself and other people makes the material intrinsically interesting. Original research reports reveal what lies behind those one- or two-sentence references found throughout your text-books. Reading the primary research literature takes you backstage at the play, to the sidelines for the sporting event, to a more revealing angle from which to observe the magician. Reading the original report allows a much greater appreciation of exactly what a study did and what the study found. Even though the vocabulary in an article may send you to your dictionary or to your instructor, and the statistics may seem like they are part of some obscure foreign language, don't be dismayed. Tenacity on your part will pay off with an appreciation of the way social psychologists attempt to find meaningful answers to meaningful questions.

One other point is important. It is often difficult to recognize our own perspective as we try to understand the perspectives of other people. Bem and Bem (1970) suggest that some of our assumptions (what they refer to as "nonconscious ideologies") are so entrenched in our culture that we are completely unaware of them. Referring to how an individual comes to have such hidden ground rules, the Bems ask:

> What happens when all [our] reference groups agree, when [our] religion, [our] family, [our] peers, [our] teachers, and the mass media all disseminate the same message? The consequence is a nonconscious ideology, a set of beliefs and attitudes which [we] accept implicitly but which remains outside [our] awareness because alternative conceptions of the world remain unimagined. As we noted earlier, only a very unparochial and intellectual fish is aware that [its] environment is wet. After all, what else could it be? Such is the nature of a nonconscious ideology. (p. 89)

We all have underlying perspectives that influence how we come to understand new material. When you read about different cultures or even our own culture at an earlier time in history, you will become more aware than usual about others' underlying assumptions. As you explore these readings, try to apply this heightened awareness to your own assumptions and basic belief structures.

What You Will Encounter in Journal Articles

Most of the readings that follow originally appeared in journals that report social psychology research. Journal studies are, however, written in a different style than the traditional textbook. The goal of the authors who write these articles is to present information clearly, and sometimes to persuade. This kind of writing requires a bit of getting accustomed to and the following should help you to get the most out of these readings.

The American Psychological Association has issued a Publication Manual with writing guidelines that most journal articles follow. Familiarity with this standardized format helps both beginners and veterans to understand an article's content.

What should you expect to find in a scientific research report? Reports of empirical studies typically include an *abstract,* an *introduction, methods, results, discussion* or *conclusions,* and a listing of *references,* although theoretical and review articles often vary somewhat from this format. It is appropriate at this point to give you a preview of what you are likely to find in each section of a typical journal article.

The Title

The title is usually a brief summary of the main idea of the article. It should, on its own, convey the fundamental issues addressed in the study.

The Abstract

The abstract is a brief overview of the entire article. Its purpose is to present the research in a nutshell. It includes the research goal, the subjects and method, the results and the conclusions, all in about 150 words or less. Since many readers skim the abstract to decide whether or not to read the full article, abstracts are usually well-written and informative, although they can also be intimidating by virtue of having packed so much information into such a small space. If you find yourself bogging down in a particular article, a quick review of the abstract is sometimes an effective way to get back on track.

The Introduction

In the introduction the author describes the reasons for doing the research, what has been done before, and how this is a new question or a novel and/or useful way to address the problem at hand. By carefully positioning the research in a historical context and selectively discussing work that has been done previously, a continuity is established between the research effort and the existing body of literature. Broad theoretical issues are often discussed early in the introduction, followed by an increasingly more specific focus.

Consider the following analogy. Your best friend has moved across the country and you embark on a motor trip to visit her. You will probably first consult regional maps, then a state map, and then a city map, and finally a neighborhood map as you try to locate your friend. The author of an article is also providing maps to readers. The directions become increasingly detailed, the research area more clearly focused. The single house you are looking for is much like the research question addressed by the report. A well-written introduction will allow you to make the trip from general questions to specific hypotheses without too much difficulty.

One thing you are sure to notice in most articles is that there are many references or citations to previously published research. Do not be intimidated by the presence of so many names and dates. Prior research provides much of the rationale for the current study. These citations are evidence that the author has been diligent in surveying the existing literature. The author's collecting and making sense of these citations can also be a time saver if you decide to continue exploring the topic on your own.

In addition to stating the general problem, the introduction describes the particular research strategy that the author uses and the specific hypotheses that will be tested. These hypotheses typically link "independent" variables, i.e., variables that the experimenter believes will affect subject behavior, with "dependent" variables, i.e., the specific subject behaviors, which hopefully are influenced by or "depend" on the independent variable. You should search for these statements of what is expected to be found, and be clear in your mind as to exactly how the hypotheses will be tested.

Remember that it is the author's purpose in this section to plead a case for the importance of the research contained in the article. You should be able to follow the logic of the study and understand precisely what the author is examining. Just as your cross-country trip to your friend's house brought you closer and closer to your final destination, so too should the introduction section of a research article guide you to the author's destination, the hypotheses proposed. These are often summarized at the end of the introduction. Thus, the final paragraphs of the introduction are often another good summary to return to if you get bogged down in an article. Now that the author has identified why the research is important and what the research questions are, the next logical step is to find out how those questions will be answered. That is the function of the method section.

The Method Section

The method section is simply a detailed description of the way the study was conducted. Sometimes complex studies will begin with an *overview,* which summarizes the method. Detailed sections about the subjects and procedure then follow.

Subjects. This section is usually a factual account of who the subjects were and how many of them there were. Additional demographic data such as age, sex, race, institutional affiliation, etc., is often included as well. This information allows you to determine the generalizability of the sample, i.e., how applicable the results may be for other populations. The way the subjects were selected is often included as well as any inducements or payments they received to take part in the study. Look for and identify any specific differences between groups, or subdivisions of subjects. Do the subjects bring any differences to the study, such as their sex or personality differences, that might influence their behavior?

Materials. If original questionnaires are used or a particular apparatus is employed, the author may provide a full description of these. The specific questions asked of the subjects are sometimes included in the text, or they may be appended at the very end of the article.

Procedure. This section should describe what happened to subjects and what was asked of them. Through a step-by-step account of the exact procedures, along with specific instructions given subjects, you should have sufficient detail so that, given the resources, you could come very close to replicating (repeating) the study. The procedure section is also important in that it allows the reader to get the feel of what it would be like to be a subject in the study.

Pay particular attention to the author's attempts to isolate or rule out alternative explanations or reasons (other than the hypothesized ones) for the behavior tested. These attempts at keeping other variables from affecting the behavior of subjects and contaminating the study are as important in a research effort as the need for a sterile environment in the surgery room.

We might consider the analogy of fine-tuning a radio so that the signal you get is static free. There are many stations out there each sending different signals but you are interested in receiving just the one that is your favorite. The better your radio is at signal detection, channel separation, and noise suppression, the better the chances are that you can receive and enjoy any output. Social psychologists are trying to receive a signal (in this case the explanation for a social behavior) in an environment that is potentially cluttered by a multitude of extraneous signals (unknown causes or explanations for that social behavior). The quality of research methodology is analogous to the quality of your radio in this example.

Continue to be an active reader and seek answers to questions. What are the independent variables or predictor variables to be tested? And what dependent behaviors will be used to test the hypotheses? How does the author try to prevent or minimize other variables from providing explanations for subject behavior that are confounded with the independent variables? You should be able to answer these questions after having read this section of the report.

Finally, you will want to compare the procedure with the stated intentions in the introduction. Given the questions identified in the introduction, and the rationale for the study, is the author appropriately measuring the variables of interest? That is, does the procedure allow for meaningful answers to the questions posed in the introduction?

While experimental research may sometimes seem overly complicated, the logic behind it is remarkably simple. Experimenters manipulate and record variables (quite literally, things that can vary between or among people, such as what happens to them and how they respond) to determine if the manipulated variables are in any way responsible for variation in subject behavior. Just as you might prepare a sauce once with butter and once with margarine, and then note differences in taste, smell, or appearance, or change brands of cat food and note differences in your cat's eating behavior, so too do experimenters look for differences. Hence, a typical experiment may entail something happening to one group of subjects that does not happen to another group. If that "something" (the independent variable) is important enough, then the behavior of the two groups (the dependent variable) should differ, assuming that the two groups were comparable to begin with. For example, in preparing the sauce above, you'd make sure that all other ingredients were the same and that the two sauces differed only by the butter/margarine variable. So the presence or absence of that "something" is the focus of an experiment. In a very real sense, the question asked is "does the difference make a difference?" The sauce made with butter may be superior in taste to the one made with margarine. And then again, it may not be. Your cat may be particularly enamored with one particular type of cat food (S. L. E.'s cat, Carmen Miranda, will only eat Friskies Buffet's Turkey and Giblets) or it may make absolutely no difference as your cat will eat anything put before it (like A. G. H.'s cat, Ananda, the epitome of an omnivore). Differences exist or can be created. You can't know whether there really is a difference until you meaningfully test the question. And that, in brief, is the logic behind experimentation.

The Results Section

This is the "how it turned out" section, in which experimenters quantitatively test their hypotheses based on the behavior of the subjects. The author should describe the results in such a way that unexpected as well as expected findings are shown. Not all hypotheses are supported; when the unexpected happens, it may be as important a finding as when the expected occurs. The numbers generated by measuring the subjects' behavior are summarized and analyzed in this section. Tables and figures often are employed to organize these numbers and the statistics generated from them, making the data easier to understand. Carefully examine all tables and figures. Read the titles of the tables or figures. Pay close attention to the column and row titles and the labels presented on figures. If you are unclear about what you are looking at, refer back to the text of the results section and determine where the reference to the table or figure is made (such as "See Table 1" or "As shown in Figure 2). Even though you may not understand the intricacies of specific statistics, you should be able to spot the patterns that emerge from the numbers and figures reported. A rudimentary understanding of statistics will enhance your understanding and ability to evaluate the results, but a good results section will be understandable even to the reader without any statistical knowledge.

An Aside About Statistics

Many students are unnerved by the statistics employed in research; students of social psychology are no exception. There is an impressive arsenal of statistical techniques and shorthand symbols that you will encounter if you spend any time reading the primary literature. Do not let these techniques and symbols deter you. The basic purpose of statistics is twofold. First, statistics are used to summarize large amounts of data in concise, manageable terms. Second, statistical techniques allow authors to determine, within certain parameters, if the results they obtained are sufficiently unlikely to have occurred by chance alone. Statistical techniques never allow us to completely rule out the possibility that a finding is merely due to chance. We can only say how unlikely it is that we have found a difference that does not, in reality, exist.

Your introductory psychology book may be a good source for the logic and meaning of statistics. If your introductory text does not have a chapter on experimental design and statistics, look for an appendix at the end of the book. Also, a brief statistical primer at the end of this chapter will help you make sense of the most frequently used terms and shorthand. In any case, no matter how exotic or mind boggling the "number crunching" you encounter, remember that statistics are used for the two basic purposes we discussed in the last paragraph: (1) to distill a quantity of numbers into more manageable and understandable form, and (2) to assess how likely it is that chance, or something other than what is hypothesized, can account for any differences obtained.

The Discussion or Conclusions Section

This is the "what this all means" section in which the results are interpreted by the author and the research is placed in perspective in light of previous findings. This section usually begins with a brief restatement of the hypotheses and the results that either support or do not support them. Be aware that the same data can be interpreted in different ways. Be skeptical. Authors usually, although not always, consider reasonable alternative explanations for their results. Even if they do not, you should.

Whereas the procedure and results sections are usually straightforward and compactly written, the discussion section typically allows a bit more expansiveness on the part of the writer. Now that the data are collected and the specific research questions have been answered to some degree, you, as a reader, are also less restrained. Don't be afraid to consider alternatives that the author has neglected. Critical thinking may also lead you to the conclusion that the author has overstated the significance of the findings. You are free to agree or disagree with the author's suggestions of "what this all means"; just be clear about your reasons and be prepared to support your own claims.

Many research reports conclude with the authors' suggestions for further research or implications for theoretical positions.

Examine these and determine whether they make sense to you. If you were the author, what would be your next research question?

References

The final section of most articles is composed of complete reference information for all the cited work contained in the article. It provides easy access to any of the articles the authors have used, and is very helpful if you would like to know more about a specific study mentioned in the article.

When psychologists discuss research, they usually refer to articles by the author(s) and year published. This convention allows credit to be given where it is due and functions as a "shorthand" way to readily convey information. . . . Each reference appears in its entirety followed by cross-referencing to all the articles within the reader that cite it.

A Reading Strategy

There is no one strategy for reading research reports that will work for everyone. Some people read an article straight through while others skip around the sections. We suggest that until you become familiar with an approach that works best for you, consider the following strategy.

First, read the title and abstract carefully. Try to identify the general questions raised. Second, skim the entire article rapidly to get an overview of what the researcher did and what the findings are. Third, read the introduction and discussion sections to understand the starting and ending points of the author's reasoning as well as the conclusions. Underline the hypotheses presented in the introduction and locate them again in the discussion section. Fourth, read the method and results sections to determine how well the procedure allows for testing of the hypotheses and whether the hypotheses were confirmed or not. Underline or make marginal notes that highlight the major points made in the article. Fifth, reread the discussion, keeping in mind the original hypotheses and the reported results. Sixth, put the article aside for a few minutes and take a break. This will allow you to clear your mind of details and focus on the issues raised by this research. Seventh, return to carefully read the article from start to finish, paying attention to your underlining and marginal notes.

Finally, when you are finished reading an article, jot down a few notes about it. Try to summarize the article briefly and assess the logic of the author's thinking from introduction to discussion. You may even write your own abstract, adding your personal questions and comments.

Now that you have the complete story, does it all make sense? You still may not be totally convinced by the data and arguments of the study.

You have that right, especially now that you have been an intelligent consumer of the research and collected and considered all the facts. Being skeptical and entertaining alternative explanations for behavior is very much a part of being a good social psychologist.

Hopefully, this strategy will help you read research reports. Each author has presented us with challenging and exciting ideas about the ways we operate as social beings. We trust you will find these studies to be a catalyst for your own thinking about and understanding of human social behavior.

A Note About Nonsexist Language

In 1977, the American Psychological Association added guidelines encouraging the use of nonsexist language in the journals it publishes. In 1982, those guidelines became a requirement. Compliance with these guidelines requires authors to designate people in less ambiguous, less stereotypical, and less evaluative ways. For instance, the word *man* may be generic and refer to all humans, or it may refer only to males and not to females. A statement such as "Man threatens his own environment" is better posed as "Humans threaten their own environment" or "People threaten their own environment." This is not a trivial issue. Words are powerful messengers of not only who or what they describe; they also may contain evaluative meaning. Consider the phrase "man and wife." It is not only semantically unbalanced, but it also makes a value judgment. A more precise and nonsexist phrase is either "man and woman" or "husband and wife." You will find few, if any, examples of sexist language in the more recent articles, although many of the older articles reflect the ideology of their times. And, hopefully, *you* will not fall into the trap of using sexist language in the psychology papers you write.

A Brief Statistical Primer

Analysis of variance (ANOVA) is a statistical technique that allows comparison between two or more group means (see Mean) to determine if there are significant differences between or among the groups. The outcome of an analysis of variance is the *"F ratio"* (usually shortened to "F") which is a ratio of explained to unexplained variance. Explained variance is attributable to the investigator's intended manipulations (independent variables) while unexplained variance results from all other reasons for subjects' behavior, including chance. *F* may be tested for statistical significance (see Statistical significance). With an analysis of variance, one can examine both main effects and interaction effects (see Main effects and interaction effects).

Chi square (X^2) is a statistical technique that assesses the degree to which two categorical or nominal variables are related. Although you could measure a person's attractiveness on a scale of one to ten, a person's eye color can only fall into one category. Most people are brown-eyed, or blue-eyed, or black-eyed, etc. For example, a chi square analysis might determine whether males or females systematically differ in their political party affiliation. Gender and party affiliation are categories.

Correlation *(r)* is a statistical technique that measures the degree of the relationship between two or more variables. The magnitude of the correlation ranges from 0 (no relationship) to 1.0 (perfect relationship) while the sign of the correlation (+ or -) indicates the direction (positive or negative) of the relationship. A positive correlation indicates that the variables change in the same direction. As one variable increases, the other variable also increases. Or, as one variable decreases, the other variable also decreases. For example, the number of years of formal education is positively correlated with income.

A negative correlation implies that as one variable increases, the other decreases. For example, an individual's credit hours earned and his or her remaining time to graduation are negatively correlated. An important point to remember is that correlation does not necessarily imply causation but rather measures degree of relatedness.

df is an abbreviation for *degrees of freedom*. Degrees of freedom reflect the number of observations that are free to vary and are important in determining statistical significance (see Statistical significance). For most statistical techniques, the larger the sample, the smaller the magnitude of a difference needs to be for statistical significance to be obtained.

Dependent variables refer to the particular behaviors of the subjects that will be measured in the study. The investigator is predicting that the subjects' behavior will be dependent upon the independent variable. For example, suppose an investigator wants to test whether the frequency of novel answers to a creativity task is influenced by the presence of an audience. The frequency of novel answers is the dependent variable, while the presence or absence of an audience is the independent variable.

Independent variables refer to the differences that are hypothesized to distinguish between or to alter the behavior of subjects. They may be "subject variables," that is, dissimilarities that the subjects bring to the study (for example, age or degree of self-awareness) or they may be the result of manipulations introduced by the investigator.

Interaction effects are possible when two or more variables are studied at the same time. They occur when one variable has a different effect based on the level of another variable. For example, suppose a hypothetical study examines the influence of two factors, subject sex and the personality variable "need for approval," on how much time is spent playing with a baby (the dependent variable). If females play with the baby more than males do, regardless of their need for approval, then there is a main effect for sex (see Main effects). And if those high in need for approval play with the baby more than those low in need for approval, regardless of sex, then there is a main effect for the personality trait of need for approval. However, if males who are low in need for approval and females who are high in need for approval play frequently with the baby, but males high in need for approval and females low in need for approval *do not* play much with the baby, then an interaction exists. Thus, in this example, subject behavior would be "dependent on" both sex (male or female) and need for approval (high or low). Neither variable alone is sufficient to predict behavior; each is dependent on the other.

Main effects occur when the mean for one level of an independent variable is significantly different from the mean for another level. For example, suppose we have an independent variable labeled "type of classroom." If children in the "cooperative learning" classroom display less racial prejudice than do children in the conventional classroom, there is a main effect for classroom type.

Mean (abbreviated *M*) is the average of a group of scores, i.e., all scores are added and then divided by the total number of scores. An example of a mean is a student's grade point average.

N or *n*, is an abbreviation for the "number of subjects."

Not significant (abbreviated *ns*) indicates that a statistical technique has determined that we cannot rule out chance as the reason for the effects obtained. This can occur when the means of two groups are not sufficiently dissimilar from one another.

Null hypothesis is the assumption that no difference exists between two or more groups in a study. It is usually the negation of the experimental hypothesis. If the investigator hypothesizes that variable X will have a significant effect on the dependent variable (subject behavior), then the null hypothesis is that variable X will have no effect on the dependent variable.

p is the abbreviation for Probability. It refers to the odds that a particular finding is due to chance (also known as "significance level"). The conventional standard for an acceptable level of significance is $p < .05$. Thus, if the study was conducted 100 times, the results obtained would be attributable to chance no more than 5 times. The smaller the level (e.g., $p < .01$ or $p < .001$), the less likely it is that the effect occurred by chance and the

more confidence we have that the finding is actually a true difference.

SD is the abbreviation for standard deviation.

Statistical significance refers to the degree to which a finding is likely to have occurred by chance. By convention, most researchers will not consider a result statistically significant unless a statistical procedure determines that the result has a probability of chance occurrence that is less than 5 percent ($p < .05$). A statistically significant difference is not guaranteed to be a true difference but has a greater likelihood of being a true one compared to a nonsignificant finding (see Probability).

t-test and *t* refer to a statistical technique that results from testing the statistical significance of the difference between the means of two groups. It takes into account how much diversity or variability there is within each group as well as how far the two means are from each other. For example, suppose we want to test the hypothesis that females smile more frequently than do males. A t-test will take into account the variability within the separate groups of males and females while it determines whether, overall, males and females differ in smiling frequency.

Validity is the degree to which a measurement evaluates what it is intended to evaluate. An honest bathroom scale furnishes a valid measurement of weight but has low validity as a measure of height.

Variance is a measure of how spread out or variable the scores are, that is, the degree to which a group of scores deviate from their mean. For example, consider the following two sets of scores: scores in Set A are 73, 74, 75, 76, and 77; scores in Set B are 55, 65, 75, 85, and 95. Although both sets have the same mean (75), Set B has a greater variability (scores are more spread out from the mean). The square root of the variance is the standard deviation, which represents the average deviation (i.e., distance) from the mean in a particular group of scores.

Reference

Bem, S. L., & Bem, D. J. (1970). We're all nonconscious sexists. *Psychology Today, 4*, 22-26.

Writing It Up[*]

Elliot Aronson, Phoebe C. Ellsworth, and Marti H. Gonzales

All the data are in. After a thorough and sensitive postexperimental debriefing, the last subject has left with self-esteem intact, confident that he or she has helped to extend our knowledge of human social behavior a little farther. The subject's job is done; as a researcher, your job continues. You have already arrived at a design appropriate to the research question, chosen or created a setting, decided on a suitable empirical realization of the independent variable, developed or chosen dependent-variable measures, and interacted with scores of subjects. *Finally,* you pour over your data, analyze and reanalyze, decide what they mean, and put pen to paper to write an article summarizing what you have learned about a particular aspect of social behavior. Thus, a research article represents the culmination of months of hard and exciting work. . . .

Readers who are new to the writing enterprise in psychology should read through the *Publication Manual* of the American Psychological Association. This valuable reference provides detailed descriptions of the recommended organization and content of a psychological journal article from the title page to the appendices, including how to format references, tables, and figures. It also contains many useful tips for improving writing style and clarity. Of course, good psychological writing is first and foremost good *prose* writing, and many researchers are familiar with good books on clear writing. We would recommend William Zinsser's (1985) *On Writing Well* and William Strunk, Jr., and E. B. White's (1979) *The Elements of Style.*

Before Sitting Down to Write

Before you can explain your research to other people, you must be able to explain it to yourself. Clear writing requires clear thinking, and many of the problems people identify as problems in *writing* actually reflect gaps and ambiguities in their understanding of just what it is they want to say. So the first step is to figure out what the main point (or points) of your article will be. What do the results mean? What do we know now that we didn't know before? Why is it interesting? What is the "story" of your article?

Sitting in a chair and staring at a blank page or screen is not generally a productive way of finding answers to these questions. It is at least as likely to produce an anxiety attack as it is to produce an insight. Before most researchers lock their doors and pick up a pen and paper or switch on the word processor, they spend a considerable amount of time thinking about the results of their studies and talking with colleagues about them. Feedback from students and colleagues is valuable once a draft has been written but is even more valuable *before* a draft has been written. When results are puzzling, colleagues can provide hunches as to what they *might* mean, and suggestions for ways to determine what they *do* mean. Often, even when the data conform to an experimenter's predictions, colleagues can suggest a slightly different context into which the completed experiment fits or point to questions that beg to be answered in a follow-up study. So it is useful to talk to others about your study, and even to try presenting it in a more or less formal talk to a group of interested people. By trying to explain your research to others, you will learn where you need to improve your own understanding.

Ultimately, however, turning thoughts into sentences is a solitary enterprise, and you alone must decide what to write and for whom to write it. Your friends and colleagues are one source of useful feedback, and they can be used throughout the writing. A second source of useful feedback, oddly enough, is the act of writing itself. Although it is important to think out what you want to say before you

[*] Excerpted from Aronson, E., Ellsworth, P. C., Gonzales, M. H. (1990). Writing it up. (Chapter 11, pp. 326-345). In *Methods of Research in Social Psychology* (2nd ed.). New York: McGraw-Hill. Copyright ©1990 by McGraw-Hill Publishing Company. Reprinted with permission of The McGraw-Hill Companies.

start writing, you will find that the order "think, then write" is an oversimplified statement of what actually happens. By writing, you continue to discover what you don't understand and to clarify your ideas (Berthoff, 1988). In the course of writing, you may find that you have to carry out new data analyses, or check out references you had previously forgotten, or go back and revise earlier parts of the manuscript.

What to Write

How should you write up your data when your initial hypothesis was disconfirmed or only partially confirmed? As Daryl Bem (1987) points out, experimenters must choose between two alternatives in deciding what to write: what they would have written at the outset of a study *or* what they would write once the data have been collected and thoroughly analyzed. More often than not, the latter is the correct choice. Often subjects' behaviors and the data they generate do not conform to even the most sensible and insightful of hypotheses. Moreover, data may reveal patterns that are exciting and provocative, even if they were not anticipated at the outset of the study. For better or for worse, data are the reality with which experimenters work: one that sometimes conflicts with their expectations. Two implications follow.

First, a great deal of time should be invested in organizing, transforming, and analyzing the data. If initial patterns in the data do not support the hypothesis, data transformations (e.g., constructing composite indices from individual dependent-variable responses) or alternative statistical procedures may be in order, and internal analyses often shed light on what would otherwise be a confusing set of findings. Of course, if initial patterns in the data *do* support the hypothesis, there is no reason to stop there. Data can be a rich source of surprises and additional hypotheses if they are exploited by a tenacious experimenter.

Second, because data sometimes yield surprising findings, it would be premature to write an article with the intention of filling in the blanks after the data have been analyzed. Far better to let the data influence the plot, at least to a limited extent. Often, the story an experimenter sets out to write has to be reworked and reframed once patterns in the data reveal themselves. Variables of primary interest may not prove as important as the experimenter predicted; variables of secondary interest at the outset of a study may prove to be more important or more interesting than the experimenter anticipated. As Bem (1987, p. 173) notes, it is better to restructure an article around unexpected findings, even to the point of forsaking the original hypothesis, than to lead readers on a meandering tour of "wrongheaded hunches only to show *viola!*-they were wrongheaded. A journal article should not be a personal history of . . . stillborn thoughts." People reading your article read it because they are interested in what you found, and your best current interpretation of the results you actually got: a story about human behavior. They are not particularly interested in a story about how you had a wrong idea and are now big enough to admit it.

Needless to say, we are *not* recommending that researchers pretend they were predicting outcomes that in actuality were unexpected. It is the obligation of the researcher to present the findings honestly and clearly, without concealing the unexpectedness of the results but without resorting to a historical account of a wrongheaded idea (for example, see Walster, Aronson, & Brown, 1966).

If the results are relevant to your initial hypothesis (e.g., they disconfirm it rather than confirm it, or they suggest a related but more complicated hypothesis), one simple solution is not to frame the introduction in terms of a hypothesis at all but simply to pose a question. If it turns out that the results provide interesting answers to a question that is *not* closely related to the one with which you started, then the introduction should be organized around the new question, the one that is actually answered, and the old question may simply be mentioned in a footnote. . . .

Writing the Article

Students who have perused as few as two or three articles in the *Journal of Personality and Social Psychology, Journal of Experimental Social Psychology,* or *Personality and Social Psychology Bulletin* already have a feel for how the typical article is organized. They have probably noticed that some articles are more clearly and engagingly written than others. In this section, we will briefly discuss the organization of the typical empirical journal article and will provide suggestions on how to write a *good* article: one that is clear, accurate, complete, and interesting to a wide range of readers. Scientific writing need not be stiff, abstruse, or lean to the point of anorexia. Good writers of journal articles are good storytellers; they engage and provoke readers, educate them, sometimes amuse them, and—when it's really done well—leave readers with a feeling of "Gee whiz! I wish I had thought of that." Being dull or overly somber need not be a prerequisite for publishing in social psychological journals.

Getting Started: Organization

The general shape of a social psychology article has four sections: an *Introduction* in which you pose the problem, explain what is known about it and what you would like to add to that knowledge, and describe in general terms how you plan to achieve your goals; a *Method* section in which you describe exactly how you carried out the research; a *Results* section in which you present the results of the data analyses; and a *Discussion* section in which you step back and say what you think the results mean and how you have added to our knowledge. For very simple, small studies, the results and discussion may be collapsed into one section called, not surprisingly, *Results and Discussion.*

For some writers, this rough outline seems to be enough. They simply sit down and knock out a first draft. In fact, this draft is usually the result of days of musing, inventing, and shaping while driving, shaving, washing dishes, or ostensibly listening to someone else talk; it only *appears* to flow effortlessly onto the page without preparation.

Other writers need something on paper from which to work. An outline of what you want to say in each section can be very useful. In the introduction, for example, you want to get from a general question about human nature to the specific context you chose for your study: What are the steps that need to come between? Writing them down can help. Or, you might want to write down the three or four main points you want to include in a given section and then figure out how you will get from one to the next. Whatever form of outline you choose serves as a reminder, a means of moving you along from one idea to the next, and a handy place to jot down additional thoughts you have about the points you want to include. It is meant to *facilitate* the writing of the paper, not be a paper in itself. Thus, unless it really helps you think, there is no point in writing down "I. Introduction. A. Opening paragraph.," and so on, following the classic outline form you learned in eighth grade. An outline is primarily helpful in forcing you to think about the organization of your paper in units larger than the single sentence and smaller than "Introduction," "Method," "Results," and "Discussion."

The Introduction

The purpose of the introduction to a journal article is to present an interesting question, to place a study within a larger context, and to give readers a sense of where the writer is headed. A well-written introduction begins by stating a problem, asking a question, or describing some social psychological phenomenon—often in very general terms at the outset. It gradually becomes more focused as related work is described and evaluated and typically concludes with a specific rationale for the current study. A good introduction not only delineates a question or problem and informs readers about what has already been learned but also convinces them that the most logical and desirable addition to the literature is the study they're now reading.

Introduce the Phenomenon of Interest. It is important in the beginning of the introduction to write in English prose, and to talk about people and their behaviors, not researchers and their findings. It is not an exaggeration to say that by the time readers have scanned the first two paragraphs, they have either become intrigued and decided to read further, or they have yawned, stretched, and set the journal aside to engage in more rewarding activities.

Very few psychologists succeed in writing good opening paragraphs, and this is not surprising. After all, writing the first paragraph is all confounded with the agony of starting the paper. For many people, the first paragraph takes an embarrassingly long time and still ends up embarrassingly bad. Many articles published in our major journals would be better if the first paragraph were simply omitted. . . .

The following illustrate some of the common problems with opening paragraphs:

1. *Too many words.* Strunk and White's (1979) most persistent command is "Omit needless words." Note how this very sentence has been shortened from "Leave out words that aren't really necessary," "Don't use a lot of words where a few will do," or "It is important that psychologists and other social science writers attend to the quantity of words employed to convey relatively straightforward ideas, and that they devote the required attention to excising those that fail to make a significant contribution to the sentence a whole." The use of too many words is particularly characteristic of first sentences, as they serve a sort of "revving the engine" function for the author. . . .

2. *Psychological jargon.* In the interest of brevity, it is tempting to introduce psychological jargon too soon. Although this specialized language serves as a useful shorthand, there is nothing like consulting a psychology dictionary at every turn to frustrate even the most motivated of nonpsychologist readers. For example, it is often useful to write about such concepts as implicit personality theories, cognitive adaptations, sex role orientation in plain English first and to follow those descriptions with the appropriate social psychological shorthand.

3. *"Research has shown."* Most of these sentences begin not by talking about human behavior but by talking about previous researchers. There is a place for this in the introduction, but ordinarily it is not the first sentence have the responsibility of making your idea interesting, and pointing out other social scientists have thought about the same issues is a rather feeble way of doing so. It is as though you're saying, "Lots of published articles address this topic, so it must be interesting." Or, "The point of this article is to place *me* in the company of (or in opposition to) Smedley, Schmolz, and

Smelch." The reader is not particularly interested in where you fit into the spectrum of psychological opinion but rather in what your study is about. Finally, the very fact that three quarters of our articles begin with references to previous research suggests that it is an overused, if not worn out, technique. For that reason alone, it is unlikely to attract the reader's attention. . . .

The following illustrate different strategies for writing an opening paragraph:

1. *The straightforward, no-nonsense description of what the article is going to do.* In the first sentence, Solomon Asch (1952) uses this technique to introduce his famous studies of conformity. . . . It looks deceptively simple, but in fact it is very hard to simply leap in and say, "I am going to tell you about X."

2. *The statement of the issue.* . . . [T]his is the classic way to introduce your topic in a straightforward manner. This study is about staring as a threat signal, commanding a person to hurt another person, the conflict between the interest of science and the interest of research subjects, people's attempts to explain why things happen. Just say it: There will be plenty of time in the next paragraph to show that you know that other important people have thought about the issue. "Just saying it" is of course extremely difficult and requires that you have a very clear idea about what "it" is. For that reason, sentences like this an their accompanying first paragraphs are often written last, after many tries, after the original first paragraph has been discarded. . . .

Note that the entire description of the problem need not be contained in a single sentence. Often it is more effective to take several sentences to lay out the problem in order to keep the first sentence from becoming overloaded with detail. . . .

3. *The example.* . . . Examples from the media, from literature, or from common experience can serve as vivid illustrations of the issue you have studied. . . . At the end of such an example, you sum up what it means psychologically and rephrase it as a research issue. . . .

4. *The question.* Your research was designed to answer a question. One of the most efficient ways of communicating to your reader what your question is is simply to ask

it. . . . When they see a question, most people will become curious and read at least the next sentence.

Develop the Background. Once the interesting phenomenon has been described, or the question raised, most writers provide a more detailed "state of the art" summary of relevant research. Commonly referred to as the *literature review,* this part of the introduction informs the reader of the contributions of other researchers. One of the hazards of being teachers and scholars is that we have a tendency to display our erudition, sometimes inappropriately. Thus, in effect, if a student or a colleague asks us the time, it is tempting to expound on a discussion of time zones and the history of time telling from the sundial to digital quartz watches. Colleagues and students may occasionally tolerate such detours, but readers almost never will. Although it is important to acknowledge the ideas and findings of other investigators, it is *more* important to limit discussion to research that is germane to the current study; research that is only tangentially related should be omitted.

Controversy is not uncommon in social psychology and makes the field exciting. Indeed, the purpose of many studies is to reconcile conflicting findings in the literature. Controversial issues should be treated evenhandedly. This is *not* to say that writers should withhold their informed opinions on an issue. However, if there are studies that conflict with other research results, or with the writer's hypothesis, they should be noted. The literature review is just that: a summary of our current state of knowledge vis-à-vis a particular question or problem, not a newspaper editorial.

State the Purpose of the Study. After the question has been posed, and after relevant literature has been reviewed, the writer sets the stage for the study that follows. By reviewing the literature, you have moved from describing what the issue is to how psychologists have studied it. Thus, it should be relatively easy to move to a summary of where we stand on this issue *in psychology* and to a somewhat more operational version of the question that was posed in general terms at the outset. This section of the introduction—seldom more

than a paragraph or two—provides for a smooth transition to the Method section that follows. One need not provide an exhaustive list of hypotheses 1, 2, 3, and 4, but one *should* provide a brief description of the study and a rationale for it. This brief overview is designed to familiarize readers with the specific question the study was designed to answer, the independent and dependent variables used, the design, and the procedure employed. In addition, a brief rationale is designed to convince readers that the question was worth asking in the first place.

Method

If the introduction establishes the underlying theme of the article, the Method section establishes the cast of characters and the plot line. That is, the Method section describes in detail the nuts and bolts of how the study was conducted. Who were the subjects? What did they experience? What was the setting like? How was the treatment administered? How was the dependent variable measured? How were subjects debriefed?

The Method section is for the most part a straightforward narrative that moves along in chronological order (with occasional digressions to describe the measuring instruments or special protections against bias or other features that are important in your particular research). The challenge of moving from general propositions to specific events or vice versa—that has to be faced in the Introduction and Discussion sections—is largely irrelevant here. Instead, the main challenge is to find a place to present detailed descriptions of those aspects of the study only you as the experimenter know about (e.g., the reliability of measures, pretest results, precautions against bias) without losing the flow of the events as they were experienced by the subjects.

Many authors write the Method section first, sometimes before the data have been completely analyzed. The story told in the introduction may depend on the actual results, but the Method section requires few modifications, even if the results are unexpected. Also, it is easiest to write a vivid, accurate description of the method if it is done shortly after the experiment is actually run.

The Method section is typically divided into several subsections, as described below.

Overview of Method and Design. Unless the design is very simple, it is often a good idea to begin the Method section with an overview so that the reader becomes familiar with the design (i.e., what conditions were run), with the basic empirical realizations of the independent variable(s) and major dependent variable(s), and often with the purpose of the experiment as described to the subject. This is like a road map that keeps the reader from getting lost in a maze of details. The overview can be very brief, almost telegraphic, but it gives the reader a framework to keep in mind while reading through the details of the procedure.

For example: "Subjects, believing that they were participating in a study of ESP, listened to persuasive arguments about political issues. We instructed half the subjects to concentrate on the content of the arguments and half to concentrate on the speaker's style. In addition, half the arguments were about topics that were highly relevant to the subjects' own lives, while the other half were peripheral. Subjects' heart rates were measured while they listened, and their memory for the arguments was measured a week later." In but four sentences, the reader is informed that a 2 x 2 factorial design was used, and that there were two dependent variables in the study.

Subjects. This subsection—typically no longer than a paragraph or two—is designed to describe participants. Who served as subjects? Was there any particular reason for choosing this kind of person for the experiment? How many subjects were there? How were they selected? Were they paid? Did any subjects fail to complete the study? If so, why? To which experimental conditions were they assigned? It is also useful to describe relevant subject demographic characteristics such as age, institutional affiliation, and gender. This section is also a good place to note relevant information about the experimenter(s).

Apparatus (or Materials). In some experiments, usually in the more biological areas of psychology, researchers include a special subsection describing the equipment used in the research: the make and model number of the polygraph, staining techniques, and particularly, any novel hardware designed for the particular study. A special subsection on apparatus rarely makes sense in the write-up of a social psychological study: first, because social psychologists seldom use complex equipment and second, and more important, because describing the equipment typically makes more sense as part of the explanation of the treatment, procedure, or measures. Thus, if the treatment is embedded in a computer game, it may be confusing to try to describe the computer program before describing the treatment itself. If unfamiliar instruments are used to measure the dependent variable, they are best described in the dependent variable subsection, along with their reliabilities.

Occasionally, the main purpose of the study is to present some new measuring device, such as a personality test, and to provide some evidence of its validity. In this case, a special section on the new test or method *does* make sense.

Procedure. The Procedure subsection provides a concrete, step-by-step description of how the experiment was executed. The reader already has an overview of the design; at this point the clearest way to proceed is to lead readers through the experiment as if they were subjects. What did you say to the subject about the purpose of the study? How did you explain what the tasks would involve? Your aim is to give readers a feel for what the experience was like for the subjects, so that readers can decide for themselves whether the procedures made sense and whether the events were engaging and meaningful. Readers should have enough information to judge whether the experimenter's conclusions about the subjects' interpretations of events and the meaning of their behaviors seem justifiable.

Often—especially in experiments with several independent variables—it is a good idea to write a brief subsection around each independent variable, and to place these subsections where they occur, chronologically, in the procedure.

. . .This technique makes a rather complex experiment easy to understand, and allows the authors to describe the actual events in great detail in a well-organized way; thus the reader does not lose sight of the design as a whole or of the point of the events.

Within each subsection, it is often a good idea to describe any verbal treatments verbatim. This makes it possible for readers to evaluate the adequacy of the experimental procedures, and to carry out an accurate replication if they so desire. It also makes the Method section vivid and interesting.

. . . It is a good idea to use concrete labels for each operation, variable, and treatment; this makes it easier for the reader to follow. . . . The Procedure subsection should be about concrete events such as reading dirty words aloud, *not* about abstractions such as cognitive dissonance. The connection between constructs and their empirical realizations can be made in the Discussion section; in the Procedure section of the article, readers want only a clear, concrete description of *what* was done and *how* it was done.

Likewise, when you get to the part of the procedure where you took your measures, use a subheading to alert the reader that you are now about to describe your important dependent variables, unless you have a very simple study with a single very simple measure. Here again, you should set off measures of different dependent variables with subheadings (e.g., Ratings of Defendants, Recommended Length of Sentence), and provide very specific descriptions of the behaviors you measured and/or actual examples of questionnaire items. Again, you thus enable the reader not only to evaluate your study, but also to see what it looked like from the point of view of the subject.

Information about the reliability of the measures, results of pretests, and equipment used can go here, where it fits the best. (Pretests of the independent variables, of course, should be described in the independent variable subsection.) It is often a good idea to describe the results of any measures designed as manipulation checks here (or in the independent variable section), rather than clutter up the Results section with methodological underbrush.

Precautions against Bias. At some point you should report any precautions to eliminate experimenter bias, reduce demand characteristics, or control for artifactual effects. Often you can work these precautions in at the appropriate point during the narrative: "Experimenter 1, blind to the subject's expectations about her partner, explained how to play the game." This method has both elegance and modesty to recommend it, but if your precautions are numerous or complex, it may be difficult to achieve. If several experimenters were used, it may be wise, when you give your overview of the design, to introduce them and to explain which ones were blind to which aspect of the procedure. If precautions against bias were elaborate, you may need to add a separate subsection after the Procedure subsection, entitled "Precautions against bias." At any rate, whatever precautions you took to rule out artifactual influences should be described in the Method section. . . .

Results

This section of the journal article summarizes the data collected, and the statistical techniques used to analyze them. When most people think of the Results section, they think of descriptive and inferential statistics, tables, and figures. And rightly so. However, as Bem (1987) notes, it is important to remember that all the information contained therein (group means, significance levels, and so on) are joined by a narrative. Tables and figures, for example, are designed to *supplement* the text; they cannot do the job of a good writer in communicating research findings.

Ideally, you want to launch into your major results as soon as possible. You have posed your question and explained how you turned it into an experiment; now the reader will be curious to know what the answer is. Often, however, you will have a number of statistical analyses that have more to do with the success of your procedures than with the answer to your question: the reliabilities of your scales or your observers, the effects of methodologically important but conceptually dull variables such as the four experimenters who ran the study, the three orders of questions used in the questionnaire, the consequences of discarding data from subjects who were dropped because they were suspicious or somehow weird, the results of your manipulation checks, the combination of various measures into a composite index measures, and so on. Beginning the Results section with a catalog of digressions from the actual results is bound to be frustrating to many readers. However, most of this information should be presented *somewhere,* and the beginning of the Results section is a common choice. . . .

Particularly with very complex analyses, you may not be able to move *all* the preliminaries away from the Results section, but it is a good idea to try. For those that remain, you might begin with a subheading such as "Preliminary Analyses" that alerts the reader that the *real* story is not yet beginning.

After the preliminaries are out of the way, writers can proceed to the main analyses. It is often useful to provide readers with an organizational overview of the analyses that follow: For example, in what order will the results be discussed? If the analytic techniques are common and familiar to most readers, an exhaustive description of the statistical procedures is unnecessary. For example, it is probably sufficient to write, "The significance of the difference between the group means was determined by an independent samples t-test"; one need not inundate readers with the theory and assumptions underlying the use of the general linear model. However, when reading about more esoteric or complicated analyses, readers often appreciate more extensive descriptions of the statistical tests, rationales for them, and references to more detailed descriptions of those techniques. If very few readers are likely to follow the statistical discussion, a long footnote or a special "statistical paragraph" may be useful.

When actually describing the data, describe the forest first, then the trees (Bem, 1987). That is, begin with the most important findings, and then proceed to secondary findings such as qualifications, elaborations, or variables of tangential interest. Throughout this section, it is important to sum up periodically and to tie the numbers to the questions you are asking. . . .

Tables and figures are valuable additions to the text, but they should not be used indiscriminately. They *can* be used to emphasize a simple but important point made in the text but are *more* useful in graphically illustrating complicated findings such as interactions among variables. Whenever possible, tables or graphs should tell their own story; readers should be able to read the title of the table or graph, look at the numbers, and immediately grasp what the data reveal. Thus, titles should be complete—even if they do look a little long—and groups should be identified with labels first used in the Method section. Notes at the bottom of the tables or figures can also remind readers what the numbers mean: *"Note.* Subject ratings of the discussion could range from a low of '0' to a high of '15.'" . . .

In summary, readers need not roll their eyes or take a deep breath before tackling the Results section. It is the writer's responsibility to keep those eyes from rolling. When the forest precedes the trees and prose precedes numbers and statistics, when the writer provides a preview of coming attractions and frequent summaries, *and* when the writer makes appropriate use of tables, figures, and concrete examples, this section can be as interesting, clear, and engaging as the rest of the article.

Discussion

After results are summarized, writers are in a position to discuss their implications, especially as they relate to the original problem, question, or hypothesis. If the Method and Results sections are the place for "Just the facts, Ma'am," the Discussion section is the place for inferences and speculations, for placing results in a larger perspective, and, occasionally, for sticking one's neck out. Presumably, you have thought more about your study and the meaning of its results than any other human being, and the Discussion section allows you some scope to communicate those thoughts.

In a well-written journal article, this concluding section becomes a mirror image of the introduction. That is, the Discussion section typically starts with a clear and succinct description of what was learned in this particular study.

What hypotheses were supported? What hypotheses were not supported? Answers to these questions should be more than a reiteration of conclusions reached in the Results section. The Discussion section provides for a description of what statistically significant differences *mean* in more general terms. That is, the writer moves from a discussion of relationships among variables described in the Results section of the article to a discussion of relationships among abstract concepts.

After the results of the study have been summarized and interpreted, it is appropriate to compare results with those obtained by other investigators. In what ways has this study advanced our knowledge? Are the implications of this study at odds with previous investigations? If so, it is useful to speculate about the sources of surprising or atypical findings. Might they be accounted for by methodological shortcomings, by a different subject population, or by specifics of the experimental procedure? Writers need not obsess on every potential flaw or shortcoming. If you are surprised or puzzled by atypical or unexpected findings, say so, and invite readers to speculate as to their source; you need not expose readers to a comprehensive list of convoluted speculations, afterthoughts, and apologies. Too many Discussion sections spend far too much time in profitless obsession over the gaps and failures of the study at the expense of a clear consideration of its successes.

No single study answers all questions related to an issue or problem. Data often reveal patterns—whether or not the results support one's original hypotheses—that suggest new research directions. The successes and pitfalls of the current study often point to better ways to tackle a research problem. Alternative experimental procedures, alternative empirical realizations, even alternative methods of research might be suggested as useful means of advancing our knowledge.

As we first pointed out in this chapter, the writer's task is to convince readers—editors, reviewers, students, psychologists and nonpsychologists alike—that the study was worth doing in the first place. Thus, although it might appear magnanimous, humble, or insightful to point to better ways to answer the question or better questions to ask, as Bem (1987, p. 188) notes, it is preferable to "end with a bang, not a whimper." Just what has the researcher contributed that others haven't? What do readers know now about human social behavior that they didn't know before they read the article? What implications do these findings have for social psychological theorizing, our understanding of the human condition, world peace, or the price of beans in Bulgaria?

After Writing the Article

It's done! After hours and hours of writing, editing, and revising, and after putting the article down for a week or two or three and picking it up again to edit and revise *some more,* is it at last time to submit the article to a social psychological journal? Not quite....[I]t is important to give a "final" draft to friends and colleagues to read with a critical eye. It is preferable that they have experience in writing for social psychological journals, but they need not be experts in the specific research area addressed by the article. Indeed, as useful critics of the writing itself, it is probably better if they are *not* well acquainted with the area, for the best index of the clarity of an article is the ease with which nonexperts understand the concepts and follow the line of reasoning. . . .

References

Asch, S. (1952). Effects of group pressure on the modification and distortion of judgments. In G. E. Swanson, T. M. Newcomb, and E. L. Hartley (Eds.), *Readings in social psychology.* New York: Holt, Rhinehart, and Winston.

Bem, D. J. (1987). Writing the empirical journal article. In M. P. Zanna and J. M. Darley (Eds.), *The compleat academic* (pp. 171-201). New York: Random House.

Berthoff, A. (1988). *Forming, thinking, writing* (2nd ed.). Portsmouth, NH: Boynton/Cook Publishers.

Strunk, W., Jr., & White, E. B. (1979). *The elements of style* (3rd ed.). New York: Macmillan.

Walster, E., Aronson, E., & Brown, Z. (1966). Choosing to suffer as a consequence of expecting to suffer: An unexpected finding. *Journal of Experimental Social Psychology, 2,* 400-406.

Zinsser, W. (1985). *On writing well: An informed guide to writing nonfiction* (3rd ed.). New York: Harper and Row.

Guidelines For Avoiding Sexism In Psychological Research: A Report Of The Ad Hoc Committee On Nonsexist Research

Florence Denmark, Nancy Felipe Russo, Irene Hanson Frieze, and Jeri A. Sechzer

This article is intended primarily for psychologists and for students of psychology who are developing skills in research design and methodology. It has become clear that much research on human and animal behavior incorporates a variety of forms of sexism. Such sexism introduces unwanted bias into the research. . . .

Whenever values and assumption—whether related to gender, race, ethnicity, disability, sexual orientation, or socioeconomic status—affect the research process, bias can operate. This article focuses on gender, but the principles illustrated here apply to other forms of bias as well.

This article provides examples of common avoidable problems as well as suggestions for eliminating such bias.

1. Question Formulation

[a.] Problem: Gender stereotypes that are associated with the topic being studied can bias question formulation and research outcomes.

i. Example: Some studies have defined leadership only in terms of dominance, aggression, and other styles that emphasize characteristics congruent with a male stereotype.

ii. Correction: Recognize the existence of a range of leadership styles, including those that emphasize egalitarian relationships, negotiation, conflict resolution, and consideration of others. The limits of any definition that is used should be specified. . . .

[b.] Problem: It is assumed that topics relevant to white males are more important and more "basic" to study, whereas topics related to white or ethnic minority females or ethnic minority males are seen as more specialized or applied.

i. Example: A topic such as the effect of television on the modeling of aggression in boys is considered as basic research whereas research on the psychological correlates of

pregnancy or menopause is seen as specialized or applied.

ii. Correction: Definitions of problems as basic or specialized should not be made on the basis of relevance to a particular group. When topics are of most interest to a particular group, this should be explicitly noted.

[c.] Problem: In formulating questions, the review of previous research is insensitive to biases in the selection of research participants or other methodological problems, leading to biased questions.

i. Example: The hypothesis that aggressive stimuli enhance sexual arousal is based on results that have been found only for male research participants.

ii. Correction: When building on previous research, formulate the question so that findings can be generalized to a heterogeneous sample or clearly state the limitations of generalizations.

2. Research Methods

[a.] Problem: The selection of research participants is based on stereotypic assumptions and does not allow for generalizations to other groups.

i. Example: On the basis of stereotypes about who should be responsible for contraception, only females are looked at in studies of contraception.

ii. Correction: Both sexes should be studied before conclusions are drawn about the factors that determine use of contraception.

[b.] Problem: The selection of research participants is limited to one sex on the basis of convenience.

i. Example: Male animals are often preferred as subjects in experiments because the estrous cycle in females disrupts responses in certain types of behavioral and biological tests. Although it may be appropriate to use animals of one sex, generalizations of results to both sexes may not always be justified.

ii. Correction: Use research participants of both sexes wherever feasible so that results can apply to males and females, and any gender differences can be noted. When subjects of only one sex are used, the researcher should indicate why this is appropriate if it is not evident by the nature of the study itself (e.g., maternal behavior; studies of male dominance, endangered species when only one sex is accessible, etc.).

[c.] Problem: When unanticipated gender differences emerge in research, researchers drop the female research participants from the analysis, rather than examining the reasons underlying the sex difference and redesigning the study.

i. Example: For years, studies of achievement behavior did not include females because in the early studies validating the theory of achievement motivation, females did not act in the expected ways.

ii. Correction: Report the gender differences as a finding and develop hypotheses and research designs to explain such differences within the theory.

[d.] Problem: The sex and race of research participants, experimenters, confederates, and persons in direct contact with the participants are not specified. Potential interactions of sex and race or other variables may create unexplained variance.

i. Example: More helping behavior by males rather than females is found in studies that use a young female confederate that needs help. Such results may be a function of the sex of the confederate or an interaction of participant and confederate rather than a difference due to the gender of the research participants.

ii. Correction: Control for or vary sex and race of persons involved in the research. Try to include experimenters and participants who are members of racial minorities. At a minimum, specify the sex and race of everyone involved in the research.

[e.] Problem: Gender is confounded with other participant variables such as job status, age, or race.

i. Example: In studies of job turnover, women are found to have higher rates of turnover than men (supposedly because of less commitment to their jobs). Other research has found that turnover is correlated with job status such that those with lower status jobs

quit more. When job status is controlled, there is no gender difference in job turnover.

ii. Correction: Select an appropriate comparison sample. For example, before asserting that differences in groups of males and females are due to gender, control for other major explanatory factors.

[f.] Problem: Selection of gender-stereotyped measures differentially affects performance.

i. Example: In studies of mathematical ability, the content of the mathematics problems (e.g., computation of baseball scores versus cooking ingredients) produced gender differences that were not found when the content was unassociated with gender-related interests.

ii. Correction: Select measures that are controlled for gender-related content or include this as a design variable. . . .

3. Data Analysis and Interpretation

[a.] Problem: Serendipitous gender differences are reported, but no report is made when differences are not found. Care must be taken to avoid giving a skewed image of the actual data.

i. Example: "In analyzing data, we found that males and females differed significantly on. . .."

ii. Correction: Any nonhypothesized sex or gender differences should be reported and the need for replication indicated to assure that the difference is not artifactual. When gender differences are not found and where such an observation is relevant, this too should be reported so that future research could confirm or disconfirm the lack of any nonhypothesized gender differences. . . .

[b.] Problem: Misleading implications of findings of gender differences are not addressed. Statistical significance is not clearly distinguished from the substantive significance.

i. Example: "The spatial ability scores of women in our sample are significantly lower than those of the men, at the .01 level." The reader is left to assume that perhaps women should not become architects or engineers.

ii. Correction: "The spatial ability scores of the women are significantly lower than those of the men, at the .01 level. Successful architects score above 32 on our spatial ability test. . .; engineers score above 31. . . . Twelve percent of the women and 16% of the men in our sample score above 31; 11% of the women and 15% of the men score above 32."

4. Conclusions

[a.] Problem: Results based on one sex are generalized to both.

i. Example: Threshold measurements in shock sensitivity for rats have been standardized for males, but are often generalized to both sexes.

ii. Correction: There should be empirically determined norms for male and female study participants that reflect differences in weight, body fat, and so on.

[b.] Problem: Gender differences in performance on a specific task or behavior are interpreted as reflecting gender differences in a global ability or characteristic.

i. Example: It is concluded that male subjects are more field independent than females, even though this is found only for embedded figures tests and rod and frame tests and not for tactile and auditory measures.

ii. Correction: Specify that males score higher on embedded figures tests or rod and flame tests, rather than making general statements about cognitive styles.

[c.] Problem: Evaluative labeling is used for results.

i. Example: Male aggressiveness is used as the standard of acceptability. Females are described as unaggressive or submissive.

ii. Correction: Use neutral, objective descriptions such as "the mean score for the aggression measure was higher for males than females."

Suggestions for Additional Reading

Caplan, P. J., MacPherson, G. M., & Tobin, P. (1985). Do sex-related differences in spatial abilities exist? A multilevel critique with new data. *American Psychologist, 40,* 786-799.

Eagly, A. H., & Carli, L. L. (1981). Sex of researchers and sex-typed communications as determinants of sex differences in influencability: A meta-analysis of social influence studies. *Psychological Bulletin, 90,* 1-20.

Eagly, A. H., & Crowley, M. (1986). Gender and helping behavior: A meta-analytic review of the social psychological literature. *Psychological Bulletin, 100,* 282-308.

McHugh, M. C., Koeske, R. D., & Frieze, I. H. (1986). Issues to consider in conducting nonsexist psychology: A review with recommendations. *American Psychologist, 41,* 879-890.

Wallston, B. S., & Grady, K. E. (1985). Integrating the feminist critique and the crisis in social psychology: Another look at research methods. In V. E. O'Leary, R. K. Unger, & B. S. Wallston (Eds.), *Women, gender, and social psychology.* Hillsdale, NJ: Erlbaum.

Wittig, M. A. (1985). Metatheoretical dilemmas in the psychology of gender. *American Psychologist, 40,* 800-811.

Everyone Can Write Better (And You Are No Exception)
Herbert H. Clark

Everyone can write better, and you are no exception. These tips illustrate a variety of common faults in academic writing.

Principle 1: Don't be pedantic.

1. Never write a word or phrase you wouldn't use in conversation.

Would you ever say aloud to anyone "the implications of these findings concern a schema" or "each of the two groups above" or "irrefutable schema-inconsistent information" or "these two seemingly contradictory components of the human organism" or "the former is more important than the latter"? I'll wager you wouldn't. If not, get rid of them. Not that writing is merely printed conversation. It isn't. Because you can edit, written language can be much more concise and precise, and so it also tends to be more formal. But it is easy to overdo the formality.... Always ask yourself, "Could I say this in a conversation or a lecture?" If the answer is no, start again.

2. Get rid of excess verbiage.

(As Mark Twain put it, "Eschew surplusage.") Excess verbiage detracts from what you have to say. Too often it puts on full display how little you have to say....

3. Never use a heavy, uncommon, or academic word or phrase where a lighter, commoner, or plainer word would do.

In academic writing, you need a certain number of technical terms, such as "schema," "mutual exclusivity," "situational," "causal attributions," and "availability," simply to make your theories clear. But these terms also make your writing hard to read. Don't compound the problem by using pedantic words and phrases where you don't need to. Here are some common offenders (many cribbed from Flesch):

Pedantic:	Replace With:
Verbs:	
acquire	get, gain
attempt, endeavor	try
concerns	is about
constitutes	is
continue	keep up
employ	use
exists	is
supplement	add to
utilize	use
Prepositions & conjunctions:	
along the lines of	like
as to	about
concerning	about, on
for the purpose of	for
for the reason that	because
from the point of view of	for
inasmuch as	because
in favor of	for, to
in order to	to
in accordance with	by, under
in the case of	if
in the event that	if
in the nature of	like
in the neighborhood of	about
in terms of	in, for
on the basis of	by
on the grounds that	since, because
prior to	before
regarding	about, on
with a view to	to
with reference to	about (or leave out)
with regard to	about (or leave out)
with the result that	so that
Connectives:	
accordingly	so
consequently	so
for this reason	so
furthermore	so
hence	so
in addition	besides, also
indeed	in fact
likewise	and, also
more specifically	for instance, for example
moreover	now, next
nevertheless	but, however
that is to say	in other words
thus	so
to be sure	of course
Other phrases that can often be omitted:	
concerned	
involved	
respectively	

Most of the pedantic expressions you will get rid of by Rule 1, since they are ones you are unlikely ever to use in conversation. Still, you *can* use any of these expressions, but before you do, make sure you have a good reason. Never put readers to extra work without a good reason.

4. *Divide complicated sentences into more than one sentence.*

Again, what you are writing about is hard enough to understand without overly complicated sentences. Get rid of them by cutting them in half or in thirds, as I have done for this example.

> Initially illusions were construed as an embarrassing error on the part of the perceiver. Later they came instead to be a more powerful and exquisitely sensitive research instrument, and still later, the very hallmark of the human being's tremendous sophistication in "creating" knowledge and actively construing reality.

This still is pretty awful. Take out the junk and here's what you get:

> At first, illusions were treated merely as embarrassing errors by the perceiver. Later, they were viewed as a powerful research instrument and, still later, as the hallmark of human sophistication in creating knowledge and construing reality.

Once you have a clear sentence, you can decide whether it is what you want to say.

5. *Root out unneeded adjectives and adverbs.*

Adjectives and adverbs weigh down a sentence faster than most other expressions, so use them sparingly. Indeed, many are redundant, and others put readers to more work than they are worth. In the passage I just revised, I got rid of "more," "exquisitely sensitive," "very," "tremendous," and "actively." The commonest offenders are: intensifiers like "very" and "extremely," which usually lead to overstatement; evaluative adjectives like *exciting, surprising, important,* and *interesting*, which presume on the reader's own judgment; and adverbs like "basically," "essentially," and "simply," which just waste space. There are many more....

Principle 2: Make your writing lively.

Some approaches to writing lead naturally to lively prose, and others to deadly prose. Here are some ways of animating what you say.

6. *Center your writing, where possible, on people and what they do.*

Most academic writing is about abstract ideas, so it is hard to be concrete. But in psychology our natural subject matter is people and what they do. Putting them at the center should make it be easy to be concrete.

6'. *Do not, however, center your writing on previous researchers and what they did.*

It is all too easy to name one scholar after another and describe what they claimed, as in these two examples:

> Tversky and Kahneman (1983) review the literature in which people making certain decisions under uncertainty fail to take base-rates into account.

> Markman (1987) points out that the way young children succeed at acquiring the concepts that their language encodes so quickly is that they are limited in the kinds of hypotheses they consider.

Ordinarily you will want to focus on how people think and behave and *not* on what scholars have to say about this. You will undermine that purpose if you place the scholars in the subject position. In the examples just cited, the sentences are about Tversky and Kahneman, and about Markman, and they shouldn't be. Put the scholars in secondary locations, in subordinate clauses or in parentheses, as in these revisions:

> People making certain decisions under uncertainty fail to take base-rates into account (Tversky & Kahneman, 1983).

> How do children succeed at acquiring the concepts that their language encodes so quickly? According to Markman (1987), it is because they are limited in the kinds of hypotheses they consider.

7. *Prefer the active over the passive voice.*

Why? The active voice is usually more concrete. It forces you to make the subject explicit—compare "when information is integrated" with "when people integrate information"—and that makes the sentence more vivid. . . .

8. Do not begin sentences with the empty "it." An example:

> It is possible that subjects evaluate their answer's correctness by the ease with which they can generate reasons that support this answer.

Sentences like this are weak. They place what is important in a subordinate position. They are easy to revise, as in this example: "Subjects may evaluate their answer's correctness. . ."

9. In reporting data, describe your findings, not your statistics.
One of the banes of good writing in psychology is statistical jargon. . . .Ordinarily, we want to know about your findings, not about your analysis of variance, so you should organize your writing around those findings.

The idea is to organize your writing around your findings and to demote statistical talk to subordinate positions—subordinate clauses, parentheses, anywhere but prominent places. And get rid of as much jargon as you can. . . .

Principle 3: Be professional.

10. Avoid sexist language, but do so unobtrusively.
There is evidence that many people interpret the generic "he" (as in "Every student should pick up his exam before leaving") to refer to males and not to males and females. How can you avoid this bias? Here is *not* a way:

> For example, in the first stage a 3-year-old child scares him/herself while telling a story about a monster.

Expressions like "he/she" and "him/herself" are abominations. They are something you would never say aloud—the ultimate in pedantic language—and, worse, they call attention to themselves and the sexism they are trying to cure. That is no way to abolish sexism.

There are three ready solutions for most sexist language. The first is to use the plural, as in this sentence from the same paper:

In the third stage, children tend to stay in the fantasy, but act as they would in reality.

"Children . . . they" covers both sexes. The second is to introduce the actual sex of the person being described, as in this revision of the passage I cited:

> For example, in the first stage a 3-year-old girl might scare herself while telling a story about a monster.

Be sure that half of your examples use males and half use females. The final option is to use "he or she." This is a bit painful to the ear, but it *is* something we could say in a lecture or conversation.

11. Check your spelling.
Nothing looks more unprofessional than a paper, even a draft, with typos and misspellings. . . . Today, with spelling checkers on every computer, there is no excuse for misspellings.

12. Put your writing in the correct format.
Papers in the wrong format also look unprofessional. Check the *Publication Manual of the American Psychological Association* for proper formats for paragraphs, tables, footnotes, titles, abstracts, references, and figures. For many readers, a sloppy form can spoil a paper, and that reflects badly on you. Nowadays, with computers and their capabilities, there is also no excuse for bad formatting.

In writing, your goal is to communicate—to get your readers to understand what you are about. The advice I have offered is to help you do that more effectively. Writing well will take work, but the rewards are great. Half of doing science is writing, so until you write well, you will never be more than half a scientist.

Useful References

Flesch, R. (1949). *The art of readable writing.* New York: Collier.
Gowers, F. (1973). *The complete plain words,* revised by Bruce Fraser. London: Her Majesty's Stationery Office.
Stone, W., & Bell, J. (1983). *Prose style: A handbook for writers.* New York: McGraw-Hill.
Zinsser, W. (1980). *On writing well.* New York: Harper & Row.

✓ PROJECT A.1
Doing Library Research In Psychology

I.   Before you begin writing your research proposal, you need to start at the very beginning—deciding what you will study. This first project is designed to help familiarize you with the existing social psychological research that is relevant to your topic of interest. In this project, you will primarily search for and read psychological journal articles. Researchers typically publish their research findings in psychological journals, so these tend to be a good source of information about the types of questions that have been asked and the types of research that has been conducted. Researchers also publish their work in books, written by them, or in books that are collections of chapters by different authors. Journal articles and books are the two primary avenues through which researchers publish their work.

II.   Before you hit the library to find these journal articles and books, you first need to think about the topic you are interested in studying. At this point, you do not need to be specific, but you do need to have a general idea. To help you generate ideas, we suggest you skim the articles in the Workbook and focus on those articles that catch your attention. Once you have narrowed in on a couple of general topics, for example, the influence of gender role expectations on female college students, you are ready to go to the library.

III.   There are several strategies for finding articles about your topic. First, each article in the Workbook has references at the end. These references are to articles and books that describe research relevant to the topic of the article in the Workbook. Referring to our example, you could look at Eccles' article on gender roles to see which articles she cites in her reference section.   Then, pick out several articles and books that look especially interesting to you.

IV.   Your reference librarian can help you find psychological articles in your library. Generally, articles are published in journals, and the volumes of the journals are typically on the shelves in your library. You can find the call number of the journals using your library catalog.

V.   A second strategy for finding articles on your topic is to use an electronic database called either *PsychLit* or *PsychInfo*. These databases include summaries and titles of articles, and you can search for articles on your topic by typing in key words. With our example, you might search for articles on "gender roles" and "college students." Your search will often yield many articles, so you will have to skim the summaries to see which are most interesting to you. After you identify the articles you want, look in *PsychLit* or *PsychInfo* to determine the journals your targeted articles are in, the volume or year of the journals, and then retrieve those volumes of the journals from your library shelves. Your reference librarian will be able to help you use *PsychLit* or *PsychInfo* for the first time, and they will often have help sheets that assist you with the terms you can use to most efficiently find articles on your topic.

VI.   A third strategy is to use your library's general catalog for books on your topic. These books are sometimes collections of chapters written by different authors, so you may sometimes be interested in only one chapter of the book.

VII.   These strategies will yield many sources of information, in fact, too many for you to read. You will need to select carefully those that look most relevant to your topic. If you still haven't narrowed in on a specific topic, skimming the many sources of information will help give you an idea of the types of questions that have been asked and the kinds of research that has been conducted on your general topic. From these, you will want to start to narrow in on several articles and books that look most interesting to you. At this point, you should re-read the article "On Reading the Research Literature" to help you with this process.

VIII.   For this project, then, you will turn in a list of five references applicable to your general topic. Before you write down these references, though, there is a specific format for you to follow in listing these references. You will list them in the same format as the references in the "Sources" section of this Workbook. As that model illustrates, for journal articles, the authors' names go first, then the year, the journal article title, the journal title, the volume of the journal, and the pages of the journal. If you are citing books or chapters from books, you will also find models for these in the "Sources" section. For more information on the proper way to cite your sources in psychology, please see the Fourth Edition of the *American Psychological Association Publication Manual*.

TOPIC: _____

_____

_____

_____

_____

REFERENCE 1: _____

_____

REFERENCE 2: _____

_____

REFERENCE 3: _____

_____

REFERENCE 4:

_____

_____

REFERENCE 5:

_____

_____

✓ PROJECT A.2
The Hypothesis

I.   You began your research project by exploring some of the social psychological literature that dealt with your area of interest. Now, you need to become clearer about what your interest is by developing a specific question. The question you settle on and will attempt to answer in your experiment will form the basis of your experimental hypothesis.

II.   In a hypothesis, you state your question so that it makes a prediction about what you think will happen in your experiment. You may be interested in the relationship between self-esteem and group identification. You may predict that people who are highly identified with a social group will have higher collective self-esteem than will those who are less identified. The point is to take your initial question and use it to develop a testable prediction.

III.   Your initial question and the hypothesis that follows from it can come from several sources. Theories are one of the most available of these sources. A theory is an organizing set of principles and predictions that is used to explain behaviors and events. Theories link individual observations to one another, allowing us to have a more general view of what is happening. You may have noticed over the course of a season that you and your roommates, who are big fans of your school's women's basketball team, are affected by whether or not your team wins or loses a big game. By linking these observations together, you may begin to create a theory of the relationship between self-esteem and social identity. This theory then permits you to propose specific and testable questions about the relationship between self-esteem and social identity and to make predictions based on those questions.

IV.   Hypotheses can also arise from existing research. Researchers will often generate questions and predictions after reading another person's or their own previous research. You may have already experienced this, deriving predictions from some of the research you have read in this Workbook. For example, an article may include speculations that there is a link between self-esteem and socioeconomic status. You might then generate a hypothesis predicting that socioeconomic status will be a factor in how well an individual copes with a threat to their self-esteem.

V.   More information about the hypothesis can be found in the articles "An Introduction to Experiments" in the section on Independent and Dependent Variables (on pp. 348-350) and "On Reading the Research Literature" in the section on the Introduction (p. 361).

VI. For this project, you will generate the hypothesis that will be the basis of the study in your research proposal. Use the lines below to write out your experimental hypothesis. Remember it should be stated as a testable prediction about what will happen in your experiment. Please turn in your written hypothesis to your instructor.

HYPOTHESIS:

_____

_____

_____

_____

_____

_____

_____

_____

✓ PROJECT A.3
The Introduction

I. In the last project, you created a hypothesis for your research proposal, which is a prediction about the outcome of an experiment that often involves specific predictions about the relationship between two or more variables. You also have done a literature search for published studies that have examined the area in which you are interested. The next step you will take is to write the Introduction section. In this step, you will pull together the literature you have read (this may require you to do more library research now that you have narrowed in on your topic) and the ideas you have about your study into a coherent and persuasive section that provides the context for your specific study.

II. In this first section of the paper, you should introduce the problem and describe the research strategy. The Introduction should include a brief literature review of relevant work, emphasizing pertinent findings or theories that contributed to your interest in the problem. After introducing the problem and relevant background, describe the rationale for developing your particular hypothesis, state your hypothesis, and summarize what you will do to test your hypothesis. Since this is the first section of your written proposal, it does not require a heading. The page length of your Introduction will be affected by the overall page length of the proposal as required by your instructor. As a general rule, the Introduction is approximately one-fourth of the overall paper length.

III. More information about the Introduction can be found in the articles "Writing It Up" (on pp. 369-371) and "On Reading the Research Literature" (p. 361) in this Appendix. Also review and follow the writing suggestions by Clark in "Everyone Can Write...." Please review these sections before you write your Introduction. After you type your Introduction, please turn it in to your instructor.

✓ PROJECT A.4
Methodology: The Nuts And Bolts Of The Study

I.   This section of your paper describes in detail how you will carry out your study. The Method section includes descriptions of the *Participants*, the *Materials* you will use, and the *Procedure* you will employ for your data collection. In your *Participants* subsection you should describe who will participate in the study, how they will be selected, and how many will participate. In your *Materials* subsection you should describe the apparatus or materials you will use to gather your data. In your *Procedure* subsection you should describe exactly what you will do to execute your project. Describe the specific experimental or observational conditions under which you will collect the data. In other words, this section should be a detailed description of *what* you will do and *how* you will it. It should be written so that someone who was not previously familiar with your experiment could carry it out without your help. Begin this section with a centered heading (Method), and include in it left-justified subsections for *Participants* (the term "subjects" is no longer used, though the articles in this Workbook often use it), *Materials,* and *Procedure.*

II.   More information about the Method section can be found in the articles "Writing It Up" (on pp. 371-373) and "On Reading the Research Literature" (pp. 361-362). Also review and follow the writing suggestions by Clark in "Everyone Can Write. . . ." Please review these sections before you write your Method section. After you type it, please turn this section in to your instructor. If you have received comments on your Introduction, please revise it and turn in the revised Introduction with your Method section.

✓ PROJECT A.5
Expected Results

I.   The Expected Results section describes all of the results you would find if you actually conducted your study. Do not discuss the implications of these results in this section, only report them. Begin the Expected Results section with a centered heading (Expected Results).

II. As before, more information about this section can be found in the articles "Writing It Up" (on pp. 373-374) and "On Reading the Research Literature" (p. 363). While both of these articles discuss the results of studies that have been conducted, the information in them should serve as a guide for the information you include in your Expected Results section.

III. After you type it, please turn this section in to your instructor. If you have received comments on the previous sections of your proposal, your instructor may request that you revise these sections before turning in the Expected Results section. You would then turn in your revised Introduction and Method sections with your newly drafted Expected Results section.

✓ PROJECT A.6
Discussing The Implications And Limitations

I.   In the Discussion section you will interpret your expected results in light of your original hypothesis. In this section, you should evaluate and qualify your expected results, as well as draw inferences from them. Remark on strengths and shortcomings of your study, and comment on similarities and differences between your expected findings and those of others who have researched a similar question. Guidelines from the American Psychological Association (APA) say that a Discussion section should be guided by the following questions: What have I contributed here? How has this study helped to resolve the original problem? What conclusions and theoretical implications could I draw from the expected results of this study? Begin the Discussion section with a centered heading (Discussion).

II.   As with the other sections, more information about this section can be found in the articles "Writing It Up" (on pp. 374-375) and "On Reading the Research Literature" (pp. 363-364).

III.   After you type it, please turn this section in to your instructor. If you have received comments on the previous sections of your proposal, your instructor may request that you revise these sections before turning in the Discussion section. You would then turn in your revised Introduction, Method, and Expected Results sections with your newly drafted Discussion section.

IV.   Finally, now that you have written all of the sections of your proposal, it is very important that you REVISE your entire proposal, making sure the sections fit together well, rewriting awkward sentences, and restructuring unclear sections. As stated in the "Writing It Up" article, have a friend look over your paper to help point out parts that are unclear. A final note—review the writing tips by Clark and make the appropriate changes in your paper.

ACKNOWLEDGMENTS

Chapter 1: Introduction to the Social Psychology of Gender, Race, and Ethnicity

Reprinted by permission of The Feminist Press of The City University of New York, from Ruth Hubbard, "Race and Sex as Biological Categories," in *Challenging Racism and Sexism: Alternatives to Genetic Explanations,* edited by Ethel Tobach and Betty Rosoff. Copyright ©1994 by Ruth Hubbard.

Excerpted from Phinney, J. S. (1996). When we talk about American ethnic groups, what do we mean? *American Psychologist, 51,* 918-927. Copyright ©1996 by The American Psychological Association. Reprinted by permission.

Excerpted from Deaux, K. (1993). Commentary: Sorry, wrong number—A reply to Gentile's call. *Psychological Science, 4,* 125-126. Copyright ©1998 by Blackwell Publishers. Reprinted by permission.

Excerpted from Caplan, P. J., & Caplan, J. B. (1994). *Thinking critically about research on sex and gender* (pp. 7-9). New York: Harper Collins College Publishers. Copyright ©1994 by Harper Collins College Publishers. Reprinted by permission of Addison-Wesley Educational Publishers, Inc.

Excerpted from Graham, S. (1992). "Most of the subjects were white and middle class": Trends in published research on African Americans in selected APA journals, 1970-1989. *American Psychologist, 47,* 629-639. Copyright ©1992 by The American Psychological Association. Reprinted by permission.

Excerpted from King, M. L., Jr. (1963). The role of the behavioral scientist in the civil rights movement. *American Psychologist, 23,* 180-186. Copyright ©1963 by The American Psychological Association. Reprinted by permission.

Chapter 2: The Power of Groups

From Jones, R. (1981). The Third Wave. In *No Substitute for Madness* (pp. 3-23). Covelo, CA: Island Press. Copyright ©1981 by Island Press. Reprinted by permission.

Excerpted from Tajfel, H., & Turner, J. C. (1986). The social identity theory of intergroup behavior. In S. Worchel & W. G. Austin (Eds.), *Psychology of Intergroup Relations* (pp. 7-24). Chicago: Nelson-Hall. Copyright ©1986 by Nelson-Hall. Reprinted by permission.

Excerpted from Saenz, D. S. (1994). Token status and problem-solving deficits: Detrimental effects of distinctiveness and performance monitoring. *Social Cognition, 12,* 61-74. Copyright ©1994 by Guilford Press. Reprinted with permission.

From *People: Psychology from a Cultural Perspective, 1st edition* by D. Matsumoto ©1994. Reprinted with permission of Wadsworth Publishing, a division of International Publishing. Fax 800 730-2215.

Chapter 3: Creating Cooperation through Group Processes

From Aronson, E., Wilson, T. D., & Akert, R. M. (1997). *Social Psychology.* New York: Longman. Copyright ©1997 by Longman Press. Reprinted by permission.

From Gaertner, S. L., Dovidio, J. F., & Bachman, B. A. (1996). Revisiting the contact hypothesis: The induction of a common ingroup identity. *International Journal of Intercultural Relations, 20,* 271-290. Copyright ©1996 by Elsevier Science Ltd. Reprinted by permission of author.

Excerpted from Kelman, H. C. (1997). Group processes in the resolution of international conflicts: Experiences from the Israeli-Palestinian case. *American Psychologist, 52,* 212-220. Copyright ©1997 by The American Psychological Association. Reprinted by permission.

Chapter 4: Who Am I? Gender, Race, and Ethnic Identities

Excerpted from Deaux, K. (1993). Reconstructing social identity. *Personality and Social Psychology Bulletin, 19,* 4-12. Copyright ©1993 by Sage Publications. Reprinted by permission of Sage Publications.

Excerpted from Bem, S. L. (1983). Gender schema theory and its implications for child development: Raising gender-aschematic children in a gender-schematic society. *Signs: Journal of Women in Culture and Society, 8,* 598-616. Chicago: The University of Chicago Press. Copyright ©1983 by The University of Chicago Press. Reprinted by permission.

Excerpted from Cross, W. E. (1994). Nigrescence theory: Historical and explanatory notes. *Journal of Vocational Behavior, 44,* 119-123. Copyright ©1994 by Academic Press. Reprinted by permission.

Excerpted from LaFromboise, T., Coleman, H. L. K., & Gerton, J. (1993). Psychological impact of biculturalism: Evidence and theory. *Psychological Bulletin, 114,* 395-412. Copyright ©1993 by The American Psychological Association. Reprinted by permission.

From Wu, S. (1990). In search of Bruce Lee's grave. *The New York Times.* New York: The New York Times Company. Copyright ©1990 by The New York Times Company. Reprinted by permission.

Chapter 5: How Should I Act? Gender, Racial, and Ethnic Social Roles

From Eccles, J. S. (1986). Gender-roles and women's achievement. *Educational Researcher, 15,* 15-19. Copyright ©1986 by the American Educational Research Association. Reprinted by permission of the publisher.

From Thompson, D. C. (1985). The male role stereotype. *As Boys Become Men: Learning New Male Roles.* New York, NY: Irvington Publishers. Copyright ©1985 by Irvington Publishers. Reprinted by permission.

Excerpted from Eisler, R. M. (1995). The relationship between masculine gender role stress and men's health risk: The validation of a construct. In *A New Psychology of Man.* R. F. Levant & W. S. Pollack. New York: Basic Books. Copyright ©1995 by Basic Books. Reprinted by permission.

From William, J. E., & Best, D. L. (1994). Cross-cultural views of women and men. In W. J. Lonner & R. Malpass (Eds.), *Psychology and Culture* (pp. 191-196). Boston: Allyn & Bacon. Copyright ©1994 by Allyn & Bacon. Reprinted by permission.

Excerpted from Taylor, S. E., Peplau, L. A., & Sears, D. O. (1997). *Social Psychology.* Upper Saddle River, NJ: Prentice-Hall. Copyright ©1997 by Prentice-Hall. Reprinted by permission of Prentice-Hall, Inc., Upper Saddle River, NJ.

Chapter 6: Categorizing + Evaluating = Stereotyping

From Heilbroner, R. L. (no date). Don't let stereotypes warp your judgments. *Reader's Digest.* Reprinted by permission of the author.

From Snyder, M. (July, 1982). Self-fulfilling stereotypes. *Psychology Today,* 60-68. REPRINTED WITH PERMISSION FROM PSYCHOLOGY TODAY MAGAZINE, Copyright ©1985 (Sussex Publishers, Inc.).

From Signorielli, N., McLeod, D., & Healy, E. (1994). Gender stereotypes in MTV commercials: The beat goes on. *Journal of Broadcasting and Electronic Media, 38,* 91-101. Copyright ©1994 by Broadcast Education Association. Reprinted by permission.

From *Sex and Gender: An Introduction, Second Edition,* by Hilary M. Lips (1988). Copyright ©1993 by Mayfield Publishing Company. Reprinted by permission of the publisher.

Excerpted from Taylor, S. E., Peplau, L. A., & Sears, D. O. (1997). *Social Psychology.* Upper Saddle River, NJ: Prentice-Hall. Copyright ©1997 by Prentice-Hall. Reprinted by permission of Prentice-Hall, Inc., Upper Saddle River, NJ.

Kevin Sullivan. (1995). In Japan, blood type can be key to success—or failure. *Washington Post.* Copyright ©1996 by The Washington Post. Reprinted by permission.

Chapter 7: The Prejudiced Mind: Biased Attitudes and Gender, Race, and Ethnicity

From Aronson, E., Wilson, T. D., & Akert, R. M. (1997). *Social Psychology: The Heart and the Mind.* New York: Longman. Copyright ©1994 by Harper Collins College Publishers. Reprinted by permission of Addison-Wesley Educational Publishers, Inc.

From THE NATURE OF PREJUDICE, by Gordon Allport; Copyright ©1954, by Addison-Wesley Publishing Company, Inc. Reprinted by permission.

From Devine, P. G. (January/February, 1996). Breaking the prejudice habit. *Psychological Science Agenda*, 10-11. Copyright ©1996 by The American Psychological Association. Reprinted by permission.

Excerpted from Taylor, S. E., Peplau, L. A., & Sears, D. O. (1997). *Social Psychology.* Upper Saddle River, NJ: Prentice-Hall. Copyright ©1997 by Prentice-Hall. Reprinted by permission of Prentice-Hall, Inc., Upper Saddle River, NJ.

From Staples, B. (September, 1986). Just walk on by: A black man ponders his power to alter public space. *Ms. Magazine*, pp. 54 and 88. Copyright ©1986 by MacDonald Communications Corporation. Reprinted by permission of author. Staples writes editorials for the *New York Times* and is the author of the memoir, "Parallel Time."

Chapter 8: The Problem of Discrimination

From Author unknown. (1981). The problem: Discrimination. From *Affirmative Action in the 1980s.* U.S. Commission on Civil Rights, *65*, January 1981, pp. 9-15. Article in public domain.

Excerpted from LaPiere, R. T. (1934). Attitudes vs. actions. *Social Forces*, 230-237. Copyright ©1934 by University of North Carolina Press. Reprinted by permission.

Excerpted from Hyde, J. S. (1984). Children's understanding of sexist language. *Developmental Psychology, 20*, 697-706. Copyright ©1984 by The American Psychological Association. Reprinted by permission.

From Landry, S. (July 17, 1996). Study: Racism is health risk to black Americans. *St. Petersburg Times*, p. 5A. Copyright ©1996 by St. Petersburg Times. Reprinted by permission.

From Swallow, D. (1984). A white man's word. From *A Gathering of Spirit: A Collection of North American Indian Women*, edited by Beth Brant. Ithaca, NY: Firebrand Books. Copyright ©1984 by Beth Brant. Reprinted by permission.

Chapter 9: Applying Research on Gender, Race, and Ethnicity: Education and the Intelligence Debate

From Serpell, R. (1994). The cultural construction of intelligence. In W. J. Lonner & R. Malpass (Eds.), *Psychology and Culture* (pp. 157-163). Boston: Allyn & Bacon. Copyright ©1994 by Allyn & Bacon. Reprinted by permission.

From "Racist Arguments and IQ," copyright ©1977 by Stephen Jay Gould. Copyright © 1974 by The American Museum of Natural History, from EVER SINCE DARWIN: Reflections in Natural History by Stephen Jay Gould. Reprinted by permission of W. W. Norton & Company, Inc.

Excerpted from Steele, C. M. (1997). A threat in the air: How stereotypes shape intellectual identity and performance. *American Psychologist, 52*, 613-629. Copyright ©1997 by The American Psychological Association. Reprinted by permission.

From Gup, T. (April 21, 1997). Who is a whiz kid? From *Newsweek*, April 21, 1997, p. 21. Copyright ©1997 by Newsweek. All rights reserved. Reprinted by permission.

Chapter 10: Applying Research on Gender, Race, and Ethnicity: The Workplace and the Affirmative Action Debate

Appendix: Guidelines for Reading and Conducting Research